Growth of banking & development
closely tied with
of security capitalism - inevitable
the philosophy of industrial
expansion and capital expansion
should be absorbed and participated
in by bankers.

The financial position of the worlds banking
systems depends on the soundness of the world p 123
of the nations holdings (Banks of the world)
bond of Govt Debt)

nations 30 10 '92 to 1910
1909 - eagle ... bonds as security
fault cred ... date 11% of
or loans on ... for purchase
(now U.S.G. at the worst
a better risk)

The stock markets and the prices of securities
are direct evidence of the difficulty of
evaluating paper claims to wealth.

① Sound private management
② Efficient public supervision

Relate index of commodity prices to a
prior period and establish real value
of savings funds by means of index (P 106)

Inflation period may encourage issue of stocks
proceeds pay off fixed debt - business not
embarrassed by it in deflation period - stock
can be revalued easier than bonds

Industry gains most from inflation - P 109
Lose working capital under stabilization - P 111

Savings must be encouraged to meet the
investment demands of the state - P 121

Compulsory Saving - Russia - P 122

THE EVOLUTION OF
FINANCE CAPITALISM

THE EVOLUTION OF
FINANCE CAPITALISM

BY

GEORGE W. EDWARDS, Ph.D.

CHAIRMAN, DEPARTMENT OF ECONOMICS, THE CITY COLLEGE,
COLLEGE OF THE CITY OF NEW YORK

LONGMANS, GREEN AND CO.

LONDON · NEW YORK · TORONTO

1938

LONGMANS, GREEN AND CO.
114 FIFTH AVENUE, NEW YORK
221 EAST 20TH STREET, CHICAGO
88 TREMONT STREET, BOSTON

LONGMANS, GREEN AND CO. LTD.
39 PATERNOSTER ROW, LONDON, E.C.4
17 CHITTARANJAN AVENUE, CALCUTTA
NICOL ROAD, BOMBAY
36A MOUNT ROAD, MADRAS

LONGMANS, GREEN AND CO.
215 VICTORIA STREET, TORONTO

EDWARDS
THE EVOLUTION OF FINANCE CAPITALISM

FIRST EDITION

PRINTED IN THE UNITED STATES OF AMERICA

RESPICE

ADSPICE

PROSPICE

PREFACE

THE title of this book, *finance capitalism,* is employed as a concession to popular usage, for this study is essentially an inquiry into the nature of the non-financial and the financial institutions of *security capitalism* which is a more accurate term. The study is based on the general theory that economic processes are determined not by laws which remain fixed but by institutions which change. The evolution of these institutions is therefore traced for the purpose of indicating the principles of private and public control which should be exercised in the future in order that the system may produce the highest results from the standpoint not only of individual wealth but also of social welfare. The non-financial institutions considered in this study include the political, social, economic, philosophic and legal forces which have moulded the evolution of the system. Analysis is made of such political institutions in the domestic field as the rise and decline of parliamentary government and in the international field as the coming and passing of world peace; of such social institutions as the rise and decline of the rate of population growth and the changes in the welfare of the various groups in society; of such economic institutions as the adjustment between production and consumption; of the schools of economic philosophy such as the rise of classicism and of such legal institutions, as the growth of corporate law. A survey is also made of the purely financial institutions such as the central bank, commercial and investment banks, and the stock exchange, as well as the force of investment and of saving in the capital market.

These institutions are treated historically, comparatively and statistically. The historical approach is used, for security capitalism should be studied in relation to the past. The dramatic financial events of recent years do not constitute an isolated episode which suddenly crashed upon an unsuspecting world in October, 1929, but rather they were the inevitable results of tendencies in operation for decades. Instead of viewing merely the recent day-to-day events of security capitalism, it is necessary to study the long-range trends which are the antecedents of the current movements. A comparative analysis is undertaken to contrast the growth of institutions in various countries. This study is also based on a statistical foundation, for the economic historian must make full use of the statistical technique developed in recent years. Particularly in the field of financial history is it necessary to apply the science of sta-

vii

tistical analysis. In recent years considerable progress has been made in developing more exact measurements, and quantitative tests have been used effectively in applied finance in analyzing the position of a particular corporation or government. This study seeks to employ in the field of social finance for the public interest, the same measurements which were heretofore utilized purely for individual gain. As far as possible the text is kept free of the statistical data which are presented either in tables accompanying the text or in appendices in those instances where the data are the basis for conclusions in more than one chapter.

Throughout the book the same general order of presentation is followed in considering each country. The stages of the rise, the development and the crisis of security capitalism are studied. Consideration is given successively to the political, social, economic, philosophic and legal background of the system, to the growth of financial organization in the form of the central bank, the commercial and investment banks and the stock exchange, to the demand for capital as expressed in governmental and corporate security investment, to the supply of capital as reflected in saving, to the various problems arising from the operation of security capitalism, to the criticism of the system and finally to the efforts at public control.

The evolution of security capitalism in leading countries, as England, France and Germany, as well as the general trends in world security capitalism are first traced. These studies serve as a setting for the comparative analysis of the evolution and the problems of security capitalism in the United States which constitutes the major part of the book. The rise and the development of the system in the United States from approximately 1820 to 1914 is first traced; consideration is given to the relation of American security capitalism to the World War and the political, economic and social background of post-war security capitalism in the United States is then surveyed. The changing function of the financial organization is presented, and a study is made of the problems arising out of the demand for capital in the fields of corporate and governmental investment. There are next presented an analysis of investment policies and a financial statement of American security capitalism. Public control of the demand for and the supply of capital is critically analyzed. The final chapter presents the principles and policies which should form the basis for reconstructing security capitalism.

The system of security capitalism is highly technical, and in practical operation is as intricate as the most highly developed industry. However, in these days of rapid change, a study of technical security practice is of little more than antiquarian interest, since the old methods are being largely discarded, and the new methods have not yet been formulated. Many parts of the financial machine have broken down, and the experts are still doubtfully experimenting with the repairs. The student of security capitalism, therefore, faces the danger of losing his way in the maze of an intricate and ever-changing financial machinery and of not arriving at an understanding of the basic forces which at first aided the development of the system and later checked it. In view of the technical and complicated nature of the subject it would be an error to oversimplify it. Persons who would hesitate to air their views on an intricate problem in physical science, think nothing of surveying the entire subject of security capitalism in a five-hundred word article or in a fifteen-minute radio broadcast. The presentation should not be brought down to the reader, but realizing the challenge to his intellectual power, the reader should rise to an understanding of the subject.

A further difficulty which obstructs an inquiry into security capitalism is that over all the years of its operation, little progress has been made in placing security capitalism on a scientific basis by developing a classified and verified body of knowledge about it. As a result of this lack of scientific progress, security capitalism is presented, and often taught, as an incoherent mass of fragmentary, unsubstantiated and confused statements. The student of the subject of security capitalism should, therefore, seek to produce a body of classified and verified facts which taken together has some coherence.

It should also be realized that security capitalism is an imperfect system which, at times, has not functioned satisfactorily from the standpoint either of the individual or of society. As a result, critics of security capitalism overemphasize the dramatic and sensational misdeeds of particular individuals. On the other hand apologists, unwilling to admit the limitations of security capitalism, seek to veil the failure of both public and private financial statesmanship by senseless propaganda. Critical iconoclasts and apologetic idolators have built up prejudices and myths which have found widespread acceptance not only among the general public but even unfortunately among professional economists. Security capitalism therefore needs understanding both from those who have little realization of the practical difficulties in finance and from those who have scant appreciation of the social consequences of their errors. Too often in recent years attack has come from those who cannot very well be considered deep students, from those who write sweepingly and condemn in broad generalization; too frequently defense has come blindly from those who lack understanding, and from those who in self-interest tolerate no honest criticism. The limitations of security capitalism should be viewed with neither destructive assault nor uncritical defense, but rather with constructive criticism and objective detachment. To the radically inclined mind the following presentation of security capitalism will seem merely another useless disclosure of the known weaknesses of the system and a futile effort to bolster up a decadent institution. To the reactionarily inclined mind the presentation will appear as just another inquisitorial venture. It is the hope of the author that the book will attain the fundamental test of scholarship in being an honest search for truth, whether pleasant or unpleasant, and based on this truth in proposing a constructive program of controlling security capitalism which, despite its imperfections in the past, has served the interests of society.

We should therefore approach the subject for the purpose of understanding the underlying principles, of grasping the significance of its complicated organization, of assembling and co-ordinating a body of classified and verified facts concerning the system and of searching out its imperfections with a view toward reconstruction.

For the general method of treatment the author is indebted to Dr. Charles A. Beard under whom he studied at Columbia University a quarter of a century ago. Dr. Beard developed a technique of historical institutional research which had been sadly lacking in financial investigation.

The manuscript has been read by Professor James D. Magee of New York University, Professor Nelson P. Mead and other members of the History Department of the City College of the College of the City of New York, Professor Joseph L. Tynan of the English Department and by Mr. Jerome B. Cohen of the Economics Department. Acknowledgment is due to Dr. Harold G. Moulton who gave the author the idea of an integrated study of the financial system. The initial compilation of the tables and appendices was undertaken by members of W. P. A. Project 165-97-6999 (6051) which I sponsored. I owe a debt to my students of the City College of the College of the City of New York who over the years have constituted a critical though always a friendly and stimulating audience. My deepest obligation is to my wife not only for her painstaking research and careful preparation of the manuscript but particularly for her encouragement and inspiration which have made the writing of this book a joyful experience.

The later chapters dealing with American security capitalism are in a large measure based on the findings of the various governmental investigations of the system. The results of these findings have been analyzed and an attempt has been made in this book to give a critical and orderly presentation of these data. The student of security capitalism is deeply indebted to Joseph Healy, Ferdinand Pecora and Max Lowenthal for the wealth of information which they have disclosed respectively in the hearings on public utility, banking and railroad finance. Liberal use has also been made of the findings of the munition industry inquiry and the reports of the Securities and Exchange Commission. In writing the chapters on the history of security capitalism on the Continent, the author was fortunate in having available the studies of Alfred Neymarck, the comments of Werner Sombart and the work of Jacob Rieser.

The source material for the early chapters was obtained over a period of years from libraries in this country and abroad, as the New York Public Library, the Congressional Library, the libraries of Harvard University, of the Federal Reserve Board, of the American Bankers' Association, of the British Museum, of the London School of Economics and of a number of French, German, Belgian, Austrian and Scandinavian banks. The general plan of this book was conceived in Germany in 1922 while undertaking a study of European financial organization and part of the data was gathered in subsequent visits to Europe. In the chapters on post-war tendencies the author has drawn upon his own direct observations in this country and abroad. He was fortunate in having had the opportunities for such direct observations through association with various departments of the federal government and also with private organizations such as in founding the Institute of International Finance for the Investment Bankers' Association of America and in working with the American Bankers' Association at various times in recent years.

GEORGE W. EDWARDS

Hartsdale, New York
    April, 1938

CONTENTS

xiii

LIST OF TABLES

THE EVOLUTION OF
FINANCE CAPITALISM

THE EVOLUTION OF
FINANCE CAPITALISM

Part I—Evolution of World Security Capitalism

CHAPTER 1

FINANCIAL INSTITUTIONS OF SECURITY CAPITALISM

THROUGHOUT its evolution, capitalism has taken various forms, and can be grouped according to its territorial extent as local, national or international capitalism; according to its relation to the state, as private or as public capitalism; according to the economic class which dominates the system as agrarian, mercantile, industrial or banking capitalism. A more important principle of classifying capitalism is according to the nature of the transfer of capital. Thus a distinction should be drawn between individual capitalism and security capitalism.[1]

Under individual capitalism the funds for financing economic activities are furnished by the entrepreneur operating as a single owner or in partnership with others. These funds may be applied either to private or to public undertakings. In the former case the funds are generally used by the entrepreneur in his own business where capital ownership and executive management are combined. In the latter the entrepreneur, singly or with a group, turns over his funds to the ruler as an individual. In private finance the single-ownership and the partnership have been gradually replaced by the corporation while in public finance the ruler, as the borrowing party, has been supplanted by a legislative body, and in both fields today the transfer of capital is largely evidenced by securities. Individual capitalism thus has given way to "stock-and-bond" or security capitalism.[2]

Individual capitalism and security capitalism differ in several essential respects. Individual capitalism depends largely on entrepreneur capital, it is personal in nature and the basis underlying

1

its capital consists largely of tangible assets as farms, factories or ships. Security capitalism rests on investor capital, it is essentially impersonal and the instruments evidencing claims to wealth are based on intangible as well as tangible assets.[3]

Under individual capitalism, the entrepreneur finances himself for short periods of time by commercial credit, while under security capitalism there is more reliance on investment credit. Under individual capitalism, labor and land are the important factors in production, but capital is dominant under security capitalism.

MEANING OF SECURITY CAPITALISM

Security capitalism may be defined as the economic system which is financed through the conversion of the saving of investors into security investment. Security capitalism is thus the system which brings together the forces of saving and of investment as far as they relate to securities.

Saving, on the one hand, results from the collective choice of individuals willing to restrict their expenditures in relation to their immediate income, while investment arises from the collective action of entrepreneurs or governments desiring to increase their expenditures beyond their current income. Saving refers to the accumulations of the consumers, whether individuals or corporations, while investment denotes the forms evidencing the transfer of the saving to entrepreneurs or governments. This investment may be evidenced in various forms such as commercial paper, mortgages and particularly securities. This study deals with the application of saving to security investment which today constitutes the greater part of total investment.

The relation between saving and investment can be studied from the standpoint of the individual saver and the individual entrepreneur. Such a treatment lies in the province of a treatise in the field of investment practice presented from the standpoint of individual profit. This book is concerned rather with the relation between saving and investment from the social viewpoint and deals with the operation of these two forces from the standpoint of public interest. Saving will therefore be considered as the excess of national income over expenditure. National income will be used in the sense of the money value of the goods and services received by the individuals composing the nation over a definite period of time such as a year.

PARTIES TO SECURITY CAPITALISM

There are three leading parties to the system of security capitalism namely the saving-investor, the saving-receiver and the saving-dealer or the investment banker.[4]   The first party, whom we will call for brevity the investor, retains the ownership of his saving, but transfers the executive management to the receiver who in exchange gives paper claims in the form of shares or of bonds.   The incentive which induces the investor to part with the control of his saving is the expectation of income in the form of dividends on stock, interest on bonds, or of profit through the appreciation of the market value of these securities.   The expectation of income by the investor is based on his confidence in the earning power of the corporation or in the fiscal power of the government.

The receiver of saving may be either a corporation which applies it to some private enterprise or a government which directs the saving to some public undertaking.   It is important throughout this entire discussion to keep in mind that security capitalism facilitates the application of saving not only to private but also to public financial operations.   The third party to the system is the investment banker.   He is not an essential party, for saving can be converted into security investment through the sale of securities by a corporation or a government directly to the investor. However, such direct sales are relatively unimportant.   The investment banker is primarily a dealer who purchases securities and sells them to the investor.   The purchasing operation of the investment banker has become an important activity in the modern capitalist system.   It is a power which has deep social and economic significance.   Through the purchasing function the investment banker exercises a selective power by which he can either grant or withhold new capital so essential to financing the needs of corporations and of governments.   By the exercise of this selective power the investment banker therefore controls the flow of new capital.

After purchasing an issue of securities, the investment banker sells them to the investor either directly or indirectly through other financial institutions, such as deposit banks, including both savings banks and commercial banks receiving savings deposits, investment trusts, or life insurance companies.   Under the direct relationship between the investment banker and the investor, the latter exchanges his saving for the securities of the receiving corporation or government.   Under the indirect system, the investor obtains a claim on a financial institution which in the case of the bank is a deposit account, in the case of the investment trust is a stock or a bond, and in the case of the life insurance company is a policy.   These institutions in turn may place the funds of the investor in securities of corporations or governments.

Old capital, as represented in securities already outstanding, is bought and sold through brokers, who act as agents, and derive their return from a commission on the purchase or the sale of securities. Such brokers are grouped in either fully organized stock exchanges which trade in listed securities or more loosely in over-the-counter markets for the purchase and sale of unlisted securities. The so-called commercial bank has also become an important party to the system of security capitalism. As mentioned before, it may serve as an institution of indirect investment. Another important function is to supply credit for carrying securities. Similarly the operation of the central bank, as the keystone of the commercial banking system, has been influenced by security capitalism. In practically every country the central bank grants advances collateralled by securities, and in certain countries it performs other security services.

RELATION BETWEEN MANAGEMENT AND BANKING

It is frequently held that the prominence of the investment banker in the financial system necessarily leads to his assuming the function of capital management. In American economic literature this extension of his function is generally described as domination by Wall Street and in European literature there is a similar criticism of the grip which the investment banker is supposed to hold over the industrial life of the nation. As will be indicated in later chapters describing the financial organization of various countries, there is not always a close relation between investment banking and industry, and banking domination is not necessarily an essential characteristic of security capitalism.

The evolution of the financial relation between capital management and investment banking generally passes through three stages. In the early history of a particular corporation or industry, or even economic system, the relation between capital management and investment banking is generally negligible. Industry finances itself internally through the reinvestment of its earnings and this policy is usually the result not of choice but of necessity, for the untried corporation or the young industry or the new system is unable to finance its growth by the sale of securities to the public. In the course of time the particular corporation or the industry or system, if operations are profitable, is in a stronger position to finance its growth by the sale of securities. At this point a close relationship between management and investment banking may develop. This tie is not a necessary result, for if the needs of the corporation are not pressing the management may readily retain control of its own business. Furthermore, the same result may follow if the supply of capital in the market is abundant, as was the case in England in the nineteenth century. If the expansion is so rapid that the corporation must have a large and continuous supply of capital, and if the supply of available capital is limited, then the investment banker may very well obtain control over the management of the affairs of the corporation. Such conditions prevailed in Germany in the period of rapid industrial expansion in the last quarter of the nineteenth century.

In the course of time there comes a third stage in the relationship between industry and investment banking. As a nation attains economic maturity the supply of capital funds directly owned by corporations increases, and under these conditions they are less dependent upon investment banking. Similarly, the increase of profits enables the management to finance its expansion more and more from the reinvestment of earnings, and as a result the control of investment banking over industry is weakened. Such was the history of the relationship of investment banking to industrial management in the post-war period in the United States when banker control was lessened. The decline of control by the banker and the re-assertion of control by industry also occurred in Germany in the post-war years, but unfortunately was accompanied by sweeping political changes. The history of security capitalism indicates that control of the management of industry by banking capitalism is but a transitory stage.

CHARACTERISTICS OF SECURITY CAPITALISM

The underlying characteristics of security capitalism may next be noted. In the first place, while the investor retains the ownership of his capital, he generally loses control over its management. This divorce of management from ownership of capital is particularly true in indirect investment where the investor turns over the disposition of his funds to the deposit bank, to the investment trust or to the life insurance company. Even under direct investment in corporate finance, the investor has frequently been separated from control of his funds through the creation of such divorcing agencies as the voting trust, non-voting class A stock and the holding company. In public finance, the investor has practically no control of his capital. Furthermore, security capitalism has led to wide diffusion of the ownership of corporations. This tendency is frequently described as the "democratization" of capitalism. It is true that security capitalism has transferred corporate ownership from the few to the many, but because of the diffusion of securities among many holders, control still continues in the hands of the few who manage not only their own capital but also that of the multitude. Security capitalism thus effects democratization of the ownership of capital but brings about monopolization of the control of capital.

A second necessary feature of security capitalism is the creation of stocks and bonds. Since the owner of capital surrenders its management, he must receive some instrument which indicates his retention of ownership and which describes the conditions governing the relation between the investor and the saving-receiver, such as that governing the payment of interest or of dividends and the ultimate repayment of the principal in the case of a bond. These stocks and bonds are the paper representatives of the assets of the corporations or of governments which have issued them.

The third characteristic of security capitalism is the impersonalization of the financial relation between the saving-investor and the saving-receiver. Their relationship is no longer based on personal acquaintance, for the two parties seldom know each other. This change in relationship has occurred both in private and in public finance. In early public borrowing the banker gave his own funds to the king, and the loan was a purely personal transaction between these two parties. Under modern security capitalism, the state by an act of the legislative body obtains funds through the sale of its bonds to investors, and the relationship has therefore become impersonal on both sides.

FINANCIAL PROBLEMS OF SECURITY CAPITALISM

Each of these characteristics of security capitalism has led to certain inevitable financial problems. The separation of the ownership of capital from its management has frequently tended toward irresponsibility in its administration. Under the system of individual capitalism where ownership and management of capital are combined in the single individual or the partnership, extreme prudence is naturally exercised by the managers in the handling of their own funds. On the other hand, under security capitalism where the owners of capital transfer its management to the directors or officers of a corporation or to the officers of a government, it is inevitable that the latter will not generally be inclined to exercise the same prudence in the handling of the funds of others as they would in the care of their own.[5]

The creation of securities based on underlying assets has given rise to the problem of capitalization, or the actual pecuniary relationship between the face or the par value of outstanding securities and the true valuation of the underlying assets of the corporation or the government. The true value of these assets in the case of a corporation is based primarily on its earning power and in the case of a government on the return from its own revenue-producing property or on the receipts from the taxable property and income of its inhabitants. Overcapitalization is the issuance of securities with a face or a par value in excess of the true value of the underlying assets. Overcapitalization is also the overstatement of this asset value and results in the creation of paper claims in the form of securities unsupported by underlying assets.[6]

A third result of security capitalism in recent years has been the growth of financial instability as reflected in the widening range of security prices. One cause has been the impersonality of the financial relations under security capitalism as described above, whereby the investor exchanges his capital either for securities under the method of direct investment or for a bank deposit, or a life insurance policy under indirect investment. Either method accelerates the shiftability of capital.[7]

Shiftability of capital is accomplished under direct security investment by the sale of a stock or a bond in the security market. Under indirect investment the conversion of a bank deposit into cash is accomplished by its withdrawal, and a life insurance policy by obtaining its cash-surrender value. This indirect method in the end necessitates the marketing of securities or other assets, since the deposit bank or the life insurance company must sell some of its assets in order to meet the demand of the depositor or of the policy holder. Economists in the past have generally looked with favor upon this increase in the shiftability of capital resulting from the wider use of securities.[8] Defenders of the stock exchange have generally pointed out that this institution, by providing a so-called free market and enhancing shiftability, tends to stabilize security values. As a matter of fact, the improvement of the machinery of the stock exchange in recent years has been accompanied by greater financial instability, as evidenced by the everwidening upward and downward swings of security prices. The increase in the shiftability of capital has been the mechanical factor leading to the instability of security capitalism.

A second factor causing instability has arisen out of the policy of recapitalization. Whether such recapitalization has meant overcapitalization or undercapitalization, the change in the capital structure creates uncertainty over the pecuniary valuation of the securities in relation to their underlying assets. The valuation of tangible assets as evidenced by a factory or a farm is hard enough, but the appraisal of securities issued on intangible assets, as good will and franchises, is much more difficult. A third factor which has increased the uncertainty of determining the value of stocks and bonds has been the growing complexity of corporate and of governmental finance. In recent years many new characteristics as the closed mortgage bond and the participating warrant have been devised for the purpose of seeking to protect or to benefit the investor. More usually such characteristics have been added to securities and placed in corporate indentures by the issuers for the purpose of obtaining a greater control of the invested capital. As a result, securities have become more complicated, and in consequence their valuation has been rendered more difficult. There has been a growing complexity also in public finance. There have been many cases of one government guaranteeing the obligations of another government or of a semi-public corporation ; of a government issuing not only general credit obligations but also bonds based on specific security ; and of a government creating overlapping political bodies with separate taxing powers.

A further problem of security capitalism is the adjustment between saving and investment in the form of the supply of and the demand for capital. A relative surplus of saving results in what may be described as capital market deflation, while a relative excess of investment really amounts to capital market inflation. It is true that theoretically the volume of investment cannot exceed the amount of saving, but actually over a short space of time such temporary excess of investment may be rendered possible through the use of credit extended for the purpose of carrying securities which have been issued but which have not yet been sold. Capital responsibility, security capitalization, financial stability and saving-investment adjustment are among the major problems relating to the financial institutions of security capitalism.

VERY IMPORTANT

CHAPTER 2

RISE OF BRITISH SECURITY CAPITALISM

IN WORLD history, economic systems pass successively through their rising, developed and declining stages. Within the framework of the declining stage of the old system appears the rising stage of the new system. In the developed stage the new system acquires the characteristics of its pure form, and in the declining stage it disappears within the framework of the rising stage of the succeeding system. The rapidity of these movements has varied. The evolution of early economic systems, as the growth and the disintegration of the Roman Empire, the coming and the passing of European feudalism and the rise of individual capitalism slipped over the centuries with the imperceptibility of a slow-moving glacier. The evolution of security capitalism however has been one of the swiftest-moving dramas in all the history of human civilization, and its course has sped onward with the rush of a fast-flowing mountain stream.

The evolution of individual capitalism in Western Europe covered the period from the thirteenth century through the first *600 years.* half of the nineteenth century. This period was marked by momentous developments in the field of politics, technology, philosophy and finance.[1]

The dominant political movement was the growth of national government in France, Spain and England. Now for the first time in centuries property received protection and as a result capital was accumulated. With the growth of towns came the rise of the middle class which in time wrested the political power from the hands of the agrarian aristocracy and later from the king. The mechanical tools of society were developed; the improvement in navigation facilitated the crossing of the oceans and the age of discovery was initiated. Technological progress also made possible the erection of public buildings. The dominant economic philosophy was that of mercantilism which preached the importance of a powerful self-sufficient state, and urged that all economic policies be directed to this end. The financial organization of individual capitalism came with the rise of the private merchant bankers, as the Peruzzi, the Medici and the Fuggers. In the later years of this period came the crude beginning of central banks as feeble organizations to bolster government treasuries and not yet institutions to

9

regulate the credit of nations, and the start of stock exchanges as mere fairs to exhibit goods and not yet powerful security markets to transfer paper claims to wealth.

DEVELOPED INDIVIDUAL CAPITALISM IN ENGLAND

In England the developed stage of individual capitalism extended from the end of the seventeenth century to the close of the Napoleonic Wars. This period included the first industrial revolution of the eighteenth-nineteenth centuries. The vast transformation in the industrial life in England over these years was financed almost entirely by entrepreneur capital. Although the canal, turnpike and dock enterprises of the later eighteenth century were organized as corporations, their securities were almost entirely held by the managers and were not usually offered for sale to the general public. By the beginning of the nineteenth century the sweeping changes in the textile and mining industries were likewise undertaken almost entirely by individuals who contributed their own capital, and the expansion of these early enterprises was financed out of the reinvestment of their subsequent earnings. Save for listing the stocks of a few mining companies, the London Stock Exchange until the first quarter of the nineteenth century had practically no contact with the vast movements which were completely transforming the industrial life of England.

From the days of Athens and Rome until the close of the eighteenth century there had been little widening in the forms of investment, for land and shipping still dominated as outlets for the placement of funds. The stock of the Bank of England and of the East India Company offered a possible but limited corporate demand for the rapidly accumulating capital of the eighteenth century. The paucity of satisfactory media of investment is well illustrated by the predicament of Alexander Pope's father who, upon retiring from his successful linen draper's business, had a considerable fund. He was apparently unable to find a suitable form of investment and so he placed his money in a strong box from which he took out sums whenever needed for his household expenses.[2]

Practically the sole form of security investment throughout the eighteenth and early nineteenth centuries was the national debt. The successive wars of the eighteenth and early nineteenth centuries necessitated extensive public borrowing, so that the national debt rose from £13,000,000 in 1709 to £900,000,000 in 1816 when Napoleon was finally banished to St. Helena.[3] As Napoleon's armies overran Europe, many capitalists transferred their funds from the Continent to England for safety and a large part was placed in

British government bonds.   National government securities constituted the bulk of the trading conducted on the London Stock Exchange.

Throughout the eighteenth century the Exchange evolved from a mercantile market essentially for the purchase and sales of goods into a true stock exchange for the transfer of securities.   Francis Hirst placed the beginning of the modern security exchange in 1773, when the brokers resolved that it should be called the "Stock Exchange." [4]   In 1802 the Exchange took over the building which it was to occupy up to the present time.   In the same year the Exchange received a deed of settlement,[5] and it was deemed unnecessary to obtain any further legal basis for its existence, such as an enabling act from Parliament or a charter under the Companies Act.   At first any one could obtain daily admission to the Exchange on payment of six pence.[6]

However, as reported in the official history of the Stock Exchange, "it became apparent that the indiscriminate admission of the public was calculated to expose the dealers to the loss of valuable property."   As a result the Exchange established a privileged group of security dealers who ultimately gained monopoly in the handling of security transactions.[7]

The Stock Exchange during this early stage, had an unsavory record.   In 1810 Abraham Goldsmid the so-called King of the Stock Exchange became involved in scandal and committed suicide.   So serious was the effect of Goldsmid's death, that the news was sent by a special messenger to the King and the Prince of Wales.   Another stockbroker, Benjamin Walsh, who had raised himself to membership in Parliament, was finally excluded from the House on the ground of fraud.   In 1814 Admiral Cochrane, prominent in the British Navy and in politics, was one of a group which circulated a false rumour concerning the death of Napoleon for the purpose of putting through a stock market deal.   For this offense the Admiral was deprived of his seat in Parliament.[8]

Thus in the developed stage of individual capitalism the system of security capitalism made its appearance in the growing volume of the national government bonds and in the formation of a market for dealing in these securities.

BACKGROUND OF RISING SECURITY CAPITALISM

The declining stage of individual capitalism in England was the period from the close of the Napoleonic wars until the middle of the nineteenth century when British security capitalism was passing through its rising stage.   The general institutional forces which brought about the growth of security capitalism may be found in fields of politics, economics, philosophy and law. International political relations, after the almost century-long duel between England and France, were fortunately quiet, and for almost a half century there were no major wars. Domestic politics in England was marked by the rise of liberalism, for suffrage was widened and with the abolition of the rotten boroughs, Parliament came to be fairly representative of the popular will. The complexion of British politics was changing, and the issues were revolving more over social welfare rather than merely private gain. The Whigs and their more progressive associates were influenced by the humanitarian movement of the day, and were gradually forcing measures for political and social betterment upon Parliament.

This changing political ideology had its effect upon England's foreign investments in stimulating particularly the flow of funds to Greece, South America and the United States. The British public sympathized deeply with Greece in its efforts to throw off the Turkish yoke, and large sums were raised to finance this movement. There was also widespread popular support for the revolutionary struggles in South America. After the successful outcome of these uprisings British investors loaned millions of pounds to the newly-founded republics. The British Whigs also felt a deep kinship with Jacksonian democracy which was sweeping away the last vestiges of federalism in the United States. In all three fields British humanitarianism was rewarded with heavy financial reverses. The Reverend Sydney Smith's "Humble Petition to the House of Congress at Washington" expressed not only the injured feelings of British bondholders who held defaulted American state obligations, but also the keen disappointment of the British liberals who regarded these defaults as a betrayal of the new political philosophy. The petition and letter read in part as follows:

Nor is it only the loss of property which your petitioner laments; he laments still more, that immense power which the bad faith of America has given to the aristocratical opinions, and to the enemies of free institutions, in the Old World. It is in vain any longer to appeal to history, and to point out the wrongs which the many have received from the few. The Americans, who boast to have improved the institutions of the Old World, have at least equalled its crimes. A great nation, after trampling under foot all earthly tyranny, has been guilty of a fraud as enormous as ever disgraced the worst king of the most degraded nation of Europe.

The letter concludes with the parting comment that:

. . . having eased my soul of its indignation, and sold my stock at 40 percent discount, I sulkily retire from the subject, with a fixed intention of lending no more money to free and enlightened republics, but of employing my money henceforth in buying up Abyssinian bonds, and purchasing into the Turkish Fours.[9]

These were years of economic progress. The industrial revolution initiated a half century before was now well under way and British mines and factories were increasing their operations enormously.[10] The increased manufacturing production was absorbed not only by an expanding domestic but also by ever-increasing overseas market.[11] Early British security capitalism was given a firm monetary foundation, for in 1821 the Bank of England resumed specie payment thus making England the first nation to adopt the modern gold standard.[12] Among the advocates of specie resumption were the Ricardos. No doubt they sincerely believed in the validity of their economic argument for specie resumption, but it is also worth noting that the stock exchange house was short on stocks and therefore stood to profit whenever specie payment was resumed by the Bank of England.[13]

British economic philosophy was travelling fast along the road of classicism as marked out by Adam Smith. By the first quarter of the nineteenth century it seemed that the majestic laws of classicism had definitely settled most of the great economic problems of the world, and that there was little further labor for future economists except to follow the beaten paths laid out by the founders of the new science. The insignificant position of security capitalism in these early years was reflected in the scanty references to it in the economic literature of the day. Adam Smith, writing in the period of developed individual capitalism, made only passing reference to the security market.[14] He failed entirely to foresee the future importance of the corporation as reflected in his statement "though such companies may not, in the present times be very oppressive, they are certainly altogether useless." [15] Malthus, although writing at the time that security capitalism was rising showed little interest in it. Even Ricardo, a leading figure in the security capitalism of his day, gave the system only passing notice. The significance of security capitalism was however appreciated by David Hume even though he was writing in the second half of the eighteenth century. In his essay "Of Public Credit." Hume wrote : "Public securities are with us become a kind of money, and pass readily at the current price as gold or silver." [16]

[margin note: Economists of the day did not recognize birth of security capitalism]

[margin note: in 1825]

Hume believed that the burden of the national debt was so heavy that the government was headed for bankruptcy.[17] Hume was critical of the stock exchange, and stated that : "What production we owe change-alley, or even what consumption except that of coffee, and pen, ink and paper, I have not yet learned."

He believed that the turnover of securities did not have the same economic significance as the turnover of commodities, a statement which was true in his day.[18]

The economic philosophy of the period generally accepted with little question the social value of individual saving. Malthus however had certain reservations on the value of thrift as may be seen in his statement that :

... if, at the very time that the supply of commodities compared with the demand for them, clearly admonishes us that the proportion of capital to revenue is already too great, we go on saving from our revenue to add still further to our capital, all general principles concur in shewing that we must of necessity be aggravating instead of alleviating our distress.[19]

DEVELOPMENT OF CORPORATE ORGANIZATION

The development of corporate organization may best be considered as a result rather than a cause of the economic changes of the period. The increasing demand for capital made necessary an improvement in the form of business organization, as the demand for capital became so great that it could no longer be supplied from resources mobilized by the forms of business organization under individual capitalism, namely, the single ownership or the partnership. It was therefore essential to develop the corporate form in order to provide co-operative capital tapped from innumerable private sources. Although the principle of corporate organization had been recognized in the eighteenth century, the number of corporations remained small and their range limited until the second quarter of the nineteenth century.[20] The formation of new corporations was still checked by restrictive legislation of the eighteenth century, particularly by the Bubble Act. Peter Moore, one of the leaders of the new security capitalism and a member of Parliament, attacked the statute, and through his leadership in 1825 it was repealed.[21] As a result corporations now grew in number and in capitalization from only 127 with a paid-up capital of £15,000,000 in 1827 to 994 with a capital of £345,000,000 in 1844.[22]

These corporations were supposed to express the general theory of democracy then being developed in the field of domestic politics. Democratic corporate control was to be achieved by giving one vote to each share, and the shareholders were to elect a board of directors at the annual meeting. In this way the principle of representative government was to apply to the field of business. However, even in this early stage of corporate history, the movement for the separation of the management from the ownership of capital developed quickly. Shareholders surrendered their proxies at the annual meetings in return for the small payment of the stamp duties by the management and so actually had little voice in the administration of their capital.[23]

FINANCIAL ORGANIZATION OF THE NEW CAPITALISM

With the close of the Napoleonic wars, the Bank of England assumed a more important position in the money market. After 1819 the membership of its board of directors improved in quality, and included persons who grasped the theoretic problems of the institution. The Bank was fortunate in having as governor, Horsley Palmer, who made a real contribution in developing not only sound banking practice but also sound credit theory. Under Palmer's guidance the Bank took recognition of the importance of the government security market by borrowing on consols, that is, selling government bonds and repurchasing an equal quantity to be paid for at a later date and following what may be today termed an open market policy.[24] However, over these years the Bank was none too successful in coping with the problems arising out of the new security capitalism, for in the crisis of 1825 and again in 1839 the Bank of England had to turn for assistance to the Bank of France.[25]

Commercial banking developed rapidly both in the provinces as well as in London. In hundreds of towns throughout England a local merchant, manufacturer or shopkeeper, having attained a measure of business success in his own field, would dabble in banking by receiving the deposits of his fellow townsmen. Since his credit was generally better known than that of the others in his community, in the course of time he would permit bills of exchange to be drawn on himself on behalf of his less-known neighbors and would charge a fee for this service. Later on he would discount or purchase bills drawn on other parties. After a while these activities increased in importance, and the individual would limit himself to these banking operations. In addition to these private banks, there was a growth in the number of incorporated banks.

The private or the incorporated commercial bank, and not the investment bank was the institution which aided in financing the industrial revolution. Capital for the new manufactures came largely from the personal resources of the individual entrepreneurs, but credit came from the commercial banks particularly in the provinces. These institutions financed the manufacturers to enable them to pay their employees and to purchase raw materials, and these loans were repaid out of the sale of the finished goods. The banks also extended credit to the merchants engaged in marketing goods to domestic and to foreign buyers.

These conditions gave rise to the so-called classical or orthodox theory of the function of the commercial bank. Adam Smith, writing in 1776 when the banks were lending mainly to merchants under individual capitalism, stated the classical theory of the function of the commercial bank as follows:

> What a bank can with propriety advance to a merchant or undertaker of any kind, is not either the whole capital with which he trades, or even any considerable part of that capital; but that part of it only, which he would otherwise be obliged to keep by him unemployed, and in ready money for answering occasional demands.[26]

In order to enable a bank to maintain a sufficiency of quick assets to meet its demand liabilities, the orthodox theory held that a bank should confine its operations to the granting of loans which were liquid in the sense of supplying their own means of self-extinguishment at maturity. Unquestionably the orthodox theory was fully justified under the financial system prevailing in England in the early nineteenth century. Credit was needed primarily over a short period of time either for converting raw materials into finished products or moving them to market whether at home or abroad. Such commercial bank credit was extended not as today by granting the borrower an increase in his deposit account, but by giving him bank notes. These continued to be the dominant form of bank credit until 1844 when the Act of that year limited the amount of the notes of the existing banks and prohibited new banks from issuing such obligations.[27]

Because of his control of credit, the commercial banker exercised an important influence on the political and social life of England. William Cobbett commented satirically on the large number of parliamentary seats which were bought up by the country bankers or "rag merchants" as he termed them.[28] A parliamentary seat was a distinct asset to a banker, for he was thereby in direct touch with the political and economic currents of the day. Even more valuable to a banker was a cabinet portfolio. The commercial banker also held a high social position. Usually the banker and the merchant classes constituted the local aristocracy, for the manufacturer had not yet been admitted to this social group.

The investment banker differed from the commercial banker in that the former granted no commercial credit and therefore issued no notes. Most of the investment banking houses did not receive deposits. In fact, with the exception of Ricardos, they did not even conduct a stock brokerage business. They performed solely the function of issuing new securities and selling them to investors, and further limited these transactions largely to government bonds. The investment banking houses had little to do with the financing of corporations or with industrial undertakings.[29] The great investment houses bitterly opposed the numerous corporate issues which were floated in 1824 and 1825. Alexander

Baring, in a speech to Parliament, strongly denounced these early issues in the statement that: "it was ridiculous to see the objects for which joint-stock companies were forming every day." [30]   The investment houses for a long time refused to take part even in the financing of the British railways. [31]

The business of investment banking was highly remunerative, for the sources of profit were quite extensive.   The investment banker first derived a large commission from the loan which he floated particularly since the commission was calculated on the par value of the issue and it was customary to issue bonds with a low coupon at a low price. [32]   The banker also usually retained a part of the issue for himself, and so controlled a large portion of the floating supply.   He was thus able to manipulate the market price, and derive profits from this speculative operation.   The banker was also generally appointed agent for the handling of the interest and sinking fund payments, and the fees for this service were high. Furthermore, he was usually given an option on subsequent flotations.   In contrast to the large number of commercial banks, the investment houses were few in number.   The leading houses were Baring Brothers, Rothschilds, Ricardos and Goldschmidts.   The record of these houses as judged by the investment experience of the foreign loans which they floated in the period from 1823 to 1825 may be seen in the following table:

TABLE 1

FOREIGN LOANS OF LEADING BRITISH INVESTMENT HOUSES, 1823-1825. [33]

NAME OF HOUSE	NUMBER DEFAULTING	NUMBER NOT DEFAULTING
Barings.............	2	0
Goldschmidts.......	3	0
Ricardos...........	1	0
Rothschilds.........	0	8
Other houses........	10	2
Total...	16	10

From this table it is seen that Rothschilds' record was perfect, since every one of its foreign loans continued to pay interest.   This record is all the more outstanding in view of the poor investment experience of other foreign loans.   Both loans made by Barings went into default, as did those of Goldschmidts, while the single foreign loan of Ricardos likewise brought loss to its holders.   If the eight successful loans of Rothschilds are omitted, all the other issuing houses had a record of sixteen defaults and only two successful issues. It is therefore little wonder that Rothschilds acquired a high reputation in these years, for they made profits not only for themselves but also for their clients. The successful operations of the Rothschilds added prestige to the entire investment banking fraternity. Contemporary recognition of the importance of the investment banker is seen in the comment of the Reverend Sydney Smith that:

If Caesar were to reappear upon earth . . . Rothschild would open and shut the Temple of Janus; Thomas Baring, or Bates, would probably command the Tenth legion, and the soldiers would march to battle with loud cries of Scrip and Omnium reduced, Consols, and Caesar.[34]

GROWING DEMAND FOR CAPITAL

Throughout the eighteenth and early nineteenth centuries the most important demand for capital, as mentioned before, came from the national government. However, after the close of the Napoleonic conflict, the national debt declined, and as this form of investment ceased to absorb the saving of the British public it turned to investment in European, South American government bonds as well as South American mining securities.[35] In 1817 the French indemnity loan was floated, and in 1818 Rothschilds placed a Prussian loan which was the first unguaranteed foreign-government issue to make its appearance on the London money market.[36] The London market also took one-half of an international Russian loan, and in 1824 made liberal advances to Greece to enable that country to free itself from Turkey. The Greek loan of 1824 was handled by a committee of which Lord Byron was a member, and the loan of 1825 was issued by Ricardos. Only a small part of the proceeds was ever applied to the lofty purpose for which the loans were issued. The greater part went to various intermediaries as the Greek commissioners to pay them for their arduous labors in negotiating the loan, several well-known English Philhellenes to compensate them for their losses in a falling security market, Admiral Cochrane to enable him to spend the rest of his life in ease and several Brooklyn shipbuilders to pay them for frigates, most of which never saw service in the cause of Greek liberty. The Greek Government did not pay the interest on these bonds for over a half century.[37] In this period of foreign loans Colombia by contracting a loan in 1820, repudiating in 1828 and settling by means of a new issue in 1845, began the succession of loan flotation, loan repudiation and loan settlement which was destined to stand as a lasting tribute to the patience and to the endurance of the internationally-minded British investor. A bond issue was even floated for the non-existent "King-

dom of Poyais."[38]   At least the South American loans floated by our
New York bankers in recent years in every case were extended to
governments which actually existed.

The demand for capital by domestic corporations was small until
the second quarter of the nineteenth century.   Until then corporate
securities were floated only by public utility (canal, dock, turnpike)
and by financial (bank and insurance) companies.   For a number
of years George Stephenson had urged the application of steam to
transportation, but his proposals were met with ridicule.[39]   However,
in 1825 Stephenson, aided by the funds of individual capitalists,
opened the first railroad from Stockton to Darlington.   By the early
forties the railroads accounted for most of the corporate securities
issued in England.

A statement of the nominal value of the total securities listed on
the London Stock Exchange in 1843 is given in Table 2.

TABLE 2

SECURITIES LISTED ON THE LONDON STOCK EXCHANGE, 1843.[40]
(pounds sterling)

CLASSES OF SECURITIES	AMOUNT	PER CENT OF TOTAL
National government........	773,000,000	69.09
Foreign governments........	121,501,410	10.86
Banking corporations........	46,449,694	4.15
Other corporations..........	177,880,070	15.90
Total.....	1,118,831,174	100.00

From this table it is seen that the securities of the national government constituted 69.09 percent of the total, while foreign government securities accounted for another 10.86 percent.   The securities of banking and other corporations amounted to only 20.05
percent of the total.

INCREASE IN CAPITAL SUPPLY

The volume of capital available for the security market increased
sharply throughout the second quarter of the century.[41]   This increase was due to the profits derived from England's rapidly expanding foreign trade, from her developing finance and particularly
from her new factory system.   Throughout the nation thousands of
small manufacturers were enlargening their shops and mills, artisans
were raising themselves to be proprietors of their own establishments, and even tenant farmers were deserting the plough to become

manufacturers. These individuals generally furnished their own initial capital, and usually preferred to reinvest their subsequent profits in their businesses rather than spend them on consumption goods. Unquestionably the expansion of British manufacture was financed by entrepreneur and not by investor capital.[42]

The expansion of manufacture brought increased income to the land-owning class. Many of these families, after struggling for years with rising taxes, suddenly found themselves wealthy, due to no effort of their own but to the increase in the rent rolls on their properties either near a newly erected factory town or a recently-opened coal mine. Thus the Earl of Derby rejoiced to see the rent rolls on his Lancashire estates rise from £14,000 a year to £180,000 a year.[43] As a result of these profits from industry and from the unearned increment on land, national wealth almost doubled from 1820 to 1840.[44]

Capital accumulation was going forward not only because of the active force of saving, but also because of the negative influence of the relative decline of government taxation as compared with the rise in national income. It was estimated that in 1815 taxation absorbed 9.0 percent. of the national income, but by 1843 this proportion had dropped to 5.5 per cent.[45]

DIFFUSION OF SECURITY HOLDINGS

Diffusion of security holdings is an inherent characteristic of security capitalism, and by the end of the second quarter of the nineteenth century both government and corporate securities were widely held. The new capitalism involved a large number of persons, and so the tendency in finance paralleled the movement in British politics. Just as suffrage, narrowly confined in the eighteenth century, was widened in the early nineteenth century, so the holding of the government's securities was similarly broadened. In the eighteenth century, according to the estimate of Hume, the number of fundholders was only 17,000,[46] but by the early part of the nineteenth century the official government figures placed it at 275,839.[47]

A similar popularization of investment holdings occurred in the new field of corporate securities. The head of Barings, in a speech to Parliament in 1825, noted that "the gambling mania that was at present abroad had seized upon all classes, and was spreading itself in all parts of the country."[48] By the forties, it was said that:

In every street of every town persons were to be found who were holders of Railway Shares. Elderly men and women of small realised fortunes, tradesmen of every order, pensioners, public functionaries, professional men, merchants, country gentlemen — the mania had affected all.[49]

According to the *London Times*, even the clergy were forsaking the scripture for script.[50]

If the demand and the supply of capital are compared, it would seem that throughout this period the latter generally exceeded the former. A vivid demonstration of the strength of the supply of capital is illustrated by an episode in 1818 when the popular demand for an issue of Treasury notes was so insistent that a mob of subscribers, assembled in front of the Bank of England at two o'clock in the morning before the books were opened, crashed the gates off their hinges, and later the entire issue was subscribed by the first ten persons in line.[51] Statistical evidence of the greater rate of saving over the rate of investment throughout the second quarter of the nineteenth century is seen in the decline in the yield on government bonds from 4.42 percent in 1820 to 3.11 in 1850.[52]

CRISES UNDER EARLY SECURITY CAPITALISM

In the second quarter of the nineteenth century British security capitalism experienced two severe speculative crises. The crisis of 1825 was brought about by the flotation of unsound and highly speculative securities of foreign governments and of domestic corporations. The promoters of one company stated that it was formed "to drain the Red Sea, in search of the gold and jewels left by the Egyptians, in their passage after the Israelites." [53] Also a company was organized, with the unconsciously true purpose of exploiting "the immense mineral wealth in Ireland which is almost unknown." [54] In a satirical novel of the day, "The Gold, Wine and Olive Joint Stock Company" is organized by a promoter who says: "Why, you talk as if we had any real business to transact. All we have to do is to puff our shares up to a premium, humbug the public into buying them, and then let the whole concern go to ruin." [55] All the elements of thin margin trading were present in this first speculative excess of the new security capitalism. The speaker of the House of Parliament saw fit to warn shareholders that they were liable on the full amount of their subscription, even though the initial deposit which they had made was only one pound of deposit for every hundred pounds of full subscription.[56]

The inevitable crash came in the autumn of 1825. The provincial banks were the first to be affected and a number failed.[57] These bank failures accompanied a sharp collapse of security prices on the London Stock Exchange and losses on securities were placed at approximately £16,000,000. Thus the new system of security capitalism experienced its initial reverse, and society faced the melancholy sight of security losses resulting from a general security panic.

1846

The next serious maladjustment in British security capitalism came in 1846. However in this case the new speculative medium was the stock of the domestic railway corporations. The leading figure in the railway development of these years was George Hudson who was characterized as "The Railway King." [58] Even in these early days Hudson developed advanced methods of railway financing, for he "maintained his popularity with the shareholders by serving them up dividends paid out of their own capital." [59]

Herbert Spencer, at that time a sub-engineer on the London and Birmingham Railway, made the following note on the rising tide of railway speculation:

During the thirties speculative local magnates and far-seeing capitalists, having projected railways which would obviously be advantageous, thereupon chose their engineers, and subsequently let portions of their work to contractors; but, as fast as there grew up considerable classes of wealthy contractors, and of rich engineers accustomed to co-operate with them, it became the habit for these to join in getting up schemes, forming companies, and practically appointing boards — a policy in all ways beneficial to themselves. Thus, by 1845, there had arisen many and various interests uniting to urge on railway enterprise; and anyone who took a broad view of the causes in operation, might have seen that great disasters were certain to ensue. [60]

Spencer's father invested in a Derby railway but his philosopher son had sufficient foresight to take him out before the crash came. [61] According to a contemporary comment: "Every nook and avenue of England which, with any shew of decency, could be described in a public print as 'an important district', abounding in traffic of a certain description, was forthwith occupied by an incipient railway company." [62]

Every symptom of a speculative security boom was present, with increasing public optimism, with rising stock prices of existing companies and with the formation of new companies. The particularly serious aspect of this speculative movement was that the investment in railways locked up large amounts of capital in fixed assets and so absorbed the liquid capital of the money market. [63] The reaction finally came in 1846 and railway securities fell sharply. The total losses on railway securities were estimated at over £100,000,000 thus far exceeding the losses in 1825. [64]

CRITICISM OF SECURITY CAPITALISM

The new system of security capitalism was subject to bitter criticism. There was considerable public opposition to stock exchange operations and particularly to speculation in government bonds which constituted the preponderant bulk of securities in this early period.   The leading critic was William Cobbett who stated that :

Such indeed, is the operation of all great capitals of credit which enable the capitalist by means of banks to multiply the natural power of his stocks even three and fourfold; to grasp, monopolize and control everything . . . Large capitals and credit . . . have a tendency to monopolization and to form a kind of bourgeois and upstart aristocracy with all the faults of the former and without any of its virtues.[65]

Cobbett's attitude has been well etched by G. K. Chesterton in the following words:

He would have been as ready as any merchant or trader to face the fact that man, as God has made him, must make money.   But he had a vivid sense that the money must be as solid and honest as the corn and fruit for which it stood, that it must be closely in touch with the realities that it represented ; and he waged a furious war on all those indirect and sometimes imaginary processes of debts and shapes and promises and percentages which make the world of wealth today a world at the worst unreal and at the best unseen . . . what he was at once predicting and denouncing, like a small cloud that had not yet become a universal fog, was that vast legal fiction which we call finance.[66]

good

The investment bankers were frequently pilloried in the public press, especially because of their loans to foreign governments. These loans were criticised particularly on the basis of their economic disadvantage for they were considered as injuring rather than helping the foreign trade of Great Britain as the funds were applied to build up competing industries.   In the House of Lords it was urged that the owner of capital should be restricted by law from sending his capital out of the country.[67]   "The profitable employment of our own," it was argued "and not foreign people nor slaves, constitutes the wealth and prosperity of the British Empire." [68]   Foreign loans were also scored on political grounds that they were "a mere prop for military despotism." [69]

This opposition to the foreign loan operations of the investment bankers came from varied sources.   At times objection came from particular classes, as the Jews and the Quakers who in 1845 bitterly opposed the loans to Russia.   The *Westminster Review* declared that "it was the duty of the inhabitants of Western Europe to endeavor to prevent further loans being made to Russia."   The article was prophetic, but about eighty years too early, in forecasting that "the spirit of Freedom has gradually but steadily marched eastward until it has at last reached the frontiers of Russia," and concluded with a forecast of a "complete revolution and a repudiation of the Russian debt tomorrow." [70]   At a meeting in the London Tavern in 1849, William Cobden, bitter opponent of the belligerent policies of Lord Palmerston, introduced a resolution that the current Austrian loan was not safe and that armament loans were "unsound in principle and injurious to the interests of nations." [71] The provincial commercial bankers as the financiers of individual capitalism also were loud in their criticism which found vent in their "Circular to Bankers," the official organ of the Association of Country Bankers. These banking critics expressed the resentment of the entrenched though passing individual capitalism in its opposition to the rising security capitalism.

EARLY FINANCIAL JOURNALISM

A necessary institution of security capitalism is its own journalism, and this institution was developed in England in the first half of the nineteenth century. The newspapers of the day, such as the *London Times* and the *Morning Herald* began their "city" article or financial column in 1825.[72] By the thirties there was a well developed financial press, and not only the London but also the provincial newspapers carried regular "city" articles. In time came publications devoted entirely to financial subjects, but they were written mainly for bankers and primarily from the professional viewpoint. A little later the financial press made a broader appeal, and catered to the general public. The *Economist,* founded in 1843 as a journal to sponsor free trade principles, gave increasing space to financial data and attained a high level of journalism.

The new security capitalism had need of developing additional journalistic aids to reach the ever-widening range of individual investors. As long as securities consisted mainly of the bonds of the national government, there was little need of an intensive system of security journalism. However, when corporate securities were first introduced in the market, it became necessary to "educate" the investing public, and thus the art of prospectus writing was born.[73] The educational work of these prospectuses was often reinforced by brief pamphlets which supposedly gave impartial economic and financial information concerning investments. A typical brochure was one entitled "An Enquiry into the Plans, Progress and Policy of the American Mining Companies," written in 1825 by Benjamin Disraeli. This pamphlet was written mainly for the purpose of keeping up the price of certain mining shares.[74]

LACK OF GOVERNMENTAL CONTROL

Notwithstanding the abuses of the rising security capitalism in issuing unsound foreign government and later over-capitalized domestic railway securities, practically no effort was made to place the system under government control. So strong was the prevailing classical philosophy of individualism and of laissez-faire in the eighteen twenties that a member of Parliament in commenting on a bill to charter a fraudulent foreign mining company, said that Parliament "had no right to take upon itself to prevent the citizens of London or the people of England, from disposing of their money in any way they might please." [75]

Opposition in Parliament to the new security capitalism came largely from the Tory members, who, however, were unable to bring about any restrictive legislation.[76]

In the forties there was a feeble effort to control the expansion of security capitalism. In 1844, Gladstone, then a Tory and President of the Board of Trade, became Chairman of the Select Committee on Joint Stock Companies. This Committee in its final report concluded that "periodical accounts, if honestly made and fairly audited, cannot fail to excite attention to the real state of a concern ; and by means of improved remedies, parties to mismanagement may be made more amenable for acts of fraud." The Committee thus accepted the principle of disclosure that protection of the investor in corporate securities rested in giving him the truth about the securities which were offered to him.[77] The Committee's report formed the basis of the Companies Act of 1844 which required the registration of prospectuses. This Act marked the beginning of legislative protection of security purchasers in England. The Committee, in general, took a narrow view of the necessary extent of governmental control in the conclusion that "the imposition of statutory regulations and prohibitions calculated not merely to put a stop to the activities of the wrong-doer but to place quite intolerable fetters upon private business."

Gladstone attempted to extend a degree of regulation over the railroads in the Railroad Bill of 1844. The original bill contained a provision giving the government a limited right to purchase the railways then being constructed, but this provision was rejected by Parliament. Probably one reason for the elimination of this and other regulatory provisions of the bill was the fact that 157 members of Parliament were listed on the registers of the new railway companies.[78] Economic self interest as well as economic reasoning thus explains the parliamentary support for a laissez-faire policy in relation to British security capitalism throughout the second quarter of the nineteenth century.

CONCLUSION

Thus throughout the eighteenth century the origins of security capitalism may be traced in the growing volume of government securities, in the increase in the number of holders of such securities and in the formation of the London Stock Exchange. Over these years individual capitalism still prevailed. However, in the period from the close of the Napoleonic wars until the middle of the nineteenth century, under favorable political and economic conditions, security capitalism made its appearance along with declining individual capitalism. At the beginning of the period the latter system was still dominant and continued to finance the economic transformation of England with capital supplied by the individual entrepreneurs and credit furnished by the commercial banks.

However, the institutional characteristics of the new system of security capitalism were taking definite shape. First came the rise of public security investment when Europe and South America floated bond issues in London. Then with the growth of corporations came private securities particularly for financing railroads, and this development of transportation with the exception of banking was the only important phase of the industrial revolution which was financed by security capitalism. Coterminously came the accumulation of funds seeking such security investment. For the first time in English history came the widespread diffusion of security holdings which is one of the fundamental characteristics of security capitalism. In order to bring together these forces of the supply of and the demand for security investment, there developed the necessary machinery in the form of investment banking houses organized to place new securities, stock exchanges operated to facilitate the purchase and sale of outstanding securities and a security journalism conducted to disseminate financial information to the investing public. The supply of capital at first exceeded the demand, and the presence of this surplus capital led to an increase in demand for new securities. The volume of these new securities increased temporarily and overinvestment led to the crises of 1825 and of 1846. In both cases the increased volume of new securities was accompanied by a decline in the quality of these securities, and eventually brought losses to the holders. However, over this period there was little governmental control of security capitalism with the exception of the adoption of the disclosure principle in the Companies Act of 1844.

A supply of savings and capital seeking investment and exceeding the demand for it encouraged an increased volume of new securities plus a decline in quality and ultimate losses.

CHAPTER 3

TRIUMPH OF BRITISH SECURITY CAPITALISM

1845-50?
1895

THE period from the end of the forties until the early nineties marked the triumph of British security capitalism. This period, which falls within the Victorian era, was the high tide of England's economic prosperity. The knowledge of her scientists, the shrewdness of her business men and the intelligence of her bankers brought to her shores a material prosperity and a social well-being never before attained in any country up to that time with the possible exception of the United States. Agriculture entered its "golden age," for farming under advanced methods of cultivation was conducted with satisfactory results. Over these years England became the manufacturer, the merchant and the banker for the world. The power which drove the wheels of industry in this period was steam, and for this purpose England possessed the richest coal deposits in all Europe.[1] The output of coal, pig iron, and steel expanded.[2] Although the output of England's factories increased, there was no oversupply of goods, as new foreign markets were continually developed. True, the Continent was also becoming industrialized, and Western European countries were now largely satisfying their needs for finished goods from their own factories and mills. England, however, found markets in other parts of the world, including her own colonies, as well as in the Far East and in the new countries in South America.

The population of England in the latter half of the nineteenth century grew rapidly and provided an ever-increasing domestic demand for British goods. The economic, financial and social system of the Victorian era thus was flexible, and was capable of adapting itself to the changes taking place in a dynamic society.

PHILOSOPHIC INTERPRETATION OF SECURITY CAPITALISM

The second half of the nineteenth century was marked by rapid intellectual progress, and there was a growing reliance on pure ratiocination as a means of solving the problems of the day.[3] Particularly was this true in the field of economic theory. A leading interpreter of developed British security capitalism was Walter Bagehot who, as a banker, was a successful practitioner and, as editor of the *Economist*, was also a keen student of the system. Another close observer was Viscount Goschen who grasped the significance of the institutions of the new system. John Stuart Mill, writing in the middle of the century, was naturally more conscious of the meaning of the new system than the earlier classicists. The growing importance of the corporation over these years may be seen by contrasting the economic views of Adam Smith and of Mill. While the former failed to foresee the future position of the corporation, the latter fully recognized its significance particularly in the field of large scale operations.[4] Mill likewise sensed the importance of capital in the new economic system.[5] He accepted the classical theory of the value of saving, but with certain qualifications. In commenting on "The Tendency of Profit to a Minimum," he observed that in developed countries capital could tend to become so great that it might threaten the extinction of profits.[6]

In general the Victorian period was an age of economic self-satisfaction and the favorable attitude of the general public to security capitalism was reflected in the following contemporary article on the growth of capital:

Millionaires benefit mankind more than themselves. In their search for new millions, they lead to universal enrichment; in themselves attaining leisure, they win it for others. They are ranged on the side of peace and good-will among men; and however greedy of wealth personally, are allied with the practical moralists of the age. The ministers and servants of economy, they throw down the ramparts erected by barbarism against the intellectual and ethical progress of our species, and proclaim the fraternity of mankind. They drag the savage from his cave and make him share in the gains of civilisation; they lift the felon from his lair and bid him toil at honest work; they bid labour economise *its* capital, and place it in the general reservoir of wealth, thereby to share yet more largely in the triumphs of trade. Thus war, pestilence, and famine disappear, and peace, health, and plenty prevail.[7]

ABSENCE OF FINANCIAL IMPERIALISM

The Continent was disturbed by a series of conflicts which had ominous political effects for the future, but in which England was not a direct participant except the Crimean War. It engaged in a number of "little" wars, and in the second half of the nineteenth century gained additional overseas territory. With the exception of the Egyptian War, these conflicts and this expansion had little relation to banking security capitalism. In fact, the Marxian charge, that security capitalism leads to "imperialistic" wars waged to advance or to protect the interests of bankers and bondholders, is not justified by the actual facts of England's financial and political history. In spite of the extensive political power and the vast economic strength of the British holders of foreign securities, they rarely forced their government into a policy of collecting unpaid debts by battleships or by bayonets. Defaults by foreign governments on the bonds floated and held in England were numerous in these years, and the circumstances of these repudiations were often exasperating. Nevertheless, the British government did little to protect the interests of British holders of foreign securities.[8]

This passive attitude of the government was severely criticised by the financial press which felt that the government was not giving sufficient protection to the holders of foreign securities.

GROWTH OF CORPORATIONS

In the previous period the corporate form of organization had grown by fits and starts. In the boom years of 1824–1825 and of 1844–1845, the number waxed considerably only to wither in the lean years which followed. Now the growth of corporate organization was continuous and sustained. The number rose from 700 in 1855 to 2,000 in 1864 and to 7,900 in 1883.[9] The impetus for this increase came in 1855 when the limited liability feature of corporate organization was definitely specified in the Companies Act of that year.[10] This statute marked the passing of the dominance of individual capitalism and the beginning of the supremacy of security capitalism. The single owner and partnership forms of business organization were at last replaced by the corporation, and the personal element in business now gave way to the impersonal character of corporate organization.[11] So reckless was the formation of many of these new companies that the master of the rolls declared : "no doubt many companies were started for the purpose of being wound up."[12]   This unsatisfactory result of the new Companies Act cast serious doubt on the advantages of limited liability which was in consequence characterized as a "pestilential principle."[13]

DEVELOPMENT OF FINANCIAL ORGANIZATION

These years witnessed a rapid development of financial institutions such as the Bank of England, the commercial banks, the overseas banks, the investment banks, the investment trusts and the stock exchange. The Bank of England continued its passive policy toward security capitalism. However, in one important respect the new system was recognized by the Bank and that was in granting loans on marketable securities listed on the London Stock Exchange except mining shares, and even on unlisted securities if they were sound and if their value could be ascertained.[14]

For a number of years the large commercial banks developed branches throughout the country, and absorbed many of the private banks. This movement was accelerated by the Companies Act of 1862 which facilitated the formation of incorporated banks. By the end of the century the large banks were absorbing not only private but also the smaller joint stock banks of the interior. Thus passed the provincial commercial banks which had financed the individual capitalism of the early nineteenth century. The new amalgamated joint stock banks, while mainly engaged in extending commercial credit, also participated to an increasing degree in the financing of security operations. By the close of the century there was a decline in the volume of commercial paper in the form of bills, and an increasing amount of bank credit was being applied to security operations. One financial commentator stated:

Turning now to the stockholders, we find that they have of late years occupied an increasing share of the portion of bank capital utilized on the Money Market, and the reason of this is to be looked for in the gradual diminution in the number of bills seeking discount happening in conjunction with, and in spite of, the rapid increase of banking funds and general business. Consequently bankers have been obliged to devote greater attention to the third division of the financial system, and lend to a greater extent on negotiable securities.[15]

Not only did this indirect participation of the commercial banks in security capitalism increase, but their direct holdings of investments also rose over these years. Thus the British banks, generally regarded as the outstanding example of pure commercial banking, actually were abandoning the orthodox theory and were becoming a part of the financial machinery of security capitalism.

Special overseas banks were also founded to facilitate the expansion of foreign trade and investment. These banks operated in undeveloped countries on the Continent, in the Near East, the Far East and Latin America.[16]

Investment banking now reached maturity. Barings and Rothschilds grew in power, but other firms also became important issuers of securities. Investment banking in this period became more aggressive in its methods. An observer remarked: "Now we have wealthy firms, with large machinery, whose whole time and staff are devoted to hunting about the world for powers to bring out loans."[17] British houses, instead of operating alone, now formed syndicates or groups for the purchase and the sale of securities, since issues became so numerous and so large that no one house was willing to assume the entire risk and by means of the syndicate it was spread over a number of distributing houses.[18] Investment banking became more impersonal in its relation to both the issuer of securities and particularly to the investing public, as securities were more widely diffused. With this growing impersonality came the inevitable weakening in the individual responsibility of the issuing bankers for their security offerings.[19]

The British investment houses, as in the previous period, continued to limit their activities mainly to the flotation of foreign government bonds. Meagre interest was shown in financing the needs of home industry. British industry was now financed largely through the issuance of securities which were handled through small promoters rather than through the great investment houses. Thus in England security capitalism did not develop a close relation between industry and investment banking. Critics of security capitalism, as Nicolai Lenin, who were more familiar with the Central European system made the error of considering this relationship a necessary feature of the system.[20]

The British investing houses, however, exerted extensive financial power. It was charged that these institutions so controlled the money market that, despite the Bank of England, they were able to keep rates low in order to facilitate the flotation of their issues. "The great capitalists," declared the *Statist*, "have strained every nerve to make money cheap, and they have succeeded. And, although the Bank of England rate of discount remained at 5 per cent, the discount rate in the open market in London on the Wednesday was barely 2⅞ percent, and last week the discount houses lowered the rates they allow on deposit ½ percent." [21]

Over these years, England also developed the investment trust as an institution of indirect investment. Investment trusts were first organized in the sixties, and until the end of the eighties their growth was gradual and on a sound basis. However the number of trusts multiplied rapidly in the years from 1888 to 1890.[22] Investors unwisely gave the managers of these trusts blanket power to operate as they saw fit. For example, the L'Association Limited was organized to carry on business "without limit or restriction . . . in any kind of business, profession or calling . . . in every part of the world." [23] The *Investors' Review* spoke of the investment trust as "really only a stock gambling and loan and company floating machine, or it is a rubbish heap which firms, overloaded with unsalable securities have established for their own relief." [24] The reaction in the security market in 1890 brought heavy losses to the investment trusts.[25] However by 1895 the trusts had recovered from these reverses, and thereafter generally followed sound policies.[26]

By the middle of the century the London stock exchange attained undisputed supremacy of the nation's security market. Through the second quarter of the century several of the provincial exchanges had developed considerable local importance, and these interior markets took an active part in financing the railroads.[27]   However, the subsequent crash in railroad securities contributed largely to the decline of these provincial exchanges.   Furthermore, as the local railroad lines were merged into major systems with terminals in London, the capital requirements for such consolidations were so large that they could be satisfied only in London.   The London Stock Exchange therefore expanded its transactions in railway secur- ities, and at the same time increased its already extensive listings of government obligations.   Thus in the period of the fifties and sixties the provincial security markets lost their significance and the Lon- don Stock Exchange came to dominate the security transactions of the entire nation.[28]

With the Bank of England assuming the note issuing function, with London commercial banks absorbing the provincial banks, with investment banking concentrated, with the investment trusts expanding their operations and with the London Stock Exchange holding undisputed sway over security transactions, London now became the financial metropolis of the world.

"PERFECTION" OF SECURITY JOURNALISM

Part of the financial press continued to serve the interests of the investment bankers faithfully, but the welfare of the investors was at times forgotten.   The city editor of the *London Times*, Marma- duke B. Sampson, was a director in the Rothschild-controlled San Paulo Railway.   Sampson seldom missed an opportunity to com- ment favorably on Brazilian and on Russian securities.   He was finally forced out in 1874, retiring with the consolation which could be derived from a large fortune—the well-earned result of his efforts in security journalism.   Fortunately another part of the press re- mained true to the standards of honest financial journalism.   The *Statist* particularly criticized many of the unsound practices of the financial market, and the *Economist* did its best to interpret fairly the important changes occurring in the financial world.

The art of prospectus writing, the crude beginnings of which were observed in the previous chapter, now attained perfection. The *Statist* described the sales-promotion method of the "financier" of the day as follows: "His [the financier's] 'literary man' has turned out the prospectus for him in fine Johnsonian periods, garnished with statistics, and illuminated with some beautiful flights of fancy."[29]   The flotation of corporate securities also gave rise to a new class of lawyers who specialized in company promotion.   "Law- yers are to be found," says a correspondent in the *Statist*, "who will lend their services to any of the most abominable schemes devised under the shelter of the Limited Liability Acts . . . the City is crammed with legal advisers who take sides with wicked promoters and dishonest directors against the poor suffering shareholder."[30]

CHANGING DEMAND FOR CAPITAL

The decline in the demand for long-term capital by the national government, in operation ever since the close of the Napoleonic Wars, continued.[31]   However this decline was more than offset by the increase in the demand from foreign governments.   After their losses in 1825 British investors were discouraged from buying the bonds of South American governments, and it was not until the sixties that these obligations were again floated on a large scale in the London market.   The history of any bond cycle shows that it generally passes through recurring stages as to the quality of bonds issued.   In a period following a financial reaction only bonds of the highest quality are taken by investors.   As these bonds rise in price and as their yields decline, investors are tempted into securities slightly below the highest quality.   In the course of time, medium-grade and finally low-grade bonds are issued.   This was true of the cycle of foreign bonds in the sixties and seventies in the English security market.   Some of these bonds issued at the later stage of the cycle were of a decidedly low-grade quality.

The demand of domestic industry for short-term capital fell off markedly in these years.   This decline was in large measure due to the improvement in international transportation and in communication.   The replacement of sailing vessels by steamships shortened the period during which goods were in transit.   The opening of the Suez Canal reduced the length of time necessary for shipping cargoes to the Far East.   As a result, capital used to finance these transactions was not tied up for so long a period.   Also the telegraph gave better control of overseas business transactions.   The effect of these mechanical improvements on methods of financing is described by the *Statist* as follows:

Active business men want less floating capital, and what has been so set free has, year after year, pressed upon the markets for fixed investments, assisting the rise in the latter, and the supply of long investments has by no means kept pace with the demand.[32]   *in 1860's*

These forces marked the decline in the demand for short-term capital and therefore the lessened importance of commercial finance. On the other hand the domestic demand for long-term capital for financing fixed improvements developed rapidly in the last half of the century as evidenced by the fact that the volume of new corporate issues rose considerably over these years.

As a result of the rapid growth of new issues, the volume of securities listed on the London Stock Exchange increased, and in 1875 the amount was as follows:

TABLE 3

SECURITIES LISTED ON THE LONDON STOCK EXCHANGE, 1875.[33]
(pounds sterling)

CLASSES OF SECURITIES	AMOUNT	PERCENT OF TOTAL
Government..............	3,030,261,594	67.95
X Railway.................	1,115,792,562	25.02
Bank (paid up)............	96,067,686	2.16
Other companies (paid up)..	217,337,286	4.87
Total.....	4,459,459,128	100.00

From these figures it is seen that government issues, both domestic and foreign still dominated the security market, but the proportion had declined from almost 80 percent in 1843 to 67.95 percent in 1875. Corporate securities increased due particularly to the large volume of railroad securities which now constituted 25.02 percent of the total. Also the total volume of securities rose from £1,118,831,174 to £4,459,459,128. The proportion of these total securities to national wealth rose from 27 percent to 52 percent. These figures give quantitative evidence of the increasing importance of security capitalism in the third quarter of the nineteenth century.

ABUNDANT SUPPLY OF CAPITAL

Ever since the end of the eighteenth century, London had been a city of refuge for foreign capital seeking to avoid loss and confiscation due to political uncertainties at home. For a time after the close of the Napoleonic Wars, the amount of such foreign capital in London declined.[34] However, the revolutionary movement of 1848 caused widespread fear among European capitalists who transferred their funds to England which seemed to stand out as the one safe haven in the disturbed world of the time.[35] Throughout the latter half of the nineteenth century the London market continued to attract large funds from abroad, even though political conditions on the Continent generally remained quiet. Of the total securities listed on the London Stock Exchange in 1875, as indicated in the preceding table, about £2,000,000,000 were held abroad.[36]

The domestic supply of capital increased rapidly over these years. National wealth rose from £4,100,000,000 in 1840 to £9,400,000,-

ooo in 1890, and national income from £335,000,000 in 1860 to £669,000,000 in 1890.[37]   Due to the decrease in commodity prices, the increase in real wealth and income was even greater.[38]   The burden of the government debt grew lighter, and the annual interest charge absorbed a declining proportion of the national income. The percentage of debt service to national income declined from 8.7 percent in 1860 to 3.7 percent in 1890.[39]

The position of the lower class improved over this period and it shared to an increasing extent in the growing wealth of the nation. In 1851 there were 1,300,000 families with incomes from £150 to £1,000, while in 1881 there were 990,000 more.   This represented a more rapid rate of increase than that of population over these years.[40] Viscount Goschen in his study, well documented by statistics of the time, concluded that there was a growth in the number of these moderate incomes greater in proportion than that of the large incomes.[41]

DECLINE IN BOND YIELDS

For certain periods of time, particularly between 1883 and 1890 when there was an investment boom, the rate of investment exceeded the rate of saving.   However, this condition was exceptional, and the rate of saving outstripped and the rate of investment.   The effect of this excess of supply over demand for capital was reflected in the decline in bond yields.   The yield on British government bonds dropped from 3.11 percent in 1850 to 2.76 percent in 1900 and in consequence the price of these securities rose sharply.[42]   Not only British government but also high-grade corporate bonds rose in price.   Evidence of this tendency is seen in the course of the debenture stock [43] of the leading British railway companies which, being irredeemable and involving only a small element of risk, reflected directly the current rate of interest.   The debenture stock of the London Southwestern railroad, a leading system, rose from a price of 93 in 1867 to 120 in 1896.[44]

The disproportion between the volume of saving as compared with the volume of investment and the decline in the rate of interest were viewed with concern by the financial press.   In 1887 the *Statist* observed that:

Every year the savings in this country are very large, and a considerable portion of those savings go into investments in Stock Exchange Securities. If the amount of Stock Exchange Securities remained constant, it is clear, therefore, that the tendency of prices would be perpetually upwards.   The money seeking investment growing larger and larger every year, while the investments themselves remained the same, price must go up; . . . outside the United States there has not been so rapid a creation of securities as would absorb all the new capital, nor even a large proportion of the new capital . . . the creation of securities is not excessive; and certainly it is moderate here at home compared with the savings of the country.[45]

In the latter part of the period under review the question was raised: "Is it that the savings of the world are becoming too great for the requirements of the world, and that capital is to depreciate so much that practically the business of banking threatens to become unprofitable, and that it will require hundreds of thousands of pounds for a private family to live out of its investments in even moderate comfort?" [46]

MODERATE CONTROL OF SECURITY CAPITALISM

Throughout this period the economic philosophy of laissez-faire was still so strong that there was only moderate governmental regulation of security capitalism. Some effort was made to eliminate the abuses resulting from the use of the corporate form of business organization. In 1867 the disclosure principle was broadened by amending the Companies Act to require that a prospectus contain a statement of the dates and the names of parties to every contract into which the promoters had entered with the company.[47]

The Stock Exchange had so far operated under the deed of settlement issued in 1802.[48] In 1877 a Royal Commission, after studying security operations recommended that the Exchange be incorporated and have the power to license brokers. The Exchange was therefore given a legalized monopoly of the stock brokerage business.[49] This change in the legal basis of the Exchange was recommended by the Commission not because it desired closer governmental regulation of the Exchange, for the Commission made it clear that regulation of the Exchange should be outside of the jurisdiction of the government. The Commission made a number of recommendations to check speculative irregularities, but urged that these reforms should be instituted by the Exchange itself. As the Exchange voluntarily accepted most of the recommendations, there was no agitation for governmental regulation of the security market. Thus British security capitalism in this period continued to operate with little governmental control.

THE BARING CRISIS — AN INTERLUDE

The suspension in 1890 of Barings, so closely associated with the London capital market since the eighteenth century, serves as a striking interlude between the passing of triumphant British capitalism and the coming of the crisis at the close of the nineteenth century. This episode was an ominous harbinger of the gloomy events that were to follow. The immediate cause of the suspension of Barings was the default of the Argentine government. The relation between Baring Brothers and Argentina had been close since the second quarter of the century. Over this entire period, according to the *Investors' Review*, "It cannot be said that the Federal Government ever met its foreign debt charges squarely from revenue. On one pretext or another the money was always borrowed." [50] In 1884 the debt of the country was £42,600,000 and by 1891 the combined internal and external debt had risen to £154,500,000 or an increase of £112,000,000 in less than seventeen years. There was, according to the *Investors' Review* :

no equivalent value of permanent public works to show in return. The Government of the country condoned an expenditure far in excess of their legitimate income. They have squandered all available assets to meet the continually accruing liabilities. They drew bills on the future until their credit became worthless.[51]

As early as 1887 the *Statist* sharply criticized Barings for its mishandling of Argentine finance, and declared that the prospectus of the Province of Buenos Aires issued by Barings was "without one word of explanation as to its object, or the slightest reference to the indebtedness and resources of the state." [52]

International economic conditions at the beginning of the nineties became unsettled and the difficulties of the London market were intensified.[53] British security capitalism, now thoroughly internationalized, suffered from these disturbed conditions throughout the world, and in 1890 Barings was forced to suspend.[54] The associates of the embarrassed house made every effort to extricate it from its difficulties. A so-called "Argentine Committee" was formed under the presidency of Lord Rothschild, and held frequent meetings at the Bank of England. The operations of this Committee were severely critized by the editor of the *Investors' Review,* who publicly accused the Committee of bad faith on the ground that:

in its short-sighted attempt to save the situation so that the big people and institutions 'caught' in the Argentine smash might unload on the public, in actual fact did its best to furnish the Argentine people with an irresistible argument in favor of open and complete default.

He added the comment that :

Their proposals fittingly crown the edifice of folly which the loan mongers had built. Primarily their motives seem to have been benevolent towards themselves alone, as creditors of the Baring estate. They wished, speaking vulgarly, to 'fake up' an appearance of solvency for Argentina in order that the balances of unplaced loans held by the Baring House, and by the maimed houses surrounding it, might be quickly sold. The investing public would have cruelly suffered by this 'deal', as it had already done by the previous financial operations, but to the loan monger the sorrows, losses, and misery of such are invisible, and therefore to be disregarded.[55]

The reserves of the Bank of England fell sharply, and again it was forced to borrow from the Bank of France.[56]

CONCLUSION

Aided by favorable economic, political and social forces, as increasing industrial production, expanding foreign trade, relative international peace and a growing population, British security capitalism attained its full development in the latter half of the nineteenth century. Although the national debt was steadily reduced, the total volume of security investment rose due particularly to the increasing amount of foreign government bonds and railroad issues. The supply of capital available for the security market was augmented, and there was a continuation of the popular diffusion of the holdings of securities. In general, the system brought economic benefits not only to investors, because of the rise in the price of their securities but to all classes because of their participation in the increase in national income and wealth. The closing years of the century, however, were marked by the suspension of Barings—which symbolized the end of the development of British security capitalism.

CHAPTER 4

PRE-WAR CRISIS OF BRITISH SECURITY CAPITALISM

JUST as the Periclean age marked the height of Athenian civilization so the Victorian era was the apogee of British security capitalism. While the last quarter of the nineteenth century in general witnessed the high tide of British economic well-being, evidences of a decline were apparent even a generation before the Golden Jubilee of Queen Victoria.[1] British agriculture faced increasing foreign competition even in the later part of the developed stage of security capitalism. The Richmond Commission, appointed to inquire into the "depressed condition of agriculture and the causes to which it is owing," reported on the unfavorable results of "foreign competition aggravated by the increased cost of production."[2] The output of the leading industries as coal, iron and steel as well as general industrial production rose over these years.[3] However, the rate of growth declined after the third quarter of the nineteenth century.[4] In contrast to this slackening rate of increase in production, other nations as Germany and the United States were experiencing a rapidly increasing rate.[5]

A large part of the well-being enjoyed by England in the period of triumphant security capitalism was based on the flourishing state of the export trade. True, the export trade of Great Britain rose, but that of other nations increased more rapidly.[6] As noted before, when the industrial revolution spread to the Continental nations, and led to the industrialization of these countries, their factories supplied their own markets and thus displaced the wares of British manufacturers. They, however, turned to the colonies and to the countries of South America and of the Far East which absorbed the increased output of the British factories, and so there had been no maladjustment between the supply and demand for British goods. Now, however, the Continental manufacturing countries and also the United States unable to dispose of the increasing output of their goods at home turned to the South American and Far Eastern markets, and so came in direct competition with British products. On this competition for overseas markets, Engels, the co-worker of Karl Marx, sarcastically commented: "Even the Negroes of the Congo are now to be forced into the civilization attendant upon Manchester calicoes, Staffordshire pottery, and Birmingham hardware."[7] New markets could no longer be found for the manufac-

tured goods of England, and as a result there was a growing maladjustment between British production and foreign demand. The
keenness of competition was evidenced by the fact that goods
stamped "made in Germany" were dumped in the English home
market.

Not only was Great Britain facing a relatively declining foreign
market but even the home market was no longer expanding at the
former rate. The birth rate in England had reached its maximum
by 1876.[8] The death rate continued to fall due to the improvement
in public health, and so there was a net increase in population.
However the decennial rate of increase tended to decline after the
decade ending in 1881. The purchasing power of the home market
was further restricted as the proportion of the unemployed to the
total employable population rose after 1890.[9]

Leading British economists and statesmen were fully conscious
of the difficulties facing their country. Inglis Palgrave, in a speech
as early as 1883, was reported as saying that "the days of great trade
profits in England were over, and there was a pause in the progress
of several great branches of industrial labor. The country might
almost be said to be entering the non-progressive state."[10] Looking
back over this period, Lloyd George in 1933 said: "If we had not
had a great war, if we had gone on as we were going, I am sure that
sooner or later we would have been confronted with something
approximately like the present chaos."[11]

These changing economic conditions influenced the trend of
British politics. In 1906 the Conservatives were forced out of office
by the Liberals lead by Asquith and Lloyd George. The new government promptly entered upon a program of social legislation including provision for an improved workmen's compensation, old
age pensions and unemployment insurance, and also increased the
scope of popular education. The resulting financial burdens were
resisted by the House of Lords, but its opposition was overcome.
Over these years the Labour Party, expressing mainly trade union
principles, grew in strength but did not attain political importance.

GROWING UNSETTLEMENT OF INTERNATIONAL POLITICS

The close of the nineteenth century was marked by growing
unsettlement in international politics. Some of these disturbances
were isolated episodes, as the Spanish-American War, the Boer War,
the Boxer Rebellion and the Russo-Japanese War. Overshadowing
all these local conflicts was the growing international tension on the
Continent which led to the Balkan War and finally to the catastrophe of 1914. None of these conflicts were caused by the actions of

the British bankers.   The Boer War to a large extent was caused by the extensive economic interests of the British in South Africa. However, these investments represented proprietary interests held by large industrial capitalists as Cecil Rhodes, who personified the revived imperialism of the late nineteenth century.[12]   Rhodes obtained the active support of an influential section of the press, particularly the *Times*.   Colonel Younghusband, correspondent of the *Times* in South Africa, carried messages for Rhodes, while Flora Shaw, writer on South African affairs for the *Times*, was confidential representative of Rhodes in London.[13]

British bankers made every effort to avoid the war with Germany up to the very day of the opening of hostilities.   It is said that in the beginning of August, 1914, a committee of bankers called on Lloyd George and notified him that "the interests both of the country and of the world at large demanded that Great Britain should stand aside and should not take part" in the conflict.[14]   Lord Morley, in describing a session at the outbreak of the War, wrote that Lloyd George "informed us that he had been consulting the Governor and Deputy Governor of the Bank of England, other men of light and learning in the city and they were all aghast at the bare idea of our plunging into the European conflict; how it would break down the whole system of credit with London as its center."

PHILOSOPHIC CRITICISM OF SECURITY CAPITALISM

The unsatisfactory trends of security capitalism over this period led to a growing literature of criticism.   J. A. Hobson was a leading critic of the system, and his study on imperialism was a caustic analysis of the effect of international capital movements on backward countries.[15]   Hobson also led the attack on the institution of saving and developed the theory of oversaving.[16]   John M. Robertson criticized the system of security capitalism on the ground that :

much of the saved claim to wealth passes to borrowing States, who spend it on implements of slaughter which in a generation grow obsolete even at that ; and to the mere buying of foreign land.   But it is further notorious that of the annual savings of claim to wealth an immense mass passes away, even on the bankers' books, in respect of futile undertakings for the production of certain forms of wealth.[17]

AMALGAMATION OF BANKS

The movement for banking concentration made rapid progress in the half century before the Great War and as a result the number of joint stock banks declined while the number of branches increased.   By 1914 the London Clearing House banks accounted for

75 per cent of all the deposits in the hands of the English banks, and under these conditions the private banks almost disappeared.[18]

Toward the close of the period before the War there was a rising opposition to the orthodox theory of the function of the British bank and a growing criticism that the British banks were not fully performing their part in the economic system.[19] Professor Foxwell was a particularly severe critic of the orthodox theory. He contended that "the proper and primary business of a banking system is to finance industry and trade," and held that the British banking system was making too great sacrifices on the altar of liquidity.[20]

MALADJUSTMENT OF CAPITAL MARKET

With the beginning of the new century the demand for capital, especially by the national government, changed markedly in nature. The decline of the British national debt in progress since the decade after the Napoleonic Wars came to an abrupt end in 1900 when England issued several loans to finance the Boer War.[21] Even after the direct war expenditures ceased, the government budget continued to show deficits caused largely by the further preparation for war.[22] The government was therefore forced to re-enter the capital market. In the field of local governmental organization, there was a trend toward consolidation. Smaller governmental units were replaced by larger units through the amalgamation of towns into county boroughs, and also through the creation of special bodies as the Metropolitan Water Board.[23] These larger local governmental units necessarily expanded their functions, and increased their borrowings. As a result the debt of the local authorities rose from £348,135,745 in 1900 to £651,768,729 in 1914.[24]

A third drain on the capital market was the borrowing of the British colonies. As part of the policy of empire building, Parliament passed an act making colonial bonds eligible as trustee securities. The creation of this artificial market for the securities of the colonies enabled them to borrow on very favorable terms, and they were quick to take full advantage of this opportunity. This step added about £300,000,000 to the volume of eligible trustee securities.[25] There was also an increased demand for capital on the part of domestic industry, particularly the new fields as electricity. Foreign borrowing in the London market increased at a rapid rate due to a number of factors. Foreign nations, particularly those on the Continent, sought additional funds to carry out social reforms and to meet their increased military expenditures. At the same time the supply of capital available on the Continent was contracting, for Germany was reducing the proportion of its foreign investment and even France, growing uneasy over disturbed international conditions, was inclined to keep its funds at home.   London, therefore, was the only available major international money market willing to meet these foreign demands.   As a result of this increased domestic and foreign demand, the annual volume of new issues in the London market rose enormously.[26]

While the rate of investment was increasing sharply, the rate of saving went forward at a slower pace.   From 1890 to 1913 the nominal amount of national wealth rose from £9,400,000,000 to £14,310,000,000   and   national   income   from   £669,000,000   to £951,000,000.[27]   However over these years commodity prices also rose, and so the increase in real wealth and real income was smaller. In fact Bowley concluded that after 1900 national income measured in pounds sterling "barely kept pace with the diminishing value of money" and that "real income increased little faster than the population."[28]   A check in the rate of saving apparently took place as early as the eighties.   Giffen, an authority on this subject, in his address as President of the Economic Science and Statistics section of the British Association stated that :

There is much prima facie evidence to begin with, that the rate of the accumulation of wealth and the rate of increase of material prosperity may not have been so great of late years, say during the last ten years, as in the twenty or thirty years just before that.[29]

One important reason for the decline in saving was the increased absorption of national income by the government through its heavier taxes.   The proportion of its total expenditures to national income rose from 12.9 percent in 1890 to 17.3 percent in 1900.[30]   The increase in government expenditures was partly due to the growing appropriations for the army and navy.[31]   The total revenues of the national government had always been below the hundred million mark until 1896, when they rose to £109,000,000, and ultimately reaching £188,000,000 in 1913.[32]   The local governments also increased their demands upon the national income.   Local taxation for England and Wales increased only slightly from £53,867,000 in 1881 to £57,558,000 in 1891, but by 1901 it mounted to £111,917,000 and by 1914 to £169,325,000.[33]

The increasing rate of investment as compared with that of saving resulted in a maladjustment in the capital market.   After the turn of the century large issues of government securities especially for financing the Boer War flooded the market.   These flotations were not well received, and the British financial press began to use the American expression of "undigested securities."[34]   In the years just before the outbreak of the War, British underwriting syndicates again and again were forced to take over securities which the invest-ing public could not absorb.[35] This unsatisfactory condition led the *Statist* to declare that :

The quantity of new securities is so vast that underwriters and others have begun to call a halt. It is true that the resources of this country in the matter of new capital are very great, but great as they are, it is obvious they have a limit. Doubtless in another generation the amount of new capital that it will be possible to raise in this country may be twice as great as the amount at present. Nevertheless, it is evident that this year we are face to face with a situation in which the amount which the world is demanding is beyond our ability to supply.[36]

Evidence of the maladjustment of the capital market is indicated in the rise in the yield of government bonds from 2.76 in 1900 to 3.39 in 1913, and the consequent fall in price of these securities.[37] The drop in consols was accompanied by a similar fall in highgrade corporate securities. The debenture stock of the London South-western railroad fell from 120 in 1896 to 84 by 1910.[38] Not only bonds but also shares declined in price and the average mean price of British railway ordinary (common) shares fell from 154.762 in 1896 to 107.910 in 1911.[39]

This decline in security prices in turn had serious financial con-sequences. The private savings banks suffered heavy losses on their portfolios and as a result some were reduced almost to a position of insolvency.[40] Commercial banks also were hard hit by this de-preciation of securities. It was estimated that British bankers in 1898 held securities with a market value of £250,000,000 and these experienced a depreciation of about twenty-eight percent over a fourteen year period from 1898 to 1912.[41] Individual investors also suffered from the decline in security values. The English middle class no longer derived an unqualified benefit from security capital-ism. Reviewing this subject in the light of post-war knowledge, John Maynard Keynes commented :

No one who has examined typical lists of investments made by middle class investors in pre-war days would lightly maintain that in practice the investor had proved capable of looking after himself.[42]

GROWTH OF CORPORATE MALPRACTICES

In the security market the period was marked by corporate frauds. Most of the old devices to trap the unwary speculator and some new practices were extensively employed. One unsatisfactory practice was the inclusion on the list of directors of the names of earls, lords and members of the nobility as window dressing.[43] Unscrupulous promoters also used the practice of rushing the public into applications for the shares of new companies by adopting the "open today closed tomorrow" subscription list system. Security prospectuses frequently overstated the facts relating to new issues.[44] The British market also suffered from overcapitalized companies.[45] Commenting on the financial results of the years from 1890 to 1897 the official receiver stated :

There has been lost to the community and gone into the pockets of the unworthy no less a sum than £28,159,482 made up of losses of creditors dealing with companies, £7,696,848, and of loss to the wretched contributors or shareholders £20,462,633.[46]

The movement to eliminate these unsound security practices led to the appointment of the Departmental Committee on Joint Stock Companies. Parliament finally passed the Companies Act of 1900 which sought to overcome some of the flagrant abuses of corporate financing.[47] Toward the close of the period the Stock Exchange itself made efforts to eliminate some of these evils. As a result of the investigation of the Marconi stock, the Exchange undertook a thorough house-cleaning in 1913.[48]

1900 / 1938 USA

1913 / 1938 USA

CONCLUSION

Thus while England was the first nation to experience the rise and development of security capitalism, it was also the first to face the crisis of the system. Already in the period before the War, there were distinct evidences of relative economic decline in agriculture, manufacture and even in foreign trade. These economic difficulties were reflected in the clash between the conservative and liberal parties on the issue of social legislation. Economic philosophy produced a literature which was critical of the institutions of security capitalism. In the field of financial organization the most important trend was the amalgamation of the commercial banks which welded them into a few institutions. These banks departed more and more from strictly commercial operations and engaged in security operations to a greater extent than in the past. There was a complete reversal in the relation of the demand for and the supply of capital with the increase in the relative demand for capital as compared with the supply. As a result, the price of fixed-interest bearing obligations declined, with losses to the individual and institutional holders. The security market witnessed widespread frauds and there was an extension of governmental regulation of corporate practices. These tendencies were symptoms of the growing crisis of British security capitalism in the pre-war period.

How many conditions here are similar to changes in U.S.A. only many years later - 25 to 70 years.

CHAPTER 5

RISE AND DEVELOPMENT OF FRENCH SECURITY CAPITALISM

THE early stage of security capitalism in France covered approximately the period from the close of the Napoleonic Wars to the middle of the nineteenth century or from the passing of the Great Napoleon to the coming of Louis Napoleon. Early French security capitalism rested primarily on the former's policies as to currency, banking, public debt and corporate law. After the disastrous experience with the assignats, French currency was placed on a sound basis in 1803 and remained so despite the costly military operations in the years which followed. The stability of the currency was in a measure due to the operation of the Bank of France which Napoleon I founded in 1800.[1] A further reason for the strength of the currency was Napoleon's policy of having his wars paid by the conquered enemy and not by the French people. Napoleon was definitely opposed to a public debt which he described as "immoral and destructive; silently undermining the basis of the State, it delivers the present generation to the execration of posterity."[2] As a result, by the close of the Napoleonic Wars, France had a much lighter debt and tax burden than England.[3]

Another Napoleonic institution which further aided French security capitalism was the Commercial Code of 1807 with its important sections concerning corporations. The code permitted the formation of a "société anonyme" or a business corporation under a general incorporation law and also recognized the principle of limited liability.[4] The Code formed the basis for the corporate law of a number of Continental countries as they came under the military jurisdiction of the Napoleonic armies.

UNCERTAINTIES OF THE RESTORATION PERIOD

It was fortunate that this foundation of French security capitalism had been firmly built, for it was forced to undergo a severe test in the Restoration period. During the years immediately following the close of the Napoleonic Wars, the position of French public credit was threatened by heavy internal and external burdens upon the public treasury. The restored Bourbons made an effort to reimburse the old nobility for losses sustained during the Revolution and sought to finance this compensation by increasing the floating debt of the government. At the same time the Allies demanded an indemnity of 700,000,000 francs. Pending its payment, France was occupied by armed forces under the Duke of Wellington, and for their upkeep France was to pay an additional sum of 400,000,000 francs.

As a result, French public credit declined, and Metternich was said to have expressed his willingness to discount Austria's share of the indemnity payment on the basis of 30 per cent of its face value if he could obtain cash. By the end of 1816 France stopped payment on the indemnity altogether. Reparations payments were finally made by the flotation of an international loan.[5] Thus the new system of security capitalism was used for the first time as a mechanism to force the vanquished to buy off the victors.

The political events from the return of the Bourbons until the middle of the nineteenth century were disturbing and at times had an unfavorable effect on the financial system of France. Political, rather than economic factors, caused most of the French financial crises of this period. The payment of the war indemnity led to a severe crisis in 1818.[6]

Again the revolution of 1830 was followed by difficulties while the revolution of 1848 caused a financial panic in Paris and later in the provinces. The industrial development of France in the second quarter of the nineteenth century was relatively slow as evidenced by the meager output of coal and pig iron particularly when compared with the output of England.[7]

The philosophic writings of this period make little mention of security capitalism. Simonde de Sismondi, in presenting his theory of crises, in part placed the blame upon the banks since they supplied funds to speculators.[8] The writings of Saint-Simon exerted a considerable influence on some of the leaders of the new security capitalism. Saint-Simon accepted in general the economic order of his day, but urged modifications. His school recognized the growing importance of the banker and advocated the reform of the economic structure through the agency of a socialized banking system.[9]

GROWTH OF FINANCIAL ORGANIZATION

The Bank of France was the dominant institution in the financial system of the nation. It was founded on sound principles and was generally well managed. The Bank recovered so rapidly after the Napoleonic wars that it was in a position to assist the Bank of England in its difficulties in 1825 and in 1839. The administration of the Bank of France was vested in a general assembly consisting of the two hundred largest stockholders who in turn elected a governing board of fifteen Regents. With the passing of the years membership on the Board of Regents came to be almost hereditary. Throughout the nineteenth century and until the reorganization of the Board in 1936, the great banking families, as the Rothschilds, the Hottingeurs and the Mallets, had almost continuous membership.[10] The financial system was largely in the hands of this group of private bankers who together constituted what was known as "La Haute Banque."[11]

The progress of incorporated banking was slow in the first half of the nineteenth century. After the close of the Napoleonic Wars there was urgent need for the development of a banking system which could mobilize capital particularly for financing the railroads. To meet this need new banking institutions were formed. Unlike the British incorporated banks these institutions combined both commercial and investment operations by receiving deposits from business houses and at the same time dealing in railroad securities. Such operations were none too carefully performed and most of these banks suspended payment in the crisis of 1848.[12] Throughout the first quarter of the nineteenth century the Paris Bourse played an insignificant part in the financial structure of the nation, as is evidenced by the slow growth in the listing of securities. By 1830 the Bourse listed only thirty securities.[13]

SMALL DEMAND FOR AND SUPPLY OF CAPITAL

In the second quarter of the century the demand for capital increased slowly. The debt of the national government over the entire period rose only moderately in spite of an initial increase at the time of the Restoration.[14] Corporate security investment was confined largely to the railroads and developed only after 1840. The French political and scientific leaders showed no enthusiasm for the new form of transporation. In referring to the railroad, Thiers, the French statesman, grudgingly said : "We must give the Parisians this as a toy, but it will never carry a passenger or a parcel."[15] A prominent French scientist opposed the building of railway tunnels on the ground that passengers would be suffocated in going through a tunnel even a few yards long.[16] It was not until well into the forties that the railroads attracted capital on a large scale. Over these years France was still a borrower of foreign capital and not a lender, and even as late as 1848 there were only six types of foreign securities traded on the Paris Bourse.[17]

The supply of capital likewise increased slowly over the second quarter of the century. From 1820 to 1850 the volume of national

wealth showed almost no change.[18]   The lack of capital in relation
to the even small demand is evidenced by the fact that the yield
on French government bonds rose from 1840 to 1850 at a time when
the yield on British government bonds was declining.[19]

A comparison of the early stage of security capitalism in England
and in France therefore shows that the latter made much slower
progress.   By the middle of the century, England possessed a clearly
defined banking system and an active capital market with a rapidly
growing demand and supply of capital.   In France on the other
hand the banking system except for the central bank was still poorly
defined, while both the demand and supply of capital was comparatively small.

DEVELOPMENT OF FRENCH SECURITY CAPITALISM

The developed stage of French security capitalism covered the
period from the middle of the nineteenth century until the Great
War.   This span of time included the Franco-Prussian War and
the Commune which together served only as a momentary interruption in the growth of the system.   The entire period can therefore
best be studied as a unit, since the various tendencies over these
years were continuous and were unchecked by the political disturbances of the early seventies.

The year 1848 marked a definite milestone in the evolution of
French security capitalism.   The system had been growing very
slowly, and the widespread political and social disturbances in this
year threatened its very existence.   The depreciation in the value
of securities on the Paris exchange within less than two months in
1848 amounted to over 4,700,000,000 francs.[20]   However, after 1848,
French security capitalism entered upon a period of rapid development.   In the second half of the century France passed through the
industrial revolution which quickened the entire life of the nation.[21]

POLITICS AND SECURITY CAPITALISM

The course of security capitalism in France as in no other country was dominated by the political trend.   From the coming of
Louis Napoleon in 1848 until the outbreak of the War in 1914, the
nature of French security capitalism was moulded to meet the needs
of domestic and international political aims.   In this sense, therefore, French security capitalism was political in nature, for it was
extensively employed as a mechanism to finance the aims of the
individuals and the groups which controlled the national government.   Security capitalism made possible Louis Napoleon's vast
schemes of domestic and overseas expansion, later financed the con-

duct and the payment of the Franco-Prussian War and maintained France's share of the armed peace which finally led to the climax of 1914. Colonial expansion in Northern Africa and in the Far East was financed largely by means of loans floated in the home security market.

SECURITY ACTIVITIES OF THE BANK OF FRANCE

Throughout the greater part of its history the Bank of France was under the close control of the government. Under Napoleon I the Bank became merely "an engine of the state." [22] The Bank was frequently forced to grant liberal advances to the national government, and at the close of the Franco-Prussian War these loans exceeded 1,400,000,000 francs.[23]

In the case of England the central bank adopted a passive attitude toward security capitalism and made little effort to guide its growth. The Bank of France, on the other hand, took an active part in aiding the growth of the new system. Under an enactment in 1834, the Bank gave positive encouragement by granting loans on securities directly to individuals.[24] At first these loans were extended only on the obligations of the national and of the municipal governments, but later they were also granted on the stocks and bonds of railroads. The Bank granted advances of from 60 to 80 per cent of the value of the pledged securities. In the early years the rate on these loans was the same as the rate of discount on commercial paper, but when security borrowings grew excessive in the sixties a higher rate was exacted.

Between the years 1858 and 1861 the Bank of France entered upon an adventure in the field of security capitalism which, to say the least, was unusual for a central bank. In these years there was increased activity in railroad building, and to finance some of the new railroad companies, the Bank, acting as an investment dealer, purchased and sold a large volume of railroad bonds.[25] These operations fortunately proved highly successful both to the Bank and to the purchasers, for the bonds experienced a sharp appreciation in price. It is questionable whether the Bank under its statute had the legal power to engage in these financial operations, but they were probably undertaken with the full understanding of the government which was anxious to further railroad building.

Toward the end of the century, the Bank, acting not as dealer but as broker, undertook the execution of stock exchange orders for its clients. Another service which the Bank performed for the growing security capitalism was to provide safe-keeping facilities for securities.[26]

After the Bank of France the most important banking institution was the Credit Foncier which was established in 1852 as a central mortgage bank.[27] Throughout its entire history this institution was under strict control of the government which named its directors and supervised its financial operations.[28] It was first organized to finance urban real estate, but later the Bank extended its activities to aid agriculture. The Bank granted loans not only to individuals but also to cities and to departments. The funds for these undertakings came in part from the Bank's own capital, but largely from the proceeds derived from the sale of its securities to the investing public. Thus the Bank performed an important service to French security capitalism by creating a continuous flow of sound securities to meet the growing volume of French saving.

SPECULATIVE BANKING

It was indeed fortunate that French security capitalism had the stabilizing influence of the Bank of France and of the Credit Foncier, for French banking in the third quarter of the century developed highly unsatisfactory tendencies. The financing of the new undertakings of this period involved a high degree of risk, and so required a large amount of speculative long-term capital. This need led to the development of speculative banks willing to furnish capital to these hazardous enterprises. Furthermore French banking in this period also possessed a peculiar non-financial nature which was destined to lead to troubled waters. In the years of recovery immediately following the disturbance of 1848, French banking under the influence of the theories of Saint-Simon started on the wierd path of basing its policy upon philosophy. Saint-Simon deeply impressed the Perèires brothers who set out to reorganize the financial system on the basis of the former's philosophy by founding the Société Générale de Crédit Mobilier in 1852. The Perèires were Jews and most of their associates were of the same faith. The Rothschilds took no part in the Crédit Mobilier which was really directed against them.[29] The institution was in effect a gigantic holding company engaged in financing and managing industrial enterprises. The securities of the controlled companies were used as assets on which the Crédit Mobilier issued its own securities, to be sold to the public. For a number of years the Bank was highly successful, and performed notable service in promoting railroads and public utilities. The Crédit Mobilier had close relations with Louis Napoleon as Emperor.[30] This relationship in one case did not redound to the welfare of the Emperor or of his Empire. The Emperor became interested in furthering the scientific studies of Alfred

Nobel for improving the manufacture of explosives. The Emperor therefore recommended Nobel to the Perèires who granted an advance to finance a factory in Sweden.[31] This very plant thus financed by French bankers was later destined to bring large profits to its owners in the sale of explosives to the Germans for killing French soldiers in the Franco-Prussian War.[32]

The Bank also extended its activities to foreign countries. It granted financial assistance to Cavour in his preparation for the struggle of Sardinia against Austria. The Rothschilds had refused to extend any funds for this purpose, but the Crédit Mobilier, at a high price for its help, aided the cause of Cavour. He commented upon this change of his financial relations by the statement that : "If after divorcing the Rothschilds we marry Mm. Perèire I think we shall get on very well together."[33] Due to its hazardous stock exchange ventures the securities of the Bank acquired a reputation of being "most dangerous papers" and the Bank itself was termed nothing more than a "gambling den where they played with marked cards."[34] The operations of the Bank proved more and more unsuccessful so that it showed heavy losses in 1866 and in the following year it failed.[35]

The period immediately after the close of the Franco-Prussian War witnessed another ambitious attempt to combine both non-financial and financial objectives in banking. In 1878 the Union Generale was founded for the purpose of attaining certain political and religious as well as financial ends. The institution was formed to support the Royalist cause against the Republic, and also to displace the Jewish bankers who held an important place in the financial system. Finance was thus to be liberated from the Jew and to be "christianized."[36]

The Bank organized a group of business enterprises, and used the simple financial device of applying its funds to purchase its own stock and that of its controlled companies. The consequent rise in the price of these securities then enabled the Bank to increase the capitalization of its companies, and the new funds were again used to purchase the outstanding securities. The market price of the Bank's shares rose sharply from 1,000 to 1881 to over 3,000 in 1882. Then followed the inevitable collapse and the price of the securities dropped to 450 in three weeks. The Bank was then declared insolvent and the officers were arrested.[37]

DEVELOPMENT OF CONSERVATIVE BANKING

In contrast to these speculative financial enterprises conservative banking was also developed. The private savings banks grew in strength, municipal savings banks were formed and in 1881 the government began a national savings bank known as the "Caisse Nationale d'Espargne." [38]

Even more important was the founding of the three conservative commercial-investment banks, the Comptoir d'Escompte, the Société Generale and the Credit Lyonnais.[39]   These banks in time developed a network of branches throughout France and were among the leading institutions in the banking system.[40]   They combined both commercial and investment banking operations.   While most of their funds were placed in commercial assets, the banks engaged actively in security operations through carrying a large portfolio of securities and through buying securities and selling them to the public.   The French investing public, consisting mainly of individuals of small means, was unwilling to trust its own judgment and came to rely on the large banks for direction in the placement of its savings.   A leading official of the Credit Lyonnais in testifying before the National Monetary Commission in 1910 frankly said :

By examining the balances of the accounts of our customers we can know whether they want to invest or not, and then we endeavor to have stocks and bonds to offer to them as they require.[41]

Thus while France developed the system of direct investment it was really controlled by the large banking institutions.   These incorporated banks were formed under the general incorporation law and not under a separate banking statute as in the United States.[42]   The banks were therefore not closely supervised by the government and were not even required to publish detailed reports.[43]

In the last quarter of the century, long-term financing on a conservative basis was developed by the so-called "banques-d'affaires" as the Banque de Paris et des Pays-Bas and the Banque de L'Union Parisienne.   The former institution was created in 1872 as a result of the merger of the Banque de Paris and the Banque des Pays-Bas, a Dutch institution.[44]   The Bank was formed by a small group of powerful industrialists who desired a financial institution of their own for forming and managing security syndicates.[45]   This institution therefore did little business with the public and its deposits were received mainly from the big industrial corporations which had promoted the Bank.[46]   The Bank undertook the financing of railroads, tramways and electrical enterprises.[47]   It therefore invaded the field occupied by La Haute Banque or the group of private bankers active in security flotations since the early stage of French security capitalism.   This group in turn formed the Banque de

L'Union Parisienne as a permanent syndicate of private bankers to protect themselves.[48] The Banque de Paris et des Pays-Bas therefore represented industrial capitalism, and the Banque de L'Union Parisienne stood for banking capitalism. The investment trust, as an institution of indirect investment, made little progress in France due to the activity of the commercial banks in caring for the investment of the funds of the small investors.[49]

IMPORTANCE OF THE BOURSE

After the middle of the century the Paris security market expanded and took an active part in the economic rehabilitation of France following the Franco-Prussian War and the Commune. Both the Bourse and the Coulisse, the Paris curb exchange, aided in floating the indemnity loans and supported the government rentes or perpetual obligations. In fact, the security market was both the means and the expression of recovery after 1871. The succeeding months witnessed a wild speculative rise which could be interpreted either as a gambling frenzy or as an economic revival of a nation arising from the throes of invasion and of social disorder. Leroy Beaulieu, writing in 1897, when the Bourse was being attacked, recalled :

the already remote years of our convalescence, after the invasion, years at once sorrowful and comforting, when with the gloom of defeat and the suffering of dismemberment, mingled the joy of feeling the revival of France. Whence came our first consolation, our first vindication before the world? Whether glorious or not, it originated on the Bourse.[50]

In the course of time, Paris obtained complete supremacy over the security markets of the nation. Lyons for a time developed an important security market, particularly due to the activity of the Credit Lyonnais, and even participated occasionally in the flotation of foreign securities. There were also small security markets in Bordeaux, Toulouse, Lille and Nantes.[51] However by the beginning of the twentieth century the Paris market accounted for most of the security transactions.[52] French financial organization was decidedly monopolistic in nature, and the security market was dominated by a so-called "money trust" which, through its control of credit, had the power to manipulate security prices. Parker in his study of the Paris Bourse claimed that it was possible for this "money trust" seriously to upset the normal market, cause widespread distrust, and demoralize the whole speculating and investing public.[53]

POLITICAL NATURE OF DEMAND FOR CAPITAL

The political nature of the demand for capital in the period immediately preceding the Great War may be seen in the statistics on the distribution of the securities listed on the Paris Bourse. The distribution of these securities by classes is given in Table 4:

TABLE 4

SECURITIES LISTED ON THE PARIS BOURSE, 1906.[54]
(million francs)

CLASSES OF SECURITIES	AMOUNT	PERCENT OF TOTAL
Rentes................................	24,915	18.81
Credit Foncier.........................	4,447	3.36
Paris, departments and colonies...........	2,915	2.20
Railway and navigation companies.........	20,964	15.83
Railways and tramways..................	2,201	1.66
Electric and industrial companies.........	4,453	3.36
Insurance companies....................	703	0.53
Banks and credit companies..............	3,102	2.34
Foreign securities......................	67,773	51.17
Miscellaneous.........................	979	0.74
Total.....	132,452	100.00

This table shows the essentially political nature of French security capitalism. The securities of the French government, the Credit Foncier, as a government institution, and the local governments together accounted for almost a fourth of the total listings. Foreign securities, mainly governmental, constituted over one-half of the total, and private securities including those of railroads, financial institutions and industrial companies together amounted to less than one fourth of the total. It is thus clear that the course of French security investment was determined largely by political forces. Louis Napoleon, unlike his uncle, appreciated the possibilities of the debt-creating power of the government, and as a result the pressure of the government on the capital market during the period of the Second Empire was heavy. Later the Franco-Prussian War and the indemnity to Prussia were financed to an extent by public loans. The ensuing armament race with Germany placed an ever-growing burden on public finance. Expenditure for armament rose sharply, and accounted for about one-fourth of the total expenditures of the ordinary budget.[55] In addition to the huge appropriations in the ordinary budget, the government also maintained a special extraordinary account for armament expenditures financed by short-term borrowing.[56]   As a result of increasing deficits in the budget the national debt rose from 5,426,000,000 francs in 1850 to 12,310,000,000 francs in 1870 and to 33,220,000,000 francs in 1913.[57]   It was estimated that armament accounted for two-thirds of this debt and that only the remaining third went into public works.[58]   Caillaux commented that as an offset for this large debt, France had "only minor industrial possessions composed of a rather poor state railroad system and certain scattered sources of credit, principally railroad companies." [59]

FLUCTUATIONS IN FOREIGN INVESTMENT

As seen in Table 4 the most important demand for capital throughout the second half of the nineteenth century came from the rapid growth in the volume of foreign securities.   After the middle of the century France became a lender in the international capital market.   In 1865 both the Paris and the Lyons markets participated with London in the flotation of an Italian loan.   The Paris market joined with London in the flotation of a Mexican loan to aid the ill-fated Maximilian, and also of a Spanish loan in collaboration with various continental money markets.[60]   As a result, by the opening of the Franco-Prussian War, the volume of foreign securities held by the French was conservatively estimated at 12,000,000,000 francs.[61] These foreign holdings stood the French in good stead, for they were used as a means of meeting a large part of the indemnity payment to Prussia.   As a result, however, the total amount of French holdings of foreign securities was sharply reduced.   The export of capital was soon resumed, and the total amount of French foreign investments rose from 15,000,000,000 francs in 1880 to 40,000,-000,000 francs in 1912.[62]

INCREASE IN SUPPLY OF . CAPITAL

In the period from the Franco-Prussian War until the Great War, the volume of French saving increased rapidly.   The wide diffusion of French saving is indicated in various statistics on indirect and direct investment.   The number of depositors in French savings banks rose from 561,000 in 1849 to 4,321,000 in 1882.   The mass of French people not only invested indirectly in savings institutions but also directly in securities.   The extent of the popularization of security capitalism in France is evidenced by the number of separate entries of holders of national securities on the government books.   There were 291,000 in 1848, over 1,000,000 in 1860,

3,500,000 in 1870 and over 4,500,000 in 1903.[63] It would seem that the rate of saving grew more rapidly than the rate of investment as evidenced by the fact that the yield on government bonds fell from 5.30 percent in 1850 to 3.00 percent in 1900.[64]

CRITICISM OF SECURITY CAPITALISM

Throughout the last quarter of the nineteenth century and the early part of the twentieth century, the attacks on security capitalism were intense. The stock exchange, the banks, and foreign lending were all subject to biting criticism. The attacks on banking security capitalism came from two widely different sources. On the one hand, the system was assailed by the radical critics who charged it with social disutility. In the period immediately preceding the War the large banks were bitterly scored. In 1907 Jaurez, an active radical member of the Chamber and a prominent leader of revisionist socialism declared that :

The public credit establishments must recognize that they cannot make many more mistakes. Their power has grown, they monopolise and centralise in blocks of milliards, the savings and the spending power of this country ; in the measure that their power has grown, so also has grown their responsibility.[65]

The policy of secrecy of the French banks was assailed in the French Chamber of Deputies where one member declared : "We must lift the veil which hides all that goes on in these establishments." [66]

On the other side, banking security capitalism was attacked by the spokesmen of industrial capitalism who directed their shafts particularly against the economic disutility of the international loans of the French banks. Raymond Poincaré, representing the interest of French industrial capitalism, urged a policy of financial and economic nationalism and opposed the export of French capital. A leading advocate of this viewpoint was a publicist named Le Tailleur who conducted a virulent campaign against foreign loans particularly to Germany. "It is thanks to French money," he declared, "treacherously surrendered by our great financial institutions, that Germany has been able to this day to develop her industries, overcome her crises, place her loans, and maintain her monstrous armaments aimed against our country." [67] Public sentiment lashed out against the banker in such statements in the financial press as:

. . . we are the richest nation of the earth ; and if I, personally, am not rich, it is because there are persons who turn these riches off toward foreign countries, whereas a part of them should belong to me. The big financiers grow wealthy at my expense ! Proper laws must be made to prevent such a state of things, and to give me back my share of those millions ! [68]

Defense of French security capitalism came from a well-subsidised press, for in no other great nation did security journalism fall so low as in France. It was a recognized practice for foreign governments borrowing in the French capital market to bribe the French press in advance of a new issue. The Serbian, Argentine, Brazilian and particularly the Russian governments contributed generous largess to the Parisian newspapers.[69]

POLITICAL CONTROL

Control over security capitalism was exercised not so much for the protection of the individual depositor or investor but rather in the interest of the state for purely political purposes. There was therefore practically no supervision over the domestic operations either of the commercial banks or the investment banks. However other institutions affected with political interest were controlled by the state. The Bank of France and the Credit Foncier were of course in the hands of the government. Likewise the state controlled the Paris Bourse and its members were governmental licensees who operated under a government monopoly.[70] In 1880, the government issued decrees giving the minister of finance the right to withhold or to grant listing privileges on the Paris Bourse.[71] Successive ministers of finance made repeated use of this power particularly to regulate the volume of foreign loans in the French money market.[72] Security transactions were further controlled by a law of 1907 which provided that announcements of all issues, sales or introductions of securities were first to be published in the official journal. Regulation was also extended over the Coulisse. In the case of this institution governmental approval for listing was not mandatory, but the government made it clear that such approval was highly desirable before securities were listed.

Denial of the listing privilege was frequently exercised to ban foreign securities from the French capital market. Thus the stock of the United States Steel Corporation was denied listing privilege. In 1908 Argentina placed an order for artillery with the Krupp concern of Germany instead of with the Schneider works of France. As a result, in the following year, when Barings sought to place an Argentine loan in Paris, its admission was prohibited by the French government. The government also banned a Bulgarian loan in 1909, because no orders were to be placed with French manufacturers.[73]

The capital market was particularly used to win the support of Italy and of Russia. Throughout the greater part of the last quarter of the nineteenth century the relations between France and Italy were unfriendly, but by the close of the century a reconciliation was attained in a large measure through the financial assistance granted by the Paris market to Italy.[74] The shortsightedness of this policy of combining international finance and international politics is well represented in the relations between the French money market and the Russian government. In 1906 the Czarist government had been weakened by the Japanese War, and the liberal elements in Russian politics were pressing their advantage for constitutional reform. For a time it seemed as if they would be successful in this objective, as the Czar, financially embarrassed, authorized the convening of a constitutional assembly in the form of the Duma. Here at last was hope that the autocratic Russian government would be reformed in keeping with the principles of western democracy. However, the French capital market granted a loan to the Russian government without waiting to obtain the consent of the Duma. The Czar then promptly dissolved the Duma, since he was no longer under the necessity of asking it for financial aid. A little over a decade later another Russian government repudiated the entire debt owing to France.

CONCLUSION

During the period from the middle of the nineteenth century until the early years of the twentieth century, French security capitalism passed through the developed stage. The period corresponds roughly to the same stage as for England but there was a difference in the rate of growth of the system in the two countries. At the beginning of the period British security capitalism had already reached an advanced state, while in France a mere start had been made. However after the middle of the century France made rapid strides and a mature system was attained by about the eighties. Louis Napoleon was the personification of developed French security capitalism and his Empire became a rococo facade of the new system. The financial institutions in each country were different in nature. The Bank of England took relatively little part in the development of security capitalism due probably to the fact that it had operated before the rise of the system. On the other hand, the Bank of France was started almost simultaneously with the beginning of security capitalism in France and grew up with it. The Bank of France therefore took an active part in the development of the new system. While British banking acquired a specialized nature, French banking tended rather to combine the functions of commercial and investment banking. British banking was actuated solely by economic motives, while French banking throughout the nineteenth century was influenced by non-financial motives as philosophic theories as well as political and even religious prejudices.

British and French security capitalism differed decidedly in the nature of their respective demand for capital over these years. On the one hand the demand for capital by the British government declined from the close of the Napoleonic Wars until the end of the nineteenth century. On the other hand the pressure of the French government on its capital market increased after the middle of the century and became particularly heavy after 1870. While the export of capital was large in the case of both countries, the foreign investments of England were economic in nature and there was an almost complete absence of political pressure. On the other hand the export of French capital was decidedly political in nature. The regulation of security capitalism was undertaken in England for the purpose of protecting the individual against loss, while in the case of France it was exercised to promote the policy of the state. The system of security capitalism in the two countries, therefore, had different characteristics.

CHAPTER 6

RISE AND DEVELOPMENT OF GERMAN SECURITY CAPITALISM

UNLIKE France and England, Germany, in the sense of Prussia and the other German states, continued in the stage of individual capitalism until the middle of the nineteenth century. This arrested development was due largely to the disturbed political history of Germany. Throughout the greater part of the seventeenth, the eighteenth and the early nineteenth centuries the economic development of Germany was checked by the succession of European conflicts from the Thirty Years through the Napoleonic Wars. At the close of this last struggle Germany was in economic ruin. The series of crushing military defeats on German soil and the later War of the Liberation left the country exhausted.

CONTINUATION OF INDIVIDUAL CAPITALISM

The years from the close of the Napoleonic Wars to the disturbances of 1848 marked a period of peace which gave the German people the opportunity for economic rehabilitation. Over these years the economic system of Germany was still very simple. The greater part of the population was engaged in agriculture, the household system of manufacture prevailed, and even textile making continued to be a home occupation. The development of steam power was slow, and as late as 1840 the number of steam engines within the industrial area of the German Zollverein was less than 500 as compared with over 5000 in England by 1810.[1] Little railway construction was started before the middle of the century, and until 1855 there were only short lines operating between the larger towns.

Until almost the middle of the nineteenth century slow progress was made in developing corporate law in most of the German states. True the Hanseatic towns adopted the French Commercial Code which recognized the principle of limited liability and permitted the issuance of corporate charters under a general company law. Due to the need of financing the new railroads, the state of Prussia in 1838 passed a railway company law based on the French Code, and in 1843 enacted a general law for the formation of joint stock companies.[2] However, in most of the other German states a corporation could be formed only by receiving a special charter from the govern-

61

ment. This policy had both an unfavorable and a favorable consequence. On the one hand, it checked the growth of corporations
needed for the financing of railroads and of industry, but at the
same time avoided the security speculation which brought such
heavy losses to both England and France during the first half of the
nineteenth century.

The nearest approach to a central bank among the German
states was the Seehandlung or the State Bank of Prussia founded
by Frederick the Great. It was little more than an adjunct of the
treasury, and its early operations were mainly for the purpose of
financing the needs of the government. After the close of the Napoleonic Wars, the Bank increased its private operations by making
extensive loans to the large landowners.[3] These operations proved
unsuccessful, and as a result over the years a deficit was accumulated
which remained concealed until 1846 when the Bank was forced to
reorganize.

The center of German private banking was the Rhine Valley particularly in the cities of Frankfurt-on-the-Main and Cologne. Frankfurt, the original home of the Rothschilds, developed in importance,
and by the middle of the nineteenth century was one of the leading
financial centers of Western Europe. Even in the eighteenth century
Cologne possessed a number of important families in the field of
banking, as the Schaaffhausen family which later founded the Disconto Gesellschaft, one of Germany's leading joint stock banks.[4]
Most of these families were originally engaged primarily in trade
and only incidentally in banking, but by the early nineteenth century their banking operations became relatively more important.
The surplus funds of the private banks which these families established were later used to finance the early manufacturing and mining
industries of the Rhine Valley. In promoting these industrial undertakings the private bankers introduced the joint-stock form of
business organization, and so they themselves accelerated the transition from individual to security capitalism.

The Berlin Bourse was organized as far back as 1685, but dealings were at first in goods and in foreign exchange. By the end of
the eighteenth century a few securities, as those of the State Bank
of Prussia, were bought and sold, but the security operations of the
Bourse were unimportant during this period.[5]

Under the simple economy of the first half of the century, capital accumulation was very small, and capital, therefore, had to be
obtained from abroad in order to finance any important undertaking. Thus the early gas plants of the German cities were financed
by British capital.

RISE OF GERMAN SECURITY CAPITALISM

German security capitalism passed through the early stage from 1848 until 1870 and the developed stage from 1870 until 1914. The political disturbances of 1848 for a time shook the German states, but after the dramatic events of that year conditions at home again became tranquil. The War of the Liberation against Napoleon had aroused a strong feeling of nationality among the Germans, and led ultimately to the formation of the German Confederation, and the Customs Union laid the basis for the economic unity of Germany.

German industrial production was still small over these years when compared with other countries. Thus in 1860 the industrial output of Germany was still only half that of France. However, moderate progress was made in some fields of economic activity. Railway construction made headway, and the short lines were gradually joined and extended. Also the number of corporations grew rapidly over these years. In the twenty-four year period from 1826 to 1850 only 102 joint stock companies of all classes with a total capital of only 638,000,000 marks were formed in Prussia, while for the nineteen-year period from 1851 to 1870, 295 joint stock companies with a capital of 2,405,000,000 marks were formed.

COMING OF THE GERMAN CREDIT BANKS

As in the case of France, the period immediately after 1848 witnessed the formation of new financial institutions, known in German financial literature as credit banks, which were to supply the foundation of the banking organization of the later period.[6] The Schaaffhausen'scher Bankverein was formed in Cologne, the Bank für Handel und Industrie in Darmstadt, and the Dresdner Bank in Dresden, while the Disconto Gesellschaft and the Berliner Handelsgesellschaft were started in Berlin. In fact, the leading banks, with the exception of the Deutsche Bank, were all founded before 1871. Eventually these institutions located their main offices in Berlin.

It is interesting to note the policy formulated by one of these early banks, the Darmstädter Bank für Handel und Industrie, in determining its relation to the system of security capitalism. According to the first report issued by the Bank, it sought on the one hand to avoid the evils of security capitalism by declaring that "it is in no way the task of the bank to pave the way for stock-jobbing operations, and to stimulate capitalists to unproductive gambling on 'change.'" On the other hand, the Bank aimed to attain for itself and for the community the advantages of security capitalism, since it went on to state that "the bank is expected to promote sound and extensive undertakings by its own participations, and by investing outsiders' funds intrusted to its care."[7] The German banks early in their history improved the methods of investment finance, and in 1859 made use of the syndicate as a method of distributing securities. The Darmstädter Bank was the first to employ this device, and in its report for 1860 declared that the syndicate was an essential device, "since it diminishes the risk of the individual participants and facilitates the accomplishment of the common task."[8]

These years also witnessed a development of a financial press. Frankfurt particularly became the leading center for publications on financial subjects. In this city the *Aktionär* was founded in 1854, and the *Frankfurter Geschäftsbericht,* which later became the *Frankfurter Zeitung und Handelsblatt,* was started in 1856. In Berlin in 1855, the *Berliner Boersenzeitung,* with the supplement of the *Berliner Boersen Courier,* was established. These publications throughout the period under review functioned as excellent organs of security capitalism.

The demand for capital increased over this period. The amount invested in the railroads rose from about a billion marks at the middle of the century to four billion marks by 1870. Also the capital of the joint stock companies increased.

Thus the third quarter of the nineteenth century marked the rise of German security capitalism. While economic progress was slow when compared with other nations, a sound financial organization was established in the form of well-managed incorporated banks which were destined to lead Germany through the period of the development of its security capitalism.

DEVELOPMENT OF GERMAN SECURITY CAPITALISM — POLITICAL SETTING

The domestic and foreign political forces exercised a strong influence on the development of security capitalism in Germany. After the Franco-Prussian War the unification of the German people was accomplished in the formation of the German Empire. Under the domination of Prussia, Germany was now a powerful state able to protect itself from foreign aggression, and capable of assuring its people of peaceful economic growth within its borders. Although provision was made for a legislative body known as the Reichstag, Germany never actually accepted the principle of parliamentary government. The philosophy of eighteenth century mercantilism continued to dominate the attitude of the German state toward economic activities and was the underlying reason for the extensive government regulation of German industry.

The overseas expansion of the German Empire was slow at the outset. Bismarck was more interested in welding the German Empire into a unit, and at first cared little for colonial possessions. However in time, influenced by bankers as Bleichröder, he yielded to the urge for foreign territory, and later Emperor William II extended German power into Africa, Asia and the Pacific until it included territory of over a million square miles and of over fourteen million people.[9] Prince von Bülow could therefore, with true national pride, just before the outbreak of the War, assert that:

The German Empire today is a great world power, not only by virtue of its industrial and commercial interests, but of its power in international politics; its power in the sense that its arm can reach to the farthest corners of the world and that German interest can be injured nowhere with impunity.[10]

INDUSTRIAL TRANSFORMATION

The economic development of Germany after 1870 was probably the most rapid of any country in any period of history until the Great War. The industrial revolution was first experienced in the mining and smelting industries. The importance of this movement was well attested by Sombart in his observation that:

In the coal and iron deposits of Germany lies . . . the explanation why the German economic world turned so decisively to industrial activity during the latter half of the last century, as well as of the intensity of Germany's capitalistic development.[11]

The output of coal, pig iron and steel ingots increased at an astounding rate.[12] The household manufacture of cotton goods disappeared completely by 1870, and thereafter the development of the textile industry was remarkable.[13] In 1879 at the Berlin exhibition the Siemens Company demonstarted the practical operation of the dynamo, and in 1883 the firm installed the world's first electric railway.[14] In the early eighties Emil Rathenau began the development of the German electrical industry through the formation of several companies which were destined to play an important part in the development of electrical power not only in Germany but throughout the world.

In the fourth quarter of the nineteenth century Germany took unquestioned leadership in the field of chemical research. The growth of this activity is well illustrated by the rise of the German dye industry. In 1880 Von Bayer produced synthetic indigo, and this step began the expansion of the German dye industry. By 1913 Germany produced over eighty percent of the world's supply of synthetic dye, while Great Britain accounted for only two percent. The profits from this industry provided the means for financing the experiments of the German chemists who now extended their researches to wider fields, not only to develop the science of industry but also to improve the art of war.[15] As a result of all this activity the general industrial production of Germany rose enormously.[16]

Manufacturing, consequently became more important than the previously dominant agriculture and commerce. In 1871 two-thirds of the population was engaged in agriculture, while in the period before the Great War less than one-third was so occupied.

Throughout the eighteenth and the first half of the nineteenth century commerce had presented the most attractive possibilities for profit, and the merchants were the most influential class in the economic society of the day. However, in the latter half of the nineteenth century, manufacture offered more opportunities, and in time commerce became relatively less important. The leaders in German economic life, in addition to the bankers, were now the industrialists as the Krupps and the Thyssens in the iron and steel industry and the Siemens in the electrical industry.[17] Thus was laid the foundation of industrial capitalism which in the post-war period was to wrest control of the economic and political life of Germany from banking capitalism.

SATISFACTORY SOCIAL CONDITIONS

The increase in population was very rapid, and provided a substantial home market for the products of German industry. At the same time the industrialization of the nation absorbed the increase in population. The opportunities for satisfactory employment in Germany improved, and as a result German emigration fell off considerably. The decline was particularly significant when compared with the increase in the excess of births over deaths.[18]

There was a difference of view among German economists as to the social distribution of income in Germany in the pre-war period. Adolph Wagner was firm in the belief that the increase in national wealth and in national income was poorly distributed. He felt that certain elements were "enriching themselves," and criticised the "constantly growing concentration of income evidenced not only in the case of some particular rich persons, but also by the constant growth in numbers of the classes occupying a high and even the highest place in the economic scale." [19] In support of this view, Wagner showed that in Prussia at the middle of the century only 100 persons were receiving an income of over 100,000 marks, while in the same territory by 1907 3,600 persons were receiving such an income.[20] Confirming this view Gustav Schmoller showed that the number of persons in Prussia paying taxes on income exceeding three thousand marks rose from 123,284 persons in 1873 to 449,741 in 1902.[21]

On the other hand, Riesser demonstrated that this increase in the number of persons receiving large incomes was due to the rise in the number of persons moving upward from the lower to the higher tax grades. He further showed that the number of non-taxpayers in proportion to the total population who were moving up into the tax paying class was increasing. The statistics, as presented by Riesser, indicated that the rise in total national income was faster than the increase in population, and that the increase in total national income was shared not only by the wealthy but also by the middle and lower classes.[22]

SUPREMACY OF THE BERLIN BANKS

German financial organization now passed through a rapid evolution. The Reichsbank, founded in 1871 from the State Bank of Prussia, grew with the development of security capitalism. As a result the Reichsbank, in the same fashion as the Bank of France, took an active part in the expansion of security capitalism. The Reichsbank granted loans on the securities of the national and municipal governments, of the railroads and even on foreign governmental and foreign railroad securities guaranteed by their respective governments.[23]

Control of the banking system passed definitely from the hands of the individual private bankers to the incorporated banks of Berlin. The leading private bankers as Bleichröders, Mendelsohns, Rothschilds and Warburgs, continued to conduct a large volume of business, and the total number of private houses even increased. But relatively they were outstripped by the "Great Banks" of Berlin which, important in the period of the rise of German security capitalism, now in the developed stage of the system, expanded rapidly. During the second half of the nineteenth century German incorporated banking developed certain marked tendencies, particularly with reference to the source of its funds, the extent of combination both in the form of concentration and integration, its relation to industry and its internationalization. A considerable proportion of the funds of the German banks came not from the deposits of customers but from the capital subscribed by the proprietors themselves. In this respect the German banks differed from the British banks which derived the greater part of their funds from the depositors.[24]

German banking experienced a rapid movement toward combination in the form of concentration through the fusion of like units. The large banks not only absorbed other institutions, but also opened branches throughout the nation. The most important factor bringing about banking concentration was the rapid formation of industrial cartels. These large units required enormous capital which could only be furnished by powerful banking institutions. A further reason was the necessity for transferring capital from places where there was an excess to those localities where capital was needed. Such mobilization was especially important in Germany where financial resources were limited in relation to the growing demand of industry and of the government.

Not only did German banking advance the movement for concentration or the grouping of like banking units, but more important it aggressively undertook combination in the form of integration or the bringing together of unlike operating units under the same management. The German banks thus engaged in mixed banking and differed from the British banks engaged primarily in specialized banking. While the French banks also engaged in mixed banking, they emphasized their commercial operations. The German banks, on the other hand, stressed investment operations and were formed not so much for receiving deposits and granting loans but rather for supplying the investment requirements of industry. The main reason for the development of mixed banking was the lack of capital which forced industry to turn to the banks for assistance.[25]

Investment operations were the dominant activity of the German banks. In general, the business of issuing new securities by the German banks was conducted on a conservative basis, as it was their policy to emit bonds and stocks only to the actual cash value of the property of the corporation being financed.[26] The Berlin banks developed an extensive stock exchange business, and the Deutsche Bank at one time had 50 members on the Bourse.

RELATION OF BANKING TO INDUSTRY

Unlike the British financial institutions the German banks directed rather than followed the industrial revolution.[27] The Dresdner Bank proudly stated that its directors were on the boards of nearly 200 corporations.[28] The extent of the power of German banks over industry was evidenced in the case of the Phoenix Steel Works. When it hesitated to join the Steel Cartel the Company was forced to enter the combine due to the pressure exerted by the Schaaffhausen'scher Bankverein which held a large financial interest in it.

However, certain powerful industrial interests retained their independence. Thus the Krupps financed their rapid expansion without banking assistance, and represented the latent strength of industrial security capitalism which in the post-war period was to triumph over banking security capitalism.[29]   German banking therefore developed a close relationship with industry which was described as follows:

the bank attends an industrial undertaking from its birth to its death, from promotion to liquidation, they stand by its side whilst it passes through the financial processes of economic life, whether usual or unusual, helping it and at the same time profiting from it.[30]

This relationship between banking and industry was effected by the mutual exchange of directors.   On the one hand the banks invited leading industrialists to their boards, but these representatives exercised little influence on banking policy.   On the other hand, the banks placed their representatives on the boards of the industrial corporations and exerted an extensive control over managerial policy.   In several cases provincial banks were dominated by industrialists, as the control of the Rheinische Bank by August Thyssen, and the Mittelrheinische Bank by Hugo Stinnes.   Toward the close of the pre-war period the formation of finance companies by the industrialists themselves tended in a measure to increase their independence from the banks.[31]   These finance companies were organized particularly in the newer industries as electric generation and electric traction.   However with such exceptions the German banks exercised a controlling influence over industry.   This movement was characterized by Lenin as "the passing of the old Capitalism and the coming of the new, the passing of the domination of capital proper and the beginning of the domination of finance capital."[32]

A further feature of German banking was the internationalization of its operations.   The early effort at overseas financial development was a failure, and brought heavy financial losses.   These misadventures were sharply criticized in the German financial press which held that the banks "intended to establish silent partnerships in the regions peopled by the Riff pirates, Kaffirs, and Blackfoot Indians."[33]   However, in the closing years of the century the German banks entered aggressively upon a policy of overseas expansion particularly through the formation of subsidiary banks which limited their operations exclusively to foreign finance.   Thus the Disconto Gesellschaft established the Brasilianische Bank für Deutschland, whose head office was in Hamburg with a number of branches in Brazil.

By the opening of the twentieth century there were six "great banks," engaged in both domestic and international financial operations. The principal members of this group were popularly known as the "D" banks from the fact that the Deutsche, the Disconto Gesellschaft the Dresdner, and the Darmstädter Banks all bore the same initial letter. In addition to these four, there were two other major financial institutions, the Commerz-und-Privat Bank and the Berliner Handelsgesellschaft. Besides these powerful Berlin Banks, there were a number of important provincial banks as the Barmer Bankverein. Most of these institutions were founded in the latter half of the nineteenth century, and like the Berlin institutions, generally operated branches at home and had extensive correspondent relations abroad.

The social position of the banker even as late as the reign of William I was not high, as evidenced by the fact that few bankers were raised to nobility during the reign of the monarch.[34] However in the reign of William II, the social status of the banker rose considerably and many of them were raised to nobility.[35]

JEWISH INFLUENCE IN GERMAN SECURITY CAPITALISM

Jewish influence in German security capitalism in the pre-war period was considerable. Table 5 shows the percentage of Jews who were managing directors and who were members of the board of directors to the total in each case in the leading industries of Germany at the close of the pre-war period:

TABLE 5

PROPORTION OF JEWS CONTROLLING GERMAN INDUSTRIES IN THE PRE-WAR-PERIOD.[36]
(per cent of total)

INDUSTRY	MANAGING DIRECTORS	MEMBERS OF BOARD OF DIRECTORS
Brewing	15.7	31.5
Cement, timber, glass and china	7.0	29.9
Chemicals	13.0	22.8
Electrical	23.1	26.8
Machinery	12.2	21.4
Metal	25.0	30.7
Mining	12.8	23.9
Potash	11.1	29.4
Textiles	13.5	13.5
Average	13.3	24.4

From this table it is seen that the proportion of Jews who were managing directors in the various industries ranked from a low of 7 percent to a high of 25 percent and averaged 13 percent. The proportion of Jews who were members of the board of directors of these industries ranged from a low of 13 percent to a high of 31 percent and averaged 24 percent. In view of the fact that the Jews constituted only about one percent of the total population of Germany, it is seen that the extent of Jewish control of German industry in the pre-war period was very high.[37] Jewish influence in German banking was likewise considerable, and this condition in the post-war period led to a social antipathy which was to have widespread political consequences.

Stock exchanges were developed particularly in Frankfurt and in Berlin. The Frankfurt exchange was more concerned with government and railroad obligations, while the Berlin Stock Exchange specialized in industrial securities.[38] Although the Frankfurt exchange continued in importance, the Berlin exchange in time came to dominate the national security market.

HEAVY DEMAND FOR CAPITAL

Throughout the latter half of the nineteenth and the early twentieth century the demand for capital by both the governments and the large industrial corporations was very heavy. The Prussian government borrowed extensively to finance its wars against Denmark and Austria and its debt rose sharply. The war against France cost Prussia relatively little, but the armed peace of the subsequent years imposed a heavy burden on the German Empire. Expenditures for armament rose sharply after 1890 and the proportion of such outlays to total ordinary expenditures increased from 23.4 percent in 1890 to over 55.7 percent in 1913. As a result the national debt mounted rapidly.[39]

The provincial governments, particularly Bavaria and Saxony, and the municipal governments, especially Bremen and Hamburg, were almost continuous borrowers over these years. The annual volume of these domestic, state and communal loans increased from 139,000,000 marks in 1895 to 1,770,000,000 marks in 1908.[40] This increased issue of municipal securities was characterized as a "sort of mania of greatness," and one German economist added,

Every mayor thinks he has failed to live up to the requirements of his office if he does not borrow a million every couple of years for slaughterhouses, sewers, the construction or purchase of electric plants and city railways, nay, even for paving and schoolhouses, the expenses for which ought to be defrayed out of current revenues.[41]

Corporate issues in the German capital market at first consisted mainly of the securities of the railroads. In time the industrial companies also entered the capital market, as the number of corporations grew and the cartel movement expanded. Indicative of this movement the number of corporations increased from 2,143 in 1887 to 5,486 by 1913 and corporate capital rose from 4,876,000,000 marks to 17,357,000,000 marks.[42]

As in the case of the other capital-accumulating countries, Germany also invested in foreign securities. The cause of this export of capital was ascribed to "the steadily diminishing yield of capital investment within our present economic area."[43] It is quite probable that a large proportion of foreign securities issued in the German market over these years was not absorbed by domestic investors but was finally placed with foreign capitalists. A large part of the export of German capital went into proprietary investment as the direct ownership of mines, factories and banks in foreign countries.

Germany in the eighties floated foreign loans with the same unrestrained enthusiasm which characterized the misadventures of the United States in the period after the World War. Germany extended loans to Greece, Portugal, Serbia, Chile and Brazil, and most of these "exotic securities" fell in price almost as promptly as they were issued. The issuance of foreign securities attained its greatest prominence in the German capital market in the eighties and thereafter declined in relative importance. In the period from 1886 to 1889 foreign issues in the German market amounted to almost one-half of the total issues; by 1905 the proportion had dropped to a little above one-third; in 1906 it was less than one-tenth and in 1907 it amounted to only about one-fifteenth of the total issues.[44] It is thus seen that, while German security capitalism became internationalized, it was not necessarily a corollary that such internationalization had to continue.[45]

INCREASING SUPPLY OF CAPITAL

The supply of German capital in the last quarter of the nineteenth century and the years until the War increased rapidly, as evidenced by the rise in the volume of saving funds.[46] The annual saving of the German people in the period of developed security capitalism was conservatively estimated at 2,500,000,000 marks.[47] It is estimated that about one-third of the annual saving was invested in securities. The total wealth of Germany was conservatively placed at 200,000,000,000 marks,[48] and the amount of securities held in Germany at 30,000,000,000 marks.[49] Such security holdings therefore represented about one-seventh of the total wealth.[50]

Notwithstanding the increase in the supply of capital, it was frequently insufficient to meet the pressing drains on the market. The demand for capital from the federal and state governments was always heavy, and when in addition the demand of private industry and to some extent of foreign borrowing became large, the combined burden caused a maladjustment in the German capital market which contributed to the periodic financial disturbances. Thus the over-rapid growth of corporations and the overissue of securities caused the panic in 1873. Again, the heavy flotation of securities in the period from 1897 to 1900 led to the crisis of 1900. Francis Hirst expressed the opinion that:

Germany's wealth was then probably increasing more rapidly than that of France, but its annual surplus was mostly absorbed by the requirements of the Imperial and State governments and of the municipalities . . . as well as by the demands of a world wide trade which was largely carried on credit.[51]

CRITICISM OF SECURITY CAPITALISM

The new security capitalism was subject to frequent criticism in German economic literature. Jhering commenting on the events which led to the crisis of 1873, stated that: "the devastations which they [the joint stock companies] caused among private property are worse than if fire and drought, failure of crops, earthquake, war, hostile occupation, had combined to ruin the national prosperity."[52] Ruhland declared: "The word capitalism denotes today a social system in which the liberty to practice usury is more or less completely legalized," and capitalists were described as "usurers in the widest sense of the word."[53] He further added "that money interests predominate and that trade and robbery, gain, usury, and extortion merge into each other."[54]

Among the industrial workers of the cities there was a strong undercurrent of radicalism and a latent opposition to security capitalism. However, the middle class, which placed more and more of its saving into securities and derived a satisfactory income and even appreciation in value from its investments, became ardent supporters of the new system.

CONTROL OF SECURITY CAPITALISM

The national government exerted extensive regulation over security capitalism with particular reference to the capitalization of corporations and the operations of the stock exchange.[55] The corporation law of 1884 sought to prevent the overvaluation of property and the concealment of promoters' profits. It required stock companies to establish a legal reserve fund to which a certain part of annual net profits and the premiums on new stock had to be transferred. The effect of this law was to force the companies to accumulate considerable reserve funds, and this policy enabled many of them successfully to withstand the crisis of 1900.

The political strength of the agrarian members of the Reichstag led in 1893 to the appointment of the Stock Exchange Inquiry Commission which undertook a comprehensive study of the stock exchange operations.[56] As a result of the report of this Commission the Reichstag passed a sweeping law controlling stock exchange operations.[57] This statute proved too drastic, and was later amended particularly by the law of 1908. This statute established boards for the admission of new securities to all the German stock exchanges. The membership of these boards included bankers and industrialists. It was the hope of the framers of the act that the boards would protect the agricultural and industrial interests of the nation from the increasing domination of the bankers. The act therefore conferred upon the boards extensive powers to exclude the listing of any security which was against the public interest. However in the end the boards apparently came under the control of the banking interests. In actual practice the boards exercised their powers very narrowly, for instead of following a broad policy of controlling security capitalism, they limited their activities to mere technical regulation as scrutinizing prospectuses for fraud or improving the collateral pledged for bond issues.[58]

The act also sought to check security speculation and stipulated that mining and industrial stocks had to be purchased on a cash basis and could not be carried on the customary monthly settlement for such transactions. The purpose of this regulation was to eliminate altogether speculation in these securities. In order to trade in other classes of securities a person had to sign an "exchange regulation." However, very few signed the regulation and speculation still continued by devices which circumvented the law so that it was repealed in 1908.[59] State governments also passed laws regulating the security markets within their respective jurisdictions but this control was not seriously invoked. Toward the closing years of the period rigorous control of the German banks was urged from various quarters. In no other country, outside of the United States, was there such a demand for government regulation of the banking system. One proposal was to fix the legal ratio of capital which banks should maintain against savings deposits. German economic thought was thus the first to appreciate the necessity for banks to maintain solvency by means of an adequate proportion of capital to deposits. Several of the expert witnesses who appeared before the Banking

Inquiry Commission of 1908 recommended that the investment of bank funds be placed under legal regulation. This proposal was urged on the ground that the administration of national saving should not be entrusted to a small group of persons without legal safeguards.

RELATION OF INTERNATIONAL FINANCE AND POLITICS

As in the case of France, there was a close relation between international investments and international politics. Riesser stated frankly that "international flotations ought to be but the means for attaining national ends and must be placed in the service of national labor." [60]   A close relation existed between German banking and the foreign office in the extension of overseas loans. Financial assistance to Italy and to Russia was encouraged by the government largely for political reasons.

In these various moves on the chessboard of international politics, the German bankers in most cases were the pawns and not the kings. In general the German bankers like the British bankers threw their influence on the side of peace. Particularly was this true in the case of the Bagdad Railroad where the Deutsche Bank showed a willingness to yield to the British in order to arrive at an amicable settlement. Von Gwinner of the Deutsche Bank, who handled these negotiations, later said: "if the question had been fully explained to the British public, and they had been made aware of the conditions offered by the Deutsche Bank, their views would have been considerably altered." [61]

CONCLUSION

Until the middle of the nineteenth century the German states continued in the stage of individual capitalism, for the institutions necessary for security capitalism had not yet been developed. Manufacture was still largely in the domestic stage and railroad construction had made little progress. The laws of most of the German states made no provision for corporate organization. The financial structure was still of the simplest form, with no central bank, with banking in the hands of private individuals, with the Bourse having only insignificant security dealings, and capital accumulation meagre. Thus while England and even France had moved along the path of early security capitalism, by the middle of the century Germany had not yet entered this stage.

The third quarter of the nineteenth century marked the rise of German security capitalism with the increase in industrial production and with the foundation of a banking system. The fourth quarter of the nineteenth century and the years until the War witnessed the full development of the system. The formation of the Imperial government laid the political basis for the system. German security capitalism in this period was dominated by the great banks which exerted control over industry to an extent found in no other country. In general the demand for capital to finance the rapid expansion of domestic industry was so heavy that there was a decline in the relative importance of exported capital. Thus developed German security capitalism, unlike British and French security capitalism, did not become increasingly internationalized. Furthermore, German security capitalism, unlike British security capitalism, operated not under laissez faire but under strict governmental regulation aimed at both economic and political objectives.

CHAPTER 7

RISE AND DEVELOPMENT OF EUROPEAN SECURITY CAPITALISM

CONSIDERATION has been given to the evolution in the pre-war period of security capitalism in England, France and Germany, which together with the United States, were the leading countries of security capitalism. No attempt will be made to analyze in detail the evolution of the system in the remaining countries of the world, for such a study would be largely a repetition of the above movements. Rather, a comparative analysis will be made of the more important general tendencies in the rise and development of European security capitalism as a whole in the prewar period.[1]

COMPARATIVE INTERNATIONAL PEACE

In general the domestic and international political conditions throughout the World from 1815 until 1914 were stable. Except for the disturbances of 1848 domestic political conditions were relatively quiet, and in most of the nations of Western Europe parliamentary government, in form if not in substance, was developed. Likewise, except for limited conflicts, international political relations were comparatively peaceful. The local revolutions and minor wars of this period were of small importance compared with the preceding French Revolution, and the Napoleonic Wars and the subsequent Great War and the Russian Revolution of the twentieth century. The hundred-year period from 1815 to 1914 was therefore a lull between two periods of major political upheaval. This condition of comparative peace was one of the most important factors making possible the growth of the modern capitalist system, for political stability in turn brought about economic and financial stability.

There were however two international political trends which were ominous for the future. In the first place, while the conflicts of this period were confined in their scope, they tended to keep Europe in a state of armed peace. Furthermore, the last quarter of the nineteenth century witnessed a revival of colonialism which added 24,600,000 square kilometers, or an area twice the size of Europe to the lands already possessed by the Great Powers.[2] This scramble for overseas territory inevitably led to international rivalry and ill will.

ECONOMIC EXPANSION

The period from the middle of the nineteenth century to the Great War was marked by rapid expansion in world production and trade. Production throughout the world increased enormously as evidenced by the rapid rise in the output of coal, pig iron and steel, and the sharp increase in the monetary value of the output of the leading basic commodities.[3] This increase in world production was accompanied by a corresponding increase in world trade which rose from £341,000,000 in 1820 to £832,000,000 in 1850 and to £3,377,000,000 in 1890.[4]

While the leading countries as England, France, Germany and the United States shared in this economic expansion the respective rate varied considerably as indicated in Table 6.

From these figures it is seen that the United States made the most rapid progress in the output of coal and pig iron, while Germany was next, then France and Great Britain last. In the increase in the output of steel Germany led France, with the United States next and Great Britain last. In the relative growth of exports, the United States was first, Germany second and Great Britain barely exceeded France. An indication of the comparative technical progress of these four leading countries of security capitalism is reflected in the number of patents granted. From 1840 to 1914 the number of patents granted in England totalled 96,510, in the United States 82,287, in Germany 56,204, and in France 42,884. However in England the number of patents showed a declining trend, while in the other countries, particularly the United States, there was a sharp rise.[6]

Throughout the period there was a rapid expansion of world population. From 1820 to 1913 it rose from 732,000,000 to 1,657,000,000 or a greater increase within the century than in all the previous period in human history.[7]

GROWTH OF CORPORATE ORGANIZATION

Over these years the corporate form of business organization was widely accepted, and special charters for joint-stock enterprises were replaced by general incorporation laws which recognized the principle of limited liability of stockholders. Throughout the nineteenth century there was a trend toward uniformity in corporate law. In the first half of the century the French Commercial Code of 1807 formed the model for the corporate laws of the Continent. In the second half of the century the British Companies Act of 1862 initiated a movement for reform of the corporate law, and resulted

TABLE 6

COMPARATIVE ECONOMIC EXPANSION OF LEADING COUNTRIES, 1870–1913.[5]

(percent)

YEAR	COAL (1870=100)				PIG IRON (1870=100)				STEEL (1870=100)				EXPORTS (1890=100)			
	England	France	Germany	United States	England	France	Germany	United States	England	France	Germany	United States	England	France	Germany	United States
1870	100.0	100.0	100.0	100.0	100.0	100.0	100.0	100.0	100.0	100.0	100.0	100.0				
1880	133.6	145.9	160.5	152.5	130.0	146.6	196.4	230.3	669.8	458.3	523.8	181.4				
1890	160.9	185.0	239.9	326.5	138.4	145.8	325.9	552.7	1707.0	631.0	1476.2	622.1	100.0	100.0	100.0	100.0
1900	204.7	242.1	373.3	575.2	150.3	226.3	416.5	827.4	2279.5	1820.2	1714.3	1481.9	110.6	114.1	138.6	162.2
1910	240.4	280.1	522.0	1069.8	168.0	342.2	1047.1	1639.7	3030.2	4107.1	10697.6	3795.6	163.5	167.5	215.5	206.3
1913	261.3	329.7	647.2	1316.8	172.1	434.2	1366.9	1859.6	3564.7	5492.9	14787.3	4552.9	199.6	191.3	259.7	291.8

in such statutes as the French Corporation Law of 1867, and the German Law of 1870 which in turn formed the basis for the Hungarian, Swiss and Italian codes.[8]

The application of the corporate form of business organization made possible the movement for industrial combination, which, by creating large issues of new stocks and bonds, contributed to the growth of security capitalism. The extent of this concentration was expressed by Walter Rathenau in his statement in 1909 that "three hundred men, all of whom know one another, direct the economic destiny of Europe and choose their successors from among themselves."[9]

MARXIAN INTERPRETATION OF SECURITY CAPITALISM

The most important interpretation of world security capitalism came from Karl Marx and his followers. Marxian literature is naturally replete with comments on security capitalism. However, this discussion of the system is lacking in agreement, and so no unified criticism of the nature and the institutions of security capitalism can be discerned in Marxian theory. One important reason is the fact that the Marxists were observing and interpreting the manifestations of security capitalism in different countries and at different times. Thus Marx himself and later Kautsky based their observations largely on British security capitalism, while Lenin and Hilferding supported their comments primarily by noting German security capitalism. As shown in the previous chapters these two types of security capitalism differed in many respects. Furthermore Marx and the later Marxists were observing the system at different periods. Thus Marx was writing at a time when security capitalism in most countries was still in its early stage, while the later writers were observing a system which had largely attained the developed stage.

Marx showed an appreciation of various aspects of security capitalism as the difference between individual and security capitalism, the distinction between industrial and banking capitalism, the power of banking capitalism and the international economic and political implications of the new system. He distinguished between individual capitalism and security capitalism in the statement that:

With the development of large-scale industry money-capital, so far as it appears on the market, is not represented by some individual capitalist, not by the owner of this or that fraction of the capital on the market, but assumes more and more the character of an organized mass, which is far more directly subject to the control of the representatives of social capital, the bankers, than actual production is.[10]

While banking capitalism was not considered as productive, industrial capitalism as employed in commerce and industry was regarded by Marx as productive.[11]   Marx described the powerful position of the leaders of the new banking security capitalism in the statement that "the most absolute monarchs became dependent upon the Stock Exchange Barons through the national debt system." [12]

Marx recognized the international economic aspect of modern capitalism in the statement that:

the expansion of foreign trade which is the basis of the capitalist mode of production in its stages of infancy has become its own product in the further progress of capitalist development through its innate necessities through its need of an ever expanding market.[13]

The political aspect of the international expansion of modern capitalism is reflected in the statement that:

. . . imperialism is at the same time the most prostitute and the ultimate form of the State power which nascent middle class society had commenced to elaborate as a means of its own emancipation from feudalism.[14]

Marx laid bare the unsatisfactory technical results of security capitalism such as overcapitalization and stock market manipulation. Overcapitalization is scored in the statement that:

Those who say that there is merely a lack of means of payment . . . are fools who believe that it is the duty and power of banks to transform all bankrupt swindlers into solvent and solid capitalists by means of pieces of paper.[15]

The evils of stock market manipulation, arising out of the difficulty of evaluating paper claims to wealth, are indicated in the following words:

Since property here exists in the form of shares of stock, its movements and transfer become purely a result of gambling at the stock exchange, where the little fish are swallowed by the sharks and the lambs by the wolves.[16]

More important were the sweeping charges of Marx that the system possessed inherent weaknesses which would inevitably lead to disastrous economic, social and political results such as crises of increasing severity, increasing misery of society and eventual world revolution.   The system, he held, contained the seed of its own destruction, and the commercial crises "by their periodical return put the existence of the entire bourgeois society on trial, each time more threateningly." [17]   Marx expressed his famous "increasing misery theory" of the laboring class in the statement that: "Accumulation of wealth at one pole is, therefore, at the same time, accumulation of misery, agony of toil, slavery, ignorance, brutality, mental degradation, at the opposite pole." [18]   The result of such increasing misery Marx held would be the disappearance of the middle class. Capitalism, according to Marx, was doomed to end in violence and revolution. This catastrophic end of capitalism, he believed to be almost at hand.

These theories of crises of increasing severity, a society of increasing misery and political revolution were not supported by the actual economic, social and political history of Western Europe until the Great War. The crises of the nineteenth century and of the years until 1914 were not of increasing severity. The early stage of security capitalism in England was characterized by a speculative excess probably unequalled in the late history of security capitalism in England. While speculation continued as a characteristic of British security capitalism in its developed and also critical stage, there is no indication that speculation tended to increase in intensity.

The Marxian forecast of the increasing misery of society and the disappearance of the middle class did not materialize in England, France, Germany or the United States in the developed stage of security capitalism. The welfare of society improved in the nineteenth century as evidenced by the increase in national wealth and national income, the widening distribution of this income among the various social classes, the satisfactory condition of employment in England, Germany and the United States, notwithstanding the rapid increase in population in these countries, and the growing diffusion of security holdings and of savings deposits. The middle class, instead of disappearing, really increased and shared extensively in the material prosperity of this period.

With the exception of the short-lived Paris Commune, the revolutionary movement in Western Europe in the latter half of the nineteenth century was unimportant, and the world enjoyed a state of comparative international peace. Thus the fundamental error of the Marxian view of capitalism was misjudgment of the time element in the evolution of capitalism. In a way it may be said that Marx mistook the sunrise for the sunset.

VIEWS OF LATER MARXIANS

This error in the time element was recognized by later Marxian writers. Engels, first believing with Marx that the new system would lead to crises of increasing severity predicted "a new world crash of unheard of violence" or a chronic rotation of crises with ever shorter and feebler business recovery and ever lengthening depression. However, by 1894 when such world crises failed to occur, Engels retreated from the theory.[19]

Influenced by the satisfactory economic, social and political trend of security capitalism in the closing years of the nineteenth century and early years of the twentieth century, the moderate or revisionist socialists rejected the catastrophic theories of the master. Bernstein denied that crises were of increasing severity and maintained that "signs of an economic world-wide crash of unheard of violence have not been established, nor can one describe the improvement of trade in the intervals between the crises as particularly short-lived." [20] Many of the later Marxists also rejected the theory of impending revolution, and felt that international peace could be attained under modern capitalism.

However, other Marxists continued an uncompromising criticism of security capitalism. These revolutionary socialists supported the catastrophic theories of Marx. Rosa Luxemburg was firm in the belief that the modern credit system accentuated speculation and crises.[21] The extreme Marxists held steadfast to the belief that social misery was on the increase and that the system would end in world-wide revolution. The later radical writers went farther than Marx in emphasizing the adverse international aspects of capitalism. As mentioned before, Marx recognized the international nature of capitalism, but did not foresee the vast overseas movement which changed the nature of modern capitalism in the last quarter of the century. His failure to note the significance of this phase of modern capitalism was due to the simple fact that the capitalist system of his day had not yet acquired pronounced international characteristics. However, the later Marxists as Rosa Luxemburg writing at a time when the Great Powers were aggressively pushing their overseas expansion gave full recognition to the so-called "imperialistic" nature of modern capitalism.

CENTRAL BANKING

During the nineteenth century the leading countries perfected their financial organization. In the period before the Great War practically every country under security capitalism formed a central bank. In most cases it was a private corporation and its capital came from the investing public.[22] The central bank generally had a monopoly of issuing circulating notes; sought to control the money market by changes in its discount rate and aided the growth of security capitalism by granting loans collateralled by securities. Such acceptable security collateral ranged from only government obligations in some cases to a wide list including even corporate securities in other cases.

In addition to the central note-issuing bank, most of the nations also organized a central mortgage bank similar to the French Credit Foncier. These institutions possessed the same general characteristics. They made conservative loans on urban and agricultural properties, required adequate margin for the safety of these advances, and the mortgage indentures made provision for rapid amortization and prompt foreclosure in case of nonpayment. The funds for these loans came from the sale of the obligations of the banks. These bonds had a high credit standing in the security market, and sold on a basis very close to that of the securities of the national government itself.[23]

HOUSE OF ROTHSCHILD

Under individual capitalism, the banking system was in the hands of the private houses and they continued in ascendency throughout the first half of the nineteenth century. The most important was the house of Rothschild. In the eighteenth century it was only of local significance, but in the first half of the nineteenth century it became the undisputed leader of the new system of security capitalism on the Continent. While the parent bank was in Frankfurt, the firm operated important branches in London, Paris, Vienna, and Naples, and was thoroughly international in character. The Frankfurt house continued as the headquarters until about 1820 when the Paris office took the leadership.[24] The growing financial importance of the Paris house was in time given social recognition when Louis Philippe, the personification of the rising French security capitalism, conferred the grand cross of the Legion of Honor upon James Rothschild.[25]

As indicated in the chapter on British security capitalism, the firm dominated the market for government loans. So strong was its grip on public credit that if a state were placed on the blackboard, or "black list," by Rothschilds, such an act meant the financial embarrassment of that government. No finance minister could survive the displeasure of this powerful house. In general the influence of the house of Rothschild was in support of international peace and of constitutional government.[26] The firm refused to finance Sardinia in its warlike preparations against Austria. The firm also threw its support in favor of parliamentary government, and, as stated by a speaker in the Reichstag in commenting on the Rothschilds, "Capital as a rule is constitutional." [27]

For a long time the house refused to take any part in the financing of the railroads. Even Nathan Rothschild, who was later to become the railway king of Europe, was at first firm in the opinion that the horse could never be effectively supplanted by the railroad.[28] A number of years passed before Nathan Rothschild came to the realization that the railway could serve as a means of widening his sources of profit. By this time railway construction had made rapid progress in England, and it was too late for the house to take an active part in that country. However, there was still time to seize the leadership in financing railway building on the Continent, and this opportunity was quickly grasped by Rothschilds. The firm advanced credit to the various governments for the financing of the early railroads, and it was said that the Rothschilds and not the state owned the railroads. The firm in time also participated in industrial financing and "scarcely a company that was started in Germany but looked to the good will of Rothschild. Those in which he had no say were not very successful, and little could be made out of them." [29]

GROWTH OF INCORPORATED BANKING

Throughout the first half of the nineteenth century the growth of incorporated banking was slow on the Continent with the exception of Belgium. The most important financial institution in the history of Belgium, and one of the great banking corporations of world security capitalism, was the Société Generale pour Favoriser le Commerce et L'Industrie. This institution had been formed by King William V of Holland for the purpose of looking after his extensive personal business interests. It maintained close relations with those corporations which it controlled, and so was the first financial institution to initiate the policy of banker domination of industry. The bank performed commercial as well as investment operations, and therefore engaged in mixed banking before it was developed even in Germany. The Société Generale thus held a unique place in the history of security capitalism in being the first important banking institution to be organized as a holding company, to engage in banker control of industry and to perform the functions of mixed banking. Other large banking institutions were founded in Belgium and by the middle of the century it was the only Continental country to possess adequate banking facilities to finance its industrial expansion.

The first stage in the development of Continental banking outside of France and Belgium came in the fifties, when banking in Central Europe fell under the influence of the Credit Mobilier movement of France. Thus the Oestereichische Credit Anstalt für Handel und Gewerbe (the Austrian Credit Institute for Commerce and Industry) was formed for the purpose of controlling the entire corporate system of Austria. While this organization was similar in nature to the Credit Mobilier of France, the directors of the Austrian bank were careful to point out that there was no business relation between the two institutions. When the French bank was encountering difficulties, the Austrian bank, in its report, emphasized "the virtue of the Austrian daughter" in contrast with "the French mother whose vice was speculation." [30] The Austrian bank grew in importance, and in time became the dominant institution in not only financing the industry of Austria but even in providing its monetary system. In most countries there was a concentrated banking system composed of a small group of joint stock banks each having its head office located in the financial center of the nation and operating a system of branches.[31] By the latter part of the nineteenth century even Russia had developed joint stock banks, and by 1914 the banking system of that country consisted of the Imperial State Bank, forty-seven joint stock commercial banks with 743 branches, 8000 savings banks and numerous other financial institutions.[32] The incorporated banks of the Continent generally followed the German rather than the British form. The Continental banks usually engaged not only in commercial but in investment operations and so were mixed rather than specialized financial institutions. In general, the banking system expanded its operations and its function broadened. Not only did investment credit increase in amount in these years, but through efficient mobilization by the banks the total volume available was rendered more effective.[33] Until the last quarter of the nineteenth century wars were still generally financed by the great banks of the nation. Even the Franco-Prussian War was largely financed by the banks, for during this conflict the Prussian government placed most of its loans with the private banks as Rothschilds, and the incorporated banks as the Disconto Gesellschaft. However, the Franco-Prussian War was the last great conflict to be financed by the resources of the banking institutions. Thereafter wars were financed by means of the resources of the general investing public mobilized by the great banks.[34]

In every Continental country of security capitalism, the function of the stock exchange was transformed. The early operations facilitating the sale of goods and foreign currency became relatively less important, as the dealing in stocks and bonds increased in volume and the exchanges became essentially security markets. Most of the Continental countries developed active stock exchanges, which became the mechanism for direct investment in securities. By the middle of the century the security markets of the Continent were beginning to be internationalized. The financial crisis of 1857 clearly demonstrated the fact that the security markets of Western Europe were tied together for better or for worse.

THE ARMAMENT RACE

The demands for capital throughout the world came from the growing needs of the business enterprises and from the governments. Under the individual capitalism of the eighteenth and early nineteenth centuries the demand by the merchant and by the small manufacturer was essentially for short-term or working capital to pay for labor and to carry inventory for a limited period of time until the goods were sold or converted into finished form.   Under security capitalism in the nineteenth and twentieth century the demand by business enterprise was essentially for long-term or fixed capital particularly for the building of railway systems and later for the expansion of industrial plants.

In the eighteenth and early nineteenth centuries the demand for capital by the governments was light, since their functions were limited in range, and their military equipment was relatively simple. In the nineteenth and twentieth centuries governments needed long-term capital in large amounts to finance their broadening social responsibilities and increasing military establishments. The governments required funds to maintain their expanding social disbursements, and subsidies were granted not only to unemployed urban workers in the form of doles but to struggling small farmers in the form of bounties. In some cases, the state took over the operation of railways and telegraph systems. Leon Say well said that "democracy tends to transfer to the State many functions with which it was not formerly burdened." [35]

The industrial revolution not only improved the technique of peace, but also of war, and the new weapons for international strife were costly. Until 1850 the expenditures of the leading nations for armament showed little growth, and the amounts remained relatively small.[36] However, after the middle of the century the erection of new fortresses and the building of new warships required more and more funds. The Crimean War marked the beginning of the race for naval supremacy. The great powers, particularly England and France, had the opportunity to compare their naval strength, and the rivalry among the leading maritime nations now developed in earnest. Wooden sailing vessels gave way to iron-hulled vessels and in time to steel-hulled warships.

The unfortunate characteristic of late nineteenth and early twentieth century security capitalism was this unsound nature of the governmental demand for capital. The most serious defect in the system was the absorption of much of the national saving, largely the result of individual thrift and self-denial, by enormous government loans which were mainly dissipated in maintaining the ever-expanding military establishment of these years. Most of the government financing over the nineteenth and early twentieth centuries diverted the flow of capital into unproductive purposes, particularly for the financial settlement of past wars, the conduct of current wars and the preparation of future wars.[37]

[handwritten marginal note:] also Now 1938

GROWTH OF DEBT

These social and military expenditures were financed largely by borrowing, and as a result the debts of the nations of the world increased enormously after the middle of the century.[38]   The aggregate of the national debts of the leading countries in 1820 was £1,-515,000,000, in 1848 it rose to £3,381,000,000 and by 1900 it reached £5,163,000,000.[39]   The trend of the national debts of the leading nations for the period until the War shows a contraction of the debt of the United Kingdom and of the United States, a moderate rise in the debt of the Netherlands and rapid expansion in the debt of Belgium, France, Germany, Italy, and Russia. It is probable that the debt structures of Germany, the Netherlands, the United Kingdom and the United States were sound. On the other hand, most likely the debt structures of Austria, Belgium, and France were unsound and those of Italy and Russia were critical.[40] By 1888 Alfred Neymarck mourned that "the finances of Europe are so involved as to make one fear lest they should fatally lead on the governments to ask whether war, with its terrible eventualities, is not to be preferred to the maintenance of a precarious and costly peace."[41] He added the prophetic statement that "all Europe, with the weight of military expenditures and burden of public debts and taxes crushing it, is marching, if it perseveres in this course, toward war, ruin, and a veritable industrial and economic revolution."   Even General von Moltke, in a statement to the Reichstag, declared that in the long run, nations would be unable to support military burdens.

Not only national but provincial and municipal governments were heavy borrowers in the capital market. The Continental municipalities, like the national governments, entered extensively upon policies of social relief and of public enterprises as gas works, electrical power stations and tramways, and for these purposes had to resort to the capital market. It was stated that the burden of municipal debts was almost equal to that of the national governments.[42]

As a result there was a rapid rise in the volume of new securities, in the last quarter of the nineteenth and the first part of the twentieth centuries. Grouped by five-year periods the total outstanding securities rose from 40,000,000,000 francs from 1891 to 1895, to 60,000,000,000 from 1896 to 1900, to 83,000,000,000 from 1901 to 1905 and to 114,000,000,000 from 1906 to 1910.[43] The total volume of securities outstanding in the leading countries by 1910 may be seen in Table 7.

From this table it is seen that by 1910 Great Britain with 24 percent was the leader of security capitalism judged from the standpoint of the largest proportion of the outstanding securities of the

TABLE 7

TOTAL SECURITIES OUTSTANDING IN LEADING COUNTRIES, 1910.[44]
(billion francs)

COUNTRY	AMOUNT	PERCENT OF TOTAL
Great Britain...........	140	24.3
United States...........	130	22.6
France.................	106	18.4
Germany...............	90	15.7
Russia.................	29	5.0
Austria-Hungary........	23	4.0
Italy..................	13	2.3
Japan..................	9	1.6
Other Countries........	35	6.1
Total....	575	100.0

world. The United States came next with 22 percent and France
with 18 percent came third while Germany with 15 percent was
fourth. These four nations together accounted for four-fifths of the
securities of the world.

MALADJUSTMENT IN THE WORLD CAPITAL MARKET

Little information is available on the supply of capital in the
Continental countries until the middle of the century. It is, however, reasonable to suppose that the volume was small due to the
simple economy of the time. Most of these countries had to import
capital from England. However, in the latter half of the nineteenth
century saving in Europe rose sharply. This accumulation of capital
in Europe in the latter half of the nineteenth century represented
one of the most important economic tendencies of the period. The
philosophy of saving dominated almost every class in economic society. The small income group had not only a comparatively satisfactory standard of living, but in addition was able to save a considerable proportion of its annual income. While each individual
amount may have been relatively small, the total saving of the ar-
tisan, the shop-keeper and the farmer was considerable. The capital
accumulation of the nouveau riche of the nineteenth century was
enormous. Aside from the spectacular few who squandered their
fortunes, the majority of the wealthy class did not increase their
standard of living in proportion to the rise in their income, and as
a result the capital accumulation of this group, added to that of
the other classes, gave a total supply which rose rapidly over these

years. Even in backward states as Russia there was accumulation of capital. From 1900 to 1912 the volume of Russian government bonds placed at home doubled in amount, and by the outbreak of the War more than two-thirds of Russia's capital issues were absorbed internally.[45]

In the closing years of the nineteenth century there was a complete change in the relation between the demand and the supply of capital in the security markets of the world. From the close of the Napoleonic Wars until the last decade of the nineteenth century there was generally a surplus of capital over the demand for it. One authority,[46] Georges De Lavaleyle, estimated that the force of European saving available for the capital market was sufficient to absorb from four to five billion francs in securities annually and that the volume of new issues until the beginning of the nineties generally fell below this range. Thus as a result interest rates continued to decline. Commenting on this downward trend, an economist of those days declared : "the question which is forcing itself home upon every civilized people to-day is, where openings are to be found in the future for the productive investment of their saved capital. Can new opening be found for investments?"[47] The decline in the rate of interest enabled the governments to convert their old high coupon issues into new lower coupon issues so that by the early nineties three percent was the usual coupon on government obligations. Thus the governments of the world, despite the fact that their borrowings were increasing, were able to raise funds at a lower cost. However, as a result of the enormous amount of public and private financing in the closing years of the nineteenth century and the opening years of the twentieth century, maladjustment between the force of investment and the force of saving developed. The capital markets of Europe before the War suffered from almost a chronic state of overissue. The financial press of this period bears evidence that there was full appreciation of "the excessive use of credit and the excessive issue of new securities."[48]

The change which occurred in the money markets of the world about the turn of the century is seen in the following table showing the changes in the yield of the bonds of leading governments from 1873 to 1912.

From these figures it is seen that throughout the seventies bond prices gradually began to rise and the yields declined until the period from 1896 to 1905, the former date marking the upturn in British bond yields and the latter the upturn in Italian yields.[50]

TABLE 8

CHANGES IN YIELD OF BONDS OF LEADING GOVERNMENTS, 1873-1912.[49]
(percent)

COUNTRY	YIELD			DATE		
	High	Low	High	High	Low	High
Austria-Hungary....	6.11	3.81	4.71	1879	1897	1912
England............	3.34	1.95	3.45	1874	1896	1912
France.............	4.95	2.86	3.40	1877	1897	1912
Germany...........	4.13	3.48	4.13	1880	1903	1912
Italy..............	7.80	3.84	3.86	1873	1905	1912
Russia.............	6.49	3.76	5.89	1877	1896	1907
United States.......	4.50	1.58	2.80	1873	1902	1910

THE COMING OF WAR

The employment of the system of security capitalism to finance the armed peace came to the inevitable end in the summer of 1914. The security markets of the world failed completely to anticipate the outbreak of the War. The significance of the murder of the Austrian archduke in the end of June was apparently not realized by the financial press. The London *Economist* the week after this event, in commenting on the London Stock Exchange, said that "The further tragedy in the House of Hapsburgs had no effect." The Berlin correspondent of the *Economist,* in his report of July 9th, noted that "the Norway voyage of the Kaiser marks the beginning of the dead season in German politics." [51] Even the Paris capital market in the beginning of July was strong. The French government issue placed on July 7th was oversubscribed many times mainly by speculators anticipating a rapid rise. The issue did actually rise in price, and it was not until the closing days of July that security prices began to fall sharply. By the closing week of July there was a complete collapse of the security markets in every country. On July 25th the rush of selling orders overwhelmed the Paris Bourse which with the Coulisse closed its doors.[52] On the last day of July the London Stock Exchange, which had never closed even in the darkest days of the Napoleonic conflict, was forced to suspend operations. A few hours later the New York Stock Exchange, which had closed only at the time of the failure of Jay Cooke, also suspended operations.[53] Thus, as Janus opened the portals of his temple security capitalism closed its doors, and the crisis was at hand.

CHAPTER 8

CRISIS OF BRITISH, FRENCH AND GERMAN SECURITY CAPITALISM

CONSIDERATION has now been given to the evolution of security capitalism of England, France, Germany, and of Europe in general in the pre-war period. The war years will not be studied in themselves since they constitute an abnormal period, but the effects of the War as reflected in the after years will be analyzed. The post-war crisis in the security capitalism of England, France, Germany, Italy, Russia and Japan and the world will be studied.

POST-WAR CRISIS OF BRITISH SECURITY CAPITALISM

The most important factor in British domestic politics in the post-war era was the rise of the Labour party, since it was to furnish the most concerted opposition to British security capitalism. In the pre-war period the membership of the Labour party was confined mainly to trade unionists but in the post-war period it broadened its appeal and gained wider social support. In 1924 the Labour party obtained control of the government, but in the following year was overthrown by the combined votes of the Conservatives and the Liberals. In 1929 the Laborites again took over the ministry. With the advent of the depression however, their difficulties were intensified, and they met with opposition in attempts to obtain financial assistance in foreign security markets, particularly New York and Paris. In 1931 the Labour Government was again overthrown by the combined opposition of Conservatives, Liberals and even some Laborites who formed a national government.[1] In the elections of 1935 the national government was continued in power.

The economic tendencies in England in the post-war period were unsatisfactory. The demand for coal was lessened by the development of new sources of energy as oil and hydro-electric power. As a result, the output of coal continued at a level below that of the pre-war period. The output of pig iron, steel ingots and of industry in general moved uncertainly.[2] The industrial expansion of England in progress from the close of the Napoleonic Wars had continued until the third quarter of the nineteenth century when the rate of increase has been retarded. It was now definitely checked in the post-war period, and many fields of economic activity registered actual declines.

In the closing years of the pre-war period, England had been facing increased trade rivalry from Germany and the United States in foreign markets. In the post-war period England encountered additional competition from France, Italy and Japan, while some of the backward countries as China, India, Russia and even South America, once extensive markets for British goods, now began to supply their own needs. In consequence, foreign trade, so essential to the very existence of England's economic life, dropped almost continuously throughout the post-war period. As a result of these unfavorable economic conditions there was a sharp increase in unemployment and throughout the post-war period it remained at a high level without precedent in British industrial history.[3]

CHANGES IN FINANCIAL ORGANIZATION

In the post-war period there were marked changes in the British financial organization particularly in reference to the Bank of England and the joint-stock banks. One of the most important tendencies was the change in the relation between the government and the Bank of England. Throughout the pre-war period the Bank had been able to maintain its traditional policy of independence from governmental control. However, the difficulties of the Exchequer in the war and post-war periods necessitated a closer relation between the Bank and the Treasury.[4] This tendency was evidenced by the fact that the directors of the Bank in the post-war period included not only representatives of the business interests, but also former government officials.

The Bank had been none too successful in coping with the problems arising out of security capitalism in the nineteenth century. After the Baring crisis, particularly in the years before the outbreak of the World War, the Bank had to seek help from the Bank of France. In the post-war period its dependence on traditional methods of control proved ineffective in meeting the difficult conditions of these years as seen in the uncertain monetary policy of England. During the War the gold standard had been abandoned but was restored in 1925. However, with the deepening of the depression the gold standard was again abandoned in 1931 and replaced by a system of managed currency. Thus the effort of the Bank to restore one of the fundamental institutions of pre-war security capitalism failed.

The movement for bank amalgamation made rapid headway. Before the War the large banks absorbed small institutions, but in the war years the large joint stock banks in several cases absorbed each other. This movement for bank amalgamation aroused concern over the possibility of a money trust, and the subject was considered by a Treasury Committee on Bank Amalgamations. The Committee reported "that the possible dangers resulting from further large amalgamations are material enough to outweigh the arguments against Government interference, and that, in view of the exceptional extent to which the interests of the whole community depend on banking arrangements, some measure of Government control is essential."[5] A bill was accordingly drafted, but was later withdrawn when the banks and the Treasury came to an agreement that there would be no further amalgamations by the former without the consent of the latter.

Notwithstanding the movement for concentration the relation between the British banks and industry was not close. Industry was not dependent upon the banks for capital due to the large supply obtainable from direct investors who generally selected securities on their own judgment and not upon the advice of the banks. As a result, although British industry obtained its short-term credit facilities from the commercial banks, the latter exercised practically no control over industrial management. This absence of close relation between banking and industry was criticised not only by business leaders but was deplored even by the MacMillan Committee, which included prominent bankers. The Committee declared:

We believe that in any community which wishes to keep in the van of progress the financial and industrial worlds should be closely integrated through appropriate organizations. In the last few exceedingly difficult years it would have been of high value if the leaders, for instance, of the steel or ship-building or other industries had been working in the closest cooperation with powerful financial and banking institutions in the City with a view to their reconstruction on a profitable basis.[6]

Even in the pre-war period the British banking system, theoretically regarded as pure commercial banking, had broadened its function. In the post-war period this tendency continued in even greater force. There was an increase in the proportion of fixed or time deposits and a consequent relative decline in current or demand deposits.[7] In the post-war period the proportion of total securities to total assets of the British banks rose sharply from 15.3 percent in 1925 to 27.2 percent in 1934.[8] This increase was due largely to the rise in the volume of government securities held by the banks.[9] The liquidity of the British banks was high as shown by the satisfactory proportion of reserve assets to total deposits which rose from 31.8 percent in 1925 to 44.2 percent in 1934. On the other hand the solvency of the British banks, or the adequacy of their capital to

TABLE 9

FINANCIAL POSITION OF BRITISH COMMERCIAL BANKS, 1925-1934.[10]
(percent)

	RATIOS	1925	1929	1930	1931	1932	1933	1934
A	Total securities to total assets...	15.3	12.7	14.6	15.9	22.6	26.8	27.2
B	Gov't. securities to total assets..	12.5	10.4	12.2	13.3	19.9	23.8	24.2
C	Reserve assets to total deposits.	31.8	28.0	31.3	31.9	39.2	42.9	44.2
D	Net capital to total assets	5.3	4.7	4.7	4.3	4.0	3.9	4.0
E	Net capital to total securities ..	34.7	37.1	32.1	26.9	17.5	14.7	14.6
F	Net capital to total deposits ...	6.1	5.5	5.3	4.9	4.4	4.4	4.5
G	Net capital to gross capital	77.8	71.5	70.1	63.0	64.4	63.6	64.7

meet losses on their assets, was unsatisfactory. The proportion of net capital to total assets was at a low level of 5.3 percent in 1925 and declined further to 4 percent in 1934.[11] The proportion of net capital to total securities dropped from 34.7 percent in 1925 to 14.6 percent in 1934.[12] A further indication of the inadequacy of the capital of the British banks is seen in the low level of net capital to total deposits which declined from 6.1 percent in 1925 to 4.5 percent in 1934.[13] As in the case of American banks, the British banks also made the error of tying up an increasing proportion of their capital in buildings and other fixed assets.[14]

OVERBURDENING THE CAPITAL MARKET

Over this period the capital market was forced to meet heavy demands of both governments and corporations. One of the most pressing problems of British security capitalism in the post-war period was the burden of the national debt. In the decade following the War the national government made an effort to contract its debt, and the total was somewhat reduced. However, during the depression it rose again, exceeding even the high level as at the end of the war period.[15] The seriousness of the burden of this national debt was due essentially to the fact that, created mainly as a result of war finance, it was a dead-weight debt in the sense of being unproductive and not providing the means of its repayment.[16] Unquestionably the payment of the service on this debt constituted a heavy burden upon the taxpayers as evidenced by the fact that the proportion of the debt service to total expenditures of the national government rose from 13.2 percent in 1913 to 42.8 percent in 1930.[17]

While the debt of the national government at least did not increase over the entire post-war period, the debt of the local authorities in England and Wales rose from £657,000,000 in 1921 to £1,393,000,000 in 1933.[18]

Opinion was divided on the extent to which this increasing local debt was unproductive. Lord Bradbury contended that the local debt was in the nature of a dead weight. The majority of the Economy Committee also expressed "grave concern" over the increase in local indebtedness, while the minority of the Committee pointed to the "increased value of the assets possessed by local authorities as a result of that expenditure."[19]

The demand for capital by private industry in the post-war period was heavy. There was a rapid growth in the formation of new companies. This movement reached a high level in 1928 when the number of new companies totaled 9,012 with a nominal capital of £220,506,126. In the previous sixty years these figures were exceeded only in 1899, in 1919 and in 1920.[20]

The nature of this governmental and corporate financing was in part reflected in the distribution of the securities listed on the London Stock Exchange as seen in Table 10 showing the listings for 1933. From this table it is seen that corporate securities constituted 56.78 percent of the total, while the issues of the national government accounted for the bulk of the public securities.

The trend of the supply of capital in the post-war period was

TABLE 10

SECURITIES LISTED ON THE LONDON STOCK EXCHANGE, 1933.[21]
(million pounds)

CLASSES OF SECURITIES	AMOUNT	PERCENT OF TOTAL
Railroads............................	1,125	6.07
Utilities.............................	872	4.70
Industrials..........................	2,176	11.75
Real estate and financial..............	683	3.69
British possessions corporate..........	401	2.17
Foreign corporate....................	5,215	28.16
Shares of no par value...............	44	0.24
Total corporate.....	10,515	56.78
British government..................	6,561	35.43
Municipal...........................	430	2.32
British possessions governmental.......	908	4.90
Foreign government..................	106	0.57
Total Government...	8,005	43.22
Grand Total........	18,520	100.00

unsatisfactory.   The nominal amount of national income moved downward from £2,462,000,000 in 1921 to £2,401,000,000 in 1924, then slightly upward to £2,531,000,000 in 1929 and to £2,725,000,-000 in 1931 and the nominal amount of saving funds over these years rose from a low of £357,000,000 in 1921 to a high of £537,000,-000 in 1934.[22]   While the nominal amount of national income and of savings funds was thus higher than in the pre-war year of 1913, the real amount compared unfavorably in view of the fall in the value of the sterling.[23]   The unsatisfactory trend of individual saving is further evidenced by the fact that from 1923 to 1927 withdrawals exceeded receipts at the post office savings banks.   The trustee savings banks showed a decrease in deposits, offset in part by an increase in the amount of government securities held for depositors.[24]   In general over the post-war years, the annual increase in the deposits of the savings banks was only equal to the interest earned on existing deposits.[25]   As in other countries, corporate saving became an increasingly important part of national saving.   It was estimated in 1924 that about 40 percent of the new accumulation of capital was in the form of profits retained by corporations and private businesses.[26]

The unsatisfactory trend in the volume of saving was due to the operation of several factors.   In the first place the heavy expenditures of the national and local governments absorbed a larger proportion of national income than in the pre-war period.   The proportion of the expenditures of the national government to national income alone rose from 19.9 percent in 1913 to 32.3 percent in 1931.[27]   In addition the expenditures of the local governments in England and Wales rose from £168,000,000 in 1910 to £566,000,000 in 1931.[28]   A further cause of the decline in saving was the unsatisfactory state of employment in the post-war years, and the resulting low level of wages which allowed little margin for saving.   As a result of these forces the proportion of saving funds to national income, which was 26.9 percent in 1913, fell to 12.9 percent in 1920 and was never higher than 16.9 percent until 1930.[29]

FINANCIAL RESULTS OF SECURITY CAPITALISM

The financial results of British security capitalism in the post-war period were unsatisfactory.   Because of the heavy demand for capital and the unfavorable trend in supply, the London capital market suffered from the overissue of securities.   One commentator declared: "The company promoters and the issuing houses float just as many issues as they think the investing public will stomach . . . the primary consideration of the market in domestic issues is not

the needs of industry but the needs of financial salesmanship." [30]
British security capitalism continued to follow the direct rather than
the indirect method of investment. In 1932 the total security holdings of the financial institutions of indirect investments as the investment trusts, the life insurance companies and the building and
loan associations, together amounted to only £1,700,000,000. As
pointed out before the official list of the London Stock Exchange
alone included securities with a nominal value of £18,371,000,000.[31]
As a result British securities were widely diffused among investors.
A study made by the *Economist* showed that £152,000,000 of common and preferred stock of some 18 companies was held by more
than 500,000 individual shareholders, each having an average of
£300.[32] In the period following the crash of 1929, the diffusion of
corporate investments continued, and the interests dominating the
corporations employed the same practices as were applied in the
United States in order to retain control. Non-voting stock was sold
to the public and shares with disproportionate voting power were
issued to the inside interests.[33] In the case of 48 issues, the investing
public contributed 93 percent of the cash but obtained less than 22
percent of the equity and would have received only 21 percent of the
prospective profits.[34]

As in other countries, the decline of security prices in the autumn
of 1929 affected all classes of issues but the securities of the old corporations depreciated less than those of the new corporations. The
former group lost but about one-fifth of their value in the decline
from the peak of prices in the fall of 1929 to the end of that year,
while the latter group experienced a depreciation of from 65 to 80
percent.[35] Losses were particularly heavy in the field of foreign
investments. The default on the principal amounted to nearly 40
percent of the total of foreign investments.[36]

The market price of British government bonds was satisfactory
during the post-war period. In 1927 the yield was 4.56 percent and
in 1931 when the government abandoned the gold standard the yield
was maintained at 4.53 percent. However, as a result of the cheap
money policy the price of government bonds rose and the average
yield in 1935 was down to a 2.91 basis.[37]

CRITICISM OF SECURITY CAPITALISM

The various financial institutions of British security capitalism
were bitterly scored in the post-war period. The Bank of England
was accused of sacrificing national for international financial interests. The joint-stock banks also were charged with favoring international business rather than domestic enterprise, with favoring the

USA
1936-7-8

security speculator rather than the industrialist and the large business man rather than the small business man.[38]   Dr. T. E. Gregory
stated that "the banker is unpopular, not merely in Labour circles,
but among the business community also, admits to-day of no dispute.
In its way it is one of the most significant of the differences between
1914 and 1927, and deserves the closest attention." [39]

The joint-stock banks, because of their prominence, bore the
brunt of the public opposition.   The short-comings of the investment houses in failing to finance domestic industry were laid at the
door of the joint-stock banks.[40]   Lloyd George criticised the large
banks in the statement that:

> The City is the stronghold of reaction.   All the time when I was
> Chancellor of the Exchequer up to 1914, I had to fight the City. . . No
> Government will ever get a big programme through unless it is pre-
> pared to face up to the reactionary money interests in the City of
> London.[41]

The *MacMillan Report* gave a tempered defense of the joint
stock banks in the statement that :

> We have in this country a great financial and banking organization
> with great experience and great traditions.   It is through and with that
> organization that we have to work, for they alone are the repositories
> of the skill and knowledge and they alone possess the equipment neces-
> sary for the management of our financial affairs.   Their views and
> opinions, however they may fail to commend themselves to enthusiastic
> reformers, are factors to be reckoned with just as much as the views
> and opinions of trade unions have to be reckoned with on questions
> of wages and working conditions.[42]

There was considerable body of opinion which held that the
Trustee Act was in error in limiting the authorized investments to
fixed-interest securities with the two nominal exceptions of the stock
of the Bank of England and the Bank of Ireland.   This limited
range was criticised on the ground that "no legislature can now
retain the impression that fixed-interest stocks, however eminent
their status, confer immunity from disturbing fluctuations in capital
values, in sympathy with changes in general interest rates." [43]   The
eligible list excluded such important securities as the prior charges
of gas companies, electrical companies, port and harbor authorities,
and of course industrial corporations.   In 1928 a committee was
appointed by the Lord Chancellor to review the subject of trustee
securities.   The committee, however, approached the subject from
a purely legalistic viewpoint and refused to recommend any drastic
change in the list.[44]

CONTROL OVER THE CAPITAL MARKET

The national government exercised a moderate control over the supply of capital through such agencies as the National Debt Commission and the Public Trustee. The National Debt Commission regulated not only the national debt but also the advances made out of the Local Loan Funds to local governments.[45] The government also influenced the flow of capital to a limited extent through the office of the Public Trustee which had been established in 1906 and which increased the volume of the trusts which it administered.[46] The Public Trustee under its administration carried about one-third of its trust funds in the securities of the national government and the remainder was distributed among domestic railroad, colonial and foreign government bonds.

A more important control of the capital market was exercised by the Government in its regulation of the demand for capital. Parliament extended its regulation of corporate financing by carrying further the principles embodied in the various companies acts of the pre-war period particularly that of disclosure in the Act of 1929. This statute required that corporations give full and accurate information of their financial position in their balance sheets and in their profit and loss accounts, and also increased the liabilities of officers and directors for misrepresentation in financial statements. The provisions of the Companies Act were applied against Lord Kylsant who was convicted on the charge of publishing a false prospectus.[47] There was, however, a growing feeling that the Companies Act was inadequate and that further control was needed particularly in protecting the public against the abuses of the holding companies.[48]

During the War the flow of capital was restricted by the government, and this control was continued in the post-war period. The government had no parliamentary authorization to prevent investment houses from floating new issues, but these houses carefully observed the restrictions "requested" by the Treasury and the Bank of England.[49] In 1925 an embargo was applied to foreign loans in order to aid the government in its policy of returning to the gold standard. In 1931 with the intensification of the world depression the embargo was extended to other forms of investment. Throughout 1933 the government continued its unofficial embargo on issues particularly those for new capital. Apparently these restrictions were not always enforced, and certain corporations placed issues which appeared to be contrary to the provisions of the embargo.[50] In 1936 the Treasury appointed a body, later known as the Foreign Transactions Advisory Committee, including representatives of the

Bank of England as well as of industry, to consult with the Chancellor of the Exchequer on the administration of the government control over the capital market.[51]   The Treasury further ordered investment trusts to limit the proportion of their foreign investments to the bare minimum necessary to conduct their business in accordance with the policy of investment trusts, to attain geographic diversification of their holdings, and recommended that if the actual proportion of foreign securities was "unusually high it should be reduced." [52]

The most drastic proposals for control of security capitalism came from the Labour Party.   At first it urged only the nationalization of the Bank of England, but in 1933 it recommended the socialization of the joint-stock banks as well.[53]   In the post-war period there was a growing conviction among students of security capitalism that the capital market ought to be more carefully controlled.[54]   E. H. Davenport wrote :

The State must supervise or direct the investment of the national savings if it is to ensure national stability . . . investment cannot safely be left to the haphazard competition of the various private agencies that now exist for the utilization of savings.   Investment must be directed by the State into fields of production which it considers conducive to the maintenance of employment at the highest possible level.[55]

This proposal for governmental control of the capital market was embodied by the Labour Party in its plan for a board of national investment which would direct the flow of capital in order to prevent its misdirection. [56]   This body was to be appointed by the government and was to co-operate closely with a nationalized Bank of England.   The proposal for a board of national investment had the approval of John Maynard Keynes who urged qualitative as well as quantitative control.[57]

CONCLUSION

Thus the crisis of British security capitalism, which had already started with the close of the nineteenth century, was intensified by the War and was deepened in the post-war period.   For the first time in the history of British security capitalism, over a period of years, industrial production not only showed no increase but actually declined.   Similarly foreign trade, the very life blood of England, also dropped in amount.   The Bank of England, never well adapted to the system of security capitalism, found itself unable to cope with the difficult problems of the post-war period.   In the field of banking the amalgamation movement made rapid progress, but the British banks continued their pre-war policy of not developing close relations with industry.   Their financial position, as reflected in their deficiency of capital was not satisfactory. The demand for capital in the post-war period was heavy. Unlike the post-Napoleonic era, the national government was unable to reduce its enormous war debt in the ensuing period, and the debt was all the more serious in view of its unproductive nature. The local governments also added to the total public debt through a continuous flow of new issues. The corporate demand for capital was also large. On the other hand the volume of capital available for the security market was unsatisfactory due to the decline in real national income and the reduction in real saving. Criticism of British security capitalism was widespread and was directed particularly against the Bank of England and the joint-stock banks. The difficulties of the post-war period led the government to extend its control over the system of security capitalism. The demand for capital was to a moderate extent controlled by the operations of such agencies as the National Debt Commission and the Public Trustee. More important was the regulation of corporate practices connected with the demand for capital in the Companies Act of 1929. Quantitative control of the demand for capital was exercised by the embargo administered by the Treasury. The Labour Party, not satisfied with this control, urged the nationalization of the Bank of England, the joint-stock banks and the establishment of a board for the control of the flow of capital.

INSTABILITY OF FRENCH SECURITY CAPITALISM

French political conditions throughout the post-war period were ominated by the fiscal difficulties of these years, and as a result one cabinet after the other was forced out of office. Immediately after the close of the War on the wave of patriotic feeling the National Bloc under the leadership of Raymond Poincaré crushed the Socialist opposition. Poincaré pursued a strongly nationalistic policy in directing France's relations with Germany, and in the dispute over reparations, sent the French army into the Ruhr. In 1924 the Left Cartel, composed largely of Socialists under the leadership of Herriot, took over the government. The new ministry followed a more conciliatory policy toward Germany, and co-operated with England and the United States in formulating the Dawes Plan. The Herriot government was unable to solve the difficult financial problems of France, and in 1926 gave way to the National Union led by Poincaré and composed of all the political parties except the extreme left. From 1924 to 1932 the foreign policies of France were guided by Briand who sought to improve the relations between France and Germany. Briand was fortunate in having the co-operation of Gustav Stresemann, Germany's foreign minister, and for a time it appeared that the two former enemy countries would come to an understanding. In 1932 the Left Cartel, headed by Herriot again returned to power, but with the deepening depression the financial condition of the government became acute, and once more Herriot was forced out of office. Again in 1934, there was a return to the National Union composed of all the parties except the Socialists and Communists. To counteract the radical elements, a fascist organization known as the Croix de Feu (Cross of Fire) supported by the powerful financial and industrial interests grew in strength.[58] However, profiting from the unfortunate experience of the radical parties of Germany and Austria, the Socialists and the Communists of France formed a common front under Leon Blum for joint action against this threat of fascism and the interests of concentrated industry. This United Front obtained control of the government in 1936 and continued in power even after the collapse of the Blum ministry in June, 1937. During this period the Croix de Feu was disbanded.

INDUSTRIAL RECOVERY

Economic conditions in France in the post-war period were directly influenced by the results of the War. The devastated areas in northern France had to be rebuilt, and this work was a heavy economic task. Another important economic consequence of the War was the acquisition of Alsace and Lorraine and also temporarily of the Saar Valley which gave France large deposits of iron and coal. As a result of these acquisitions industrial production in France increased sharply in the post-war period particularly the output of coal, pig-iron and steel.[59]

During the period under review France encountered serious currency difficulties, and, in 1926 and again in 1936 the government was forced to devaluate the franc. These successive devaluations, by reducing the gold value of the franc, brought losses to the holders of fixed obligations, and struck at the very foundation of French security capitalism.

DOWNFALL OF THE "FINANCIAL BASTILE"

An important trend in post-war French security capitalism was the conflict between the radical government and the Bank of France. In the post-war period the various radical governments met bitter opposition from the Bank's Board of Regents whose members were elected by the two hundred largest stockholders or the so-called "two hundred families." The bitterness between the radical cabinets and the Regents was mainly political in that the Regents were generally members of the conservative parties. However, the immediate issue between the radical governments and the Bank of France concerned the extent to which the Bank should grant accommodations to the national government. On the one hand the government, hard pressed by its budgetary difficulties demanded liberal advances, while the Regents, concerned primarily with the solvency of the Bank, were reluctant to accede. Hence the almost continual clash between the radical cabinets and the Bank.

In 1924 the issue was sharply drawn when Herriot, as leader of the Left Cartel, demanded liberal financial aid from the Bank, but in the end he was defeated and later forced out of office. In 1935 the government again attacked the Bank, and Premier Flandin removed Governor Mauret of the Bank of France and placed Jean Tannery in charge. The latter, however, followed a conservative financial policy and joined with the Board of Regents in resisting the efforts of the government to obtain more liberal accommodation.[60] Throughout the depression the Bank stood firm for a policy of deflation. Unlike other central banks, it gave relatively little help to the public treasury and discounted only a comparatively small amount of short-term notes.[61] As an aid in carrying out its deflationary policy the Bank won the support of the financial press by liberal distribution of money.

With the coming of the popular cabinet under Leon Blum in 1936, the attack on the Bank and particularly on the Board of Regents became stronger. The Board was bitterly indicted in the speeches in the Chamber of Deputies, and the minister of finance declared that "the Government of France is democratic and renewable by popular suffrage. The economic and financial government of the nation is hereditary, oligarchic and of divine right." As a proof of these charges it was pointed out that the two hundred largest shareholders included the leading elements of French security capitalism. Of the six banking members of the Board of Regents five were descendents of the leaders of security capitalism during the First Empire.[62] Five more seats were held by the leaders of French industrial security capitalism such as Francois de Wendel, President of the powerful Comité des Forges.[63] Together twelve Regents directly or indirectly were directors in ninety-five huge corporations which had grown out of the war and post-war concentration movement. These corporations were gigantic industrial units wielding extensive political and economic power.

The attack on the Bank of France as the symbol of security capitalism was conducted with the same ardor as the eighteenth century assault on the Bastile, the symbol of the privileged aristocracy. In July, 1936, the Parlement overwhelmingly voted reform of the Bank.

The law provided that the Regents were no longer to be elected by the two hundred largest stockholders, but by all, with one vote for each share irrespective of the number of shares held. The "financial Bastile" had fallen so it was thought.

CHANGES IN THE BANKING STRUCTURE

In the post-war period the banking structure underwent considerable change. There was a movement toward banking concentration through consolidation of individual banks and through the extension of the branches of the Paris banks over the country. The number of actual bank failures in France was small, but this apparently satisfactory result was achieved through the absorption of weaker units by stronger banks and through government assistance.[64]

In the post-war period the distinction between the credit banks and the banque d'affaires became less pronounced.[65] Even before the War the former had engaged in underwriting and in marketing securities, and this function increased considerably in later years. At the same time the banque d'affaires, essentially investment institutions, in the pre-war period expanded their commercial operations and financed a considerable part of French business.

The French overseas banks became an important factor in the financial machinery of the nation. These banking institutions were of two kinds. Those which operated in the French colonies, as Indo-China and Morocco, were called colonial banks, and those which operated in foreign countries, were outright overseas banks. The colonial banks had extensive powers which included not only those of deposit and discount, but also the right of issuing notes for circulation. The French overseas banks, operating in foreign lands, were usually owned or closely controlled by the large banks of Paris.

CHANGES IN THE CAPITAL MARKET

The capital market in the post-war period was dominated almost entirely by the demands of the national government. The French national debt rose enormously during the war and post-war years, and the expenditure for debt service increased sharply.[66] The burden of this expenditure for debt service had always been high and in 1934 constituted over 54 percent of total expenditures.[67] The volume of foreign loans in the post-war period was much smaller than that in the pre-war period.[68] To a large extent these loans continued to be made for political reasons, and the members of the Little Entente particularly were granted liberal financial support.[69] The uncertainty of the currency had a direct effect upon the nature

England
42.8% in
1930

of corporate financing in the post-war period. Because of losses in fixed-interest bearing obligations due to devaluation the French investor favored stocks over bonds. Bowing to this changing demand, French corporations modified their policy and issued a greater proportion of stock than in the past.

The supply of capital in the years immediately following the close of the War was small. The nominal value of national income was 208,000,000,000 francs in 1926, as compared with 36,000,000,000 francs in 1913. However, in view of the fact that the index of commodity prices in 1926 was 812 as compared with 116 in 1913, therefore the real value of the national income in 1926 was only 29,610,000,000 francs or below the level of 1913. Similarly the nominal value of saving funds in 1926 was 15,700,000,000 francs but the real value of these saving funds in 1926 expressed in terms of the franc of 1913 was only 2,200,000,000 francs as compared with 5,800,000,000 francs in 1913.[70] The proportion of new securities to such saving over these years was large, and was reflected in the high yields on government bonds which rose to 6.17 in 1926.[71]

With the de facto stabilization of the franc in 1927 there was once more a growth in saving and an increase in the supply of capital. National income rose to 228,000,000,000 francs in 1931 and then fell to 178,000,000,000 francs in 1934 but saving funds however rose continually from 15,700,000,000 francs in 1926 to 60,700,000,000 francs in 1934.[72] Over this period total accumulated saving funds to national income rose from 7.5 percent to 34.1 percent.[73] In the depression period the valume of new securities declined sharply and the proportion of new securities to saving funds fell.[74] Thus the demand for capital was small in relation to its supply, and the cost of capital, as reflected in the yield on government bonds, dropped to 3.88 percent in 1935.[75]

CONTROL OF SECURITY CAPITALISM

As in the case of England, the French government exercised a veto power over the exportation of capital. However, in the case of France this power was exercised not by an informal embargo but as a result of a formal act of the Chamber of Deputies. The listing of foreign issues had to have the approval of the minister of finance. The exercise of this power to control foreign securities led to the serious political scandal of the Snia Viscosa, an Italian company manufacturing artificial silk. This company was highly speculative in nature and its listing was attained through the bribery of the minister of finance himself.

CONCLUSION

In the post-war period the position of French security capitalism was unstable. The political ferment of the post-war years was caused in a large measure by the unsatisfactory budgetary position of the national government. The movement for business concentration made rapid headway and the leaders of this new industrial capitalism were also active in French politics. This conservative force was met in later years by a radical opposition, and so France did not follow the path of Germany in falling under the political control of industrial capitalism. The radical groups were even victorious in wresting control of the Bank of France from the influence of the banking and industrial capitalists.

French security capitalism was confronted by an almost intolerable burden in the form of an enormous public debt—the heritage of the pre-war and post-war periods. The failure of the attempts to collect full reparations from Germany placed the burden of the debt squarely on the French people, and notwithstanding the increased industrialization of the nation the load was very heavy.

STRUGGLE BETWEEN GERMAN INDUSTRIAL AND BANKING SECURITY CAPITALISM—POLITICAL FERMENT

The history of German security capitalism in the post-war period can best be understood in relation to the struggle between the industrialists and the bankers. This conflict passed through three successive stages. The period from 1920 to 1923 marked the ascendancy of industrial security capitalism; from 1924 to 1929 the temporary victory of banking security capitalism, and finally after 1930 the triumph of industrial capitalism.

In the closing days of the War the monarchy came to an end, and in 1919, under the Weimar Constitution, the government was formally declared a republic with Franz Ebert as provisional President. The new socialist government made commendable efforts to establish a middle class democracy but was beset by powerful political opposition both on the left and on the right. In 1919 the Spartacists actuated by the principles of communism rebelled against the socialist government, but the movement was crushed and many of the leaders, including Carl Liebknecht and Rosa Luxemburg, were killed. On the other side, the socialist government was faced by a powerful reactionary opposition which expressed itself in the uprising of 1920 headed by General Kapp and that of 1923 in which General Ludendorf and Adolph Hitler participated, but these assaults were also suppressed. Even after the crushing of the communists and the reactionaries, the German socialists continued to be seriously divided within their own ranks. The Independent Socialists at the party Congress in 1920 voted for adhesion to the Third Internationale and accepted the conditions dictated by Moscow, calling for a rejection of the revisionist socialism of Kautsky and Hilferding. The Revisionist Socialists did not agree among themselves on their policy toward capitalism and at their Congress at Cassel in 1920 there was a sharp clash of views between those who urged "full socialization" or the complete conversion of private-owned concerns into public-owned corporations and those who argued for a system carefully controlled by the government but operated under private ownership.

THE CARTHAGINIAN PEACE

As in the case of France after the close of the Napoleonic Wars, Germany after the Great War was forced to pay reparations to the victors. Under the terms of the Armistice of 1918, Germany agreed to make compensation for the damage wrought on French and Belgian soil during the War. In the following year in the Treaty of Versailles, Germany formally assumed sole responsibility for the War and agreed to pay such damages as might be fixed by the Reparations Commission. The exact amount of compensation was not determined by the Treaty, and Germany practically signed a blank check. The Conference of London held in 1921 wrote the sum of 132,000,000,000 gold marks into this check which Germany was then asked to honor. In vain, Germany pointed out the impossibility of paying this amount. To France the imposition of this huge financial burden was the means of keeping her former enemy crushed under the terms of a Carthaginian peace. For a short time Germany paid the required sum, but in 1923 she defaulted and Allied armies occupied the Ruhr Valley, the industrial heart of Germany. The results of this effort to collect reparations at the point of the bayonet proved futile for France but disastrous for Germany. The German mark, which had already depreciated because of the unbalanced budget at home, now collapsed. The conflict in the Ruhr threatened to bring about not only disorder in France and Germany but throughout the Continent.

Banking security capitalism in England and the United States, now thoroughly alarmed, intervened. In November 1923, the Reparations Commission appointed committees to investigate the problem and report their findings. That, headed by General Charles E. Dawes, made the first attempt at a rational solution of the reparations problem. The Dawes plan, without fixing the total amount, provided for reasonable annual payment of reparations to the Allies. The Dawes plan recommended the transfer of the control of the German railroads from the German government to a private corporation, and provided for Allied control over German industry and banking. German political sovereignty over the Ruhr was restored, but the Allied armies continued to occupy part of the Rhineland. The respite given by the Dawes plan enabled the Reichsbank under the leadership of Dr. Schacht to stabilize the currency.

EFFECTS OF CURRENCY DEPRECIATION

The currency depreciation over these years had significant effects on the various classes in German economic life as the industrialists, the bankers and the middle class. The industrialists were the chief beneficiaries of the collapse of the mark. From 1920 until the end of 1923 industrial production rose sharply.[76] In financing these operations most of the great industrial corporations shaped their policies so as to take full advantage of the depreciation of the currency. On the one hand they obtained liberal short-term loans from the banks, and these loans were paid at maturity in depreciated currency. At the same time long-term debts, incurred in the pre-war period in gold currency, were now paid off in paper money worth only a fraction of the amount originally received. Hugo Stinnes, a power in the pre-war period, became the leader of German industrial capitalism, and extended his control into the field of banking by seizing the Barmer Bankverein and by acquiring a third interest in the Berliner Handelsgesellschaft.[77]

By the end of the inflation period the capital of the large industries had increased, while that of the banks had decreased. On the one hand the gold mark capital in 1924 as compared with 1913 in the case of the textile industries had increased by 124.5 percent, in the mining industries by 135 percent and in the chemical industries by 189.5 percent.[78] On the other hand, the inflation of the currency sharply reduced the capital of the great banks. The gold mark capital and reserves in 1924 as compared with 1913 of the Darmstädter Bank dropped to 29.9 percent, the Dresdner Bank to 38.2 percent, the Disconto Gesellschaft to 47.6 percent and the Deutsche Bank to 64 percent, or an average of 42.8 percent.[79] Unquestionably many individual bankers, particularly the private bankers, personally gained by the collapse of the mark, but German banking as a whole suffered from the decline in the currency.

The depreciation of the currency brought ruin to the middle class including the small businessmen, professional persons, government employees, clerks, pensioners, and farmers. In the pre-war period this class had been the bulwark of German security capitalism. The middle class through its frugality had accumulated savings, had invested them in bank deposits and in securities and thereby had supplied funds for German pre-war industrial expansion. The value of these direct and indirect investments was now largely swept away with the depreciation of the currency.

The middle class, which in the pre-war period had been opponents of Marxism, not only continued its opposition but now developed a new and bitter hostility to banking security capitalism which was held responsible for the collapse of the mark and accused of engaging in speculative activities. This attitude of the middle class expressed itself in the formation of the National Socialist Party which first became a political factor in the national elections of 1924.

It was naturally difficult for the middle class to express itself against an abstract system, and so it gave vent to its feelings concretely in its hostility to the Jews who, since the beginning of the nineteenth century, personified banking security capitalism. Unquestionably in the pre-war period the influence of the Jews over security capitalism had grown out of proportion to their number, and in the post-war period their power continued to be extensive. It was stated that in 1928 fifteen Jews held 718 directorships of German companies and that in 1931 nearly 89 percent of the Berlin stockholders were Jewish.[80]

POLITICAL AND ECONOMIC RECOVERY

From 1924 to 1930 German banking capitalism regained some of its former power due to more favorable political and economic conditions. Over these years domestic as well as international political conditions remained relatively quiet. In 1925 on the death of Ebert, the elections were won by the monarchist groups headed by General Von Hindenburg who, however, loyally supported the republican form of government. Over these years Germany's foreign relations were skillfully handled by Gustav Stresemann with the cooperation of Briand, and the Locarno Pact brought Germany back into the family of nations. Economic recovery was rapid. From the low level of 1923 industrial production rose sharply until the end of 1927.[81]

With the stabilization of the currency the relative positions of banking and industrial capitalism were reversed. On the one hand the shrinkage of bank capital came to an end, and bank deposits increased. On the other hand the industrialists found themselves without working capital due to the sudden deflation following the revaluation of the mark and to the fact that their assets were im-

[handwritten marginalia: tion. ... leaving them without ... bank capital to water fixed capital which had been magnified during the period of currency depreciation and inflation.]

mobilized in the form of fixed capital. Industry again had to accept the dictation of the German banks, and for a while they were able to regain some of their control over industry. The great Stinnes concern suffered severe reverses, and after the death of Hugo Stinnes in 1923 his son Edmund was forced to give up most of his business interests.[82]

With the end of the inflation movement in 1923, Germany was in urgent need of capital not only to pay reparations but also to meet the domestic requirements of industry.[83]   However, the domestic supply of capital was badly depleted.   From 1913 to 1922 there was a sharp drop in national wealth, national income and national saving, and the proportion of saving to income showed a marked decrease.[84]   Under these conditions Germany had to import capital.

Throughout the nineteenth century nations with developed systems of security capitalism had obtained control over the economic systems of undeveloped countries.   Now for the first time in history a nation with a developed security capitalism was in danger of being financially controlled by other countries.   Imperialism thus took a new form and for a time there resulted the exploitation of not a backward but of a highly developed economy.   Due to the depreciation of the mark, investors with foreign currencies were able to obtain large interests in German corporations with only a small investment of their funds.[85]   In 1932 it was estimated that foreign capitalists held a total participation of 1,553,000,000 marks in corporations with nominal capital of 5,534,000,000 marks.[86]   However, this danger of alienation was overcome by various protective devices, as the issuance and retention by the German management of preference stock with multiple voting power.[87]

Between 1924 and 1930 Germany's import of capital amounted to nearly three times the sum paid in reparations.   The greater part of these funds were applied to accumulate reserves in the form of working capital and to the rationalization of German industry through the application of scientific management.[88]

DECLINE OF BANKING CAPITALISM

Notwithstanding this financial assistance from abroad German economic conditions became unsatisfactory as early as 1928 and were already desperate by the coming of the world depression.   General production declined continuously from 1928 through 1932.   Unemployment rose from 16.7 percent of the population in 1928 to the staggering figure of 43.7 percent in 1932.[89]   Again it became necessary for international banking capitalism to intervene in an effort to support the weakening structure of German capitalism. An international committee was formed under the leadership of Owen D. Young, and composed of prominent representatives of banking capitalism. This committee made an earnest effort to overcome the political and financial difficulties which were confronting Germany. The Young plan ended the occupation of the Rhineland five years ahead of its schedule and also terminated the irksome Allied control over German banking and industry which had been imposed by the Dawes plan. The financial provisions of the Young plan were likewise sensible. The total amount of reparations was fixed for the first time at eight billion dollars. Provision was made for possible postponement of payment of part of the debt if circumstances necessitated. Furthermore, the Young plan established the Bank for International Settlements to bring about more effective international cooperation among the various systems of security capitalism.

All this effort was doomed to failure as a result of the deepening of the depression. Finally, in June 1931, President Von Hindenburg personally informed President Hoover that: "The whole world lacks confidence in the ability of the German economic system to work under the existing burdens." [90] President Hoover then proposed a moratorium which postponed both reparations payments by Germany as well as the war debt payments by the Allies. In 1932 the Lausanne conference made an effort at a further solution of the reparations problem but in vain, for German banking security capitalism was doomed.

The depression ushered in the third and final stage of the struggle between German banking and industrial security capitalism. Already in the closing years of the 1920's the contest between the two systems was being fought over economic, religious and political issues. In the economic field banking and industrial security capitalism struggled to control the United Steel Works, the great metallurgical trust of Germany. In this contest the forces of banking capitalism were led by the directors of the Deutsche Bank and by Otto Wolff, an industrialist of the Rhineland, closely associated with the banking interests.[91] The forces of industrial capitalism were captained by Fritz Thyssen.[92] The banking group was willing to make concessions to the French steel interest, particularly the Schneider-Creusot and the de Wendel groups in order to attain closer cooperation among the continental steel companies. The industrial group also realized the necessity for international cooperation, but insisted that Germany have the dominant position in any such continental combine. The two opposing forces carried the fight into the religious and political fields. The Deutsche Bank represented the Jewish interests, and gave its backing to the republican parties. Otto Wolff was a Catholic and supported the Center party which joined with the republicans in a bloc against both extreme right and left parties. Thyssen and his associates gave active support to National Socialism.[93] In 1929 Thyssen brought Adolph Hitler to Düsseldorf and introduced him to several hundred leading industrialists of the Ruhr.[94] With this support Hitler confidently entered the political campaign of 1930. In the campaign of that year Hitler denounced all the past efforts of international security capitalism at solving Germany's difficulties in the following searing words :

. . . with lies our people were led into the Dawes Pact, with lies we were induced to sign Locarno, and lies, lies and yet more lies have now given us the Young Plan. Germany has been doped with illusion after illusion; Spa, Brussels, Versailles, Geneva, Paris, London, Locarno, the League of Nations, and now the Young Plan—all were illusions, and under the curse of these illusions Germany has lost her freedom, she has lost her moral prestige and, having no longer any political honour she has now even sacrificed her economic substance.[95]

While National Socialism was an expression of mass protest against the unnecessary humiliation and the shortsighted blow to German national pride contained in the provisions of the Versailles Treaty, the movement was also directed against banking security capitalism. National Socialism was fundamentally anti-socialist in that it opposed international Marxism, but at the same time it was anti-capitalist in that it equally opposed international banking security capitalism.[96] The system of banking capitalism in its developed stage naturally becomes international in nature. In the pre-war period the German banks therefore had developed close relations with the banks in other financial centers, particularly London, New York and Paris and in the post-war period the German banks were forced to renew this relationship with their former enemies. This international aspect of German banking capitalism became the target of the bitter attacks by the National Socialists. The struggle between German banking security capitalism and National Socialism was thus a conflict between the necessary international relations of modern capitalism and the nationalistic characteristics of the new party which sought to revert to the economic nationalism of individual capitalism.

The elections of 1930 recorded the first major victory of the National Socialists, and again in 1932 they were successful. The Catholic-Liberal group, which had sought to retain control of the government under Dr. Brüning, now turned to General Schleicher who was closely connected with Otto Wolff. The Schleicher government was short-lived, and in 1933 the National Socialists came into power. The Reichstag then suspended the constitution and granted Adolph Hitler dictatorial powers. At the same time control of the United Steel Works passed into the hands of the Thyssen interests.[97]

This triumph of industrial capitalism was made complete by the collapse of German banking capitalism. With the intensification of the depression the position of the German banks became critical as may be seen in Table 11 showing their reserve position in 1929 and 1931.

TABLE 11

RESERVE POSITION OF GERMAN BANKS, 1929 AND 1931.[98]
(million reichmarks)

NO.	ITEMS	1929	1931
1	Total deposits..........................	10,965	7,041
2	Cash..................................	258	237
3	Rediscounts............................	−1,816	−1,912
4	Net cash (2−3)........................	−1,558	−1,675
5	Due from banks.......................	1,948	996
6	Due to banks..........................	3,270	2,546
7	Net due from banks (5−6).............	−1,322	−1,550
8	Government securities..................	29	345
9	Guarantees............................	−828	−703
10	Reserve assets [(4+7+8)−9]............	−3,679	−3,588
	Reserve assets to total deposits (10÷1)[(a)]..	−29.84	−50.96

[a] In percent.

From this table it is seen that the cash of the German banks was more than offset by rediscounts representing borrowings largely from the Reichsbank, and the balances due from banks were likewise more than offset by the balances due to banks mainly foreign financial institutions. As a result the German banks had a deficit in their reserve assets of 3,679,000,000 marks in 1929 and of 3,588,000,000 marks in 1931. The ratio of reserves to deposits shows a deficit of 29.84 percent in 1929 and of 50.96 percent in 1931, a condition almost without precedent in banking history. The German banks made every effort to save themselves, but unfortunately adopted desperate policies which in the end only served to intensify their difficulties. Most of the banks followed the policy of buying back their own stock, so that by July, 1931, the Deutsche Bank and the Disconto Gesellschaft owned 36.8 percent of their own stock, the Dresdner Bank 55 percent and the Darmstädter Bank 58.3 percent.[99]

The failure of the Darmstädter Bank, and later the Dresdner Bank in 1931 signalized the collapse of the German banking structure. The government made drastic efforts to aid these institutions, and contributed funds extensively to the Darmstädter Bank which was merged with the Dresdner Bank, and also gave support to the Deutsche Bank which was merged with the Disconto Gesellschaft.[100]

FINANCIAL POLICIES OF THE NATIONAL SOCIALISTS

The National Socialists completely reversed the financial policies of the previous government. The latter had followed a policy of credit contraction, which had resulted in a marked rise in the volume of unemployment. The National Socialists now entered upon a program of credit expansion, whose two-fold aim was reemployment and rearmament. Under the National Socialist regime there was a marked recovery in industrial production; unemployment was reduced and the first objective of the Party's program was attained.[101] The second fundamental aim of rearming Germany was also achieved, for the shackles of the Versailles Treaty were shattered by blow after blow, and after 1934 Germany entered upon a drastic program of augmenting her naval and military forces. As a result armament expenditures rose sharply, and the proportion of armament to total expenditures increased.[102] In consequence the total indebtedness of the federal government rose from 11,992,000,000 marks in 1932 to 20,833,-000,000 marks in 1936.[103] This rearmament program in a large measure was responsible for the increase in production and the reduction in unemployment. The total public debt including that of the local as well as the federal government in 1937, was about 37,-000,000,000 marks as compared with 27,000,000,000 marks in 1933 and 33,000,000,000 marks in 1914.

There are varying conclusions as to the financial effects of this program. The German government contended that these policies did not cause an excessive credit expansion, and in an official publication stated that "the credit indebtedness" in the sense of bonds, mortgages, short-term credits, had changed only slightly.[104] However these official figures were disputed by outside commentators on German finance.[105] It is however probable that the total public debt, although increasing, in 1937 was not a serious burden in relation to Germany's economic and financial resources. The one weakness in the public debt was the rapid increase in the short-term debt.

Over these years there was an increase in national income and national saving. The official reports indicated a rise in national income from 45,200,000,000 marks in 1932 to 61,500,000,000 marks in 1936.[106] This increase in income was largely caused by the rise in employment and the recovery of industrial production.[107] However an increasing proportion of national income was absorbed by taxation. In addition, the German people paid so-called "voluntary" contributions and semi-official taxes which were practically forced levies upon national income. Notwithstanding these payments the saving of the German people increased considerably. Deposits in German saving banks rose from 11,400,000,000 in 1932 to 14,600,-000,000 by the end of 1936, and over the same period receipts from life insurance premiums rose from 749,000,000 to 940,000,000 marks.[108] This increase in saving was, however, largely accomplished by the conscious policy of the government in limiting the standard of living.

CONTROL OF SECURITY CAPITALISM

The National Socialists extended the power of the government over the various financial institutions of security capitalism including the Reichsbank, the banks, the stock exchange, the capital market and the corporations. The Reichsbank was placed under the direction of Dr. Schacht. The granting of credit to the government was facilitated by the extension of liberal security loans. These loans, important in the pre-war period, had been restricted under the Banking law of 1924, but in 1933 were expanded so as to give the Reichsbank increased powers in dealing in the securities of the German national, state and government railroads in the open market.

As a result of the extensive government aid to the banks, the Reich for a time owned over 70 percent of the capital of all the large German banks. However, by 1936, a considerable part of these bank shares were returned to private ownership.[109]

The National Socialists appointed a commission to study the entire subject of banking. The report of this body opposed the nationalization of credit, but urged closer government supervision of banking operations and also a separation of the commercial and investment functions which had been jointly exercised by the German banks from their inception in the middle of the nineteenth century. The German banking law of 1934 permitted a bank to carry assets in fixed property and investments, but such investments could not exceed its capital. This law also recognized the necessity of maintaining an adequate relation of capital to depreciable investments. Assets in the form of securities, not quoted on the German stock exchanges, could not exceed a fixed percentage of total capital.[110]

The National Socialists also extended the control over the stock exchanges by a decree of March, 1933. Under this law the Berlin Exchange was placed under the supervision of the Prussian state commissioner and the Chamber of Industry and Commerce of Berlin and was managed by a board of directors whose members had to be approved by the Chamber of Industry and Commerce.[111]   The capital market was closely controlled, and the government's consent had to be obtained for all private issues. These were restricted mainly to corporations manufacturing materials needed by the government.

The National Socialists bitterly attacked the whole principle of incorporated business particularly its impersonality and the so-called "democratic" system of control of management by shareholders, and in its place urged the principle of "personal responsibility" and "leadership."   National Socialism not content with abolishing democracy in German political life, also sought to eliminate "shareholders parliamentarianism."   As a result a law was passed which transferred the control of German corporations from stockholders, and placed these powers in the hands of salaried directorates.   Furthermore, the boards of supervision, which in the past had controlled the affairs of German corporations, were deprived of all powers of management.[112]

ATTITUDE TOWARD CAPITALISM

There was a difference in the theory of National Socialism toward capitalism and its actual policy toward the system.   While National Socialism favored the principle of private property, the increasingly difficult economic conditions forced the government into a policy of what amounted to partial confiscation of private property.[113]   Although the means of production were still privately owned, they were placed under rigorous state control, and the output of almost all raw and semi-manufactured materials as well as food products was placed under government supervisory boards. The government also followed a policy of practically drafting capital whenever funds were needed for public works and rearmament. Companies were prohibited from paying dividends in excess of 6 percent, with certain exceptions when an 8 percent rate was permitted, and profits in excess of this amount had to be turned over to the Golddiskontbank to be placed in government bonds for a period of three years.[114]   The government also compelled the "investment" of capital in industries which were essential to the state even though unprofitable in operation.[115]   Dr. Dietrich, Chief of Press of the National Socialist Party stated that: "The capitalist system has been replaced by the National Socialist System."[116]   This statement was really incorrect for German capitalism was not "replaced" or "destroyed" but rather modified in that there was an increase in the public or governmental nature of the system.   Security capitalism still continued in Germany though under strict government control.

CHAPTER 9

CRISIS OF WORLD SECURITY CAPITALISM

THE PREVIOUS chapter has traced the crisis of security capitalism in England, France and Germany in the post-war period. This chapter will continue the analysis of the crisis by studying the leading trends in Italy, Russia and Japan and finally the general movement of world security capitalism.

MODIFICATION OF ITALIAN SECURITY CAPITALISM

The position of Italy in the years immediately following the War was highly unsatisfactory. The territorial gains from the War were disappointing, for the newly-acquired lands did not provide the basis for profitable colonial expansion. After the close of the War industrial disorders became widespread and the nation was faced with growing radicalism. Italy was in a state of economic deadlock, as strikes increased in violence and disturbed the industrial and financial systems. The middle class of Italy, with large holdings of securities, bank deposits and real property, had a pencuniary stake in the maintenance of Italian security capitalism, and threw its support on the side of the large industrial and banking interests to prevent the possibility of a proletarian uprising. The combined forces of the middle and upper classes formed the social basis of the movement which beginning with the march on Rome in 1922 was to sweep Parliamentary government away and to replace it with Fascism. Mussolini, as the leader of Italian fascism, expressed very definite views on the evolution of capitalism.[1] The system, he held, passed first through the dynamic period from 1830 to 1870, which marked the beginning of the factory system, short wars, short depressions and an inactive government motivated by the theory of liberalism. The static period, he held, began in 1870 with the growth of cartels and trusts, the end of free competition and government intervention. These conditions, he maintained, lead to the period of decline, of "decadence" and of the crisis of capitalism. It was the purpose of Fascism to save Italy from a repetition of this cycle of capitalism.

The Facist government now proceeded to change the nature of Italian security capitalism. Economic and financial life was organized into unions which in turn were bound together into national confederations in the various fields of activity.

WEAKNESS OF THE BANKING STRUCTURE

The first serious problem of Italian security capitalism was the weakness of the banking structure, impaired by the ravages of war and post-war finance. As in the case of Germany, in Italy in the immediate post-war period there was a struggle between banking and industrial security capitalism. In the pre-war period Italian banks had controlled many of the important industries. However in the post-war period there were continual attempts by the industrial interests to obtain control of the leading banks by purchasing their shares in the open-market and then forcing the banks to grant liberal credit accommodation. Thus the Perrone interests acquired a dominant position in the Banca Italiana di Sconto, and also expanded their holdings in the Banca Commerciale Italiano, and the Fiat Company sought control of the Credito Italiano. The Banca Commerciale Italiano and the Credito Italiano, despite efforts to protect themselves, were forced to compromise with the industrial capitalists.[2]

As in the case of Germany, the Italian banks had to write down a large proportion of their capital after the financial disturbances of the immediate post-war period.[3] By 1921 the banking structure was near collapse, the Banca Italiana di Sconto failed, and the Banca di Roma was on the verge of failure due largely to "speculative investment."[4] The Fascist Government had to grant liberal assistance to support this weakened banking structure. It created a new bank out of the Banca Italiano di Sconto and granted assistance to the Banca di Roma. Notwithstanding this aid by the government, the Italian banking structure was not soundly reorganized and this defect was apparent in the crisis after 1930. Once more the Italian government had to support the banks. So serious was the financial position of the Italian banks that in March, 1935 the shares of the four big banks were removed from the stock exchange list.[5] Because of the weakness of the banking system the government had to form a number of public financial institutions for the purpose of completing the liquidation of weakened industries and re-establishing essential economic activities. The Instituta de Constructional Industrial was established to wind up companies which were insolvent and no longer necessary to the nation. The Instituto Mobiliare Italiano granted long-term loans for the rebuilding of important concerns.[6]

INCREASE IN NATIONAL DEBT

The second pressing problem of Italian security capitalism was the national debt. Statistics on the Italian national debt vary widely. According to official figures it rose during the Fascist regime from

95,000,000,000 lire in 1923 to only 106,563,000,000 lire in the first quarter of 1935.[7] These figures, however, did not present the full national debt, for actually it rose much faster. Moody's Investment Service stated that the total internal debt rose from 91,000,000,-000 lire in 1925 to 128,000,000,000 lire in 1935. In addition in 1935 there was an external loan of $82,000,000 and also a small sterling loan.[8] Dr. Salvemini, a sharp critic of Fascist policies, but a well-known student of public finance, in his study of Italian debt, contended that it rose from 93,275,000,000 lire in 1922 to 148,646,-000,000 lire in 1934.[9] *Fortune* in an article on Italy in 1934 placed the total debt at the higher figure of 170,000,000,000 lire, exclusive of war debts.[10]

The financial position of the government was aggravated by a continual deficit since 1931. Thus for the fiscal year of 1935–1936, expenditures of the ordinary budget amounted to 20,000,000,000 lire and resulted in a net deficit of over 3,000,000,000 lire. In a special budget the total expenditures of operations in East Africa incurred in that year amounted to another 9,000,000,000 lire.[11]

REBUILDING OF RUSSIAN SECURITY CAPITALISM

An important movement in modern history was the destruction of the old and the building of the new Russian capitalism. The capitalism of Imperial Russia was essentially the same in nature as that of other countries. However the system was seriously shattered by the War. Kerensky with his moderate policies was unable to maintain the tottering structure, and the revolution in 1917 brought the nation under the control of the Soviet government headed by Lenin, a devout follower of Marx, and an active critic of private security capitalism. The Soviet government swept away the old Russian capitalism. All industrial properties, including railways, factories and mines, were confiscated and turned over to the state, and the obligations of the Czarist government were repudiated.

In place of the old system an entirely new financial structure was established by the reorganization of the banking system and by the restoration of the capital market. The Soviet government developed an entirely new banking system centered mainly around the Gosbank or State Bank, the Prombank or Industrial Bank, and the State Savings Bank.[12] The Gosbank operated several thousand branches and carried the short-term deposits of the state industrial enterprises.[13] The Prombank was a corporation whose stock was owned by the Supreme Economic Council, the commissariat of finance, or secretary of the treasury and several other government institutions.[14] Russian industries were required to pay 25 percent of their profits into the capital funds of the Prombank and also had to keep their long-term accounts with this institution.[15] The Bank in turn was empowered to grant loans up to a period of four years, and the borrowers were required to amortize these loans after the first year. The interest rate on these loans varied according to the rate of return of the industry and ranged from six percent for the oil industry to two percent for the coal industry.

RESTORATION OF THE CAPITAL MARKET

From 1918 to 1922 the Soviet Government struggled along without utilizing the capital market. Over these years, the Soviet government employed the crude mechanism of individual capitalism by issuing paper money for the purpose of financing itself. As a result, by 1922, the financial position of the Soviet government was unsatisfactory, as evidenced by the declining value of its monetary unit and by the increasing deficit in its budget. In order to check these unsound tendencies the government made use of the capital market in 1922 when it issued a short-term grain loan.[16] However, after the devastating influences of the war and the postwar period the available supply of capital in the hands of the public was negligible, and there was no market for the issue. The government therefore had to follow a policy of a compulsory distribution of the bonds among the populace. Under these conditions, the cost of the first loan was high. Notwithstanding these difficulties, the mechanism of security capitalism proved more satisfactory than that of individual capitalism and in the following years the Soviet government continued to secure funds to finance industry by issuing bonds instead of paper money.

The next step in the return to security capitalism was the abolition at least in name of the compulsory distribution of bonds and the institution of a so-called voluntary distribution of securities. The commissar of finance entered the market to regulate the price of government bonds by repurchasing them from unwilling holders and selling them to willing investors. As a result the bonds rose in price until they reached 95 in 1926.[17]

The next step in the restoration of the capital market came when the Soviet government, in spite of its political philosophy, realized that saving had to be encouraged in order to mobilize capital to meet the investment demands of the state.[18] Even under communism there was machinery for the accumulation of saving in the form of the State Saving Bank with 20,000 branches including the local post-offices. Saving under private security capitalism is essentially voluntary in nature and is undertaken by individuals and to a growing extent by corporations. Under public security capitalism, saving becomes involuntary in character and is undertaken by individuals and by government-controlled agencies which make repayments of their surplus to the treasury; these two forms may be described respectively as private and social saving.[19]

Saving under a communist system must naturally be largely compulsory in nature, since there are not the same motives for saving as under private capitalism. There is supposedly no need to save in order to provide for old age or incapacity, since these contingencies are provided for by the state. Furthermore there is no incentive to save to enter business, since enterprise is publicly controlled. Private saving is accomplished by the direct investment in government loans, and by indirect investment through deposits in savings banks and through the purchase of shares in co-operative organizations. To a large extent this private saving is compulsory rather than voluntary, since the purchase of shares in the co-operatives is really required, and the purchase of state bonds is made by monthly deductions from wages. Furthermore, state bonds can only be sold after permission is granted by government authorities.[20] Saving deposits, however, are superficially voluntary in nature. The Soviet government followed a conscious policy of encouraging saving banks for the purpose of increasing the supply of capital funds. To this end workers in certain factories were paid with deposit accounts in the saving banks.[21]

As a result of an intensive campaign to mobilize the saving of the people, from 1928 to the beginning of 1933 the number of saving bank depositors increased from 3,500,000 to 24,000,000, and deposits rose from 213,200,000 roubles to almost 1,000,000,000 roubles. Over the same period the number of state loan subscribers rose from 8,000,000, to 40,000,000, and the amount of the bonds distributed among the population from 411,000,000 to 5,442,000,000 roubles.[22] It was estimated that in 1937 there were 45,000,000 Russian bondholders.[23] The internal holding of the national debt rose from 1,422,000,000 roubles in October, 1928 to 22,813,700,000 roubles in January, 1937.[24]

Thus communism, after seeking to destroy pre-war Russian security capitalism and after its unsuccessful attempt to revert to the financial mechanism of individual capitalism returned to security capitalism. The banking structure was rebuilt by the formation of several powerful state banks. Also the capital market was restored through the issuing of government securities and the encouragement of saving. Since all the banks were owned by the government and all the securities in the capital market were those of the government, the Russian system represented the extreme form of public security capitalism.

RISE OF JAPANESE SECURITY CAPITALISM

While the evolution of the nations of western Europe from feudalism to security capitalism required several centuries, the same transition took place in Japan in less than three-quarters of a century. In fact Japan really never passed through the stage of individual capitalism but evolved directly from feudalism to security capitalism. Japan therefore missed the benefits of the transition stage of individual capitalism which in other countries led to the growth of a middle class and provided a stabilizing force in the evolution of economic society. For several centuries Japan continued in a stage of political and economic feudalism, and was governed by a military and agricultural aristocracy living on hereditary pensions and supported by the masses who were practically serfs. The dominant political figure was the Shogun, the head of the leading clan, the Emperor possessing little actual power.[25] This feudal system was swept away by the revolution of 1868 which was largely an alliance of the merchant class with one of the feudal groups against the ruling clan.[26] As a result, the Shogun was displaced and the Emperor restored to power. Japan now entered the stage of political nationalism, and a strong central government sought to overcome the power of the feudal nobles.

A determined effort was made by the Emperor to introduce the political and economic institutions of western security capitalism. In the first place he endeavored to establish the system of parliamentary government. Voting power was first bestowed cautiously but in time culminated in widespread suffrage.[27] In 1871 Japan adopted the gold yen as the nominal standard, although in actual practice the nation continued on an inconvertible paper basis. Japanese security capitalism was given a powerful stimulus when the government began the practice of giving bonds to the Samurai in payment of their hereditary pensions.[28] Thus their income under security capitalism consisted of the return on these securities.[29] For most of the lower Samurai this new return was small, but for many of the upper group it was large. In a number of cases these bonds were used to provide the capital for founding banks, and as a result the banking system came into the hands of the old aristocracy. Thus Japanese security capitalism did not grow as a result of natural evolution but was introduced and nurtured largely through governmental action.

SLOW ECONOMIC AND FINANCIAL PROGRESS UNTIL THE WAR

Economic progress was at first slow, and the transition from feudalism to early security capitalism was not completed until the nineties. The war with China brought about a rapid expansion of manufacture and foreign trade.[30] Railroad development came much later than in the other capitalist countries, for it was not until 1873 that the first railroad was constructed.[31] Private capital took an active part in railway development in the eighties, but the government assumed leadership which became increasingly important after the Russo-Japanese war so that in time the government owned the trunk lines and the private corporations operated only the feeder lines.[32] After 1890 the textile industry made progress.[33] It was not, however, until after 1900 that the steel industry expanded.[34]

In most countries, the coming of security capitalism was accompanied by an improvement not only in manufacture and in commerce but also in agriculture. However, in the case of Japan agriculture continued in an almost primitive state.[35]

The period from the closing decade of the nineteenth century until the Great War witnessed rapid economic expansion. The number of factories increased from 9,234 in 1904 to 17,062 in 1914; railway mileage rose from 2,118 miles to 7,074 miles from 1894 to 1914; over the same period foreign trade rose from a gross value of 235,000,000 yen to 1,223,000,000 yen and the number of corporations from 2,844 to 16,858.[36]

THE FINANCIAL SYSTEM

The evolution of the financial system was at first very halting. The government established a central bank, the Bank of Japan, modelled after the Bank of Belgium, and also a banking structure in imitation of the national banking system of the United States.[37] However, these steps in financial organization at first were unsuccessful due to the fact that they represented an effort to impose the banking institutions of a developed security capitalism on a country which had scarcely passed out of feudalism.[38] The system of specialized investment banking did not develop, and the distribution of securities was undertaken by the commercial banks. Stock exchanges were established in Tokio in 1877 and later in Osaka, but the security markets made slow progress until the beginning of the twentieth century.[39] It was not until 1870 that the Japanese government floated its first bond issue.[40] The wars with China and Russia led to further issues in the foreign markets, and as a result the total debt rose sharply. While most of the proceeds of the public debt were applied to war at the same time a part was productive in that it was used in railway expansion.

It was not until 1890 that the state and local governments were organized separately and exercised their debt-creating powers.[41]

Municipal borrowing first began in 1899 when the city of Kobe obtained a small loan in London, but in later years the large cities floated extensive loans in foreign markets particularly for public utility development.   Corporate borrowing came late, and it was not until 1906 that the first corporate issue was floated in the foreign market.   While Japan made progress in corporate organization, many of the large companies were owned and controlled by family interests which possessed large capital resources and had no need of obtaining additional funds from the security markets.[42]

The domestic supply of capital in Japan was small.   Defeated politically in 1868 the landowner class retained most of its economic power and commanded a large part of the domestic supply of capital, but very little of this capital was placed in the security markets.[43] The scarcity of capital in Japan was evidenced by the high interest rates which prevailed in the Japanese money markets.   As a result, the greater part of the Japanese public debt was floated in foreign countries.

EXPANSION AFTER THE WAR

In the post-war period there was considerable social unrest particularly among the laborers, the farm hands and the intellectuals. This growing radicalism was opposed by a rising tide of fascism which represented the revival of agrarian feudalism in its struggle against industrial and banking security capitalism.   The fascist movement made further progress in 1936 when the military coup brought in the Hirota Government.[44]   However in the elections in 1937 the anti-fascist parties increased their representation in Parliament.   The demonstration of the strength of the labor party was favorably regarded by the bankers who welcomed any aid against the military power.[45]   The World War gave a powerful stimulus to Japanese industry which furnished the Far East not only with war supplies but with manufactured goods.[46]   Industrial production increased in the post-war period as evidenced by the rise in the output of pig iron, steel and to some extent coal, while the index of general production increased sharply particularly after 1932.[48]   From 1914 to 1930 the number of factories rose from 17,062 to 62,234, and the number of corporations from 16,853 to 51,910.[49]

DEVELOPMENT OF FINANCIAL ORGANIZATION

In the post-war period there was a marked trend toward banking concentration as evidenced by the fact that between 1919 and 1930, the number of banks decreased while the capital funds (paid in capital and reserve fund) of the remaining institutions rose.[50] By 1932 five large institutions controlled the banking structure of

TABLE 12

EVOLUTION OF JAPANESE SECURITY CAPITALISM, 1920–1935.[47]

YEAR	PRODUCTION				EXPORTS (million yen)	NATIONAL DEBT (million yen)	ARMAMENT EXPENDITURES (million yen)	TOTAL EXPENDITURES (million yen)	TOTAL REVENUES (million yen)	ARMAMENT EXPENDITURES TO TOTAL EXPENDITURES (percent)	SAVING FUNDS (million yen)
	COAL (million tons)	PIG IRON (thousand tons)	STEEL (thousand tons)	INDUSTRIAL (1929=100)							
	1	2	3	4	5	6	7	8	9	10	11
1920	29	721	811		1,948	3,668	650	1,360	2,000	47.8	1,711
1921	26	637	832		1,252	4,085	731	1,490	2,066	49.1	1,597
1922	28	702	909		1,597	4,256	605	1,430	2,087	42.3	1,555
1923	29	809	959	69.1	1,414	4,425	499	1,520	2,045	32.8	1,550
1924	30	833	1,099	70.3	1,761	4,770	449	1,625	2,127	27.6	1,721
1925	31	838	1,200		2,220	5,026	444	1,525	2,071	29.1	1,995
1926	31	822	1,548	77.9	1,973	5,162	434	1,579	2,056	27.5	2,226
1927	34	910	1,728	82.9	1,912	5,172	492	1,766	2,063	27.9	2,668
1928	34	1,111	1,955	89.7	1,909	5,398	517	1,815	2,006	28.5	2,994
1929	34	1,112	2,343	100.0	2,101	5,831	495	1,737	1,826	28.5	3,479
1930	31	1,187	2,328	94.8	1,431	5,959	443	1,558	1,597	28.4	3,890
1931	28	934	1,914	91.6	1,118	6,154	455	1,477	1,531	30.8	4,252
1932	28	1,037	2,441	97.8	1,362	6,412	686	1,950	2,045	35.2	4,381
1933	33	1,470	3,261	113.2	1,827	7,375	873	2,255	2,332	38.7	4,623
1934	36	1,772	3,923	128.7	2,134	8,683	938	2,163	2,247	43.3	4,831
1935				141.8		9,613	1,022	2,215	2,215	47.8	5,157

the nation.[51]   There was also a growing concentration in the under-writing and purchasing of corporate bonds in the hands of powerful syndicates composed of the larger banking institutions.[52]   It is esti-mated that 62 per cent of the bond issues were taken up by the business banks, 15 percent by the savings banks and the remainder by security dealers, trust and insurance companies and government institutions.[53]   Another estimate claims that 90 percent of all do-mestic issues were taken up by institutions of indirect investment.[54] By 1930 there were six security exchanges, of which those in Tokio and Osaka were the most important.   Some of these exchanges continued to deal both in securities and in produce thus indicat-ing that the security markets had not yet reached the stage of spe-cialization of operation characteristic of developed security capital-ism.   The operations of even the leading exchanges were small when compared with those of other countries.[55]

LIMITATIONS OF THE CAPITAL MARKET

The demand for capital came largely from the national and local governments.   Although the budget of the national government nominally showed surpluses the government continually entered the capital market.[56]   The national debt rose moderately to 3,668,-000,000 yen in 1920 and then continuously to 9,613,000,000 in 1935.[57]   In addition the debt of the local governments reached 3,187,-000,000 yen by 1935.[58]   Corporate finance remained relatively unim-portant in Japan.   The government owned and operated the im-portant public utilities, railways, telegraph and telephones, and through public monopolies administered the sale of many necessities. Another factor which further restricted the private demand for capital in the security market was the fact that many of the large corporations were controlled by family interests, as the Mitsui and the Mitsubishi, which had no need of securing capital from the security market.[59]   In the post-war period the supply of capital in-creased.[60]   National saving funds rose from 1,597,000,000 yen in 1921 to 5,157,000,000 yen in 1935.[61]   Capital was largely concen-trated in the hands of a small proportion of the population.   Japan lacks almost completely a middle class which through its saving contributed to the supply of new capital.   Although the income tax was levied on all incomes above 1,200 yen there were only 569,046 such taxpayers in 1931.[62]   Direct security ownership did not become popular in Japan, and there was no wide diffusion of securities as found in other capitalistic countries.[63]

MILITARY CHARACTER OF JAPANESE CAPITALISM

The striking feature of Japanese capitalism in recent years was the extensive application of capital to war purposes. The budgetary expenditure for armament was 650,000,000 yen in 1920, fell to 434,-000,000 yen in 1926 then rose to 1,022,000,000 yen in 1935.[64] The proportion of stated armament expenditures to total expenditures dropped from 48 percent in 1920 to 27.5 percent in 1926 but rose to 47.8 percent in 1935.[65] In addition to the stated budgetary appropriations for war, it is charged that there were also large indirect expenditures which did not appear in the budget as armament items.[66]

The Japanese government placed the task of supporting the burden of armament expenditure squarely upon security capitalism. The tax policy, as stated in 1936, was a "re-distribution of the tax burden as equitably as possible over the whole nation so that the incidence may fall heavier on the urban rather than the rural population, on corporations than on individuals and on personal than on real property." [67] As a result the government derived its revenues essentially from income, inheritance and corporate taxes.[68] In 1937 the struggle between the military and financial interests became intensified. On the one hand the military interests sought to revive the feudal system of the Shogun abolished in 1868, while the bankers sought to retain their influence through remnants of the nominal parliamentary form of government. Since government bonds and corporate securities were almost entirely held by the large industrialists and bankers, they had the greatest stake in maintaining Japanese security capitalism and supporting the credit of the government. These groups therefore opposed the extreme steps of the military class. In recent years the Mitsubishi group favored a moderate policy, while the Mitsui gave some backing to the military class. The former, in general, urged financial stability, while the latter was willing to lend an ear to inflationary policies.[69]

CONCLUSION

Because of the rapidity of the changes which occurred since 1868, the Japanese economic system contained the survival of feudal characteristics as well as the features of early and developed security capitalism. This confusion in the economic system led to the adoption of national and international political and economic policies which may prove serious in the coming years. Japanese capitalism entered upon imperialism without having first developed the necessary institutions to support such a program. Imperialism demands the continuous export of large amounts of capital.   Thus the exploitation of Formosa, Manchukuo and China demanded an enormous flow of capital from Japan which has not even a sufficient supply to complete the financing of her own industrial revolution.[70] An incompletely developed security capitalism is thus being used as a mechanism to carry out an ambitious policy of international expansion which threatens eventually to cause Japan serious economic and political difficulties.

CRISIS OF INTERNATIONAL SECURITY CAPITALISM

The background of world security capitalism following the Great War was entirely different from that after the Napoleonic Wars and throughout the remainder of the nineteenth century, for the political, financial, economic and philosophic setting was now distinctly unfavorable.   Parliamentarianism in a number of nations was replaced by authoritarism in the form of communism or fascism.   The period of comparative international peace gave way to international hostility which led to the Great War and in the post-war period to the French invasion of the Ruhr, the Japanese occupation of Manchuria and invasion of China, the Italian conquest of Ethiopia and the Spanish civil war.

In the Napoleonic period the great nations of the World were still largely in the stage of individual capitalism which constituted a relatively simple economy.   Wars were financed largely by the issue of paper money, and the financial and economic resources of the nation were only partly mobilized so that the adverse effect on the economic system was relatively small.   On the other hand, in the period until the Great War, most of the major nations had acquired the highly complicated structure of developed security capitalism. The financial system was perfected to a point where most of the resources of the nation could be fully mobilized for war purposes. The shock of war, therefore, was far more serious to the highly organized and integrated structures of these nations.   The carefully wrought interrelations not only within the national economy but with other nations were seriously disturbed.   Furthermore, the deficits of the national governments were now no longer financed by the issuance of paper money, but through the flotation of governmental securities.   England had been the first nation to utilize the machinery of security capitalism on a large scale to finance her wars, and the successful conflict against Napoleon was made possible through the sale of governmental securities.   After the Napoleonic wars, a few of the Continental nations also issued securities, but these were sold largely in the London market.   It was not until the second half of the nineteenth century that the system of security capitalism was widely applied to war financing. As noted before security issues were utilized to finance the Franco-Prussian War and to maintain the vast armies in the years which followed. The Great War however was the first general conflict in which security capitalism, in addition to paper money, was universally employed by the belligerents to obtain the necessary purchasing power to maintain their armed forces. The significance of the system of security capitalism was not understood in 1914 by those who predicted the conflict would be short because of the impossibility of supplying sufficient financial means to continue a prolonged war. These prophets failed to realize that the perfection of the financial machinery of developed security capitalism, by fully mobilizing the resources of the nations, made possible the prolongation of modern warfare. However this very prolongation in the end brought about an exhaustion which impaired not only the financial but the entire economic structure.

UNSATISFACTORY SETTING OF POST-WAR CAPITALISM

After 1918 every effort was made to rebuild the monetary foundation of pre-war security capitalism. The gold standard, the monetary basis of nineteenth century security capitalism, was restored in England and in most of the Continental countries. The restored gold standard, however, was maintained only by liberal loans of Great Britain and of the United States. The depression forced the abandonment of the international gold standard, and most countries of the world adopted a system of controlled or managed currency. The monetary mechanism now became a weapon to be used by the nations of the world in their political and economic struggles against each other.

In the period of the rise and development of security capitalism world production stimulated by the industrial revolution rose sharply, but after 1913 the rate of increase declined.[71] After 1934 there was a recovery in production induced largely by the activities of the heavy industries to meet the needs of increasing armament. While this artificial stimulus had an immediate favorable effect, the ultimate results in bringing about a one-sided expansion and unproductive capital expenditure are bound to be serious.

One of the basic factors which favored the progress of security capitalism throughout the nineteenth century was the satisfactory adjustment between world production and world trade, for the expansion of industrial production was absorbed by widening foreign markets. In the post-war period, the neo-mercantilist policies involving quotas, tariffs and controlled exchange, all tended to check the expansion of foreign trade. In the period from 1932 to 1935 inclusive there developed a growing maladjustment between world production and world trade, as may be seen in table 13.

TABLE 13

PRODUCTION AND TRADE OF THE WORLD, 1932–1935.[72]
(percent, 1929 = 100)

YEAR	PRODUCTION	TRADE
1929	100	100
1932	69	74
1933	78	75
1934	85	77
1935	95	79

From these figures it is seen that production of the world dropped to 69 percent in 1932, and then recovered sharply to 95 percent in 1935. On the other hand world trade dropped to 74 percent in 1932, and showed little recovery in the following years.

An important social difference between security capitalism in the post-Napoleonic period and to-day has been the change in the trend of population. In the early and developed stages of security capitalism, the population of the world more than doubled. After 1913 the rate of increase in world population slackened.[73]

In the pre-war period the attitude of economic philosophy was generally favorable to the development of security capitalism. The prevailing classical philosophy preached laissez faire and in general favored the operation of a system untrammeled by government regulation. True, the growing Marxian philosophy attacked the entire system, but with the exception of the disturbances of 1848 and of 1871, the political structure of security capitalism was never seriously menaced. In the post-war period there was a complete change in the philosophic attitude toward security capitalism. Laissez faire gave way to a revival of mercantilism which extended governmental regulation to almost every institution of security capitalism. Furthermore, world security capitalism was now threatened by militant international Marxism. As noted before the revisionist socialists, influenced by the generally satisfactory conditions in the latter half of the nineteenth century, had departed from the extreme views of the master and had even recognized the beneficial characteristics of security capitalism. Another group had held uncompromisingly to the revolutionary principles of Marx, and believed that the peaceful stage of the latter nineteenth century was merely a passing episode in the evolution of modern capitalism. Revolutionary socialism found expression in communist philosophy expounded particularly by Nicolai Lenin. As the leading nations passed from the developed to the critical stage of security capitalism, economic crises became more intense, social welfare declined and political revolutionary movements as that in Russia grew in severity. These tendencies disillusioned the moderate socialists and strengthened the extremists.

CHANGING NATURE OF THE FINANCIAL SYSTEM

The post-war period brought about drastic changes in the central banks, the private banks, the incorporated banks and the stock exchanges. A leading tendency in European central banking in the post-war period was the initial relaxation and the subsequent renewal of regulation by the national governments. The necessity during the War of obtaining unlimited advances from the central bank naturally led to increased control by the state. Such control militated against the interest of private security capitalism, and in the years immediately following the close of the War a vigorous effort was made to break the grip of the governments over the central banks. This attitude of international private security capitalism was expressed in the resolution of the Brussels conference of 1920 "that banks and especially banks of issue should be free from political pressure and should be conducted solely on the lines of prudent finance." [74] This policy was followed by the League of Nations in its financial reconstruction of Austria and of Hungary and in the establishment of central banks in Esthonia and in Greece. All these efforts were nullified with the coming of the depression, and as a result almost every central bank came to be closely controlled by the national government.

In almost every country the financial organization of the old individual capitalism was controlled mainly by the private banker. However, in the developed stage of security capitalism the private banker was replaced by the incorporated bank. The post-war period swept away this vestige of individual capitalism in the eclipse of the private bank. The Krueger and Toll Company, in its last annual report of 1931, claimed that one of the dominating forces in the crisis was the "disappearance of the great merchant houses and private bankers who had a wide latitude in the choice of their investments, and the substitution for them of industrial corporations, large deposit banks, and insurance companies more restricted in the use of their funds to clearly specified investments." [75]

In the post-war period the large joint-stock banks tended more and more to perform the operations of both commercial and investment banking.   During the first post-war depression the banks, in order to recover their loans, were compelled to take over the control of many industries.   Due to the tardiness of the recovery in the following years the liquidation of these frozen assets moved very slowly, and was only partially completed when the second post-war depression began in 1928.[76]

The movement for bank concentration made rapid headway in the depression period, since it frequently became necessary for the strong institutions to take over the weaker ones.   Thus in Belgium the Société Generale absorbed a number of other Belgium banks, and as a result controlled a major part of the aggregate bank assets of the nation.[77]   Throughout the depression there was a sharp decline in the proportion of loans and discounts to total assets, and a marked increase in security holdings.[78]   With the growth of public as compared with private security capitalism, the banks by necessity were forced to take over an increasing proportion of government securities, and so the financial position of the banking system became dependent upon the credit of the national government. Today with the leading banks of the world holding so large a proportion of the national debts, the very future of security capitalism rests on the maintenance of the soundness of national credit.

The stock exchanges of the world held a less significant position in the financial organization.   Even before the War the importance of the stock exchange had been diminishing in a large measure due to the effect of banking concentration since the amalgamated banks cancelled out the buying and selling orders of securities within their own organizations.   Throughout the depression period, the stock exchange was further weakened by the decline in the amount of corporate financing for in many cases the volume of security transactions was placed under an embargo in order to conserve capital resources for the government issues.[79]

FAILURE OF CO-OPERATIVE EFFORTS

In the post-war private security capitalism was confronted with a serious menace in the form of communism.   Not only did communism capture Russian security capitalism, but, through its support of the Third Internationale, waged war against security capitalism in other countries.   Thus the manifesto of the Third Internationale in 1919 in summary stated that:

Finance-capital which has flung mankind into the abyss of war, has also suffered.   The complete deterioration of paper money reflects the general deadly crisis of capitalist commodity exchange.[80]

In the face of this threat the leaders of security capitalism realized the necessity of cooperating to maintain the system throughout Western Europe. This motive was an important factor influencing the flow of international capital in the years immediately following the close of the War. Thus Herbert Hoover in 1921 stated:

The whole of American policies during the liquidation of the Armistice, was to contribute everything it could to prevent Europe from going Bolshevik or being overrun by their armies.[81]

Sir William Goode, British Director of Relief in Central Europe, in his official report declared:

. . . half of Europe had hovered on the brink of Bolshevism. If it had not been for the £137 million in relief credits granted to Central and Eastern Europe between 1919 and 1921, it would have been impossible to provide food and coal and the sea and land transport for them. Two and one-half years after the Armistice the back of Bolshevism in Central Europe had been broken, largely by relief credits. . . The expenditure of £137 million was probably one of the best international investments from a financial and political point of view ever recorded in history.[82]

Through the League of Nations, international security capitalism made drastic efforts to buttress the system of private security capitalism. Loans were extended to Austria, Hungary, Bulgaria, Greece, the Free City of Danzig and Esthonia, under a system of drastic financial control by the League.[83] The immediate result of this international financial cooperation was satisfactory. However, in the end the movement failed, for it served only as a basis for over-lending. The efforts at cooperation were rendered ineffective by the unrestrained competition among the international money centers.

In the pre-war period the investment banks of London, Paris, Berlin and later New York respected each other's fields of operation. In the post-war period such restraint was abandoned, and unrestricted competition marked the relations among the financial centers. In a large measure this change of policy was brought about by the action of the New York banking houses in their efforts to conquer new fields abroad. However, the Continental financial centers also entered into the new competition, and Paris, Zurich, Amsterdam and even Stockholm became serious competitors of the London investment houses.

In 1930 the leaders of security capitalism made an effort to attain closer cooperation among the central banks of the world through the formation of the Bank for International Settlements. It was hoped that this institution would play an important part in the development of the system of international security capitalism, since the Bank was given the right to issue not only short but also long-term obligations and was granted extensive open market powers. However, the nationalistic interests of the leading countries doomed this institution to failure, and its accomplishments were insignificant.

With the intensification of the depression the struggle of international security capitalism against the forces of political nationalism became more serious. The first ominous rift of the international banking structure came with the failure of the Austrian Creditanstalt.[84] This bank along with other Viennese institutions, had been facing serious difficulties for several years. However, the extent of its reverses was not realized by the general public until the publication of its financial statement in May 1931.[85] Again, international security capitalism made every effort to prevent the collapse of the Bank, but in vain, for the political rivalry between Germany and France nullified every effort at financial cooperation. Throughout the depression and even in the recovery after 1932 international banking capitalism made little headway in attaining close cooperation among the great financial centers of the world.

INCREASING CAPITAL DEMAND

The demand for capital in the post-war period was heavy. The requirements of corporations were considerable in order to make up for postponed maintenance and also to modernize plants. While it is true that the demand for capital for the development of new countries and for the building of railroads declined, nevertheless in view of the speeding up of the tempo of industrial activity there was a heavy demand for capital to overcome obsolescence. The demand for capital by the governments, particularly after 1930, in almost every country was even greater than that of private industry. The demand was caused first by the increase in armament expenditures. Modern armament, being essentially mechanized in nature, required large outlays of capital to pay for heavy artillery, battleships, tanks, and aeroplanes together with the auxiliary equipment in the form of docks, hangars and landing fields.

During the War period armament expenditures accounted for the greater part of total expenditures. In the case of England it amounted to as much as 89 percent and in the case of France it reached 82 percent.[86] The proportion fell off sharply in the years following the War but after 1930 the disbursements for armament again increased very rapidly. The report of the Bank for International Settlements stated that "for the world as a whole, the level of armament expenditure in 1936 was, on a gold basis, three times higher than in 1913."[87] Due to the severity of the depression and the serious social distress which followed, the various governments were forced to use their credit to grant direct relief to the unemployed or to maintain public works to supplement the declining activity of private industry.

As a result of this financing for armament and relief purposes, the proportion of government issues to the total of security offerings in mo. of the leading capital markets of the World increased sharply. The proportion for England rose from 26 percent in 1929 to 74 percent in 1933. Over the same period the proportion for the United States rose from 7 percent to 96 percent. For Germany the proportion rose from 1 percent in 1931 to 60 percent in 1933. In the case of France over the period from 1930 to 1933, the proportion declined from 23 per cent to 14 percent.[88]

As a result the aggregate national debts of the leading countries of the world expanded from £5,163,000,000 in 1898 to £24,408,000,-000 by 1935.[89] The debt of Great Britain, France, Italy and the United States particularly rose.[90]

The burden of this national debt may be seen from Table 14 which shows the decline in the extent to which wealth covered national debt in the leading countries of the world in the pre-war and post-war periods.

TABLE 14

CHANGES IN PROPORTION OF NATIONAL WEALTH TO
NATIONAL DEBT OF LEADING COUNTRIES [91]
(percent)

COUNTRY	PRE–WAR 1913	POST–WAR *
England...........................	2,022	238
France...........................	921	266
Germany..........................	6,719	4,435
United States....................	40,611	2,045

Explanation:
  * Post-War figure for
     England is 1928
     France is 1928
     Germany is 1928
     United States is 1930

From this table it is seen that there was a decline in the extent to which national wealth covered national debt in the post-war period as compared with the pre-war period. The largest drop took place in the United States where the coverage fell from 400 times to 20 times. In the case of England the coverage fell from 20 times to only a little over 2 times. In the case of France the coverage fell from 9 times to a little over 2 times. Only in Germany was the change relatively small, with a decline from 60 times to 40 times.

As a result of these various forces, there was an increase in the public element in the security capitalism of almost every leading nation, due to the necessity of financing the War, and later of alleviating the depression. In the case of some countries, as Russia and Germany, this public nature of security capitalism was carried to an extreme form. However, even in other countries, as England and the United States which retained the democratic form of government, the necessities of the war and depression similarly placed emphasis on the public aspect as evidenced by the increasing proportion of government securities to total securities outstanding.

CONTROL OF SECURITY CAPITALISM

In the post-war period, there was a general extension of the control of the government over the institutions of security capitalism. There was a widespread movement to reform the corporate law. New statutes governing corporations were passed in almost every country.[92] These laws sought to protect the investor in corporate securities by prohibiting stock watering, the issuance of stock below par, and by requiring compulsory reserves. In some cases corporate law was liberalized to recognize such practices as the issue of non-voting shares and convertible bonds.

A complete change took place in the relation between the banks and the government throughout Europe. Before the War the system of government supervision, as developed in the United States, was practically non-existent in Europe. This situation changed entirely in the post-war period, and the intimate relationship between banking and government became an important feature of present-day world banking. This movement began with the outbreak of the War, when the belligerent governments promptly exercised control over all forms of finance. During the inflation period which accompanied the War, governments made every effort to sustain their depreciated currencies by a system of rigid exchange control which brought the operations of the banks under direct supervision of the government. A more serious form of regulation occurred in the first post-war reaction. The depression at first swept away many of the smaller banks in several countries, but as the crisis continued, some of the larger institutions were also threatened with failure. The amalgamation movement of the preceding years had developed institutions of such size that their downfall would have involved the financial structure of the entire nation, and would have impaired the national credit at home and abroad. It was therefore necessary for the government to give financial assistance in one form or another.   In some cases it was accomplished by the central bank extending liberal rediscounting privileges to the particular banks in difficulty.   In other cases a special organization was formed as the Kreditkassen which helped embarrassed Swedish banks.   When the leading bank in Copenhagen failed, it was necessary for the Danish parliament to come to the rescue and guarantee a large proportion of the obligations.   A similar procedure had to be followed by the Norwegian government which was forced to take over the liquidation of the failed banks and guarantee their future obligations.

In several countries the failure of these big banks and the consequent danger to public credit brought about a change in government policy toward banking.   Whereas before the War the governments had pursued a laissez-faire policy, they now adopted a program of supervision.

During the depression in a number of countries, the governments were again forced to support the tottering banking structure.   In Switzerland in 1932 the Federal government established a Caisse des Prêts for the purpose of granting advances to illiquid banks.   The government purchased the stock of a number of banks in order to provide them with the necessary capital to write off assets.[93]   Similarly the Swedish government, in 1932 had to assist the Scandinavian Credit Corporation which had suffered serious reverses through the failure of Ivan Krueger.   The Austrian government, and foreign creditors, became the joint owners of the Creditanstalt.   The Austrian government was also compelled to give financial assistance to other Viennese banks, through the formation of a trust company, to purchase the frozen assets of the banks and to furnish them with new capital.[94]

As a result of the depression of the thirties control over the financial system was further extended.   The legislation on banking was based on the orthodox theory which sought to attain greater liquidity and to separate commercial from investment banking operations. The Swiss bank law of 1934 provided for a fixed minimum proportion of reserve assets to short-term liabilities; the law also sought to increase solvency by prescribing a minimum percentage between capital funds and total liabilities.[95] The Swedish bank law was amended in 1934 to forbid banks to acquire shares in industrial concerns except when such acquisition is necessary to protect the bank from loss.   The Finnish bank law of 1933 limited the extent to which banks could participate in industry.[96]

CONCLUSION

World security capitalism, which had passed through its rise and development in the nineteenth and the early twentieth centuries, now faced its critical period in the post-war years. The background of security capitalism was distinctly unfavorable with the rise of dictatorships, the growth of international hostility, the decline of production and trade growth, the slackening of the growth of world population, the rise of an aggressively hostile economic philosophy, the failure of international banking cooperation and the expansion of unproductive national debts unsupported by national production or national wealth. The critical hour of world security capitalism had arrived.

Part II — Evolution of American Security Capitalism

CHAPTER 10

RISE OF AMERICAN SECURITY CAPITALISM

UNTIL the end of the second decade of the nineteenth century the United States remained in the stage of individual capitalism. In fact the period of colonial economy lasted until after the second war with Great Britain, for the economic life of the American people continued to be dominated by its relations with England and with the Continent. Financial organization until the end of the second decade of the nineteenth century was simple in nature, and only in the large cities as New York, Philadelphia and Boston was there the semblance of a banking structure. Capital was invested mainly in local business enterprises, and before 1815 eastern capital was not applied to the settlement of the West and the development of its resources.[1] Although the corporate form of organization had received legal recognition in the eighteenth century, its application was limited to a small number of what we would now call public utility corporations as turnpike and canal companies.[2] There were a few industrial corporations, but these were small in size. The volume of corporate securities in the hands of the public was therefore insignificant, and the security market played an important part in the economic life of the American people.

While there was investment in land and commodities, federal government bonds were about the only form of security investment.[3] Due in a large measure to the policy of Alexander Hamilton the credit of the federal government was placed on a sound basis. His proposal that the federal government assume not only its own domestic and foreign debts but also those of the states, and refund them by means of federal bonds was an important step from the standpoint of security capitalism.

By giving the powerful minority of wealth in the country a financial stake in the continuance and maintenance of a strong central government, Hamilton felt that he had insured the survival of the government at a very inexpensive price. This view was expressed by a contemporary publication in the statement that ". . . we hope that all true friends to our republican union will do all they can to extend the system of banks, insurance companies, canals, turnpikes, bridge companies and all other such useful commonwealth associations with small shares."[4] Elsewhere, however, Hamilton seems to have cautioned against excessive debt and urged a policy of debt reduction in the following words: "as the vicissitudes of nations beget a perpetual tendency to the accumulation of debt, there ought to be, in every government, a perpetual, anxious and unceasing effort to reduce that which at any time exists, as fast as shall be practicable, consistently with integrity and good faith." [5]

The financing of the federal government during the War of 1812 clearly showed the extent to which the United States was still in the stage of individual capitalism. The securities of the federal government were sold not to the general public but mainly to a small number of wealthy individuals. In 1813 the federal government was able to place with the public only $6,000,000 of its $16,000,000 issue, and the remainder had to be purchased by individual capitalists as Stephen Girard, John Jacob Astor and David Parish. [6]

THE WESTWARD MOVEMENT

The rise of security capitalism in the United States falls in two phases, interrupted by the Civil War, namely from about 1820 to 1860 and from 1865 until 1873. The vital factor which brought about the rise of security capitalism in the United States in the first period was the westward movement which, although in progress for a number of years, gained momentum only in the second quarter of the nineteenth century. The economic life of the United States now changed its entire course, and turned from Europe to the West. This movement marked definitely the end of economic colonialism and the beginning of nationalism.

The westward movement was facilitated by the improvement in transportation which was no longer a local matter, but was now undertaken on a national scale. Turnpikes, canals and railroads were extended from one state to another. So rapid was the expansion of the railroads that by 1843 the United States had 3,688 miles of road as against 2,069 miles in Great Britain. [7] In the following years until the Civil War the mileage in the United States was increased eight fold. [8] The steamboat was also an important instrument in the opening of the interior waterways, and helped to bring the West into closer communication with the Atlantic seaboard. The invention of the telegraph further improved communication by making possible the expansion of the railroad system and by bringing about closer relations between the business men of the new western towns and those on the Atlantic seaboard. [9]

An important social effect of the westward movement was the growth of the total population, for the opening of a vast new area of profitable farming not only encouraged immigration from abroad but also tended to raise the native birth rate. There was a great

increase in the concentration of population in urban areas. While
in 1830 only 6.72 percent of the population lived in communities of
more than 8,000 inhabitants, by 1850 the proportion had risen to
12.49 percent.[10] While the total population rose 85 percent between 1840 and 1860, that of New York City increased 300 percent.
and that of Philadelphia increased 166 percent.[11] Thus by the outbreak of the Civil War, the United States had developed a considerable urban population which is an essential characteristic of security capitalism. The concentration of thousands of persons in
cities made necessary the assumption of municipal functions requiring fixed capital, such as street lighting and water supply, and these
undertakings were largely financed by the issue of bonds.

The settlement of the West brought with it the rise of Jacksonian democracy which became an aggressive opponent of security
capitalism. The Whig party on the other hand was the political
organ of the new security capitalism of the Northeast. These years
were marked by considerable social unrest, as evidenced by the Dorr
rebellion in Rhode Island, and the Anti-rent troubles in New York.
There was a scattered movement of communism as seen by experiments as Brook Farm which had the active support of Emerson and
Hawthorne and New Harmony, where Robert Owen attempted to
apply his utopian socialism. The first labor party in world history
was formed in Philadelphia in 1828. In 1835 the Equal Rights
party, later known as the Loco Focos, was formed, and forced the
New York legislature to pass the banking act of 1838 which established a general banking incorporation law, shattering the previous
banking monopoly.[12]

Paradoxically enough, this measure, demanded by the opponents
of security capitalism, contributed greatly to the growth of the system before the Civil War. This "free" banking act, as it was known,
provided for a bond-secured currency. Any banker who wished to
issue bank notes would have to deposit an equal amount of bonds
with the state comptroller. If the banks failed the bonds were sold
by the comptroller and the proceeds used to pay off the note-holders.
By 1850 sixteen states had adopted this system which became the
model for the National Bank Act of 1863. A widespread market
was thereby opened for securities, particularly state bonds and their
quality tended to deteriorate. Thus a measure originally intended
to break up banking monopolies provided a very great stimulus to
security investment and aided the development of security capitalism.

It was not until the second quarter of the nineteenth century
that the corporation attained its present-day characteristics. Thus
the Massachusetts trust as a quasi-corporation had legal recognition

as early as 1827.[13] The practice of securing bonds by mortgages developed some time between the close of the eighteenth and the end of the second decade of the nineteenth century.[14] So widespread had the acceptance of the principle of the limited liability of corporate organization become by the middle of the century, that it was a subject of special comment by the British commissioners returning from the New York exposition in 1854.[15]

EARLY FINANCIAL ORGANIZATION

The financial organization of the United States in this early period consisted of the Second Bank of United States which acted as a kind of central bank; a group of private bankers who, besides their mercantile operations, were mainly concerned in obtaining foreign capital by selling American government securities abroad; a growing number of state-incorporated banks which, in addition to their extension of credit for mercantile transactions and land speculation, in part financed the operation of American security capitalism by investing in securities and by furnishing credit for security speculation; and finally several stock exchanges located in the more important financial centers on the Atlantic seaboard. The dominant institution was the Second Bank of the United States. Because of its rapid expansion, the West was primarily interested in a liberal credit policy which the Bank's conservative directors and officers in the East were unwilling to follow. The struggle between the Western interests and the Bank, crystallized in the Jackson administration, became the dominant issue in the election of 1832. Clay, with the support of Biddle and the Northeastern Whigs, defended the Bank against the attacks of the Jacksonian Democrats, but was overwhelmingly defeated. The Bank's charter expired in 1836 and was not renewed. Thus from 1836 to 1913 there was no central bank in this country.[16]

The private banks were an important element in the financial system, and in the beginning performed a wide range of operations as engaging in lotteries, in foreign exchange as well as in stock brokerage.[17] In 1837 George Peabody founded the private banking house which was later to be J. P. Morgan and Company. George Peabody was at first mainly concerned in creating a market for Maryland securities, and it was largely through his efforts that the necessary financial support for the construction and expansion of the Baltimore and Ohio Railroad was obtained. Alexander Brown and Sons of Baltimore was also an important house engaging in both mercantile and financial operations.[18] In the City of Washing-

ton there were several prominent banking firms as Corcoran and
Riggs which floated the $16,000,000 issue of the federal government
in 1848. Another prominent house was E. W. Clark and Company
with whom Jay Cooke was associated in his early years.[19]

As a result of the dependence upon British capital the financial
organization of the United States was influenced by that of England. Barings were agents for the United States government until
1835 when Rothschilds took over this function.[20] Rothschilds
operated their own offices in New York, Boston, Philadelphia and
Baltimore. The close relation between American and British security capitalism was described by a member of Congress in the
observation that "the barometer of the American money market
hangs up at the stock exchange in London."[21] Another American
commentator, in discussing the Bank of England, declared that:

This immense engine of finance is now so intimately connected with
monetary matters in our own country that the slightest throb of its
quickening pulse has a controlling influence on movements in State or
Wall Street.[22]

Incorporated commercial banks increased rapidly in number
with the adoption of the principle of "free" banking which permitted any group of persons to apply for a charter under the general
banking law of the state. In theory the incorporated banks were
supposed to confine their activities to commercial operations, and
the economic literature of this period accepted with little question
the orthodox theory of the function of the commercial bank.[23] In
actual practice the banks performed both commercial and investment operations, for they held not only state and municipal bonds
but also stocks. The proportion of such securities to the total assets
of the banks over this period averaged somewhat over 7 percent.[24]
The incorporated banks also granted a large volume of loans based
on security collateral. In fact the system of call loans existed in
New York before 1837, for in that year a special committee of
the New York legislature presented a report opposing such loans.[25]
The bank commissioners of Massachusetts in their report for 1837
also scored the practice of banks in making call loans.[26] After the
panic of 1857 security loans were again severely criticised. One
writer considered the "treacherous resources of call loans delusive
alike to the banks and to the public" as "the great panic-making
power."[27] Throughout this entire period there was no distinct group
of investment bankers, for this specialized form of banking was undeveloped until the large bond issues of the federal government during
the Civil War made necessary the creation of such specialized financial machinery.

Over these years security markets developed in the large eastern cities as Philadelphia, Baltimore, Boston and particularly New York.[28] The New York Stock Exchange organized in 1816 soon became the leading security market. Trading on the security markets was at first confined largely to dealings in the federal and the state debts, for there was only a very small volume of corporate securities in existence, mostly shares of bank and insurance companies. Later, there were transactions in the stocks of canal and gas light companies, but it was not until the listing of railroad stocks that corporate security operations really became important. The volume of trading was very small, as for example on March 16, 1830 when only 31 shares changed hands and $3,470.25 was sufficient to buy all the stock.[29]

PUBLIC NATURE OF CAPITAL DEMAND

The demand for capital over these years was mainly public in nature and came from the federal, state and municipal governments. The War of 1812 was financed partly by public credit, and by 1820 the federal debt amounted to $91,000,000. The debt reduction policy formulated by Alexander Hamilton was carefully followed by the national government, and by 1835 the debt was entirely extinguished. However, the Mexican War was financed by credit, and so by 1850 the debt rose to $63,000,000.[30]

State debt increased rapidly over these years, in view of the fact that the states engaged extensively in public enterprises. The strict interpretation of the constitution barred the federal government from participating in internal improvements. The assumption of such powers by the state governments was also due to the weakness of the structure of private security capitalism over these years. The expansion of the West made necessary the development of transportation and of internal improvements, but these undertakings required a large amount of capital which could not be obtained by private corporations, since their financial position had not yet grown to a point where they inspired the confidence of either domestic or foreign investors. Capital in large amounts for internal improvements therefore could be obtained only on the credit of the state governments in the form of their own direct obligations or of their indirect obligations created by guaranteeing the bonds of public corporations. This situation was well stated in a contemporary report that:

The public are now firmly convinced that, in the United States, where the fortunes of private individuals are limited in amount, great public works can only be accomplished by the expenditure of the public treasury.[31]

The era of such state borrowing began on a large scale with the New York State bond flotation for the purpose of financing the state-constructed and state-owned Erie Canal. Between 1817 and 1825 a large amount of these bonds were sold,[32] and after the construction of the Canal, revenues from it accumulated so rapidly that in 1834 the state, in retiring its bonds, was forced to pay a premium of from 5 to 9 percent.[33] This financial success of the Erie led to the construction of other trunk canals in the middle, southern and western states. Maryland, with the aid of George Peabody, gave support to the Chesapeake and Ohio Canal in order to maintain the prestige of Baltimore. Pennsylvania likewise aided the building of canals to assist Philadelphia in its competition against New York. The Southern states also entered the race for internal improvements. In 1838 the Governor of North Carolina admitted that the people of his state were too poor to finance internal improvements from their own resources, but urged the sale of the state securities in foreign markets on the ground that this policy held "no higher terror to a mind of enlarged and patriotic views." [34]   In the case of Kentucky, notwithstanding the fact that the state program would result in a debt of $6,000,000 the governor declared: "What is this sum to the resources and wealth to the State of Kentucky whose taxable property is now valued at $275,000,000." [35]   The Western states, particularly Michigan, Ohio and Illinois entered upon the unrestrained building of internal improvements. The proceeds of these state loans were applied to a variety of purposes, canals constituting the most important single purpose especially in New York and Pennsylvania. The creation of banks, next in importance, was confined to the Southern states. These were essentially land banks of which the most important was the Planters Bank of Louisiana. In most cases the stock was subscribed by local planters, and the bonds, guaranteed by the state, were sold in the East and in London. The state loans for railroads were well distributed among almost all the states, while the debts incurred for turnpikes were confined almost entirely to Pennsylvania, Kentucky and Indiana.[36] In general the New England states had the smallest debts while the Southern states had the largest.[37]

The demand for capital by the municipalities remained small until the close of the third decade of the nineteenth century. Washington placed a loan in Amsterdam in 1830, and Philadelphia and Boston obtained capital from London in 1833. New York City was the largest borrower and accounted for $13,000,000 of the total of $27,500,000 of aggregate municipal debt in 1842.[38] From 1840 until the Civil War the increase in urban population necessitated considerable local borrowing, and by 1860 municipal indebtedness was estimated at $200,000,000.[39]

In the early part of the period under review, the volume of corporate investment remained unimportant. Most corporations were small in size, and these were largely public or semi-public utilities, such as banking, insurance, water, steam boat, turnpikes, bridge and canal companies.[40] Corporate financing in the capital market did not become important until about the middle of the century when the railroads were able to float their issues. By 1858 the sum of $90,000,000 had been invested in 26,000 miles of railway.[41] Corporate financing took the form of bonds, common stock and even preferred stock. Preferred stock was issued as early as 1836 for financing railroads, canals and for industrial enterprises.[42]

SUPPLY OF CAPITAL

Capital for these various undertakings of governments and of corporations came in part from domestic sources but also from abroad. The supply of domestic capital over these years was unquestionably increasing, as evidenced by the rise in national wealth and in national income.[43] Domestic capital for the security market came mainly from the merchant and the manufacturing classes of the North. The merchant class included both the small storekeepers of the interior and the wealthy importers of the seaboard who placed a considerable proportion of their saving in securities. The manufacturers of the Northeast derived large profits from their operations as evidenced by the high dividends which they were able to declare.[44] In fact some of the manufacturers themselves financed the building of railroads. Thus Connecticut brass manufacturers financed the Naugatuck Railroad as an auxiliary to their enterprises, and the owners of mills on the Merrimac River promoted the railroad from Boston to Lowell.[45] The profits of the industrial revolution led to the accumulation of large individual fortunes.[46]

The rapid increase of wealth in the northeastern states is evidenced by the increase in the value of taxable property in the larger states and cities of this section. Valuation of real and personal property in New York State rose from $101,160,046 in 1825 to $235,960,047 in 1844.[47] The value of taxable property in Massachusetts rose from $153,545,171 in 1820 to over $299,880,338 in 1840.[48] However, capital accumulation in the South was small in view of the limited returns on cotton planting.[49] In the Northeast there was also a growing diffusion of capital ownership as evidenced by the widespread holdings of bank deposits and of securities. In 1860 the aggregate deposits of the savings banks in New York State, amounting to over $58,000,000, were held by over 273,000 persons, and total savings deposits in Massachusetts, exceeding $39,000,000, were held by over 205,000 depositors.[50] The stock of the Merrimac Company of New England was held by 390 people including 68 "females," 52 retired business men, 40 clerks, students and unspecified, 18 physicians and 15 farmers.[51] The securities of the New York Central railroad were held by 2,445 investors.[52]

Notwithstanding the increase in the supply of domestic capital, it was insufficient to meet the pressing demand for capital to finance the industrial revolution of the period. Early American security capitalism was therefore forced to look for funds from abroad. The greater part of this foreign capital went into governmental rather than corporate securities. In 1828 $14,000,000 of the federal debt was held by British investors, and $5,000,000 was held by Continental investors.[53] Most of the state debt was held abroad, while municipal securities were largely owned in this country. American corporate securities found little favor abroad, and the stock of both the First and the Second Bank of the United States was the earliest important form of American corporate investment of British capital.[54] Even as late as 1840 only about a dozen American corporations had been able to place their securities abroad.[55] The unfortunate investment experience of British investors in American public securities in the thirties restricted the subsequent flow of British capital into American corporate securities, and so the financing of American railroads attracted little foreign capital before the Civil War. In the fifties a few railways such as the Erie and the Illinois Central were able to place their securities in the British market. In 1854 the secretary of the treasury presented a detailed statement of American government and corporate securities held abroad, and according to this report almost one-half of the federal debt and well over one-half of the state debt was held abroad, while only about a quarter of the municipal debt was in foreign hands. Only a very small amount of the capital for railway, bank, insurance, canal and navigation financing came directly from foreign sources.[56]

CRISES UNDER EARLY AMERICAN SECURITY CAPITALISM

The financial structure of early American security capitalism, although containing several elements of weakness, was generally sound. The credit position of the federal government was high as seen by the low per capita debt, the declining proportion of debt service to total expenditures and the large coverage of wealth to debt.[57] On the other hand the financial position of the states varied considerably. The financial position of the northeastern states was strong, while that of the southern and particularly of the western states was uncertain. The municipal debt was contracted on a sound basis, and in the entire period before the Civil War there were only four important municipal defaults, namely those of Mobile in 1839, Detroit in 1841 and Chicago and Philadelphia during the depression of 1857.[58]

The corporate structure of early American security capitalism was satisfactory. The industrial corporations of the Northeast made large profits and were soundly capitalized. The railroads in the East were likewise on a firm financial basis, if the present-day financial standards are applied. Thus the railroads of Massachusetts in 1846 had a net income of 6.89 percent on their total capitalization as compared with an average of 5.2 percent for the Class I railroads for 1890–1929.[59] In 1859 the Massachusetts railroads had 29.5 percent of debt to total capitalization which was low compared with 61.5 percent for the Class I railroads from 1890–1929.[60] On the other hand many western roads were not soundly financed, and due to hasty construction through sparsely settled territory the earning power was frequently insufficient to meet the interest on the debts.

The early stage of American security capitalism was marked by financial crises in 1837, 1857 and again in 1860. The crisis of 1837 was particularly serious for the new system, and in the five-year period from 1837 to 1841 state securities depreciated $100,000,-000 and corporate securities $80,000,000.[61] During the depression following the panic of 1837 early American security capitalism, based largely on the creation of public debt held mainly abroad, was badly shaken as one state after another including even Pennsylvania defaulted on its debt. In most cases the taxing capacity of a state was insufficient to meet the debt service and default was inevitable. At times the default was defended by the local officials on high moral principles. Thus Governor McNutt of Mississippi, in vetoing legislative resolutions which recognized the validity of a particular state bond issue, declared that:

The Bank [i. e.–of the United States] . . . has hypothecated these bonds, and borrowed money upon them of the Baron Rothschild. The blood of Judas and Shylock flows in his veins, and he unites the qualities of both his countrymen . . . He has advanced money to the Sublime Porte, and taken as security, a mortgage on the Holy City of Jerusalem and the Sepulchre of our Saviour. It is for the people to say whether he shall have a mortgage on our cotton fields, and make serfs of our children.[62]

An effort was made to induce the federal government to assume the state debts. This proposal arose out of the difficulties of Nicolas Biddle and his United States Bank. A friend of Biddle suggested the idea in a letter to Barings and then induced Daniel Webster to sponsor the assumption proposal.[63]   As a result of correspondence with Webster, Barings issued a circular urging such assumption by the Federal government.   The proposal was supported by the Whig newspapers, as the New York *Herald,* while the Democratic press branded the proposal to transfer the defaulted states debts to the national government as a devious plot between Barings and Webster.[64]   The assumption plan became an issue in the elections of 1840, and Harrison was accused of having the support of the British banks.[65]   A House committee presented a report in favor of the assumption plan, but it was not approved by Congress.

The repudiation of state debts and the failure of the assumption plan for a time weakened the credit of even the federal government in the European capital markets.   In 1842, when the federal government sent its representative to Paris to negotiate a loan, he was told by Baron Rothschild to report that the man who was the head of the finances of Europe had said "you cannot borrow a dollar not a dollar." [66]   The London *Times,* consistently hostile to the United States, declared : "The people of the United States may be fully persuaded that there is a certain class of securities to which no abundance of money however great, can give value and that in this class their own securities stand pre-eminent." [67]

The second financial crisis in the early stage of American security capitalism occurred in 1857.   The sudden discovery of gold led to an overexpansion of credit used for speculation on the stock market and brought about a rapid rise in security prices.   In the beginning of 1857 the stocks of the new railroad system showed weakness, but the real crash came in August with the suspension of the Ohio Life Insurance Company.   It had conducted large financial operations in the West and in New York, and had made extensive loans to the Western railroads.   By the end of the year, a number of the leading railroads, including the Erie, Reading, Illinois Central and Michigan Central, failed to meet their obligations and as a result security prices virtually collapsed.   Because of these conditions the New York *Times* described the New York Stock Exchange as an "enormous gambling establishment." [68]

The third financial crisis came at the outbreak of the Civil War when the South repudiated its debt to the northern capitalists.[69]   The London *Economist* stated that:

many voices have been heard clamoring for secession as an excuse for repudiating the debts, private and commercial, as well as public, which they owe to the wealthier classes of the North.[70]

Because of these successive crises the trend of both government and corporate security prices were very irregular.   The 6's of 1862 of the United States Government rose from par in 1841 to 124 in 1853 and then sold off to a low of 109 in 1857. The prices of the bonds of the state governments showed wide variation. On the one hand the 5's of Massachusetts sold as high as 117, and the 6's of New York and of Ohio sold at high prices but were very irregular. On the other hand the bonds of Pennsylvania sold down to 40, Maryland to below 50, Kentucky to 67, Indiana to 171/2 and Illinois to 163/4. However all these issues recovered their values in the later years.[71] The trend of equities over these years is reflected in the prices of the stocks of banks, and railroad companies. In general bank shares were fairly stable, while railroad shares fluctuated markedly and their trend was generally downward.[72]

CRITICISM AND CONTROL OF SECURITY CAPITALISM

The rising system of security capitalism was the subject of sharp criticism. The opposition to corporations was exceedingly bitter. The labor press contended that capital was unduly favored by the granting of "charters for monopolizing companies," while the "interests of labor" were not sufficiently recognized by legislators.[73] The corporation was condemned in the economic theory of the day. Thus, Daniel Raymond, whose *Thoughts on Political Economy* published in 1820 was the first book of its kind written in the United States, declared that:

Every money corporation is *prima facie* injurious to national wealth, and ought to be looked upon by those who have no money with jealousy and suspicion. They are, and ought to be considered, as artificial engines of power, contrived by the rich for the purpose of increasing their already too great ascendency and calculated to destroy that natural equality among men which God has ordained and which government has no right to lend its power in destroying. The tendency of such institutions is to cause a more unequal division of property and a greater inequality among men than would otherwise take place.[74]

Incorporated banks in particular were singled out for attack. *The New York Working Man's Advocate* stated that the bankers were "the greatest knaves, imposters and paupers of the age." [75] A meeting of "mechanics and other working men" declared that the banks

under the administration of their present directors and officers and by the concert of auctioneers and foreigners, aided by custom house credits, form a monopoly that is hostile to the equal rights of the American merchant manufacturer, mechanic and laboring man; and the renewal by the legislature, of the charters prayed for, will confirm and perpetuate an aristocracy which eventually may shake the foundations of our liberties and entail slavery on our posterity.[76]

The opposition to rising security capitalism came not only from the working class of the North, but also from the landed class of the South. In general the South continued in the stage of agrarian capitalism throughout the first half of the nineteenth century. Thus within the United States there were two different economic systems; in the South a developed agrarian capitalism largely based on slave labor and in the North mainly a rising security capitalism. The issue between these two systems was defined with truly remarkable insight by one commentator in 1837 as "whether cotton shall control exchanges and importations or whether the banks and the stock interest shall do it." This commentator added "The struggle is for ascendancy . . . break down the swindling of bankers, and the capitalists of the South will control the confederacy. Drive out to a great extent paper credits, except upon bona fide capital, and cotton will do the exchanges of the commercial world. . . The capitalists of the North have by their corporations concentrated their power as in one man. . . The South will be more prosperous under cotton at ten cents, and no banks connected with the government, lending its credit and power to the stock interest than we would be under the latter at thirteen cents, and the reverse of these things." [77]

This conflict of interest between the agrarian South and the industrial North was reflected in the decisions of the Supreme Court in the period before the Civil War. In its early years dominated by the Federalists the Court merely upheld the will and intent of the founders of the Constitution. They had set out to construct a government which would protect property from the onslaughts of radical agrarian majorities bent upon debtor and agrarian legislation.[78] John Marshall, in his long career as Chief Justice, with irrefutable logic carried out the intent of the framers of the Constitution to the letter. In a series of notable decisions he aided in building a strong central government capable of protecting property. He ordered the State of Georgia to fulfill a land sale, put through by a bribed legislature because he was unwilling to permit a state to engage in a breach of contract. As a recent commentator accurately noted: "It was at the power of the States, not that of Congress, that he struck with all the weight of remorseless logic and unbending will." [79] Contrary to popular opinion, in the course of his entire career only one act of the federal government was declared unconstitutional.[80] In his seventy-seventh year in 1832, wearily surveying his accomplishments and grimly speculating on the future, he wrote: "I yield slowly and reluctantly to the conviction that our constitution cannot last . . . the Union has been prolonged thus far by miracles. I fear they cannot continue." In 1837 the number of justices on the Court was increased from seven to nine. During the course of his two administrations Jackson had the opportunity to fill six vacancies on the Court. A social lag came to an end. Federalist domination, which in the legislative and executive branch had ended with Jefferson's election, was driven from its last outpost. The Supreme Court fell to the agrarians, and their forces controlled all three branches of the government until the Civil War. Wildcat banking flourished, tariffs were reduced, slavery upheld. Manifest destiny and "black imperialism" added vast additional territories and though less united there came to be more states.[81]

Over these years there was little attempt by either the federal or state governments to regulate the financial institutions of security capitalism. Among the few instances of government regulation of security capitalism was the law of Massachusetts passed in 1837 which authorized a specified list of local securities as investments for some of the funds of life insurance companies. In 1849 New York, and a year later Wisconsin similarly prescribed the investments of life insurance companies.[82] In order to restrict the growing security operations of the banks, New York State passed a law stipulating that incorporated banks should "not directly or indirectly deal or trade in . . . buying or selling any stock created under any Act of the United States or any particular State unless in selling the same when truly pledged by way of security for debts due."[83] New York State in 1855 established a State Board of Railroad Commissioners who were empowered to regulate railroads, but the railroad interests proved too powerful and in 1857 the Board came to an end.[84] As a result of the excessive expansion of state debt, restrictions were embodied in the constitutional provisions limiting the amount of debt that might be contracted.[85]

Thus in the second quarter of the nineteenth century and until the Civil War, the United States as a whole passed from colonialism to nationalism; the Northeast from individual to security capitalism; while the South continued in the stage of agrarian capitalism. In time the West became more and more interrelated with the new form of capitalism of the Northeast.

GOVERNMENTAL POLICIES IN THE RECONSTRUCTION PERIOD

The years immediately following the Civil War until the panic of 1873 marked a continuation of the rise of security capitalism.[86] The economic policies of the national government underwent drastic changes, particularly in relation to tariff, currency, banking, private property and railroads. Northern security capitalism victorious in the Civil War, was determined to reap the full fruits of its victory over the crushed agrarian capitalism of the South. As a result high protective tariffs were passed successively over these years, and these acts safeguarded the home market for the products of the northern industrialists. Notwithstanding strong pressure from various groups, Congress with hesitating feet moved along the path which led to sound currency. This policy had the support particularly of the bankers. Thus financial history repeated itself, and as British banking influence in the period immediately after the Napoleonic Wars was successful in forcing a sound currency policy on England, so a half a century later in the post-civil war period American banking security capitalism likewise threw its influence on the side of sound currency. In the throes of the Civil War Congress enacted the National Bank Act primarily as a temporary measure to provide a market for United States Government bonds. While this purpose was not well attained during the War, nevertheless the Act accomplished the more permanent aim of supplying the United States with the framework for developing a national banking structure. Economists have generally been over-critical of the limitations of the National Banking system as established under the Act of 1863, and have been too ready to point out its weaknesses, particularly the inelasticity of the currency, the difficulty of mobilizing reserves and the costliness of the exchange system. However, the National Banking system over the years created a safe and uniform currency in place of the diversified and generally unsafe state currency of the pre-civil war period. The Act also established standards of banking as to capitalization, and provided for a national system of control in the form of examinations and reports.

The fourth important economic policy of the federal government was the passage of the fourteenth amendment and its application by the Supreme Court to the protection of private property. It is not clear whether the framers of this section sought merely to protect the rights of Negroes or whether they had a broad economic view in mind.[87] Whatever may have been the motive behind this constitutional change, its actual effect was to give extensive protection to private property interests and to provide a firm legal foundation for security capitalism. Without this legal protection, it is doubtful whether the rapid flow of capital into corporate securities over this period would have been possible. A further important economic policy was the liberal aid given to the railroads in the form of lands and subsidies. Railroad development was helped by extensive land grants and public subsidies.

The industrial revolution swept over the United States and touched all fields of economic activity, including manufacturing, agriculture, foreign trade. The factories of the Northeast turned out their goods in ever-increasing volume. Agriculture in the middle western states, under the influences of machine methods, increased its produce many times over. The frontier was pushed westward, and new lands were brought into cultivation. During these years there was little concern about overproduction, and the increased output of American factories was absorbed at home, while surplus farm products found outlets in the foreign markets. Transportation bound the various parts of this new economic empire, and moved the enormous agricultural surplus to the eastern seaboard for shipment to foreign markets. Population in these years increased rapidly.

In this period the United States had not yet developed an economic philosophy of its own. In this respect the early stage of security capitalism in the United States was unlike that of British security capitalism which had a well developed economic philosophy as expressed by the classical economic writers of that period. For a number of years American economic policy followed closely the classical school of laissez faire and of individualism. This tendency found expression in the absence of federal regulation of economic activity outside the banking field. The federal government refrained from active interference and adhered to the classical doctrine of laissez faire in the relation between the state and industry.

EARLY INDUSTRIAL CAPITALISTS

In the period following the Civil War the corporation came to be more widely used in organizing business enterprise and therefore led to the creation of an ever-increasing volume of securities, particularly of railroads. This activity was directed not by the banker but by the industrial capitalists as Cornelius Vanderbilt, Leland Stanford and Collis Huntington. They had large personal resources, but even these were inadequate to finance their enormous expansion programs, and so it was necessary to attract the funds of the public. The security market therefore became the institution which supplied these industrial capitalists with the necessary funds for their vast undertakings.

The operations of this early security capitalism was not altogether beneficial to the investing public, as its interests in the railroads exceeded that of the speculative capitalists. A number of the latter, such as Daniel Drew and James Fiske, came to realize that greater stakes could be won by clever security manipulation than by sound operating management of the railroads. This choice of policy led to overcapitalization.

The Erie was an illustration of the unsound railroad financing of these years. The road in a short period of four years was recapital-

ized from $17,000,000 to $78,000,000. In one case of Erie financing
Daniel Drew and his "brother directors" purchased for themselves
a worthless road, the Buffalo, Bradford and Pittsburgh, for $250,-
000, and then in the name of this company issued bonds to the
amount of $2,000,000. The road was thereupon leased to the Erie
for 499 years, and the latter agreed to assume the bonds of the
former.[88] Because of such operations, the property of the Erie railroad was poorly maintained, and according to an official report to the
Railroad Commission of the New York State legislature:

the iron rails have broken and laminated and worn out beyond all
precedent until there is scarce a mile of your road, except that laid
with steel rails, between Jersey City and Salamanca or Buffalo, where
it is safe to run a train at the ordinary passenger or train speed, and
many portions of the road can only be traversed safely by reducing the
speed of all trains to 12 to 15 miles per hour . . .

Jay Gould in testifying as to the value of Erie stock, was therefore
undoubtedly correct in stating that "there is no intrinsic value to
it probably; it is speculated in here and in London and it has that
value." [89]

Another instance of railway overcapitalization was the case of
the New York, West Shore and Buffalo. This road was built along
the west bank of the Hudson River in order to give it a "nuisance
value" against the New York Central. The West Shore failed in
1884 with a capitalization of $40,000,000 of stock and $70,000,000 of
bonds based on a non-paying line of 475 miles.[90] Such operations
were bitterly scored in the financial press. The *Nation* claimed
that the cause of the panic of 1873 was the closing of the English
markets to American railway securities under the influence of repeated cases of American rascality.[91] The London *Statist* held that
"no railroads in the world have the earning power of the American,
and none have been from first to last such scandalously bad investments." [92]

JAY COOKE

In American financial history the regime of Jay Cooke represents the passage of the control of security capitalism from the
speculative capitalist to the investment banker. Jay Cooke was the
outstanding security banker of what we may describe as the pre-
Morgan period in American security capitalism.[93] His distinctive
service to American finance was the successful flotation of the United
States Government bonds during the Civil War. It was largely
through his efforts that in the difficult days of the War the government was able to find a market for its bonds in this country and
abroad. To the ringing slogan that a "national debt is a national

blessing," he sold government bonds in every part of the North and even in Europe.[94]   Jay Cooke unquestionably was the father of the system of American security banking, for he was the first to introduce the modern methods of purchasing and distributing securities.   He noted the underwriting syndicate in France when he was negotiating the sale of Northern Pacific bonds in European markets and used this financial device in the purchase and sale of new issues.[95]   In selling securities, Cooke used a large number of salesmen.[96]   An extensive sales force was also used in the sale of the Northern Pacific bonds, and in this campaign, clergymen, lawyers, storekeepers and postmasters acted in communities which did not have banking facilities.[97]   The efforts of these agents were personally supervised by Cooke who gave them generously of his counsel. "Hold levees," he advised, "as I do every afternoon with the brokers and bankers of the street and go into a thorough explanation after a thorough reading of the documents.   Spread out your maps so that they can see them."   At times he himself would take the field to reinforce the efforts of his agents, and would frequently address small groups of local bankers and capitalists.   Cooke also enlisted the services of financial journalism; "I have great faith in being kind to editors," wrote Cooke.   In the summer of 1871 he organized a party of journalists including Charles A. Dana of the New York *Sun* and other leading writers of the larger papers.   These individuals took part in an editorial excursion to look over the property of the Northern Pacific, but the group was unable to go beyond the Red River Valley since the secretary of war would not agree to provide an escort any further due to the danger of Indians.[98]

The essential function of the conservative investment banking houses even before the Civil War was to facilitate the importation of foreign capital.   Cooke, therefore, sought to extend his financial empire abroad, and so formed the firm of Cooke, McCulloch and Company in London by taking the former Secretary of the Treasury as a partner, since his name "suggested an alliance with the government which was likely to impress Europe very favorably." [99] Cooke tried to locate his London branch near the Bank of England, but failing in this effort he nevertheless had the consoling thought "that it was not farther away from the 'Old Lady' than Morgans' or Barings'." [100]

Cooke developed close relations with the political powers in Washington.   His name was prominent on the circular of business men and bankers in 1872 urging the continuation of Grant's administration and warning the public that the election of Horace Greeley would bring "widespread ruin." [101]   The secretary of the treasury carried a balance with Jay Cooke without offering United States bonds or any other security to cover these deposits. The firm also made liberal loans to some of the leading political figures of the day without requiring any security. Blaine obtained a loan from Jay Cooke which was not adequately covered by collateral, and in correspondence on this subject Cooke stated:

Blaine will be a hard nut to crack. He ought certainly to pay the note as the loan was too much on such a property. But you will have to be very careful not to offend him. He is figuring for the Presidency. Has he paid his interest? [102]

Fresh from his triumphs in the sale of the federal securities Cooke sought other worlds to conquer, and in 1869 he undertook the financing of the Northern Pacific which was to bring his firm to its end in the crash of 1873. The Northern Pacific had been chartered during the Civil War, and had obtained from Congress a grant of over 47,000,000 acres of public lands or an area about the size of New England. The original speculators lacked the financial resources to carry through the development of the road, and Cooke, by making a small advance, was able to obtain the business of financing the road and selling its securities. Notwithstanding the extensive selling organization both in this country and abroad, the distribution of the securities of the Northern Pacific encountered increasing difficulties. The advice of his more conservative partners was disregarded, and Cooke plunged deeper and deeper. The firm, unable to carry the burden of the Northern Pacific, finally crashed on September 18, 1873. That night the Fifth Avenue Hotel, the social center of the financial world, was crowded with "all the magnates in the commercial, financial and political world," and President Grant with his Secretary of the Treasury, Richardson, made their headquarters there to relieve the financial emergency.[103] The Philadelphia press wrote the following obituary on the firm of Jay Cooke:

The most enterprising and renowned of American monetary institutions, its name was everywhere the synonym for strength and solidity. An hour before its doors were closed, the Bank of England was not more trusted. The disaster was as unexpected as an earthquake is to-day.[104]

SUPPLY OF AND DEMAND FOR CAPITAL

During the Civil War the volume of governmental and corporate security investment developed rapidly. Over these years the leading form of security investment was the United States Government bonds. These issues, however, became smaller in amount after the Civil War and the net total of the national debt declined steadily. The borrowings of the state governments were relatively unimportant. The volume of municipal financing increased rapidly and by 1870 the municipal debt rose to $516,000,000.[105] Over this period industry, except for petroleum, was financed largely by entrepreneur capital, and so the volume of industrial securities was small. Likewise utility financing, with the exception of the Atlantic Telegraph and other international cable companies, was still in swaddling clothes. Railroad securities dominated the capital market throughout this entire period.

The supply of domestic capital available for security investment grew rapidly during the third quarter of the century. Profits in the North were considerable during the Civil War, and in the ensuing period these accumulated funds sought investment in the security market. National wealth and national income in these years rose rapidly.[106] Capital accumulation was fairly widespread as evidenced by the increasing number of individual investors.[107] The import of foreign capital to the United States revived, and came both from England and from the Continent. The total amount of foreign capital in 1869 was estimated at $1,465,000,000 of which $1,000,000,000 was placed in the United States Government bonds, $243,000,000 in railroad securities, and the remainder in miscellaneous public and private securities.[108]

RESULTS OF SECURITY INVESTMENT

Judged from the standpoint of the investor, the financial results of security capitalism over these years were mixed. On the one hand the securities of the national government brought large returns to the holders. These bonds were issued at prices at times to yield 7 percent and even higher. From the levels of the dark days of 1863, they rose in value with the successes of the Northern army. The instability of the currency caused sharp fluctuations in the price of the bonds, but they finally reached par and even rose to a premium. The obligations of the Northern and Western states generally were free of default. During the Civil War the governments of the Southern states and of the Confederacy expanded their debts to finance the secession movement. These debts were abrogated and their payment prohibited by the fourteenth amendment to the Constitution. In the reconstruction period, the carpet-bag governments in a number of the Southern states expanded their debts which were generally repudiated on the overthrow of these governments.

The period immediately following the Civil War was marked by extensive municipal defaults. A number of Southern cities expanded their debts under the carpet-bag governments, and these obligations were later repudiated. A number of Western cities like-wise increased their debts for the purpose of granting aid to the railroads and subsequently defaulted. By 1870 one-fifth of all the municipal indebtedness of the United States was in default.[109] In-glis Palgrave warned the British investing public that American municipal securities were "hardly in a position which renders it desirable for private persons to invest in them. . . A small munici-pality in the West has apparently no idea of what credit means or how vital it is to stand in good credit. Investors find to their annoyance that there is apparently no idea in the minds of those responsible that it is necessary to be up to date in the payment of the coupons or the bonds." [110]

The domestic and foreign holders of American railroad bonds at times fared poorly due to the depredations of the security specu-lators. Bond yields were high until 1876 due to the uncertainty of the currency. In these years bonds were necessarily speculative in nature, for the railroads, which were the largest issuers of these se-curities, had not yet established themselves on a sound credit basis. As a result yields ranged from 7 to 9 and even 10 percent.[111] The obligations of even the best roads were on about a 7 percent basis.[112]

CONCLUSION

In the period from the close of the Civil War to the early seven-ties the American economic system acquired more definitely the char-acteristics of security capitalism. Its growth was aided by govern-mental policies particularly those relating to money and banking. Unfortunately the new system fell under the control of the specu-lative capitalist. The first effort of investment banking to dominate the new system ended in disaster with the failure of Jay Cooke. The tendencies in the form of security investment were parallel to those in England in the early stage of security capitalism following the Napoleonic War. In the case of both countries a severe war had increased the public debt, but in the post-war period the debt was reduced and the funds thus released were absorbed in the financing of railroad development. As in England speculative excess was a characteristic of early American security capitalism. Despite the ir-regularities in the new security capitalism, there was almost no move for control by the federal government which scrupulously followed the policy of laissez faire.

CHAPTER 11

DEVELOPMENT OF AMERICAN SECURITY CAPITALISM

THE years following the panic of 1873 to the crisis of 1907 marked the developed stage of security capitalism in this country. The period may justly be called the Morgan Era for over these years the House of Morgan came to dominate the financial system. In general, the economic tendencies operating in the previous period continued over these years. American manufacture increased its output, and technical improvements transformed both production and consumption. Free land was still available, and thousands of new acres were brought into cultivation. Foreign trade changed in nature, for, where formerly exports consisted largely of raw materials and foodstuffs, there was now a growing increase in the proportion of manufactured goods. In the railroad field, the great trunk lines were formed.

The struggle for a gold currency continued, and the sound money program supported by Eastern bankers was finally adopted by Congress. In the words of the secretary of the treasury, on the day of the resumption of specie payment "By five o'clock the news was all over the land and the New York bankers were sipping their tea in absolute safety."[1] However, in the ensuing years the supporters of sound money were hard pressed to hold their gains. Uncertainty as to the future of the currency, due to the passage of the Bland-Allison Act in 1878 and the Sherman silver legislation in 1890, continued over this period, and at times checked the flow of capital.

At the height of the political campaign of 1896 the *Chronicle* observed that :

There has been no lack of investment funds any more than there has been a lack of capital to engage in reproductive enterprises. The real trouble has been that in view of the pending uncertainty—an uncertainty at once menacing the standard of values and threatening to derange all values—neither the investor nor the capitalist was willing to tie up his money or to let it go far out of his reach.[2]

The Gold Standard Act of 1900 placed the United States on a sound money basis where it remained until March 1933.

In this period the social opposition to security capitalism became intense and the system was attacked in granger acts, and also federal legislation particularly against the trusts. These laws came under the critical review of the Supreme Court, which, by weakening the impact of the Sherman Act, restricting the operations of the Interstate Commerce Commission and the Federal Trade Commission, limiting federal taxation and railroad legislation, became a most important bulwark protecting developed security capitalism from the attacks of its enemies.[3]

DEVELOPMENT OF CORPORATE ORGANIZATION

While the corporation had existed in the period before the Civil War and had developed in the years immediately following, it was however only after the panic of 1873 that this form of business organization came not only to dominate the economic structure but to be "the master institution of civilized life."[4] Corporate financing was stimulated by the development of bond issues secured by the corporate mortgage. This instrument now included careful provisions for foreclosing on pledged property in case of default and for enabling a company to redeem its bonds prior to maturity through the use of call features, and by the nineties the corporate mortgage reached its modern form.[5]

Another important change in corporate practice was replacing the individual trustee by the corporation, generally a trust company organized specifically for this purpose. The unreliability of an individual as a transfer agent for bonds was demonstrated in the heavy reverses suffered from fraudulent transactions, and the investing public lost confidence in individuals as trustees.[6] There was also a growing practice of issuing collateral trust bonds supported by a block of stocks or bonds which had to be deposited with a trustee acting in behalf of the bondholders.[7] Individual trustees were therefore replaced by corporate trustees.

Another development in corporate organization was the growing use of the holding company. This legal device had already been used in railroad finance as early as 1833, but the first pure holding company in the modern sense of the term was developed between 1868 and 1872 by special acts of the Pennsylvania legislature.[8] These companies were given "full power and authority to hold and own securities of any form, either as collateral or otherwise, and to dispose of the same at pleasure."[9] A number of these holding companies played an important part in the railroad and the utility industries. The Pennsylvania Company was formed to aid the financing of the Pennsylvania Railroad system, and the United Gas and Improvement Company developed the first permanent gas and electric system. The State of Massachusetts also granted a special charter for the formation of the American Bell Telephone Company.[10]

Holding companies were created by special legislative acts until 1889 when New Jersey amended its general corporation law permitting a corporation to hold the stocks of other companies, and in time other states followed the same practice.[11] The significance of this measure is well stated by Meade:

> For momentous consequences, this statute of New Jersey is hardly to be equalled in the annals of legislation . . . the little state of New Jersey, containing 2 percent of the population and 1 and 3/10ths percent of the wealth of the United States, by the simple act of amending its corporation law, nullified the anti-trust laws of every State which had passed them.[12]

The growing intricacies of corporate practice developed a class of lawyers who specialized in this field. John B. Dill began his lecture at the Harvard Law School with the statement that "I am the lawyer for a billion dollars of invested capital."[13] William Nelson Cromwell, of Sullivan and Cromwell, in the biography which he prepared for *Who's Who* stated that he was an "officer or counsel of more than twenty of the largest corporations of the United States and one of the organizers of the United States Steel Corporation" and that he had "reorganized Northern Pacific Railway and many others and put all on a paying basis."[14] Another important corporation lawyer was Joseph Choate who performed what was then considered a great service for security capitalism in presenting the arguments in favor of invalidating the income tax.[15]

OPPOSITION TO SECURITY CAPITALISM

The period was marked by widespread social unrest, and probably at no time in American history was the class struggle sharper. The opposition to security capitalism expressed itself in national politics. Bryan was the leading spokesman of this opposition, and at the Democratic convention of 1896 his ringing words, "You shall not press down upon the brow of labor this crown of thorns. You shall not crucify mankind on a cross of gold," were aimed probably at the corner of Wall and Broad Streets.[16] The campaign was fought over the issue of financial concentration as well as that of monetary policy. Singling out the United States Government bond issue of 1895, Bryan declared, "the people will vote against bond syndicates and trusts."[17] Wall Street was quick to take up the challenge. On the Saturday before the election an anti-Bryan demonstration of 80,000 persons marched from morning until night. Wall Street was bedecked with flags, and the Morgan banking house "made the finest and most ornate show."[18] One section of the parade consisted of 5,000 bankers and brokers, and as they passed the reviewing stand there was a cry "where is Pierpont Morgan?" but he was not in the parade.[19] Bryan's defeat was an important political victory for security capitalism. In 1900 Bryan was again a candidate for the presidency, but this time he was crushingly defeated.

The system encountered its most aggressive foe not in the ranks of the Democratic party but in the Republican party in the person of Theodore Roosevelt. Drawing a distinction between "good" and "bad" trusts, he exerted every effort to effect governmental control over the giant industrial corporations then being formed. He directed his shafts particularly against J. P. Morgan, and between these two personalities there was a bitter feud. An attempt was made to bring them together at the Gridiron Dinner in 1906, but this effort at reconciliation failed dismally when Roosevelt, after explaining his policy of business control, shook his fist in the banker's face and shouted : "if you don't let us do this, those who will come after us will rise and bring you to ruin." [20] Wall Street made a vain effort to set up Mark Hanna in opposition to Roosevelt for the Republican nomination in 1908, but Hanna died a few months before the convention.[21] The New York *Sun* expressed its choice of Roosevelt over Alton B. Parker in the following words : "We prefer the impulsive candidate of the party of conservatism to the conservative candidate of the party which the business interests regard as permanently and dangerously impulsive." [22]

The Democratic convention of 1912 was the scene of a bitter assault on security capitalism. Bryan, still smarting from his past defeats, forced through a resolution that :

As proof of our fidelity to the people, we hereby declare ourselves opposed to the nomination of any candidate for President who is the representative of or under obligation to J. Pierpont Morgan, Thomas F. Ryan, August Belmont, or any other member of the privilege-hunting and favor-seeking class. That we demand the withdrawal from this convention of any delegate or delegates constituting or representing the above-named interests.[23]

This resolution was passed by an overwhelming vote, and August Belmont and Thomas Fortune Ryan, at whom the above resolution was directed, were expelled. The convention under Bryan's guidance then nominated Woodrow Wilson who was to continue the work of Theodore Roosevelt as the leader of the political opposition to concentrated security capitalism.

INTERNATIONALIZATION OF AMERICAN SECURITY CAPITALISM

The United States was evolving from the stage of purely national to that of international capitalism, and in consequence its foreign political relations were becoming more important. It is generally held that the stage of international economy of the United States began during the Great War, but actually it was under way two decades earlier. Even before the turn of the century the United States entered upon a policy of overseas expansion which extended its power to the Caribbean and to the Pacific. American security capitalism, similar to British security capitalism, did not stand to gain from an aggressive foreign policy. In 1896 the United States in supporting the Monroe Doctrine came close to conflict with British internationalism over Venezuela. American banking security capitalism strongly opposed the belligerent stand of its government. Commenting on Cleveland's ultimatum to Great Britain, J. P. Morgan said:

I have labored to build up such relations of confidence between the United States and the money markets of Europe that capital from there could be secured in large sums for our needs, and here is a threatened disaster that will put an end to our borrowing.

Fortunately the clash was averted.[24]

Following the Spanish-American War, the American government took an active part in the financial affairs of Cuba. The Platt amendment provided that the Cuban government was not to contract any public debt if its ordinary revenues were inadequate, and also that the United States Government could intervene for the preservation of Cuban independence in the maintenance of a government adequate for the protection of life and property. The amendment gave the United States control over the finances of Cuba, and this power was exercised on several occasions. Likewise the United States Government intervened in Santo Domingo in 1907 when its finances were in a demoralized condition. The United States Government facilitated the flotation of a loan by the National City Bank to the government of Haiti, and also took a hand in the reorganization of the finances of Nicaragua. In almost every case American intervention resulted in a settlement of the financial difficulties of the country and in the improvement of the credit position of the nation. Unlike the policies of the European powers, the protectorates established by the United States over foreign territories were temporary. In the Far East, American banking capitalism came near being seriously involved in an imperialistic venture but fortunately did not carry the policy through. In the period immediately preceding the Great War, the State Department for a time took an active interest in regulating the flow of American capital to China. "That diplomacy" noted one writer, "represents the maximum point to which diplomatic assistance to private investments has been extended by the American Government." [25]

CHANGING FUNCTION OF COMMERCIAL BANKING

The trend of commercial banking in this period may best be traced by studying the changing financial position of the national banks.[26]   The national banks at first made extensive use of the privilege of issuing circulating notes permitted under the National Bank Act, and these notes constituted about 20 percent of the total liabilities of the national banks.[27]   However, the proportion declined sharply, and by 1910 was only about six percent of the total liabilities.   The deposits of these institutions were almost entirely in the form of demand deposits.[28]   In 1905 the comptroller of the currency ruled that national banks were not prohibited from operating savings departments, but little advantage was taken of this ruling.[29] The proportion of securities to total earning assets reached a high figure in 1870 due to the large holding of government bonds after the Civil War; the proportion dropped until 1890, and thereafter moved irregularly upward.[30]   A growing proportion of the loans of the national banks were based on stocks and bonds as collateral.   By 1892 security loans constituted 29.72 percent of total loans, in 1901 they reached a peak of 41.47 percent and then receded but by 1910 still accounted for 37.17 percent.[31]   The exact proportion of the security investment assets in the form of direct security holdings and security loans of all the commercial banks of the United States to their total assets in the period before the passage of the Federal Reserve Act has been variously estimated.   Dr. Anderson in his study of bank earning assets for 1909 estimated that, exclusive of real estate loans, more than one-half of bank credit was applied to the purchase of bonds or the granting of loans on stocks and bonds.[32]   Writing in 1914, C. W. Barron, a financial editor, claimed that two-thirds of the funds extended by commercial banks were used for investment purposes and only one-third for commercial transactions.[33]   It is thus clear that even before 1914, as a result of the changing nature of the entire financial system, the so-called commercial bank was broadening its function and was becoming an important institution of developed security capitalism.

American economists and bankers themselves generally accepted the orthodox theory of banking which maintained that commercial banking must be conducted separately from investment operations.[34] However, A. Barton Hepburn, Chairman of the Chase National Bank, as far back as 1893 properly stated that "the purely commercial function as formulated in text books and laid down by the course as the business of the bank, fails fully to describe the banking of today.   Banks of discount and deposit have become large owners of securities." [35]

GROWTH OF THE STOCK EXCHANGE

Over these years the stock exchanges also expanded rapidly. The successful opening of the Atlantic cable in 1866, the adoption of the stock ticker in 1867, and the installation of telephones on the floor of the New York Stock Exchange in 1878 were mechanical improvements which accelerated the growth of security capitalism.[36] The Open Board of Brokers was formed in 1864 as a competitive organization to the New York Stock Exchange, and there was also a Government Bond Department which traded in the securities of the federal government. In 1869 the Exchange, the Open Board and the Government Bond Department, all merged into the New York Exchange. The Exchange now grew in importance, and from 1870 to 1910 the number of stocks listed on the Exchange rose from 143 to 426, while the number of bonds increased from 200 to 1,013.[37] The volume of trading on the Exchange, although small when compared with that of later years, nevertheless, showed a rapid increase. The volume for a single day rose to an early peak of 700,000 shares on November 28, 1879. In December 1886 the million-share mark was attained, and on April 30, 1913 the volume rose to 3,281,226 shares, a record that was to stand until 1916.[38]

In addition to the New York Stock Exchange there were several other security markets in New York City. The New York Mining Stock Exchange traded in mining and other stocks from 1876 to 1883 when it became the New York Mining and National Petroleum Exchange of New York. This financial market later added other securities as those of the railroads, and by the nineties its business was about a third of that of the New York Stock Exchange. The Curb Exchange also expanded its volume of business.[39]

Unlike European financial centers, New York in the period of developed security capitalism did not absorb the interior stock exchanges and these have continued in importance particularly in Baltimore, Boston, Chicago, Philadelphia and San Francisco.[40]

RISE OF INVESTMENT BANKING

The most important change in financial organization occurred in the field of investment banking. The significant trend of this period was the transfer of the control of American capitalism in many fields from speculative capitalists to banking capitalists. In this respect American differed from British security capitalism, and partook rather of the nature of German security capitalism. To a large extent this difference was due to the relative extent of the supply of capital. In England there was sufficient capital even in the early years to finance the needs of industry, which obtained its funds largely from the resources of individual entrepreneurs. On the other hand, in Central Europe and in the United States, the financial resources of the industrialists were insufficient to meet the needs of the vast enterprises being formed. It was therefore necessary for the investment banker to mobilize not only the funds of the public but also to contribute a proportion of the necessary capital out of his own resources. Under these conditions, it was inevitable that the banker should obtain extensive control over the managerial policies of the enterprises in which he placed his own funds. Thus close relations between industry and investment banking became at first a dominant feature of American security capitalism in the developed stage.

The course of security capitalism in the years immediately after the Civil War was marked by the private wars of the Fiskes and the Drews which may be likened to the anarchy prevailing under feudalism of the Middle Ages, with the distinction that, whereas under the feudal system the people lost their lives, under security capitalism they lost their money. The investment banker brought a semblance of order out of this chaos, and for a time was able to restrain the ruthless feuds of security capitalism. The transfer of control from the speculative capitalist to the investment banker meant the transition from financial feudalism to financial nationalism. As the growth of nationalism in the fifteenth and sixteenth centuries ended the private wars of the barons, and at least within the confines of the nation brought law and order, so the coming of banking capitalism in the eighties instituted a system of stabilized finance. The captains of industry were no longer sovereigns in their own right but now ruled by the grace of the higher power of the investment banker.

This close relation between industry and finance brought about the combination movement in both fields. The expansion of industry was made possible by the development of intercorporate relations through agreements, pools, interlocking directorates, voting trusts and holding companies. At the same time, to raise the funds for these giant corporations it was necessary to mobilize the financial resources of the nation into concentrated financial combinations. This combination movement was brought about not so much by concentration, that is, the fusion of like units in the form of a number of investment banks, but rather by a policy of integration or the development of a close relation among unlike financial units. Thus the large investment banking houses extended their influence over insurance companies and trust companies in order to obtain dominance over capital resources and over commercial banks to

direct their credit resources.[41]   By 1912 integration had progressed
to the point where 180 individuals representing 18 investment banking houses, commercial banks and trust companies, through holding
341 interlocking directorates controlled 112 corporations with total
resources of over $22,000,000,000.[42]

A number of investment banking houses gained in strength over
these years.   Palgrave, writing in the New York *Forum*, recognized
in addition to the Morgan firm the importance of other houses,
as Kuhn Loeb, Speyer, J. & W. Seligman and Brown Brothers, in the
comment that "there is a considerable moral fibre in the United
States, and it would be difficult to find higher examples of business
qualities than among its first-rate men." [43]

RISE OF THE HOUSE OF MORGAN

Until almost the end of the seventies the house of Morgan was
conducted as an old-style private banking establishment.[44]   Its primary function was to place American securities among foreign investors.   At home it participated in the various syndicates which
handled United States Government bonds, but in these groups it
was still a follower and not yet the leader.   The Morgan firm was
unsuccessful against Jay Cooke in bidding for the issue of United
States Government bonds in 1871.   But in 1873 it broke the Cooke
monopoly by forcing the secretary of the treasury to provide for
equal participation in the flotation of the loan between the Morgan-
Morton syndicate (including Barings) and the Cooke syndicate (including Rothschilds).   It was thus a Morgan victory, since the house
had asked only for equal participation while Jay Cooke had opposed
any division.[45]   In 1877 the house of Morgan took part in the refunding of the Government bonds, but the banking group was
known as the "Belmont Syndicate." [46]   This transaction was, however, important in that Drexel, Morgan took the place of Jay Cooke,
and became the American associate of Rothschilds.

The eighties however, marked the early preeminence of the Morgan firm.[47]   In addition to its normal banking operations, the firm
now initiated policies which were to influence the entire economic
system of the United States.

INFLUENCE OVER SUPPLY OF CREDIT AND CAPITAL

The broad significance of Morgans in the development of American security capitalism can best be understood by noting the two
underlying policies of the house.   The first policy advanced its influence over the supply of the credit and the capital resources of the

financial system; the second policy extended its influence over the sources of the demand for capital. While a growing proportion of the capital of the American investing public was placed directly in securities, most of these resources continued to be invested indirectly through investment institutions such as savings banks, commercial banks, trust companies and life insurance companies. For the most part, the Morgan firm made little or no attempt to tap the capital resources of the savings banks and they generally remained independent of investment houses. However, other institutions of indirect investment, as commercial banks, trust companies and life insurance companies, came under the influence of the Morgan firm. This relationship was aided by the fact that the American financial system in practice followed the Continental system of mixed rather than the British system of specialized finance. In the course of time, trust companies extended their activities to include both commercial as well as investment banking operations, and life insurance companies in turn, through buying control of trust companies and of commercial banks, indirectly performed the operations of these institutions. This mixed financial system therefore made possible the extensive integration of the structure which took place in the closing decade of the nineteenth century. Influence over these institutions of indirect investment was needed to give the investment banker the assurance of a market for new issues, and syndicate subscriptions were allotted to these financial institutions.

It was particularly advantageous for investment houses to gain control of commercial banks and trust companies. These institutions were important not only because they possessed capital resources but also credit facilities essential for carrying securities until finally marketed. Influence over the banks was exercised through interlocking directorates. J. P. Morgan became vice-president and director of the National Bank of Commerce, and thereby gained close contact with that institution. This bank in turn was closely interlocked with the First National Bank headed by George F. Baker an ally of Morgan. The Morgan firm through stock ownership and interlocking directorates also obtained an interest in the Chase, the Liberty, the Hanover and the Astor National Banks, and in addition developed a considerable interest in a number of out-of-town banks.[48] Interest was also extended to a group of important trust companies. J. P. Morgan & Company had representation on the boards of directors of the Union, the Commercial and the Fidelity Trust Companies, and in addition organized the Bankers Trust Company. Through the First National Bank a close relation with the Manhattan Trust Company was maintained.[49] In 1909 the

Morgan firm obtained an interest in the Guaranty Trust Company which was then added to the Morgan group.

To meet the government attack on the security operations of the national banks connected with Morgans and other investment banks, separate companies known as affiliates were formed. In 1908 the First National Bank, the keystone of the Morgan system of commercial banks, organized the First Securities Company by declaring a dividend of 100 percent which was issued in the form of stock in the securities company. The two organizations were bound together under an organization agreement between George F. Baker on behalf of the trustees and J. P. Morgan acting for the stockholders. In similar manner in 1911 the National City Bank formed the National City Company by paying a 40 percent dividend to the stockholders, and thus providing $10,000,000 of stock in the new institution.[50]

The great life insurance companies were veritable reservoirs of financial resources, and the large investment houses made every effort to develop close contacts with these companies. Because of this resultant intimate relationship the insurance companies were described as "the financial annexes to Wall Street interests" in the "Armstrong Report" on insurance companies.[51] The house of Morgan developed connections with the Mutual Life Insurance Company, and acquired an interest in the New York Life Insurance as well as in the Equitable Life Assurance Company.[52] The latter institution had been controlled by Thomas F. Ryan who, in the words of the biographer of Dwight Morrow, "was not considered a man of sufficient calibre to execute so large a responsibility."[53] Morgan, therefore, assisted by George Baker and James Stillman, took over Ryan's interests.[54]

INVESTMENT BANKING AND FEDERAL GOVERNMENT FINANCING

The investment banker is primarily a middleman, or a merchandiser of securities and thus he desires to obtain as large a supply of securities as he can market. The Morgan firm, therefore, developed relations with three sources of demand, the United States Government, the railroads, and industry. As mentioned before, the firm took an active part in the flotation of the various issues of the federal government after the close of the Civil War. The influence of the Morgan firm in floating federal government securities became increasingly important with the passing of the years, from its competition against Jay Cooke, its secondary position in the Belmont syndicate to its leadership in the critical federal financing of the nineties.

The relations between the Morgan firm and the federal government in the famous "gold loan of 1895" were the subject of bitter controversy. From the perspective of over forty years it is now possible to view the episode objectively.[55] The panic of 1893 was followed by one of the worst depressions in American history. Unemployment gripped the industrial centers, a large number of the railroads were in receivership and the confused currency legislation of Congress raised serious doubt as to the ability of the United States to maintain the gold standard.

Financial conditions abroad were unsatisfactory as an aftermath of the Baring failure, and Europe was drawing heavily on our supply of gold. Throughout 1894 the gold reserves of the treasury at various times were seriously depleted.[56] In order to replenish the government's gold stock, the treasury throughout 1893 sold several bond issues to the public, but they were not well received.[57] These public issues gave no relief since they did not replenish the government gold fund, and the gold supply fell to the desperately low level of only $42,000,000 in February, 1895. In this crisis President Cleveland and Secretary Carlisle were forced to decide whether to obtain the necessary financial relief through another public loan sold to the investors at large or through a private loan by a banking syndicate. The latter policy alone would give the assurance of obtaining the necessary gold from abroad. The government in despair turned for help to Morgan who rushed to Washington to confer with Cleveland and Carlisle. As a result of these negotiations Morgan agreed to raise a private loan of $50,000,000 with the understanding that the payment should be made in gold of which half was to be obtained from abroad. Morgan was aided by the Deutsche Bank, by August Belmont and by James Stillman, President of the National City Bank.[58]

When the details of the negotiations were announced, bitter criticism was levied at both Cleveland and Carlisle. In these negotiations one senator saw "the iron band of contraction wielded at the dictation of England," and the *New York World* held that the syndicate was made up of Jews and non-Americans. It was particularly charged that the terms of the loan were exorbitant.[59]

The actual terms of the issue were on a 3.75 percent basis, while the outstanding bonds of the United States Government were selling on a 3 percent basis. The issue however was conditioned by the requirement that one-half of the gold had to be obtained from abroad.[60] The action of the Morgan syndicate enabled the federal government to avoid the step of suspending gold payment and abandoning the gold standard. Cleveland and Carlisle on their part, in seeking to maintain the gold standard, had no alternative but a private loan from the banking syndicate. The fact that the country, at that time, had no central bank, made it necessary to deal with a banking syndicate having sufficient foreign support to import gold.

REBUILDING OF RAILWAY FINANCE

The original reason for Morgan's active participation in railroad finance was primarily due to his realization of the need of protecting the interests of the investors, particularly foreign investors, in American railroad securities. Throughout the seventies losses were heavy, and in 1876 39 percent of all the railroad bonds were in default, while in 1879, 65 roads with capitalization of $234,000,000 were sold under foreclosure.[61] As a result of these conditions, the European market for American railway securities was practically closed, and the free flow of capital from Europe to America was checked. A German banker stated that an American railroad bond could not be sold "even if signed by an angel." [62]

In this emergency the house of Morgan determined to take the leadership in the financial reorganization of the railroads. In the end this policy was to lead the house not only to take merely an external financial interest in the railroads but also to participate actively in the managerial policy of many of the systems. Throughout the sixties the railroads were mainly controlled by the speculative capitalists. The only important invasion of this field by banking interests was the ill-fated venture of Jay Cooke in obtaining control of the Northern Pacific. For years Gould and Fiske not only ruled their own railroad domains absolutely, but even made successful forays into the territories of other powerful railroad barons, including that of Cornelius Vanderbilt, who notwithstanding all his financial strength was forced to give ground. The conservative bankers of the East strongly disapproved of these financial raids, but lacked the courage to check them.[63] Morgan, however, was determined to meet force with force, and with his intervention the Gould-Fiske interests were thoroughly whipped in the battle for control of the Albany and Susquehanna Railroad.[64] The defeat of the Gould-Fiske interests brought relief to harassed security capitalism, and this contest waged not only by litigation but by force of arms made Morgan the acknowledged leader of the new banking capitalism.[65] The victory of the security banker over the speculative security capitalist was decisive, and the latter now disappeared as an important factor in the railroad field.

With his influence over a number of eastern lines now established, Morgan gradually extended his sway over the western roads. Many roads were in a demoralized financial position. To a large extent this condition was due to the economic feudalism which permitted ruthless competition among systems dominated by separate railroad presidents acting as lords over their respective territories. There was urgent need of replacing this chaos with order, and the strong hand of Morgan forced many of the railroad barons to accept his sovereignty. In January 1889 the leading railroad presidents assembled in the Madison Avenue home of Morgan, and at the conclusion of this meeting Morgan made the following significant public announcement:

I am authorized to say, I think, on behalf of the banking houses represented here that if an organization can be formed practically upon the basis submitted by the committee, and with an executive committee able to enforce its provisions, upon which the bankers shall be represented, they are prepared to say that they will not negotiate, and will do everything in their power to prevent the negotiation of, any securities for the construction of parallel lines, or the extension of lines not approved by that executive committee. I wish that distinctly understood.[66]

The financial press of the time referred to this meeting as "the bankers' triumph and the presidents' surrender." This conference signified the transfer of the control of the railroads from the hands of the industrial capitalist to those of the investment banker. Not only were the finances of many of the railroads to be directed by the bankers but also the management of these vast systems passed into their hands.[67]

STRUGGLE WITH HARRIMAN

The supremacy of banking security capitalism in the railroad field met its most serious challenge from Edward H. Harriman. There was a vast difference between the speculative capitalist as Fiske and the industrial capitalist as Harriman. The former used the railroads merely as a convenient vehicle for deriving profits from the manipulation of the securities of the roads on the stock exchange. Although they dominated and controlled the management of these roads, the speculative capitalist gave little attention to maintaining satisfactory operations. Harriman, on the other hand, possessed all the virtues of the industrial capitalist, and sought his profits mainly from the more efficient management of the roads under his control. Moody in commenting on this point stated that Harriman "had early adopted the theory that the first duty of railroad management was to maintain the character of the physical property. . . Thus in the management of the Illinois Central he never 'skinned' the road to pay dividends, he never allowed the roadbed or equipment to become inefficient."[68] The struggle between

Harriman as the protagonist of industrial capitalism in the railroad field and Morgan as the leader of banking capitalism was waged in three successive battles over the Illinois Central, the Erie and finally the Northern Pacific. In the skirmish over the Illinois Central, Harriman, with the aid of Stuyvesant Fish, defeated Drexel, Morgan & Company.[69] The next battle was fought over the Erie. This road went into the hands of the receiver during the panic of 1893, and in the following year Drexel, Morgan & Company proposed a plan of reorganization. Harriman was the owner of a small block of the junior securities of the road, and opposed the Morgan plan for reorganization on the ground not only that the holders of the junior securities were forced to make heavy sacrifices, but on the additional basis that the plan was financially unsound. Harriman, together with other holders of securities, including Kuhn, Loeb & Company, August Belmont and representatives of the Astor estate, sent a scathing protest to Morgan & Company.[70] This protest was ignored and the original reorganization was approved at a meeting of the Erie stockholders. Harriman, however, refused to deposit his bonds and brought suit to the Supreme Court which, finally, denied his appeal.[71] However, the Erie defaulted on the payment of the very first coupon of the new bonds, and so demonstrated the truth of the criticism of Harriman and his associates that the Morgan plan was unsound. The new reorganization plan recognized the criticism of the protesting committee.[72]

The supreme struggle between Harriman and Morgan was waged for the control of the Northern Pacific. This road had come under the management of James J. Hill, the "Empire Builder," and was largely financed by Morgan & Company. Harriman, aided by Kuhn, Loeb & Company, leading rival of Morgans in the investment banking field, and the National City Bank, strongest competitor of Morgans in the commercial banking field, carried the offensive into the enemy camp. Harriman mobilized his own capital by drawing upon the cash resources of the Union Pacific Railroad. Altogether the sum of $78,000,000 was needed to purchase the control of $155,-000,000 of the stock of the road in the market.[73] In the beginning the market campaign was so cleverly handled by the Harriman interests that they were even able to purchase 10,000 shares of stock directly from J. P. Morgan & Company itself, and 13,000 shares from the Northern Pacific Company.[74] The rise in the price of the stock, however, stirred the suspicion of Hill who personally confronted Jacob Schiff and then communicated with J. P. Morgan.[75] The Morgan interests, now aroused, entered the market, and the competitive bidding of the opposing camps forced the price of Northern Pacific stock up to unprecedented heights but at the same time depressed the prices of other securities.   The struggle, according to the *Chronicle,* caused "one of the most serious and yet most un-necessary panics New York has ever experienced." [76]   In the end the Morgan interests retained control of the common stock, while the Harriman forces gained a majority of the preferred stock which had equal voting power with the common.   However, the board of directors of the Northern Pacific had the right to retire the pre-ferred stock, and threatened to take this step in order to maintain control.[77]   At this point the two forces reached a settlement and agreed to leave the composition of the Northern Pacific board in the hands of J. P. Morgan personally. [78]   The settlement made by Morgan created five vacancies on the board of directors of the North-ern Pacific and the new appointees included both Hill and Harri-man but the control of the board was retained by Morgan.[79]

THE NEW HAVEN DEFEAT

The most serious reverse suffered by J. P. Morgan in the field of railway finance came toward the close of his career in the unsatis-factory results of his plan to combine the transportation system of New England.   Morgan had been a director of the New York, New Haven and Hartford Railroad for a number of years, and under his guidance the road prospered until the close of the century.   Mor-gan then decided to apply his policy of railroad combination suc-cessful in the past in other territories to the entire New England area.   To carry out the plan the resources of the New Haven, then in an excellent financial position, were used.   All forms of trans-portation, including railroads, steamship lines and trolley lines were bought up.[80]   The most important acquisition was that of the Boston and Maine which was soundly capitalized and efficiently managed.[81]   On the other hand, worthless property was also purchased.   One railroad operating at a loss, was acquired at a cost of $1,500,000.[82]

The effect of these operations may be seen in table 15 on page 177 showing the financial position of the New Haven in 1903 and in 1909.

From this table it is seen that in 1903 the financial position of the New Haven was excellent, with the ratio of funded debt to total capitalization at a low of 7.93 percent and with fixed charges fairly well covered at 184.21 percent.   By 1909 the funded debt had been increased to $234,900,000, and consequently the ratio of funded debt to total capitalization rose to 52.15 percent while fixed charge cover-age fell to 149.08 percent.   Dividends on the inflated stock were at first paid from surplus, then from short-term borrowings, were later reduced and finally suspended altogether.   The press and the Inter-

TABLE 15

FINANCIAL POSITION OF THE NEW HAVEN RAILROAD.[83]

(1903 and 1909)

ITEMS	(MILLION DOLLARS)	1903	1909
1	Operating revenues..................	47.3	54.3
2	Total income........................	10.5	24.3
3	Fixed charges[a].....................	5.7	16.3
4	Funded debt........................	14.5	234.9
5	Total capitalization[b]...............	182.9	450.4
RATIOS	(PER CENT)		
A	Total income to fixed charges..........	184.21	149.08
B	Funded debt to total capitalization.....	7.93	52.15
C	Total income to total capitalization.....	5.74	5.39

Explanation:

For meaning of these items and ratios see pp. 370-371.

[a] includes rents for leases.

[b] includes capitalization of leased rentals at rate of 6 per cent.

state Commerce Commission were bitter in their denunciation of the Morgan policy. The critical but calmer conclusion of Professor W. Z. Ripley on the New Haven episode was as follows:

The New Haven disaster goes far to justify the popular distrust of any undue concentration of power, . . . Once and for all in New England the question seems to be settled that even an honest transportation monopoly is inimical to the best public interest.[84]

INFLUENCE OVER INDUSTRY

In addition to the extension of influence over the forces of the demand for capital in the field of national government and of railroad financing, Morgan & Company also extended its power to certain fields of industrial financing, particularly the steel business. In this field Morgan encountered another powerful leader of industrial capitalism in the person of Andrew Carnegie who was a firm believer in the competitive system, and who entered into bitter competitive fights. In a memorandum to his partners Carnegie wrote:

Put your trust in the policy of attending to your own business in your own way and running your mills full, regardless of prices and very little trust in the efficacy of artificial arrangements with your competitors, which have the serious result of strengthening them if they strengthen you. Such is my advice.[85]

Carnegie threatened Morgan with competition not only in steel but in railroads, for he instituted surveys for his own road from Pittsburgh to the Atlantic seaboard.[86] Morgan then determined to buy out Carnegie. After considerable negotiation, Carnegie agreed to take $447,000,000 for his properties.[87] Thus a leading industrialist capitalist passed from the scene.[88] The Carnegie properties now formed the basis of the billion-dollar United States Steel Corporation, whose board of directors included a large representation of Morgan interests.[89] This deal was another victory for banking capitalism over industrial capitalism, and was so recognized by the press of the day.

Outside of the steel business Morgan & Company in these years made little effort to penetrate the other major fields of industry. The petroleum industry by this time was dominated completely by John D. Rockefeller. An industrial capitalist he differed from Carnegie in that the latter believed in competition while the former aggressively pushed the policy of monopoly. The enormous profits from the petroleum industry furnished sufficient resources to finance the expansion of the Rockefeller interests, and thus they were independent of the bankers. The Rockefeller interests even entered the banking field, and obtained a substantial interest in several financial organizations, particularly the National City Bank.[90]

Henry Clews paid tribute to the financial power of the Standard Oil group in the statement that "This combination controls Wall Street almost absolutely. Many of the strongest financial institutions are at their service in supplying accommodations when needed." [91]

Rockefellers and Morgans, as the respective leaders of industrial and banking capitalism, at times had conflicting interests and came close to open warfare, particularly during the fight over the Northern Pacific, but in every case an open clash was avoided.

In this period Morgan and Company made little effort to finance the new industries which were then coming into existence. For example, in 1908 the Morgan firm was offered the financing of William C. Durant who was a leader in the new automobile industry. Durant was seeking additional capital and asked Morgan and Company to underwrite $500,000 for which loan he offered stock in his company as collateral.[92] Durant fell into a controversy with E. L. Stetson, counsel for Morgans, and with George W. Perkins, an active partner of the firm. In the conversation Durant stated that the time would come when 500,000 automobiles would be sold annually. Perkins commented: "If he has any sense he'll keep such notions to himself if he ever tries to borrow money." The underwriting was therefore denied. In the course of time the stock which Durant offered as collateral for the loan was to pay $35,000,000 in dividends and was to attain a value of over $200,000,000. Durant in later years founded the General Motors Company and became its President. However, during the difficulties of 1920 control of the company passed from Durant to the DuPont interests.[93] Even in the pre-war period Henry Ford became the leading industrial capitalist in the automobile field. In the post-war period he not only retained his independence of banker control, but even extended his influence over certain major banking institutions. Like Carnegie, Henry Ford was an outspoken critic of banking capitalism.

GROWING DEMAND FOR CAPITAL

The demand for capital came to some extent from the federal, state and municipal governments but largely from the railroad, industrial and utility corporations and from real estate. The trend of the national debt over these years was generally downward.[94] This decline was checked by the financing of the Spanish-American War, the indemnity to Spain and the construction of the Panama Canal. All told, however, the national debt increased but slightly.

Table 16 shows the trend of state government debt from 1870 to 1913.[96] The debt structure of the state governments was very sound. The unfunded debt showed no increase and the proportion of the unfunded to gross debt was never high.[97] The net debt generally declined and showed little increase until the turn of the century when it began the rise which continued throughout the war and post-war period.[98] However, population also increased over these years, and as a result the net debt per capita remained at a low figure.[99] The state governments always had a goodly amount of assets which could be deducted from their gross debt, and the proportion of such deductions to the gross debt was always high.[100] The statistics on the amount of the tax base or the assessed valuation of the property on which taxes could be levied are incomplete, but they indicate the rapid increase in assessed valuation of such taxable property.[101] As a result of the more rapid increase in the tax base compared with the increase in the net debt of the states, the tax base covered the net debt at a rising ratio.[102] Thus the various trends in the finances of the state governments were very satisfactory.

Municipal debt rose sharply. In 1870 the total debt was $516,000,000 and by 1880 it had increased by $305,000,000, but over the next decade municipalities adapted a pay-as-you-go policy and debt rose only by $105,000,000. After 1890, however, municipal borrowing rose sharply and by 1902 the total debt was $1,630,000,000. The 1912 figures showed a municipal debt more than double that of 1902 or $3,476,000,000.[103]

TABLE 16

STATE GOVERNMENT DEBT, 1870–1913.[95]

YEAR	(MILLION DOLLARS)						(PER CENT)			
	UN-FUNDED DEBT (a)	FUNDED DEBT	GROSS DEBT	DEDUC-TIONS (b)	NET DEBT (c)	TAX BASE (d)	UN-FUNDED DEBT TO GROSS DEBT $1 \div 3$	DEDUC-TIONS TO GROSS DEBT $4 \div 3$	TAX BASE TO NET DEBT $6 \div 5$	NET DEBT PER CAPITA (g)
	I	2	3	4	5	6	A	B	C	D
1870	11	341	352	..	352	14,179[e]	3.1	....	3,240.3	$9.15
1880	19	286	305	31	274	17,140	6.2	10.2	4,028.1	5.48
1891	19	238	257	46	211	25,473[f]	7.4	17.9	12,072.1	3.37
1892	19	230	249	43	206		7.6	17.3		3.14
1893	19	220	239	38	201		7.9	15.9		3.03
1894	12	220	232	37	195		5.2	15.9		2.88
1895	13	212	225	31	194		5.8	13.8		2.80
1896	13	213	226	28	198		5.8	12.4		2.81
1897	14	222	236	28	208		5.9	11.9		2.90
1898	15	238	253	30	223		5.9	11.9		3.06
1899	12	248	260	32	228		4.6	12.3		3.07
1900	11	253	264	29	235		4.2	11.0		3.10
1901	10	251	261	33	228		3.8	12.6		2.95
1902	12	261	273	34	239	35,338	4.4	12.5	14,785.8	3.03
1903	9	257	266	34	232		3.4	12.8		2.88
1904	9	262	271	36	235		3.3	13.3		2.86
1905	11	267	278	39	239		4.0	14.0		2.85
1906	11	270	281	42	239		3.9	14.9		2.79
1907	10	269	279	44	235		3.6	15.8		2.70
1908	12	277	289	50	239		4.2	17.3		2.70
1909	10	290	300	59	241		3.3	19.7		2.67
1910	11	311	322	66	256		3.4	20.5		2.78
1911	13	333	346	71	275		3.8	20.5		2.95
1912	13	362	375	76	299	69,453	3.5	20.3	23,228.4	3.15
1913	19	403	422	76	346		4.5	18.0		3.57

Explanation:
(a) Total of current and floating debt.
(b) Sinking fund assets.
(c) Unfunded and funded debt less sinking fund assets.
(d) Assessed valuation of all property subject to ad valorem taxation. U.S. Census Bureau *Wealth, Debt* and *Taxation*, 1913, Vol. I, p. 747.
(e) Currency not gold basis.
(f) 1890.
(g) In dollars.

FINANCIAL POSITION OF THE RAILROADS

The volume of railroad financing was by far the most important form of corporate investment over these years. The statistics on American railroads before 1890 are incomplete, and owing to differences in the methods of keeping accounts, it is unwise to compare the financial statements before and after this date. The following ratios show the financial position of the railroads from 1880 until 1889.

TABLE 17

RAILROAD FINANCE, 1880–1889.[104]

(percent)

YEARS	TOTAL INCOME TO INTEREST	FUNDED DEBT TO TOTAL CAPITALIZATION	PROPERTY TO FUNDED DEBT
	A	B	C
1880	236.58	48.36	194.54
1885	189.46	49.65	186.88
1889	186.73	51.78	178.07

From 1880 to 1890 the financial position of the railroads was not satisfactory, as may be seen by the fact that the total income to interest declined. The proportion of the funded debt to total capitalization increased and the property protection of their funded debt declined.

The trend of railway finance may be studied more accurately after 1890, for after that date the Interstate Commerce Commission presented annual figures for all the Class I railroads.[105] Due to the rapid extensive development of the United States the operating revenues of the railroads from 1890 to 1910 expanded to 261 percent, while operating expenses were at about the same level (263 percent) and so the ratio of operating expenses to operating revenues remained fairly satisfactory at an average of 66.2 percent for the period.[106] Also the ratio of operating income to operating revenues was maintained at the high average of 33.7 percent for the period.[107] This ratio indicated that the roads had the satisfactory sum of 33 cents of operating income left over from the revenues after paying for all operating expenses. Total income rose to 244.9 percent or greater than the upswing in fixed charges which rose to only 159.3 percent.[108] As a result the ratio of the total income to fixed charges rose from 132.6 percent in 1890 to 204 percent in 1910 which was very satisfactory.[109] Also the amount of net income or the balance left over after fixed charges rose more sharply than operating revenues and so the ratio between these two items increased from 9.6 percent in 1890 to 18.8 percent in 1910.[110] This ratio signified that operating revenues could fall 18.8 percent before the coverage of the fixed charges was impaired and indicated a satisfactory margin of safety. While net income, or the balance available for dividends, rose to 511.9 percent, the dividends actually paid by the roads increased to 402.3 percent, and so the ratio of net income to dividends paid rose from 127 percent in 1890 to 147 percent in 1910.[111] This ratio shows that the roads more than earned their dividends over these years.

It was fortunate that the course of earning power was satisfactory, for the trend of railroad capitalization over these years was unsound. From 1890 to 1910 the roads increased their funded debt from $4,462,000,000 to $10,388,000,000, their total debt including capitalized leased rentals from $5,978,000,000 to $12,638,000,000 and their total capitalization from $10,157,000,000 to $20,700,000,000.[112] As a result of the greater increase in the total debt as compared to total capitalization, the ratio between these two items rose from 58.8 percent in 1890 to 61.0 percent in 1910.[113] By 1890 the proportion of debt to total capitalization was already high but increased further in the years which followed. Fortunately the total income increased rapidly and it was possible at the time to carry the heavy debt without serious difficulty.

In part, the increase in total capitalization was due to the need of funds for the construction of additional operating mileage which rose from 163,597 in 1890 to 240,831 in 1910.[114] The total stated value of railroad property over these years rose from $7,755,000,000 to $14,387,000,000.[115]

FOREIGN FINANCING

The trend of the capital movement between the United States and foreign countries began to change in the early eighties. The first important foreign loan was made in 1879 when an issue of $3,000,000 was granted to the Province of Quebec.[116] Between the years 1896 and 1900 $100,000,000 of American capital was exported to Canada.[117] In 1899 Morgans floated a loan to the Mexican Government and there was also considerable American investment in Mexican railroads.[118] In the early years of the century the New York market granted loans to various continental countries as Germany, Russia and Sweden.[119] The most important single case of foreign financing in these years was America's extensive participation in the flotation of the British government loans issued to finance the Boer War. During 1900 and 1901 Morgan and Company floated successive loans in large amounts for this purpose.[120] Later England bought back a large part of her securities, and by 1903 the *Chronicle* expressed the opinion that "practically all these securities have gone back to England." [121]

After the beginning of the century the United States took an active though generally unsuccessful part in financing the Far East.

Kuhn Loeb and Company and Edward Harriman participated extensively in financing Japan during its conflict with Russia.[122] Harriman apparently had a grandiose plan of a round-the-world railroad, and for this purpose negotiated with both the Japanese and Russian Governments. In 1905 Morgan and Company took over the Belgian interest in the American China Development Company, but later the entire American participation in the Company was bought out by the Chinese Government.[123] An American banking group headed by Morgan and Company, including Kuhn Loeb, the National City Bank and Edward Harriman, on the insistence of the state department, and even of President Taft personally, gained its admission into the international banking loan to China in 1911.[124] In 1913 President Wilson withdrew all official support of American banking in its far-eastern financial operations and thus forced the American group to retire from this field.[125]

CHANGING SOURCES OF CAPITAL SUPPLY

Throughout this period foreign capital in the United States continued large in amount but of declining importance. While foreign capital had a large and even a majority interest in the leading railroads in the early nineties this participation was sharply reduced by 1905.[126]

In the last quarter of the century the supply of domestic capital increased rapidly, coming both from the profits of the wealthy class and particularly from the growth in the material prosperity of the middle class. As in other countries this group formed the social foundation of developed security capitalism. National wealth rose from $43,600,000,000 in 1880 to $65,000,000,000 in 1890 to $88,-500,000,000 in 1900 and to $186,300,000,000 in 1910 and likewise national income rose from $7,400,000,000 in 1880 to $31,400,000,000 in 1910.[127] Estimates of the total volume of saving are always difficult but the trend may be seen in Table 18 which indicates the total assets of the financial institutions of the United States from 1873 to 1911. The assets of these institutions including banking institutions as national banks, savings banks, private banks, loan and trust companies and also life insurance companies, rose slowly from a total of $3,091,000,000 in 1873 to only $3,817,000,000 in 1880. However by 1890 the total rose to $7,096,000,000, by 1900 it was $12,-528,000,000 and by 1910 it reached $26,326,000,000.[129] These institutions of indirect investment over the years transferred a growing proportion of their assets into security investment. The total for all the financial institutions rose from 18 percent in 1890 to 24.7 percent by 1910.[130]

TABLE 18

TOTAL ASSETS OF FINANCIAL INSTITUTIONS, 1873–1911.[128]

(million dollars)

YEAR	BANKING INSTITUTIONS	LIFE INSURANCE COMPANIES	TOTAL
1873	2,731	360	3,091
1874	2,890	387	3,277
1875	3,205	403	3,608
1876	3,183	407	3,590
1877	3,204	396	3,600
1878	3,081	404	3,485
1879	3,213	402	3,615
1880	3,399	418	3,817
1881	3,869	429	4,298
1882	4,031	450	4,481
1883	4,208	472	4,680
1884	4,221	491	4,712
1885	4,427	524	4,951
1886	4,522	560	5,082
1887	5,204	596	5,800
1888	5,470	642	6,112
1889	5,941	697	6,638
1890	6,343	753	7,096
1891	6,562	819	7,381
1892	7,245	904	8,149
1893	7,192	972	8,164
1894	7,291	1,056	8,347
1895	7,610	1,142	8,752
1896	7,554	1,228	8,792
1897	7,822	1,334	9,156
1898	8,869	1,463	9,531
1899	9,905	1,595	11,500
1900	10,786	1,742	12,528
1901	12,358	1,911	14,269
1902	13,364	2,092	15,456
1903	14,303	2,265	16,568
1904	15,199	2,499	17,698
1905	16,918	2,706	19,624
1906	18,148	2,924	21,072
1907	19,645	3,053	22,698
1908	19,583	3,380	22,963
1909	21,095	3,644	24,739
1910	22,450	3,876	26,326
1911	23,631	4,164	27,795

A growing proportion of individual investors turned from indirect to direct investment and from real estate mortgages to securities. Until the end of the nineteenth century only fragmentary figures on the distribution of security holdings are available. In 1880 it was estimated that the public debt was held by 71,587 individuals.[131] The shares of the national banks in 1886 were held by 223,583 persons of whom 117,974 or more than one-half held ten shares or less.[132]   In 1897 war loans of $200,000,000 issued by the United States Government were taken up in 320,000 separate allotments.[133]   The first extensive figures on security holdings, as compiled in 1899, showed that 54 railroad companies reported 282,160 stockholders and 56 industrial companies showed 338,824 stockholders or a total of 110 corporations with 626,983 stockholders.[134]   The number of bookholders of corporate shares in the United States rose from 4,400,000 in 1900 to 7,500,000 in 1913.[135]   Over the same period the average number of one hundred dollar par value shares per stockholder declined from 140 shares to 87 shares.[136]   These figures indicate the growth of the popularization of security capitalism in the pre-war period.

There was also a widening of the geographic distribution of security holdings.   This distribution of security holdings was no longer confined to the East, but began to spread throughout the West.   Frank A. Vanderlip, as vice-president of the National City Bank, stated in 1905 that :

The whole great Mississippi Valley gives promise that at some day distant perhaps it will be another New England for investments.   There is a developing bond market there which is of constant astonishment to Eastern dealers.[137]

Public interest in security investment varied with the course of security prices, but since the general trend of security prices over these years was upward, a favorable public attitude towards security capitalism was created.

As a result of the rapid conversion of the assets of the institutions of indirect investment into securities, and the growth of direct investment in securities by individual investors, the proportion of securities to total wealth rose sharply.   It was estimated that the outstanding securities amounted to one-third of the total national wealth.[138]   This proportion was about equal to that of the leading nations of Europe and thus the United States, by the beginning of the century, had reached about the same maturity in the evolution of security capitalism as these older countries.

RESULTS OF SECURITY CAPITALISM

The developed stage of security capitalism brought with it the usual evils of overcapitalization of assets, deterioration in the quality of the securities based on these assets, the issuing of fraudulent statements, consequent security price depreciation, intermittent maladjustment between saving and investment with the resultant sharp security price fluctuations and financial panics.

In the case of certain specific railroads there was serious over-capitalization. Within a seven-year period the bonded debt of the Chicago and Alton was raised from $33,900,000 to $114,000,000.[139] Within a ten-year period the bonds of the Cincinnati, Hamilton and Dayton were increased from $12,000,000 to $48,000,000, while the unfunded debt rose from $200,000 to $10,000,000.[140] In neither case was there any corresponding increase in earnings to justify the higher capitalization. In fact, the underlying assets often depreciated in value and as Sterne declared:

The original bonded indebtedness, representing ties that have rotted, rails that have been sold, cars that have broken up, bridges and engines that have disappeared, remains a charge upon the road in the shape of bonds bearing interest.[141]

Overcapitalization was also a characteristic of much of the industrial financing of the late nineteenth and early twentieth centuries. In the case of the so-called "Sugar Trust," the outstanding bonds of $10,000,000 were based on plants estimated at $7,740,000 and the additional capital stock of $75,000,000 represented no tangible value.[142]

A further illustration was the United States Steel Corporation which had a total capitalization of $1,403,450,000 consisting of $303,-450,000 in bonds, $550,000,000 in preferred stock and $550,000,000 in common stock. The physical valuation of the property, as estimated in the report of the United States commissioner of corporations, was placed at $682,000,000 which did not even cover the bonds and preferred stock.[143] This corporation is a good illustration of the interpretation of overcapitalization as given in the introductory chapter. It was there stated that the test of overcapitalization is whether or not the future earning power of the corporation is adequate to support the volume of securities which have been issued. During the early years the earnings of the United States Steel Corporation were insufficient to justify the heavy capitalization. However, in time the expanding profits of the Corporation were sufficient to place even the common stock on a satisfactory earning basis. Judged therefore by actual earnings the United States Steel Corporation eventually was not overcapitalized. The conservative financial press was strong in its denunciation of overcapitalization, and the *Chronicle* stated that:

the floating of many of these concerns, however, at enormously inflated valuations and the issue of stocks upon such fictitious basis cannot be too strongly condemned—a more forceful objection to these combinations can be found in the extravagant overcapitalization adopted by the promoters. In most of the schemes offered to the public for subscription the bonded debt and preferred stock are fully equal to, and often in excess of, the real value of the property represented, while the common stock is simply a bonus which is divided between the promoters and the original proprietors.[144]

The course of a security boom is generally marked by a deterioration in the quality of new securities and the widespread speculative trend of these years was no exception. Conant writing in 1904 stated that :

In the case of industrial securities issued on the American market, the character of those issued has tended in many cases to become worse as the issues have increased. When this demand for new securities was small, it was necessary that they should be of the highest character to find a market ; when the demand became apparently insatiable, it was natural that shrewd and sometimes unscrupulous promoters should set themselves to provide a supply.[145]

Financial statements in this period were unreliable, and the issuing of untrue earning statements was a common practice. When the Atchison, Topeka and Santa Fe went into receivership in 1894, an independent audit revealed that while the statements from 1891 to 1894 showed satisfactory surpluses, actually the books had been falsified to cover an average annual deficit of over $1,250,000 for these years.[146]

As a result of unsound financial practices there were frequently serious losses to the holders of securities.

Losses were especially heavy in oil and in mining stocks. Marvin Scudder who compiled lists of obsolete and extinct securities stated in 1904 that "out of something over one million face value of such old mining stocks which have come to hand from estates in the past ten years, I have recovered exactly $12 on one certificate." [147] Real estate bonds also brought heavy losses. One company placed on its bonds in large letters, the words : "United States of America" and in even larger letters the words "savings bonds." The company even employed clergymen to sell its bonds, and when it failed the receiver was not able to find sufficient money in the treasury even to retain an accountant to go over the books.[148]

In the last quarter of the nineteenth century a number of cities overexpanded their debt and in many cases defaults followed. After the panic of 1873 Houston, Pittsburgh, Elizabeth and Rahway defaulted on their obligations. The panic of 1893 again precipitated extensive municipal default but from that year until 1926 the volume of municipal default was relatively small. There was also a marked drop in municipal defaults arising out of acts of invalidity due to technical legal irregularities. In the seventies and even eighties many municipalities took advantage of some small irregularity in the issuing of their bonds subsequently to declare their obligations void. However, these acts in time decreased and by the beginning of the century the practice was negligible. As early as 1885 the

American investor began to suffer losses on foreign government bonds and the *Chronicle* for that year bemoaned the fact that : "For the first time a large body of American investors find themselves affected in purse by the action of a foreign government." [149]

Notwithstanding their considerable losses on individual securities, the holders of American issues as a class derived a net gain over these years. The value of common and preferred stocks appreciated markedly over these years. An investment in the stock of the average corporation which had both common and preferred stocks listed on the leading stock exchanges showed a growth in value from 100 in 1886 to 1,102 for common stocks and to 822 for preferred stocks by 1910.[150]

RELATION BETWEEN SAVING AND INVESTMENT

The trend of the relation between saving and investment in the United States in general followed the same movement as that in other countries in the developed stage of security capitalism. While the demand for capital continued very strong, there was a relative increase in the supply. The increasing supply of capital is reflected in the almost continuous decline of interest rates throughout the eighties and nineties. Between 1875 and 1890 railroad bonds with 7 and 8 percent coupons were refunded at 4 and 5 percent, and in 1901 and 1902 issues were emitted with 3½ percent coupons.[151] One railroad had the opportunity to put out an issue on a 3½ percent basis for a 100-year period but preferred to issue 25-year bonds in the belief at the end of that period they would be able to refinance on a 3 percent basis.[152]

As close a student of finance as Jacob H. Schiff made the following forecast :

To me it appears almost certain that the rate of interest on investments such as a conservative corporation will be willing to make, must further decline. The amount of available railroad bonds which have heretofore offered so large a field to draw upon for investment, is becoming more and more reduced, and the new railroad construction to be undertaken in the future will not be very considerable and will almost entirely be done in the way of extensions to existing companies. I have very little doubt that the rate of interest on such investments will, before long, decline to 3 percent, while upon state and municipal bonds this has already become the top rate.[153]

However, the opening of the century brought a change in the money market. Money rates moved upward, and even the soundest corporations and municipalities were forced to borrow at higher rates. New York City in 1902 borrowed on a 3.194 basis, but by 1905 was forced to pay 3.499.[154] The income on the bonds of twenty leading cities rose from 3.00 percent in 1900 to 3.40 percent in 1905 and to 4.00 percent in 1910.[155]

This trend, as in foreign countries, was a direct result of the world-wide maladjustment between the force of investment and saving. Recognition of the fact that the American financial market was suffering from overinvestment may be found in the financial press of the day. J. P. Morgan described the unsatisfactory condition as due to "undigested securities," and James J. Hill modified the terminology by calling it a case of "indigestible securities." [156] After a number of unsuccessful issues, the *Chronicle* complained of the "apathetic investment market," [157] Alexander Noyes writing in the *Forum* commented : "The public absolutely refused to subscribe for the new securities, and the reckless underwriters accordingly found themselves compelled to take up millions upon millions of securities whose salable value was entirely uncertain." [158] The *Chronicle* added that "there was no surplus capital available to support a further expansion and advance." [159]

PANICS OF 1903 AND 1907

By the beginning of the century it was hoped that the integrated financial structure of developed security capitalism would be able to safeguard the economic system against the recurrence of panics. This thought was expressed at a dinner given in 1901 in honor of J. P. Morgan when John B. Claflin was quoted as saying :

With a man like Mr. Morgan at the head of a great industry, as against the old plan of many diverse interests in it, production would become more regular, labor would be more steadily employed at better wages, and panics caused by over-production would become a thing of the past.[160]

However, the panic of 1903 marked the first check encountered by the house of Morgan. The large volume of new securities, "undigested" or "indigestible," could not be absorbed, and it was necessary for Morgans to mobilize all possible financial resources, and every ally had to be pressed into financial service.[161]

The panic of 1907 further demonstrated the inability of even highly organized finance to control the conditions which lead to boom and subsequent collapse. By active support of the stock market the financial interests did succeed in checking the drastic liquidation of securities and these interests took over large blocks of securities held in weak hands, such as the stock of the Tennessee Coal, Iron and Railroad Company. This stock had been pledged by Moore and Schley, a leading brokerage house, which was being hard pressed for cash by the banks holding their collateral. It was a critical moment, for the failure of Moore and Schley would probably have carried down other brokerage houses weakened by the already sharp drop in security prices. In this emergency the Tennessee Company was merged with the United States Steel Corporation. The deal was first presented by Elbert Gary and Henry C. Frick to President Roosevelt who stated that he "felt it no public duty . . . to interpose any objections." [162]

There was a widespread popular belief that the panic of 1907 had been brought on by the great financial interests to crush their opponents, and the above transaction was frequently cited as proof of this assertion. The opposite view was expressed by Horace White, that :

The Samsons of Wall Street did not pull down the temple of finance on their own heads in order to slaughter a countless number of Philistines. They suffered mortal terror while the panic continued, and they did not escape wounds and bruises, which some of them are still carrying.[163]

Although organized financial power was thus able to check the extent of stock market liquidation and prevent the sharp downward course of security values, nevertheless, the same power was unable to bring about a revival of economic activity. Concentrated finance could stabilize conditions after a panic but could not bring about an upturn. The years immediately following the panic of 1907 saw little business revival and production remained at a low level as compared with the previous years. It was not until 1915 when the Great War gave the United States an artificial prosperity that business again revived.[164]

The panics of 1903 and 1907 are generally regarded as minor flurries in the financial history of the United States but considered in the perspective of the evolution of security capitalism in other countries, these disturbances take on a more serious significance. The British crisis of 1890 and the American panics of 1903 and particularly of 1907 have several striking characteristics in common. Both marked a turning point in the economic and financial life of the respective countries.

CRITICISM OF SECURITY CAPITALISM

As noted before, the period was marked by intense social unrest and class feeling against security capitalism. Thus Mary E. Lease declared that : "Wall Street owns the country. It is no longer a government of the people, by the people and for the people but a government of Wall Street, by Wall Street, and for Wall Street." [165] The Knights of Labor conceived the economic conflict as a struggle against the "money power" rather than against employers, and declared in its preamble :

The recent alarming development and aggression of aggravated wealth, which, unless checked, will invariably lead to pauperization and hopeless degradation of the working masses, render it imperative if we desire to enjoy the blessings of life, that a check should be placed upon its power and upon unjust accumulation. . .[166]

The organization according to its by-laws excluded permanently from membership only "bankers, lawyers, stockbrokers, gamblers and those making or selling intoxicants." Actually, the banker capitalist was generally more willing to see the public aspect of the labor question than the industrial capitalist. This difference of view between the banker capitalist and the industrial capitalist was illustrated in the coal strike of 1902. George Baer, famous for his statement on the holding of property by divine right, as the leader of the coal operatives adamantly refused to arbitrate with John Mitchell and the representatives of the unions. The Morgan firm, on the other hand, made strenuous efforts to bring about such arbitration, and J. P. Morgan himself went to Washington to discuss the matter with President Theodore Roosevelt.[167] Some of the so-called literature of exposure which crowded the journals of this period was based on an emotional appeal and had little substance.[168] There were however, a number of thoughtful works such as Henry George's *Progress and Poverty*, Edward Bellamy's *Looking Backward*, Henry Demarest Lloyd's *Wealth against Commonwealth*, and Ida Tarbell's *History of the Standard Oil Company*. The most penetrating criticism of security capitalism was that of Louis D. Brandeis who evidenced a clear understanding of security capitalism and the various institutions connected with the system.[169] The monumental study of the United States Industrial Commission, which gave Thorstein Veblen material for his comments on institutional change, stands as a most important source book on the development of American security capitalism.

The governmental attack on security capitalism began in the administration of Theodore Roosevelt. In 1904 the administration took active step against the system in dissolving the Northern Securities Company. Advance information of this move was kept secret even from the cabinet, and the announcement was a complete surprise to Morgan and Company and to Wall Street. The security market acted badly, and the *Detroit Free Press* stated that "Wall Street is paralyzed at the thought that a President of the United States would sink so low as to enforce the law." [170] Roosevelt was bitterly attacked by New York corporation lawyers on the ground that he "had shown lack of respect for the Supreme Court since the legal device on which the Northern Securities Company was based, had already been held valid in a preceding case." [171] Roosevelt's messages to Congress for legislation to regulate trusts and his bitter speeches against financial concentration were blows at developed security capitalism. These attacks on the trusts were regarded in the financial press as the cause of the uncertain condition in the stock market in the early years of the new century. "Hail, Caesar, we who are about to bust, salute thee," proclaimed the New York *Sun*.[172] "Many investors have already lost much," said the *Chronicle*, "and not knowing what Mr. Roosevelt may do or say next, are getting extremely nervous, afraid if they hold on much longer they may see the little of value left vanish." [173]

Roosevelt replied to this criticism in the following words:

. . . You say that the fear of investors in railway securities must be dispelled; and you say that the people now have the impression that the greatest business interests (those of railroads) are imperiled. I am inclined to think that this is the case. If so, the responsibility lies primarily and overwhelmingly upon the railway and corporation people—that is, the manipulators of railroad and other corporation stocks—who have been guilty of such scandalous irregularities during the last few years.[174]

Elihu Root tried to assure Wall Street that they had nothing really to fear from Roosevelt, in the statement to the Union League Club in 1904: "You say Roosevelt is an unsafe man. I tell you he is a great conservator of property and rights." [175] The President himself made his position clear in a letter to Jacob Schiff, in the following words:

It is difficult for me to understand why there should be this belief in Wall Street that I am a wild-eyed revolutionist. I cannot condone wrong, but I certainly do not intend to do aught save what is beneficial to the man of means who acts squarely and fairly.[176]

With the passing of Theodore Roosevelt as President the attack on security capitalism continued but was given added impetus under Woodrow Wilson. In some of his statements while still in the academic world he had adhered closely to the classical theory of laissez faire and had condemned government regulation of business as socialistic in nature.[177] However, by 1908 he was an outspoken critic of security capitalism. As President of Princeton University, in an address to the American Bankers Association, he stated:

For the first time in the history of America there is a general feeling that issue is now joined, or about to be joined, between the power of accumulated capital and the privileges and opportunities of the masses of the people. The power of accumulated capital is now, as at all other times and in all other circumstances, in the hands of a comparatively small number of persons, but there is a very widespread impression that those persons have been able in recent years as never before to control the national development in their own interest.[178]

As President of the United States his attacks became even more bitter, and in this capacity he proclaimed that :

The great monoply in this country is the monopoly of big credits. So long as that exists, our old variety and freedom and individual energy of development are out of the question. A great industrial nation is controlled by its system of credit. Our system of credit is concentrated.[179]

THE PUJO COMMITTEE

The high tide of the criticism of security capitalism came in the hearings held by the House Committee on Banking and Currency, popularly known as the Money Trust Investigation, headed by Arsene Pujo of Louisiana. The inquiry was authorized by a resolution of the House "to obtain full and complete information on the banking and currency conditions of the United States for the purpose of determining what regulation is needed." [180] The resolution called for an inquiry into the charges against the "management of the finances of many of the great industrial and railroad corporations of the country." The attack of the Pujo Committee was directed mainly against the combination movement which extended the control of banking security capitalists over industry and finance.[181] The chief investigator of this committee was Samuel Untermyer, and before him appeared J. P. Morgan, George Baker and other leading representatives of security capitalism. The pages of these hearings are replete with the clash of conflicting financial philosophy. The significance of this report has been underestimated in financial literature, for it constitutes one of the most important documents in American financial history.

The Committee attacked the system of affiliates by which the investment houses had extended their control over the commercial banks and in its report stated that :

The national banks in the great cities are exceeding their charter powers in the character of the business they are conducting and from which their principal revenues are derived. They are acting as promoters, underwriters, and houses of issue for the securities of railroad and industrial corporations.[182]

Formation of security affiliates was also attacked by Frederick W. Lehman, then solicitor general of the United States. His opinion rendered to the attorney general, held that the formation of the National City Company was in violation of the existing law. In the hearings of the Senate Committee on Banking and Currency in 1932 it was charged that this opinion was suppressed.[183]

DEFENSE OF SECURITY CAPITALISM

The financial press made desperate efforts to battle against this rising tide of popular disapproval. The public was assured that:

Wealth and production are good, and the law should do for them the best it can, namely, let them alone. Rich men are valuable in any community, and they are more and more disposed to treat their wealth as a public trust; it is short-sighted to discourage that. Property is a good thing; let everybody respect it and do his best to get it for himself.[184]

Regulatory legislation was condemned as "revolutionary" [185] and "socialistic," and the *Chronicle* added: "Every man's property is threatened; all securities are under a ban." [186] Prominent spokesmen made every effort to defend the institutions of security capitalism.[187] Otto Kahn, a leading member of Kuhn, Loeb and Company, stated that there were "very few financial houses of great wealth. All of the very greatest fortunes of the country, and in fact most of the great fortunes have been made, not in finance, but in trade, industries and inventions."[188] In another speech he described the New York Stock Exchange as "the most efficient and best conducted organization of its kind in the world." [189]

GOVERNMENTAL CONTROL OF DEMAND AND SUPPLY OF CAPITAL

Over this period there was a strong public demand for the extension of control by the state governments. Such control was exercised over the demand for capital, or the flow of security investment, by regulating new issues of corporations and governments, and also over the supply of capital and credit, or the direction of saving, by supervising the operations of the financial institutions. There was a determined move to regulate the financing of the railroads which were then the largest issuers of corporate securities. Certain states, as New York, sought to regulate the issuance of securities by public utilities corporations under their respective jurisdictions. For a number of years there had been agitation for such control in order to check the large volume of watered stock and fictitious securities which had brought heavy losses to investors.[190] Finally in 1905 the Gas Commission of New York State was given power to regulate the securities issued by gas and electric companies under its jurisdiction.[191] In 1906 New Jersey created a state public utility commission which was empowered to control the flotation of securities issued by public utilities within the state, and the scope of the original law was later extended by an act passed in 1910.[192] By 1917 every state, except Delaware, had such a commission. About one-half of the states conferred upon these commissions the power to regulate the issuance of public utility securities.[193]

There was an extension of state control also over the financial operations of local governments. A number of states either through their constitutions or their statutes placed restrictions on the debt-creating power of their municipalities. Most of these limitations imposed a maximum percentage of debt in relation to the assessed valuation of local property.[194]

The state and federal governments also extended their control over the direction of the supply of capital and credit of the financial institutions, as the life insurance companies, the trust companies and the commercial banks. The investment operations of the insurance companies were subjected to close scrutiny in the Armstrong insurance investigation of 1905.[195] The investigation disclosed certain practices which were technically against the law. For example, the New York Life Insurance Company in order to conduct its business in Prussia was required officially to state in its annual report that "the company does not invest in stocks of any kind." Nevertheless, the company invested in stocks by making a loan of $1,857,000 to a bond clerk and another loan of $1,150,000 to a messenger.[196] Again the New York State insurance law (section 35) provided that "a director who derived a profit by selling or aiding in the sale of any stocks or securities to or by such a corporation shall forfeit his position — and be disqualified from thereafter holding any such office in any insurance company." Notwithstanding this law, during the years that Mr. Jacob Schiff was a director of the Equitable Life Assurance Company, it purchased from Kuhn, Loeb and Company, of which Mr. Schiff was a member, securities to the value of over $47,-000,000.[197] Also the New York Life Insurance Company, on whose board of directors were members of the Morgan firm, subscribed to International Mercantile Marine bonds, which were floated by Morgan and Company.[198]

REGULATION OF BANK INVESTMENTS

In the northeastern states the mutual savings banks developed rapidly and became the leading institutions for receiving the saving of the mass of the population. For a time practically no restriction was placed on them. As a result of unsatisfactory experiences most of the northeastern states placed drastic restrictions on the investment of their savings banks.[199] During this period of severe restriction the state laws permitted the mutual savings banks to invest only in the bonds of the government of the United States, of the state in which a bank was located and of the municipalities within the state. These limitations, while assuring safety, at the same time restricted the scope of legal investment. The field was further narrowed by the policy of the federal government and of many of the eastern states in reducing their debts.[200] Thus there was need of widening the investment base and a number of states began to liberalize their laws on savings bank investments. In 1893 New York permitted its savings banks for the first time to invest in municipal securities outside the state but under careful restrictions.[201] During the panic of 1893 the savings banks of New York were forced to meet heavy withdrawals of deposits, and at the same time found it difficult to market their holdings of municipal bonds.[202] The Savings Banks Association of the State of New York urged the enlargement of the security list so as to permit the investment in railroad bonds which were considered more marketable. Subsequently New York permitted the investment of savings funds in the securities of railroads located within the state.[203]

Until the opening of the century, most states prohibited their savings banks from investing in street railway bonds.[204] However, in 1902 Masachusetts passed a law permitting its savings banks to invest in the first mortgage bonds of street railway companies.[205]

Over this period a number of states also extended their control over the investment operations of the commercial banks within their jurisdiction. Several states sought to check the policy of combining both commercial and investment operations within the same institutions.[206] New Hampshire adopted the principle of segregating savings deposits from the ordinary deposits of commercial banks. The law required that the savings deposits of trust companies should be segregated into a separate department and these funds were to be invested only in securities which were legal for mutual savings banks of the state. The Michigan Bank Act for a number of years had specified the securities which were eligible for the investment of savings deposits, and in 1899 the Act was further amended so that "all the investments relating to the savings department shall be kept separate from the other investments of the bank."[207] The principle of segregation and specified investment for savings deposits was adopted in Connecticut in 1907, in Massachusetts and Rhode Island in 1908 and in Texas and California in 1909. California adopted the principle of segregating banking operations by dividing institutions within its jurisdiction into commercial banks, savings banks and trust companies. A bank was permitted to perform all three functions but each class of business had to be kept separate and distinct.

ANTECEDENTS OF THE FEDERAL RESERVE SYSTEM

The federal government made no effort to regulate the investment operations of the national banks, but there was a determined move to reform the entire commercial banking system.[208] The defects in the commercial banking system became more and more apparent with each recurring financial panic and ensuing business depression, and so toward the end of the nineteenth century the demand for a revision of the banking system became insistent. The panic of 1893 particularly demonstrated the inelasticity of the national bank currency. The first step in the movement toward banking reform was taken in 1894 by the American Bankers Association at its convention in Baltimore. This meeting adopted the so-called "Baltimore Plan" which proposed the issue of a new currency protected by a joint guaranty fund to which all the issuing banks were to make a contribution. The plan, however, was not adopted.

Internal and external political events in the next few years drew public attention away from the pressing need for banking reform. At home there was a battle between the advocates of cheap money marshalled by William Jennings Bryan and the supporters of sound money led by William McKinley. This conflict attracted the public mind to the more spectacular issue of a currency standard rather than the technical but fundamentally more important matter of banking reform. It was further forgotten in the excitement over the war with Spain.

However, the movement for banking reform made progress with the work of the Indianapolis Currency Commission, which had been appointed at a convention of business organizations for the purpose of undertaking a broad and scientific study of the entire banking problem. The Commission made its report in 1898 and recommended not only the adoption of the gold standard but in addition made an important contribution to the movement for banking reform by proposing that bank notes should be secured by commercial paper rather than by bonds.

The next important step was the passage in 1900 of the Gold Standard Act which placed the United States on a monometallic basis. While this legislation itself did not directly effect any improvement in the banking structure, nevertheless, it was important in that, by settling the question of the monetary standard and by removing this issue from public attention, the passage of the Act cleared the way for the consideration of banking reform. Then came several years of inaction due to the general prosperity of the country.

However, the panic of 1907 which created a shortage of national bank currency, a scattering of reserves and consequent bank failures throughout the land, at last focused public attention upon the urgent need for reforming the banking system. The psychological time for action had at last arrived. In the following year, Congress passed the Aldrich-Vreeland Act which created an emergency currency in the form of bank notes to be secured by state and municipal bonds and even by commercial paper. The new currency was created solely as a temporary means of overcoming the shortage of circulating currency arising out of the panic of 1907. It was hoped that its use would give the nation time to analyze more carefully the entire banking problem with a view of solving it by carefully planned federal legislation.

For this reason the Aldrich-Vreeland Act also provided for the establishment of the National Monetary Commission composed of members of Congress. The Commission was to make a scientific study of currency and banking conditions not only at home but also abroad, and, based on these studies, was to recommend suitable legislation. The Commission under the chairmanship of Senator Aldrich conducted extensive investigations, had monographs compiled by financial experts, heard testimony of leading bankers and economists, and issued a forty-five volume report. This report gave a careful and painstaking analysis of the banking systems of almost every civilized nation of the world, and is today a classic in banking literature since it has retained for posterity a well-etched picture of the financial systems of Europe at a time when they had attained their highest development just before they were destined to be shaken by the Great War. While the report of the Commission has thus today an important historical interest, it had little practical value at the time in the movement for American banking reform, since few of its recommendations were followed by Congress.

The Commission gave its support to the Aldrich bill which was sponsored by Senator Aldrich and presented to Congress in 1911. This bill proposed a reorganization of the banking system along the lines of the best European models described in the report of the Commission. The plan, as presented in the bill, provided for a National Reserve Association with the main office in Washington and branches in the leading cities of the United States and so proposed what was practically a central banking system. The Aldrich plan was indorsed by many individual leaders in banking and business, but found little favor with the public which viewed central banking as un-American and remembered Senator Aldrich as the father of a none too popular tariff act. As a result the bill was never reported out of the congressional committee. The significance of the plan, however, is not to be underestimated. Modeled after the

German banking system the proposed central bank was to have control over all phases of the financial structure. Not only commercial banking, but also investment banking and stock market credit operations were to have been subject to central banking control. Thus the financial system would have been well integrated, and official leadership over financial resources firmly established.

Public opposition to banking centralization was further intensified in 1912 by the findings of the Pujo Committee. The same year saw the passing of national political power from the Republicans to the Democrats, and the new administration under President Wilson gave prompt and serious consideration to the subject of banking reform. Leadership in the movement was taken by the Banking and Currency Committee of the House of Representatives of which Carter Glass was the dominant figure. He was assisted by a committee of experts headed by Dr. H. Parker Willis which analyzed the mass of financial data already assembled. The committee finally drafted a measure which was amended and passed by Congress and became known as the Federal Reserve Act of 1913. In contrast to the Aldrich plan, the Federal Reserve System was empowered to control only the commercial banking system. The orthodox theory of banking was accepted and written into central banking practice. There was to be little or no control over investment banking and investment operations. Operations of the Federal Reserve banks were to be confined to the financing of short term loans, used largely, as was discovered later, by the consumer goods industries. There was a definite attempt to divide existing financial funds and resources equitably between investment and commercial banking. Later, the justice of this distribution was questioned, and a further allotment was made to the investment interests. Some attempt was made in the Reserve Act to prevent these interests from absorbing, as they had frequently in the past, the free financial resources of the community, but aside from this rather nebulous negative restriction, no attempt was made to regulate, supervise or control investment credit. The consequences of this failure to provide for central banking control of investment banking and investment operations was to become tragically apparent in the late twenties and early thirties.

REGULATION OF THE STOCK EXCHANGE

The stock exchange conducted its operations with little interference by the state or federal governments. In 1881 the legislature of the State of New York gave serious consideration to taxing security transactions.[209] This proposed legislation was bitterly opposed by the New York Stock Exchange, and the *Chronicle,* expressing financial sentiment, made the following threat:

We might proceed further and trace the practical effect of this raid on brokers, by showing how evidently its tendency would be to drive business from the State and drive brokers into the business of evading the tax. If a title to a stock cannot be perfected without a stamped transfer, it can be transferred in Boston, or perhaps it could be dated at Jersey City.[210]

Governor Hughes of New York State appointed a committee for the purpose of determining what recommendations "were advisable in the laws of the state bearing upon speculation in securities and commodities," and the following year the committee submitted an extensive report on the entire field of stock exchange regulation. The committee held extensive hearings and considered the subject not only from the standpoint of financial practice but also of public welfare. It conceded that a substantial part of the transactions on the stock exchange were virtually gambling, yet the report added that speculation "in some form is a necessary incident of productive operations," and "when carried on in connection with either commodities or securities, it tends to steady their prices." [211] It concluded that:

We are unable to see how the State could distinguish by law between proper and improper transactions, since the forms and mechanisms used are identical. Rigid statutes directed against the latter would seriously interfere with the former. The experience of Germany with similar legislation is illuminating. But the Exchange, with the plenary power over members and their operations, could provide correctives.[212]

Because of this favorable view of the New York Stock Exchange, the committee made practically no recommendations for legislative action. However, the Exchange itself took recognition of some of the irregular practices brought out in the committee hearings, and undertook a number of internal reforms such as the abolition of the unlisted department,[213] and the amendment of its constitution so as to give the law committee the power to scrutinize the dealings of any member and the order forbidding members to have relations with bucket shops.[214]

The federal government in general adopted a laissez faire attitude toward the stock exchanges. For revenue purposes during the Civil War brokers had to pay a license fee and also a tax on all sales of securities. This legislation, however, was discontinued after the close of the Civil War.[215] It was not until a half century later that the federal government gave serious consideration to regulating the security markets. The Pujo Committee made drastic recommendations for legislative control of the stock exchanges, such as their incorporation under state laws, complete reports of corporations applying for listing of their securities, and the requirements of margins of at least 20 percent. In 1914 most of these recommendations were incorporated in a bill introduced by Senator Robert Owens. The bill was opposed by a number of important witnesses, while Mr. Untermyer supported the bill particularly the proposal to incorporate the stock exchange.[216] The bill failed to pass, but Mr. Untermeyer continued his campaign for several years for the regulation of the stock exchange. In vain Untermyer pleaded that :

The time will come, and before long, after regulation has been enforced, when those who are now bitterly assailing the champions of this legislation in the vain hope of thereby diverting the issue will find that it has marked the dawn of a new era of usefulness and prosperity for them, and that the Exchange will feel grateful to those who have pointed the way.[217]

However the coming of the War turned the attention of the nation from financial reform. With the return of prosperity, due to orders from abroad, energies were concentrated upon earning higher profits or receiving higher wages.

CONCLUSION

With the close of the Civil War, the nation was ready to enter the stage of economic maturity. Its vast natural resources were open to development. Its manufactures expanded and the search for world markets began. The railway system became a spidery network encompassing the entire nation, knitting together distant regions and opening the whole domestic market. The railroads were among the first enterprises financed by the system of security capitalism. In the beginning the roads fell into the hands of speculative capitalists who were concerned only in the attainment of quick profit from the market manipulation of the securities of these enterprises. The first efforts of banking capitalism to finance the railroads ended in the failure of Jay Cooke. Once more the speculative capitalist was free to continue his exploitations with disastrous results in ruinous competition among the roads, their physical deterioration and serious financial consequences as overcapitalization, defaults on bonds issues, and eventual receivership. The railway system of the nation suffered from the worst sort of financial feudalism. Out of this chaos the house of Morgan brought some degree of order ; and the security capitalists were routed, and the financial rehabilitation of the railroads was attained.

American industry turned to large scale production and consequently required an enormous amount of credit and capital. In some fields, as petroleum and steel, these financial resources were furnished by powerful industrial capitalists who in turn financed themselves by the mechanism of security capitalism. However, the demand for credit and capital was largely met in most fields by the banker capitalist who gave to these enterprises not only his own funds but also the mobilized resources of the investing public. In the case of both the railroads and some of the industries, the house of Morgan replaced competition with monopoly, and instability with stability. For this purpose the house extended its influence over the various institutions of indirect investment as the life insurance companies and the credit institutions, including national banks, state banks and trust companies. The Pax Morgana was extended over both the forces of the demand and the supply of capital. This expanding power of banking capitalism encountered opposition from leading industrial capitalists. Some were overcome ; others, if not conquered, had to recognize the imperial edicts. However, on the fringe of the Empire remained the unconquered Parthians of industrial security capitalism, the Rockefellers.

By the opening of the twentieth century the extensive development of the United States was passing. The very rapidity of the development brought with it new economic and financial difficulties which impeded progress. The panics of 1903 and 1907 were manifestations of these maladjustments.

CHAPTER 12

AMERICAN SECURITY CAPITALISM AND THE WORLD WAR

AFTER the financial disturbances of 1907 the United States experienced a period of unsatisfactory business activity.[1] Steel production made little advance and industrial production moved uncertainly, while only the new industries as automobile manufacture moved forward.[2] The formal statement of Morgan and Company, made in 1936 to the Senate Committee, summarized conditions immediately before the outbreak of war in the comment that : "Business throughout the country was depressed, farm prices were deflated, unemployment was serious, the heavy industries were working far below capacity, bank clearings were off."[3]

Within a few months after the outbreak of the Great War in 1914, these conditions were entirely changed. The prices received by the farmers for their agricultural products rose sharply as reflected by the increase of the index of farm purchasing power, industrial production expanded sharply and in consequence wages increased.[4] This prosperity was built essentially on the sharp rise in American exports which became more and more confined to the Allied countries.[5] The War thus lifted the United States from a condition of depression to that of prosperity. Only a small part of the American people questioned the fact that this prosperity was based on the destruction of human life and of property and the great mass rejoiced only that the depression was over. This war trade was financed at first by the shipment of gold from London to New York and by the sale of American securities held abroad and their repatriation to the United States. In time these means were exhausted and the trade ultimately had to be financed by the resources of American security capitalism mobilized by American bankers. Before the War American banks had developed financial relations with the banking systems of England and of France as well as Germany, but the ties with the Allied countries were much closer.[6] The members of the Morgan firm, due to their close contracts with the British banking system for almost a century, were naturally strong supporters of the Allied cause. Henry P. Davidson, a member of Morgans declared : "Some of us in America realized that this was our war from the very start."[7] As European nations declared war against each other and mobilized their forces, the

Rothschilds of Paris suggested to Morgan, Harjes, the Paris office of Morgans, that a hundred million dollar loan be issued in New York to pay for purchases by the French government in the United States.[8] Morgan, Harjes immediately cabled this request to Morgan and Company of New York which, however, replied that:

conditions here make transactions suggested quite impossible for present. United States Government strongly disinclined send more gold abroad. We are using every effort assist in this and therefore could not properly undertake transaction indicated. Believe, however, after little while might be very possible.[9]

On August eighth the Paris office of Morgans again pressed the New York office for the establishment of a French credit, and added: "fear that if we do not forestall others, it is probable that such houses as Kuhn, Loeb and Company may try to do something for other nation." [10] The New York office thereupon took up the matter with the State Department, and asked whether there would be any objection to their making a loan to the French Government.

UNCONDITIONAL FINANCIAL NEUTRALITY

Bryan, then Secretary of State, referred the request to Robert Lansing, at that time counsellor to the Department, who replied that he knew of no legal objection to the loan.[11] Bryan, not satisfied with this legalistic opinion, presented the matter to President Wilson and urged that the United States Government "take the position that it will not approve of any loan to a belligerent nation." [12] In support of this proposal, Bryan argued that: "money is the worst of all contrabands because it commands everything else" and added that "I know of nothing that would do more to prevent war than an international agreement that neutral nations would not loan to belligerents."

He then applied this general thesis to the immediate position of the United States in the reasoning that "we are the one great nation which is not involved and our refusal to loan to any belligerent would naturally tend to hasten a conclusion of the war." A further reason advanced by Bryan for his proposal that the government disapprove foreign loans was the prophetic statement that "the powerful financial interests which would be connected with these loans would be tempted to use their influence through the newspapers to support the interests of the government to which they had loaned because the value of the security would be directly affected by the result of the war."

President Wilson apparently accepted Bryan's proposal for a ban on all loans, for on August 15th Bryan replied to Morgans that "there is no reason why loans should not be made to the Governments of neutral nations, but in the judgment of this Government loans by American bankers to any foreign nation which is at war are inconsistent with the true spirit of neutrality." [13]   Lansing at the time, was apparently in full agreement with this position for Bryan, in the postscript of his letter to the President, added that : "Mr. Lansing calls attention to the fact that an American citizen who goes abroad and voluntarily enlists in the army of a belligerent nation loses the protection of his citizenship while so engaged, and asks why dollars, going abroad and enlisting in war, should be more protected." [14]   In its statement of August 15, 1914, the United States Government therefore banned all forms of loans by American bankers to belligerent nations and took the position of unconditional financial neutrality.   Thus in the first tilt over financial neutrality Bryan was victorious against his arch-enemy, Morgan and Company.[15]

CONDITIONAL FINANCIAL NEUTRALITY

In October, 1914, came the first retreat of the American Government from its original stand on financial neutrality.   The need of obtaining the means to finance the flow of munitions and of raw materials from this country to the belligerents was pressing.   The urgency of the matter was presented in a letter to Lansing from the National City Bank pointing out that manufacturers, who were customers of the Bank, and in "some cases representatives of the foreign governments," were requesting the Bank "to provide temporary credits for these purchases."   The letter stated that it was "the desire of the National City Bank to be absolutely in accord with the policies of our own Government," but added "the Bank is disposed to grant short time banking credits to European governments, both belligerent and neutral."   The letter concluded with the statement that "this business was deemed necessary to the general good" and that the Bank would "proceed along the lines indicated unless it is objectionable from the Government standpoint." [16]

On October 23, 1914, Lansing, apparently ignoring his superior, since there is no mention that Bryan was consulted, took up the matter of "loans and bank credits to belligerent governments" directly with President Wilson.[17]   According to Lansing, President Wilson now held that :

There is a decided difference between an issue of Government bonds, which are sold in open market to investors, and an arrangement for easy exchange in meeting debts incurred in trade between a government and American merchants.

The sale of bonds draws gold from the American people.   The purchasers of bonds are loaning their savings to the belligerent government, and are, in fact, financing the war. . .

The acceptance of Treasury notes or other evidences of debt in payment for articles purchased in this country is merely a means of facilitating trade by a system of credits which will avoid the clumsy and impractical method of cash payments. As trade with belligerents is legitimate and proper it is desirable that obstacles, such as interference with an arrangement of credits or easy method of exchange, should be removed.[18]

The original position of the government of unconditional financial neutrality which placed a ban on all loans was now qualified by drawing a distinction between a so-called publicly offered bond and privately-granted bank credit. While the former was still proscribed, the latter was now permitted. Thus Bryan's position of unconditional financial neutrality of August 15, 1914 was superseded by Lansing's stand for conditional financial neutrality of October 23, 1914.

MISAPPLICATION OF THE BANKERS' ACCEPTANCE

The fallacy in the fine distinction between a loan and a credit as drawn by President Wilson becomes clear from the review of the actual transactions which were undertaken by the American banks as a result of the new position of the government. With the virtual approval of the national government, the large New York banks extended liberal credits to the Allied governments.[19] Within a few months these credits became so large that it was no longer possible for the New York national and state banks to continue them for both legal and practical reasons. National and also most state banks were limited by law as to the maximum amount of credit which they could extend to any one borrower. Besides, it was becoming unwise financially for the New York banks to extend so large a proportion of their funds to one interest.

In order to relieve this situation, a move was made to spread the financial burden from the New York institutions to the entire banking system of the nation. The vehicle for such a transfer was the bankers' acceptance or time draft drawn on a banking institution and accepted by it. This instrument had been introduced into the United States with the formation of the Federal Reserve system, and students of finance had hoped thereby to improve the quality of American commercial paper. The Federal Reserve Act had established careful regulations as to the characteristics of the bankers' acceptance with respect to its purpose, security and maturity. The acceptance under the provisions of the Reserve Act was to be created only for a strictly productive purpose, as financing the sale of readily marketable staples from seller to buyer, or aiding a manufacturer who would work up the raw materials into finished goods of higher value. The acceptance was to be secured at all times by the underlying goods. Furthermore, the acceptance was to be limited to a period of not more than three months and was not to be renewed. The bankers' acceptance was therefore to serve a commercial purpose, be fully secured and limited as to its maturity.

The practical application of this instrument in the war period proved to be one of the worst perversions of a sound mechanism to an unsound use in all the history of finance,[20] for the bankers' acceptance was utilized in such a way that each sound characteristic mentioned above was grossly violated. The instrument in actual practice was employed for the commercial purpose of financing the export of munitions and supplies to belligerent nations. The security underlying the instrument was a shell, torpedo, tank or other supply either subsequently sent to the bottom of the ocean or more productively liquidated on the war front. The acceptance nominally had a maturity of three months, but actually it was now allowed to run for several periods of three months, since each member of the banking group would generally take up the acceptance of another bank at maturity. Furthermore the acceptance became an investment instrument which was distributed through syndicates among banks seeking to invest their surplus funds and no longer bore any resemblance to a commercial credit. The bankers' acceptance in fact became a bond, and partook of the characteristics of the proscribed bond as defined in the very words of President Wilson's statement of October 23, 1914, since the acceptance was "sold in the open market to investors," while the banks purchasing such acceptances were "loaning their savings to the belligerent government" and so were "in fact, financing the war." [21]

ABANDONMENT OF FINANCIAL NEUTRALITY

For almost a year the government followed the policy of conditional financial neutrality by maintaining this official distinction between a credit and a loan. However, in the summer of 1915 the government completely abandoned financial neutrality. By this time the financial position of the Allied countries experienced definite signs of strain. Sterling exchange dropped sharply during the latter part of August and this decline, by requiring more British pounds to purchase American dollars, threatened to reduce the volume of American goods that could be purchased by the Allies.[22] Under these conditions it now became necessary to mobilize additional financial resources through the public sale of the bonds of the Allied governments issued directly to American investors. However, such a direct public offering of bonds had been banned by the American government in its statement of October 23, 1914.

The leading members of the cabinet as McAdoo, Secretary of the Treasury and Lansing, who by this time had replaced Bryan as Secretary of State, now urged President Wilson to change this policy.[23] Lansing in a letter to President Wilson reviewed the economic position of the United States since the outbreak of the War and added that:

> If the European countries cannot find means to pay for the excess of goods sold to them over those purchased from them they will have to stop buying and our present export trade will shrink proportionately. The result would be restriction of outputs, industrial depression, idle capital and idle labor, numerous failures, financial demoralization and general unrest and suffering among the laboring classes.

Both he and Secretary McAdoo were convinced that "there is only one means of avoiding this situation which would so seriously affect the economic conditions in this country, and that is the flotation of large bond issues by the belligerent governments."[24] President Wilson thus pressed by his closest advisers agreed to this proposal, for in his reply he wrote: "I have no doubt that our oral discussion of this matter yesterday suffices. If it does not, will you let me know that you would like a written reply."[25] Thus the government first committed itself to a policy of financial neutrality by banning all financial assistance to the belligerents, later conditioned this stand by distinguishing between credits and loans, and then completely abandoned its original position of financial neutrality by permitting the public offering of the bond issues of the Allied governments.

ALLIED BOND FLOTATIONS

For several months before this change in the policy of the American Government toward publicly-offered bonds, Morgan and Company had been preparing for such an event and had sounded out the probable attitude of the investing public. However, such inquiries "about the street, especially among the bond houses, had not shown any great enthusiasm."[26] The First National Bank of Chicago notified Thomas Lamont that "the middle West would take little, if any of such loan."[27] Lee Higginson and Company informed Morgans that "after a campaign of education the bonds could be sold but without such a campaign they would be unwilling to make firm commitment to any amount whatever."[28] Nevertheless the opinion of Lee Higginson was that the loans should be made, even though it would take a little time, "owing to the importance of filling in the lacks of education, in the central and western part of this country." Discussion of the loans continued, and an Anglo-French financial mission headed by Lord Reading came to New York to complete the arrangements. The American government itself took a part in these negotiations for McAdoo requested Lansing's aid in making the work of the mission a success.[29] After negotiating with the mission, Morgans floated the Anglo-French loan of 1915 which was an issue of $500,000,000 at 5 percent interest with a maturity of 5 years. The issue was purchased by the buying syndicate at a price of 96 and was sold to the public at 98.

Then came the task of placing the issue with the investing public. For this purpose Morgans formed a syndicate consisting of 1,570 members, the largest in American financial history until that time.[30] Of the total amount $98,000,000 or about one-fifth was placed among individual manufacturers and industrial corporations which were selling war supplies.[31] The greater part of the issue, however, was placed with the investing public.[32] The issue met with strong opposition from the German and Irish elements in the population particularly in the Middle West.[33] Partly because of this opposition and partly because of the lack of organization of the American security market at that time, the issue proved one of the most difficult that the house of Morgan ever attempted to place.

In the following months a United Kingdom loan amounting to $300,000,000 was offered and was well received, for by this time in the words of Lee Higginson "the lacks of education" of the public had been filled. Other Allied loans followed in quick succession.[34] Even the Imperial Russian Government was able to float a bond issue in 1916 with a prospectus which stated that: "These bonds are the direct general credit obligation of the Imperial Russian Government whose faith and credit are pledged to the prompt payment of principal and interest when due."[35] By December 1, 1916, the total loans to belligerents reached $1,794,000,000.[36]

ATTEMPTED RETURN TO FINANCIAL NEUTRALITY

In the closing months of 1916, the administration made a belated effort to return to its original position of unconditional financial neutrality by checking the granting of financial aid to both belligerents. Kuhn, Loeb was planning the flotation of a public bond issue for Germany, but on November 24, 1916 President Wilson personally advised against the issue. At the same time the administration took action against the granting of further assistance to the Allies.[37] In November Lloyd George informed Morgans that the British government needed $300,000,000 a month for the next five months and that if this credit were not available for the Allies they would be forced to suspend their purchases in America. To meet this demand the American banking houses decided to place issues of short-term treasury bills, and on November 24, 1916 Morgans made a public announcement "that the British and French Government Treasuries had each authorized the sale in this market of a limited amount of their short-term bills running at various maturities from thirty days to six months." These short-term treasury bills were to be drawn in dollars and at maturity were to be met by the issue of new bills. It was planned to place these bills among the banks throughout the country. They however, would absorb the bills only if rediscountable at the Federal Reserve banks.[38] However, on November 29th, the Federal Reserve Board issued a public statement squarely opposing such purchases, declaring "the board deems it therefore its duty to caution the member banks that it does not regard it in the interest of the country at this time that they invest in foreign treasury bills of this character." [39] This statement was a serious blow to the whole structure of Allied financing in the American market. It was not only an official notice that the Federal Reserve system would not rediscount the treasury bills but was really a public pronouncement barring the Allies from American financial resources including both private bank acceptance credits and public bond issues, since in the face of a hostile Reserve Board the interior banks would not be likely to absorb further issues of either credits or bonds.[40]

This position of the Federal Reserve Board was probably part of President Wilson's effort to force peace upon the belligerents, for in the next month he issued his famous peace message.[41] This statement resulted in the most violent slump in the New York Stock Exchange since 1907.[42] The index of stock prices in December fell from 99.26 to 83.88, and Bethelehem Steel a favorite war stock dropped 72 points in one day.[43] If the government had returned to its original position of unconditional financial neutrality and had prohibited all forms of American aid to finance the export trade, this policy would have brought about a major economic recession in the United States. At the same time had the United States returned and adhered to this policy, it is quite probable that the War would have come to an end in 1917. Andre Tardieu, later French High Commissioner in the United States, observed that if the Federal Reserve Board had maintained its position toward the British treasury bills "the defeat of the Allies would have been merely a question of months, as they could neither have supplied their armies nor fed their peoples." [44] The weakening of the credit of the Allied governments was reflected in the change in the financial market from 1915 to 1916. While the 1915 loans were unsecured and bore an interest rate of 5 percent, the 1916 issues were secured by collateral and bore a rate of 5½ percent.[45] Unquestionably the fiscal position of the Allies, embarrassed in 1914, strained in 1915, was serious by the end of 1916.

ENTRANCE INTO WAR

During the early months of 1917 the United States took the fateful steps which lead to the abandonment of political neutrality. On March 5, 1917 Ambassador Page who, as well stated, "was less interested in his own country than in the success of what he supposed to be a crusade for civilization," warned the Department of "international conditions most alarming to the American financial and industrial outlook." [46] He added that unless the United States granted financial assistance "there may be a world wide panic for an indefinite period," and expressed the opinion that "the pressure of this approaching crisis has gone beyond the financial ability of the Morgan financial agency for the British and French governments. The need is becoming too great and urgent for any private agency to meet." He therefore urged "that our going to war is the only way in which our present preeminent trade position can be maintained and a panic averted" and urged this policy on the ground that we should "thus reap the profit of an uninterrupted, perhaps an enlarging trade over a number of years." [47]

This letter of Page stated exactly the position in which the United States found itself at the opening of 1917. Since August, 1914, the United States had been experiencing a prosperity based essentially on exports to the Allied governments. These exports had been made possible largely by private bank loans and public bond issues based on the credit of the Allied governments. The credit of the Allied nations as judged by their ability to command purchasing power in the United States was practically exhausted, for both American banks and American investors were unwilling to grant further financial assistance to the extent necessary for the continuance of vast purchases in this market. Such continued purchases by the Allies and the resulting prosperity for the American people could have been sustained only by the employment of the credit of the United States Government itself through the sale of its own obligations to American banks and investors. The use of such credit was possible only if the United States cast aside its position as a political neutral and itself became a belligerent on the side of the Allies. This was the economic factor which brought about the entrance of the United States into the War.[48] No clearer recognition of the economic cause of our entrance into the War can be found than in the triumphant paens of the New York financial press at that fateful moment, when President Wilson was about to call the nation to war. The New York *Sun* declared: "leading bankers expect that the entrance of the United States into the War will result in a material increase in orders placed here for shells and other munitions. . . Munition companies which have been closing their plants and discharging employees by the thousands are expected to resume operations on a large scale." The *Wall Street Journal* added that "the coming loan of the United States government has put new life into the War order companies." [49]

CONCLUSION

The preceding review seems to indicate that entrance of the United States in the War was not the result of financial machinations of a small group of bankers, but came about because the great mass of American people had acquired an important economic interest in the success of the Allied cause. Their desire for the continuation of prosperity arising from the sale of their goods abroad made it difficult for the administration to take those steps which though insuring neutrality would have brought on depression. Once the exports to the Allied nations assumed a large volume, they had to be financed by the United States, and to maintain financial neutrality, as was attempted in the Bryan declaration of August, 1914, was politically and economically impossible. The economic pressure for the maintenance of the purchasing power of our foreign market therefore nullified every effort to maintain financial neutrality.[50] This pressure drove the administration to recede step by step from its original policy of unconditional financial neutrality, from the futile distinction between a credit and a loan, which permitted the banking system ultimately to extend financial assistance by means of bankers' acceptances which were practically loans, and in time forced the abandonment of the distinction entirely by sanctioning the public issuing of the bonds of the Allied governments directly to the American public. Finally when the credit of the Allied nations was no longer sufficient to continue their purchases in the American market, the United States entered the war as an actual belligerent and so made possible the utilization of its credit to finance a continuation of the war prosperity. It is doubtful whether the American people, who as a whole in 1916 and 1917 favored the continuation of political neutrality, would have supported the maintenance of American financial neutrality in view of the economic sacrifices which such a policy would have involved. However, in the end the abandonment of financial neutrality, dictated by economic considerations, made impossible the maintenance of political neutrality.

The lesson to be learned from the study of these events is therefore clear. In any major international conflict in the future it will be again impossible for the United States to maintain political neutrality, for the inexorable sweep of events will successively break down economic, financial and later political neutrality. All efforts to stem the tide of these events *after* the outbreak of a World War by such policies as mere financial neutrality are bound to be futile. It is therefore necessary for the United States to realize that positive measures must be taken *in advance* to prevent this country from once more being drawn into the next conflict. President Wilson was only too right in his statement made in the fall of 1916 that "this is the last War of this kind or of any kind that involves the world that the United States can keep out of." [51]

CHAPTER 13

CRISIS OF AMERICAN SECURITY CAPITALISM

IN THE years immediately following the World War political conservatism dominated the mind of the American people and the period of political crusading for the time was over. The Socialist party, shaken by the War, showed little strength in the post-war period, for Eugene Debs and later Norman Thomas obtained small popular votes. The Communist Party, led by William Z. Foster, likewise received little popular support. Thus over the period the parties of protest were completely ineffectual.[1]

The period was one of general self-satisfaction, and social unrest was largely local in nature. The Sacco-Vanzetti case aroused curiosity among the American public which, however, remained somewhat apathetic and was quite mystified at the commotion which the case of the two condemned men aroused in foreign countries. The troubles in the textile mills of Gastonia, North Carolina, and in the coal mines of Harlan County, Kentucky, resulted in no popular action. Organized labor made little progress in this period. The American public over these years were thus not class conscious.

TRIUMPH OF LAISSEZ FAIRE

In the post-war period laissez faire dominated the minds of the American people from Main Street to Pennsylvania Avenue. He who dared propose that the government extend its control over security capitalism was a prophet crying futilely in the wilderness. Professor William Z. Ripley pointed out that corporate statements were inadequate, and maintained that the Federal Trade Commission had power to require the filing of more satisfactory reports.[2] However, the "spokesman" of President Coolidge promptly put the Professor in his place by stating that:

> Mr. Coolidge is not convinced that the Federal Trade Commission has the power to control reports of corporations doing inter-State commerce, even though they have control of the products in inter-State commerce.
>
> In the opinion of the President it is difficult to determine what is a good or a bad stock. Publicity as to the financial strength of corporations, he thinks, has usually been left to the jurisdiction of the States, many of which have blue-sky laws which assure the public adequate information.[3]

The chief counsel of the Federal Trade Commission considered Professor Ripley's proposal "too sweeping." This position was supported by state officials, and the special deputy attorney general of New York declared that the application of the state blue-sky law was "the best argument in favor of President Coolidge's contention that State laws best protect the American investor in securities and against bond and stock swindles and a timely answer to Professor Ripley." [4] However some of the states, as California, even weakened their laws regulating new corporate securities on the ground that :

it does not prevent fraud as intended, that there is no provision for the extension of its scope or jurisdiction to regulate corporations issuing securities or to the development of a prosecutions department of research and public relations, that it is actually burdensome and harmful to organizations coming under its scope and has actually driven financial and corporate business in huge amounts from the state and that it has created unnecessary barriers to new business and modern financial operations.[5]

ECONOMIC BACKGROUND—MALADJUSTMENT OF AMERICAN AGRICULTURE

By the beginning of the twentieth century the last western frontier had been conquered. In the post-war period American agriculture suffered the cumulative blows of a war-shaken world economic system. The historic cause of the troubles of the American farmer may be found in the unwise expansion in the nineteenth century. The federal government had acquired public lands amounting to millions of acres which were sold too rapidly and without classification, and this unsound policy placed too many acres in cultivation. The adverse effects of those events bore down upon the American farmer with all the heavier weight in the post-war period when as an aftermath of artificial agricultural expansion other unfavorable factors began to extend their baneful influences.

There was a growing discrepancy between the prices of agricultural and of manufactured products. Both tended to fall, but the drop of the former was more rapid than that of the latter. Because of this greater decline in the prices received by the farmer as compared with the prices paid by the farmer, his purchasing power declined.[6] Even before the depression the woes of the farmer were further accentuated by the contraction in the domestic and foreign markets for agricultural products. The change in traction power from the horse to the automobile substituted a demand for gasoline instead of oats and grain, and changes in the food styles of American people reduced the demand for meat and for wheat. Far more serious was the decline in the foreign demand for American farm products. During the War the American farmer had produced for Europe as well as the United States. With the close of the War and the rehabilitation of European agriculture, the foreign demand fell off sharply, but this drop was not followed by a curtailment of American production. In addition the depreciation in the value of foreign currencies and the consequent appreciation in the value of the dollar required the payment of more dollars for American foodstuffs and led to a decline in the demand for them.

DECLINE IN THE RATE OF INDUSTRIAL EXPANSION

The industrial production of the United States remained high in the post-war period. The relative importance of the leading industries underwent considerable change, for the motor-vehicle industry gained on the iron and steel industries, and the petroleum industry expanded. Automobile production was one of the mainstays of the prosperity of the post-war period and the output rose sharply. The steel industry likewise increased its production enormously over these years, and petroleum production expanded without interruption, while exports, particularly of manufactured goods, rose sharply. In order to overcome the housing shortage resulting from the cessation of building activity during the war years, there was a sharp recovery in building construction.[7]

Notwithstanding the industrial expansion over the post-war years the rate of growth showed evidence of decline when compared with previous periods in the industrial history of the nation. The Standard Statistics index of the secular trend of general industrial production showed a general declining rate of growth.[8] Cotton consumption which had expanded at the rate of 4 percent yearly from 1885 to 1900 showed a yearly expansion of only 2 percent from 1915 to 1925.[9] Coal production, which had grown at a rate of 5 percent from 1900 to 1910 and 4 percent from 1910 to 1920, showed practically no growth after 1920. The annual rate of growth of pig iron, which was 6 percent until 1900, thereafter fell to 3 percent. The automobile industry which expanded at the rate of 35 percent from 1905 to 1910, and 18 percent from 1915 to 1920, showed the reduced rate of 8 percent for the decade ending 1930.[10] Railroad freight traffic, increased at an annual rate of 7 percent from 1890 to 1910, 6 percent from 1910 to 1920 but only one percent in the following years.[11] In general the leading manufactures grew at the decennial rate of about 6½ percent yearly until 1890, at the rate of 5 percent until 1920 and at 4½ percent until 1930.[12] Clearly American security capitalism in the post-war period was experiencing the same declining rate of industrial expansion as occurred in England in the fourth quarter of the nineteenth century.

DECLINING RATE OF POPULATION GROWTH

The growth in the population of the United States has been one of the most significant social movements in world history. From 1840 until 1920 the general rate of growth of the population was about 2.3 percent annually, but from 1920 to 1930 the rate of growth was only 1.5 percent.[13] This change in the rate of population growth was a social factor of real economic significance. The continuous development of railroads, the expansion of the electric light and power companies and the output of manufacturing concerns in the past had consciously or unconsciously been based on the assumption of an ever-increasing rate of population. This premise could no longer be accepted for the future. Overequipment and overproduction were problems which now had to be anticipated. Also real estate valuation had to be adjusted to the theory that the ever-increasing rate of population would not continue.[14]

The drift of population in the past had been toward the cities. Immigration had further contributed to the increased population of American cities but it was now checked by restrictive legislation. The drift of population was partly halted by certain economic forces. Inter-connected electric systems were able to carry power long distances, and small localities could obtain power at rates which were almost as low as those charged in large cities. The disappearance of this differential advantage and the increasing costs of production in large cities [15] tended to check the rate of urban growth.

UNSATISFACTORY LABOR CONDITIONS

The trend in the position of labor, when analyzed by itself, improved in the post-war period. The index of employment and of payrolls rose, and wages paid by the manufacturing industries increased moderately.[16] However, this improvement was not as rapid as the increase in production as may be seen in Table 19 showing the increase in the indices of industrial production as compared with those of labor from 1921 to 1929.

From these figures it may be seen that, with the exception of only two, the indices of production rose much faster than the indices of labor. Unemployment, until the close of the nineteenth century, was not a pressing problem. After the Civil War the United States had experienced intermittent waves of unemployment caused by cyclical movements beginning particularly in 1873 and in 1893. Added to such periodic cyclical unemployment, with the twentieth century there came continual technological unemployment brought

TABLE 19

LABOR AND PRODUCTION, 1929.

(percent 1921 = 100)

INDICES OF LABOR	Sources [a]	PERCENT IN 1929
Employment..............................	13	127.3
Payrolls..................................	14	143.2
Wages paid by all manufacturing industries...	15	141.8
INDICES OF PRODUCTION		
Industrial production......................	4	188.7
Automobile production......................	5	334.3
Steel ingot production......................	6	284.8
Coal production...........................	7	127.8
Petroleum production.......................	8	213.4
Building contracts awarded.................	9	169.4
Building expenditures.......................	10	102.6

[a] Numbers refer to columns in Appendix VI.

about by the introduction of labor-saving machinery, the extension of scientific management, the growth of mergers and the changing whims of consumers' demands.[17] For a time, workers discharged as a result of these forces found employment in the new industries as the automobile, radio, aviation and motion picture fields and in service employment as gasoline workers. However, unemployment in the depression of 1921 rose to 5,500,000 and in May 1929 at the height of industrial activity, it was estimated that 2,000,000 persons were out of work.[18] Meagre savings were insufficient to meet the emergency of unemployment in the case of many families, for a large proportion of the workers did not receive sufficient income in good years to build up adequate surpluses for the bad years. To make up this deficiency, recourse was had to private charity, but this method of relief proved inadequate.

The volume of consumption expanded rapidly from the close of the nineteenth century and for the first two decades of the twentieth century, and in consequence the standard of living of the American people in general rose sharply. In the third decade consumption was held up by various artificial supports. Installment selling gave a temporary fill-up to domestic purchasing power. Paper profits from the rising stock market created a false sense of prosperity, and since the public felt rich it spent more freely. Over-liberal foreign loans tended to support the foreign consumption of American goods and sustained exports over these years, but these foreign sales crumbled when the export of American capital ceased.

VOICES OF CRITICISM AND OF OPTIMISM

Here and there a few farseeing individuals at the time noted these unsatisfactory trends. In 1927 Melvin A. Traylor, Chairman of the First National Bank of Chicago and an able leader of banking capitalism said:

> Every kind and character of combination and consolidation was made, regardless of economic advisability or the possibility of economics in management or increased profits therefrom. Little or no consideration was given to the nature of the business involved: in one instance, for example, soaps and candles were united. Such combinations and mergers were promoted and securities were sold on the theory that temporary earnings derived from a false demand would not only continue, but would forever increase. . . Was such financial leadership calculated to inspire confidence or make for an economic stability which insures social welfare?
>
> I believe that without the proper education and direction of human conduct, economic depressions will inevitably continue to recur with ever-increasing social and political disaster.[19]

However, the general chorus struck a note of continuous optimism. Otto Kahn maintained that there was "widely diffused prosperity, percolating through all sections of the country, benefiting the people, adding to the contents not merely of their pocketbooks, but of their lives."[20] E. H. H. Simmons, President of the Stock Exchange stoutly declared "I cannot help but raise a dissenting voice to statements that we are simply living in a fool's paradise, and that prosperity in this country must necessarily diminish and recede in the future."[21]

PANIC OF SECURITY CAPITALISM

September, 1929, marked the high tide of the stock market and the closing months of the year witnessed successive collapses of security prices. The methods of 1907 were applied on an even grander scale and banking support, which had in the past checked security price declines, was once more mobilized. October 24, 1929 was one of the landmarks in the history of security capitalism. So-called "air pockets" developed in the market, and there was no bid for some of the most active stocks. The heads of the leading New York banks met in the office of Morgan Company and formed a banking pool with reserves in excess of $240,000,000.[22] This organized financial power was, however, unable to check the decline in security prices, and accomplished nothing more than a rear guard action which covered the none-too-orderly retreat of American security capitalism. About $100,000,000 of securities were purchased, and for a time were placed in the portfolios of the security affiliates. By February, 1930, the banking pool was dissolved and all the security holdings were liquidated without loss to the banking group.[23]

The latter part of 1930 dragged along wearily with complete lack of profit for agriculture, manufacture and transportation throughout the world. This discouraging economic situation laid the basis for the banking troubles serious even before 1929. By the end of the year New York City experienced a serious disturbance when the Bank of United States failed. Only half-hearted efforts were made to save this institution, and today, with the benefit of aftersight, it is clear that the full salvaging of this institution by other New York banks should have been the course pursued if only in self interest. The year 1931 was marked by widespread banking embarrassment abroad. In May the Austrian Creditanstalt closed its doors. This failure was practically unnoticed by Wall Street, too deeply engrossed in reading the ticker recording the security price changes of the moment. By July, the German banks were tottering; the British financial interests made desperate efforts to check the collapse of the German financial system only to become involved themselves; by September the Bank of England would no longer pay out gold for its notes, and by December the United States was shaken by numerous bank failures throughout the country. In the summer of 1932 the United States experienced an incipient industrial revival which, however, was checked by the uncertain political trend of the early fall and now the very props under American security capitalism began to give way.

Agriculture, industry, trade and labor were all suffering grievously. From 1929 to 1932 the index of farm purchasing power fell from 95 to 61. Industrial production declined from 108 to 54; automobile production from 5,622,000 cars to 1,431,000 cars; steel production from 56,400,000 gross tons to 13,700,000 gross tons; the output of petroleum from 1,007,500,000 barrels to 785,200,000 barrels; the index of building contracts from 89 percent to 17 and exports from $5,241,000,000 to $1,611,000,000. In consequence employment fell from 104 to 64 percent in 1932; payrolls from 109 to 46.1 percent and wages in the manufacturing industries were cut from $11,620,000,000 to $4,925,000,000.[24] Agriculture was weakened by thousands of foreclosures, industry discouraged and consuming power slashed by millions of unemployed, the banking system impaired by the failure of thousands of institutions, commerce decimated by the collapse of exports, the capital market at a standstill, over two thousand municipalities in bankruptcy, a large number of the railroads in receivership and commodity prices, national income and national wealth were sharply reduced.

The cumulative effect of these combined blows brought American security capitalism to the brink of collapse by March, 1933. The investor lost faith in his security investments and in the entire system of security capitalism, and in open revolt withdrew his funds from the banks and from the security markets. The darkest hour in the history of security capitalism had struck. American security capitalism, the bulwark of world security capitalism, was in panic. A few more days and the entire machinery of commercial banking would have been unable to meet the demand for the withdrawal of deposits, and the investment system would have been unable to withstand the pressure of the flood of securities thrown upon the market. In this crisis it was necessary for the government to act and to act quickly. On a bewildering March noon, Franklin D. Roosevelt the incoming President in his first official utterance denounced security capitalism in these searing words:

Primarily this is because the rulers of the exchange of mankind's goods have failed through their own stubbornness and their own incompetence, have admitted their failure and abdicated. Practices of the unscrupulous money changers stand indicted in the court of public opinion, rejected by the hearts and minds of men.

True, they have tried, but their efforts have been cast in the pattern of an outworn tradition. Faced by failure of credit, they have proposed only the lending of more money.

Stripped of the lure of profit by which to induce our people to follow their false leadership, they have resorted to exhortations, pleading tearfully for restored confidence. They know only the rules of a generation of self-seekers.

They have no vision, and when there is no vision the people perish.

The money changers have fled from their high seats in the temple of our civilization. We may now restore that temple to the ancient truths.[25]

In the succeeding weeks and months the Roosevelt Administration proceded to enact the New Deal legislation which checked the panic but which at the same time modified American security capitalism.

RECOVERY AND DEPRESSION

After 1932, notwithstanding relapses, there was a general economic recovery. In this period prices received by the farmer rose more rapidly than prices paid by the farmer and as a result the index of farm purchasing power increased. There was a similar improvement in general production; automobile, steel ingot, coal and petroleum output rose and the index of building contracts increased.[26]

As a result of this improvement, labor benefited as evidenced by the fact that the indices of employment and of payrolls mounted and wages paid in manufacturing industries increased sharply.[27] However, by 1937 this upward movement had been in operation for five years and was in its advanced stages. In 1937 there was evidence of the approaching end of the cycle, and the harbingers of the coming depression were already visible.[28]

CONCLUSION

From this review of the background of American security capitalism in the post-war period, it is clear that there was a definite change in the broad economic and social forces which had brought about the rise and development of American security capitalism until the beginning of the twentieth century. The maladjustment of agriculture, the declining rate of industrial growth after the turn of the century and the drop in the rate of the growth of population were similar to the trends which were in evidence in England in the closing years of the nineteenth century. Furthermore the uncertainty of security prices, the inability of banking capitalism to stabilize the financial system, and the uneven nature of economic activity in the post-war years all gave evidence of the crisis confronting American security capitalism.

Part III— Problems of American Security Capitalism

CHAPTER 14

FINANCIAL ORGANIZATION

THIS chapter will trace the evolution of the financial organization of American security capitalism in the post-war period with particular reference to commercial banking, the Federal Reserve system, investment banking and the stock exchange.

CHANGING NATURE OF COMMERCIAL BANKING

The development of commercial banking in the post-war period can best be understood by continuing the study of the financial position of national banks as presented in Chapter 11 which traced their development from 1870 through 1913. In the post-war period the national banks reduced the volume of their circulating notes, and the proportion of such notes to their total liabilities became almost negligible.[1] Another significant tendency was the decline in the proportion of demand deposits and the consequent growth of the proportion of time to total deposits.[2] The deposits of national banks were almost entirely payable on demand until the end of 1913, when the Federal Reserve Act permitted national banks legally to accept time deposits and fixed lower reserve requirements for them. Economists are not in agreement on the causes of this increasing proportion of time deposits. It is held by some that this tendency was due largely to mere bookkeeping entries caused both by the expansion of bank credit and by the transfer of corporate accounts from a demand to a time basis in order to take advantage of the higher interest rate allowed on the latter.[3] It is believed by others that the increase in time deposits over these years reflected the rise in the actual saving of American people.[4]

The rise in time deposits was one of the factors which in turn induced the banks to increase the proportion of their assets in the form of securities and of loans on securities. For the national banks, the proportion of securities, including both United States Government and other securities, to total earning assets rose considerably.[5] Similar to national banks, most of the other classes of financial institutions, as state banks, private banks, savings banks and insurance companies, increased the proportion of their security investments to their total assets.[6]

still payable on demand

INCREASE IN SECURITY LOANS

Not only did the direct security investments of banks increase, but their indirect investments in the form of loans on securities also rose. The proportion of the security loans of national banks to their total loans and discounts rose from 22.5 percent in 1921 to 36.2 percent in 1928.[7] The increase in security loans was not confined to banks in New York City but was general throughout the United States. From the beginning of 1921 to the beginning of 1930 in the Federal Reserve district of San Francisco security loans rose 133 percent, in Chicago 129 percent, in Dallas 126 percent and in Boston 121 percent which exceeded the 100 percent increase in the New York district, while the average for the United States was 98 percent.[8] It is thus clear that the entire banking system of the United States, and not merely the financial center, was influenced by the rapid expansion of security capitalism in the post-war period.

This increase in security loans was sharply attacked, and various arguments were presented by the critics of this phase of security capitalism. It was frequently contended that security loans lacked marketability.[9] As a matter of fact in the two financial crises in the post-war period, security loans possessed a high degree of marketability for in the 1920-1921 crisis when commercial loans were generally frozen and again in the 1929-1930 crisis banks were readily able to convert their security loans into cash.[10] By the end of 1930, even after the drastic reduction of these security loans and after the sharp recession in the market value of the underlying collateral, only 4 percent of all the customers' security loans of 18 large New York City banks and only 6 percent of such loans of 26 large banks elsewhere were secured by collateral whose market value was less than 110 percent of the amount of the loan.[11]

The second criticism leveled against security loans was that they absorbed bank credit needed for the financing of legitimate business activity. Various economists as Rogers, Calvin Hoover, Reed and Roelse, attempted to refute these charges.[12]

TREND IN LIQUIDITY AND SOLVENCY

A further pronounced tendency in the national banking system was the trend in liquidity. The liquidity of a bank, or its ability to meet current liabilities, is tested by the proportion of its reserve assets to deposit liabilities. Such reserve assets include cash and other assets convertible into cash quickly and without loss of value.[13] In the post-war period the ratio of such reserve assets to total deposits increased sharply.[14] Notwithstanding this increasing reserve ratio and satisfactory liquidity of the system as a whole, the national banks experienced a continuous series of failures not only in the depression years but throughout the entire period of the twenties.[15]

The fundamental cause of the bank failures over these years was rather the lack of solvency. This term refers to the capacity of a bank to meet losses arising from the depreciation in the market value of its assets. The solvency of a bank is determined by the proportion of its net capital to its depreciable assets.[16] In the post-war period many banks followed unwise policies regarding their capital funds in the form of their capital, surplus and undivided profits. They failed to build up adequate surplus and undivided profits, but instead paid out overliberal dividends, and applied a large proportion of their capital funds to the erection of elaborate bank buildings. These beautiful Greek temples of the nineteen-twenties frequently became lugubrious mausoleums in the nineteen-thirties. As a result of these unsound building and dividend policies, there was a sharp decline in the proportion of net capital to the gross capital funds of the national banks.[17]

This immobilization prevented the banks from having adequate net capital to meet losses arising from the depreciation in the value of their assets particularly their direct security investments. The decline in the market value of commodities, securities and real estate impaired a large part of the collateral underlying the loans of the banks, but this loss was carried primarily by the customers and only secondarily by the banks, and as seen on p. 224 their losses on loans collateraled by securities were small. However, the depreciation in the value of their direct security investments fell squarely upon the banks themselves.

As a result of the relative decrease in net capital and of the increase in holdings of securities, the proportion between these two items declined sharply.[18] The proportion of net capital of national banks to their securities other than United States Government bonds dropped from 118.23 percent in 1920 to 91.26 percent in 1923 and to 56.06 percent in 1932. In other words, by 1932 the national banks as a whole had only $56.06 to meet losses resulting from the depreciation on every $100 of their securities other than United States Government bonds.[19]

It is thus clear that the commercial banking system, as evidenced by the national banks, continued to operate on the theory that its protection rested solely on the maintenance of liquidity. This was the traditional policy of commercial banking in England in the eighteenth and early nineteenth centuries. This policy, however, was inadequate under a system of developed security capitalism which forced the banks to shift from short-term commercial assets

which usually remained relatively stable in value to long-term security investment assets which continually fluctuated in value. Unmindful of this change in the nature of their assets the commercial
banks failed to realize the importance of the principle of solvency,
and possessed inadequate capital resources to meet the possible losses
on their security assets.[20]

EXPANSION OF INVESTMENT AFFILIATES

Not only did the commercial banks to an increasing extent become investors in securities but many also became dealers in such
securities through operating either bond departments or separate
investment affiliates. In describing the evolution of security capitalism in the United States, the growth of affiliates before 1914
was traced. In subsequent years these institutions increased rapidly
in number and in importance.[21] The importance of the affiliate
in the post-war period may be seen in the increasing proportion
of the originations and participations in new security issues floated
by the commercial banks to the total flotations in the period
from 1927 to 1930. The commercial banks, either through bond
departments or affiliates, in 1927, accounted for 22 percent of the
originations of new issues, and by 1930 the proportion had risen to
44.6 percent or almost one-half of the total. Similarly, the commercial banks in 1927 accounted for 36.8 percent of the participations in new issues and by 1930 the proportion had increased to 61.2
percent or over three-fifths of the total. Thus by 1930 the commercial banks had taken over the greater part of the mechanism of
issuing new securities.[22]

At first the affiliates confined their activities to the flotation of
bonds, but in time they also sold preferred stock and later common
stock. In the course of time they extended their operations and
began playing the market on their own account, purchasing shares
which were considered low in price, and hoping to sell at a higher
figure. The affiliates even went to the extent of speculating in the
stock of their parent banks.[23] It was the practice of certain commercial banks, when asked for disinterested investment advice by
their customers, to refer them to their affiliates, and these institutions
at times unloaded their own securities on these applicants instead
of providing the unbiased information sought.[24] Time and again
the banks granted to their affiliates loans which were not justified
either as to the amount or as to the quality of the collateral pledged
for the loans. In general, however, the securities issued by the
affiliates were no worse than those of other investment houses.[25]

While the commercial banks thus increased their extension of investment credit, they did not at the same time strengthen their control over industry.[26]   Therefore although the American banks followed the same policy as the German banks in increasing the amount of investment credit extended to industry, they did not obtain domination over industry.   The probable reason for this difference in policy was the fact that in Germany, as mentioned on pages 68–69, the scarcity of capital gave the industrialist in the pre-war period little choice but to accept the sovereignty of the banker, while in the United States in the later period the abundance of available capital enabled the industrialist to retain his independence.

Not by any conscious policy on the part of the bankers themselves, but by the relentless force of changing capitalism therefore did the so-called commercial banking system alter its function by reducing its commercial and increasing its investment assets, and by engaging in investment as well as commercial operations.   American banking thus became essentially mixed rather than specialized.   In actual practice it departed far from the classical or orthodox theory and followed the anti-classical or liberal theory.[27]   The liberal theory realistically expressed the actual function of the commercial bank under the security capitalism of the present, while the older orthodox theory defined the function of banking under the individual capitalism of the past.

EFFECT OF CHANGING BANKING FUNCTION ON THE FEDERAL RESERVE

The Federal Reserve system, as established in 1913, was based essentially on the orthodox theory of commercial banking.   The original act restricted rediscounts by member banks to commercial paper and carefully defined the paper acceptable as security for Federal Reserve notes.[28]   However, the changes in the assets of commercial banks in the post-war period had a direct effect on their rediscounts with the Federal Reserve system.   There was a steady decline in the holding of paper eligible for rediscount, and in the case of the national banks eligible paper to total loans and discounts dropped from 30.2 percent in 1923 to 15.9 percent in 1933 from which there was a rise to 19.2 percent in 1935.[29]

GROWTH OF COMPETITION IN INVESTMENT BANKING

Investment banking in the United States since the Civil War passed through three successive stages which may possibly be described as the pre-Morgan, the Morgan and the post-Morgan eras. The later part of the pre-Morgan period was marked by the activities of the speculative capitalists and the rise and decline of Jay Cooke. In the second stage, the house of Morgan came to dominate the sys-

tem of security capitalism, and the supremacy of the firm was complete until the third decade of the twentieth century.   Over these
years the Appian Way of finance led to the corner of Wall and Broad
Streets, and the Pax Morgana gave stability to the financial world.
Investment banking was in the hands of a few large houses and even
these were bound in close alliances with Morgans.   Kuhn, Loeb and
Company alone was in a position to dispute the sway of Morgans,
but, with the exception of the aid given to Harriman in the battle for
the control of the Northern Pacific, open warfare between the two
houses never materialized.

As is seen in Chapter 11 the preeminence of the Morgan firm was
due largely to influence over the supply of capital through its relations with institutions of indirect investment as commercial banks
and life insurance companies.   Although there was an increase in
the amount of such indirect investment after the beginning of the
century, there was relatively greater increase in the volume of direct investment by individuals in stocks and later on in bonds.   This
popularization of security investment was the underlying factor
which weakened the relative control of Morgans over the supply
of capital.   The firm followed a policy of selling not to the general
public but rather of distributing securities to wholesale houses or
to a small group of large individual or institutional buyers.   The
distribution of securities under the Morgan regime rested primarily
on the system of indirect investment where the investor entrusted his
saving to institutions which in turn invested these accumulated
funds.   The growth of direct investment resulted in diffusion of
security ownership, and so made it more difficult for one firm, even
though powerful, to influence the investment of funds.   The Morgan
group of banks, including J. P. Morgan and Company, the First
National Bank, Guaranty Trust Company, Bankers Trust and Bonbright & Company, together accounted for $15,693,000,000 or only
14.73 percent of the total of $106,567,000,000 of new issues placed by
leading syndicates over a period from 1927 to 1932 inclusive.[30]

The growth of direct security investment in turn brought about
a complete transformation in the organization of investment banking.   In place of a few large houses located mainly in New York,
Boston, Chicago and Philadelphia, there were now many investment
banks operating in almost every city of any size from coast to coast.
The increase in the number of investment concerns may be seen in
Table 20 showing the membership in the Investment Bankers' Association of America.

Table 20 shows that the total of the main office and branches of
members of the Investment Bankers Association rose from 277 in
1912 to 810 in 1921.   By 1928 the total had risen to 1072 and to

TABLE 20

MEMBERSHIP IN THE INVESTMENT BANKERS ASSOCIATION, 1912–1936.[31]

(number of members)

YEAR	NUMBER OF MEMBERS		
	MAIN OFFICES	BRANCH OFFICES	TOTAL
1912	257	20	277
1913	354	42	396
1914	356	63	419
1915	340	176	516
1916	361	....	....
1917	407	204	611
1918	399	194	593
1919	433	186	619
1920	485	203	688
1921	552	258	810
1922	584	....	....
1923	607	....	....
1924	617	....	....
1925	620	312	932
1926	664	340	1004
1927	676	377	1053
1928	690	382	1072
1929	665	1237	1902
1930	615	1231	1846
1931	533	969	1502
1932	421	657	1078
1933	375	570	945
1934	495	558	1053
1935	621	665	1286
1936	751	795	1546

1902 by 1929 due to the expansion of branch offices. In the depression period many of the branch offices were closed, and so the total dropped to 945 in 1933 but after that year the total again rose to 1546 in 1936.

RESULTS OF OVERCOMPETITION

This increase in the number of investment houses brought about significant changes in the two essential operations of investment banking, namely the purchasing of new issues from corporations and governments and the selling of these securities to investors. The new competitive condition brought about unsatisfactory consequences in the underwriting of securities such as in the relation of investment banking to corporations and governments, the growth of irresponsibility of the investment banks for their issues, the increase in bond defaults and the overissue of new securities.

The growth in the number of new investment houses resulted in a change in their relations to corporations and governments. British and generally continental investment bankers recognized and avoided each other's territory. Likewise in the pre-war period the large American investment houses were usually careful to respect the financial relations which each firm had established over the years. Corporations and even governments in most cases developed a closed or continuous relationship with one investment house which came to know intimately the financial position of the particular corporation or the government, and was able to offer constructive advice on the latter's general financial policy. In Congressional investigations, this relationship was bitterly attacked, and every effort was made to break up what was considered a monopolistic arrangement. The Interstate Commerce Commission particularly made serious efforts to force competitive bids for the financing of the railroads, but this field continued to be handled by the leading investment houses.[32]

However, in other fields of financing the former closed relation of investment houses to corporations and governments gave way to open competition. There followed a mad scramble for business between the older investment houses and the new. No longer was there any respect for each others' field, but instead investment houses offered corporations and governments almost any inducement to win them away from long-established contacts with the older firms. The competition for new issues was particularly severe in the rush for domestic utility and for foreign government financing. For example the representatives of fifteen American banking houses, with their respective retinues, taxed the limited hotel capacity of Belgrade in the rush to obtain the Yugoslavian government financing.[33]

A further result of the overcompetition among investment banking houses was the revival of the speculative capitalist. He now found himself happily besieged by a horde of investment bankers who forced upon him financial resources entirely unjustified by his true credit position. Thus Alfred Lowenstein obtained the means of financing his ill-fated venture into international power.[34] Likewise the operations of Ivan Krueger and of Samuel Insull were made possible because of the competition among the investment houses which pressed funds into the hands of these individuals to finance their speculative enterprises.

The shift from the closed to the competitive or open relation also led to a change in the responsibility on the part of the investment banker for the issues which he had financed. In the past the investment banker had generally continued his interest in the securities which he had floated. J. P. Morgan, son of the elder Morgan, in his testimony before the Committee on Banking and Currency in 1933, stated:

If he (the banker) makes a public sale and puts his own name at the foot of the prospectus he has a continuing obligation of the strongest kind to see, so far as he can, that nothing is done which will interfere with the full carrying out by the obligor of the contract with the holder of the security.[35]

This old-fashioned philosophy was discarded by the new investment bankers. In many cases they made no effort to see that the corporations or governments which they financed continued in a sound financial condition. Not only did investment houses fail to exercise control over the financial policy of corporations and governments whose securities they had issued, but at times did not even continue to keep on file current information on the financial position of these corporations and governments. An individual investor who had purchased securities and who applied to the issuing house for information was frequently unable to obtain it, for the simple reason that the issuing house once having put out the loan was no longer interested in it.

DECLINE IN QUALITY OF SECURITIES

Under these conditions of overcompetition and irresponsibility, the purchasing function of investment banking was poorly performed. Capital was frequently raised for corporations and for governments whose financial position did not warrant such financial assistance. The inevitable consequence of overcompetition among investment houses in these years was the deterioration in the quality of the bonds which they issued. As a result a large proportion of the issues floated in these years went into default in the depression period. The author made a study of the investment experience of th 4,398 bonds listed in the Fitch Bond Record in the critical market at the close of December, 1931. The results of the study appear in Table 21.

The table shows that of the bonds issued in 1927, 1928 and 1929, 31 percent were in actual or pending default by the end of 1931 as compared with a much lower percentage for the bonds issued in

TABLE 21

DATES OF ISSUE OF DEFAULTED BONDS, DECEMBER 1931.[36]

DATES OF ISSUE	NUMBER OF BONDS ISSUED	PERCENT OF BONDS DEFAULTING
Before 1900...............	70	14.3
1900–1913.................	419	14.5
1914–1919.................	206	10.1
1920–1922.................	263	18.6
1923–1924.................	637	18.4
1925–1926.................	371	21.6
1927–1928.................	1,118	31.8
1929.....................	267	31.1
1930–1931.................	496	11.9
No information............	551	22.0
Total.......	4,398	20.2

previous years. In contrast to the general trend the issue credit of Morgans continued to remain high. In the nineteen twenties in the railroad field Morgan and Company floated 77 issues of which 5 went into default. The firm floated 23 utility issues and 11 industrial issues without a single default. It floated 40 foreign issues of which two, the German loans of 1924 and 1930, went into default.[37]

OVERISSUE OF NEW SECURITIES

A further unsatisfactory result of the intense competition among investment banking houses was the overissue of new securities. In 1924 the municipal bond market became overexpanded, and the *Chronicle* complained that the favorable money market conditions had "led dealers to take more and larger issues from smaller communities than conservative financing would warrant."[38] In 1927 there was a particularly serious congestion in the bond market, and it was estimated that in June of that year nearly a billion dollars of new securities held by dealers remained unsold.[39] Again in 1929 the bond market was so heavily overloaded with securities that it was necessary for the dealers to make "a concentrated drive resulting in wholesale liquidation of unsold newly issued securities."[40] A financial writer in February, 1929, estimated that from 10 to 20 percent of brokers' loans was extended to carry undigested securities.[41] In March of that same fateful year the amount of undigested securities was estimated as high as $600,000,000 as compared with a normal amount of from $250,000,000 to $300,000,000.[42]

UNSOUND SELLING PRACTICES

The transition from the Morgan-dominated system of investment banking era to the competitive system of the post-Morgan era led also to the employment of unsound selling practices.[43] The disposition of a large issue of new securities required the formation of a syndicate or group of investment banks. Such a group had only an informal legal nature and was bound together by a mere syndicate agreement. Frequently the intensity of the competition among the investment houses induced them to violate their pledged word. Under these syndicate agreements they promised not to sell an issue to the public below a stipulated price. However, price cutting, both direct and indirect, was a frequent practice. Thus an investment house would agree to take a customer's old bond in exchange for a new issue at a valuation of $\frac{1}{2}$ point above the market price of the old bond, and in this way the customer would really obtain $\frac{1}{2}$ point concession on the new bond. Another violation of the syndicate agreement was "beating the gun," or offering customers a new issue before it had been released for actual sale by the syndicate manager.[44] The erring syndicate participant therefore obtained an unfair advantage for himself, since he was thus able to obtain orders for the issue in advance of other syndicate members who were more scrupulous in observing the terms of the agreement but who therefore unfortunately found that the demand for their bonds had already been met by their less ethical associate.

Another unsound practice in the sale of securities over these years was "pegging" the market for new issues. In the pre-war period in the United States and in England investment houses generally followed the policy of permitting new issues to find their true market level whether above or below the issuing price. After the War the frequent overissues of securities led to weak markets, and investment bankers followed the practice of trying to stabilize the market for new issues at a fixed price by means of supporting orders. Syndicates generally supported their issues for a period of a month, but when market conditions were unfavorable the support was continued for as long as six months.[45] Otto Kahn defended this policy on the ground that it was the duty of the originating banker to make a market "for a reasonable length of time for the people at large, including distributors, to make up their minds whether these bonds are really definitely placed." [46] He further added that :

a bond issue is not placed to our satisfaction or to the satisfaction of the corporation until it has found its level in the hands of ultimate investors, and that sometimes takes a little time, and sometimes you have overestimated the market value which is properly placeable upon these bonds, and sometimes conditions change. We are not pegging, we are not supporting, we are trying to aid the distribution of bonds which is our duty as agents for the corporation, and it is our duty toward investors, to help them, if need be, to get those bonds placed that for one reason or another, they may try to get rid of.[47]

However, this manipulation or rigging of the market created a fictitious price, and gave the appearance of a stable market which deceived no one except the individual investor unacquainted with the technique of security distribution. Sometimes this support prevented the temporary undervaluation in the market of a sound issue which later rose in price. But, in many cases, after "the pulling of the peg" or the withdrawal of artificial support, the issues declined to low levels.[48] In general the results of the practice of pegging securities in the post-war period proved not only unsatisfactory to the investing public but frequently unprofitable to investment banking itself.

CHANGE IN RELATION OF BANKER TO SECURITY PURCHASERS

The new competitive system also changed the relation of the investment banks to the purchasers of securities. Formerly the banking house of the old type rarely solicited new accounts, and bonds were sold to a selected group of long-standing customers who were invited personally to purchase the securities. Many conservative houses objected even to sending out typewritten letters for fear that their clients would infer that the need of selling was due to pressure, and so letters were generally written in long hand and signed by the senior partner. In this letter the customer was informed that the firm had carefully investigated a new issue and would be glad to discuss its terms personally at the office of the banking house. Every effort was made to keep the business upon a basis of strictest integrity, absolute straightforwardness and unimpeachable respectability.

In the new era these old fashioned methods were discarded and were replaced by the rapid-fire, high-speed sales program which aimed to sell out an issue on the day of its flotation. The new investment banking house organized a corps of security salesmen often recruited from the graduating classes of prominent colleges. These recruits were then given a brief training in security selling, and were turned loose on the investing public. These salesmen were frequently directed to sell the issues regardless of their merit. Thus the instructions of a large New York house to its salesforce on a certain date read:

We anticipate a reasonable supply of new issues. Some of them will be easy sellers and some will be difficult, but for us to do our full duty, it is essential that we be prepared to sell any issue of securities which this company buys, regardless of whether it is hard to sell or easy to sell.[49]

TWILIGHT OF THE GODS

In brief in the post-war period, the supremacy of Morgans in the investment field was shaken on the one hand by governmental opposition to banking concentration and on the other hand by the system of direct investment which led to the formation of new firms and the expansion of the older firms. In the financial Valhalla there came to be too many Gods, and a large number turned out to be Lokis.

DECLINE OF THE STOCK EXCHANGE

The growth of indirect investment and the popularization of the ownership of stocks as well as of bonds led to a rapid increase in the volume of the transactions on the stock exchanges. The number of different stocks listed on the New York Stock Exchange mounted from 612 in 1919 to a peak of 1,308 in 1931, and bond listings from 1,131 to 1,607 over the same period.[50] Notwithstanding this rapid increase, the New York security market never attained complete domination over the national security market as in the case of the other leading metropolitan exchanges of security capitalism. Thus in 1935 the New York security market accounted for 1,483,-000,000 of 3,213,000,000 shares listed on the registered national security exchanges, or 46 percent. It accounted for $24,453,000,000 bonds at par value out of $31,478,000,000 listed on all the exchanges or 78 percent.[51]

As in Europe, with the coming of the depression the importance of the stock exchange in the financial system of this country declined.[52] The volume of new financing, particularly of stocks declined because of the unwillingness of the investing public, mindful of its past losses, to absorb such issues. The number of stock listings fell from 1,308 in 1931, to 1,185 in 1936, while the number of bond listings declined from 1,607 to 1,463. The volume of transactions dropped from the peak of 1,124,608,910 shares of stock in 1929 to 323,845,634 shares in 1934.[53]

CHAPTER 15

CORPORATE INVESTMENT

THE next two chapters undertake a qualitative analysis of the trend of corporate and of governmental security investment in the post-war period. This chapter will trace in order, the trend in railroad, utility, industrial, real estate, holding company and trust investment. Consideration will be given to each field of corporate security investment as a whole to observe whether the application of capital was sound or unsound. In order to pass judgment with any degree of accuracy on the trends of security investment in these respective fields, exact tests of measurement will be utilized and the methods of applied finance will be employed in this study of social finance.[1]

TREND OF RAILWAY FINANCE

Until the second decade of the century, the unsound trend of the debt structure of the railroads had been overcome by the satisfactory course of earning power.[2] However, after 1910 the trend of earning power gradually reversed itself, and became less and less satisfactory.[3] Operating revenues continued to rise from 1911 to 1926 when they turned downward, but operating expenses rose more sharply from 1911 to 1923 and thereafter were somewhat reduced.[4] Throughout the entire period the increase in operating expenses was greater than that of operating revenues, and as a result the ratio of operating expenses to operating revenues was less satisfactory in the period from 1911 to 1929 averaging 75.2 percent than it was in the period from 1890 to 1910 when it averaged 66.7 percent.[5] This unsatisfactory trend in operations was further reflected by the drop in the ratio of operating income to operating revenues. For the period from 1911 to 1929 the average was only 24.8 percent as compared with 33.5 percent for the years from 1890 to 1910.[6]

The trend in the protection of the fixed charges of the roads in the period from 1911 to 1929 requires careful analysis. Over these years the ratio of total income to fixed charges moved irregularly upward and attained an average of 200 percent as compared with 155.3 percent in the period from 1890 to 1910.[7] Superficially it would seem that the fixed charges of the roads were being protected at a rising and even more satisfactory margin but this traditional test failed to show the real lack of improvement in the protection of the fixed charges of the railroad system. The real condition is reflected in the absence of an advance of the proportion of net income to operating revenues.[8] This ratio showed an average of 12.6 percent from 1890 to 1910 and remained about the same, roughly 13 percent, from 1911 to 1929. Thus the net income, or the balance after fixed charges, as the margin of protection for these fixed charges, failed to show improvement. Contrary to the general impression the dividend policy of the railroads continued sound. Net income rose more rapidly than dividends paid and so the ratio of net income to dividends paid was well maintained.[9] The trend of the capital structure of the railroads in the post-war period was also contrary to the generally-stated view. Even careful students of railroad finance have failed to realize that the increase in railroad debt was not a recent but a long standing trend. Thus a member of the Interstate Commerce Commission said: "I think probably one of the worst things that has happened since 1920 to railroad finance, one of the most disastrous things, has been the increase in debt on the railroad as a whole."[10] Actually the total debt of the roads, as compared with 1890 as a base, increased from 224.5 percent in 1920 to only 249.6 percent in 1929.[11] Total capitalization likewise showed only a small increase of from 203.8 percent in 1910 to 220.4 percent in 1929.[12] As a result of these various changes in both items, the ratio of total debt to total capitalization rose only slightly from 61 percent in 1910 to 62.8 percent in 1920 and to 63.4 percent in 1929.[13] However, the high level of debt accumulated before 1910 became top-heavy in the period after 1910 when the operations of the railroads and their consequent earning power became less satisfactory.[14]

In the depression after 1929, the unfavorable tendencies in the operating results of the previous twenty years were accentuated. Compared with 1910 as a base, operating revenues dropped more rapidly than operating expenses, and the ratio between these two items was at the unsatisfactory high average of 75.1 percent for the period from 1930 to 1934.[15] Also operating income to operating revenues remained at the low average figure of below 25 percent.[16] The drop in operating revenues cut deeply into total income which fell sharply, while fixed charges could not be reduced.[17] As a result of the fall in total income and the inflexibility of fixed charges, the proportion of total income to fixed charges dropped precipitously.[18] More significant was the collapse in the ratio of net income to operating revenues which disappeared entirely, and the margin of safety of the fixed charges of the railway system as a whole was wiped out in the depression.[19] Although the roads cut dividend payment sharply after 1930 even these were not covered by net income,[20] and were paid out of surplus. There was little effort to reduce the debt of the railroads during the depression period, and the ratio of the total debt to total capitalization remained at the high level of previous years.[21] The fundamental mistake in the railroad field was the assumption that a high ratio of debt to total capitalization could be maintained due to the assumed stability of earnings. Since earnings in the railroad field, however, fluctuate directly with business activity, the assumed stability never actually materialized, and the debt proved far too large. In industry, as shown on page 241, debt held to a low level, since the instability of earnings in this field was clearly recognized. In the railroad field, early recognition of the character of earnings would have avoided eventual difficulties.

TREND OF PUBLIC UTILITY FINANCE

Public utilities, as the term is used in limited investment terminology, include electric light and power, traction, gas, water, telephone and telegraph companes. Consideration will be given only to the electric light and power and the traction utilities. There is herewith given an abbreviated form of the consolidated financial statement of electric light and power companies from 1912 to 1931.

Table 22 shows clearly the trend of the capitalization of electric light and power companies, but the items and ratios deserve careful study. The items themselves show that funded debt, total capitalization and property [23] all experienced considerable increases in amount from 1912 to 1931, and these increases would normally indicate debt, capital and property inflation. However, the actual trends are seen when these increases are compared to the fundamental item of earning power as expressed by total income. Thus, from 1912 to 1931 the funded debt increased to 535.05 percent, total capitalization increased to 602.28 percent and property increased to 585.99 percent. Nevertheless over the same period, total income increased to 658.18 percent, or more than any of the previous items. Thus the increase in funded debt, total capitalization and property, while superficially showing corporate inflation, did not actually constitute inflation because the increase in these items was based on a more than corresponding rise in earning power. A further indication of the absence of corporate inflation is seen in the fact that the total income covered interest requirements satisfactorily and even provided increasing protection in the period under review.[24] Furthermore, the satisfactory trend of electric light and power finance is seen in the reduction of the proportion of the funded debt to total capitalization and the increase in the extent to which property protected the funded debt.[25] The only indication of overcapitalization is evidenced in the trend of total income to total capitalization which

TABLE 22

ELECTRIC LIGHT AND POWER FINANCE, 1912–1931.[22]

ITEMS (MILLION DOLLARS)	1912	1922	1929	1931
1. Total income [a]	$ 110	336	714	724
2. Interest...................	48	138	269	307
3. Funded debt..............	1,084	2,040	5,075	5,800
4. Total capitalization........	1,926	3,968	10,150	11,600
5. Property [b]..............	2,099	4,290	10,400	12,300
(PERCENT, 1912 = 100)				
1. Total income..............	100	305.45	649.09	658.18
2. Interest...................	100	287.50	560.41	639.58
3. Funded debt..............	100	188.19	468.17	535.05
4. Total capitalization........	100	206.02	526.99	602.28
5. Property.................	100	204.38	495.47	585.99
RATIOS (PERCENT)				
A. Total income to interest (1 ÷ 2).................	229.17	243.48	265.43	235.83
B. Funded debt to total capitalization (3 ÷ 4)...........	56.28	51.41	50.00	50.00
C. Property to funded debt (5 ÷ 3).................	193.63	210.29	204.92	212.06
D. Total income to total capitalization (1 ÷ 4)........	5.71	8.47	7.03	6.24

Explanation:
[a] Technically known in utility finance as " net earnings prior to fixed charges."
[b] Technically known in utility finance as " plant investment."

rose from 5.71 percent in 1912 to 8.47 percent in 1922 and then fell to 7.03 percent in 1929 and to 6.24 percent in 1931.[26]

In sharp contrast to the financial trends of the electric light and power companies are those of the electric railway companies as seen in Table 23.

The table shows that the funded debt, the total capitalization and the property of the traction companies were reduced in dollar amounts from 1922 to 1931. These reductions might on the surface reflect trends toward debt, capitalization and property deflation. Actually in these respects there was resultant inflation for the total income declined much more rapidly. The further unsatisfactory trend in traction finance is seen in the decline in the coverage of interest by total income and in the protection of the funded debt by property.[28] This trend is demonstrated by the decline in the ratio of total income to interest which dropped from 164.76 percent in 1912 to 96.27 percent in 1931.[29] The proportion of property to

TABLE 23

ELECTRIC RAILWAY FINANCE, 1912–1931.[37]

ITEMS (MILLION DOLLARS)	1912	1922	1929	1931
1. Total income............	$ 173	213	133	129
2. Interest.................	105	156	123	134
3. Funded debt............	1,823	2,500	2,280	2,480
4. Total capitalization.......	3,602	4,288	3,800	4,205
5. Property................	4,597	5,059	4,000	4,100
(PERCENT, 1912 = 100)				
1. Total income............	100	123.12	76.87	74.56
2. Interest.................	100	148.57	117.14	127.61
3. Funded debt............	100	137.13	125.06	136.03
4. Total capitalization.......	100	119.04	105.49	116.74
5. Property................	100	110.05	87.01	89.18
RATIOS (PERCENT)				
A. Total income to interest (1÷2).................	164.76	136.54	108.13	96.27
B. Funded debt to total capitalization (3÷4)...........	50.61	58.30	60.00	58.97
C. Property to funded debt (5÷3).................	252.16	202.36	175.43	165.32
D. Total income to total capitalization (1÷4).........	4.80	4.97	3.50	3.07

funded debt fell from 252.16 to 165.32.[30] There is also evidence of a trend toward overcapitalization in the proportion of total income to total capitalization which dropped from 4.80 percent in 1912 to 3.07 percent in 1931.[31]

INDUSTRIAL FINANCE — CAPITALIZATION OF MANUFACTURING CORPORATIONS

In the field of applied finance, industrial securities include those of corporations engaged in extractive operations as coal and oil production; transportation operations as steamship companies and carriers other than steam and electric railroads; manufacturing operations as automobile and textile making and trading corporations as chain and department stores.

The two most important groups are the manufacturing and trading corporations and their financial position will be studied. The financial trends of manufacturing corporations in the post-war period are presented in Table 24.

TABLE 24
MANUFACTURING FINANCE, 1924–1933.[32]

ITEMS (MILLION DOLLARS)	1924	1929	1931	1933
1. Total income..............	$3,687	5,793	292	957
2. Fixed charges.............	608	712	598	454
3. Funded debt.............	3,753	5,449	5,579	5,022
4. Total capitalization........	39,820	58,141	53,216	48,363
5. Net property.............	22,410	28,235	28,285	24,384
RATIOS (PERCENT)				
A. Total income to fixed charges (1 ÷ 2).................	606.41	813.62	48.83	210.79
B. Funded debt to total capitalization (3 ÷ 4).........	9.42	9.37	10.48	10.38
C. Net property to funded debt (5 ÷ 3).................	597.12	518.17	506.99	485.54
D. Total income to total capitalization (1 ÷ 4)........	9.26	9.96	0.55	1.98

Table 24 shows that the fixed charges of manufacturing corporations were well covered except in 1931.[33] The proportion of the funded debt to total capitalization was at a very low figure, and so was satisfactory.[34] Property covered the funded debt at a very high level even though it declined somewhat over the period.[35] The total income to total capitalization was high at 9.26 percent in 1924 and 9.96 percent in 1929, but fell sharply in the depression years due to the drop in earnings.[36] Considering these figures as a whole the capital structure of manufacturing companies was sound.

CAPITALIZATION OF TRADING COMPANIES

The financial trend of trading companies is presented in Table 25. The capital structure of trading corporations was less satisfactory than that of the manufacturing companies. While the fixed charges of the trading corporations were well covered in 1924 and 1929,[38] there was a deficit in 1931.[39] Fortunately the ratio of funded debt to total capitalization was low, although the level rose somewhat in the depression years.[40] Property covered the funded debt at a high level which however declined over these years.[41]

DEBT STRUCTURE OF INDUSTRY

In presenting the trend in railroad and in utility finance consideration was given essentially to the problem of capitalization in

TABLE 25

TRADING FINANCE, 1924–1933.[37]

ITEMS (MILLION DOLLARS)	1924	1929	1931	1933
1. Total income..............	$1,064	1,077	−245	183
2. Fixed charges.............	219	276	209	147
3. Funded debt..............	679	1,252	1,314	1,127
4. Total capitalization........	11,278	14,771	13,760	11,014
5. Net property.............	3,053	4,966	4,728	3,809
RATIOS (IN PERCENT)				
A. Total income to fixed charges (1 ÷ 2)..................	485.84	390.22	−117.22	124.49
B. Funded debt to total capitalization (3 ÷ 4).........	6.02	8.42	9.55	10.23
C. Net property to funded debt (5 ÷ 3).................	449.63	396.65	359.82	337.98
D. Total income to total capitalization (1 ÷ 4)........	9.43	7.29	−1.78	1.66

relation to earning power. In industrial finance, consideration must be given not only to the problem of the relation of capitalization to earnings but also that of the maturity of debt. The debt of a corporation may be either unfunded or funded depending upon whether it matures before or after the period of one year. Unfunded debt consists largely of bank loans and of bonds which have been issued in past years but which have less than a year to their date of payment. The railroads and the public utilities, since their operations are largely non-seasonal and are on a cash basis, have little need of obtaining loans from commercial banks. On the other hand, the operations of industrial corporations generally are seasonal in nature and to a large extent are conducted by granting credit to their customers. Thus industrial corporations have in the past been large users of bank credit.

However, an important tendency in the post-war period was the decline in the volume of such bank credit used by industrial concerns. This significant trend was due largely to changes in the business organization and in the management policies of industrial concerns. The corporate form of organization completely dominated the railroad and the public utility fields almost from the very start due to the need of capital in so large an amount that it could not be raised by individuals but had to be obtained from the investing public through the sale of securities. On the other hand until the end of the nineteenth century the industrial field continued to be organized in the form of the individual ownership, the partnership and to some extent the small-scale corporation. Thus individual capitalism continued as a factor in the field of industry long after security capitalism had dominated the other fields of business activity.

However, after the turn of the century large-scale corporations began to attain domination in the industrial field. In 1904 all corporations, both large and small, accounted for 73.7 percent of the volume of the products of manufacture; in 1914 this figure rose to 83.2 percent and by 1929 it was 92.1 percent.[42] Moreover, the larger corporations shared to a greater extent than the smaller corporations in the expansion of the post-war period. In 1923 the 1,240 largest manufacturing companies received 69.4 percent of all corporate net income, while in 1929 the 1,289 largest corporations accounted for 75.6 percent.[43]

This growth of large-scale corporations in industry had a direct effect on the method of financing in this field, and particularly upon the relation between the industrial concern and its bank. The small firm since it could not sell its securities in the capital market by necessity continued to borrow from its local bank. On the other hand the large corporation, since it was able to sell its securities in the capital market, generally utilized this means of financing and reduced its bank loans. There was thus a definite tendency for large corporations to replace bank funds with capital funds. The method of corporation finance changed from a temporary to a more permanent form, and the obligations of corporations were converted from short-term bank loans into long-term bonds or even into stock.

A further factor in reducing the volume of bank credit employed by industrial concerns was the change in their management policies. After the financial disturbances of 1920, business firms followed the policy of carrying small inventory and so there was a less demand for bank credit.[44] For years it had been customary for business firms to carry large inventories of goods to meet the needs of their customers. This policy brought heavy losses in 1920 when prices fell sharply, and merchandise depreciated in value. To prevent a recurrence of such events, business firms followed a policy of carrying small inventories sufficient to meet only current needs. They were aided in this policy by the improvement in transportation which made possible prompt delivery of goods when ordered by dealers and retailers, and therefore they had less need of bank credit. Another change in managerial policy was the attempt to reduce seasonal peaks in industrial production and merchandising by spreading business over the entire year. With a reduction in seasonal peaks came a corresponding reduction in the volume of bank credit needed.[45]

The large corporations also made less use of the commercial paper market.[46] In consequence the volume of commercial paper outstanding in the New York market declined from the peak of $1,019,000,000 in January, 1920, to a low of $60,100,000 in May, 1933.[47] By 1936 the market for bankers' acceptances also declined, and the American Acceptance Council, which for many years had sought to propagandize the instrument, was dissolved.[48]

This decline in the use of bank credit, by reducing the unfunded debt of the borrowing corporations, had a beneficial effect on their financial position as may be seen by contrasting their position in the depression of 1920–1921 with that in 1929–1934. The current debt of large industrial corporations had risen from $8,544,000,000 in 1913 to $16,750,000,000 in 1920.[49] When the financial crisis broke in 1920, many industrial corporations, notwithstanding their underlying soundness, faced serious financial difficulties due to the large volume of their unfunded debt. Had the depression been of longer duration many would have been forced to the wall. Profiting by this experience industrial corporations generally followed a conscious policy of reducing their bank debt out of the proceeds derived from the sale of their securities. As a result, from 1921 to 1932 the unfunded debt of a large group of industrial corporations fell from $13,700,000,000 to $10,800,000,000 and funded debt rose from $4,800,000,000 to $10,400,000,000. The ratio of unfunded debt to total debt dropped from 74 percent to 51 percent.[50] As a result of this policy, most of the large industrial corporations entered the crisis of 1929 with a much sounder capital structure from the standpoint of maturity, and few were forced to reorganize. It is therefore clear that the debt structure of American industrial corporations improved considerably because of the policy of financing by the sale of securities rather than by bank loans. It would therefore be financial folly for industrial corporations to return to the outmoded system of bank loans and surrender the more beneficial policy of financing through securities. Unquestionably the rapid development of security capitalism in the post-war period greatly improved the debt structure of American industry.

REAL ESTATE FINANCE

Individual capitalism obtains most of its financial assistance for short-term periods from bank loans and for long-term periods from mortgage loans. Until recent years real estate operations were financed by the single mortgage whereby the funds were advanced by one mortgagee to one mortgagor. Thus this important financial activity lay within the field of individual capitalism and outside of the scope of security capitalism. However, by the beginning of the century the erection of large buildings in urban communities began to be financed by means of the multiple mortgage held by a number of persons who joined in the investment, and their participation was evidenced by real estate bonds as instruments of security capitalism. These bonds were handled by financial houses which were really investment banks specializing in the flotation of real estate securities, and generally confining their business to the financing of large urban properties.

Various methods were used in real estate security finance. One method was for the real estate bank, acting as a dealer in the same capacity as an investment bank, to buy an issue of bonds floated for the purpose of providing funds to erect a building and to sell the bonds to individual investors. For these bonds the real estate investment bank assumed no legal obligation, but since the bonds were sold on the reputation of the bank, it really gave its implied or moral guarantee to the issue. A second method of real estate finance was for the bank, acting as guarantor, to assume the liability for the mortgage, and thus to become legally the secondary obligor of the certificates of participation in the guaranteed multiple mortgage.

A third method was for the real estate bank, acting as an investment trust, to issue its own bonds based on real estate as collateral, and so these collateral mortgage bonds became the direct obligations of the real estate bank.[51]

The application of these methods of security capitalism brought about a complete change in the capitalization of real estate in general as may be seen in the following table showing the trend of urban real estate finance from 1913 to 1931.

Table 26 presents the trends in the funded debt, property value and rentals of urban real estate. In 1913 the amount of the funded debt represented only 13.1 percent of the total value of urban real estate.[53] By 1921 the amount of the funded debt had increased,[54] but likewise had the property value of urban real estate[55] and the ratio between the two remained roughly about the same.[56] Over this period the index of rentals had increased to 159 percent as compared with an increase to 174 percent for the funded debt, and to 164 percent for property value.[57] Thus the funded debt was still fairly well protected by both rental power as well as by property. However, by 1929 the amount of the funded debt rose to over $27,-616,000,000 while the value of urban real estate rose to $73,700,000,-000 and the proportion of funded debt to property value rose to 37.5 percent.[58] However by 1929 the index of rentals had declined

TABLE 26

URBAN REAL ESTATE FINANCE, 1913–1931.[52]

ITEM	UNIT OF MEASURE-MENT	1913	1921	1929	1931
1. Funded debt..........	{million dollars}	5,151	8,968	27,616	27,554
2. Property value........	{million dollars}	39,300	64,600	73,700	61,300
3. Index of rentals.......	1913 = 100	100	159	154	142
4. Index of funded debt...	1913 = 100	100	174	536	535
5. Index of property value	1913 = 100	100	164	188	156
6. Funded debt to prop-erty value (1÷2)....	percent	13.1	13.9	37.5	44.9

to 154 per cent while funded debt remained almost the same for the next two years and the value of property dropped. The ratio of funded debt to property value rose to 44.9 percent,[59] and the index of rentals declined to 142 percent.[60] As a result 60 percent of the outstanding real estate bond issues were in distress.[61]

HOLDING COMPANY FINANCE

Expansion and concentration of business in the United States led to the development of various forms of intercorporate relationships as the trade association, the trade agreement, the pool, the trust, the community of interest, the holding company, the lease of assets, the sale of assets, the merger and amalgamation. The trade associations, the simplest form of intercorporate relations, developed in the post-war period in many fields for the purpose of performing statistical research, financial and legislative services for members.[62] Trade agreements also were extensively employed to maintain uniform prices, limit output or restrict the marketing area of the parties involved. In the post-war period pools were revived to regulate output, territory, distribution of income among the members and to provide for the common use of patents.[63] The trust based on a trust agreement as a device for effecting relations among corporations had been generally outlawed and was not widely employed. The community of interest which brought about close relations through placing the same directors and the same officers on the boards of the various corporations, despite legal restrictions, in many fields brought about unity of management. Close intercorporate relations were attained through the leasing of properties, the out-right sale of these properties and finally consolidation or the complete fusion of the companies into a single unit either through merger or amalgamation.[64]

However, the most important agency employed in the post-war period for accomplishing close intercorporate relations was the holding company. It was employed in railroad, industrial and banking finance, but in the post-war period it was most extensively applied in utility finance.

In the post-war period this instrument of corporation finance was used particularly to bring together electric light operating companies all over the United States. Critics of the holding company frequently failed to see the possible benefits which could be derived, and at times were derived, from well-managed holding companies. The holding company could make avaible to operating companies certain definite financial and technical services. Holding companies with efficient administrators could enable operating companies to finance their needs at more reasonable interest rates than the latter could have obtained from issuing their own securities in local capital markets. Also a holding company with a well-trained staff could furnish operating units within its system with valuable technical aid in solving the complicated engineering construction and management problems which arise in such a rapidly expanding industry as electric light and power.

However, these benefits, actually extended by well-managed holding companies, were only too often offset by the unsound financial and technical policies of unscrupulous holding companies. There was no field in which overcapitalization was carried further than in the financing of public utilities by holding companies in the post-war period. The holding companies competed with each other, and in the mad scramble for operating properties paid prices far above true value based on earning power. These properties were then written up to the high purchase prices, and such overrated assets were used as the basis for issuing the securities of the holding companies.[65] In many cases holding companies were dominated by super-holding companies, and through the issuance and sale to the public of preferred and common shares with non-voting power, control was retained by a small block of closely held voting stock. Thus several million dollars of common stock frequently controlled an entire system with a capitalization of several hundred million dollars. The effect of such pyramiding through holding companies may be illustrated by tracing the relationship of a single company in the Insull system. The top holding company was Middle West Utilities which owned a controlling interest in fourteen large companies, of which one was National Electric Power Company. In turn it controlled National Public Service Corporation which in turn controlled Seaboard Public Service, which in turn controlled Georgia Power Company, the only operating company in the entire chain so far mentioned. As a result, one dollar invested in the common stock of Middle West Utilities Corporation controlled $350 of Georgia Power common stock and controlled $1,750 of its assets.[66] Another way of illustrating the control over vast operating company assets through a small holding company investment is to compare the amount of the controlled assets with the dominating investment. Thus the vast Associated Gas and Electric Company system in 1929 was controlled by an investment of only $298,318.[67] Another unsound practice was the unwise use of the sound credit of the operating company to support the weakening credit position of the holding company, particularly during the depression years.[68]

A further unsound financial policy was the "milking" of the operating subsidiaries by the transfer of their accumulated surpluses to embarrassed holding companies which temporarily tided over such concerns but depleted the working capital of the operating companies. That is in order to maintain the tottering structure of the holding company, the operating companies were frequently forced to pay out dividends not covered by actual earnings but obtained from the surpluses accumulated in past years. As a result the financial resources of these operating companies were often seriously weakened.

The relation between the holding companies and the investment banks which handled their securities was frequently marked by serious irregularities.[69] The promoters of the Insull Utilities Investment Corporation from the time of its organization followed an over-liberal policy of distributing free stock to insiders. For purchasing the debentures of Insull Utilities, one investment firm received 57,000 shares of common stock for which it paid nothing. If all the stock of the Insull Company had been sold in the market at prevailing prices from December, 1928, when it was organized, to August, 1930, the Company would have received $231,387,442 while actually it realized only $101,845,293.[70] On August 2, 1929, several months after the corporation was formed, the stock sold for $149 a share, and its shares had a market value of $302,044,754, which was 7½ times the amount of the capital actually placed in the Company. To earn even 6 percent on this market value, the Company would have had to show a net income of more than $18,000,000 which would have been 44 percent of the actually invested capital. Actually the net income of the Company for the entire year of 1929 was only $1,948,265.[71]

INVESTMENT TRUST FINANCE

In theory the investment trust was to bring to the American investor the advantage of safety through diversification of risk and the benefit of expert knowledge in the selection of the securities in the portfolio of the trust. <u>In practice just the opposite results were frequently attained</u>, as illustrated in the case of one trust which had been formed by an investment bank. The officers of these two institutions became favorably impressed in the fall of 1929 with the outlook for the railroads, and together they determined to acquire a substantial holding of railroad stocks.[72] This joint account terminated on November 9, 1929, and by that time securities costing $10,891,578 had been acquired both by the investment trust and by the banking house. On November 11, 1929, two days after the termination of the joint trading account, the investment trust purchased from the investment bank, 13,700 shares of Chicago, Rock Island and Pacific Railway common stock at $114.25 for $1,565,225 and 16,050 shares of St. Louis and San Francisco Railway common stock at $111.25 for a total of $1,793,587.[73] On December 31, 1932, the investment trust had in its portfolio 45,000 shares of Chicago, Rock Island and Pacific Railway common stock at a cost of $5,566,366 and St. Louis and San Francisco common at a cost of $5,820,883.[74] The average price paid by the investment trust for Chicago, Rock Island and Pacific was $138.36 and the average price paid for St. Louis and San Francisco was $130.39. These roads eventually went into default.[75] These two holdings represented almost twenty percent of the entire capital of the investment trust, and so violated the principle of diversification.[76] In the post-war period investment trusts were too often used as a convenient dumping ground by investment banking houses for securities which could not be marketed.[77] The loading charges imposed for organizing an investment trust frequently were very high. During the Senate hearings, in reply to a criticism of the excessive profits to organizers, one banker testified, "We could have taken 100 percent, we could have taken all of the profit. We could have bought all of the common stock for five million dollars"; to which one of the investigating senators replied, "Do you remember that Lord Clive said 'When I consider my opportunities, I marvel at my moderation.'"[78]

In general the financial operations of investment trusts were unsatisfactory. Even after the sharp break in the security markets in the fall of 1929, the net assets of the leading investment trusts showed a further decline of over 62 percent in the years from 1930 to 1932 inclusive, and despite the rise after 1932 their assets for the entire period from 1930 to 1936 showed a net decline of over 23 percent.[79]

CONCLUSION

This chapter has now reviewed the trend of corporate security investment in the post-war period in the field of railroad, utility, industrial, real estate, holding company and investment trust finance and particular attention was given to the problem of overcapitalization. In the railroad field there was no trend toward overcapitalization, although the general financial position of the roads became less satisfactory particularly in the depression. In the case of the public utility operating companies, little evidence of overcapitalization was found in the field of the electric light and power companies, but it was noted that the traction field, due to declining earnings, was overcapitalized. The application of security capitalism to industrial finance had satisfactory results, since this field had a sound capitalization and a satisfactory debt structure. However, the intrusion of security capitalism into real estate finance was disastrous. Furthermore while utility operation itself was sound, the application of the holding company to utility finance led to serious overcapitalization. The financial operations of investment trusts were generally unsound.

CHAPTER 16

GOVERNMENT INVESTMENT

THIS chapter continues the examination of the trends of security investment in the post-war period, and presents a qualitative analysis of the tendencies in federal, state, municipal and foreign government financing in the American security market.[1] In analyzing the trend of governmental finance, this study will group the various governments on the principle of legal classification into sovereign governments, including, the true sovereign government as the United States, the quasi-sovereign government as the state governments and the non-sovereign bodies or municipalities, including primarily cities and other local governments, such as counties, towns, villages and tax districts.[2]

FEDERAL GOVERNMENT FINANCE

In 1916, the year before the entrance of the United States into the World War, the financial position of the federal government was excellent.[3] The budget was balanced and expenditures for debt service amounted to only $22,900,000.[4] This small sum was the result of the almost continuous policy of debt contraction followed after the Civil War, so that the gross debt was only $1,225,000,000 in 1916. To offset even this small gross debt the federal government had accumulated sinking funds of $1,052,000,000 so that the net debt of the Federal Government was only $173,000,000.[5] Meantime the tax base of the United States as expressed in national wealth had risen to over $251,000,000,000.[6] As a result of these trends, the expenditure for debt service amounted to only 3.1 percent of total expenditures, and national wealth covered the total debt of the federal government over 1454 times.[7] These figures show clearly the satisfactory condition of the finances of the federal government until the coming of the War. The United States, with a minimum national debt in 1916, had approached the millennium of public finance.

Then came the stage of debt expansion which covered the period from 1917 to 1919 inclusive. The deficit in the budget in 1918 amounted to over $9,000,000,000 and in 1919 to over $13,000,000,-000.[8] The gross debt reached a record figure for those years of over $25,000,000,000 which, by deducting the sinking fund accumulated in past years, was reduced to a net debt of about $24,000,-

251

000,000.[9] By 1920 national wealth covered the total debt 20 times. Thus in the short period of three years the financial position of the federal government was changed from soundness to uncertainty from which it never fully recovered.[10]

In the period from 1919 to 1930, the Republican administration made strenuous efforts to correct this unsatisfactory condition. Expenditures were reduced from $18,523,000,000 in 1919 to $3,795,-000,000 in 1922 and were held well below the four billion mark until 1931.[11] Revenues were maintained about up to four billion, and as a result there was a continuous surplus over these years.[12] The large debt of the federal government required a heavy payment of interest which rose to over a billion dollars in 1923. At the same time the administration undertook a drastic reduction of the debt as reflected in the large item of public debt retirements which ranged from $422,300,000, in 1921 to $554,000,000 in 1930.[13] Consequently the expenditures for debt service rose to $1,459,000,000 in 1923 and remained at a high level throughout the period. This item constituted about one-third of the total expenditures.[14] As a result of this large allowance for debt retirement, the net debt was reduced from $24,298,000,000 in 1920 to $15,797,000,000 in 1930. Most of this reduction was in the unfunded debt which was cut from $8,521,000,000 in 1919 to $3,894,000,000 in 1931.[15] This decline in the unfunded debt was reflected in the drop in the proportion of unfunded debt to gross debt from 34 percent in 1920 to 23 percent in 1931.[16] By 1930 the national wealth again covered the total debt 20 times.[17]

In the period from 1930 to 1936 the financial position of the federal government fell back into the uncertain position which had prevailed at the close of the War. Since these unfavorable trends began in 1930 under the Hoover administration and were continued under the Roosevelt administration, the period must be considered as a unit regardless of the political change which occurred in 1933. Revenues declined sharply from 1930 to 1933, while expenditures increased and the deficit rose from $902,000,000 in 1931 to $3,989,-000,000 in 1934, after which year the deficit was reduced through an increase in revenues.[18] Expenditure for debt service increased, but not in the same proportion as in the rise in the debt, due to the abnormally low rates prevailing in the money market. During the Hoover administration gross debt increased from $16,185,000,000 in 1930 to $20,935,000,000 by March 1, 1933 and during the Roosevelt administration the gross debt reached $33,545,000,000 in 1936.

The increase occurred particularly in the unfunded debt which rose from $4,673,000,000 in 1930 to $15,876,000,000 in 1935.[19] The ratio of unfunded to gross debt rose from 28.9 percent in 1930 to

55.3 percent in 1935.[20]   In addition, the federal government assumed the obligations of a group of quasi-public corporations, as the Reconstruction Finance Corporation, the Federal Land Banks, and the Home Owners Loan Corporation.   This indirect debt added another $4,151,000,000 to the federal debt.[21]   Quasi-government obligations, although extensively used by continental countries as well as by Great Britain, were practically unknown in the United States until the post-war period.   For a time because of the unfamiliarity of these obligations, there was a wide differential between their yield and that on the direct obligations of the national government.   However, Congress by successive legislation placed both the direct and the guaranteed obligations on the same basis in almost every respect. Guaranteed obligations were made eligible as collateral for advances from Federal Reserve banks, legal as security for trust funds and exempt as to both principal and interest from federal, state and local taxation except sur-tax, estate, inheritance and gift taxes. The greater part of the assets of these public corporations will probably prove to be sound, and so it is unlikely that the federal government will be called upon actually to assume much of this indirect debt.   Thus these obligations are contingent rather than actual.

Due to the more rapid increase in total expenditures than in debt service, the proportion of the latter to the former declined.[22] The coverage of national wealth to total debt declined from 20 times in 1930, to 9 times in 1935.[23]   By 1936 the net federal debt increased to $33,275,000,000 as a result of the cumulative force of both war and depression finance.   It is essential to realize that, while the original Liberty loans were gradually retired through repayment and through refunding, only about one-third of these war loans were completely retired.   The remainder was merely transformed as to maturity.   Therefore $15,872,000,000 or about 47 percent of the direct debt of the federal government even in 1936 was attributable not to the depression but to war finance.   The trend of the federal finances, weakened as a result of the War, showed further maladjustment because of the cumulative force of the depression.

STATE GOVERNMENT FINANCE

The trend of state government finance is indicated in Table 27. From this table it is seen that revenues and total expenditures[25] of state governments increased rapidly over these years, but generally remained nearly balanced.   The proportion of the interest on debt to total expenditures remained at a low figure,[26] never going higher than 4.8 percent for 1926.   It is thus clear that the budgetary policies of state governments as a whole were satisfactory.

TABLE 27
STATE GOVERNMENT FINANCE, 1915–1932.[24]

ITEMS (MILLION DOLLARS)	1915	1921(d)	1922	1923	1924	1925	1926	1927	1928	1929	1930	1931	1932
1. Revenues	458	521	1,159	1,247	1,370	1,485	1,655	1,758	1,935	2,059	2,243	2,325	2,208
2. Total expenditures	495	521	1,280	1,310	1,514	1,615	1,615	1,726	1,889	2,061	2,290	2,509	2,506
3. Balance	−37	......	−121	−63	144	−130	40	32	46	−2	−47	−184	−298
4. Interest on debt	19	13	41	50	56	68	77	79	87	94	101	111	112
5. Unfunded debt (a)	101	92	202	255	289	238	142	159	164	212	238	299	302
6. Funded debt	479	376	1,064	1,165	1,449	1,508	1,610	1,726	1,867	1,971	2,094	2,259	2,499
7. Gross debt	580	468	1,266	1,420	1,738	1,746	1,858	1,995	2,144	2,300	2,444	2,666	2,896
8. Sinking fund assets	88	94	227	254	311	347	378	402	411	444	450	496	535
9. Net debt (b)	424	298	879	956	1,183	1,249	1,328	1,445	1,585	1,662	1,833	1,977	2,361
10. Debt base (b)	75,527	48,220	106,878	108,676	131,318	136,184	142,092	146,432	155,465	163,683	165,727	166,048	163,317
RATIOS (PERCENT)													
A. Revenues to total expenditures (1÷2)	92.5	100.0	90.5	95.2	90.5	92.0	102.5	101.9	102.4	99.9	97.9	92.7	88.1
B. Interest on debt to total expenditures (4÷2)	3.8	2.5	3.2	3.8	3.7	4.2	4.8	4.6	4.6	4.6	4.4	4.4	4.5
C. Unfunded debt to gross debt (5÷7)	17.4	19.7	16.0	18.0	16.6	13.6	7.6	8.0	7.6	9.2	9.7	11.2	10.4
D. Sinking fund assets to gross debt (8÷7)	15.2	20.1	17.9	17.9	17.9	19.9	20.3	20.2	19.2	19.3	18.4	18.6	18.5
E. Debt base to net debt (10÷9)	17,813.0	16,181.2	12,159.0	11,367.8	11,100.4	10,903.4	10,699.7	10,133.7	9,808.5	9,848.6	9,041.3	8,399.0	6,917.0
F. Net debt per capita (c)	$4.31	5.17	8.12	8.72	10.64	11.09	11.46	12.32	13.35	13.77	15.03	16.04	19.07

Explanation:
(a) Unfunded debt includes current and floating debt. From 1926 to 1932 inclusive special assessment bonds were not included in either the unfunded or funded categories in the reports, and this omission explains why the total of the unfunded and funded debt does not equal the gross debt.
(b) Debt base includes assessed valuation of real and personal property.
(c) Net debt per capita is in dollars.
(d) Includes only 30 states.

Likewise, the state debt structure was generally sound. The proportion of unfunded debt to gross debt which rose to the level of 19.7 percent in 1921, was held to below 10 percent by 1930.[27] Also the proportion of deductions in the form of sinking fund assets to the gross debt was high from 17.9 percent in 1922 to 20.3 percent in 1926.[28] This figure indicates that about one-fifth of the debt of the state governments was covered by assets and could actually be reduced by that amount. The net debt of the state governments was well covered by the debt base in the form of the taxable property.[29] It should however, be noted that the ratio of this coverage declined from 178 times in 1915 to 69 times in 1932, due to the more rapid increase of net debt as compared with the debt base.[30] Also the net debt rose faster than the increase in population and so the per capita net debt moved from $4.31 in 1915 to $19.07 in 1932.[31] Thus the budgetary position and the debt structure of state governments showed satisfactory trends in the war and post-war periods.[32]

MUNICIPAL GOVERNMENT FINANCE

The trend of municipal government finance may be traced in Table 28.

In contrast to state government finance the trends in city government finance were unsatisfactory.[34] Revenues were generally exceeded by total expenditures[35] and so over the period there were almost continual deficits.[36] This unsatisfactory budget situation is also shown by the low ratio of revenues to total expenditures[37] which was continually below 100 percent, except in 1933, due to drastic reductions in expenditures. The proportion of interest on debt to total expenditures[38] was high, and averaged about 10 percent as compared with an average of about 4 percent for the state governments. The budgetary position of the cities became critical in the depression when they were confronted by the added problem of tax delinquencies. Cities could order tax levies, but it was another matter actually to collect them. Many taxpayers did not pay their bills, and there was thus a sharp rise in tax delinquencies. The percentage of such delinquencies of total tax levies rose from 10 percent in 1930 to a high of 26 percent in 1933 and then fell to 18 percent in 1935.[39] The debt structure of the cities also showed unsound tendencies. The proportion of the unfunded debt to the gross debt was generally high, and rose from 5.9 percent in 1927 to 12.3 percent in 1933. A number of cities followed the imprudent policy of increasing their unfunded debt by issuing short-term notes in the anticipation that these would be replaced at maturity with long-term bonds. However, unsatisfactory conditions in the money

TABLE 28

CITY GOVERNMENT FINANCE, 1915–1933.[33]

ITEMS (MILLION DOLLARS)	1915	1921	1922	1923	1924	1925	1926	1927	1928	1929	1930	1931	1932	1933
1. Revenues	940	1,280	2,007	2,132	2,323	2,509	2,739	2,946	3,120	3,075	3,419	3,420	2,597	2,507
2. Total expenditures	1,080	1,416	2,223	2,361	2,642	2,912	3,053	3,324	3,402	3,435	3,811	3,743	2,843	2,464
3. Balance	−140	−136	−216	−229	−319	−403	−314	−378	−282	−360	−392	−323	−246	43
4. Interest on debt	129	146	214	228	242	266	294	319	342	366	405	400	355	355
5. Unfunded debt (a)	240	385	412	467	473	456	494	466	502	667	828	859	1,006	1,045
6. Funded debt	2,900	3,174	4,629	4,862	5,325	5,828	6,376	6,895	7,332	7,755	8,612	8,175	7,055	7,125
7. Gross debt	3,305	3,704	5,268	5,580	6,096	6,651	7,284	7,848	8,308	8,961	10,018	9,587	8,427	8,489
8. Sinking fund assets	630	848	1,092	1,173	1,264	1,355	1,469	1,582	1,683	1,776	1,933	1,137	1,051	1,064
9. Net debt (b)	2,355	2,474	3,612	3,876	4,226	4,059	5,122	5,479	5,828	6,130	6,857	7,249	6,289	6,361
10. Debt base (b)	26,800	28,922	41,932	43,983	47,746	51,503	55,739	61,620	64,577	66,833	71,723	71,886	56,217	52,027
RATIO (PERCENT)														
A. Revenues to total expenditures (1÷2)	87.0	90.4	90.3	90.3	87.9	86.2	89.7	88.6	91.7	89.5	89.7	91.4	91.3	101.7
B. Interest on debt to total expenditures (4÷2)	11.9	10.3	9.6	9.7	9.2	9.1	9.6	9.6	10.1	10.7	10.6	10.7	12.5	14.4
C. Unfunded debt to gross debt (5÷7)	7.3	10.4	7.8	8.4	7.8	6.9	6.8	5.9	6.0	7.4	8.3	9.0	11.9	12.3
D. Sinking fund assets to gross debt (8÷7)	19.1	22.9	20.7	21.0	20.7	20.4	20.2	20.2	20.1	19.8	19.3	11.9	12.5	12.5
E. Debt base to net debt (10÷9)	1138.0	1169.0	1160.9	1134.8	1129.8	1105.5	1088.2	1124.7	1108.0	1090.3	1046.0	991.7	893.9	817.9
F. Net debt per capita (c)	$75.56	85.68	93.24	98.96	105.71	114.33	122.42	128.27	134.16	138.32	144.57	150.14	166.66	169.70

Explanation:

(a) Unfunded debt includes current and floating debt. From 1922 to 1933 inclusive special assessment bonds were omitted. See Table 27 Note (a).

(b) Debt base includes assessed valuation of real and personal property.

(c) Net debt per capita is in dollars.

market during the depression made it frequently impossible to carry out such refunding operations, and a number of cities faced serious financial embarrassment. The net debt per capita rose sharply from $75.56 in 1915 to $169.70 in 1933.[40] The unsound position of city debt is also seen in the fact that the coverage of the net debt by the debt base dropped from 11 times in 1922 to 8 times in 1933.[41] In the depression period in the case of certain cities there was a particularly sharp decline in assessed valuation.[42]

In this study consideration has been given only to the debt of cities. The same unsatisfactory trend of debt expansion occurred in the case of all classes of municipalities, including counties, towns, villages and school districts. The net debt of all municipalities rose from $3,476,000,000 in 1912 to $15,216,000,000 in 1932.[43]

These unsound trends in municipal finance inevitably led to widespread defaults. Even before the coming of the depression, there were two important series of defaults, for in 1926 and 1927 in the State of Washington 55 municipalities were forced into arrears on special assessment bonds which they had issued for street and road improvements.[44] The year 1927 marked the default on the bonds of a number of Florida municipalities which had over-extended their debt in relation to a debt base contracted by the collapse of real estate values. These two sets of defaults were merely the preliminaries of the more serious impairment of municipal credit which occurred in the depression years. By 1934 municipal defaults amounted to $2,000,000,000 out of a gross municipal bonded debt of $18,500,000,000 [45] and involved 2,000 out of a total of 175,000 local governments. In addition to these actual defaults, there were numerous cases of municipal insolvency since local governments all over the United States frequently committed technical defaults in using sinking funds to meet current expenses or in failing to turn over funds which were due to other governments.[46] However, unlike previous municipal defaults, there were few cases of outright repudiation, and most of the cities made commendable efforts to rehabilitate their financial position. After 1934 there was an improvement in municipal finance for the recovery in general business and the partial restoration of former real estate values enabled municipalities again to collect taxes. Also the cities generally made serious efforts to balance their budgets and to bring about a better adjustment between expenditures and revenues. The improvement in the capital market also enabled many cities to meet their maturing obligations and to convert their short-term notes into long-term issues at low rates of interest. These low rates, however, were the expression of an artificial money market and not the reflection of an actual improvement in municipal credit. In fact, American municipalities had not learned the lesson of the post-war and the depression years, for many cities again plunged into a new period of debt expansion and continued the same unsound tendencies which led to the difficulties after 1929. As a result, the way has been prepared for an even greater collapse of municipal debt in the coming years. Considering all these facts it is clear that the municipalities constituted one of the weakest elements in the debt structure of the United States.

TREND IN FOREIGN FINANCE

As noted in Chapter 11 the United States had invested in foreign securities as early as the last quarter of the nineteenth century, and by the beginning of the twentieth century it had purchased a considerable volume. During the Great War the American capital market absorbed a large volume of European government bonds, and in the decade of the twenties the volume of foreign investment was heavy. In various fields these investments did not bring losses. Canadian investments, outside of certain local issues, brought good returns, and, with the exception of China, the investments in the Far East as Japan and in Australia proved satisfactory. In general our security investments in the Scandinavian countries likewise proved safe, and those in France, Belgium and even Italy gave the holders a good return. On the other hand the security investments in Central and Eastern Europe and South America brought heavy losses to American holders. Since the financial position of the leading European countries were studied in Chapters 8 and 9, consideration will be given only to the quality of the investment in South America. The quality of such investments may be judged from Table 29 which presents the financial position of leading South American countries for the period from 1920 to 1930 when most of our investments were made.

In general Argentina was the soundest of all the South American governments which borrowed in the American security market. However, there were several flaws in the financial position of even this country. Total expenditures [48] increased faster than revenues,[49] showing a chronic deficit in the budget. The proportion of expenditures for debt service to total expenditures was large.[50] A further weakness was the large unfunded debt to total debt.[51] Although the government reduced the proportion from 36.8 percent in 1920 to 27.8 percent in 1930, the unfunded debt was still excessive and caused embarrassment in the depression when a considerable part of this debt matured. However a fairly diversified economy and the large white population enabled Argentina to bear the heavy per capita debt.

TABLE 29

SOUTH AMERICAN GOVERNMENT FINANCE, 1920 AND 1930.[47]

(changes in 1930 in percent as compared with 1920
as base = 100).

NUM-BER	ITEMS	COUNTRY					
		ARGEN-TINA	BOLIVIA	BRAZIL	CHILE	COLOM-BIA	PERU
1	Revenues....................	159.9	118.3	198.3	239.4	190.7	176.0
2	Total expenditures............	195.7	154.4	192.3	239.3	159.0	168.6
3	Debt service.................	185.3	188.0	270.2	188.2	138.5	430.5
4	Unfunded debt...............	125.7	56.8	476.0	.....	1300.0	913.0
5	Funded debt.................	190.7	240.2	170.6	291.5	200.0	413.2
6	Total debt...................	166.8	212.9	194.4	341.4	224.2	425.4
7	National wealth..............	72.4	120.0	89.7	115.4	160.0	.....

	RATIOS IN 1920 AND 1930							
A	Debt service to total expenditures (3÷2).....	1920	22.4	31.4	18.4	19.6	17.2	9.3
		1930	21.2	38.3	25.8	15.4	15.0	23.7
B	Unfunded debt to total debt (4÷6).........	1920	36.8	14.9	7.8	.....	2.2	2.4
		1930	27.8	4.0	19.1	14.6	12.7	5.2
C	National wealth to total debt (7÷6).........	1920	1038.1	1693.0	2756.7	1983.8	7692.3	.....
		1930	450.5	954.4	1271.5	670.4	5490.2	3735.1
D	Total debt per capita [(a)].	1920	$256.00	31.60	171.90	319.70	7.70	16.30
		1930	$288.40	62.86	239.44	1040.70	12.10	64.80

Explanation:
[(a)] Total debt per capita in dollars.

Bolivia had the poorest credit of any South American government. The budgetary situation, unsatisfactory from the start, became worse as total expenditures[52] rose faster than revenues.[53] Because of the increase in the debt, the expenditures for debt service absorbed over 38 percent of total expenditures by 1930.[54] Over the same period the total debt[55] more than doubled to 212.9 percent, while national wealth[56] rose only to 120 percent. The debt per capita rose to $62.86 which was a serious load for an almost improverished population.

Brazil had an uncertain financial history as a borrower even before it entered the New York security market. However, in the post-war period Brazil increased its debt service to 270.2 percent[57] as against an increase in revenues to only 198.3 percent.[58] Debt service, which had been responsible for 18.4 percent of total expenditures in 1920, accounted for 25.8 percent in 1930.[59] A further unsound tendency was the growth of the unfunded debt to 476.0 percent,[60] causing the proportion of the unfunded debt to total debt to rise from 7.8 percent to 19.1 percent.[61] The per capita debt in 1930 reached the high figure of $239.44.[62] These unfavorable tendencies were already apparent by 1926 and at that time the financial position of Brazil was doubtful.[63]

Chile for many years, had an excellent record in meeting its obligations. However, in the decade from 1920 to 1930 it expanded its total debt to 341 percent,[64] while national wealth rose only to 115.4 percent.[65] The per capita debt reached the abnormally large figure of $1,040.70 by 1930 and default soon followed.[66]

The statistics on the national government of Colombia do not indicate the true financial position of the country, due to the heavy financing undertaken by the provinces and cities. While the position of the national government was fairly satisfactory, the local governments borrowed without reason and so impaired the entire structure of Colombian credit.

Peru represented a flagrant case of overborrowing. While revenues increased only to 176 percent,[67] expenditures for debt service rose to 430.5 percent,[68] and by 1930 accounted for 23.7 percent of all expenditures.[69]

In general South American financing, undertaken mainly in the New York capital market in the nineteen-twenties, resulted in unsound debt expansion. Interest charges on these debts were so heavy that in most cases they could not possibly be met from revenues and were maintained for a time only by new loans from abroad. When the flow of new capital ceased default on the old loans was inevitable.

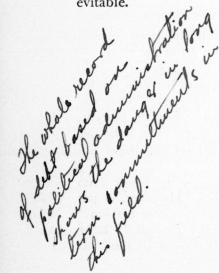

The whole record of debt based on our administration of political administration is long shows the danger in term commitments in this field.

CHAPTER 17

SECURITY POLICIES

THE two previous chapters undertook a qualitative analysis of the trends of the demand for capital by corporations and governments in the post-war period. This chapter presents a qualitative study of the trends of the supply of capital in the post-war years as expressed in the security policies of investors. Consideration will be first given to the distribution of the various types of securities among the several classes of investors, to their investment policies and finally to whether these policies were successful in maintaining the principal of these investments.

DISTRIBUTION ACCORDING TO SECURITIES

The distribution of securities among investors may be studied according to the securities and according to the investors. According to securities, the distribution may be analyzed first by the various classes of securities, as those of the railway and public utility corporations or the federal and local governments, and by the form of securities as stocks or bonds. Statistics on the distribution of the classes of stocks are not available but data on the distribution of the classes of bonds are obtainable. Table 30 shows the distribution of the holdings of the funded debt of various classes of issuers as of 1932.

From this table it is seen that the banks held about one-half of the federal debt in 1932. Large holders of state, city and local governmental bonds were the banks which naturally grant liberal advances to their own local governments. Individuals with net income above $5,000 also were large holders of local government bonds because of their tax-exempt features. Life insurance companies owned the largest proportion of railway bonds, banks came next in importance, and a considerable portion of the railroad debt was held in trust funds. Trust funds accounted for the largest proportion of utility bond holdings, while banks and insurance companies held almost the same amount. The proportion of the total of utility bonds held by the banks and life insurance companies was much smaller than the proportion of the total of railroad bonds held by these institutions. In the case of each class of bonds, the issuers themselves possessed a portion of their own obligations. The

TABLE 30

DISTRIBUTION OF HOLDINGS OF FUNDED DEBT IN THE UNITED STATES, 1932.[1]
(percent)

HOLDERS	FEDERAL[a]	STATES, CITIES AND LOCAL	RAILWAY	PUBLIC UTILITY
Issuers themselves...............	5.68[b]	19.4[c]	7.6[d]	2.98[e]
Mutual savings, national and other banks.................	48.83	15.5	19.6	10.05
Life insurance companies[j]......	4.07	4.7	23.3	11.87
Other insurance companies......	1.70	5.1	3.8	2.38
Philanthropic institutions[k].....	.34	....	4.1[(f)]	3.45[(f)]
Trust funds...................	.85[g]	....	12.0[h]	17.52
Individuals with net income $5000 or over...............	6.85[i]	14.4	....	....
Unaccounted for..............	31.68	40.9	29.6	51.75
Total.................	100.00	100.00	100.00	100.00

Explanation:

[a] As of June 30, 1934.

[b] Funds administered by the Treasury and held by governmental corporations and credit agencies.

[c] State, local government and public trust funds.

[d] Railways other than issuing companies.

[e] Public utilities other than issuing companies.

[f] Public welfare foundations and educational institutions.

[g] Includes investments of states and municipalities.

[h] Individual trust accounts.

[i] Figure for 1933.

[j] Legal Reserve Life Insurance Companies holding 92 percent of assets of all legal reserve life insurance companies.

[k] Universities, foundations and charitable institutions.

federal government invested a large part of its surplus funds in its own obligations, the state, city and local governments, particularly, purchased a large volume of their own bonds especially for their sinking funds, and the railroads held a considerable volume of the securities of other roads, while utilities had only a small proportion of their funds in utility bonds.

The changes in the distribution of security holdings from year to year may be traced in the case of the bonds of the federal government, and these changes indicated in Table 31 show the distribution in the holdings of the United States government bonds from 1917 to 1934 in percent of the total.

This table groups the holders of United States Government securities into three classes, namely Federal Reserve banks, all other banks and "others" or non-banking holders which include individuals, corporations, and non-banking investment institutions as life insurance companies. From these figures it is seen that the distribution of the holdings of the federal debt from 1917 passed through three successive stages, namely from 1917 to 1920, 1920 to 1930 and from 1930 to 1935. During the first stage, the debt was

TABLE 31

DISTRIBUTION OF HOLDINGS OF UNITED STATES GOVERNMENT BONDS, 1917–1934.

(percent of total)

YEAR (JUNE 30)	FEDERAL RESERVE BANKS	BANKS[a]	OTHERS[b]
1917	2.39	33.01	64.60
1918	2.11	21.01	76.88
1919	.91	16.33	82.76
1920	1.45	13.76	84.79
1921	1.08	16.15	82.77
1922	2.42	15.24	82.34
1923	.46	18.84	80.70
1924	2.03	21.71	76.26
1925	1.72	20.38	77.90
1926	1.96	20.67	77.37
1927	2.00	20.69	77.31
1928	1.34	23.59	75.07
1929	1.28	23.76	74.96
1930	3.65	23.77	72.58
1931	3.98	34.03	61.99
1932	9.15	33.13	57.72
1933	8.87	34.59	56.54
1934	8.99	43.11	47.90

1940

Explanation:
[a] Includes national banks, state banks, loan and trust companies, stock savings, mutual savings, private banks in the United States and possessions.
[b] Obtained by deducting holdings of Federal Reserve banks and of banks from the total.

held mainly by non-banking investors. During the War the federal government distributed its issues as widely as possible. The first loan had 4,000,000 subscribers but by the fourth the number of subscribers had increased to 22,700,000.[3] As a result, in 1920 almost 85 percent of the federal debt was held by investors other than the banks and the Federal Reserve banks.

The second stage in the distribution of the federal debt came in the period from 1920 to 1930. As the total of the federal debt declined from 1920 to 1929, there was relatively little change in the holdings by the Federal Reserve banks, while non-banking investors reduced and banking institutions increased their holdings.

The third stage in the distribution of United States Government bonds in the post-war period came after 1930. While there was an increase in the dollar amount of holdings by non-banking investors, the percentage held by this group dropped after 1930, the amount held by the Federal Reserve banks and particularly by banking institutions rose sharply. In other words, the enormous increase in the federal debt after 1930 was largely absorbed by the banking institutions of the country.[4]

SECURITY DISTRIBUTION ACCORDING TO FORM

The distribution of securities may be viewed not only from the standpoint of the various classes of issuers but also from the standpoint of the form of securities, as stocks or bonds. The direct investment by individuals in stocks developed rapidly after the beginning of the century. It was estimated that the number of book stockholders in the United States increased from 8,600,000 in 1917 to 12,000,000 in 1920 and to 18,000,000 in 1928.[5] These figures contain a margin of error, for the same individual may appear a number of times as a stockholder in different companies. Joseph S. McCoy, actuary in the United States Treasury Department, made an estimate based on income tax returns in 1924 that only 2,358,000 separate individuals owned stocks.[6] Another estimate placed the number of actual stockholders at the higher figures of from 5,000,000 to 6,000,000 in 1927 and from 9,000,000 to 11,000,000 in 1930.[7]

These direct holdings of stocks were widely diffused among the American people and were owned not only by persons with large incomes but also by those with moderate incomes. Warshaw claimed that persons with incomes under $20,000 in 1921 were receiving 53.2 percent of dividends paid by corporations.[8] McCoy estimated that persons with incomes of less than $12,500 in 1924 owned 50 percent of all the corporate stock.[9] Although there is thus a difference in maximum income figures, it would seem from both studies that the middle class in economic society in the period preceding the depression possessed about one-half ownership in American corporations, and this movement constituted an important change in the history of property ownership. The trend toward the diffusion of security ownership continued in the period after 1929. R. G. Dun & Company in a study of the trend in security ownership from the fall of 1929 to 1932 for more than 400 corporations showed that the holders of the common stock of these companies increased

by more than 40 percent.[10]   In the case of 50 leading corporations
the number of book stockholders increased about 100 percent from
1929 to 1932.[11]

The holding of bonds was less diffused than that of stocks.
McCoy estimated that only 1,300,000 persons held bonds in 1924.[12]
In the depression period the study of R. G. Dun & Company
showed that the number of registered bondholders decreased.[13]

SECURITY DISTRIBUTION ACCORDING TO INSTITUTIONAL HOLDERS

The distribution of securities in the post-war period may also
be studied by viewing the subject from the standpoint of the institutional holders of the securities, as trustees, philanthropic institutions, national banks, savings banks, and insurance companies.
Not only was security investment becoming more widespread among
individual holders but also among institutional investors. With the
exception of the mutual savings banks, financial institutions including national banks, state banks, loan and trust companies, private
banks, stock savings banks, increased the proportion of security investments to their total assets. The proportion for all these financial
institutions rose from 25 percent in 1920 to 42 percent in 1935.[14]

The proportion of security investments to the total of trust funds
of a large group of trusts rose from 82 percent in 1920 to 97 percent
in 1931.[15]   These trusts for the years 1919 to 1931 on the average
placed 27.2 percent of their total investments in bonds, 7.0 percent
in preferred stock, 33.5 percent in common stock 18.7 percent in
real estate obligations, 11.0 percent in real estate directly and 2.6
percent in miscellaneous assets.[16]   The obligations of the federal
government composed only 3 percent of their total investments while
state and municipal bonds averaged 9 percent, railroad bonds 7.5 percent and utility bonds 4.5 percent.

The distribution of the investments of institutions of higher education is difficult to study, because of the lack of published data.
The leading universities and colleges in 1929 invested up to 49.8
percent of their endowment funds in bonds. Of this total only 3.3
percent was placed in United States Government and 0.9 percent in
municipal bonds. On the other hand, utility bonds accounted for
17.9 percent and railroad bonds 16.2 percent, while real estate obligations amounted to 0.8 percent, industrial bonds 8.3 percent and
foreign bonds 2.5 percent. Preferred stock constituted 7.8 percent,
and common stock only 10 percent. Real estate mortgages, a survival
of the investment of individual capitalism, still accounted for 13.5
percent.[17]

TABLE 32

DISTRIBUTION OF SECURITY INVESTMENTS OF NATIONAL BANKS, 1910–1935.[18]

(percent of total security investments)

YEAR	RAILROAD	UTILITY	OTHER SECURITIES	STOCK	UNITED STATES GOVERN- MENT	MUNICIPAL	FOREIGN
1910	18.5	9.5	13.0	2.3	45.8	10.0	0.9
1915	18.3	10.6	12.0	7.1	37.9	11.8	2.3
1920	9.9	6.8	12.5	2.7	54.2	8.1	5.8
1921	10.1	6.9	14.7	3.3	50.1	9.8	5.1
1922	10.7	7.0	14.8	2.8	50.1	9.1	5.5
1923	9.9	6.6	14.9	2.8	53.1	7.9	4.8
1924	11.2	7.7	15.0	2.9	48.3	9.8	5.1
1925	11.8	8.6	15.9	2.7	44.3	10.4	6.3
1926	10.8	9.3	17.2	2.9	42.3	11.1	6.4
1927	10.3	10.2	17.9	2.7	40.6	11.6	6.7
1928	9.5	10.4	17.4	2.7	40.5	11.8	7.7
1929	8.9	10.4	16.9	2.9	42.1	11.4	7.4
1930	9.6	11.4	16.7	3.1	40.0	11.5	7.7
1931	9.4	10.8	15.4	2.8	42.4	13.0	6.2
1932	9.1	9.5	12.9	2.8	46.6	14.3	4.8
1933	7.2	7.2	10.2	2.6	54.7(a)	14.5	3.6
1934	5.7	5.6	4.5	2.5	66.5(a)	13.1	2.1
1935	5.5	5.0	3.8	2.2	69.0(a)	13.1	1.4

Explanation
(a) Includes quasi-public obligations.

INVESTMENTS OF NATIONAL BANKS

The distribution of the security investments of commercial banks may be studied from Table 32 which shows the distribution for national banks only.[19] National banks wisely reduced their holdings of railroad bonds, while the proportion of utility securities rose. The proportion of all other bonds and stocks which included industrial and investment trust securities rose from 12 percent in 1915 to a high of 17.9 percent in 1927 and then declined sharply to only 3.8 percent in 1935.

The holdings of United States Government bonds were always large in the case of national banks, due to the use of these bonds as a basis for issuing circulating notes and for obtaining advances from the Federal Reserve banks. The proportion increased from 37.9 percent in 1915 to 54.2 percent in 1920 as the national banks absorbed a large proportion of the government bonds issued during the War. The proportion declined to 40.5 percent in 1928 and then rose to 69 percent in 1935. The holdings of municipal bonds increased from 10 percent in 1910 to a high of 14.5 percent in 1933. The proportion of foreign bonds including Canadian securities rose from 0.9 percent in 1910 to a high of 7.7 percent in 1928 and then declined to 1.4 percent in 1935.

TABLE 33

DISTRIBUTION OF SECURITY INVESTMENTS OF MUTUAL SAVINGS BANKS, 1890–1935.[20]

(per cent of total security investments)

YEAR	RAILROAD	UTILITY	OTHER SECURITIES	UNITED STATES GOVERNMENT	MUNICIPAL	FOREIGN
1890	$14.3^{(c)}$	....	20.3	22.0	43.4	...
1895	$16.3^{(c)}$	....	15.1	15.3	53.3	...
1900	$20.4^{(c)}$	....	24.6	9.8	45.2	...
1905	$22.1^{(c)}$	....	67.6	.9	9.4	...
1910	45.2	5.2	$5.4^{(d)}$	1.4	42.7	.1
1915	43.7	5.8	4.1	.9	45.5	...
1920	19.5	3.9	56.1	13.6	6.9	...
1921	30.7	4.0	11.7	31.4	22.2	...
1922	20.1	4.7	51.0	15.9	8.3	...
1923	18.4	4.6	53.8	16.7	6.5	...
1924	31.4	6.7	6.6	36.3	19.0	...
1925	18.9	7.0	51.4	18.0	4.7	...
1926	19.0	8.1	51.5	14.8	6.6	...
1927	18.5	10.6	51.6	6.3	13.0	...
1928	$18.4^{(e)}$	12.7	50.7	5.4	12.8	...
1929	$31.1^{(e)}$	....	49.0	4.7	13.5	1.7
1930	$32.2^{(e)}$	....	49.9	4.0	12.2	1.7
1931	$30.5^{(e)}$	....	52.9	3.5	11.5	1.6
1932	$52.2^{(e)}$	....	7.2	12.7	26.3	1.6
1933	$52.0^{(e)}$	....	6.0	13.4	26.9	1.7
1934	$51.6^{(b)}$	....	....	$25.3^{(a)}$	21.5	1.6
1935	$43.9^{(b)}$	....	....	$35.1^{(a)}$	19.6	1.4

Explanation:
(a) Includes quasi public obligations.
(b) Includes utility and other securities.
(c) Includes railroad stocks.
(d) Includes stocks.
(e) Includes utilities.

INVESTMENTS OF MUTUAL SAVINGS BANKS

The distribution of the security investments of mutual savings banks is shown in Table 33. These banks carried a large proportion of their funds in railroad bonds despite the weakening credit of the carriers. When utility bonds were made legal for investment, they became an important part of the portfolio of the mutual savings banks. In the post-war period they reduced their holdings of United

States Government bonds to a low of 3.5 percent until 1931, after which year the proportion rose to over 35 percent. The proportion of municipal bonds fluctuated widely but later increased and constituted about a fifth of the total security investments. Foreign bonds were negligible.

INVESTMENTS OF LIFE INSURANCE COMPANIES

The distribution of the investments of life insurance companies is presented in Table 34.

TABLE 34

DISTRIBUTION OF SECURITY INVESTMENTS OF LIFE INSURANCE COMPANIES, 1924–1935.[21]

(per cent of total security investments)

YEAR	BONDS							STOCK		
	RAIL-ROAD-	UTILITY	INDUS-TRIAL	UNITED STATES GOVERN-MENT	MUNICI-PAL	FOR-EIGN	TOTAL	PRE-FERRED	COM-MON	TOTAL STOCK
1924	51.8	11.3	2.5	17.2	8.6	6.7	98.1	0.3	1.6	1.9
1925	51.3	14.5	2.6	14.7	8.3	6.6	98.0	0.3	1.7	2.0
1926	52.4	18.1	2.6	10.8	7.6	6.5	98.0	0.3	1.7	2.0
1927	50.9	21.3	3.2	8.8	7.1	6.8	98.1	0.5	1.4	1.9
1928	48.5	23.0	4.2	7.1	7.5	6.7	97.0	2.1	0.9	3.0
1929	46.5	22.7	4.1	5.3	9.1	6.9	94.6	3.9	1.5	5.4
1930	44.0	23.8	4.8	4.7	9.0	6.7	93.0	5.4	1.6	7.0
1931	41.9	23.8	4.9	5.1	10.0	6.8	92.5	6.0	1.5	7.5
1932	40.9	23.5	4.8	6.0	10.6	6.8	92.6	6.0	1.4	7.4
1933	38.0	22.5	4.5	10.9	11.0	6.2	93.1	5.5	1.4	6.9
1934	32.5	20.2	4.7	19.9	11.7	5.2	94.2	4.7	1.1	5.8
1935	28.1	20.1	5.2	24.8	11.7	4.8	94.7	4.3	1.0	5.3

From this table it is seen that the funds of life insurance companies, notwithstanding the liberal provisions in the laws governing their investment, were largely placed in bonds rather than in stocks. The insurance companies wisely decreased the proportion of their holdings of railroad bonds and increased the proportion of utility bonds. Their holdings of federal bonds declined relatively in importance from 17 percent in 1924 to a low of 4.7 percent in 1930, after which the proportion began to rise again reaching 24 percent in 1935. There was also a moderate rise in the holdings of municipal bonds through the depression years. The holdings of foreign bonds remained fairly constant and unimportant. The equity holdings of the insurance companies consisted mainly of preferred stocks, of which the proportion rose to 6 percent in 1932 and then declined slightly. Common stock holdings were insignificant.

RESULTS OF POLICIES OF FINANCIAL INSTITUTIONS

The purpose of this section is to determine whether or not the various groups of investors in recent years were able successfully to shape their policies to meet the changing conditions of the security markets so as to retain the principal of their security investments. In other words, were the results of the system of security capitalism in the post-war period satisfactory from the standpoint of the investors?

It is impossible to appraise precisely the results of the investment policies of individuals, corporations, trustees and philanthropic institutions as groups. However approximations of the results of the policies of the various classes of financial institutions may be made.[22]

The security investments of each group of financial institutions, including mutual savings banks, stock savings banks, state banks, national banks, loan and trust companies, and life insurance companies, as reported in various statistical publications, were tabulated according to the forms of securities, namely, bonds, common and preferred stock, and these in turn were separated into classes of issuers as United States and municipal government, railroad, utility and industrial corporations as well as foreign issuers. The average prices of each of these classes of securities for the years from 1920 to 1935 were obtained from the Standard Statistics Service. These average security prices were then used to compute the probable appreciation or depreciation in the value of each class of investment a year later. An obvious margin of error lies in the assumption that holdings did not change in the year. However, this margin of error is probably small, in view of the relatively limited variation in the holdings throughout the year compared with the total of the holdings. A second margin of error lies in the assumption that the securities held by the institutions varied with the Standard Statistics index. However, this index was composed largely of high-grade active securities, while many of the institutions held medium and even low-grade securities, and so the variation in price may have been even greater. Therefore this margin of error would tend to strengthen rather than weaken the conclusions which follow.

The results of this study are given in Tables 35 and 36 showing the net change in dollars in the investments of financial institutions in the period from 1920 to 1934 by years and by securities as determined by the net change in dollars.

Table 35 shows that the financial institutions suffered losses in 1922 arising out of the primary post-war depression. The next four years showed a moderate appreciation but in the two years before the crash of 1929 the investment experience of financial institutions

TABLE 35

INVESTMENT EXPERIENCE OF FINANCIAL INSTITUTIONS, BY YEARS, 1920–1934.[23]

(Net change in million dollars)

YEAR	NATIONAL BANKS	STATE BANKS	LOAN AND TRUST COMPANIES	STOCK SAVINGS BANKS	MUTUAL SAVINGS BANKS	LIFE INSURANCE COMPANIES			TOTAL
						BONDS	STOCKS	TOTAL	
1920	51	26	23	3	41	260	....	260	404
1921	435	254	210	7	338	99	6	105	1349
1922	−76	−28	−27	−4	−34	−30	....	−30	−199
1923	111	31	33	5	74	98	....	98	352
1924	89	60	62	7	56	39	12	51	325
1925	24	31	33	3	49	87	5	92	232
1926	46	13	16	2	56	117	23	140	273
1927	−13	−15	−10	−1	5	−138	24	−114	−148
1928	−195	−75	−84	−9	−117	−33	−12	−45	−525
1929	179	67	69	8	95	98	−51	47	465
1930	149	−37	−74	−7	−5	−834	−114	−948	−922
1931	−1276	−703	−820	−97	−789	32	−47	−15	−3700
1932	592	312	373	57	311	143	77	220	1865
1933	469	146	238	28	374	714	81	795	2050
1934	299	66	131	16	83	157	61	218	813
Net change	884	148	173	18	537	809	65	874	2634

TABLE 36

INVESTMENT EXPERIENCE OF FINANCIAL INSTITUTIONS, BY SECURITIES, 1920–1934.

(Net change in million dollars)

CLASSES OF SECURITIES	NATIONAL BANKS	STATE BANKS	LOAN AND TRUST COMPANIES	STOCK SAVINGS BANKS	MUTUAL SAVINGS BANKS	LIFE INSURANCE COMPANIES			TOTAL
						BONDS	STOCKS	TOTAL	
Railroad ...	16	−4	9	....	204	134	−14	120	345
Utility.....	78	25	39	2	133(b)	182	−4	178	455
Industrial..	11	−44	−130	−12	−270(b)	54	22	76	−369
U. S. Govt..	607	108	204	16	186	188	....	188	1,309
Municipal..	200	71	67	12	276	218	....	218	844
Foreign....	−28	−8	−16	....	8	33	....	33	−11
Total...	884	148	173	18	537	809	65(a)	874(a)	2,634(a)

Explanation:
   (a) Includes gain of $61,000,000 in preferred shares held by insurance companies.
   (b) In the case of securities carried by mutual savings banks as "all other stocks and bonds," the index for all bonds was taken since it was assumed that most of these securities were bonds and not stocks.

was unsatisfactory owing to the drop in bond prices. The losses in
1930 were heavy but in 1931 they were staggering and for this year
alone amounted to $3,700,000,000. Over the next three years there
was a considerable recovery, and these losses were overcome.

Table 36 shows the investment experience of financial institutions according to the classes of their securities. From this table it
will be seen that the absolute dollar losses on foreign bonds were
small while the losses on industrial securities were high.[24] Railroad,
utility and municipal securities showed good results. The most satisfactory investment experience of financial institutions came from
their holdings of United States Government bonds. In fact the
rapid recovery in the price of these bonds in the period after 1932
was the determining factor in bringing about a net appreciation in
the value of the investments of the financial institutions.

Table 37 shows the proportion of the losses of these various

TABLE 37

LOSSES ON SECURITIES TO NET CAPITAL OF FINANCIAL INSTITUTIONS, 1931.

INSTITUTION	NET CAPITAL[b] (MILLION DOLLARS)	LOSSES ON SECURITIES (MILLION DOLLARS)	LOSSES ON SECURITIES TO NET CAPITAL (PERCENT)
National banks...........	$2,704	$1,276	47.19
State banks..............	1,288	703	54.58
Stock savings bank.......	49	97	197.96
Mutual savings banks......	945	789	83.49
Loan and trust companies..	2,227	820	36.82
Life insurance companies[a].	1,277[c]	948	74.24
Total................	$8,490	$4,633	54.57

Explanation:
[a] For 1930.
[b] Net capital is capital, surplus and undivided profits less bank buildings and real estate.
[c] In the case of the life insurance companies, the net reserves are considered as a basis for net capital, and losses are those on all operations.

classes of financial institutions in relation to their net capital for the
year 1931 when losses were heaviest.

From this table it is seen that the losses on securities in 1931
absorbed 47.19 percent of the net capital of the national banks as a
whole, 54.58 percent of the state banks, 197.96 percent or a sum
almost twice as large as the net capital of the stock savings banks,
83.49 percent of the mutual savings banks and 36.82 percent of the
capital of the loan and trust companies.[25] The table also reveals

that the life insurance companies by 1930 had lost approximately 74.24 percent of their net reserves.

The conclusion derived from this study indicate that the system of security capitalism from the standpoint of the various classes of institutional investors functioned very uncertainly in the post-war period. A continuation of the depreciation in security prices after 1931 would have seriously impaired the solvency of the financial institutions.

It seems true these analyses show clearly that in the case of every form of financial institution — none of them bought heavily of Governments when they should have, in preference to other forms of securities.

CHAPTER 18

A FINANCIAL STATEMENT

THE trend of corporate and of government finance was analyzed by presenting a financial statement and by applying ratios to this statement. In similar manner a financial statement of American security capitalism in the post-war period may be presented, and ratios may be employed to study the trends of the system. Such a financial statement of American security capitalism in the post-war period is presented in Table 38.

NATIONAL INCOME

The national income of the American people, after dropping from $75,000,000,000 in 1920 to $59,400,000,000 in 1921, rose to the high of $84,100,000,000 in 1929. With the coming of the depression the total fell to $73,300,0000,000 in 1930, to $56,000,000,000 in 1931 and to a low of $38,800,000,000 in 1933. The ensuing business recovery brought national income back to $47,800,000,000 in 1934 and to $53,100,000,000 in 1935.[2]

SAVING FUNDS

There are as yet no complete statistics which state the exact amount of national saving available for security investment, but the trend may be studied from the volume of the saving funds with financial institutions including the various classes of banks, life insurance companies and building and loan associations. This total rose sharply from $20,900,000,000 in 1920 to $52,600,000,000 in 1931 and fell to $44,500,000,000 in 1933 [3] with a recovery to $46,-000,000,000 in 1934. Under security capitalism saving comes not only from individuals but also from corporations. Corporate saving is the amount of annual net earnings of domestic corporations and other business organizations not declared as dividends but credited to surplus. According to the estimates of Fabricant the total annual corporate saving was generally above $2,000,000,000 annually from 1920 to 1929, but in the depression years there was a continuous deficit which amounted to over $7,000,000,000 in 1932.[4]

273

TABLE 38

FINANCIAL STATEMENT OF AMERICAN SECURITY CAPITALISM, 1920–1935.[1]

(billion dollars)

YEAR	NATIONAL INCOME (a)	SAVING FUNDS (b)	NEW SECUR-ITIES (c)	INTEREST ON BONDED DEBT (d)	BONDED DEBT (e)	TOTAL SECURITIES OUT-STANDING (f)	NATIONAL WEALTH (g)
	1	2	3	4	5	6	7
1920	75.0	20.9	3.6		55.7		488.7
1921	59.4	24.2	3.6	4.3	58.4		317.2
1922	60.3	25.4	4.3	4.3	61.0		320.8
1923	70.8	28.0	4.3	4.6	64.1		339.9
1924	71.3	30.5	5.6	4.7	67.0		337.9
1925	75.6	33.5	6.2	4.8	61.2	136.2	362.3
1926	80.2	38.8	6.3	5.2	61.6	146.2	356.5
1927	78.1	43.1	7.8	5.6	67.7	159.6	346.4
1928	81.0	48.0	8.1	5.7	73.3	169.1	360.1
1929	84.1	50.1	10.2	6.1	76.9	182.1	361.8
1930	73.3	52.0	7.0	6.0	81.4	187.6	323.1
1931	56.0	52.6	3.1	5.6	81.7	180.7	275.1
1932	39.2	48.1	4.3	5.1	83.5	181.0	246.4
1933	38.8	44.5	3.7		85.2	177.7	252.3
1934	47.8	46.0	6.2		92.3		289.2
1935	53.1		4.9		96.9		308.9

(percent)

YEAR	NEW SECURITIES TO SAVING FUNDS (3 ÷ 2)	INTEREST ON BONDED DEBT TO NATIONAL INCOME (4 ÷ 1)	BONDED DEBT TO TOTAL OUTSTANDING SECURITIES (5 ÷ 6)	NATIONAL WEALTH TO BONDED DEBT (7 ÷ 5)	TOTAL SECURITIES OUTSTANDING TO NATIONAL WEALTH (6 ÷ 7)
	A	B	C	D	E
1920	17.2			877.4	
1921	14.9	7.2		543.2	
1922	16.9	7.1		525.9	
1923	15.4	6.5		530.3	
1924	18.4	6.6		504.3	
1925	18.5	6.3	44.9	592.0	37.6
1926	16.2	6.5	42.1	578.7	41.0
1927	18.1	7.2	42.4	511.7	46.1
1928	16.9	7.0	43.3	491.3	47.0
1929	20.4	7.3	42.2	470.5	50.3
1930	13.5	8.2	43.4	396.9	58.1
1931	5.9	10.0	45.2	336.7	65.7
1932	8.9	13.0	46.1	295.1	73.5
1933	8.3		47.9	296.1	70.4
1934	13.5			313.3	
1935				318.8	

1940

NEW SECURITIES

The demand for capital comes from sources which may or may not issue securities for the purpose of obtaining such capital. This study is concerned only with the demand for capital through the issue of securities. Securities may be issued for the purpose either of obtaining new capital or of refunding issues which have matured. These refunding issues do not represent the absorption of new capital and so are not included in the computation given in Table 38. The deduction of this item from the total of new security issues gives the amount of net capital demand arising from the issue of securities as shown in column 3 of Table 38.[5]

From these figures it is seen that the volume of new securities rose almost continuously after 1920, reaching a peak of $10,200,-000,000 in 1929 and then fell off sharply.

Table 39 shows the items which made up the total of new securities and indicates in detail the trend of the capital market in the post-war period according to issuers both in dollar amounts and in percent. The volume of securities issued by the railroads remained comparatively steady with the exception of the years 1924 and 1930. On the other hand, the volume of securities placed by the utilities increased rapidly from a low of $382,000,000 in 1920 to a high of $2,365,000,000 in 1930. The volume issued by industrial corporations was well sustained from 1925 to 1930 at over a billion dollars annually and rose to $1,928,000,000 in 1929. Real estate securities, which had been small until the post-war period, rose to $715,000,000 by 1925, and continued at a high level through 1928 when the realty boom began to slacken. Investment trust securities, practically unknown before 1925, rose to $787,000,000 in 1928 and to a peak of $2,222,000,000 in 1929. After 1930, the volume of railroad, utility, industrial, real estate and investment trust issues fell off sharply. The issues of the Federal government dropped continuously until 1930 and then rose sharply to $3,152,000,000 in 1932 and $5,164,-000,000 in 1934. Municipal financing from 1921 to 1930 held at a level of well over a billion dollars annually. Foreign securities moved irregularly upward until 1927 when they rose to $827,000,000. In the following years they moved intermittently and were negligible after 1930.[7]

The percentage distribution of these securities indicates several interesting trends in the capital market in the post-war period. Railroad securities, after 1924, with the exception of 1930, were a minor factor in the capital market. This situation was in direct contrast to the pre-war period, and when railroad issues had dominated the capital market. Their place in the corporate field was taken mainly

Table 39

New Securities—According to Issuers, 1920–1935

(million dollars)

YEAR ENDING DEC. 31	RAIL-ROAD	PUBLIC UTILITY	INDUS-TRIAL	REAL ESTATE	INVESTMENT TRUST	UNITED STATES GOVERNMENT (a)	MUNIC-IPAL (b)	FOREIGN GOVERNMENT (a)	MISCEL-LANEOUS	TOTAL
1920	322	382	1,593	91	...	16	672	236	322	3,634
1921	353	492	784	50	...	147	1,194	411	144	3,575
1922	524	721	675	162	...	395	1,060	489	247	4,273
1923	465	888	896	251	...	346	1,043	213	202	4,304
1924	780	1,326	690	333	...	188	1,354	706	193	5,570
1925	380	1,481	1,098	715	15	177	1,352	590	411	6,219
1926	346	1,598	1,197	709	71	102	1,344	542	436	6,345
1927	506	2,065	1,280	630	175	98	1,475	827	734	7,790
1928	364	1,811	1,407	716	787	70	1,379	586	994	8,114
1929	547	1,932	1,928	520	2,222	5	1,418	120	1,490	10,182
1930	797	2,365	1,070	245	233	97	1,434	548	234	7,023
1931	346	949	272	129	4	77	1,235	41	63	3,116
1932	13	274	17	8	1	3,152	761	26	12	4,264
1933	12	34	113	1	1	3,087	483	0	1	3,732
1934	73	49	26	0	19	5,164	803	0	11	6,145
1935	73	84	213	2	2	3,638	855	0	30	4,897

(percent of total)

1920	8.86	10.51	43.85	2.50	....	0.44	18.49	6.49	8.86	100.00
1921	9.87	13.76	21.94	1.40	....	4.11	33.40	11.50	4.02	100.00
1922	12.26	16.87	15.80	3.79	....	9.24	24.82	11.44	5.78	100.00
1923	10.80	20.63	20.82	5.83	....	8.04	24.24	4.95	4.69	100.00
1924	14.00	23.81	12.39	5.98	....	3.38	24.30	12.68	3.46	100.00
1925	6.11	23.81	17.66	11.50	0.24	2.85	21.73	9.49	6.61	100.00
1926	5.45	25.19	18.87	11.17	1.12	1.61	21.18	8.54	6.87	100.00
1927	6.50	26.50	16.43	8.09	2.25	1.26	18.93	10.62	9.42	100.00
1928	4.49	22.32	17.34	8.82	9.70	0.86	17.00	7.22	12.25	100.00
1929	5.37	18.97	18.94	5.11	21.83	0.04	13.93	1.18	14.63	100.00
1930	11.35	33.68	15.24	3.49	3.32	1.38	20.41	7.80	3.33	100.00
1931	11.10	30.46	8.72	4.14	0.13	2.47	39.64	1.32	2.02	100.00
1932	0.30	6.43	0.40	0.19	0.02	73.92	17.85	0.61	0.28	100.00
1933	0.32	0.91	3.03	0.03	0.03	82.71	12.94	0.00	0.03	100.00
1934	1.19	0.80	0.42	0.00	0.30	84.04	13.07	0.00	0.18	100.00
1935	1.49	1.72	4.35	0.04	0.04	74.29	17.46	0.00	0.61	100.00

Explanation:

(a) Includes U.S. Government, Farm Loan and Government agencies as well as U.S. Possessions.

(b) Municipal securities include state issues.

(c) The *Chronicle* carries Canadian securities separately, but for the purpose of this table they have been included with foreign securities.

by the utilities which accounted for the largest percentage of all the corporate issues. Industrial issues after 1920 ranged from a high of 20.82 percent in 1923 to a low of 0.40 percent in 1932. Investment trusts experienced only one big year, 1929, when they accounted for 21.83 percent of the total. The proportion of federal government issues fell from 9.24 percent in 1922 to .04 percent in 1929, rose to 73.92 percent in 1932 and to 84.04 percent in 1934. Municipal securities continued to account for a high proportion of the total throughout the entire period.[8]

INTEREST ON BONDED DEBT

The interest payment on the bonded debt in the United States was $4,299,000,000 in 1921, rose to a high of $6,062,000,000 in 1929 and then fell to $5,109,000,000 in 1932.[10] The separate amounts which composed these totals are presented in Table 40. The trend of interest payment on corporate debt rose from $3,069,000,000 in 1922 to a high of $4,924,000,000 in 1929. This rapid increase was due to the extensive issuance of new corporate securities over these years. On the other hand the trend of interest payment on the federal debt reached a high of $1,056,000,000 in 1923 and then declined to $599,000,000 in 1932. The decline until 1930 was due to the reduction of the Federal debt, while the drop from 1930 to 1932 was due to the lower cost at which the government was able to undertake its borrowing. Although the total of the federal debt expanded in 1931 and 1932, the government floated a large proportion of short-term issues on which the rate of interest was low. However, after 1932 the interest burden on the federal debt rose, and reached $689,000,000 in 1933 and was $757,000,000 in 1934. The interest charge of the state debt rose very sharply from $13,000,000 in 1921 to $94,000,000 in 1929 and in the depression period continued upward to $112,000,000 in 1932. Likewise the interest charge on the municipal debt rose from $146,000,000 in 1921 to $366,000,-000 in 1929 and continued upward to $355,000,000 in 1932. A study of the percentage distribution of these interest payments indicates that the corporations accounted for a rising proportion of from 71.1 percent in 1922, to a high of 81.2 percent in 1929 and a slight decline to 79.1 percent in 1932. Conversely the proportion of the interest payment on the federal debt dropped from 23.2 percent in 1921 to 10.9 percent in 1931 and rose to only 11.7 percent in 1932.

BONDED DEBT

The bonded debt, including both corporate and governmental, in the United States rose from $61,225,000,000 in 1925 to $81,447,-

TABLE 40

INTEREST ON BONDED DEBT IN THE UNITED STATES, 1921–1933.[9]

(million dollars)

YEARS	GOVERNMENT				CORPO-RATE[c]	GRAND TOTAL
	Federal[a]	State[b]	Munici-pal[b]	Total		
1921	$999	$13	$146	$1,158	$3,141	$4,299
1922	991	41	214	1,246	3,069	4,315
1923	1,056	50	228	1,334	3,278	4,612
1924	941	56	242	1,239	3,445	4,684
1925	882	68	266	1,216	3,617	4,833
1926	832	77	294	1,203	3,989	5,192
1927	787	79	319	1,185	4,375	5,560
1928	732	87	342	1,161	4,581	5,742
1929	678	94	366	1,138	4,924	6,062
1930	659	101	405	1,165	4,861	6,026
1931	612	111	400	1,123	4,492	5,615
1932	599	112	355	1,066	4,043	5,109
1933	689	...	...	....	3,511	....
(percent of total)						
1921	23.2	0.3	3.4	26.9	73.1	100
1922	23.0	1.0	5.0	28.9	71.1	100
1923	22.9	1.1	4.9	28.9	71.1	100
1924	20.1	1.2	5.2	26.5	73.5	100
1925	18.3	1.4	5.5	25.2	74.8	100
1926	16.0	1.5	5.7	23.2	76.8	100
1927	14.2	1.4	5.7	21.3	78.7	100
1928	12.7	1.5	6.0	20.2	79.8	100
1929	11.2	1.6	6.0	18.8	81.2	100
1930	10.9	1.7	6.7	19.3	80.7	100
1931	10.9	2.0	7.1	20.0	80.0	100
1932	11.7	2.2	7.0	20.9	79.1	100

000,000 in 1930 and then continued upward to $85,158,000,000 in 1933.[10]

Table 41 presents the various classes of corporate and governmental debt which make up the total bonded debt. The table shows the dollar amount of each class and also the percentage of each class to the total bonded debt for each year from 1925 to 1933 inclusive. From this table it is seen that the bonded debt of the railroads re-

+4,000
+2,800
+7,300
+6,000
+3,500

TABLE 41

BONDED DEBT IN THE UNITED STATES, 1925–1933.[11]

(million dollars)

CLASSES OF ISSUERS	1925	1926	1927	1928	1929	1930	1931	1932	1933
Railroad	11,305	11,404	11,380	11,427	11,467	11,880	11,830	11,836	11,656
Utility	7,730	5,367	9,218	11,419	12,181	14,118	12,387	11,910	11,902
Industrial	7,858	7,502	8,524	9,517	10,262	10,837	10,450	11,282	10,645
Financial and real estate	1,596	4,740	6,047	8,103	10,135	11,079	11,000	9,307	8,652
State and municipal	11,771	12,657	13,746	14,670	15,611	16,575	17,289	17,577	17,551
Federal land bank	982	1,059	1,139	1,175	1,188	1,184	1,170	1,147	1,242
U.S. Government	19,983	18,823	17,687	16,991	16,029	15,774	17,528	20,448	23,450
Grand Total	61,225	61,552	67,741	73,302	76,873	81,447	81,654	83,507	85,158
Total governmental	32,736	32,539	32,572	32,836	32,828	33,533	35,987	39,172	42,243
Total corporate	28,489	29,013	35,169	40,466	44,045	47,914	45,667	44,335	42,915

(percent of grand total)

CLASSES OF ISSUERS	1925	1926	1927	1928	1929	1930	1931	1932	1933
Railroad	18.5	18.5	16.8	15.6	14.9	14.6	14.4	14.2	13.7
Utility	12.6	8.7	13.6	15.6	15.8	17.3	15.2	14.3	14.0
Industrial	12.8	12.2	12.6	13.0	13.4	13.3	12.8	13.5	12.5
Financial and real estate	2.6	7.7	8.9	11.0	13.2	13.6	13.5	11.1	10.2
State and municipal	19.2	20.6	20.3	20.0	20.3	20.3	21.2	21.0	20.6
Federal land bank	1.6	1.7	1.7	1.6	1.5	1.5	1.4	1.4	1.5
U.S. Government	32.7	30.6	26.1	23.2	20.9	19.4	21.5	24.5	27.5
Total governmental	53.5	52.9	48.1	44.8	42.7	41.2	44.1	46.9	49.6
Total corporate	46.5	47.1	51.9	55.2	57.3	58.8	55.9	53.1	50.4

mained almost unchanged. On the other hand, the amount of utility bonds outstanding increased considerably, and the bonded debt of industrial corporations likewise increased. The amount of financial and real estate bonds showed the greatest increase of any class of corporate obligations. State and municipal debt increased rapidly until the end of 1931. The debt of the federal government declined until 1930 but from that year it increased precipitously. Total corporate debt over the period rose from $28,489,000,-000 in 1925 to $42,915,000,000 in 1933. The total governmental debt rose from $32,736,000,000 to $42,243,000,000 over the same period and the grand total of both corporate and governmental debt increased from $61,225,000,000 to $85,158,000,000.

The proportion of railway debt dropped sharply to the total bonded debt while the proportion of public utilities rose until 1930 and then declined in relative importance. In general, the proportion of the industrial debt remained steady. On the other hand, the proportion of the debt in the form of financial and real estate securities increased sharply until 1930 and then declined. The total corporate debt rose from 46.5 percent in 1925 to a high of 58.8 percent in 1930 and then dropped to 50.4 percent in 1933. State, county and municipal bonds rose sharply to a high of over 21 percent in 1931 and then declined slightly. The federal government debt declined from a high of 32.7 percent in 1925 to a low of 19.4 percent in 1930 and then rose to 27.5 percent by 1933. Throughout the depression period, the proportion of the bonded debt in the form of total government securities, including federal, state and municipal, rose from 44.1 percent in 1931 to approximately 49.6 percent by 1933. These figures confirm the fact that in the United States, as in foreign countries, there has been a relative decline in private and an increase in public security capitalism.

TOTAL SECURITIES OUTSTANDING

The total securities including both bonds and stock outstanding rose from $136,159,000,000 in 1925 to a high of $187,647,000,000 in 1931 and then fell to $177,658,000,000 in 1933.[13] Table 42 presents the various items which make up the total securities outstanding. From this table it is seen that preferred stock outstanding showed little change, rising from $15,947,000,000 in 1925 to a high of $19,700,000,000 in 1929, and then a relatively small recession to $18,400,000,000 in 1933. On the other hand the volume of common stock increased sharply from $58,987,000,000 in 1925 to a high of $87,100,000,000 in 1930 and then dropped to $74,100,000,-000 in 1933. Corporations accumulated a large total surplus which

TABLE 42

Total Securities Outstanding in the United States, 1925–1933.[12]

(million dollars)

YEAR	CORPORATE				Total capitalization (1+2+3+4)	Governmental bonded debt (a) 6	Total bonded debt (a) 7 (4+6)	Total securities outstanding 8 (1+2+4+6)	Corporate bonded debt to total capitalization	Corporate bonded debt to total bonded debt
	Preferred Stock 1	Common Stock 2	Surplus 3	Bonded debt (a) 4					Percent of Total	Percent of Total
									A (4÷5)	B (4÷7)
1925	15,947	58,987	37,567	28,489	140,990	32,736	61,225	136,159	20.2	46.5
1926	17,100	67,500	34,600	29,013	148,213	32,539	61,552	146,152	19.6	47.1
1927	17,800	74,100	40,500	35,169	167,569	32,571	67,740	159,640	21.0	51.9
1928	18,500	77,300	47,200	40,466	183,466	32,836	73,302	169,102	22.1	55.2
1929	19,700	85,500	55,100	44,045	204,345	32,828	76,873	182,073	21.6	57.3
1930	19,100	87,100	55,100	47,914	209,214	33,533	81,447	187,647	22.9	58.8
1931	19,200	79,800	44,400	45,667	189,067	35,987	81,654	180,654	24.2	55.9
1932	19,100	78,400	36,100	44,335	177,935	39,172	83,507	181,007	24.9	53.1
1933	18,400	74,100	35,100	42,915	170,515	42,243	85,158	177,658	25.2	50.4

Explanation:
(a) Excludes foreign governmental and foreign corporate bonds.

rose from $37,567,000,000 in 1925 to a high of $55,100,000,000 in 1929, but in the depression this was sharply reduced to $35,100,000,-000. Over these years the corporate bonded debt rose sharply from $28,489,000,000 in 1925 to a high of $47,914,000,000 in 1930 and then declined slightly to $42,915,000,000 in 1933. Total corporate capitalization rose sharply from $140,990,000,000 in 1925 to a high of $209,214,000,000 in 1930 and then fell to $170,515,000,000 in 1933. Because of the relatively greater decrease in the preferred stock, common stock and surplus of corporations as compared with their bonded debt, the proportion of this debt in the total corporate capitalization showed an unsatisfactory increase from less than one-fifth in 1926 to more than one-fourth in 1933.

In contrast to the variations in the total of corporate issues on the other hand governmental securities, after remaining steady at $32,-000,000,000 from 1925 to 1929, rose sharply to $42,243,000,000 by 1933. The proportion of corporate bonded debt to total bonded debt, after rising from 46.5 percent in 1925 to a high of 58.8 percent in 1930, dropped to 50.4 percent in 1933.

WEALTH

National wealth of United States was estimated at $317,200,000,-000 in 1921 and $361,800,000,000 in 1929. With the coming of the depression, national wealth dropped to a low of $246,400,000,000 in 1932 and then recovered to $308,900,000,000 in 1935.[14]

ANALYSIS OF RATIOS

The various items thus far studied individually are now used to compute ratios which indicate significant relationships in the financial system. Consideration will be given to the following ratios:

A. New securities to saving funds
B. Interest on bonded debt to national income
C. Bonded debt to total securities outstanding
D. National wealth to bonded debt
E. Total securities outstanding to national wealth.

NEW SECURITIES TO SAVING FUNDS

The ratio of new securities to saving funds shows the relation between the amount of the net capital demand in the form of new security issues to the total volume of saving. A more accurate ratio would be the volume of new securities issued to the amount of saving available for the security market, but the latter item has never been computed.[15] This ratio is a corollary of total investment to total saving.[16] The amount of investment and the amount of saving tend to equal each other over a long period of time, but over a short period of time there may be a definite maladjustment between these two forces.

It has been maintained that saving in the United States grew more rapidly than the volume of new securities in the post-war period until the depression of 1929, and as a result there was an excess of such saving. This redundant saving, it is contended, then flowed into foreign securities and into investment trust issues, and the proceeds of the latter were applied to bidding up the prices of outstanding securities. This inflation of security values, it is held, finally resulted in the collapse of the security market in 1929.

That there was not an excess of saving in relation to security investment but rather an excess of such security investment in relation to saving in the years immediately preceding the crash of 1929 seems clear from an examination of the conditions of the capital market over these years. In the first place the proportion of new securities to total saving funds rose from 14.9 percent in 1921 to a high of 20.4 percent in 1929. In other words, new securities were absorbing only a little more than one-seventh of total saving funds in 1921 but by 1929 were absorbing well over one-fifth.[17] Though the value of this ratio is limited, in that it shows the relationship between the annual amount of new securities and the volume of saving funds accumulated over a period of time, nevertheless an examination of the figures on new securities and saving funds shows that the increase in the latter figure rises less than the former. While, again, the crudeness of these figures imposes limitations, nevertheless they are an indication of the general trend.

Evidence of the excess of new securities in relation to available saving is found in the unsatisfactory condition of the bond market in the post-war period. In describing the trend of investment banking over these years [18] it was seen that the dealers in new securities were continuously forced to resort to artificial support for their issues in order to prevent a fall in price. Despite this support, the bond market over these years, particularly from 1927 to 1929 inclusive, suffered from an almost chronic condition of undigested securities.

The excess of security investment in relation to saving may have been a factor in the increase in the yield of bonds in the closing years of the period. The bond price index of the Standard Statistics Corporation declined from 102.1 in March, 1928, to 96.6 in September, 1929 and the yield on these bonds rose from 4.53 percent to 4.91 percent. Over the same period the municipal bond price index fell from 97.9 to 92.0 and the yield on municipal bonds rose from

3.89 percent to 4.32 percent. The Liberty Bond price index fell from a high of 104.1 in December, 1927, to a low of 99.3 in October, 1929. Moreover, the average yield on preferred stock rose from 5.18 percent to 5.65 percent over the years from April, 1928 to November, 1929.[19] On the other hand, the average yield on common stocks fell from 5.02 percent in January, 1927 to 3.36 percent in January, 1929.[20] However, it may be argued that common stocks do not represent the cost of capital since they are generally purchased for price appreciation rather than for a return on capital.

In view of the fact that in theory the force of the supply of saving in relation to demand must necessarily equal each other, how then was this excess of demand in the form of new securities over the flow of saving overcome? Temporarily it was met by the use of bank credit. For a short period of time, bank credit can carry unsold securities and keep them off the market. In the long run these securities must be absorbed by actual saving, otherwise when they are thrown on the market prices will decline sharply. Month after month in the twenties, the increasing issues of new securities were carried by bank credit in the form of brokers' loans, which rose from $2,000,000,000 in 1925 to $3,000,000,000 in 1927 and to $8,000,000,000 in the fall of 1929 when the security market collapsed.[21] It was impossible for the saving available for the security market to keep pace with the ever-mounting volume of new securities, and the collapse of October, 1929 was inevitable. In other words, in the period immediately preceding the collapse of 1929, there was an excess of the demand for capital in the form of new issues in relation to the supply of new capital in the form of saving available for the security market. The United States was therefore suffering not from oversaving but from overinvestment.

After 1930 the relation between the volume of saving and new security issues was reversed. While the federal government increased its demand for capital, corporate demand fell off very sharply. As a result the ratio of new securities to saving funds dropped from 20.4 percent in 1930 to 8.3 percent in 1934.

INTEREST ON BONDED DEBT TO NATIONAL INCOME

From 1921 through 1925 the amount of interest payments rose but national income increased more rapidly, and thus the ratio between these two items dropped from 7.2 percent to 6.3 percent. However, after 1925 and through 1929, interest payment increased more rapidly than the rise in national income, and so the ratio rose to 7.3 percent in 1929.[22] After 1929 the decline in national income was more rapid than the drop in interest payment and the ratio rose sharply to 13.0 percent in 1932. In other words, in that year, the interest payment on the bonded debt was absorbing over one-eighth of national income and thus constituted a heavy burden.

BONDED DEBT TO TOTAL SECURITIES OUTSTANDING

The ratio of bonded debt to total securities outstanding shows the capital structure of security capitalism. The proportion of bonded debt to total corporate and governmental securities showed a satisfactory decline from 44.9 percent in 1925 to 42.2 percent in 1929.[23] However, in the period from 1929 to 1933 the proportion rose from 42.2 percent to 47.9 percent, and this unsatisfactory increase was due to the rise in the governmental debt.

WEALTH TO BONDED DEBT

The proportion of wealth to bonded debt is comparable to the ratio showing the extent to which property or the debt base covers the debt in the case of a corporation or a government.[24] In general the trend of total wealth to bonded debt in the post-war period was decidedly downward. In 1920 it was at the satisfactory level of 877 percent. However from 1921 to 1924 it moved irregularly downward to 504 percent. In the depression with the inflexibility of debt and the decline in national wealth, the ratio dropped to a low level of 295 percent in 1932. This downward trend was unsatisfactory and reflected the weight of the debt burden.

SECURITIES OUTSTANDING TO WEALTH

The ratio of securities outstanding to wealth indicates the extent of the development of security capitalism. The proportion of securities to wealth in the United States was 33⅓ percent in 1904,[25] while in the post-war period the proportion rose sharply from 37.6 percent in 1925 to 50.3 percent in 1929. Due to the increase in government debt in the depression the total securities outstanding decreased relatively little, while national wealth dropped sharply. As a result the ratio of securities to wealth reached the high figure of 73.5 percent in 1932.[26]

The consequences of this increase in the proportion of total wealth in the form of securities are of vital importance. A century ago, ownership of wealth took the form largely of the possession of physical assets, such as mills, ships and merchandise. Capital was not as shiftable as it is to-day, but its value was more stable. In recent years ownership of wealth has come to mean ownership of paper claims representative of physical property; of securities indicative of ownership, but very often possessing values apart from the physical property underlying them. This change in the nature of maintaining and holding wealth from the direct possession of physical assets to the indirect ownership of such assets by means of paper claims in the form of securities, has increased the shiftability of capital, but it has at the same time led to serious instability of values. The value of the paper claims evidencing ownership of property often fluctuates quite apart from fluctuations in the value of the property itself. This ownership of wealth and capital no longer carries with it the stability which previously characterized it. This change in the shiftability and stability of wealth has in turn had serious consequences. As values become more unstable and fluctuate widely from one extreme to another, the stability of financial institutions, such as commercial banks, saving banks, investment trusts, and insurance companies, is threatened, and their continual existence becomes uncertain. Fluctuating security values and losses to institutional investment holders tend to weaken and endanger the very foundation of the whole financial structure.

CONCLUSION

Thus a financial statement of American security capitalism for the post-war period reveals certain unsatisfactory tendencies. American security capitalism experienced overinvestment rather than oversaving. The burden of interest payment to national income became increasingly heavy and the former absorbed an ever-growing proportion of the latter. The capital structure of American security capitalism became more and more unsound due to the increase of bonded debt in relation to total securities outstanding. This debt was heavy and became less protected in view of the fact that it was covered by a smaller proportion of wealth. Finally the increasing proportion of securities to wealth added to the instability of the system.

CHAPTER 19

PUBLIC CONTROL

THE tendencies of American security capitalism described previously gave rise to pressing problems, and consideration will now be given to the efforts of the government to cope with these problems by public control and regulation. This chapter will analyze critically control through monetary action, Federal Reserve policy, banking supervision, federal support of the financial institutions of security capitalism through direct assistance or through guaranteeing their obligations, and specific and general control over the demand for capital.

CONTROL THROUGH MONETARY POLICY

The drastic economic disturbances of the depression after 1929 led to an insistent demand for a change in the traditional monetary policy of the United States.[1] As shown in Chapter 11 the struggle over the monetary policies in the United States during the nineteenth century was won by the supporters of the gold standard, and the fruits of this victory were embodied in the Gold Standard Act of 1900. Over the next three decades the gold standard came to be accepted with little question except by a small group of currency reformers in academic circles and by some of the agricultural interests which grievously felt the burden of debt after the commodity deflation of the early twenties. It was not until the coming of the depression after 1929 which intensified the burden of debt that any serious question rose over the acceptability of the gold standard. As the depression deepened and as the burden of debt became heavier, the demand by inflationary interests for the abandonment of the gold standard became stronger. Accordingly, one of the first acts of the Roosevelt administration was to abandon the gold standard. This cutting loose from old moorings was accomplished by the successive steps of suspending gold payments at home in the Act of March 6, 1933, by requiring the delivery for the account of the government of all domestic gold to the Federal Reserve banks in the Act of April 5, 1933 and finally by the embargo on gold exports in the Act of April 20, 1933. The Thomas Amendment to the Agricultural Adjustment Act gave permissive rather than mandatory power to take various inflationary steps. The Federal Reserve banks might purchase $3,000,000,000 of government securities in the open market for the purpose of increasing the supply of money through the expansion of Federal Reserve credit. The President was also given the power to issue $3,000,000,000 of fiat money without gold cover for the purpose of retiring the interest-bearing debt. The President was further given the power to devalue the dollar by reducing the gold content to no more than fifty percent of its current value, and finally there was also permissive legislation to coin silver. The Federal Reserve banks had already increased their holdings of government securities to $2,400,000,000, while the second power of issuing fiat money was not exercised. The third provision formed the basis for the Gold Reserve Act of 1934. This Act provided, first, for the reduction of the gold content of the dollar, which was accomplished by lowering it from 23.22 grains of fine gold to 13.71 grains, thus reducing the dollar to 59.06 per cent of its former value. At the same time the Act provided for the nationalization of the gold holdings of the Federal Reserve banks which were to receive gold certificates in exchange. The Act thus transferred the ownership and possession of the nation's gold from the Federal Reserve banks to the Treasury. The reduction of the gold content and the seizure of the gold holdings gave the government a stabilization profit of $2,793,000,000 which represents a nominal appreciation in the value of the gold holdings from $4,029,000,000 to $6,822,000,000. The transfer of gold signified the passing of the largest single supply of gold, representing about two-thirds of the world's total, from private hands, since the Federal Reserve banks are really private corporations, to the Treasury, a public body. Furthermore, the stabilization profit from the appreciation of gold redounded entirely to the government. These were two important steps in the direction of public security capitalism. A further monetary step was the Silver Purchase Act.[2] The statute itself was of no specific significance from the standpoint of security capitalism beyond the fact that it represented another step in the general movement to reduce the value of the dollar.[3] The motive underlying the monetary policy of the New Deal was to decrease the value of the dollar in order to raise commodity prices, which in turn would relieve the burden of debt and stimulate business recovery. To the inflationist the debtor represented a harried producer, particularly a farmer, who was burdened with a large mortgage and who required government protection against an aggressive creditor. The inflationist argued that the pressure of debt by forcing debtors to throw their goods on the market was the underlying cause of depression and that the reduction of the debt burden would therefore bring about business revival. This theory failed to recognize the true nature of debt under the system of security capitalism. Debtors under security capitalism are no

longer only individuals but are mainly corporations and governments. Few of these corporate and governmental debtors to any
extent possessed inventories of goods which they could throw on
the market to meet their obligations with the possible exception of
industrial corporations. However, as pointed out on page 244, the
debt burden of industrial corporations was not serious as evidenced
by the fact that few major industrial corporations carrying inventory
were forced into receivership throughout the depression. Obviously
the argument, that the burden of debt, by forcing the liquidation
of commodities, intensified the depression was unfounded. Creditors, on the other hand, who are adversely affected by the forced
alleviation of debt, are to a large extent the indirect investors who
hold bank deposits and life insurance policies.

The argument that reduction of debt starts a nation back to prosperity is refuted by the actual experience of European countries in
the post-war period. Debt reduction through inflation obtained its
highest perfection in Central European countries, but they did not
as a result of the drastic application of inflation enter a new era
of prosperity. In fact drastic inflation resulted in discouraging thrift
and in reducing the volume of capital available for investment.
Control of capitalism through monetary manipulation is therefore
a futile policy.

GOVERNMENTAL DOMINATION OF RESERVE ORGANIZATION

Public control of security capitalism was also exercised over
the organization and the operation of the Federal Reserve System.[4]
In tracing the growth of security capitalism in England, France and
Germany, it was noted that the financial power came to be concentrated in the leading metropolis of each of these countries. This
movement naturally met with opposition from the non-metropoli-
tan interests, but in time it proved ineffective, and London, Paris
and Berlin came to be the centers for conducting both national and
international financial transactions. By the end of the second quarter of the nineteenth century New York City became the leading
financial center in the United States, but rival markets continued to
flourish in Boston, Philadelphia and later in Chicago. In time the
American financial metropolis was faced with a powerful social and
political opposition unparalleled in any other capitalist country.
In most of these other countries there came to be a general acceptance of the need of a strong financial center, but in the United States
the opposition to the so-called "Wall Street" interests grew rather
than weakened in intensity. This opposition found expression in
the formation of the Federal Reserve System. The Pujo hearings

and the report on the "Money Trust" [5] publicized the concentration of financial power in New York City, and consolidated the determination both of the public and of Congress that the new banking system should not come under control of "Wall Street." As a result Federal Reserve organization was based on the two underlying principles that the system should be controlled by the government rather than by the bankers and that it should be regional rather than centralized.

William Jennings Bryan remembered his defeat at the hands of security capitalism in the elections of 1896 and of 1900, and cast his influence in favor of government and against so-called banker control of the Reserve System. As a result of his support of the nomination and the later election of Woodrow Wilson, Mr. Bryan exerted a powerful influence in the administration and was successful in winning over President Wilson, Secretary McAdoo, and Senator Owens who was directing banking legislation in the Upper House. At first Carter Glass, who was then guiding banking legislation in the lower house, opposed Bryan's view but later accepted it.[6]

As a result of this opposition to so-called banker control the members of the Federal Reserve Board in the original act were appointed by the President, with the consent of the Senate. The act, however, specified that at least two members should be "persons experienced in banking or finance."[7] However, in 1923, even this requirement was dropped from the Act. In later years there was a persistent effort to re-introduce the requirement that some of the members of the Federal Reserve Board should have banking experience. In 1932 Senator Glass, in his draft of a bill to change the organization of the Federal Reserve system restored the provision that two of the appointed members of the Federal Reserve Board should be persons of tested banking experience.[8] This provision, however, was left out of the final form of the Banking Act of 1933. Again in the discussion of the Banking Act of 1935 this provision was revived. The special committee of the American Bankers Association, in its recommendation on the Banking Act of 1935, urged that two members of the Federal Reserve Board should be selected when possible from persons who had banking experience. However, no such provision was incorporated in the final draft of the Act. Due to the inherent fear of so-called banker control, the qualification of banking experience is still not required of any member of the Board of Governors (the former Federal Reserve Board), even though the position calls for the highest degree of technical skill and expert knowledge. Although these qualifications were not mandatory, nevertheless the Roosevelt administration appointed several members possessing seasoned banking experience.

In the Congressional discussion of the Banking Act of 1935 a determined move was made to augment governmental control of the Board of Governors. The earlier draft of the bill contained the provision that the chairman of the Board, as the acting executive officer, was "to serve until the further order of the President." The early drafts of the Act were not clearly worded and were susceptible to curious interpretations. In fact, it would have been possible for a governor of the Board to be advanced to the position of chairman, removed as chairman and so automatically removed as a governor of the Board. This provision was later reworded and the danger to the tenure of board members was eliminated. For a time it was insisted that the chief executive officer of the Board should serve at the pleasure of the President on the ground that the latter had a right to appoint an officer in sympathy with administrative policy as to public and private finance.[9] It was, however, felt that such a policy would have placed the chairman in the position of merely a cabinet member and would have made it impossible for the Board of Governors to constitute itself as an independent body, and so the final provision gave the chairman a tenure of a full term of years.

STRUGGLE FOR DOMINATION OF RESERVE BANKS

The second element in the organization of the Federal Reserve system is the group of Federal Reserve banks. In order to carry out the will of Congress that the new system should be regional rather than centralized in New York City, twelve Federal Reserve banks were established. The operations of each bank were to be administered by a board of nine directors. Three directors were to be appointed by the Federal Reserve Board to represent the interests of the public, of which one was to be chairman and was to be designated as the Federal Reserve agent. Six members, three representing banking and three others representing commerce, agriculture and industry, were to be elected by the member banks. The bankers were therefore supposed to have only minority representation. Although only three members of the board of directors of the Federal Reserve banks were to voice the interest of the banks, the three representatives of industry were also appointed by the member banks. It was therefore entirely natural for the member banks, in selecting the three industrialists, to choose those who would be friendly to the interests of the banking institutions. Thus in the course of time the banking interests controlled six out of the nine directors of the Federal Reserve banks.

A second institutional change which brought about a shift from governmental to banker control over the Federal Reserve banks was the creation of the office of governor of the Federal Reserve banks. The original Federal Reserve Act made no provision for this office, and so it had no de jure but only a de facto basis. In the course of time the governor of a Federal Reserve bank came to be more important than the Federal Reserve agent. As the governor had no legal existence, he could not be a member of the board of directors, but it became the practice for the board of directors to appoint an executive committee composed of a small group of its membership. The governor was then appointed to serve as a member of this committee which came to be the active and controlling body of the Federal Reserve banks.[10]

In the Banking Act of 1935, an effort was made to extend the control of the federal government over the appointment of the governor of a Reserve bank, but this proposal met with strong opposition. As a result the final act was a compromise which gave the Board of Governors the right to approve the governor (now called president) of a Federal Reserve bank, but at the same time, permitted the president to serve for a term of five years before the Reserve Board of Governors could again pass on his reappointment. Although the president is not legally a member of the board of directors of a Reserve bank he can still be a member of the executive committee in accordance with the practice in force in most Federal Reserve banks.[11]

OPEN MARKET COMMITTEE

The third important institution in Federal Reserve organization has been the open market committee. Ever since the inception of this committee unfortunately it provided a battleground between the government and the banking forces.[12] The original Federal Reserve Act provided that open market purchases and sales of the Federal Reserve banks were to be subject to the "rules and regulations prescribed by the Federal Reserve Board." [13] However, almost from the start the actual control over these operations was exercised by the Federal Reserve Bank of New York. In 1914, the Bank made its first open market operation in purchasing a block of the warrants of New York City. The other Federal Reserve banks joined in this transaction and requested the New York bank to act as agent for them in the purchase of these warrants.[14] In the following year the Federal Reserve banks also appointed the Reserve Bank of New York as their agent in purchasing commercial paper in the open market.

The federal government made an effort to assert its control over open market operations in 1915 when the Reserve Board gave notice that it would exercise its right to regulate such transactions if they should develop along undesirable lines.[15]

With the increased importance of open market operations after 1920, the struggle between the Federal Reserve Bank of New York and the Federal Reserve Board for control became more intense. The Federal Reserve banks appointed an open market committee of their own with the governor of the Federal Reserve Bank of New York as chairman. In the following year the Federal Reserve Board asserted its authority by replacing this committee with a new "open market investment committee for the Federal Reserve system" having the same membership but appointed by the Federal Reserve Board. In time this committee was replaced by a new group known as the Open Market Policy Conference, which included representatives of the twelve Reserve banks, but the Reserve Board retained final approval of all policies.

All these open market committees were really extra-legal institutions created merely by agreement between the Reserve banks and the Reserve Board. The Banking Act of 1933 legalized this open market group and provided for a "Federal Open Market Committee" which as later revised consisted of seven members of the Board of Governors and five representatives of the Reserve banks. No Federal Reserve bank was to engage in open market operations except in accordance with the regulations of the open market committee.

Under Section 14-b defining open market operations, a Federal Reserve bank is permitted to undertake open market operations not only at home but also abroad. Under this power, the Federal Reserve Bank of New York gradually established financial relations with the Bank of England, the Bank of France and other important central banks of the world. This again was a natural development of international security capitalism. The Banking Act of 1933 however definitely vested the administration of these international relations with the Reserve Board.[16] Thus in the post-war period the Federal government extended its control over the various organisms of the central banking system such as the Reserve Board, the Reserve Banks and the Open Market Committee. This trend was similar to the movement of the extension of governmental regulation of the central banks in France, and Germany.

REGULATION OF FEDERAL RESERVE OPERATIONS — RETREAT FROM THE ORTHODOX THEORY

The original Federal Reserve Act was based on the orthodox theory of banking and the Reserve authorities made every effort to operate the system on this theory.[17]   The Federal Reserve Act of 1913 permitted the Reserve banks to rediscount only commercial paper which met definite tests of eligibility relating to maturity and purpose.   However, early in the history of Reserve practice there was a gradual departure from this limited basis.[18]   In 1917, under the exigencies of war finance, the Federal Reserve Act was amended to permit the Reserve banks to make advances to member banks not only on eligible commercial paper but also on their promissory notes secured by United States obligations.   This amendment was the first legislative recognition of the impracticability of the original provision limiting reserve credit to the rediscounting of eligible commercial paper.   In the years after the close of the War, the Federal Reserve banks began to rediscount eligible paper on condition that additional collateral be provided by the borrowing banks.[19]

Throughout the post-war period, the volume of eligible paper declined sharply.   With the coming of the depression many banks were hard pressed to meet the demands of their depositors, but were unable to receive adequate assistance from the Federal Reserve banks because of the lack of acceptable assets for rediscounts.   However, until 1931 the leading officials of the reserve system clung stoutly to the orthodox theory, and opposed the liberalization of the eligibility requirements.[20]

By 1932 conditions were so serious that Congress had to broaden the base of rediscounts, and Senator Glass, the leading supporter of the orthodox theory in banking legislation, introduced legislation recognizing the liberal theory.   The Banking Act of 1932 provided that in an emergency whenever a member bank with capital not exceeding five million dollars had no further eligible assets to obtain adequate credit accommodation from a Federal Reserve bank [21] the latter, on the affirmative action of not less than five members of the Federal Reserve Board, could make an advance to the member bank on its note collateralled by ineligible assets.   In the hearings on the Banking Act of 1935, a determined effort was made further to broaden eligibility.   This movement was led by Marriner S. Eccles, Governor of the Reserve Board.   He argued convincingly against limiting the Federal Reserve banks to the rediscounting of only eligible paper by testifying that $300,000,000 of ineligible paper had been rediscounted by the Federal Reserve banks and all but $1,500,000 had been repaid up to the time when he testified.[22]   The Banking Act of 1935 in its final form eliminated the provision that advances on collateralled notes should be made only during an emergency and when the member bank has no further eligible assets. The effect of this elimination was to transform such advances from emergency to regular accommodation which a member bank might receive from its Federal Reserve bank. This was one of the most significant changes made by the Banking Act of 1935 in the powers of the Federal Reserve banks, for the Act rejected the orthodox theory and forwarded the movement for the liberalization of Federal Reserve credit.

In the entire movement toward liberalization there was only an occasional voice raised to urge the granting of advances collateralled by securities. In 1918 this matter was presented to the Senate Banking Committee in its hearings on the establishment of the War Finance Corporation.[23] W. P. G. Harding, former Governor of the Reserve Board, favored the liberalization of the rediscounts of the Reserve banks to the extent of granting advances on high-grade bonds.[24] The proposal, however, was opposed by the Economic Policy Commission of the American Bankers Association.[25]

The leading figures in the controversy over the liberalization of the eligibility requirements in 1935 apparently had only in mind non-security assets such as ineligible commercial paper and real estate. Neither the opponents nor the proponents in their public utterances gave any indication that they were considering the inclusion of loans collateralled by stocks and bonds. The nature of the assets which may be offered as collateral for advances to banks on their notes is not specified in the Banking Act of 1935, but this decision is left to the satisfaction of the Federal Reserve bank. The way therefore is left open for a Federal Reserve bank to grant advances based on stocks and bonds as collateral. It is probably doubtful that the framers of this provision had in mind the admission of such collateral as the basis for advances by the Federal Reserve banks to member banks[26] but unconsciously they at last gave legal permission to the granting of advances on security collateral. In the coming years this provision will undoubtedly be utilized. If properly administered, it can be developed into one of the most effective methods of directing the flow of credit into sound channels.

CONTROL OF SECURITY OPERATIONS OF COMMERCIAL BANKING

Control over security capitalism was also exercised through regulating the security operations of the commercial banks. These operations were bitterly attacked after the stock market crash of 1929. The Senate Committee on Banking and Currency which drafted the Banking Act of 1933 was determined to separate the commercial and investment operations of banks and to restore commercial banking to its supposedly "pure" pre-war form. The spokesmen for the bankers argued desperately against restricting the security operations of the commercial banks. The Board of Directors of the Federal

Reserve Bank of New York addressed a carefully drawn memorandum to the Senate Committee on the subject of the relations between the commercial banking system and the capital market.[27] The
memorandum conceded "certain past defects and the need for the
prevention of possible future abuse of the capital market," but
urged "that any material disorganization of that market would be
most unfortunate." The memorandum stated the issue in the following words :

The broad question to be determined is the extent to which the
capital market should be divorced from the banking system and removed
from all supervision, or whether its relations with the banking system
should be maintained and placed under appropriate supervision.

This was a clear statement of the issue, and public interest would
have been better served had Congress decided to supervise rather
than divorce the capital market from the commercial banking system. Certainly it would have saved Congress the inevitable task of
retracing its course in the years which are yet to come. However,
in 1932, the plea of the New York Reserve Bank fell on deaf ears.

Over the years there had developed in the United States really
two interrelated banking systems. The commercial banking system composed largely of national and state banks, headed by the
Federal Reserve banks and the Board, was under careful governmental supervision. The investment banking system, composed of
investment dealers (including the security affiliates), and brokers
capped by the stock exchanges, was largely outside government control. Over the years the relations between the two systems had become closely intertwined. The Banking Act of 1933 sought to perform the major operation of severing these relationships which had
largely been the result of the natural evolution of security capitalism.
The most important objective was the amputation of the security
affiliates from the commercial banks. The Act prohibited any financial institution from simultaneously engaging in investment banking operations such as underwriting or dealing in securities and in
commercial banking operations such as receiving deposits. The Act
further required that bank officers were not to be associated with
any partnerships or corporations, except mutual savings banks, which
obtained loans on stocks or bonds. This section was aimed to
strengthen the Clayton Act of 1914 which had prohibited interlocking directorates but which had been amended in 1916 so as to give
the local Federal Reserve bank the power to grant exemptions in
exceptional cases. In time such exemptions became the rule, and
the Banking Act of 1933 sought to end them.

In drafting the Banking Act of 1935 efforts were made to retrace some of these steps. The Senate draft of the Banking Act of 1935 (section 308) sought to restore the underwriting powers of national banks subject to regulations by the comptroller of the currency. Senator Glass, in urging this proposal, admitted the failure of the restrictive measures which he had included in the Banking Act of 1933, in the statement that:

We prohibited outright any underwriting, by a commercial bank. We did it with the avowed hope and expectation that thereafter there would be organized in this country underwriting houses such as exist in Great Britain and continental Europe . . . That did not take place.[28]

This provision was not included in the final draft of the Act. However, the Banking Act did in a measure weaken the original provisions of the Clayton Act regarding interbanking directorates, for the Board of Governors of the Federal Reserve system was authorized by general regulation rather than individual permit to allow interlocking directorates. Furthermore, the prohibition against interlocking relationships between banks and trust companies and institutions which made loans secured by stock or bond collateral was repealed. Thus year after year there was a continual struggle arising from the efforts of financial evolution to free itself from legislative restraints which have sought to mould the course of banking organization into a legal form contrary to the natural trends of developed security capitalism in this country and abroad. This conflict brought loss not only to the individual banker but also to the public as a whole.

CONTROL OVER SECURITY LOANS

The Banking Act of 1933 corrected one of the most flagrant abuses of the capital market by restricting the use of bank credit for the purpose of carrying securities. The Act (section 3) directed that each Federal Reserve bank should keep itself informed on "the general character and amount of the loans and investments of its member banks, for the purpose of determining whether undue use is being made of bank credit for the speculation, carrying or trading in securities, real estate or commodities." Any member bank which made undue use of reserve credit for speculative purposes was, upon the judgment of the Federal Reserve Board, to be denied further credit facilities. Furthermore under section 7 of the Act the Federal Reserve Board was further empowered to fix the amount of credit which might be extended by member banks for speculative purposes. Again, section 9 provided that if a member bank was obtaining accommodation from a Federal Reserve bank and at the same time was increasing its security loans, the reserve accommodation to the bank should become immediately due and payable and the bank should become ineligible as borrower for as long a period as the Federal Reserve Board might determine.

REGULATION OF BANK INVESTMENTS

The federal government made little effort to regulate the quality of the investments of member banks. In 1927 the comptroller was given the power to define the "investment securities" held by national banks [29] but he took a limited view of his powers by merely ruling that such investment securities must be "marketable." In the Banking Act of 1933,[30] the comptroller was again given power to define the scope of the term "investment securities," but again he merely reiterated the same feeble regulation on marketability.[31] However, in 1936 the comptroller made the first attempt to control the quality of the investments of the commercial banks,[32] and prohibited member banks of the Federal Reserve system, including not only national but also state banks and trust companies, from purchasing securities "in which the investment characteristics are distinctly or predominantly speculative or investment securities of a lower designation standard than those which are distinctly or predominantly speculative." This ruling therefore required that bank officers and also bank examiners study the statistical information on a bond and determine whether it was either of investment or speculative character. In case of doubt reference could be made to the rating manuals of the statistical agencies. This regulation was undoubtedly a step in the right direction in seeking to raise the quality of bank investments.

STATE REGULATION OF INVESTMENTS OF FINANCIAL INSTITUTIONS

In general the investments of state banks which were not members of the Reserve system continued to be unregulated. Several states regulated the investments of the savings deposits of commercial banks, and the investments of the mutual savings banks of the northeastern states were prescribed in a state legal list. These legal lists generally permitted the investment of savings funds in railroad, utility and municipal and real estate bonds, while industrial bonds and all forms of stock, except stock of banks, located with the state, were barred. The investment standards established by the states were in many cases based on the investment experience of the nineteenth and early twentieth centuries in the period of developing security capitalism and proved inadequate in the critical years of the nineteen thirties. There was a growing consciousness of these defects of the legal list, and most states made progress in revising their standards to meet the new conditions in the investment market.[33]

The state laws governing the investment of trust funds varied widely as to the types of securities which were legal. Alabama took the extreme position in its state constitution which provided: "that no act of the legislature shall authorize the investment of any trust funds by executors, administrators, guardians or other trustees in the bonds or stocks of any private corporation."[34] Thus, at one sweep, Alabama settled the issue of legal investments by prohibiting the investment of trust funds in any corporate security whatsoever. At the same time Tennessee permitted the investment of trust funds in securities of any foreign government which maintained diplomatic relations with the United States. Louisiana prohibited the investment of trust funds in railroad bonds but allowed the investment in railroad stocks selling at or over par and regularly paying a dividend of 4 percent annually for at least five years before the date of investment. Corporate trustees were also permitted to invest in the bonds of any county or municipality anywhere in the United States, with the only restriction that the bonds must be selling at or above par and show no default in interest for two years before the date of investment. The state thus set up simple investment tests and refused to concern itself with all the technical investment standards such as the relation of debt to assessed valuation, and the burden of overlapping debt which should be carefully considered in investing in municipal securities.

The laws of the State of New York regulating the investment of trust funds were probably more rigid than those of any other state. However, in discussing these laws George A. Slater, Surrogate of Westchester county uttered the following note of criticism: "The Legislature while protecting savings banks depositors threw open to a wide degree, the throttle of safety of the machinery of the law, for the protection of testamentary trusts and guardian funds," and added that "it would appear that the Legislature lacked vision."[35]

The regulation of the security investments of insurance companies also varied considerably. Certain states, as Connecticut and Virginia, permitted insurance companies to invest their funds in all securities not definitely prohibited. Conversely, other states as New York, prohibited companies from investing in any securities not definitely authorized. In later years there was a movement to liberalize these statutes. In 1929 the states of Georgia and Minnesota permitted life insurance companies to invest in bonds and preferred and common stock of all solvent institutions.[36] Likewise Vermont and South Dakota for the first time permitted the investment of life

insurance funds in public utility and railroad bonds.[37]   New York
State even permitted insurance companies to invest in guaranteed
and preferred stock.[38]   This step was particularly significant in view
of the fact that New York State ever since the Armstrong investigation of 1905 had followed a conservative policy in regulating the
investments of insurance companies.   The action was also important
because a large part of the insurance funds of the United States come
within the scope of the jurisdiction of New York State.   Though
New York permitted investment in preferred stock, it continued to
prohibit investment in common stock.

In reviewing the course of state government regulation of the
investment of saving, trust and life insurance funds, it is evident
that there was a general trend toward liberalization and a widening
of the volume of securities available for such investment.   At first
such legal investments were limited to government securities, and
then to railroad bonds.   In time public utilities, particularly electric light and power companies, were included.   Eventually there
was a gradual departure from this limited base and investment was
permitted not only in bonds, but also in preferred stock and even
in common stock in some instances, for trust and insurance funds.
It is not entirely unreasonable to anticipate that industrial securities
in the course of time will also be legal, particularly in view of the
increased stability of large industrial corporations in the post-war
period.

SUSPENSION OF REGULATION OF INVESTMENTS

The successive financial crises of recent years brought heavy
losses to banks on their investments.   These reverses were so severe
that they forced the supervising governmental bodies to suspend the
operation of their regulations in order to save many of the financial
institutions from receivership.   In the fall of 1917 there was a sharp
drop in the value of bonds, particularly of railroads and so on October 15, 1917 the comptroller made the following statement:

In view of all conditions, the Comptroller of Currency has in-
structed National banks holding high grade bonds of unquestioned intrinsic value and merit, not to charge such investments down to present
abnormal figures; but an intelligent and conservative discretion will
be exercised as to the prices at which National banks can safely and
reasonably be permitted to carry such high class securities, and as to
what proportion of the depreciation should be charged off in any six
months' period.[39]

State banking departments followed a similar policy.[40]   The collapse
of the bond market in 1920 again forced the federal and state banking departments to pursue a similar policy.

With the collapse of bond prices in 1931, the national and state banking departments, in order to prevent widespread bank closings, were again forced to adopt drastic policies. The comptroller ruled that national banks were permitted to refrain from writing off depreciation on their high grade corporate bonds and on all the state and municipal bonds if they were not in default. These assets could be entered at their full value, on the ground that the depreciation of high grade securities was due purely to momentary market fluctuations.[41] On speculative and inferior grade bonds, the banks were required to make a reasonable reduction for depreciation. This policy was adopted "in the public interest," and bank examiners were given wide latitude in applying the ruling. Where a severe write-off would have impaired the capital of a bank, and therefore its solvency, the comptroller required only reasonable depreciation charges on bonds which had declined in value but which were not speculative or in default on interest.

The closing weeks of 1931 witnessed a virtual collapse of the bond market, and the comptroller, in issuing his call for the end of the year, advised examiners "to use their discretion in virtually all types of bonds, other than those which actually had been defaulted in fixing values that are considered fair." The comptroller held the view that in many instances prices that had been quoted on the exchange were "perfectly absurd." [42] In the beginning of 1932, the comptroller continued his policy because he was satisfied that the prices at which many types of bonds frequently sold in the market did not represent their true value.[43]

Thus the government regulatory bodies in order to avoid a recognition of the impairment of the banking system were again and again forced to pose as investment experts, to issue wise proclamations on investment values and to engage in metaphysical discussions of intrinsic values of which they would have been hard pressed to explain the meaning. They were also forced to adopt policies based on legal fiction in order to keep open banking institutions actually insolvent due to the impairment of their capital resulting from losses on their security holdings.

The same policy had to be followed in the case of the investments of the insurance companies. In 1931 the National Convention of Insurance Commissioners adopted a general resolution permitting insurance companies in their annual statements of December 31, 1931 to carry their securities at the higher market values which had prevailed as of June 30, 1931. As the security market continued to fall, the Convention in December 1932, permitted the companies to carry their securities at practically the same valuation as in 1931.[44]

GOVERNMENTAL SUPPORT OF FINANCIAL INSTITUTIONS

As seen before the European governments were forced to come to the aid of their financial institutions in the crisis of 1920-1921 and again in the crisis of 1929–1933. The United States Government took similar action through the formation of the War Finance Corporation, the Reconstruction Finance Corporation and the Federal Deposit Insurance Corporation.

The first step of the government in granting direct financial aid to private industry came in the formation of the War Finance Corporation.[45] Owing to the financial uncertainty of the war period, commercial banks were unwilling to tie up a large part of their assets in securities or ineligible paper. There was also uncertainty over the position of the savings banks, since they could not be members of the Federal Reserve system but at the same time faced the possibility of heavy withdrawals by their depositors. To meet these needs Congress created the War Finance Corporation. Its stock was subscribed by the treasury, and the Corporation was managed by a board of directors appointed by the President, with the secretary of the treasury as chairman. The Corporation was empowered to grant loans to commercial banks extending credit to borrowers whose operations were necessary to the prosecution of the War and to savings banks facing heavy withdrawals by their depositors. The quality of the collateral for such loans was not carefully defined, and so the Corporation was really an agency whose purpose was to grant loans for war purposes and to rediscount the ineligible paper of hard-pressed banking institutions.[46] However, little use was made of the resources of the War Finance Corporation during the period of hostilities.[47] The savings banks did not avail themselves of this assistance, since the necessity for it did not materialize. In the period immediately following the War, the Corporation extended advances to the railroads due to the failure of the passage of the Congressional appropriation bill which contained provision for the governmental operation of the roads. In 1920 the Corporation granted export credits to stimulate international trade and in 1921 it extended advances to finance agriculture. In 1925 it began the liquidation of its operations.

It was not, however, until the depression after 1929, that the federal government granted direct financial assistance on an extensive scale. For this purpose Congress created the Reconstruction Finance Corporation to aid practically all forms of financial institutions, as commercial banks, trust companies, savings banks, building and loan associations, and insurance companies, as well as railroads, cities, states and agriculture. The loans were to have a maturity of not exceeding three years and the security was to be adequate. The procedure for granting such a loan required first a formal application together with detailed financial statements. Based on credit analysis, the loan was then approved by the Reconstruction Finance Corporation, the collateral to secure the loan was deposited and the funds were then made available to the applying institution. The Reconstruction Finance Corporation was similar to the institutions formed in various European countries to overcome serious weaknesses in the financial structure resulting from the adverse effects of the prolongation of the depression.

According to radical economic philosophy, the Reconstruction Finance Corporation represented "State financial aid to sustain tottering private industry," and it was considered as "definite evidence of the decline of American capitalism." [48] This interpretation was too pessimistic, since a large part of the advances made by the Reconstruction Finance Corporation was repaid, and it is probable that most of the remaining loans are recoverable due to the care exercised in obtaining sound collateral.

While the actual experience of the Reconstruction Finance Corporation does not substantiate the Cassandra prophecies of its critics, nevertheless the Corporation must be regarded as a public financial institution created to perform a function which private financial institutions were unwilling or unable to perform. [49]

FEDERAL DEPOSIT INSURANCE CORPORATION

Not only did the federal government grant direct assistance to the financial institutions of security capitalism but it also guaranteed some of the liabilities of the banking institutions through the creation of the Federal Deposit Insurance Corporation. It was established under the Banking Act of 1933 and revised by the Banking Act of 1935. The revised system provided for a Federal Deposit Insurance Corporation headed by a board of directors consisting of three members, including the comptroller of the currency and two other members, appointed by the President, with the approval of the Senate. [50] The funds of the Corporation were derived from contributions by the treasury and by the Federal Reserve banks, and from assessments on the member banks in the system. Compulsory insurance was required of all banks which were members of the Federal Reserve system. These banks were assessed at the rate of one-twelfth of one percent of their total deposits and insurance protection was extended only to deposits up to and including $5,000.

The plan served to strength public confidence in the commercial banking system and for this reason alone the Act justified itself.

However, the fundamental weakness of the plan was its failure to make adequate financial provision to meet the risks which commercial banking faces under security capitalism due to the increased holdings of securities whose values fluctuated markedly. A recent study shows that the funds of the Corporation would have been insufficient to meet losses of failing banks, assuming that the existence of the Corporation had no effect on the number of bank failures. This conclusion is based on a comparison of a hypothetical assessment of one-twelfth of one percent on the total deposits of active commerical banks with the actual losses on *total* deposits in suspended banks from 1865 to 1934. Such an assessment would have been insufficient in the difficult years of the seventies; generally sufficient after 1878 with the exception of the depression years of 1882, 1896 and 1907; and entirely insufficient after 1919. The cumulative losses above the assessments from 1930 to 1934 alone would have amounted to $2,300,000,000.[51] It must however be noted that these are losses on *total* deposits whereas only deposits less than $5000 are insured. However the losses on deposits of less than $5000 in closed banks between January 1, 1931 and March 15, 1933 alone amounted to $1,500,000,000 as compared with the capital of $326,000,000 of the Deposit Insurance Corporation.[52]

In the event of the deficiency in the fund of the Corporation, no additional sum may be collected from the Federal Reserve banks, since under the Act they are not apparently liable beyond their original assessments. It would, however, be possible under the Act for the secretary of the treasury to purchase an additional sum of $250,000,000 par value of the obligations of the Corporation when required for insurance purposes. It would therefore seem that the funds of the Deposit Insurance Corporation have so far come largely from the government, and in the future in case of emergency would be derived largely from the federal treasury which would then seek repayment through assessment on the banks in future years.

CONTROL OVER DEMAND FOR CAPITAL — MUNICIPAL FINANCE

The Federal government exercised little control over municipal finance. An effort in this direction was made in the passage of the National Municipal Bankruptcy Act which was to facilitate insolvent municipalities in adjusting their debts by agreements with the majority of their creditors. The Supreme Court, however, declared the act unconstitutional on the ground that it thus constituted interference in the affairs of the local government and thus impaired state sovereignty.

For many years most of the states had exercised some form of control to limit the debt-contracting power of the municipalities within their jurisdictions. New Jersey, particularly, established a comprehensive limitation of municipal debt, and Massachusetts also enacted a drastic law for the purpose of restricting the incurrence of municipal debts.[53] These limitations generally required that the municipal debt could not be extended beyond a certain percentage of the assessed valuation of local property. Some states also limited the debt in relation to the annual revenues of the municipality. In other states restrictions were also placed on the maximum period within which the debt must mature. Limitations were also placed on taxation which was usually restricted to a certain percentage of the assessed valuation of property within the confines of the municipality. Students of municipal finance were generally in agreement that such debt and tax limitations were ineffective in maintaining sound municipal finance.

Municipal defaults became particularly serious after 1929, and as a result, there was a considerable extension of control over municipal finance by such states as Massachusetts, New Jersey and North Carolina. Due to loss of revenue-producing power caused by the decline of the textile industry in the years before the depression, Fall River faced serious difficulties after 1930. Massachusetts, therefore, instituted what amounted to a state receivership in 1931, and appointed a "state board of finance." [54]

In 1931 New Jersey passed a law creating a State Commission on municipal finance for the purpose of administering the numerous local government defaults within the state.[55] Under this law either a holder of a defaulted bond or a municipality itself could apply to the State Commission for the appointment of a receiver. This official was then given extensive control over the budget and over the debt of the defaulted municipality. He was expected to rehabilitate the finances by reducing expenditures and by obtaining tax payments either through compromises on delinquent taxes, or, if such compromises were unavailing, through the enforcement of tax sales. In this way, the receiver was expected to bring about the payment of the municipal debt without reduction of the capital sum.

The most extensive form of state control over local finance was instituted in the Municipal Finance Act of North Carolina passed in 1931.[56] Under this Act the State Commission possessed not only temporary administrative power in time of default but exercised continuous supervision over local finance. The Commission was vested with complete control over debt creation and in order to issue notes or bonds local governments had to obtain the approval of the state commission. In arriving at its decision, the Commission was to consider such factors as whether the amount of the proposed bond issue was excessive, whether the resulting increase in the tax rate would be burdensome and whether the local government was in default on any of its existing indebtedness. The Commission also supervised the investment of the sinking fund assets of the local governments. The maladministration of sinking funds has been one of the most serious abuses of municipal finance throughout the United States, for time and again local officials had placed these funds in improper assets. The North Carolina Commission was given the power to designate the assets eligible for the investment of sinking funds. The Commission was also empowered to bring about uniform municipal accounting and to institute a system of regular reports and examinations.

REGULATION OF RAILWAY AND UTILITY FINANCE

In the post-war period, the federal government extended its control over railway financing under the Transportation Act of 1920.[57] One of the fundamental purposes of this Act was to maintain the credit of the railroads and so attract capital for the improvement of railway service. The Transportation Act gave the Interstate Commerce Commission control over the issue of new securities by the railroads. The only excepted securities were those which had a maturity of less than two years and which were less than five percent of the par value of a company's outstanding securities. The Commission also had the power to fix the minimum price which a railroad was to receive for a new issue.[58] The Commission could also scrutinize the profits of the bankers underwriting railroad issues, and at various times tried to prevent excessive fees. In the railway field for many years it was the practice of a road to float all its issues through the same banking house. The Interstate Commerce Commission opposed this system of closed relationship between railroads and banking houses, and insisted upon the policy of open competitive bidding whenever the railroads sought to obtain new capital through equipment trusts.[59]

Over these years the state public utility commissions continued to exercise extensive control over the financing of these corporations.[60] The commissions regulated particularly the capitalization of the utility companies, and determined the amount of stock which could be issued in relation to the volume of bonds or to the earnings of the company. Holding company control has often obstructed regulation by public service Commissions. Through service contracts, overcapitalization and other means, holding companies have frequently rendered such control ineffective and at times even impossible.

REGULATION OF FOREIGN FINANCE

With the growth in the volume of new foreign securities the federal government began to exercise control over this type of financing. At first this regulation was for the purpose of supporting the interests of American bankers in their competition for such loans.[61] In the period from 1914 until 1917 the national government also attempted to control the sale of the bonds of the belligerent nations in the New York market.[62] A definite statement of the policy of the American government toward the growing volume of capital export in the post-war period was enunciated in 1922. In 1921 several members of President Harding's cabinet held a conference with a group of investment bankers interested in international finance. At this meeting the government expressed the desire to be kept informed of the future capital movements from this country, and the banking group was asked to cooperate in furnishing the government with this information.[63] Under date of March 3, 1922, the government issued its "Statement for the Press on Flotations of Foreign Loans" which declared that: " . . . it is hoped that American concerns that contemplate foreign loans will inform the Department of State in due time of the essential facts and subsequent developments of importance." This statement became known as the "ruling of 1922" and formed the basis of the government's policy regarding the control of our foreign loans in the twenties. Under this ruling a definite procedure of control over the flotation of foreign loans was established.[64] An American banking house, contemplating the flotation of a foreign loan, would send to the State Department a written memorandum giving the important details of the prospective loan and asking whether there were any objections to it. Thereupon the State Department with the cooperation of other departments, undertook an investigation of the loan from the standpoint of public policy. Various government agencies particularly the Commerce Department began to collect data on foreign financial developments, and usually there was adequate information available to serve as a basis for judging whether the proposed loan was in accordance with public policy.

Attempts were made by Congress to supplement or supersede the informal executive ruling of 1922 by a formal act of the legislature. Senator Glass particularly attacked its legality and insisted that the practice of the State Department amounted to approval of the issuance of foreign bonds, and criticized the Department for "usurping of a banking function and engaging in lawless activities." He added that "the foreign bonds were sold to the investors of this country with moral sanction of the government." [65]

In general governmental control over foreign investment in the case of the United States was relatively slight. The American government did not use its power to derive any direct political advantage for the United States. Furthermore, the policy of the American government did not result in political complication. Although American investors in the post-war period lost millions of dollars in the defaults by South American and by European governments, in no case did such action bring about American intervention or direct political action.

GENERAL REGULATION BY STATE BLUE SKY LAWS

In addition to the regulation of specific classes of securities as municipal, railway, utility and foreign issues, the state and the federal governments also exercised general control over the demand for capital. Such general regulation by the state government was expressed in the passage of the so-called "blue sky" laws to prohibit the sale of fraudulent issues.[66] A series of proceedings were instituted to test the constitutionality of the state blue sky laws and at first the courts took an unfavorable view. However, after a number of contradictory opinions in the lower courts, the constitutionality of the basic principle of the blue sky legislation was upheld by the Supreme Court of the United States.[67]

The regulation of securities under these statutes was at first very limited. Although the United States as a whole had experienced a rapid development of security capitalism, the system was largely concentrated in a small number of security markets. Throughout the rest of the country the financial machinery was still undeveloped and most of the states did not have important security markets. However, after 1920 with the extension of security capitalism the need of state regulation over security issues became pressing, and so state laws were more fully developed. These state laws may be classified in two groups. Fraud acts sought to punish fraud in the sale of securities and general blue sky laws attempted to regulate the sale of all but certain exempted securities.[68] The fraud act generally requires no registration of securities and is not in the true sense a blue sky law. An example of this type is the Martin Act of New York under which criminal action can be brought against the issuers and dealers in fraudulent securities. On the other hand, a real blue sky law makes it unlawful to issue or sell securities without first obtaining permission of the state within which the securities are to be sold. Exemption is granted to certain classes of securities, as the issues of the United States Government, a state, a political subdivision, a friendly foreign government, or a public utility company supervised by a state government. Because of the variation in the blue sky laws, the National Conference of Commissioners on Uniform State Laws in 1922 began the preparation of a uniform blue sky law, which in 1930 was finally adopted by the Conference and later approved by the American Bar Association.[69]

In explaining the state laws on security regulation the officials generally went out of their way to indicate that such legislation was limited in scope and did not extend to the control of the quality of the securities being issued. Thus, Attorney-General Albert Ottinger of New York, in explaining the Martin Fraud Act to the National Association of Security Commissioners, stated that:

It, (the Martin Act) does not create the licensing system because we believe in this state the volume of business is so vast that it would be absolutely impossible to pass upon the merits of particular securities, and that being so, it would be most unfortunate for investors to be seized by the notion that there was a state guarantee or a state sanction or a state approval of the particular security which is being sold to the people.[70]

However, in the actual administration of the law, the attorney-general of New York was often forced to exercise wide discretion which came close to qualitative control, as indicated by the fact that he drew up definite rules of practice for certain classes of securities "in the public interest."[71] Thus, in 1926, the attorney-general formulated definite rules regarding real estate mortgage bonds which went far beyond merely the elimination of fraud, and established rules of quality for the protection of investors in this type of security. Again, in a report on investment trusts, the attorney-general included specific statements as to the tests which this type of security should pass.

GENERAL REGULATION BY THE FEDERAL GOVERNMENT — CAPITAL ISSUES COMMITTEE

The first effort made by the federal government at general regulation of the demand for capital occurred during the War through the agency of the Capital Issues Committee. The operation of this little-known organization was of deep significance, since it constituted a general regulation of both the quality and the quantity of the demand for capital.[72] The first intimation that the government was planning to control the capital market came in June 1917 in the press statement that "the closing of money markets to further foreign government bond issues is regarded as imperative if the Government is to remain master of the financial situation."[73] The increasing pressure of government financing brought about a better realization of the need of regulating new financing.

The first exercise of formal governmental control over the flotation of new capital issues was evidenced in a letter written by Secretary McAdoo to the Miami conservation district which was planning to float a large bond issue for flood control purposes. Mr.
McAdoo made the following statement :

It is my hope that others charged with similar responsibilities in
respect to the financing of enterprises both public and private will make
it their practice to consult with the Secretary of the Treasury before
undertaking any new financing, or indeed before making commitments
or expenditures that would require it to be financed by borrowings.[74]

This publicly-stated wish of the treasury was generally respected,
and so corporations and local governments submitted their requests
to the federal government.

The work of passing on these new issues was referred to a committee consisting of three members of the Federal Reserve Board
assisted by an advisory committee of three bankers. In each Federal
Reserve district there was a local committee consisting of the chairman and the governor of the Federal Reserve bank, and three other
members including usually a banker, a public utility official and a
manufacturer. These local committees were consulted by the committee of the Federal Reserve Board in determining whether a new
issue was "compatible with the public interest." [75]

This informal organization was given official status as the Capital
Issues Committee. The formal organization of this government
agency for control of the capital market was the same as the previous
informal system. There was a national Capital Issues Committee
composed of three members of the Federal Reserve Board and three
advisory members, and in addition in each district there was a local
sub-committee.[76]

The primary purpose of the Capital Issues Committee was to
control the volume of securities floated. As one official declared,
"the first direct reason for having the control of capital issues is to
prevent competition in the money markets."[77] In addition, however, the agency also exercised qualitative control over new issues.
This is evident from an official statement that in performing their
work the local committee members

consider whether that corporation embarking in time of war is apt to
achieve financial success, or whether it is not ; whether the men engaged
in it are of the proper character ; whether the subject-matter of the new
corporation is one which serves a war purpose. And then, over and
beyond that, they also consider the plan and method whereby the moneys
are to be obtained by that particular corporation to finance its work.[78]

The reports of the local committees were carefully studied by the
Capital Issues Committee which was "thinking in national terms

and acting in national terms." The Committee was advised by well qualified experts. Thus both the local and the national committees, in addition to considering merely the question of the "compatibility" of a particular issue in relation to war finance, actually undertook a study of the credit position of the prospective issuer of securities. The significant feature of the Capital Issues Committee was the fact that it undertook both quantitative and even qualitative control of the capital market.

The Committee, however, made it clear that its approval of a proposed financial undertaking was not to be construed to mean "that the committee had passed upon the credit standing of the company issuing the securities, or that it was recommending the security to the public as a desirable investment." [79] In another statement the Committee said that it would not "express any opinion upon the intrinsic merits of the securities to be offered for sale," and it was concerned only with whether the issue was timely in respect to the financial operations to be undertaken by the government and whether the purposes for which the funds were to be raised, were compatible with national interest.[80]

The work of the Capital Issues Committee was considerable. Between May 17, 1918 when the formal committee was organized and November 11, 1918 when the Armistice was signed, the Committee passed upon 2,289 applications involving new securities with a par or face value of $2,564,021,000.[81] In addition to this volume of securities which were approved, the Committee considered numerous issues which were not approved. In many cases applications were voluntarily withdrawn, and thus the Committee exercised considerable influence in restricting the unnecessary use of capital.

With the close of the War, the Committee unanimously recommended that "federal supervision of security issues here undertaken for the first time should be continued by some public agency." [82] However, there was a general feeling, as stated by Dr. Willis, that the "limitation of investment had undoubtedly caused considerable hardship." During the administration of Secretary of the Treasury Glass, the Committee was advised that it might be well to reduce its activities" and soon thereafter was abolished entirely.[83]

FEDERAL SECURITIES ACT

The move for general federal regulation of the demand for capital came in 1918 when the Capital Issues Committee proposed a federal securities act which was recommended to Congress by President Wilson.[84] This bill also had the support of Secretary of the Treasury Glass but the bill was not reported out of Committee.[85]

Other bills to regulate the sale of investment securities were introduced in Congress, particularly in the years immediately following the close of the War, but were not enacted. The most important of these early bills was that of E. T. Taylor, of Colorado.[86] This bill was not passed by Congress but it later formed the basis for the Securities Act of 1933.[87]

In 1933 Congress passed the Securities Act designed "to provide full and fair disclosure of the character of securities sold in interstate and foreign commerce and through the mails and to prevent frauds in the sale thereof."[88] The purpose of this Act was not to replace state laws regulating securities but rather to supplement them, and in addition to furnish the investor with more detailed financial information, statistics and data. The fundamental part of the statute (Section 12) provided severe penalties if a prospectus "includes an untrue statement of a material fact or omits to state a material fact necessary in order to make the statements not misleading." The Act, following the general content of state blue sky laws, exempted from its provisions a number of securities such as those issued or guaranteed by the United States, by any state, or by any political subdivision of a state or territory, those issued by a corporation organized for non-profit making purposes, by a building and loan or similar association, or by a common carrier subject to the Interstate Commerce Commission, certificates issued by a receiver in bankruptcy, insurance policies issued by a corporation operating under a state insurance commission, and notes or drafts with maturities not exceeding nine months. The federal act also exempted various types of financial transactions, such as those conducted by persons other than issuers, underwriters, or dealers and transactions not involving any public offering, brokers' transactions executed upon customers' orders, and the exchange of securities without payment of a commission.

With the exception of these exempted securities and transactions, the law applied to all securities in the sense of notes, bonds, debentures, transferable shares, or certificates of interest in property, tangible or intangible. All such securities were to be registered with the Securities and Exchange Commission, which administers the Act.[89]

The Securities Act was based on the first premise that the investing public had suffered losses on securities because it had received fraudulent (that is, untruthful) and inadequate information regarding new securities offered for sale. The Senate Committee on Banking and Currency, made the statement that "the exposure at the subcommittee hearings of flagrant misrepresentations and concealment in these prospectuses upon which members of the investing public implicitly relied, to their detriment, furnished one of the most important grounds for the passage of the Securities Act of 1933." The Committee added that the Securities Act was passed "to prevent a recurrence of these gross frauds." [90] In passing the Securities Act, it was also the accepted view of Congress that the losses experienced by investors in securities had been due mainly to the failure of the issuing bankers to tell the "truth about securities." [91]

The Securities Act was based on the second premise that the investing public would be protected if it received truthful and adequate information regarding securities offered for sale. Publicity was therefore the remedy offered by the Securities Act. Mr. J. P. Kennedy, as Chairman of the Securities and Exchange Commission, stated that "the greater the publicity, the more protected the public will be and the more corrective the influence upon the financiers." [92]

Both of these premises are questionable. In the first place, the losses on securities caused by fraud as defined in the New York State law were relatively small compared with the vast total of securities issued.[93] Very few cases of fraud were actually proved against investment bankers. The various federal hearings on financial legislation did not disclose conclusive proof of fraud, with the possible exception of one instance in the case of the securities listed on the New York Stock Exchange. Even in the case of foreign bonds there were only a few cases of misrepresentation which would have brought such issues within the scope of the Securities Act had it been in operation at the time, according to an analysis, made by the author, of the prospectuses of which public notice was given in the leading New York City newspapers for the years from 1925 to 1929 inclusive.[94]

Secondly, this study of the prospectuses showed that the investing public did receive truthful and adequate information which disclosed the inherent weaknesses in most of the bonds eventually in default. In most cases a careful reading of the prospectus by the investor would have indicated the unsound financial position of the bond which was being offered for sale. Again and again the prospectus truthfully and adequately stated that the earning power of the corporation was insufficient, that the security pledged for the bonds was inadequate, that the past financial record of the corporation was bad, or that the corporation was reserving for itself powers which might adversely affect the investment position of the bond. As shown on pages 370–371 the financial position of a corporation, and therefore the investment status of its bonds, can best be determined by its income account, and so the Securities Act requires that a true statement of the income account must be given to the public. In the past such statements were frequently included in the prospectuses, and repeatedly these figures clearly showed that the income of the corporation was so meager that even a small reduction in income would have made it impossible for the corporation to meet the interest on the bonds which were being offered to the public. A large steamship company offering its debentures showed that the operating ratio of the company was 93 percent and that the balance after the interest on the funded debt to gross earnings was only 3.2 percent. In other words the prospectus clearly showed that a drop of 3.2 percent in gross earnings would have impaired the protection of the interest payment.[95]

Investment houses frequently demonstrated their complete lack of respect for the intelligence of the investor by showing truthfully and adequately that the property pledged as security for the bond issue was entirely insufficient. An illustration was the twenty year 6½ percent sinking fund gold debentures of the Lincoln 42nd Street Corporation which, the circular stated, "will be a direct obligation of the Lincoln 42nd Street Corporation subject only to the $16,000,000 first mortgage issue." The prospectus further showed that these two issues amounted to $21,500,000 or over 84 percent of the estimated value of the unconstructed building.[96] The holders of these bonds certainly could not claim fraud under the Securities Act, for the prospectus truthfully stated the material facts necessary to show the unsoundness of the bond issue and was neither fraudulent nor misleading in the literal sense of the Act.

One would generally believe that a corporation which had previously defaulted on its bonds would make every effort to conceal this condition from the investing public. As a matter of fact, a number of corporations truthfully and accurately gave the investing public the full details of their previous bankruptcy, and even emphasized this fact as an argument for their present strong credit position. A certain Southern railroad, in its prospectus describing its $4,136,000 first mortgage 20-year 6 percent gold bonds, frankly stated that "the recently consummated reorganization, by extinguishing the lien of $8,000,000 mortgage debt of the old company and providing the new company with $1,550,000 of new money, besides the proceeds of these Series A bonds, will have reduced fixed interest bearing debt from $11,692,000 to $5,742,000." This road for a number of years had poor earning power and as a result in October, 1929 it again went into receivership.

Of the various prospectuses which truthfully and adequately told the investor the unfavorable terms of the issue, a common type openly proclaimed that the borrowing corporation was reserving for itself without restriction certain powers which might adversely affect the investment position of the bond. A spectacular illustration of such a grant of unrestricted power by the bondholders to an issuing corporation was the $50,000,000 5 percent secured sinking fund gold debenture of the Krueger and Toll Company issued on March 1, 1929. The prospectus contained a clause that "in view of the nature of the business of the Company the Debenture Agreement will contain broad provision in regard to withdrawal and substitution of pledged securities." The agreement merely provided that such substitutions should not impair the required ratio of 120 percent between the par value of the eligible securities on deposit and the principal amount and interest payable on all the outstanding debentures.[97] The agreement further provided that the trustee was to rely upon the Krueger and Toll Company for proof that the securities were eligible and that the ratio was being maintained. The debenture agreement specified the original collateral which secured this issue, and included a number of sound bonds such as French 3's and 4's. In the course of time these sound securities were withdrawn and there was substituted Yugoslavian and other bonds which were on the verge of default.[98] It is doubtful whether Ivan Krueger in this case could have been convicted under the Securities Act, for, as mentioned above, the agreement contained "broad provisions in regard to withdrawal and substitution of pledged securities." [99]

It is doubtful whether the flotation of the above issues could have been prevented or the corporate issuers or the investment bankers punished under the Securities Act. Yet all these issues brought heavy losses to the investor, and such losses can legally be repeated in the future. The Securities Act relies on publicity as the sole protection against loss, but the previous cases show that, even when the truth regarding an investment is given, the investor is unable to understand the significance of this information. The Securities Act fails to recognize the highly complicated nature of the modern investment system and the extreme technicality of security analysis.[100] The Securities Act of 1933 therefore embodied little more than the early Victorian principle of publicity laid down by Gladstone's Committee in 1844.[101] This principle, possibly adequate for the early period of security capitalism, was certainly inadequate in its critical stage.

The Securities Act was therefore based on questionable premises, since the major losses on securities were not caused by the investing public receiving fraudulent and inadequate information, and the investing public was not protected by merely receiving truthful and adequate information regarding securities. As shown in Chapter 16 losses on corporate and governmental securities were caused by the unsound trends in private and in public finance. This fundamental defect in the present investment system is entirely ignored by the Securities Act.[102] Therefore it will still be possible for investment bankers under the stress of competition to issue bonds which meet every provision of the Securities Act but which are of uncertain quality. As long as all of the material facts are given, investment bankers can still legally issue bonds of foreign governments with budgetary deficits, and real estate bonds resting on overappraised properties. Also the Securities Act does not check the overproduction of securities. In short, the main errors of post-war financial policy namely, the issuing of securities of poor quality and in excessive amount are still outside the scope of the Securities Act.[103] A further weakness of the Securities Act lies in the fact that state and municipal financing is exempt from its provisions. This vast field has been marked by unfavorable financial practices which have brought loss to investors. As emphasized in this study, it is essential for the government to consider the evils not only in corporate, but also in governmental finance.

REGULATION OF THE STOCK EXCHANGE

The heavy losses sustained by the public after the stock market collapse of 1929 led to a popular demand for drastic control of the security market. In response to the public demand for action, legislators at times sought extreme forms of action. Thus one leading senator, stirred by heavy losses of the public but unmindful of the experience of King Canute, sent the Stock Exchange the following telegram:

Today's activity in your Exchange demonstrates absolute necessity for immediate adoption of a rule limiting amount of loss on any stock during any one session. The country is not prepared to withstand the effect of a repetition of what happened today. Unless a rule is adopted and published establishing a reasonable amount of depreciation in any one session, campaign for reform will immediately take shape with possible result either closing Exchange entirely or placing same under Government supervision.[103]

In 1934 Congress passed the Securities and Exchange Act. To enforce the Act a Securities and Exchange Commission was created consisting of five members appointed by the President for a term of five years. Each securities exchange had to file a registration statement in a form prescribed by the Securities and Exchange Commission. In that statement the exchange agreed to comply with the provisions of the Act and to require compliance by its members. The rules of each exchange provided for the expulsion, suspension, or disciplining of members whose conduct was inconsistent with equitable principles. Margin requirements were established by the Federal Reserve Board, with provision to be made especially for undermargined accounts and for the withdrawal of funds or securities pledged as collateral for loans. Members of the exchanges and brokers or dealers operating through these exchanges could borrow on a registered security from member banks of the Federal Reserve System or from non-member banks complying with the Securities Exchange Act, the Federal Reserve Act and the Banking Act of 1933. However the Securities and Exchange Commission was given power to permit a broker to borrow elsewhere with its approval. The total debt of a broker, exclusive of his fixed assets and the value of his exchange membership, was not to exceed such percentage of his net capital as the Securities and Exchange Commission prescribed and in no case was to be over 2,000 percent of such capital. Moreover, no broker could lend securities carried for the account of any customer without the latter's written consent.

The Act forbade manipulation of security prices by various devices as the transfer of securities involving no change in beneficial ownership, the dissemination of rumors about the market movement of a security to enable a group to buy or sell a security on favorable terms, and the employment of a manipulative practice in contravention of the rules of the Securities and Exchange Commission.

The Securities and Exchange Act, like the Securities Act, sought to aid the security purchaser by giving him detailed information regarding stocks and bonds. Corporations whose securities are listed or registered on exchanges must submit annual reports prescribed by the Securities and Exchange Commission. However the Securities and Exchange Act has been more effective than the Securities Act in correcting abuses of the investment system. The Securities and Exchange Act has made progress in correcting unfair practices as security manipulation through pools, wash sales and matched orders which characterized many of the stock market operations of the past. Also the efficient administration of the Act has regulated the use of credit in financing security trading and has reduced the instability arising out of inadequate margins.

CONCLUSION

Governmental control of security capitalism in the post-war period varied in its effectiveness. Legislation aiming to bring about business revival and the relief of the debt burden by monetary action rested on a misconception of the debtor class under security capitalism. The Federal Reserve system became the battleground for the conflicting forces of the governmental and banking interests which fought to gain possession of the Reserve Board, the Reserve banks and the Open Market Committee, and this internecine war proved harmful to both sides. The full operation of the Reserve system was restricted by its adherence to the orthodox theory of commercial banking. This theory led to congressional legislation separating commercial from investment banking and the abolition of the security affiliates of the commercial banks. The Banking Act of 1933 made excellent provision for checking the use of credit by commercial banks for speculative purposes and in other ways overcame a number of the unsound practices which had crept into the commercial banking system. The regulation of the quality of the security investments of the financial institutions by the federal government was negligible, while such regulation by the state governments was marked by a lack of uniformity and a failure to realize the changing conditions in the security market. The federal government in later years came to the aid of the financial institutions through national organizations created to grant direct assistance or to guaranty the liabilities of these institutions. Both the federal and state governments exercised public control over the demand for capital. Specific control was exercised by some of the states in regulating municipal and utility investments and by the federal government in controlling railroad and foreign investment. In addition, general control was exercised by the state governments in blue sky laws and by the federal government in the Securities Act. While the Securities and Exchange Act proved useful, the Securities Act was inadequate to correct the fundamental unsound tendencies in the capital market. The Capital Issues Committee, formed during the War, was the only organization of public control which provided for quantitative and qualitative control of the capital market. In general, federal legislation failed to realize that the United States had passed out of agricultural and town economy and into the stage of security capitalism which required a financial machinery carefully controlled for the purpose of attaining not only profit for the individual but also welfare for society as a whole.

CHAPTER 20

RECONSTRUCTION

OUR survey has now traced the evolution of security capitalism in the leading countries of the world. Let us consider therefore the general policies necessary for the reconstruction of security capitalism as well as a specific program for the control of the financial institutions of the system.

NON-FINANCIAL INSTITUTIONS OF SECURITY CAPITALISM — DEMOCRACY

In the case of most countries, parliamentary government was the political institution which nurtured the growth of security capitalism. Democracy was a potent factor in the growth of security capitalism in the nineteenth century in England, the United States and to a lesser degree in France. However, democracy is not an absolutely essential condition for the existence of security capitalism. In the case of Germany in the pre-war period, parliamentarianism was a form rather than a fact, but nevertheless security capitalism attained a high degree of development. During the post-war period, in the case of Russia, Germany, Italy and Japan, security capitalism existed under political institutions from which parliamentarianism was largely or completely eliminated. The experience of security capitalism under such conditions of authoritarianism has been for so short duration that no definite conclusion can be drawn as to the relative social and economic progress which security capitalism has made in these countries. However, the results of security capitalism under both fascism and communism furnish no ground for the belief that these political systems would enable security capitalism to bring individual or social benefit to the United States to the extent now derived under a democratic form of government. As far as the United States is concerned, security capitalism can best be served by maintaining and strengthening our present democratic system of government.

In certain countries security capitalism has exerted an unfortunate influence upon domestic politics, particularly in the struggle between industrial and banking security capitalism. The conflict between these two types of security capitalism was sharpest in the case of Germany where the former supported National Socialism and obtained political domination. The struggle was also waged in Italy.

319

In the case of Japan it has become rather a conflict of agrarian forces against both banking and industrial capitalism. In England, and to a less degree in France, banking capitalism has been dominant throughout the evolution of security capitalism. In the United States, banking security capitalism triumphed in the pre-war period. However, as a result of the depression after 1929, banking capitalism has been weakened, while on the other hand industrial capitalism is today relatively stronger than in the nineteenth century. Fortunately the issue between these two types of capitalism has not been joined in the United States, and every effort should be made to avoid such a struggle which would inevitably have serious economic and social consequences.

NECESSITY FOR INTERNATIONAL PEACE

While no particular domestic political institution is absolutely essential to security capitalism, there is no question that international peace is a necessary political condition for the satisfactory operation of world security capitalism. Throughout the period of comparative international peace from the close of the Napoleonic Wars to the outbreak of the Great War, security capitalism flowered in England, France, Germany and the United States and to a lesser degree in other countries. As a result of the World War, the developed stage of world security capitalism was checked and the system as a whole entered its critical stage.

The relation of American security capitalism to the Great War demonstrated beyond question that this nation, notwithstanding every intention to keep aloof from the next conflict, will abandon its economic, financial and eventually political neutrality and finally become an active participant. It is therefore clear that the United States should take active and positive measures to join with other nations in the removal of the political and economic factors which are driving the nations of the world to another world conflict.

Developed security capitalism also requires the expansion of its international economic operations as evidenced by the growing volume of the export of goods, services and of capital. In recent years the free flow of goods between nations has been seriously restricted by tariff barriers and currency regulations, and the volume of world trade has declined in relation to world production. This maladjustment is one of the most serious problems of developed security capitalism. The readjustment of world trade and world production is highly important for American security capitalism, since it became internationalized earlier in its history than is generally realized. This characteristic of American security capitalism was carried further by the events of the war and post-war periods. As a result of the growing importance of such internationalization, the United States during the depression was directly affected by the adverse conditions of security capitalism in other countries, and notwithstanding its own vast economic and financial resources was able to make only moderate progress toward recovery. It would therefore be to the interest of the United States to remove the barriers hindering the free flow of goods and capital, and bring about a revival of both international trade and international investment.

MONETARY POLICY

Throughout the nineteenth century the growth of security capitalism was facilitated as a result of the adoption of the gold standard by the leading countries of the world. Until the outbreak of the War, these nations were favored by a comparatively stable monetary unit. In the war and the post-war periods the gold standard was abandoned, and the currencies of most of the countries were devalued. These policies had an adverse effect upon security capitalism, since such manipulation injected an element of uncertainty in monetary value and intensified the instability of the system. Moreover, the devaluation of the currencies dealt serious blows to those classes in economic society which had accumulated capital and therefore held fixed-interest bearing securities or bank deposits.

It is therefore clear that a policy of monetary stabilization is desirable and essential.

Stabilization within a nation may be attained after any one of three possible steps, namely, repudiation, restoration or devaluation. Repudiation, really a prelude to permanent stabilization, as in the case of Germany and Austria, implies the complete abandonment of the old form of currency and the adoption of a new monetary unit. Such a drastic policy becomes necessary only in cases of extreme depreciation of the currency and so is unthinkable for the United States. The second policy may be that of restoration or bringing the dollar back to its former gold content of 23.22 grains of gold. Devaluation is the policy of reducing the monetary content of the standard.

The choice for the United States lies between the policy either of restoration or of devaluation. From the standpoint of the parties to security capitalism, a policy of restoration would in general benefit the holders of high-grade fixed-income securities and injure the holders of equities and low-grade securities. Raising the value of the dollar from its present level to the previous par would multiply the burden of debt. The added interest payment on this debt

—(and further)

might even prove intolerable, for it must be remembered that in the last analysis such interest and principal payments represent transfers of purchasing power from debtors and tax payers to creditors. It would therefore seem that restoration is impossible, and that a policy of permanent devaluation is the only recourse for the United States. Furthermore, it is highly essential that such a policy of permanent stabilization at about the present levels be carried out with international cooperation as soon as possible in order to eliminate one of the most serious uncertainties in the economic system of the world.

DECLINE IN RATE OF POPULATION GROWTH

The developed stage of security capitalism was marked by a sharp increase in industrial production. During the first industrial revolution the output of the mines and factories of England expanded enormously, and in the course of the second industrial revolution at the close of the nineteenth century the plants of France, England and the United States multiplied their operations. The domestic demand for their products was increased to a large extent by the rapid rate of growth in population. However, the rate of population increase in England dropped in the eighties; was checked in Europe during the War and declined even in the United States in the nineteen-twenties.

This change in the population trend was a social factor of deep significance for the system of security capitalism. In the past the growth of the railroads, the expansion of the electric light and power companies and the increasing output of the manufacturing concerns had consciously or unconsciously been based on the ever-increasing rate of population growth. This basis can no longer be accepted in the future. Under these conditions is has become necessary for the United States to adjust its production, whether in agriculture or in manufacture, and its plant expansion to meet present day market conditions.

SOCIAL SUPPORT OF SECURITY CAPITALISM

The benefits of the developed stage of security capitalism were widely shared by economic society. Not only did the upper class in economic society gain from the system, but the middle and even the lower classes shared in the growth of national income and national wealth. The middle class derived increasing returns from their business enterprises and from their security operations due to the appreciating value of their stocks and bonds. While unemployment increased in England after the nineties, in other leading countries, particularly Germany and the United States, the condition of the laboring class improved. It is therefore little wonder that not only the upper, but the middle and lower classes gave strong social support to security capitalism.

In the post-war period, this support was seriously weakened. In almost every country business profits were sharply reduced or entirely eliminated. The middle class saw its direct investment in securities as well as its indirect investment in bank deposits and life insurance policies swept away in the case of Germany, decimated in the case of France and depreciated in the case of the United States and England. The laboring classes suffered severely from unemployment even in the United States. In the post-war period there was probably no decline in the proportionate share of national income available to the middle and lower class, but there was a sharp reduction in the total national income available to all classes. As a result, social support for security capitalism gave way to social hostility. This opposition gave vent to the espousal of National Socialism in Germany and the encouragement of fascist and communist movements in other countries.

Private security capitalism, if it is to survive, must regain broad social support. Not only the upper, but also the middle and lower classes, must derive full economic benefit from the system. This end can be obtained by both an increase in the national income and a more equitable distribution of this income.

PHILOSOPHIC BASIS OF SECURITY CAPITALISM

Over the years a consciously-formulated economic philosophy exercised little influence in shaping the course of security capitalism. The classical economists in the early nineteenth century failed to understand the nature of the system, and the socialist writers of the middle nineteenth century were naturally hostile to it.

The modern schools of economic thought have made little progress in the field of financial philosophy. Monetary and banking theory have largely been based on the policies of the old individual capitalism and not of the new security capitalism. Furthermore, this theory has failed to consider the effect of the non-financial factors in modern civilization on financial institutions. There is therefore urgent need for the formulation of a realistic financial theory based on an appreciation of the changes in our financial institutions, and a recognition of the influence of the non-financial forces on monetary and banking policies. As in Plato's republic of old, so today, the constructive economic philosopher should take an active part in reconstructing security capitalism.

The growth of corporate law furnished a further institutional basis for security capitalism. The legal recognition of the principle of limited liability, the incorporation by general rather than by special charters, the sanctioning of the holding company, the refinement of the corporate mortgage, and the development of the various forms of stock and bond instruments made possible the flotation of securities and their sale to the investing public. Over the years these legal devices in every country were frequently misapplied as evidenced by the abuses of the holding company by the separation of capital management from ownership and by the evils of overcapitalization, and resulted in widespread violation of property rights. In recent years progress has been made in purifying corporate activities but there is still need of drastic recodification and further regulation to overcome many of the abuses which still exist and to protect the holders of corporate securities.

In summary, the non-financial institutions of security capitalism in the United States can be strengthened by maintaining a democratic system of government, avoiding the clash between banking and industrial security capitalism, taking positive measures to promote world peace, reviving international trade and investment, securing international monetary stabilization, adjusting production to changing markets, widening the social support of security capitalism, developing a realistic financial philosophy and recodifying the laws relating to security capitalism.

FINANCIAL INSTITUTIONS OF SECURITY CAPITALISM — CENTRAL BANK

Consideration has thus been given to the broader political, economic, social, philosophic and legal institutions of security capitalism, and the policies in these respective fields which should be carried out. Attention will now be directed to the recommendations concerning purely financial institutions of the system, as the central bank, the stock exchange, banking organization and the supply of capital.

The keystone in the financial organization of security capitalism is the central bank. The extent to which this institution aided the progress of security capitalism varied considerably. On the one hand, the Bank of France and the Reichsbank actively aided the growth of the system, while on the other hand, the Bank of England and the Federal Reserve system following slavishly the British traditions of central banking took only a passive part in the movement. In the United States the Federal Reserve should take an active not a passive role in the future in influencing the course of American security capitalism.

Over the years a complete change has taken place in the relation between the government and the central bank. In the case of France and Germany, there was a close association even before the War. In the post-war period in almost every country the banking and the political forces struggled for control over the central bank. In France the fight was particularly bitter and led finally to the diminution of the hereditary banking control over the Bank of France. A similar, though fortunately milder, struggle was waged for control of the Federal Reserve system, and legislation finally brought about an extension of public control. Unquestionably such increase of government control carries with it certain dangers, but it must be frankly recognized that in these days of fiscal difficulties the federal government is justified in its demand for increased control over the central bank. A rational policy would bring about a proper balance between the banking and the public control over the central bank by recognizing the respective interests and needs of both the banks and of the government.

STOCK EXCHANGE

In the course of time in each country, the stock exchange of the leading financial center developed more rapidly than the interior exchanges, and became the dominant security market. The extent of such domination was carried to a marked degree in England, France and Germany, and to a lesser degree in the United States. Throughout the nineteenth century the stock exchange played an important role not only in the financial but also in the economic and political life of the nation. However, after the Great War, the stock exchange became relatively less important due to the trend of banking concentration, to the relative decline in the volume of corporate financing, to the increase in government financing which was generally undertaken directly with investors and to the closer governmental regulation of security operations.

The stock exchange is still a financial institution of major importance in the economic life of modern capitalism. Unquestionably its operations must be regulated either by within or by the government. Such regulation should be directed toward checking as far as possible price fluctuations, for instability of security value is one of the major unsolved problems of security capitalism.

NEED FOR BANKING RESPONSIBILITY

An important change in the financial system before the War was the decline in the relative importance of the private bank, a vestige of individual capitalism, as compared with the incorporated bank. This decline of the private bank was indicated by the lessening importance of Rothschilds on the Continent and of Morgans in the United States. In general these powerful private banks in their time exerted a stabilizing influence over the system of security capitalism. Throughout the nineteenth century Rothschilds aided the rise and development of world security capitalism by throwing its influence on the side of peace and by supporting the principle of parliamentary government, and in the capital market by floating issues of high quality. Similarly Morgans in the United States replaced instability with stability, gave active assistance to the government in its financial difficulties during the nineties, and issued sound securities.

However in the course of time these single private houses, though possessed of considerable financial resources, were unable to influence either broad public or banking policy due to the decline in their relative importance as compared to that of incorporated banking.

Unfortunately incorporated banking did not develop a consciousness of its public responsibility. Incorporated banking came into possession of tremendous power, without realizing the significance of this power. It is therefore necessary for incorporated banking, since it has definitely replaced private banking to realize its social responsibility and to aid constructively in shaping public and banking policies which will strengthen rather than weaken the structure of security capitalism. In recent years the American Bankers Association representing commercial banking has made an effort in this direction.

On the other hand, practically no progress has been made in the field of investment banking where the need of such a constructive policy has been all the greater. After the War the dominance of Morgans over investment banking declined and was replaced by a competitive array of houses which had little or no sense of the social importance of their operations. This competition time and again led to serious evils in the overissue of securities and in the emission of low-grade securities. The investment banker too frequently concerned himself rather with financial salesmanship than with financial statesmanship. The post-war period brought not only banking irresponsibility in the field of national banking, but also in international banking relations. There is therefore need of promoting close international banking cooperation to cultivate a higher responsibility among the banking systems of the world, in view of the fact that modern capitalism is essentially international in nature and can function best if there is close coordination among the financial systems of the leading nations.

RECOGNITION OF CHANGING NATURE OF COMMERCIAL BANKING

With the development of security capitalism the function of commercial banking changed. This change was brought about not by conscious banking policy but by the sweep of broad economic movements. The improvement in transportation and communication helped to bring about a change in the method of financing business operations. On the one hand, the need of short-term capital was diminished, since the period of time required for the shipment of goods was reduced. This was true of the developed stage of British security capitalism in the middle of the nineteenth century with the replacement of sailing vessels by steamships and with the opening of the Suez Canal. It was similarly true of developed American security capitalism in the nineteen-twenties with the introduction of the improved devices of communications. Furthermore with the increase of the corporate form of business organization and the rise of the large business units, industry obtained its funds through securities sold to the public rather than through bank loans.

As a result, not only in the United States but in almost every other country of developed security capitalism there was an increase in time as compared with demand deposits, and an increase in the proportion of investment assets of banks particularly in the form of securities as compared with commercial assets in the form of loans and discounts. In addition the commercial banks performed investment operations by engaging in the purchase and sale of securities.

It is essential that the inevitability of these changes be recognized in government regulation. The function of a banking system should be to mobilize not only commercial but also investment credit, and legislation should be directed not to prohibit but rather to control this mobilization which in the future will be needed to meet the heavy demands of industry and of government.

A further change in the nature of commercial banking, particularly in recent years, has been the increase in the proportion of the assets of the commercial banks in the form of the securities of the national government. This movement has developed to such an extent that the financial position of banking is directly dependent upon the soundness of the credit of the national government. This close relationship between the banking system and public credit must be fully recognized by the government for it must be realized that the safety of the banking system is dependent upon the soundness of public credit. The weakness of the banking structure under security capitalism in foreign countries as well as in the United States lies in the lack of solvency or the insufficiency of capital resources to meet losses on depreciating assets particularly securities. It is therefore urgent that banks be encouraged and even required to build up their capital resources.

ADJUSTMENT OF THE CAPITAL MARKET

The history of security capitalism since the beginning of the nineteenth century shows two secular trends in the supply of capital in relation to the demand. The secular trend of the supply of capital was upward until the closing years of the nineteenth century, while thereafter the secular tend has been downward. A careful examination of the available data leads to the conclusion that the World as a whole to-day faces a shortage rather than a surplus of capital. This condition is particularly true with governments absorbing an increasing proportion of total capital accumulations and using a large part for unproductive expenditure on armaments. The peoples of the world are pinched, and their standards of living lowered in order that a larger proportion of their annual return may be absorbed by governments and applied to unsound and destructive purposes.

It is also important to recognize that the sources of saving have changed, and that under security capitalism saving emanates not only from individuals but also from corporations. With government demand for capital expanding and a larger percentage of the total accumulation being absorbed by tax levies, it seems illogical to discourage the source of such accumulations. In this country there exists a serious maladjustment in the supply of capital. There appears to be an abundance available for seasonal enterprise, but a great dearth for new risks. Commercial banking channels are choked with excess funds, but investment banking resources are insufficient to meet the real needs of American industry. Consumer goods industries apparently are able to obtain necessary short-term credit, but long-term capital is not available particularly for the durable goods industries.

Obviously the problem of capital supply is closely related to that of capital demand, since both forces are in effect playing upon the same situation. It becomes apparent from this study that the maladjustment between the force of capital supply, or saving, and that of capital demand, or investment, has been a fundamental cause of economic crises. This conclusion simplifies of course, that it is necessary to look behind the forces of both saving and investment to determine the causes of their relative movements, but it suggests that this may be the fulcrum point at which to apply the lever of control in order to achieve a degree of stabilization.

PUBLIC NATURE OF SECURITY CAPITALISM

An important trend of security capitalism has been the growing public nature of the system. This movement is evidenced first in the growing proportion of governmental to total securities. In the early stage of security capitalism it was mainly public in nature, since the government alone was in a position to float securities. This condition was true of England until the second quarter of the nineteenth century, and of the United States until the middle of the nineteenth century. However, in the developed stage of security capitalism, there was a relative increase in the volume of the securities of the railroads and of other corporations. Modern industry with its enormous plants and machinery required essentially fixed capital. Such capital could only be supplied through the issue of stocks and bonds which brought about the growth of private security capitalism.

However, the large volume of bonds issued by the national and local governments in the war and the post-war periods increased the proportion of such public securities, and in the case of most countries they constituted the larger part of the total. In view of this fact, any program of control must be extended to the regulation not only of corporate but also of public securities, since it would be futile to maintain standards for corporate financing if at the same time no similar standards were established for public financing.

As a result of the increase of debt, particularly of governments, the structure of security capitalism has been weakened. This unfavorable trend is evidenced by the increase of debt to total securities, the increase in the proportion of such debt to wealth and the increase of debt service to national income.

Adam Smith and David Hume were firmly convinced that the burden of the British national debt resulting from the wars of the eighteenth century could not be borne and would be repudiated. However, the debt, though heavy, was successfully carried and reduced due to the satisfactory political and economic conditions after the Napoleonic Wars. This study has similarly emphasized the burden of debt from the Great War and the depression, and has likewise indicated the possibility of eventual reduction or repudiation. Repudiation is inevitable particularly if the debt continues to be

incurred for armament and other unproductive purposes. The present debt can only be successfully carried provided the favorable
political and economic conditions of the post-Napoleonic period are
repeated, and the World enters into a new era of peace and of an
expanding industrial production and international trade.

ATTITUDES TOWARD SECURITY CAPITALISM

Toward the system of security capitalism itself, several possible
attitudes may be adopted. The first or ultra-conservative attitude,
based on the narrowest possible interpretation of laissez faire, would
be to permit the continued operation of the system without regulation and with financial competition unrestrained by either external
government regulation or internal control. This policy today is no
longer possible, for there is a general acceptance of the theory that
the evils of unrestrained security capitalism must be regulated either
by the parties to the system themselves or by the government. The
other or extreme radical policy would be to consider that security
capitalism has outlived its usefulness, that it is no longer able adequately to meet the requirements of a modern economic society and
therefore should be replaced by an entirely new economic system.
This policy likewise is not desirable in view of the advantages
to be derived from the efficient operation of security capitalism.

The third, or liberal policy, is opposed to the abolition of security capitalism but at the same time is based on the conviction
that the system cannot function without control. The liberal theory
aims rather to develop a proper mechanism of control by private
and public agencies which will overcome the evils of security capitalism and at the same time retain the benefits which the system
yielded to society in leading capital-accumulating countries of the
world throughout the nineteenth century.

Certain students, impressed by the gloom of the crisis of security
capitalism have discussed the future of modern capitalism in the
same general philosophy of pessimism expressed by Spengler in his
Decline of Western Civilization. This attitude of mind is in contrast
to the feeling of unrestrained optimism set forth by the classicists basking in the glow of rising security capitalism. While we
must necessarily recognize the fact that the system is already well
advanced, it has not as yet entered into what critics would call the
"decadent stage." True the system of private security capitalism
entered the critical stage even before the War, and was further
weakened by the conduct and the results of the War. It is still possible for private security capitalism to continue and regain its

strength under carefully conceived government control and consciously directed private management.

It is essential for bankers in Wall Street as well as Main Street and legislators on Pennsylvania Avenue to appreciate this distinction between democratically controlled capitalism and authoritarian capitalism. There should be a clearer realization that, as much as it may be regretted, uncontrolled security capitalism is a thing of the past. Bankers and capitalists should realize that a controlled security capitalism under a liberal democracy is far more desirable than a drastically regimented system under an authoritarian form of government. This so-called liberal view has come to be accepted by a wide range of individuals who have given thought to the subject. The necessity for a reform of the system is recognized not only by forward-looking economists but also by progressive bankers. As a result of his observations in Europe, Mr. Rudolph Hecht, former President of the American Bankers Association, in its convention of 1936 emphasized:

The need of our gracefully accepting some of the more moderate evolutionary changes going on at home, lest we, too, may face some of the social upheavals which have taken place and are still taking place throughout Europe today.[1]

Raymond N. Ball, President of the New York State Bankers Association, declared that:

The maladjustments created by the World War have caused revolutionary changes in the political social and economic life of the peoples of the world. . . There has been a growing movement on the part of the people, even ante-dating the World War for better social conditions. This movement has been expressed in various forms in different countries. In attempting to accomplish the expressed desires and needs of the majority for better social conditions I do not believe we are headed for Communism, Socialism or Fascism in this country. I am not disturbed, as yet, about a radical change in our form of government. We should be greatly disturbed however unless we face the facts and recognize that the desire for these changes are world-wide in their roots.[2]

A FINANCIAL PROGRAM

In the past too much reliance has been placed on the efficacy of regulating the financial system through credit control by the central bank. An almost childish faith has been placed in the efficacy of control through changes in the rediscount rate and even through open-market operations which by influencing the cost of money were supposed to ease or to tighten the money market. The limitations of these traditional methods of control were demonstrated by the experiences in the post-war period. Monetary manipulation is too weak a machine to control the powerful forces of disintegration which in recent years have shaken the financial system to its very foundation, nor can these forces be checked merely by applying the disclosure principle as embodied in the Securities Act. A more comprehensive mechanism must be set up to regulate the financial institutions of security capitalism. There is herewith presented a system for controlling these institutions of security capitalism. The plan proposed is not original but rather eclectic in nature in that it seeks to bring together the ideas and practical devices for the control of the financial institutions as evolved not only by the federal and state governments but also by bankers in their efforts to restore order from within.

There is first a need of unifying the various governmental agencies which regulate the operations of security capitalism particularly the Federal Reserve, the Federal Deposit Insurance Corporation, the Comptroller of the Currency, the Reconstruction Finance Corporation, the Interstate Commerce Commission (in its financial activities) the Securities and Exchange Commission and the Treasury Department. It would be well if all these federal agencies were unified into a Federal Finance system which would exercise all the powers now performed by these separate agencies.

The organization of the Federal Finance system should be built around the present Federal Reserve system which consists of a Board of Governors, Advisory Council, an Open Market Committee, twelve Federal Reserve banks and the commercial and the savings banks as members of the system. A Federal Finance Board could be formed by merging the present federal agencies into a single supervising body. This board and the system controlled by it should be divided into two parts, commercial and investment. Similar to the present Federal Advisory Council which confers with the Board of Governors on matters of commercial credit policy, there should be a Federal Advisory Council for Investment, appointed in the same manner as the present Advisory Council by the nomination of one member by each of the boards of directors of the twelve Federal Reserve Banks. However, the Federal Finance Board and the Federal Advisory Council for Investment should include not only representatives of banking, but also of the railroads, public utilities, industry, labor and agriculture.

The Federal Finance Board would do well to revive the local machinery of the former Capital Issues Committee. As described on pages 332–333 this agency operated through a local committee in each Federal Reserve District. Such a local committee would pass on the credit position of the corporation or government proposing to float an issue of securities in the national capital market. The report on this corporation or government would then be referred to the Investment Division of the Federal Finance Board which would consider not only the applicant's credit position but would also study the application in relation to the demand and supply in the national capital market.

The fundamental object of such control should be the proper direction of the flow of capital in order to avoid waste in its use. The social direction of capital is essential for national economic stability. National saving must be regarded as a public utility whose flow can no longer be left to haphazard competition but must be subject to careful guidance in the public interest.

The Finance Board would budget the capital market by watching the volume of new financing, particularly in relation to the amount of saving. If the volume of new issues continued to exceed the amount of saving available for the capital market over a long period of time, the Board would then either ration or prevent entirely further new issues until equilibrium between the demand and supply of capital has again been restored. Theoretically equilibrium may be maintained by controlling either the rate of saving or the rate of investment.[3] Practically however the former is hard to control and is the more constant factor, while the latter is the variable one which should therefore be regulated.

The Federal Finance Board should also have the power to control the quality of security investment.[4] The Board would determine the quality of investment credit by establishing minimum standards and by defining the purposes of new bond issues. These standards in the case of a corporation would be based essentially on its earning power. In the case of a government the standards would be determined by its revenue-producing power. Such minimum standards should be based on the experience of bonds which held their value throughout depressions. Critics of this policy of establishing minimum standards based on the experience in depression years may contend that such standards are too severe and that there will not be another reaction as severe as the past. There is no assurance against a recurrence of a similar financial crisis and in the future bonds should be required to meet the tests of safety derived from the bitter experience of these years. As the engineer develops higher structural standards after a serious railway catastrophe, so it is the duty of the financier to raise his standards after the calamitous crises of recent years.

Furthermore the Board should have the power to determine whether the issue will be applied to a productive purpose which is a vital factor. Productivity for investment credit is parallel to liquidity for commercial credit. In other words, as the Federal Reserve system now has the power to define the eligibility of commercial paper which may be rediscounted, so the Finance Board should have the power to determine the desirability of investment paper offered to the public.

The prospectus of every bond issue would therefore contain the statement that the issue has met the minimum standards as established by the Board and was for a productive purpose.[5] Objection may be raised to such qualitative control on the ground that it would seem to imply the guarantee by the government of such a bond. The above plan, however, merely certifies that, at the time of issue, the bond met certain minimum requirements. Qualitative control in no way determines the price which is a matter of bargaining between the dealer and the buyer.

The Finance Board would thus have control over the quantity or volume of both bonds and stocks, and the determination of the quality of bonds only. Stocks, both common and preferred, would be issued without regulation as to quality except as specified in the Securities Act, for it is necessary to permit freely the financing of new enterprises which involve an element of risk and which require financing by stocks of varying grades.

Such qualitative control by the Federal Government should be closely coordinated with the existing state regulation of securities. The principle of the legal list which prescribes the investments of savings banks should be preserved. However, there is an urgent and immediate need of revising legal lists to the end that there be a new set of standards based on the investment experience of recent years, and that these standards be uniform throughout the entire United States. To this end it is recommended that such standards should be adopted not only by the federal government, but also that there should be a uniform law on the legal list formulated by the commissioners of the forty-eight states, similar to the uniform law on bills of lading and warehouse receipts. A uniform code should be applied not only to the investment of saving but also to trust and insurance funds. Naturally greater latitude in the type of investment should be allowed, in the case of trust and insurance funds and the purchase of preferred or even common stock should be permitted. Over the years not only has there developed in this country a set of conflicting laws on legal investments for trust funds within the various states, but this confusion has been further accentuated by the continual outpouring of opinions made necessary in order to explain the complicated technical provisions of these laws. For this reason, there is need of a complete revision of state laws to the end that simplicity and clarity in these statutes may be obtained.

In exercising qualitative control over the capital market, the Finance Board should work closely with the existing state agencies now controlling the supply of new securities. There should be particularly close cooperation with the state commissions regulating the issue of securities of public utilities and also those established in certain states to supervise municipal finance. It should be remembered that the securities of the public utilities and municipalities are not generally sold to investors within these states, but are distributed in the national capital market. It would therefore be highly advisable that state control over the financing of public utilities and municipalities be made more nearly uniform. The states would do well if the present regulations governing the financing of public utilities were carefully examined in the light of the changes in public utility financing in recent years. Furthermore, the entire system of state control over municipal financing should be reorganized. In most states restrictions on municipal financing in the form of tax and debt limitations established in some cases over a half a century ago are today obsolete. The state law of North Carolina could well serve as a model for other states particularly its provisions for regular reports and examinations of municipal accounts, for a uniform system of municipal accounting, and for conservative investment of sinking fund assets.

Under the new system each Federal Reserve bank would be divided into two separate divisions, one for granting commercial credit in the form of rediscounts of commercial paper and the other for extending investment credit in the form of advances on bonds. Each division would have its own capital, and the assets and reserves of each would be entirely distinct. However, both departments of a Reserve bank would be under the same administration, and the Finance Board as the unifying force would supervise both activities of the revised system. The investment division of a Reserve bank would obtain its funds from its own capital, deposits of members and long-term bonds sold to the public. Each member would contribute to the capital stock of the Reserve bank. Also each member would carry a reserve balance in proportion to its own liabilities. Furthermore, in case of need, the Reserve banks would be able to issue obligations based on the underlying security of standard bonds. In this way investment division would have time liabilities in the form of its bonds while the commercial division would have demand liabilities in the form of its circulating notes.

Under the present provisions of the Federal Reserve Act, commercial banks are required to meet certain reserve requirements in order to maintain their liquidity. However one of the most important lessons of recent years is the fact that a bank must possess not only liquidity but also solvency, or the ability to meet losses on depreciated assets. Banks should therefore be required to maintain on account with the investment division a certain percent of net capital funds in relation to the quality and quantity of their assets. The law should prohibit the payment of dividends or the increase of assets until this minimum percent has been met.

The funds carried in savings accounts should be invested only in safe and liquid assets and in minimum standard bonds. Against these savings acounts the commercial bank should maintain a reserve with the investment division of the Federal Reserve bank. The member bank would also be permitted to conduct an investment department for dealing in securities. This department would likewise have its separate capital and assets. It would have relations with the investment division of the Federal Reserve bank which could grant advances and at the same time would be required to purchase stock of the Federal Reserve bank in proportion to the capitalization of the investment department of the member bank and require the maintenance of reserve balances in proportion to the amount of securities underwritten by the department of the member bank.

All investment dealers who buy, underwrite and sell directly to the public should become members of the new system and should be supervised by the investment division of the Reserve bank which would locally take over the powers of the Securities and Exchange Commission. Investment dealers would be required to incorporate and to possess a minimum paid-up unimpaired capitalization in relation to their underwritings before they could sell securities in interstate commerce. These dealers, similar to the investment departments of commercial banks, would then be required to purchase in proportion to their capitalization a certain amount of stock of their Federal Reserve bank and to maintain the required reserve against their underwriting liabilities.

Such investment banks would be required to make reports of their inventory of securities to the Federal Reserve bank of which they would become members. This information on individual houses would be kept confidential by the local Federal Reserve bank, but the composite national figure would be published weekly. The publication of these figures would be a guide to investment banks in determining their policy; and with self control on the part of the bankers themselves there would be need of regulating the quantity of investment credit by the Board only in case of emergency. Not less than three detailed reports should be made annually on call of the Federal Reserve bank on dates to be fixed by the Federal Reserve Board. As a privilege of membership, such investment banks would be able to obtain from the Reserve banks advances on their notes collateralled by bonds which met the minimum standards.

In other words, commercial, savings and investment banking could be conducted as departments of a single institution or as three separate banks depending upon the needs of each locality.

Insurance companies, building and loan, and mortgage banks should also be eligible as members of the investment division of the Federal Finance system and so could obtain advances enabling them to meet sudden demands for cash by their claimants. These advances have been granted by the Reconstruction Finance Corporation, but this function should be taken over by the Federal Finance system. Control over the entire financial structure, particularly over the investment system, would thus be attained. The attempt to confine central banking control to commercial operations alone failed dismally in the past two decades. It is now time to recognize the error, and try the alternative which was proposed in 1912 in the Aldrich Bill, but rejected because of public fear of undue concentration. Such fear led to political action in 1913 which resulted in extreme competition in the investment field in the twenties with consequences already too familiar to require further elaboration.

TWILIGHT OR DAWN

American financial history since the beginning of the century clearly demonstrates that security capitalism cannot be controlled alone from within. In 1903 and in 1907 organized finance, even when captained by intelligent leadership, was able to accomplish little more than check the downward plunge of the stock market, and could not bring about an upswing in economic activity. Again in October, 1929, the bankers by themselves were able to do little more than fight a none-too successful rearguard action to halt momentarily the collapse of security values. Outside of such technical support they were powerless to restrain the forces which were swiftly bringing about a collapse of the entire economic system. It is therefore clear that in the future, control needs the cooperation of both public and private agencies.

The reform of security capitalism is unquestionably the most pressing problem of the day. It is a standing challenge to all persons who are concerned not only in the advancement of individual profit but also of social welfare. Security capitalism stands today at the crossroads. If the forces of disintegration now in operation for a number of years continue unchecked in their ravages, then society will fall back to an economic status comparable only to the dark ages of a thousand years ago. On the other hand, intelligent leadership based on sound private management and efficient public supervision can lift security capitalism to a new economic renaissance, for a carefully directed security capitalism can well serve as a mechanism for a new industrial revolution which could give society an economic welfare not attained by any previous civilization. Such a program for control of security capitalism is a matter which cannot wait, for there is need of an immediate adoption of such a program to control not only the financial institutions but what is more important the non-financial institutions.

The first thought expressed in this study was the swiftness of the entire movement of the rise, development and crisis of security capitalism. Feudalism lasted for a thousand years, and individual capitalism covered three centuries. In the case of most countries, the social, political, and economic institutions necessary for the growth of security capitalism were not present until the middle of the nineteenth century. A little more than a century encompassed the entire cycle of security capitalism even in England where it had its longest history. In Japan, where it developed last, the entire period of security capitalism covered little more than a half century. The lesson to be derived from this rapid tempo of security capitalism is that sound comprehensive and intelligent private and public control must be instituted immediately to check the disintegrating forces which are undermining the system and to raise it to a new high level of social service. It would be well for those who are concerned with the future of security capitalism to remember that the "hours pass and they are counted against us."

NOTES

CHAPTER 1

[1] These various principles of classification overlap each other for there is industrial security capitalism and also banking security capitalism. Capitalism can, of course, be classified according to other characteristics depending upon the viewpoint being presented. The characteristics herewith mentioned alone are needed for the special purpose of this study.

[2] This term is used by Robert Liefmann, *Beteiligungs und Finanzierungsgesellschaften*, 5th ed. Jena 1931, p. 29, where he discusses "effektenkapitalismus." The expression "security capitalism" is preferable to the term "finance capitalism" as used by Rudolf Hilferding, *Das Finanzkapital*, Vienna 1910, and by Nicolai Lenin in his *Imperialism, the Final Stage of Capitalism*, Petrograd 1917, translated by André Tridon, Boston 1917.

[3] The distinction between tangible and intangible assets is well drawn by Thorstein Veblen in his discussion on the nature of capital in *The Place of Science in Modern Civilization*, New York 1919, pp. 352-353.

[4] "Saving-receiver" is a more accurate term than "borrower," for it is technically erroneous to call him a "borrower" when saving is exchanged for stock. The term "saving-receiver" applies to the conversion of saving both into shares as well as into bonds. A chart giving a dynamic picture of the operation of the financial system is presented by Harold G. Moulton in his *The Formation of Capital*, Washington 1935, p. 103.

[5] This resulting misuse of capital by imprudent corporate managers has long been pointed out in economic literature, particularly in such studies as Brandeis, Louis D. *Other People's Money and How the Bankers Use It*, New York 1932 ; Veblen, Thorstein B. *Absentee Ownership and Business Enterprise in Recent Times*, New York 1923 ; Ripley, William Z. *Main Street and Wall Street*, Boston 1927 ; Berle, Adolph A. Jr. and Means, Gardiner C. *The Modern Corporation and Private Property*, New York 1932. Insufficient emphasis has been placed upon the similar evil in the field of public finance.

[6] A distinction should be drawn between overcapitalization and recapitalization, for they are not necessarily the same. As mentioned before, overcapitalization is the overissuance of securities in relation to the value of the underlying assets. Recapitalization may likewise bring about an absolute increase in the face or par value of securities, but if, as a result of the issuance of additional securities, the earning power of the corporation or the revenue-producing and taxing power of the government is increased, the true value of the underlying assets is therefore enhanced, and so the result is not overcapitalization. Recapitalization may result also in undercapitalization or the reduction in the volume of securities to a face or par value less than the true value of the underlying assets.

[7] A distinction should here be made between the term "shiftability," "mobility" and "liquidity." Shiftability refers to the marketability of an asset as measured by the ability to transfer it to some other party. Mobility of capital refers to its movement from one place to another. The greater transferability of securities, since it widens the field of investment beyond the mere locality of the investor, may increase the mobility of capital. Shiftability of securities and mobility of capital are therefore two different economic phenomena. Liquidity in the strictest sense of the term, may be defined as that quality of an asset, whereby the obligation, since it is based on an actual sale of goods from a seller to a buyer, possesses the ability of repayment or self-extinguishment at maturity without loss of value.

[8] See for example, Lavington, Frederick, *The English Capital Market*, London 1921, pp. 186-187.

CHAPTER 2

[1] The evolution of individual capitalism is well described by Ehrenberg, Richard, *Capital and Finance in the Age of the Renaissance ; A Study of the Fuggers and Their Connections* London 1928.

2 Bagehot, Walter, *Lombard Street*, London New York 1873, p. 133.

3 Mulhall, Michael George, *Industries and Wealth of Nations*, London and New York 1896, p. 106.

4 Hirst, Francis Wrigley, *The Stock Exchange; A Short Study of Investment and Speculation*, London 1932 (Rev. Ed.) p. 45.

5 Twentieth Century Fund, Inc. *The Security Markets*, New York 1935, p. 510.

6 Hirst, op. cit. p. 43.

7 Ibid. pp. 45–46.

8 Halevy, Elie, *A History of the English People*, New York 1924, Vol. 1, p. 315.

9 Smith, Rev. Sydney, *Letters On American Debts*, New York 1844, pp. 3–4, 13.

10 Appendix I, "Evolution of British Security Capitalism, 1820–1935"; columns 1 and 2 show the rise in production of coal and pig iron.

11 Ibid. column 5 shows the growth of exports.

12 Gilbart, James Wm., *History and Principles of Banking*, London 1837, Vol. I, p. 57.

13 Jenks, Leland Hamilton, *The Migration of British Capital to 1875*, New York and London 1927, p. 27.

14 Smith, Adam, *Lectures on Justice, Police, Revenues, and Arms*, Oxford 1896, p. 251.

15 Smith, Adam, *An inquiry into the nature and causes of the Wealth of Nations*, Cannan 5th Ed. London 1930, Vol. II, p. 226.

16 Hume, David, *Essays and Treatises on Several Subjects*, Edinburgh 1825, Vol. I, p. 347.

17 Ibid. p. 360. This was also the view of Adam Smith in his *Wealth of Nations*, pp. 744–745.

18 Hume, David, *Political Discourses*, Edinburgh 1752, p. 127

19 Malthus, Thomas Robert, *Principles of Political Economy Considered with a View to Their Practical Application*, London 1820, p. 505.

20 The term "corporation" is here used broadly to include not only true but also quasi-corporations as joint stock associations which were the historic predecessors of the true corporation.

21 Hunt, Bishop Carleton, *The Development of the Business Corporation in England, 1800–1867*, Cambridge, Mass. 1936, pp. 40–41.

22 Todd, Geoffrey, "Some Aspects of Joint Stock Companies, 1844–1900," in the *Economic History Review*, Vol. IV, October 1932, pp. 46–71.

23 Jenks, op. cit. p. 133.

24 Dodwell, David William, *Treasuries and Central Banks Especially in England and the United States*, London 1934, pp. 58–60; Hawtrey, Ralph George, *The Art of Central Banking*, London 1932, pp. 144–145, 151 and 188–189.

25 Powell, Ellis, T., *The Evolution of the Money Market*, London 1915, pp. 329–340; Halevy, op. cit. Vol. 3, p. 286.

26 Smith, op. cit. Vol. I, Book II, Chapter II, p. 287.

27 Dunbar, Charles F., *Chapters on The Theory and History of Banking*, New York 1929, p. 145.

28 Cobbett, William, *Rural Rides in the Counties of Surrey, Kent, etc.*, New Edition, London 1908, Vol. I, pp. 17 and 48.

29 Barings and Rothschilds did however promote the Alliance British and Foreign Life and Fire Insurance Company. Hunt, op. cit. p. 32.

30 Hansard, T. C., *The Parliamentary Debates*, London 1825, p. 1064.

31 Jenks, op. cit. p. 130.

32 Thus the French loan of 1817 with a coupon of 5 percent was issued at a net price of 53, and the commission to the bankers was 2½ percent on the par value of 100,000,000 francs. Ibid. pp. 34–35.

33 Based on figures "extracted from the appendix to the Report of the Secret Committee on the Bank of England Charter" and reproduced in Doubleday, Thomas, *The Political Life of the Right Honourable Robert Peel*, London 1856, Vol. I, p. 326.

34 Smith, Rev. Sydney, op. cit. p. 9.

35 A detailed statement of the foreign loans raised in England in 1824 and 1825 is given in Hansard, op. cit. Vol. XIV Feb. 20, 1826, pp. 591–592.

36 Jenks, op. cit. pp. 34–38.

37 Ibid. p. 51.

38 Ibid. p. 47.

39 Corti, Egon C., *The Reign of the House of Rothschild*, New York, 1928, p. 77.

40 Compiled and adapted from Jenks, op. cit. pp. 373–374.

41 *The Annual Register*, London 1824, p. 2.

[42] Sir Josiah Stamp correctly said: "The small-scale individual unit in the textile industries, the backbone of Victorian advance, depended for its continuous progress upon the supplies of personal capital provided by abstemious living proprietors." quoted in Thomas, Samuel E., *British Banks and the Finance of Industry*, London 1931, p. 116; *see also* Wilson, James, *Capital, Currency, and Banking*, London 1859, Article XIII.

[43] *Money Market Review*, December 10, 1864, cited by Jenks, op. cit. pp. 72, 360.

[44] Appendix I, column 17.

[45] Baxter, R. Dudley, *National Debts*, London 1871, p. 18.

[46] Hume, op. cit. p. 514.

[47] Figures stated by Cobbett as cited in Doubleday, Thomas, *Financial Monetary and Statistical History of England*, London 1847, p. 264.

[48] Hansard op. cit. March 1825, p. 1063.

[49] Tooke, Thomas and Newmarch, William, *A History of Prices*, London 1857, Vol. 5, p. 234.

[50] Hunt, op. cit. p. 106.

[51] Turner, B. B., *Chronicles of the Bank of England*, London 1897, pp. 107-108.

[52] Appendix I, column 24.

[53] Francis, John, *History of the Bank of England, Its Times and Tradition*, London 1847, Vol. II, p. 3.

[54] Smart, William, *Economic Annals of the Nineteenth Century 1821-1830*, London 1917, p. 187.

[55] Francis, op. cit. p. 2.

[56] Hansard, op. cit. p. 3.

[57] Halevy, Vol. II, op. cit. pp. 224-226.

[58] Lambert, Richard S., *The Railway King, 1800-1871*, London 1934.

[59] Ibid. p. 126.

[60] Spencer, Herbert, *An Autobiography*, New York, 1904, Vol. II, p. 326.

[61] Ibid. Vol. 2, p. 332.

[62] *The Bankers Insurance Manager's and Agent's Magazine*, London 1845, Vol. 3, p. 75.

[63] Ibid. 1848, Vol. 8, pp. 243-4.

[64] Crump, Arthur, *The Key to the London Money Market*, 6th Ed., London 1877, p. 33.

[65] *Annual Register*, Chapter X, 1810, *Parliamentary History*, Vol. XXXIV, p. 23.

[66] Chesterton, Gilbert Keith, *William Cobbett*, London 1925, New York 1926, pp. 32-33.

[67] Hansard, op. cit. Vol. N. S. 35, pp. 226-232, 428-435.

[68] *Morning Herald*, January 9, 1822, cited by Jenks, op. cit. pp. 36-37.

[69] *The Bankers Magazine*, London 1849, Vol. 9, pp. 619-620.

[70] "Loans and Standing Armaments," in the *Westminster Review*, Vol. 52, October 1849, pp. 210-216; *see also* account of speech of J. Mitchell against the Russian Loan, *Jewish Chronicle*, London, Vol. VI, January 25, 1850, No. 16, p. 125.

[71] Jenks, op. cit. p. 402; for discussion of the struggle of Cobden against Palmerston, *see* Bowen, Ian, *Cobden*, London 1935, pp. 102-120.

[72] Jenks, op. cit. p. 347.

[73] Files of these early prospectuses are in the British Museum and in the archives of the London Stock Exchange.

[74] Cited by Jenks, op. cit. p. 354.

[75] Hansard, op. cit. N. S. Vol. 12, p. 1048.

[76] *See* speeches of Lord Chancellor Eldon, a prominent Tory, who bitterly denounced the abuses of the new corporations, Hansard, op. cit. London 1825, N. S. Vol. 12, pp. 31, 127, 1195, 1277-8.

[77] This principle was embodied in the American Securities Act of 1933; *see* p. 315.

[78] Lambert, op. cit. p. 115.

CHAPTER 3

[1] The importance of coal in England's economic supremacy is well explained by André Siegfried in his *England's Crisis*, London 1933, pp. 11-12.

[2] Appendix I, columns 1, 2, 3, 4.

[3] Wallas, Graham, *Human Nature in Politics*, New York 1921, p. 170.

[4] Mill, John Stuart, *Principles of Political Economy with Some of Their Applications to Social Philosophy*, New York, Ashley Ed. 1909, pp. 137-140.

[5] Ibid. pp. 74-75.

6 Ibid. pp. 506–507.

7 *Chambers Journal*, Vol. 19, London June 3, 1882, p. 348.

8 Feis, Herbert, *Europe the World's Banker 1870–1914*, New Haven 1930, p. 85.

9 *The Statist*, Vol. 23, 1889, p. 15.

10 Hunt, op. cit. p. 133.

11 This change was recognized in Shaw, Bernard and others, *Fabian Essays in Socialism*, London 1920, pp. 26–27; preface written 1889.

12 Cited by Powell, op. cit. p. 396.

13 Cited by Andreades, Andreas Michael, *History of the Bank of England*, London 1909, translated by Meredith, Christobel, London 1924, p. 355.

14 United States National Monetary Commission, *Interviews on Banking in England, France, Germany, Switzerland and Italy*, Vol. I, Washington 1910, p. 20.   While the studies made by the National Monetary Commission had little effect on American banking legislation, they constituted excellent sources of information on pre-war security capitalism.   The volumes of the Commission have preserved for the future a careful and minute description of the system at its highest state of perfection just before it was impaired by the devastating influence of the World War.

15 Cole, William Alfred, "The Relation Between Banks and Stock Exchanges," in the *Journal of the Institute of Bankers*, London 1899, p. 409.

16 Baster, A. S. J., *The International Banks*, London 1935.

17 Crump, Arthur, *The Theory of Stock Exchange Speculation*, New York 1887, p. 116.

18 *Economic Journal*, London 1891, p. 392.   In underwriting securities the syndicate agreed to purchase for its own account the securities which the public did not absorb.

19 *The Statist*, Vol. 22, November 10, 1888, p. 538.

20 Lenin, op. cit.

21 *The Statist*, op. cit.

22 *The Economist*, Vol. 46, July 21, 1888, p. 915; Vol. 47, April 6, 1889, p. 433.

23 *The Statist*, Vol. 23, March 23, 1889, p. 348.

24 *The Investor's Review*, Vol. I, London 1892, p. 26.

25 *The Economist*, Vol. 49, May 2, 1891, p. 562.

26 Ibid. Vol. 53, June 1, 1895, p. 713.

27 The Leeds Exchange for a short time even out-stripped London in the number of transactions in railway securities. Jenks, op. cit. p. 131.   The Manchester Exchange in 1845 quoted 148 British railway companies and twenty three foreign railway securities. Powell, op. cit. p. 539.

28 Powell, op. cit. p. 370, places this movement between 1847 and 1866.

29 *The Statist*, Vol. 18, July 24, 1886, p. 91.

30 Ibid. Vol. 20, August 27, 1887, p. 237.

31 *See* Appendix I, column 8.

32 *The Statist*, Vol. 10, September 30, 1882, p. 373.   For a study of the same tendency in our own time *see Recent Economic Changes in the United States*, New York 1932, Vol. I, p. 7.

33 Compiled from the *Stock Exchange Year-Book and Dairy for 1875*, London 1875, Preface p. iii.

34 Hobson, C. K., *The Export of Capital*, London 1914, pp. 237–238.

35 *The Economist*, Vol. IX, August 30, 1851, p. 949.

36 *Stock Exchange Year-Book*, op. cit. preface, pp. iv–v.

37 Appendix I, columns 17 and 18.

38 Appendix I, column 6.

39 Appendix I, column 14.

40 *British Review*, May 22, 1897.

41 Goschen, Viscount, *Essays and Addresses on Economic Questions*, (1865-1893) London 1905, p. 260.

42 Appendix I, column 24.

43 British term for bonds.

44 MacDonald, Robert A., "The Rate of Interest Since 1844" in the *Royal Statistical Society Journal*, March 1912, Vol. 75, pp. 375–377.

45 *The Statist*, Vol. 20, July 23, 1887, p. 97.

46 Ibid. Vol. 35, June 22, 1895, p. 784.

47 English Companies Act of 1867 (Sec. 38).

48 See p. 11.

49 Great Britain, Reports from Commissioners, Inspectors, and Others, Vol. XIX, Session 17, January–August, 1878.   *Report of London Stock Exchange Commission*,

presented to both Houses of Parliament by command of Her Majesty, London 1878.

[50] *The Investors' Review*, Vol. I, London 1892, p. 32.

[51] Ibid. p. 6.

[52] *The Statist*, Vol. 20, October 15, 1887, p. 429.

[53] Stevens, Albert C., "Analysis of the Phenomena of the Panic in the United States in 1894," in *The Quarterly Journal of Economics*, Vol. 8, 1894, p. 120. *The Statist*, Vol. 29, May 28, 1892, pp. 602–603.

[54] Andreades, op. cit. p. 365.

[55] *The Investors' Review*, Vol. I, 1892, pp. 7–8.

[56] André Liesse, *Evolution of Credit and Banks in France,* National Monetary Commission, Vol. 15, p. 189. Washington 1909. Several commentators have maintained that the Bank of England was able to survive the various crises after 1890 only with the help of the Bank of France. R. S. Sayers in his *Bank of England and its Operations 1890–1914*, London 1936, Chapter V., rejects this view. However the actual facts indicate that the Bank of England did receive repeated assistance over these years. It would appear that the Bank of France also aided the Bank of England in 1906 and 1907. See Patron, M., *The Bank of France in its Relations to National and International Credit*, National Monetary Commission, Washington 1910, pp. 143–145; White, H. D., *French International Accounts 1880–1913*, Cambridge 1933, p. 194.

CHAPTER 4

[1] Tougan-Baronowsky expressed the view that the year 1875 signalized the turning point in the industrial history of England. Tougan-Baronowsky, Michel, *Les Crises Industrielles en Angleterre*, Paris 1913, p. 22.

[2] Great Britain, Agriculture, *Royal Commission, Final Report*, 1897, p. 6.

[3] Appendix I, columns 1, 2, 3, and 4.

[4] Tougan-Baronowsky's statistics indicate that the rate of increase in the production of iron throughout the decades from 1871 to 1880, 1881 to 1890, and 1891 to 1900, fell from 40 to 20, and to 3 percent respectively. Over the same decennial periods the rate of increase in the production of coal fell from 35 to 25 to 18 percent, but in the decade from 1901 to 1910 the rate of increase was accelerated. Tougan-Baronowsky, op. cit. p. 24.

[5] Ibid. p. 24.

[6] Appendix I, column 5; see Table 6, p. 79.

[7] Engels, Fredrich, preface to *Condition of the Working Class in England in 1844,* London 1892, p. XVI.

[8] Beveridge, Sir William, *Causes and Cures of Unemployment*, London 1931, p. 16.

[9] Appendix I, column 7.

[10] Cited by Engels, op. cit. p. XVII.

[11] Speech at Cambridge, reported in the *Manchester Guardian Weekly*, Vol. 28, April 7, 1933, No. 14, p. 278.

[12] See Burns, C. D., "Effects of Foreign Investment," in the *International Journal of Ethics*, Vol. 32, July 1922, p. 370.

[13] Staley, Eugene, *War and the Private Investor*, New York 1935, p. 201.

[14] Lyon, Laurence, *The Pomp of Power*, New York 1922, p. 20; Lord Revelstoke stated that the British bankers were unprepared for the war. *The Statist*, Vol. 88, July 1, 1916, p. 14.

[15] Hobson, John A., *Imperialism*, New York 1902.

[16] Hobson, John A. and Mummery, A. F., *The Physiology of Industry*, London 1889. Keynes described this publication as "an epoch in economic thought." Keynes, John M., *General Theory of Employment — Interest and Money*, New York 1936, p. 365.

[17] Robertson, John M., *The Fallacy of Saving; A Study in Economics*, London 1892, pp. 93–94.

[18] Pownall, George H., *English Banking*, London 1914, p. 62; see Sykes, Joseph, *The Amalgamation Movement in English Banking*, London 1926, pp. 47–62.

[19] Perry, S. E., "English and American Banking Methods" in *The Journal of the Institute of Bankers*, Vol. XXX, November 1909, p. 553.

[20] *The Economic Journal*, London, Vol. XXVII, pp. 501–511.

[21] See Appendix I, column 8.

[22] Ibid. column 11, 12.

[23] Slater, Gilbert, *The Growth of Modern England*, London 1932, p. 476.

[24] Great Britain Statistical Department, *Statistical Abstract for the United Kingdom, 1892–1906*, Vol. 54, Table 23A; Vol. 66, Table 24.

25 Hirst, op. cit. p. 70; for criticism of this policy see article by John Maynard Keynes, in the *Manchester Guardian Commercial*, August 7, 1924, p. 176.

26 Appendix I, column 20.

27 Ibid. columns 17 and 18.

28 Bowley, Arthur L., *The Change in the Distribution of the National Income, 1880-1913*, Oxford 1920, pp. 26-27.

29 *The Statist*, Vol. 20, September 3, 1887, p. 262.

30 Appendix I, column 16.

31 Ibid. column 15.

32 For the years 1896 and 1902 see Page, William, *Commerce and Industry*, London 1919 Vol. 2, pp. 32–33; for the year 1910 see Appendix I, column 12.

33 Page, op. cit. Vol. 2, p. 64.

34 *The Commercial and Financial Chronicle*, Vol. 77, October 3, 1903, pp. 797–798. Hereafter this publication is abbreviated as the *Chronicle*.

35 Ibid. Vol. 94, June 15, 1912, p. 1591; June 29, 1912, p. 1729; *The Statist*, Vol. 76, May 31, 1913, p. 592.

36 Ibid. Vol. 76, May 31, 1913, p. 592.

37 Appendix I, column 24.

38 MacDonald, op. cit. p. 377.

39 *The Economic Journal*, Vol. 22, June 1912, p. 223.

40 National Monetary Commission, *The English Banking System*, Washington 1910, p. 59.

41 *The Statist*, Vol. 76, London April 5, 1913, p. 29.

42 *Manchester Guardian Commercial*, August 7, 1924, p. 176.

43 *The Statist*, Vol. 42, November 26, 1898, p. 791.

44 Ibid. Vol. 38, October 10, 1896, pp. 549–550.

45 See criticism of overvaluation of intangible assets as good-will and patent rights. *The Economist*, Vol. 58, April 14, 1900, p. 532.

46 Quoted in Webb, Sidney and Beatrice, *The Decay of Capitalist Civilization*, New York 1923, p. 138.

47 Barnett, George E., "The Securities Act of 1933 and the British Companies Act" in the *Harvard Business Review*, Vol. 13, October 1934, p. 3.

48 *Chronicle*, Vol. 97, December 20, 1913, p. 1776.

CHAPTER 5

1 Dunbar, op. cit. New York 1929, pp. 179–180.

2 Cited by Birck, Lauritz Wilhelm, *The Public Debt: The Scourge of Europe*, New York 1927, title page.

3 Hansard, op. cit. Vol. XXIX, February 22, 1815, p. 982.

4 Levasseur, Émile, *Histoire du Commerce de la France*, Paris 1912, Part II, p. 48.

5 Nicoll, André, *Comment la France a payé après Waterloo*, Paris 1929, pp. 163–165.

6 Liesse, op. cit. p. 45.

7 Appendices I and II, columns 1 and 2.

8 Simonde de Sismondi, J. C. L., *Nouveau Principes d'Economique Politique*, Vol. II, Paris 1827, p. 92.

9 Gide, Charles and Rist, Charles, *A History of Economic Doctrines*, New York pp. 206, 210.

10 *The Economist*, Vol. 124, July 25, 1936, p. 170.

11 Rogers, James H., *The Process of Inflation in France 1914–1927*, New York 1929, p. 25.

12 Liesse, op. cit. p. 75.

13 Neymarck, Alfred, *Une Nouvelle Evaluation du Capital et du Revenu Des Valeurs Mobilières en France*, Paris 1893, p. 5.

14 Appendix II, "Evolution of French Security Capitalism 1820–1935," column 8.

15 Corti, op. cit. pp. 104–105.

16 Ibid. p. 105.

17 Clapham, J. H., *The Economic Development of France and Germany, 1815–1914*, Cambridge, England 1921, pp. 133–134.

18 Appendix II, column 17.

19 Appendix I and II, column 24.

20 *The Bankers Magazine*, London, May 1848, Vol. 8, p. 311.

21 See rise in output of coal, pig iron, steel and iron castings, Appendix II, columns 1, 2, 3.

22 Dunbar, op. cit. p. 182.

23 Ibid. p. 193.

24 Liesse, op. cit. p. 129.

25 Vidal, Emmanuel, *The History and Methods of the French Bourse*, National Monetary Commission, Washington 1910, pp. 178–179.

26 Ibid. p. 188.

27 Ibid. p. 185.

28 Ibid. pp. 184–185.

29 Sombart, Werner, *The Jews and Modern Capitalism*, London 1913, p. 107.

30 Corti, op. cit. p. 270

31 Lewinsohn, Richard, *The Profits of War Through the Ages*, London 1936, pp. 124–125.

32 In 1868 the Krupp firm was saved from financial difficulties by a loan from another internationally-minded French banking house. Noel-Baker, Philip, *The Private Manufacture of Armaments*, Vol. I, London 1936, p. 37.

33 Corti, op. cit. p. 349.

34 Kulisher, Joseph M., *Allegemeine Wirtschaftsgeschichte der Mittelalters und der Neuzeit*, Munich 1928, Vol. II, Book 4, p. 538.

35 Liesse, op. cit. p. 106.

36 *The Statist*, Vol. 40, September 18, 1897, p. 444.

37 The legal aspects of the collapse of this bank are explained by Arthur Nussbaum in his article "Acquisition by a Corporation of Its Own Stock," in the *Columbia Law Review*, Vol. 35, November 1935, p. 972. The collapse of the Union Generale is dramatically described in Emile Zola's *L'Argent*.

38 Rogers, op. cit. New York 1929, p. 30.

39 Vidal, op. cit. p. 192.

40 The provincial banks continued to retain their position in local finance and played a more important part in the financial system than did the interior banks in either England or Germany.

41 *Interviews on Banking and Currency Systems*, National Monetary Commission, Washington 1910, p. 233.

42 Ibid. p. 219.

43 *The Statesman's Year-Book* reported that the statistics on French banking were so incomplete that they were not worthy of publication. *The Statesman's Year-Book* for 1912, London, p. 794.

44 *Interviews*, National Monetary Commission, op. cit. p. 275.

45 Kaufmann, E., *La Banque en France*, Paris 1914, p. 124.

46 *Interviews*, op. cit. p. 268.

47 Ibid. p. 272.

48 Rogers, op. cit. p. 26.

49 *Federal Reserve Bulletin*, January 1921, p. 63.

50 "Le Regne de L'Argent," in the *Revue des Deux Mondes*, February 1897, p. 894.

51 Parker, William, *The Paris Bourse and French Finance*, New York 1920, p. 24.

52 Neymarck, writing in 1907 stated that 150,000,000,000 francs out of 155,000,000,000 francs of negotiable securities were listed on the Paris market. Neymarck, Alfred, "La Statistique International des Valeurs Mobilières" *Bulletin de L'Institut Internationale de Statistique*, 1907, Report XVI, p. 49.

53 Parker, op. cit. p. 68.

54 Neymarck, Alfred, op. cit.

55 Appendix II, columns 10 and 15.

56 Martin, Germain, *Les Finances Publiques de la France et La Fortune Privé (1914-1925)*, Paris 1925, p. 49.

57 Appendix II, column 8.

58 Fisk, Harvey, *French Public Finance*, New York 1922, p. 200.

59 Caillaux, Joseph, *Whither France? Whither Europe?* New York 1923, p. 28.

60 Hobson, C. K., *The Export of Capital*, London 1914, p. 138.

61 Ibid. p. 139.

62 Neymarck estimates that about 10 percent of this total was held by foreigners. Neymarck, Alfred, *Bulletin de L'Institut Internationale de Statistique*, 1913, Report XX, Part II, p. 91.

63 Vidal, op. cit. p. 172. These figures show only the book entries and do not indicate the actual number of separate bondholders. Leroy-Beaulieu estimated that, while there were 1,254,000 entries in 1869, there were only from 700,000 to 800,000 actual owners of the government debt. Leroy-Beaulieu, *Traité de la Science des Finances*, Vol. 2, Paris 1879, p. 543. The previous figures on holders of savings de-

posits have not been adjusted to avoid duplication among the holders of two or more accounts by the same depositor.

[64] Appendix II, column 24.

[65] Quoted in Chastenet, J. L., *The Bankers' Republic*, London 1926, p. 16; see also Guillaume, A., *L'Epargne Francaise et les Valeurs Mobilières*, Geneva 1907; and Wuarin, A., *Essai sur les Emprunts d'Etats*, Paris 1907.

[66] Chastenet, op. cit. p. 68.

[67] Le Tailleur, Eugène, *Contre L'Oligarchie Financière en France*, Paris 1911, p. 6 ; see also his *Les Capitalistes Francais Contre La France*, Paris 1916 ; Becque, Emile, *L'Internationalisation des Capitaux*, Montpellier 1912 ; and Seilliere, Ernest, *La Philosophie de L'Imperialisme*, Paris 1903.

[68] Quoted by Guyot, Yves, "The Amount, Direction and Nature of French Investments" in *Annals, American Academy of Political and Social Science*, Vol. 68, November 1916, p. 37.

[69] Feis, op. cit. p. 158.

[70] Parker, op. cit. p. 30.

[71] Vidal, op. cit. p. 100.

[72] Guyot, op. cit. p. 46.

[73] The close relation between French international politics and finance has been generally recognized by students of the subject. See Viner, Jacob, "International Finance and the Balance of Power Diplomacy, 1880–1914" in the *Southwestern Political and Social Science Quarterly*, Vol. IX, March 1929, pp. 407–451 ; Feis, op. cit. pp. 124–126.

[74] Feis, op. cit. pp. 239–241.

CHAPTER 6

[1] Riesser, Jacob, *The German Great Banks*, Washington 1911, p. 27–30. The period of the rise and development of German security capitalism is also well covered by Von Waltershausen, A. Sartorius, *Deutsche Wirtschaftsgeschichte, 1815–1914*, Jena 1930.

[2] Clapham, op. cit. p. 152.

[3] Ibid. p. 122.

[4] Hartsough, Mildred L., "Business Leaders in Cologne in the Nineteenth Century" in the *Journal of Economic and Business History*, Vol. 2, February 1930, p. 338.

[5] Twentieth Century Fund Inc., *The Security Markets*, New York 1935, p. 539.

[6] The term "credit bank" was applied to the German incorporated financial institution which engaged both in commercial and investment banking operations.

[7] Riesser, op. cit. pp. 48–49.

[8] Ibid. 396–397.

[9] See Townsend, Mary Evan, *Origins of Modern German Colonialism, 1871–1885*, New York 1921, pp. 109–110; and Dobb, Maurice, *Capitalist Enterprise*, London 1925, p. 341.

[10] Von Bülow, Prince Bernhard, *Imperial Germany*, New York 1914, p. 98.

[11] *Deutsche Volkswirtschaft*, 2nd ed. 1903, p. 111.

[12] Appendix III, "Evolution of German Security Capitalism, 1870–1935," columns 1, 2 and 3.

[13] Sinclair, H. M., *A Preface to Economic History*, New York 1934, page 154.

[14] Slater, op. cit. pp. 454–455.

[15] Ibid. pp. 456–457.

[16] Appendix III, column 4.

[17] An illustration of the relative decline in the social importance of domestic commerce as compared with manufacture is given in the act of Werner Siemens in refusing the honorary title of Kommerzienrat, because he did not consider himself a merchant but in accepting instead the honorary title of Geheimer Regierungsrat which, to him, implied the concept of a producer.
Wiedenfelt, W., *Die Rheinprovinz, 1815–1915*, pp. 64–65.

[18] The excess of births over deaths rose from 5,500,000 in the decade from 1881 to 1890, to 8,670,000 in the decade from 1901 to 1910 while emigration from Germany in these two periods declined from 1,342,000 to 220,000. Hellfferich, Karl, *Germany's Economic Progress and National Wealth, 1888–1913*. New York 1914, p. 17.

[19] *Zeitschrift des Kgl. Preussischen Statistischen Büreaus*, Berlin 1904, p. 92.

[20] *Die Reichsfinanznot u. die Pflichten des Deutschen Volks wie seiner politischen Parteien. Ein Mahnwort eines alten Mannes*, Berlin 1908, p. 14.

[21] *Grundriss*, II, p. 460, cited by Riesser, op. cit. p. 98.

[22] Riesser, op. cit. p. 99.

[23] *Interviews*, National Monetary Commission, op. cit. p. 344.

[24] Thomas, Samuel E., *British Banks and the Finance of Industry*, London 1931, p. 134.

[25] This explanation was questioned by Adolph Weber who held that the German banks at the end of the nineteenth century had reached the stage where they should have been able to limit their function to that of specialized banking. *Depositen Banken und Spekulations Banken*, Munich and Leipsig 1915, pp. 66–67.

[26] *Interviews* op. cit. p. 403.

[27] Schuster of the Dresdner Bank in 1908 stated: "In Germany our banks are largely responsible for the development of the Empire, having fostered and built up its industries" quoted by Clapham, op. cit. p. 390.

[28] Dresdner Bank, *Germany's Economic Forces*, Berlin 1913, p. 29.

[29] See article by Landsburgh, Alfred, in *Die Bank*, November 1908, pp. 1079 and 1083; see also his *Das Deutsche Bankwesen*, Charlottenburg 1909, pp. 48, 49 and 52.

[30] Jeidels, Otto, *Das Verhaltnis der deutschen Grossbanken zur Industrie*, Leipzig 1905, p. 50.

[31] Liefmann, op. cit. p. 491. Liefmann disputes the conclusion of a growing influence of the banks on German industry.

[32] Lenin, op. cit. p. 35.

[33] Riesser, op. cit. pp. 422–424.

[34] There was a close personal relation between Chancellor Bismarck and Gerson Bleichröder who was court banker and administered Bismarck's private fortune. Lewinsohn, op. cit. pp. 97–100. Bleichröder considered himself an unofficial member of the foreign office and was the only person admitted unannounced to the office of the Chancellor.

[35] Ibid. p. 100.

[36] Compiled from Sombart, Werner, *The Jews and Modern Capitalism*, London 1913, p. 113.

[37] The proportion of Jews to the total population in Germany reached its highest mark in 1880 when it stood at 1.09 percent. *Wirtschaft und Statistik*, February 1935, Part II, p. 147.

[38] Wormser, O., *Die Frankfurter Börse*, Tubingen 1919, in Table XII p. 210, gives a statement on the listings of the Frankfurt exchange.

[39] Appendix III, columns 10 and 15.

[40] Riesser, op. cit. p. 381.

[41] Müller, Waldemar in the *Bank-Archiv*, Vol. 8, No. 8, January 15, 1909, p. 118.

[42] Hellfferich, op. cit. p. 44.

[43] "Why World Power? The Significance of Our Colonial Policy," article in *Kölnische Zeitung*, August 4, 1881. See also Townsend, Mary E., op. cit. p. 99.

[44] Riesser, op. cit. p. 395.

[45] This was the error made by Otto Jeidels when he predicted that in the evolution of capitalism German banks would be forced by necessity "to exert their activity abroad" in order to find opportunities for the profitable investment in foreign countries for unemployed German capital. Jeidels, op. cit. p. 270. Lenin in turn, following Jeidels made the same error. In general Lenin's study on *Imperialism* must be judged as essentially a political document for its consideration of international economics is inferior to other works on this subject.

[46] Appendix III, column 19.

[47] This is the lowest estimate of Schmoller who placed the upper range at 3,000,000,000 marks. *Grundriss*, 6th ed. Vol. II, p. 184; another estimate placed the figure at 3,700,000,000 marks and Hellfferich's calculation was even higher, op. cit., p. 118.

[48] Riesser, op. cit. p. 92. Hellfferich's estimate was 310,000,000,000 marks, and another estimate was at a high of 360,000,000,000 marks.

[49] *Deutsche Oekonomist*, June 27, 1908, p. 305. Another estimate placed this total at 44,000,000,000 marks. Appendix to *Reichstagsdrucksachen* No. 1087 of 1908, pp. 247–248.

[50] The proportion is placed at the higher figure of one third in a German study. See Ernst V. Halle, *Die Deutsche Volkswirtschaft an der Jahrhundertwende*, Berlin 1902, pp. 56–57.

[51] Hirst, op. cit. pp. 91–92.

[52] Jhering, Rudolph, *Der Zweck in Recht*, Leipsig 1884–1886, Vol. I, p. 223.

[53] Ruhland, G., *System der Politischen Oekonomie*, Berlin 1908, Vol. III, p. 302.

[54] Ibid. p. 116.

55 For description in English of the system of governmental control of the German stock exchange in the period immediately before the War, see Parker, Carl, "German Banks and Stock Exchange Speculation" *Proceedings Academy of Political Science,* Vol. I, 1910–1911, p. 449, et. seq.

56 See *Bericht der Börsen Enquete Commission,* Berlin 1893. This study represents the first scientific survey of stock exchange operations.

57 Lexis, W., "The New German Exchange Act" in the *Economic Journal,* London, Vol. VII, 1897, p. 368.

Emery, Henry C., "Ten Years Regulation of the Stock Exchange in Germany," in the *Yale Review,* Vol. 17, May 1908, p. 7.

58 Jacobs, P., *Die Zulassung von Wert Papieren sum Börsenhandel,* Berlin 1914, and Zichert, H., *Die Kapitalsanlage in Auslandischen Wert Papiern,* Berlin 1911, Jacobs cites the refusal to admit a Mexican loan in 1896 because of the doubtful legality of the pledges made for the loan, and the demand that the prospectuses be improved in the cases of the Turkish loan of 1905 and of the Canadian Pacific issue of 1913.

59 See summary of the German Government Report of 1907, Emery, op. cit. p. 19.

60 Riesser, op. cit. p. 384.

61 *British Documents on the Origins of the War,* Vol. II, p. 195 ; Ross, J. S., *Trade Rivalry, 1875–1914,* Philadelphia 1933, p. 148.

CHAPTER 7

1 Special comment should however be made of Holland which was the first to enter upon security capitalism. This country was really the morning star of security capitalism, for, during the late seventeenth century and early eighteenth century, the Dutch granted security loans to foreign countries on an extensive scale. See discussion in Hobson, C. K., *Export of Capital,* London 1914. However, in the last quarter of the eighteenth century the financial power of Holland was weakened by the policy of over-lending, and signs of financial distress were distinctly evident. See letter from John Adams to the Continental Congress, cited in article by Nathaniel T. Bacon in the *Yale Review* 1900, p. 277. The occupation of Holland by Napoleon I, the levy of a French indemnity, the collapse of the Bank of Amsterdam and the failure of the East India Company all served to impair Dutch security capitalism. More than one-half of the population of Amsterdam in 1805 was receiving poor relief, and in 1808 a contemporary historian wrote that "the country resembles a hollow willow ; it only lives in the bark." *Economist* February 15, 1913, p. 334. After the Napoleonic wars Holland made rapid recovery. In 1814 a new state bank, the Bank of Netherlands, was begun. Private banking revived, and the firm of Hope & Company of Amsterdam was the one Continental banking house associated with Barings and Rothschilds in the flotation of the loan for the payment of the French indemnity. Clapham, op. cit. p. 133.

In 1830 came the separation of Belgium from Holland. This political move was followed by the rapid economic development of Belgium. Due to the extent of her mineral resources, her favorable location on the Channel and the energetic character of the population, Belgium was the first continental country which passed through the industrial revolution. As in the case of England, the cotton and the metallurgical industries expanded rapidly. Belgium also led the Continent in the formation of corporations. These were organized for such purposes as the building of water works, canals, railroads and financing foreign trade, and were generally conducted on a sound basis.

2 See table in Bukharin, Nikolai, *Imperialism and World Economy,* New York 1929, p. 86.

3 See Appendix IV "Evolution of World Capitalism, 1820–1935," columns 1, 2, 3 and 4.

4 Ibid. column 5.

5 The actual figures on which these indices are based are given in the appendices and tables showing the evolution of security capitalism in the individual countries.

6 Bukharin, op. cit. pp. 29–30.

7 Appendix IV, column 8.

8 Feller, A. H., "The Movement for Corporate Reform: A Worldwide Phenomenon," in the *American Bar Association Journal,* Vol. 20 1934, p. 347.

9 Lowenthal, Marvin, *The Jews of Germany,* New York 1936, pp. 321–322.

[10] Marx, Karl, *Capital*, Moore and Aneling edition from the Untermann translation, Chicago 1912, Vol. III, p. 433.

[11] Ibid., Chapter XIX.

[12] *Gesamtausgabe*, Vol. I, Chapter 6, pp. 306–307. Marx and Engels in the Communist Manifesto, recognizing the power attendant upon the control of the banking system, recommended the "centralization of credit in the hands of the State by means of a national bank with State capital and an exclusive monopoly." Marx, Karl and Engels, Fredrich, *Manifesto of the Communist Party*, New York 1902, 2 ed., p. 41.

[13] Marx, *Capital*, op. cit., Vol. III, p. 278.

[14] Marx, Karl, *The Paris Commune and The Civil War in France*, New York 1920, p. 73.

[15] Marx, *Capital*, op. cit. p. 606. This statement may also be interpreted as referring to the function of the commercial banker in issuing his notes.

[16] Marx, Ibid. pp. 520-521.

[17] *Communist Manifesto*, paragraph 3, p. 14.

[18] Marx, *Capital*, op. cit., New York 1936, p. 709.

[19] Laidler, Harry, *A History of Socialist Thought*, New York 1927, p. 307.

[20] Bernstein, Edward, *Evolutionary Socialism*, New York 1909, translated by Edith Harvey, p. 79.

[21] Luxemburg, Rosa, *Die Akkumulation des Kapitals*, Berlin 1913.

[22] The only important exception was the Riksbank of Sweden which was founded in the seventeenth century when private capital was not available, and so the government, contributing the necessary funds owned and controlled the Bank. Kisch, C. H., and Elkin, W. A., *Central Banks*, London 1928, p. 44.

[23] See discussion by Gray, John H. and Terborgh, George W., *First Mortgages in Urban Real Estate Finance*, Brookings Institution, Washington, D. C. 1929, pp. 21–23.

[24] Birck, op. cit. p. 213.

[25] Corti, Egon C. *The Reign of the House of Rothschild*, New York 1928, p. 49.

[26] A brief exception to this policy was the policy of the house during the American Civil War. Having acquired large commercial interests in the Southern States, the Rothschilds were consequently pro-Confederate; but this attitude did not prevent them, in alliance with Jay Cooke, after the close of the Civil War, from participating in the financing of the federal government.

[27] Cited by Steefel, Lawrence, "The Rothschilds and the Austrian Loan of 1865," in the *The Journal of Modern History*, Vol. VIII March 1936, p. 38.

[28] Corti, op. cit. p. 78.

[29] Sombart, *The Jews and Modern Capitalism*, pp. 104–105.

[30] Kulisher, op. cit. p. 540.

[31] Italy was an exception to this rule, since its banking system was decentralized and there was a large number of private and incorporated banks. There were several major institutions as the Banca Commercile Italiano, the Credito Italiano and the Banca di Roma. The first two institutions were located in Milan which was the industrial and the financial center, while only the Banca di Roma had its main office in Rome.

[32] Raffalovich, Arthur, *Russia, Its Trade and Commerce*, London 1918, pp. 380–385.

[33] Economists have fully emphasized the importance of the improvement of the banking system in increasing the velocity of commercial credit, but insufficient attention has been directed to the similar effect of the improvement of financial organization on the mobility of investment credit.

[34] Lewinsohn, op. cit. pp. 104–105.

[35] Cited by Neymarck, Alfred, *French Savings and Their Influence Upon the Bank of France and Upon French Banks*, National Monetary Commission, Washington 1910, pp. 178–179.

[36] Appendices I, II, III, column 10.

[37] Baxter, writing in 1871, estimated that only 12 percent of the total national debts of the World had been raised for productive purposes, while the remaining 88 percent had been applied to war and other unproductive purposes. Baxter, op. cit. p. 83.

[38] The details of governmental securities in the first half of the century may be found in Fenn, Charles, *Compendium of the English and Foreign Funds* first issued in 1837. This work was later edited by Robert L. Nash and is more briefly described as *Fenn on the Funds*.

[39] Baxter, op. cit. pp. 76–77 and 79; Mulhall, *Dictionary of Statistics*, London and New York 1899, pp. 699–706.

[40] Appendix V, "National Debts of Leading Countries, 1870–1935."

41 Neymarck, Alfred, *The Public Debts of Europe*, New York 1888, pp. 78–79; see also "The Growth of Expenditure on Armaments" in the *Quarterly Review*, Vol. 126, January 1912, p. 224.

42 Birck, L. V., op. cit. p. 217.

43 Neymarck, Alfred M., "La Statistique Internationale des Valeurs Mobilières" in the *Bulletin Institut Internationale de Statistique*, Vol. 19, Book 2, p. 206.

44 The lowest estimate is taken in each case. Ibid. p. 223.

45 Lawton, Lancelot, *An Economic History of Soviet Russia*, Vol. I, London 1932, p. 56.

46 Georges De Laveleyle in his annual compilation in the *Moniteur des Interêts Materiels*, Brussels 1892.

47 Conant, Charles A., "Can New Openings Be Found for Capital" in the *Atlantic Monthly*, Vol. 84, October 1899, p. 600.

48 Comment of Arthur Raffalovich, reproduced in the *Chronicle*, Vol. 91, September 3, 1910, p. 556.

49 Compiled from Raymond, William L., *American and Foreign Investment Bonds*, Boston 1916, p. 77.

50 The extent of the subsequent increase in yield was the greatest in the case of England and the least in the case of Italy. The smaller increase in the case of Italy may have been due to the over-liberal loans received from France and Germany extended not so much on the basis of Italy's credit but rather for the purpose of wooing her political support.

51 *The Economist*, Vol. 79, July 4, 1914, p. 36; see also July 11, 1914, p. 73.

52 Ibid. August 1, 1914, p. 231.

53 *Chronicle*, Vol. 99, August 1, 1914, p. 314.

CHAPTER 8

1 The ultimate overthrow of the Labour Party was blamed on the bankers. Cole, G. D. H., "A Socialist View" in *The Economist*, Vol. 113, October 17, 1931, p. 697; see also Radek, Karl, "Britain and American Finance Capital," in *The Labour Monthly*, Vol. 13, October 1931, p. 625.

2 Appendix I, columns 1, 2, 3 and 4.

3 Ibid. column 7.

4 See statement of Sir Ernest Harvey, Deputy Governor of the Bank, *Report of the Committee on Finance and Industry* (MacMillan Report), London 1931, p. 454.

5 *Report of the Treasury Committee on Bank Amalgamations* (Colwyn Report), London 1918, p. 7.

6 MacMillan Report, op. cit. pp. 164–165.

7 According to the calculations of Keynes the proportion of demand to total deposits of three of the leading British banks declined from 66 percent in 1919 to 52 percent in 1929. Keynes, John Maynard, *A Treatise on Money*, New York 1930, Vol. 2, p. 9.

8 *See* Table 9 "Financial Position of British Commercial Banks 1925–1934," Ratio A.

9 Ibid, Ratio B.

10 For explanation of ratios see pp. 225–226. Computed from the League of Nations, *Commercial Banks*, Geneva, 1934, p. 215.

11 Table 9 op. cit. Ratio D.

12 Ibid. Ratio E.

13 Ibid. Ratio F. The ratio of capital to deposits for British banks was declining even in the pre-war period. Colwyn Report, op. cit. p. 5.

14 Ibid. Ratio G.

15 Appendix I, column 8. For discussion see Sykes, Joseph, *British Public Expenditure, 1921–1931*, London 1933.

16 Lord Bradbury in his memorandum of dissent to the MacMillan Report expressed the view that the burden of this unproductive debt was the main cause of the economic troubles of Great Britain in the post-war period. MacMillan Report, op. cit. p. 280.

17 Appendix I, column 13.

18 *The Economist*, Budget Supplement, April 5, 1930, p. 11; April 9, 1932, p. 12; April 18, 1936, p. 10.

19 Ibid. Vol. 113, August 8, 1931, p. 265.

20 Ibid. Vol. 108, January 26, 1929, p. 170.

21 Compiled from *The Economist*, Vol. 119, Aug. 4, 1934, p. 232. Based on nominal amount. Includes only official list.

[22] Appendix I, columns 18 and 19.

[23] The Colwyn Committee estimated with allowance for the change in the value of money and of population that the national saving in 1913 would have been the equivalent of £650,000,000 in 1927 compared with actual saving of £399,000,000 in that year. *The New Statesman*, Vol. 30, December 24, 1927, p. 350.

[24] *The Economist*, Vol. 108, February 23, 1929, p. 388.

[25] Paper read by Ashton, T. S., to the Manchester Statistical Society, cited in *The Economist*, Vol. 110, February 22, 1930, p. 406.

[26] See article "Are We Short of Capital?" in *The New Statesman*, December 24, 1927, p. 349.

[27] Appendix I, column 16.

[28] *Statistical Abstract for the United Kingdom*, Vol. 77, p. 203.

[29] Appendix I, column 21.

[30] Davenport, E. H., "The Control of National Investment" in *The New Statesman*, Vol. 2, No. 33, October 10, 1931, p. 429.

[31] *The Economist*, Vol. 117, November 11, 1933, p. 918.

[32] Ibid. Vol. 108, March 30, 1929, p. 691.

[33] Ibid. September 15, 1928, Vol. 107, p. 475 and Vol. 108, March 30, 1929, pp. 691–692. An analysis made by *The Economist* of 210 companies which financed themselves in this period showed that out of over 158,000,000 votes the public exercised 88,000,000 or only 56 percent. Ibid. December 14, 1935, Vol. 121, p. 1211.

[34] Ibid. Vol. 107, September 15, 1928, p. 475.

[35] Ibid. Vol. 110, February 15, 1930, p. 363.

[36] Ibid. Vol. 115, September 10, 1932, p. 476.

[37] Appendix I, column 24.

[38] *The Economist*, Vol. 109, October 19, 1929, p. 701.

[39] Gregory, T. E., cited by Thomas, op. cit. p. 15.

[40] "The Banking Inquiry" in *The Economist*, Vol. 109, October 19, 1929, p. 701.

[41] *Forward*, July 6, 1931, cited by Johnston, Thomas, *The Financiers and the Nation*, London 1934, p. 138; see also criticism by Bevin, E., and Cole, G. D. H., *The Crisis*, London 1931.

[42] MacMillan Report, op. cit. p. 5.

[43] *The Economist*, Vol. 119, October 13, 1934, p. 687.

[44] Ibid. Vol. 106, June 2, 1928, p. 1127.

[45] "The Control of Capital" in *The New Statesman*, Vol. 30, No. 776, March 10, 1928, p. 687.

[46] "The Public Trustee: A Study in Socialization," in Ibid. Vol. 8, No. 192, October 27, 1934, p. 577.

[47] *The Economist*, Vol. 113, August 1, 1931, p. 212.

[48] Ibid. Vol. 117, September 9, 1933, p. 499; Wilmot, John, *Labour's Way to Control Banking and Finance*, London 1935, p. 117.

[49] Royal Institute of International Affairs, *The Problem of International Investment*, London 1937, pp. 76–79; Richardson, J. H., *British Economic Foreign Policy*, London 1936, pp. 69–75.

[50] *The Economist*, Vol. 116, January 7, 1933, p. 35.

[51] Ibid. Vol. 123, April 11, 1936, p. 86.

[52] Ibid. Vol. 126, March 20, 1937, pp. 654–655.

[53] "Labour and the Banks" in *The New Statesman*, Vol. 6, No. 138, p. 437.

[54] Hobson, J. A., *Economics and Ethics*, London, 1929, p. 287.

[55] Davenport, op. cit., October 10, 1931, p. 429.

[56] "The Control of Capital" in *The New Statesman*, Vol. 30, No. 776, March 10, 1928, p. 686; Cole, G. D. H., *The Socialisation of Banking*, London 1931, p. 7.

[57] Keynes, John M., "A New Economic Policy for England" in the *Economic Forum*, Winter 1932–1933, pp. 29–37.

[58] Colonel de La Roque the leader of the Croix de Feu was backed by Jean Allier, a prominent banker connected with the Schneider Company, the great munition firm, by James Rothschild and by Guy de Wendel, a member of a family prominent in the industrial life of France. *Fortune*, June 1937, p. 82 et. seq.

[59] Appendix II, columns 1, 2 and 3.

[60] *New York Times*, June 14, 1936.

[61] Boris, Georges, "Reforming the Bank of France" in *Foreign Affairs*, Vol. 15, October 1936, p. 160.

[62] *The Economist*, Vol. 124, July 25, 1936, p. 170.

[63] Boris, op. cit. p. 157.

[64] League of Nations, *Commercial Banks, 1925–1933*, Geneva 1934, p. 98.

[65] See pp. 53–54 for explanation.

[66] Appendix II, columns 8 and 9.

[67] Ibid. column 13.

[68] Myers, Margaret S., *Paris as a Financial Centre*, London 1936, p. 141.

[69] *The Economist*, Vol. 112, May 16, p. 1045.

[70] Appendix 11, columns 18 and 19.   The real value of national income and saving is computed on the basis of the change in commodity prices given in column 6.

[71] Ibid. columns 22 and 24.

[72] Ibid. columns 18 and 19.

[73] Ibid. column 21.

[74] Ibid. columns 20 and 22.

[75] Ibid. column 24.

[76] See increase in pig iron, steel and general production Appendix III, columns 2, 3 and 4.

[77] *The Economist*, Vol. 101, August 22, 1925, p. 308 and Hartsough, Mildred, "The Rise and Fall of the Stinnes Combine" in the *Journal of Economic and Business History*, February 1931, p. 287.

[78] Computed from Warriner, Doreen, *Combines and Rationalization in Germany*, London 1931, p. 9.

[79] Computed from the *Journal of the American Bankers Association*, January 1925, pp. 433–444.

[80] Hausheer, H., "The Social Economic Background of Nazi Anti-semitism," in *Social Forces*, Vol. 14, March 1936, p. 347.   Marvin Lowenthal claims that the number of Jews in the banking business was small and estimates that in 1925 only 3.3 percent of all German bankers and brokers were Jews. Lowenthal op. cit. p. 275.   In 1925 the proportion of Jews to the total population was 0.90 percent ; in the large cities 2.1 percent and in Berlin it was 4.3 percent. *Wirtschaft und Statistik*, February 2, 1935, Part II, p. 147.   According to Lowenthal's figures the proportion of Jews in the banking field would thus not be abnormally high when compared with the percentage of Jews in the large cities and in Berlin.   Lowenthal fails to note that the proportion of Jews in the executive positions of the German banks was very high.   From the author's personal contact with the large Berlin joint-stock banks in the postwar period, it seemed evident that the Jews dominated the policies of these institutions.   They completely controlled the private banks.

[81] See increase in output of coal, pig iron, steel and production, Appendix III, columns 1, 2, 3, 4.

[82] *The Economist*, Vol. 101, August 22, 1905, p. 308.

[83] Ibid. Vol. 114, January 16, 1932, p. 104.

[84] Appendix III, columns 17, 18, 19, 22.

[85] *Manchester Guardian Commercial*, April 5, 1923, p. 449.

[86] *Statistische Amt*. Vol. 42, III, p. 70.

[87] *Manchester Guardian Commercial*, November 29, 1928, p. 603.

[88] As a result of the depreciation of the pound and of the dollar, it was estimated that the total of Germany's foreign indebtedness by the beginning of 1934 had been reduced to less than half of the original amount borrowed.   *The Economist*, Vol. 121, September 14, 1935, p. 506.

[89] Appendix III, column 1, 2, 3, 4 and 7.

[90] *New York Times*, December 17, 1931, p. 18.

[91] Henri, Ernest, *Hitler Over Europe*, New York 1934, p. 11.

[92] Pinner, Felix, *Deutsche Wirtschaftsführer*, Charlottenburg 1925, pp. 66–74.

[93] Henri, op. cit. p. 11.

[94] Ibid. p. 11; also Schuman, Frederick, *The Nazi Dictatorship*, New York 1935, p. 141.

[95] Cited by Eddy, Sherwood, *The Challenge of Europe*, New York 1933, p. 21.

[96] National Socialist leaders in their speeches and writings distinguished between banking and other forms of capitalism.   Goebels assailed "Börsenkapital" (Stock Exchange Capital) and "international Jewish high finance": *see also* Gottfried Feder in his *Der Deutsche Staat*, Munich 1932, pp. 135–142.

[97] Henri, op. cit. p. 14.

[98] Compiled from League of Nations, *Commercial Banks 1925–1933*, Geneva 1934.

[99] Nussbaum, Arthur, "Acquisition by a Corporation of its own Stock" in the *Columbia Law Review*, Vol. 35, November 1935, p. 973.

[100] League of Nations, *Commercial Banks, 1925–1933*, Geneva 1934, pp. 44, 116–117.

[101] Appendix III, columns 1, 2, 3, 4 and 7.

[102] Ibid. column 15.

103 Trivanovitch, Vaso, *Economic Development of Germany under National Socialism*, New York 1937, p. 139.

104 "The Credit Indebtedness of the German Economy" as cited in *The Economist*, Vol. 126, January 23, 1937, p. 173.

105 *The Economist*, Banking Supplement, Vol. 123, May 16, 1936, p. 16. Notwithstanding the increase in the federal debt, the yield on German government bonds under the National Socialist regime fell from 8.72 in 1932 to 4.86 in 1935. Appendix III, column 24.

106 *Wirtschaft und Statistik*, September 2, 1936 and Reichskredit Gesellschaft *Germany's Economic Situation at the Turn of 1936–1937*, p. 36. It was claimed that national income in 1937 reached 68 billion marks. Speech of Adolph Hitler as reported in *The New York World-Telegram*, February 21, 1938, p. 6.

107 Ibid.

108 *Weekly Report* of the German Institute for Business Research, February 10, 1937.

109 *The Economist*, Banking Supplement, Vol. 123, May 16, 1936, p. 16.

110 League of Nations *Commercial Banks, 1929–1934*, Geneva 1935, pp. 50–51.

111 United States Department of Commerce, Special Report No. 218, May 23, 1933. Groves, Lawrence H., *Functioning of the Berlin Stock Exchange*, Washington, D. C. 1933, p. 541.

112 *The Economist*, Vol. 126, February 6, 1937, p. 299.

113 Ibid. March 6, 1937, p. 524.

114 *Reichsgesetzblatt*, Part I, 1934, p. 1222.

115 Ibid, Cf. Law of September 28, 1934, and executive decrees of October 23, 1934.

116 Cited by an anonymous author of "The Destruction of Capitalism in Germany," in *Foreign Affairs*, Vol. 5, July 1937, p. 595.

CHAPTER 9

1 Mussolini, Benito, "Speech upon the Constitution of the Corporations" in the News Notes on Fascist Corporations, No. 11, November 1933, pp. 1–7; *see also* Haider, Carmen, "The Meaning and Significance of Fascism" in the *Political Science Quarterly*, Vol. 48, No. 4, December 1933, pp. 558–559.

2 *The Economist*, Vol. 91, August 7, 1920, pp. 27–28.

3 *Manchester Guardian Commercial*, January 25, 1923, p. 161.

4 See extract from speech of President of Banca di Roma, Ibid. October 11, 1923, p. 392.

5 League of Nations *World Economic Survey, 1934–1935*. Geneva, 1935, p. 241.

6 "Fascist Finance," in *Fortune*, Vol. 10, July 4, 1934, p. 74; *European Finance Notes*, United States Department of Commerce, August 9, 1937, p. 15.

7 The League of Nations *Statistical Year Book, 1934–1935*. Geneva, 1935, p. 289.

8 Moody's *Manual of Investments—Governments*, 1937, p. 2830.

9 Salvemini, Gaetano, "Twelve Years of Fascist Financing" in *Foreign Affairs*, Vol. 13, April 1935, pp. 473–482.

10 *Fortune*, op. cit. p. 74.

11 Moody's *Manual of Investments, Governments*, 1937, p. 2829. This section does not consider the economic results of Italian security capitalism due to the difficulty of obtaining complete data. In general industrial production rose sharply from 1921 to 1929. Over these years the output of coal rose from 114,000 tons to 223,000 tons, pig iron from 61,000 tons to 727,000 tons and steel from 714,000 tons to 2,122,000 tons, while exports increased from 8,272,000,000 lire to 15,236,000,000 lire. League of Nations *Statistical Yearbook* for respective years. However in the depression from 1929 through 1932, production declined, excepting coal, with the output of pig iron down to 495,000 tons, steel to 1,396,000 tons and the export trade to 6,812,000,000 lire while the general index fell from 100 to 66. From these low levels there was a recovery by 1934 in the production of coal to 374,000 tons, pig iron to 581,000 tons and steel to 1,832,000 tons, and the general index rose to 80. However exports declined further to 5,224,000,000 lire. One of the most satisfactory trends was the marked increase in saving funds which rose from 13,-150,000,000 lire in 1920 to 40,005,000,000 lire in 1934.

12 For studies of the Soviet financial system see Arnold, Arthur Z., *Banks, Credit and Money in Soviet Russia*, New York 1937; Dobb, Maurice, *Russian Economic Development Since the Revolution*, London 1928; Hubbard, L. E., *Soviet Money and Finance*, London 1936; Katzenellenbaum, S. S., *Russian Currency and Banking, 1914–1924*, London 1925; Pasvolsky, Leo and Moulton, Harold G. *Russian Debts and*

Russian Reconstruction, New York 1924; Sokolnikov and associates *Soviet Policy in Public Finance 1917–1928*, edited by L. Hutchinson and Carl C. Plehn, California 1931; *Soviet Year Book for 1930* which was the last one published.

[13] Webb, Sidney and Beatrice *Soviet Communism: A New Civilization*, Vol. I, New York 1935, pp. 118–119.

[14] Hoover, Calvin B., *The Economic Life of Soviet Russia* New York 1931, p. 188.

[15] Ibid. p. 189.

[16] Sokolnikov and Associates, op. cit. p. 261.

[17] Ibid. p. 265.

[18] Hoover, op. cit. pp. 50–51.

[19] Ibid. p. 57.

[20] Ibid. p. 59.

[21] Ibid. p. 201. See also Haensel, Paul *The Economic Policy of Soviet Russia*, London 1930, pp. 93–94. This book is critical of Soviet finance.

[22] From figures computed by Arnold, op. cit. p. 503.

[23] *The Economist*, Vol. 126 March 27, 1937, p. 705.

[24] Ibid. p. 705.

[25] Hara, K. *An Introduction to the History of Japan*, New York and London 1920, p. 360; Utley, Freda, *Japan's Feet of Clay*, New York 1937, p. 226.

[26] Honjo, Eijiro, *The Social and Economic History of Japan*, Kyoto 1935, p. 83; see also Tanin, O., and Yohan, E., *Militarism and Fascism in Japan*, New York 1934, p. 53. The date of the passing of feudalism is placed at 1871. Ishii, Ryoichi, *Population Pressure and Economic Life in Japan*, London 1937, p. 19.

[27] Moulton, Harold G., *Japan, An Economic Appraisal*, Washington 1931, p. 346.

[28] Utley, op. cit. p. 232.

[29] Ibid. p. 233.

[30] Moulton, op. cit. p. 283.

[31] Ibid. p. 68.

[32] Ibid. p. 69.

[33] Ibid. p. 106.

[34] Ibid. p. 112.

[35] Saburo, M., "A Historical Study of Japanese Capitalism" in *Pacific Affairs*, Vol. 7, March 1934, p. 75.

[36] Ishii Ryoichi, op. cit. p. 24–25.

[37] Araki, Mitsutaro *Financial System in Japan*, Tokyo 1933, p. 3.

[38] Moulton, op. cit. p. 428.

[39] Araki, op. cit. p. 22.

[40] Moulton, op. cit. p. 237.

[41] Ibid. p. 315.

[42] Araki, op. cit. pp. 28–29.

[43] Tanin, and Yohan, op. cit. pp. 15–16.

[44] *China Weekly Review*, Vol. 76, March 21, 1936, p. 76.

[45] *New York Times*, May 3, 1937, pp. 1 and 5.

[46] Moulton, op. cit. pp. 100–101 and 553.

[47] *Financial and Economic Annual of Japan*, Department of Finance of Japan; League of Nations, *Statistical Yearbook*; Moulton, op. cit.

[48] Table 12, "Evolution of Japanese Security Capitalism, 1920–1935," columns 1, 2, 3 and 4.

[49] Ishii, op. cit. p. 24–25.

[50] Araki, op. cit. p. 2.

[51] Ibid. p. 60.

[52] *Transpacific*, Vol. 22, November 29, 1934, p. 22.

[53] Mitsubishi, *Economic Research Bureau*, cited by Utley, op. cit. pp. 371–372.

[54] *Japanese Advertiser, Annual Review*, 1928–1929, cited by Utley, op. cit. p. 211.

[55] Moulton, op. cit. p. 157.

[56] Table 12, columns 8 and 9.

[57] Ibid. column 6.

[58] Sansom, George *Report on Economic and Commercial Conditions in Japan*, Department of Overseas Trade Report London 1936, p. 15.

[59] Araki, op. cit. pp. 28–29. It was estimated that the Mitsui family owned about 20 percent and the Mitsubishi about 16 percent of the share capital of the country. Utley, op. cit. pp. 241–242.

[60] Mitsubishi Economic Research Bureau, *Japanese Trade and Industry*. London 1936, p. 82.

[61] Table 12, column 11.

[62] Utley, op. cit. pp. 211–212.

[63] Araki, op. cit. p. 29.

[64] Table 12, column 7.

[65] Ibid. column 10.

[66] Hamadau, A., "How Japanese Imperialists are Preparing for the Great War," in the Moscow *Pravda* February 4, 1936. Cited in *The China Weekly Review*, March 14, 1936, p. 58.

[67] *The Economist,* Vol. 125, November 7, 1936, p. 260.

[68] *See* Tax Reports in the *Japan Year Book,* Tokio.

[69] Utley, op. cit. p. 377.

[70] Ibid. p. 214.

[71] General production, as measured by the output of basic commodities, rose from a monetary value of $35,000,000,000 in 1913 to $40,000,000,000 in 1934. If the same rate of increase in production in operation from 1850 to 1913 had been continued, the production in 1934 would have reached the hypothetical amount of $66,400,-000,000. There was therefore a differential of $26,400,000,000 between the actual and the hypothetical production in 1934. This hypothetical figure was computed by plotting actual figures from 1850 to 1913 on a semi-logarithmic scale. A straight line trend was found to be the best fit for the years from 1850 to 1913 and was projected until 1934. Based on Appendix IV, Column 4.

[72] League of Nations, *World Economic Survey, 1935–36,* p. 13; The *Times Annalist,* Sept. 18, 1936, p. 389, using 1928 as a base, shows a much wider discrepancy between world production and world trade with production in 1935 at 92 percent and world trade at only 35 percent.

[73] Appendix IV, column 8; League of Nations, *World Economic Survey*, 1933–1934 Geneva 1934, p. 60.

[74] Resolution 3, proposed by the Commission on Currency and Banking, and adopted by the Brussels Conference, 1920. *Federal Reserve Bulletin,* December, 1920, Vol. 6, pp. 1284–1285.

[75] *The Economist,* Vol. 112, April 11, 1931, pp. 780 and 802.

[76] League of Nations, *Commercial Banks, 1913–1929,* Geneva 1931, pp. 13–14.

[77] Ibid. p. 66.

[78] League of Nations, *World Economic Survey, 1934–1935,* Geneva 1935, p. 237.

[79] Grebler, Leo, "The Changing Significance of the Stock Exchange," in the *Index* of the Svenska Handelsbanken, Vol. XI, April 1936, p. 78.

[80] Laidler, Harry W., *History of Socialist Thought,* New York 1927, p. 469.

[81] Letter of Herbert Hoover to Oswald Garrison Villard, 1921, cited by Fischer, Louis, in his article "Recognize Russia Now" in the *Nation,* Vol. 135, December 28, 1932, p. 633.

[82] Quoted in Dutt, R. P., *Fascism and Social Revolution,* New York 1935, p. 47.

[83] League of Nations, *Ten Years of World Cooperation,* London 1930, p. 190.

[84] Einzig, Paul, *World Finance, 1914–1935,* New York 1935, p. 217.

[85] League of Nations, *Commercial Banks, 1925–1933* Geneva 1934, p. 18.

[86] Computed from *The Statesman's Year Book.*

[87] *New York Times,* May 4, 1937, p. 43.

[88] League of Nations, *World Economic Survey, 1933–1934,* pp. 286–289.

[89] Mulhall's *Dictionary of Statistics,* pp. 699, 706; *Statesman's Yearbook,* 1936.

[90] Appendix V.

[91] Appendices I, II, III, and VII.

[92] Feller, A. H., "The Movement for Corporate Reform: A World-Wide Phenomenon" in the *American Bar Association Journal,* Vol. 20, June 1934, p. 347.

[93] League of Nations, *Commercial Banks, 1925–1933,* p. 201.

[94] Ibid. p. 44.

[95] Bank for International Settlements *Fifth Annual Report,* 1934–1935, Basle 1935, p. 53.

[96] League of Nations, *Commercial Banks, 1929–1934,* Geneva 1935, p. 30.

CHAPTER 10

[1] Callendar, G. S. "The Early Transportation and Banking Enterprises of the States in Relation to the Growth of Corporations" in the *Quarterly Journal of Economics,* Vol. XVII, November 1902, pp. 131–133.

[2] Davis, Joseph S., *Essays in the Earlier History of American Corporations,* Cambridge Mass. 1917, Vol. II, p. 33.

[3] Smith, Walter and Cole, Arthur, *Fluctuations in American Business, 1790–1860*, Vol. I, Cambridge Mass. 1935, p. 7.

[4] Blodgett, Samuel, Jr., *Economica: A Statistical Manual for the United States of America*, Washington, D. C. 1806, p. 200.

[5] Hamilton, Alexander, *Report on the subject of Manufactures, December 5, 1791*, Boston 1892, p. 40.

[6] *Bankers Magazine*, New York Vol. I, November 1846, pp. 257–258.

[7] *The Merchants' Magazine and Commercial Review* conducted by Freeman Hunt, (hereafter cited as *Hunt's Merchants' Magazine*), Vol. 14, New York January 1846, p. 100.

[8] Smith and Cole, op. cit. p. 88.

[9] Simons, A. M., *Social Forces in American History*, New York 1911, p. 240.

[10] Weber, Adna F. *The Growth of Cities in the 19th Century*, New York 1899, p. 22.

[11] Smith and Cole, op. cit. p. 87.

[12] Commons, John R. and Associates, *History of Labour in the United States*, New York 1918, Vol. I, pp. 169–462–464.

[13] Burchett, Floyd F., *Corporation Finance*, New York and London 1934, p. 288.

[14] Coote, R. H., *Treatise on the Law of Mortgages*, New York 1821, p. 45.

[15] Whitworth, Joseph, *New York Industrial Exposition of 1853, Special Report*, p. 9.

[16] The Bank continued to operate under a charter from Pennsylvania until its failure in 1841. Catterall, Ralph C., *The Second Bank of the United States*, Chicago 1903, p. 375.

[17] See interesting description of the firm of S. & M. Allen by Henrietta M. Larson, *Journal of Economic and Business History*, Vol. III, May 1931, p. 424.

[18] Brown, John B. *One Hundred Years of Merchant Banking*, New York 1909, pp. 10–45.

[19] Larson, Henrietta M., "E. W. Clark & Company, 1837–1857" in the *Journal of Economic and Business History*, Vol. IV, May 30, 1932, p. 429.

[20] *Niles Weekly Register*, December 13, 1834, p. 234.

[21] *Financial Register of the United States*, Vol. I, p. 83.

[22] Martin, Joseph G. *Twenty-one Years in the Boston Stock Market*, Boston 1856, p. 70.

[23] Adams, C. F., *Further Reflections Upon the State of the Currency in the United States*, Boston 1837; Gallatin, Albert, *Suggestions on Banks and Currency of the Several United States*, New York 1841; Colwell, Stephen, *Ways and Means of Payment*, Philadelphia 1859.

[24] Computed from the House *Executive Documents* from 1835 to 1855. The annual reports of the secretary of the treasury include statistics on banking but they are incomplete and contain many inconsistencies, since they were in turn compiled from state sources which were not uniform.

[25] Report of the special bank examiner of Ohio, in *Public Documents* (1854) XVIII, pp. 356, 401.

[26] *Massachusetts, Report of the Bank Commissioners*, December 1838, p. 21.

[27] Dwight, E. "The Financial Revulsion and the New York Banking System" in *Hunt's Merchants' Magazine*, Vol. 38, February 1858, p. 159; See also Seaman, E. C., "The Panic and Financial Crisis of 1857" Ibid. Vol. 37, December 1857, p. 660.

[28] Callendar, op. cit. pp. 149–150.

[29] Stedman, Edmund C. *The New York Stock Exchange*, New York 1905, Vol. I. p. 85.

[30] See Appendix VII, "Evolution of American Security Capitalism, 1820-1935" column 11.

[31] "Facts and arguments in favor of adopting Railways in preference to Canals in the State of Pennsylvania" p. 10 cited by Bishop, Avard L., *The State Works of Pennsylvania*, New Haven 1907, p. 188.

[32] Callendar, op. cit. pp. 139–140.

[33] Ibid. p. 143.

[34] *North Carolina Senate Document*, 1838, No. 1, p. 19.

[35] *Kentucky State Journal*, 1839, p. 25.

[36] *Hunt's Merchants' Magazine*, Vol. I, August 1839, p. 179.

[37] *Statistics of Public Indebtedness*, United States Census Office 10th Census, 1880, Washington 1881, p. 25.

[38] These first official figures on municipal debt are given in 27th Cong. 3rd Sess. H. *Report* 296, Report of W. C. Johnson, Washington, D. C. 1843, pp. 104–106.

[39] Hillhouse, A. M., "Lessons from Previous Eras of Default" included in Chatters, Carl H., *Municipal Debt Defaults*, Chicago 1933, p. 10.

40 Davis, op. cit. p. 291.

41 Bloomfield, Joseph E., "Canals of the United States" in *Hunt's Merchants' Magazine*, Vol. 42, January 1860, p. 54.

42 Evans, George H., "Early Industrial Preferred Stocks in the United States," in *The Journal of Political Economy*, Vol. 40 April 1932, p. 227.

43 Appendix VII, columns 14, 15; the effect of the discovery of gold in increasing supply of domestic capital is noted in *Hunt's Merchants' Magazine*, Vol. 23, July 1850, p. 205.

44 Clark, Victor S., *History of Manufactures in the United States, 1607–1860*, Washington 1916, p. 377. New England manufacturing showed average annual dividends of about 10 percent.

45 Lathrop, William G., *Brass Industry in Connecticut*. Conn. 1909, p. 81; see also Clark, op. cit. p. 353.

46 It was reported in 1846 that in the city of Boston there were 314 persons with estates from $100,000 to $200,000, 9 persons with estates of over one million dollars and one with an estate of over six million dollars. "The Wealthy Men of Boston" in *Hunt's Merchants' Magazine*, Vol. 15, October 1846, p. 424.

47 Ibid. Vol. 13, September 1845, p. 260.

48 Ibid. Vol. 16, May 1847, p. 436.

49 DeBow, J. D., *The Industrial Resources etc. of the Southern and Western States*, New Orleans 1852, p. 100. For example in 1848, it was estimated that cotton planting in the Carolinas did not yield a return of more than 3 or 4 percent upon the investment. Clark, op. cit. p. 368. The returns in the Southwestern states were probably higher.

50 *Hunt's Merchants' Magazine*, May 1860, Vol. 42, pp. 601–602.

51 Ware, Caroline F., *Early New England Cotton Manufacture*, Boston 1931, p. 150.

52 Stevens, F. W., *The Beginning of the New York Central Railroad*, New York 1926, pp. 352–382.

53 *Report of the Secretary of the Treasury*, October 15, 1828.

54 Catterall, op. cit. p. 108.

55 Callendar, op. cit. p. 153.

56 *Secretary of the Treasury to Congress, Report of Foreign Holdings of American Securities*, 1854.

57 See Appendix VII, Ratios F, B and E.

58 Chatters, op. cit. *Public Administration Service No. 33*, p. 10.

59 *Hunt's Merchants' Magazine*, Vol. 16, 1847, p. 418; Appendix IX "Financial Position of the Railroads, 1890–1934" Ratio G.

60 Computed from *Hunt's Merchants' Magazine*, Vol. 42, 1860, p. 373; Appendix IX, ratio F.

61 McGrane, Reginald C. *Panic of 1837*, Chicago 1924, p. 141.

62 Hansard op. cit., Vol. III, pp. 273–277.

63 Barings frequently granted financial assistance to Webster. See letter in the Baring manuscript cited by McGrane, Reginald C., *Foreign Bondholders and American State Debts*, New York 1935, p. 22.

64 Ibid. pp. 23–25.

65 See letter of Huth and Company, a London banking house, to the State Bank of Missouri, Ibid. pp. 29–30.

66 Ibid. p. 34.

67 Jenks, op. cit. p. 106.

68 Cited by Pratt, Sereno, S., *The Work of Wall Street*, New York 1903, pp. 16–17.

69 The debts of the Southern planters and merchants to the northern capitalists in 1860 were variously estimated at from $40,000,000 to $400,000,000. Schwab, John C., *The Confederate States of America*, New York, 1901, p. 111.

70 *The Economist*, January 12, 1861, Vol. 19, p. 30.

71 For these quotations see *Bankers Magazine*, Vol. 12, pp. 334–35; *Hunt's Merchants' Magazine*, Vol. 8, p. 462; Vol. 10, p. 74; Vol. 13, p. 84; Martin, op. cit. pp. 51, 183–184; Stedman, op. cit. Vol. 1, pp. 117–118.

72 Smith and Cole, op. cit. Table 62, p. 174; see also tables 69 and 70 pp. 183–184.

73 *Mechanics Free Press*, May 30, 1829.

74 Raymond, Daniel, *Thoughts on Political Economy*, Baltimore 1820, Part II, Chapter X, p. 429.

75 *New York Working Man's Advocate*, October 31, 1829.

76 *Proceedings of a Meeting of Mechanics and Other Working Men*, December 29, 1829.

77 *Pickens to Hammond*, July 13, 1837, Hammond MSS. cited in McGrane, *Panic of 1837*, pp. 158–159.

78 Beard, Charles A., *An Economic Interpretation of the Constitution of the United States*, New York 1913.

79 *New York Times Magazine*, June 30, 1935.

80 See *Marbury vs. Madison*, 1 Cranch, 146.

81 Parrington, V. L., *Main Currents in American Thought*, New York 1927, Vol. II, pp. 67–69, 145–150.

82 Halaas, E. T., "Legal Control of Life Insurance Company Investments" in *The Journal of Business of the University of Chicago*, Vol. 5, No. 4, Chicago October 1932, p. 321.

83 Willis, H. Parker and Bogen, Jules I., *Investment Banking* (Revised Edition), New York 1936, p. 217.

84 New York Public Service Commission, 1st District *Annual Report* for 1907, Vol. I, p. 451, gives an account of the statutory regulations of utilities in New York State.

85 Secrist, Horace, *An Economic Analysis of the Constitutional Restrictions upon Public Indebtedness in the United States*. University of Wisconsin Bulletin, Madison 1914, p. 54.

86 No detailed consideration of the war years is given, but rather the effect of the Civil War on security capitalism is traced.

87 The Supreme Court held to the narrow interpretation in the Slaughter House cases in 1873, but later followed the broad view. In the Slaughter House cases the court declared: "We doubt very much whether any action of a state not directed by way of discrimination against the negroes as a class, or on account of their race, will ever be held to come within the purview of this provision. It is so clearly a provision for that race and that emergency, that a strong case would be necessary for its application to any other." 16 *Wallace*, 81; In contrast see *New State Ice Company vs. Liebman*, 285 U.S. 262.

88 Adams, Charles Francis, Jr. and Henry, *Chapters of Erie and Other Essays*, Boston 1871, p. 19.

89 Railroad Committee of the New York State Legislature *Proceedings*, January 14, 1869, pp. 23–24.

90 Dewing, A. S. "Theory of Railroad Re-Organization" *American Economic Review*, Vol 8, December 1918, pp. 784-785.

91 *Nation*, Vol. 17, September 25, 1873, p. 206.

92 *The Statist*, 1885, p. 485.

93 Ellis Paxton Oberholtzer's *Jay Cooke, Financier of the Civil War*, Philadelphia 1907, is the best descriptive presentation of Jay Cooke's activities, while the most penetrating critical interpretation is Henrietta M. Larson's *Jay Cooke, Private Banker*, Cambridge, Mass. 1936.

94 This business brought Jay Cooke and his associates commissions amounting to over $7,000,000. Oberholtzer, op. cit. Vol. II, p. 34.

95 Ibid. p. 275.

96 Minnigerode, Mead, *Certain Rich Men*, New York 1927, p. 65.

97 Oberholtzer, op. cit. pp. 239-240.

98 Ibid. pp. 237–238.

99 Ibid. Vol. II, p. 202. Even Chief Justice Chase considered the possibility of becoming a "sleeping partner" in the London house. Larson, op. cit. p. 459.

100 Oberholtzer, op. cit. p. 206.

101 *The New York World*, Oct. 6, 1873.

102 Oberholtzer, op. cit. Vol. II, p. 416.

103 Minnigerode, op. cit. p. 78.

104 Oberholtzer, Vol. II, op. cit. p. 425.

105 *Chronicle*, Vol. 92, 1911, p. 1406, *Valuation Taxation and Public Indebtedness*, United States Bureau of the Census, Tenth Census, 1880, Washington 1884, Vol. VII, p. 284.

106 Appendix VI, columns 14 and 15.

107 See article by E. L. Godkin, "Who are the Bondholders?" in the *Nation*, February 6, 1868 Vol. VI, p. 104.

108 41st Congress, 2nd Session, *House Executive Doc.* 27, p. XXVII and XXVIII.

109 Shanks, Sanders, "The Extent of Municipal Defaults" in the *National Municipal Review*, Vol. 24, January 1935, p. 32.

110 Palgrave, R. H. Inglis, "An English View of Investments in the United States, in the *Forum*, Vol. 15, April 1893, p. 197.

111 See Arens, Hermann, and Bancroft, James, "History of Bond Prices," in *The Annals of American Academy of Political and Social Science*, Vol. 88 March 1920, p.

189 ; The Hannibal and St. Joseph Railroad in 1867 issued a 10 percent bond which matured in 1892. *Chronicle,* op. cit. Vol. 48, March 30, 1889, p. 414.

112 New York Central 7's sold at 103 in 1872 and the Harlem 1st 7's were at par in the same year. Ibid. February 22, 1879, Vol. 28, p. 183.

CHAPTER 11

1 Beard, Charles A. and Mary R. *The Rise of American Civilization* New York 1927, Vol. II, p. 331.

2 *Chronicle,* Supplements Vol. 63 October 17, 1896, State and City Supplement—"The Municipal Bond Market," p. 4.

3 Lerner, Max, "The Supreme Court and American Capitalism" in the *Yale Law Review,* 1933, pp. 668–701 ; Smith, James Allen, *The Spirit of American Government,* New York 1907, and *The Growth and Decadence of Constitutional Government,* New York 1930. An extreme economic interpretation of the decisions of the Supreme Court is that of Myers, Gustavus *History of the Supreme Court of the United States,* Chicago 1912.

4 Veblen, Thorstein, *Absentee Ownership and Business Enterprise* New York 1923, p. 86.

5 Stetson, Francis L., and others, *Some Legal Phases of Corporate Financing, Reorganization and Regulation,* New York 1917, p. 13.

6 Smith, James G., *The Development of Trust Companies in the United States,* New York 1927, pp. 291–295.

7 Noyes, Alexander D., *Forty Years of American Finance,* New York and London 1909, p. 296.

8 Bonbright, James C. and Means, Gardiner C. *The Holding Company,* New York 1932, p. 59.

9 Ibid. p. 59.

10 Ibid. pp. 61–64.

11 Ibid. p. 64.

12 Meade, Edward, *Trust Finance,* New York 1903, p. 39.

13 Sullivan, Mark, *Our Times,* vol. II, New York 1927, p. 318.

14 Ibid. p. 319.

15 *Pollock* vs. *Farmers Loan and Trust Co.,* 157 U. S. 429.

16 See graphic description of convention by Harry Thurston Peck reproduced by Mark Sullivan op. cit. Vol. I, pp. 123–124.

17 *New York Journal,* November 3, 1896.

18 Ibid. October 31, 1896.

19 Ibid. November 1, 1896.

20 Wister, Owen, *Roosevelt, The Story of a Friendship* New York 1930, p. 212.

21 Sullivan, op. cit. Vol. II, p. 447.

22 Ibid. p. 460.

23 Bryan, William Jennings, *Memoirs of William Jennings Bryan,* Chicago 1925, pp. 174–175.

24 Seitz, Don Carlos, *Joseph Pulitzer,* New York 1927 pp. 201–205. J. P. Morgan was also opposed to the war with Spain. Seldes, George, *Iron, Blood and Profits,* New York 1934, p. 6.

25 Finch, George A., "American Diplomacy and the Financing of China," in the *American Journal of International Law,* Vol. 16, January 1922, p. 25 ; see above p. 165.

26 Appendix VIII "Financial Position of National Banks, 1870 to 1935."

27 Ibid. Ratio A.

28 Ibid. Ratio B.

29 Willis, H. Parker, and Steiner, William H., *Federal Reserve Banking Practice,* New York 1926 p. 659. State banks, on the other hand, increased the proportion of their time deposits to total deposits from 11 percent in 1896 to 16 percent in 1909. Compiled from *Statistics for the United States* by A. Piatt Andrews for the National Monetary Commission, Vol. XXI, p. 151.

30 Appendix VIII, Ratio C. Dr. Jacob Hollander commented on the increase in the security investments of commercial banks in "The Security Holdings of National Banks" in the *American Economic Review,* December 1913, p. 793.

31 Computed from *Report of the Comptroller of the Currency,* 1920, Vol. II, p. 774.

32 Anderson, Benjamin, *The Value of Money,* New York 1936, pp. 510–511.

33 Barron, C. W., *The Federal Reserve Act* Boston 1914, pp. 68–69.

[34] See views of William Scott, E. M. Patterson, and F. A. Cleveland. Cited in Moulton, Harold G., *Principles of Money and Banking,* Chicago 1916 Part II, pp. 456–460.

[35] Hepburn, A. Barton "State and National Bank Circulation" in the *Annals of the American Academy of Political and Social Science,* Vol. 3, p. 577.

[36] Meeker, J. Edward, *The Work of the Stock Exchange,* New York 1930, p. 68.

[37] *New York Stock Exchange Bulletin,* Vol. 3 February 1932, p. 1.

[38] *Chronicle,* Vol. 29, supplement, November, 29, 1879, p. III; Ibid. Vol. 43, December 18, 1886, p. 739; Ibid. Vol. 72, April 30, 1901, p. 865.

[39] No definite figures are available for the Curb, as the volume of sales was not reported before 1921.

[40] *Chronicle,* Vol. 46, 1888, p. 304. A study of the amount of the listings of these exchanges made by the *Chronicle* in 1888 showed that the Baltimore exchange on its complete returns had listings of $9,875,000 in bonds and $2,802,000 in stocks. Boston, on incomplete figures, showed $13,141,000 in stocks.

[41] 62nd Congress, 2nd and 3rd Sessions, Banking and Currency Committee, United States Congress, House of Representatives, "Money Trust Investigation," 1912, pp. 89–90.

[42] United States Banking and Currency Committee (House, 62nd Congress, 2nd and 3rd Sessions) *Investigation of the Financial and Monetary Conditions of the United States, Hearings,* hereafter called *Money Trust Investigation.*

[43] *Forum,* April 1893, p. 198.

[44] Drexel and Company of Philadelphia was really the parent firm, and Drexel, Morgan & Company the New York firm was started in 1871. By 1894 the importance of the former firm had declined, and J. P. Morgan the elder then formed the firm of J. P. Morgan and Company of New York. See testimony of J. P. Morgan, the younger, before the Senate Committee on the Munitions Industry, *Hearings* S. Res. 206 Part 25, p. 7479. The outstanding study of the firm is Lewis Corey, *House of Morgan,* New York 1930.

[45] Oberholtzer, op. cit. Vol. II, p. 366.

[46] *Bankers Magazine,* July 1877, p. 172.

[47] Recognition of its growing importance is seen in the cable sent by Cyrus W. Field to Junius Morgan as follows: "Many of our business men seem to have lost their heads. What we want is some cool-headed strong man to lead. If you should form a syndicate in London to buy through Drexel, Morgan & Company good securities in this market I believe you would make a great deal of money and at the same time entirely change the feeling here." Corey, op. cit. p. 132.

[48] *Bankers Magazine,* Vol. 63, September 1, 1900, p. 434.

[49] *Chronicle,* February 17, 1900, p. 306, July 28, 1900, p. 163; *Bankers Magazine,* Vol. 63, November 1901, p. 880.

[50] Money Trust Investigation, Part 20, p. 1423.

[51] See State of New York—*Report of the Joint Committee of the Senate and Assembly of the State of New York Appointed to Investigate the Affairs of Life Insurance Companies,* 1907.

[52] For an account of the internal controversy over the Equitable Life Assurance Society, see Sullivan, op. cit. Vol. III, pp. 41–44.

[53] Nicholson, Harold George, *Dwight Morrow,* New York 1935, pp. 152–153.

[54] In 1915 these holdings were turned over to T. Coleman DuPont, and later through the efforts of Dwight Morrow the Equitable was converted from a stock to a mutual company. Ibid. p. 154.

[55] New light is thrown on these negotiations by the careful study of James A. Barnes *John G. Carlisle, Financial Statesman,* New York 1931.

[56] McElroy, Robert, *Grover Cleveland, the Man and the Statesman,* Vol. II, New York 1923, pp. 78–79.

[57] *Chronicle,* January 20, 1894, pp. 105–106; February 3, 1894, p. 199.

[58] Stillman claimed considerable credit for the success of the negotiations. Burr, Anna R., *Portrait of a Banker—James Stillman 1850–1918,* New York 1927, p. 116.

[59] Even Alexander Dana Noyes, financial editor of the *New York Times,* felt that the bankers had driven a hard bargain. See Noyes, op. cit. pp. 234–235. This opinion of Noyes, a conservative commentator, is frequently quoted in radical literature. See also Nevins, Allan, *Grover Cleveland,* New York 1932, pp. 662–665.

[60] The banking syndicate made its profit mainly from the appreciation of the issue in the open market, since it was purchased at a price of 104 and rose as high as 123. *New York Tribune,* May 11, June 27, September 22, 1895.

[61] *Bankers Magazine,* Vol. 34 February, 1880, p. 654; British *Bankers Magazine,* 1876, Vol. 36, p. 141.

[62] Oberholzer, op. cit. Vol. II, p. 418.

63 Corey, op. cit. pp. 111–112.
64 Ibid. pp. 110–112.
65 Ibid. p. 112.
66 Corey, op. cit. p. 170.
67 Dewing, op. cit. p. 779.
68 Burr, op. cit. p. 127.
69 Kennen, George, *E. H. Harriman*, New York and Boston 1922. Vol. I, p. 80.
70 *Chronicle*, Vol. 58, February 10, 1894, p. 264.
71 Daggett, Stuart, *Railway Reorganization*, Boston 1908 p. 65.
72 Ibid. p. 69.
73 Pyle, Joseph Gipin, *Life of James J. Hill*, New York 1936, Vol. II, pp. 144–146.
74 Corey, op. cit. p. 298.
75 *Chronicle*, Vol. 72, May 11, 1901, p. 900.
76 Ibid.
77 *New York Tribune*, May 14, 1901.
78 Ibid, May 15, 1901. Sombart, in reviewing this episode, describes it as Harriman's "brutal campaign against Morgan." Sombart, Werner, *Quintessence of Capitalism*, New York 1915, p. 186.
79 Corey, op. cit. p. 302.
80 Brandeis, Louis D., *Other People's Money*, New York 1914, pp. 179, 193.
81 *Interstate Commerce Commission Reports*, Vol. 31, June–October 1914, p. 47.
82 *New York Times*, May 20, 1914, November 10 and 23, 1915.
83 Compiled from Poor's *Manual of Railroads*, 43rd Annual Number, 1910, p. 64.
84 Ripley, William Z., *Railroads, Finance and Organization*, New York 1915, p. 473.
85 Tarbell, Ida M., *Life of Elbert H. Gary*, New York 1933, p. 114.
86 Sullivan, op. cit. Vol. II, pp. 347–349.
87 Tarbell, op. cit. p. 121.
88 Carnegie in retirement continued to criticize banking security capitalism severely, lashing out against the "Wall Street gamblers." *Chronicle*, Vol. 48, March 30, 1907, p. 714.
89 Tarbell, op. cit. p. 118.
90 Money Trust Investigation, Part 22, pp. 1581–1591.
91 Clews, Henry, *Fifty Years in Wall Street*, New York 1908, p. 702.
92 McManus, Theodore F., and Beasley, Norman, *Men, Money and Motors*, New York 1924, pp. 103–104.
93 Nicolson, op. cit. p. 156.
94 Appendix VII, column 11.
95 For detailed explanation of these terms see p. 374.
96 *Chronicle*, 1914, Vol. 99, Part I July–Sept. p. 511.
97 Table 16, column 1 and Ratio A.
98 Ibid. column 5.
99 Ibid. Ratio D.
100 Ibid. column 4, Ratio B.
101 Ibid. column 6.
102 Ibid. Ratio C.
103 Hillhouse, Albert M., *Municipal Bonds*, New York 1936, pp. 34–35.
104 Compiled from Poor's *Manual of Railroads* for these years.
105 Appendix IX "Financial Position of the Railroads, 1890–1934."
106 Ibid. columns 1 and 2, Ratio A.
107 Ibid. Ratio B.
108 Ibid. columns 4 and 5.
109 Ibid. Ratio C.
110 Ibid. columns 1 and 6, Ratio D.
111 Ibid. columns 6 and 7, Ratio E.
112 *Statistics of Railroads*, Interstate Commerce Commission, 1890, p. 12; 1910, p. 15.
113 Appendix IX. Ratio F.
114 *Statistics of Railroads*, op. cit.
115 Ibid.
116 *Bankers Magazine*, Vol. 33, April 1879, p. 745.
117 Ibid. *The Economist*, Vol. 59, January 26, 1901, p. 119.
118 *Chronicle*, April 27, 1901, Vol. 22, p. 60.
119 *Bankers Magazine*, October 1900, pp. 496, 637.
120 *Chronicle*, Vol. 71, August 11, 1900, pp. 258, 261; Ibid. Vol. 72, August 27, 1901, p. 796; Ibid. Vol. 74, April 19, 1902, pp. 802–803; See speech of Chancellor of the Exchequer, April 23, 1903; *Economist*, Vol. 61, May 9, 1903, p. 832.
121 *Chronicle*, Vol. 77, December 5, 1903, p. 2132.

122 Croly, Herbert David, *Willard Straight,* New York 1924, pp. 239, 297. Willard Straight, consul general at Mukden, later acted for Morgans in their Far-eastern financial operations.

123 Ibid. p. 287; Nearing, Scott and Freeman, Joseph, *Dollar Diplomacy,* New York 1925, p. 37

124 MacMurray, John, *Treaties and Agreements with and Concerning China,* Vol. I, New York 1921, p. 800.

125 The statement of President Wilson is reproduced in the *American Journal of International Law,* Vol. 7, pp. 338–339.

126 Ripley, op. cit. p. 5.

127 Appendix VII, columns 14 and 15.

128 Banking institutions include national banks, savings banks, private banks, loan and trust companies. *Report of the Comptroller of the Currency,* 1912, pp. 39–40. The assets of these institutions include the influence of their credit operations and are not the most reliable series for indicating the trend of saving. However, these are the best consecutive series available for these years. The statistics on life insurance companies were obtained for 1872 to 1897 from the bulletin *Wealth Accumulation through Life Insurance* compiled by the Massachusetts Bureau of Statistics of Labor, summarized in the *Chronicle,* Vol. 66, 1898, p. 1025, and for 1898 to 1911 from the *Insurance Yearbook* of the Spectator Company, summarized in the *Statistical Abstract of the United States,* Washington 1912, p. 640.

129 Some students of the subject believed that the increase in saving funds as indicated in these figures did not represent a growth of the actual saving of the lower classes. It was pointed out that the size of deposits in Connecticut banks from 1880 to 1910 showed that the total of accounts less than $1,000 decreased from nearly one-half of the total amount of deposits in 1880 to a little over one-third by 1910. This decrease, it is stated, took place notwithstanding the fact that total saving increased almost 400 percent and that the number of depositors increased nearly 200 percent. Epstein, Abraham, "Darker Phases of American Prosperity" in the *New Republic,* Vol. 57, February 6, 1929, p. 314.

130 Appendix X "Proportion of Security Investments to Total Assets of Financial Institutions, 1890–1935."

131 Adams, Henry C., *Public Debts,* New York 1887, p. 47.

132 *Chronicle,* Vol. 43, December 11, 1886, p. 685.

133 *Annual Report of the Secretary of the Treasury,* 1898, p. XXXVIII.

134 *Chronicle,* 1909, p. 521.

135 Estimates of Warshow, H. T., "Distribution of Corporate Ownership in the United States" in the *Quarterly Journal of Economics,* Vol. 39, November 1924, p. 28.

136 Ibid. p. 28.

137 *Chronicle,* Supplement Vol. 81, Bankers and Trust Section, October 21, 1905, p. 94.

138 Conant, Charles A., "The World's Wealth in Negotiable Securities," in the *Atlantic Monthly,* Vol. 101, January 1908, p. 97.

139 Ripley, op. cit. p. 112.

140 Ibid. p. 113.

141 Sterne, Simon, "Recent Railroad Failures and Their Lessons" in the *Forum,* 17, March 1894, p. 27.

142 Lloyd, Henry Demarest, *Wealth Against Commonwealth,* New York 1894, p. 33.

143 Cotter, Arundel, *United States Steel,* New York 1921, p. 201.

144 *Chronicle,* Supp. Vol. 69, July–December, 1899, Bankers and Trust Supplement, p. 25.

145 Conant, Charles A., *Wall Street and the Country,* New York 1904, pp. 24–26.

146 Dewing, op. cit. p. 788.

147 *Chronicle,* Vol. 78, May 28, 1904, pp. 199.

148 Atwood, Albert W., "Unsound Real Estate Bonds," *Harper's Weekly,* Vol. 59, August 29, 1914, p. 214.

149 *Chronicle,* op. cit. Vol. 41, July 18, 1885, p. 62.

150 Bosland, C., *The Common Stock Theory of Investment,* New York 1937, p. 23.

151 *New York Times Annalist,* Vol. I, May 26, 1913, p. 583; *Chronicle,* Vol. 45, September 3, 1887, p. 287; Statistical data on the movement of bond prices is given by Mitchell, Wesley C., "Rates of Interest and the Price of Investment Securities," in *The Journal of Political Economy,* Vol. XIX, April 1911, p. 272, and "Security Prices and Interest Rates," Vol. XXI, June, 1913, p. 510; *New York Times Annalist,* Vol. I, May 19, 1913, pp. 549–550 and May 26, 1913, p. 583. Macaulay has charted the movement for 1856–1911; Macaulay, Fred K., "Construction of an Index

Number of Bond Yields in the United States," in the *Journal of the American Statistical Association*, Vol. XXI, March 1926, p. 27.

[152] Arens, Hermann and Bancroft, James, "History of Bond Prices," in the *Annals*, Vol. 88, March 1920, p. 191.

[153] Rose, Dwight C., *A Scientific Approach to Investment Management*, New York 1928, p. 274.

[154] *Chronicle*, Vol. 82, February 24, 1906, p. 421.

[155] Ibid. Vol. 102, April April 15, 1916, p. 1397.

[156] *New York Times*, March 31, 1903, p. 1, column 7. Interview at St. Paul, Minnesota, July 19, 1903, quoted by Noyes, op. cit. p. 309.

[157] *Chronicle*, Vol. 82, June 30, 1906, p. 1468.

[158] Noyes, Alexander D. "Finance," in the *Forum*, Vol. 38, April 1907, p. 498.

[159] *Chronicle*, Vol. 83, December 29, 1906, p. 1555.

[160] Ibid. Vol. 72, March 2, 1901, p. 416.

[161] *Wall Street Journal*, April 1, 1903; *Times*, March 31, 1903.

[162] Bishop, Joseph Bucklin, *Theodore Roosevelt and His Time*, New York 1920, Vol. 2, p. 55.

[163] White, Horace "The Hughes Investigation" in the *Journal of Political Economy*, Vol. 17, October 1909, p. 528.

[164] See pp. 203-4.

[165] Quoted by Kirkland, Edward C., *A History of American Economic Life*, New York 1932, p. 629.

[166] Powderly, T. V., *Thirty Years of Labor*, Columbus 1889, p. 243.

[167] Sullivan, op. cit. Vol. II, pp. 425, 439-442.

[168] A survey of the literature of protest is given by Regier, C. C., *Era of the Muckrakers*, University of North Carolina, Chapel Hill 1932.

[169] Brandeis, op. cit.

[170] Sullivan, op. cit. Vol. II p. 415.

[171] Ibid. Vol. II. p. 415.

[172] "Topics of the Day" in the *Literary Digest*, Vol. XXXV, November 9, 1907, p. 671.

[173] *Chronicle*, Vol. 85, September 7, 1907, p. 550.

[174] Bishop, op. cit. pp. 39-40.

[175] Kirkland, op. cit. p. 640.

[176] Bishop, op. cit. pp. 40-41.

[177] Wilson, Woodrow "Politics (1857-1907)" in the *Atlantic Monthly*, Vol. 100, pp. 635-646.

[178] *Chronicle*, Supplement Vol. 87, October 10, 1908, p. 94.

[179] Quoted by Isaac, C. P., *The Menace of Money Power*, London 1921, p. vii.

[180] H. R. Res. 429, afterward extended by H. R. Res. 504, February 24, 1912.

[181] Money Trust Investigation, Part I, p. 4.

[182] Ibid., p. 151.

[183] *Stock Exchange Practices*, Part 6, p. 2030. Summary of Hearings Before Senate Committee on Banking and Currency—72nd Congress, 2nd Session, Report No. 1455.

[184] *Chronicle*, Vol. 85, November, 1907, p. 1109.

[185] Ibid. Vol. 85, December 21, 1907, p. 1547.

[186] Ibid. Vol. 82, March 24, 1906, p. 656.

[187] See statement of James Beck, Ibid. Vol. 79, December 31, 1904, p. 2770.

[188] Ibid. Vol. 102, April 29, 1916.

[189] Ibid. Vol. 104, January 27, 1917, p. 309.

[190] New York Public Service Commission, 1st District, *Annual Report* for 1907, Vol. I, p. 451.

[191] New York Laws, 1905, C. 737, paragraph 12, amended by New York Laws, 1907, C. 429, paragraph 55, 69; Rosenbaum, Irwin S., and Lilienthal, David E., "Issuance of Securities by Public Service Corporations," *Yale Law Journal*, Vol. 37, April 1928, p. 719.

[192] Waltersdorf, M. C., *Regulation of Public Utilities in New Jersey*, 1936, p. 105.

[193] Barron, Mary L., "State regulation of the securities of railroads and public service companies," *Annals of the American Academy of Political and Social Science*, Vol. 76 March, 1918, p. 167 ; see also Frederick, John H., Hypps, Frank T. and Herring, James M., *Regulation of Railroad Finance*, New York 1930, p. 145.

[194] Secrist, op. cit. For discussion of this subject see *Bankers Magazine*, Vol. 30, June 1876, p. 947, Vol. 31, September, 1876, pp. 181-183; Dillon, John F., *The Law of Municipal Bonds*, St. Louis 1876, p. 5 ; see also Van de Woestyne, Royal S., *State Control of Local Finance in Massachusetts*, Harvard Economic Studies, Cambridge Mass. 1935, p. 23.

195 Price, William H., *Life Insurance Reform in New York*, Cambridge 1909.

196 State of New York, *Report of the Joint Committee of the Senate and Assembly Appointed to Investigate the Affairs of Life Insurance Companies* so-called "Hughes Report," pp. 66–67.

197 Ibid. p. 139.

198 Ibid. p. 68.

199 *Chronicle*, Vol. 58, April 21, 1894, p. 657.

200 See p. 179.

201 *Chronicle*, State and City Supplement, Vol. 52, April 11, 1896, p. 5.

202 Ibid. Banking Convention Section, Supplement Vol. 101, September 18, 1915, p. 167.

203 Ibid. Supplement Vol. 68, State and City Supplement, April 15, 1899, p. 3.

204 Ibid. Vol. 70, State and City Supplement, April 14, 1900, contains an analysis of the laws relating to street raiway investments, pp. 3–5.

205 Ibid. Vol. 75, August 9, 1902, p. 264.

206 Barnett, George E., *State Banks and Trust Companies Since the Passage of the National Bank Act*, National Monetary Commission, Washington 1911, p. 21.

207 Ibid., p. 22.

208 An attempt was also made to place the trust companies under federal supervision. The secretary of the treasury in his annual report of 1904 made such a recommendation, but the plan was abandoned in 1905. The opinion was expressed that the federal government did not have the power to regulate trust companies. Ridgely, William B., "Government Control of Banks and Trust Companies," *Annals of the American Academy of Political and Social Science*, Vol. 24, July, 1904, pp. 17–26. However, a bill for this purpose was introduced in the House. Kilburne, Frederick C., "Control and Supervision of Trust Companies," *Annals* op. cit. pp. 29–42. During the panic of 1907 President Roosevelt again gave serious consideration to such supervision. However, in the end the regulation of these institutions was left to the states.

209 New York State *Senate Document* 106, Session 1883, Vol. 5, No. 45; *Chronicle*, Vol. 32, May 14, 1881, p. 511.

210 *Chronicle*, Vol. 32, May 14, 1881, p. 511. It is interesting to note that the same tactics were used by the New York Stock Exchange in opposing local restrictive legislation in recent years.

211 Ibid. Vol. 88, June 19, 1909, p. 1533 ; see also article by White, Horace, "The Hughes Investigation," in the *Journal of Political Economy*, Vol. 17, October 1909, pp. 528–540. Horace White was a member of the Hughes Commission.

212 Ibid. op. cit. Vol. 88, June 19, 1909, p. 1533.

213 Ibid. Vol. 90, April 2, 1910, p. 891.

214 U. S. 63rd Congress, 2nd Session, *Hearings before the Senate Committee on Banking and Currency on Regulation of the Stock Exchanges*, pp. 544–9.

215 Annual Report of the United States Internal Revenue Commissioner, 1864–66, *Annual Report of the Secretary of Treasury*, 1867.

216 *Hearings*, op. cit. pp. 544–550.

217 Untermeyer, Samuel, "Speculation on the Stock Exchange and the Public Regulation of the Exchanges" in the *American Economic Review*, Supplement, March, 1915, p. 68.

CHAPTER 12

1 Thorp and Mitchell described 1908 as a year of "depression," 1909 as "revival and mild prosperity," 1910 as "recession," 1911 as "mild depression," 1912 as "revival : prosperity," 1913 as "prosperity and recession" and 1914 as "depression." Thorp, Willard and Mitchell, Wesley C., *Business Annals*, New York 1926, pp. 140–142.

2 Appendix VI, columns 4, 5 and 6.

3 Special Committee on Investigation of the Munitions Industry, S. Res. 206, 73rd Congress, 2nd Session, *Hearings* No. 944, p. 2. This chapter is largely based on these hearings. The agents of this Committee went through the private papers of Morgan and Company and examined numerous letters, cablegrams and other documents bearing on the firm's activities during the period from 1914 to the end of the War. The Committee also examined the public records of various governmental agencies, including the State Department, the Treasury Department and the Federal Reserve Board. As a result, the Committee disclosed private and official documents hitherto unavailable to the public. In addition the Committee called the leading bankers and industrialists as witnesses, and their testimony added further information on the policies of American security capitalism during the war years.

[4] Appendix VI, columns 1, 3, 4, and 15.

[5] Ibid. column 11; *Munitions Report*, op. cit. Part 5, p. 55.

[6] See comment by Low, Alfred Maurice, *Woodrow Wilson*, Boston 1918, p. 119.

[7] Kerney, James, *The Political Education of Woodrow Wilson*, New York 1936, p. 395.

[8] *Munitions Report*, Exhibit 2030, Part 25, p. 7658.

[9] Ibid. Exhibit 2031, p. 7658.

[10] Ibid. Exhibit 2032, p. 7659.

[11] Ibid. Exhibit 2046; Bryan, William Jennings, *Memoirs of William Jennings Bryan*, Chicago 1925, pp. 365–376.

[12] *Munitions Report*, Exhibit 2046, p. 7665.

[13] Ibid. Report on Legislation, p. 60.

[14] Ibid. Exhibit 2046, pp. 7665–7666. Bryan in his personal memoirs states that Lansing "endorsed the position as sound in principle." Bryan, op. cit. p. 376.

[15] In reviewing the developed stage of American security capitalism Bryan seems to stand out as the bitterest opponent of the system, for he sensed its significance and its limitations as few men either in public or in private life. In 1896 Bryan was fighting the domestic advance of security capitalism and in 1914 its overseas expansion, but in both conflicts he was doomed to defeat. However, in the end many of his proposals were recognized; for example, in 1937 the *Munitions Report* recommended the very policies which Bryan urged in 1914. See comments by Borchard, Edwin and Lage, William P., *Neutrality for the United States*, New Haven 1937, p. 43.

[16] *Munitions Report*, Exhibit 2045, p. 7664.

[17] Memorandum dated October 23, 1914, made by Lansing of conversation with President Wilson that evening "relative to loans and bank credit to belligerent governments." Ibid. Exhibit 2047, p. 7666.

[18] Ibid. Exhibit 2049, p. 7666.

[19] Ibid.

[20] Ibid. Part 27, pp. 8215–8237.

[21] The Neutrality Act of 1937 (section 3a) provided that, upon the proclamation of the President it would be unlawful to deal in the obligations of a belligerent state with the exception that "if the President shall find that such action will serve to protect the commercial or other interests of the United States or of its citizens he may in his discretion, and to such extent and under such regulations as he may prescribe exempt from the operation of this section, ordinary commercial credits and short time obligations in aid of legal transactions and of a character customarily used in normal peacetime commercial transactions." Senate Joint Res. 51 *Congressional Record*, April 29, 1937, p. 3397, Vol. 81, Part 4, 75th Congress, 1st sess. It is thus seen that the Neutrality Act again committed the fundamental error of futilely distinguishing between short term credits and long term loans.

[22] During the hearings of the Munitions Committee it was charged that sterling exchange had been deliberately permitted to fall in order to create an exchange crisis as a means of compelling the American government to permit the flotation of public loans for the Allies. *Munitions Report*, Part 26, p. 7867. The original documents, particularly the confidential cables between Morgans and the British government, do not substantiate this view, but indicate that the unsatisfactory balance of international payments of Great Britain created by the large excess of imports over exports was the actual cause of the drop in sterling exchange.

[23] Ibid. Part 5, p. 161; Part 26, pp. 7882–7883.

[24] Ibid p. 7882.

[25] Ibid. p. 7884.

[26] Ibid. Exhibit 2192, p. 8112.

[27] Ibid. Exhibit 2194, p. 8113.

[28] Ibid. Exhibit 2211, p. 8121.

[29] Ibid. Part 5, p. 15.

[30] Lamont, Thomas W., *Henry P. Davison*, New York 1933, pp. 195–196.

[31] Senator Clark of the Committee implied that the investment banking houses "put the heat" on these purchasers, but Mr. Morgan (son of J. P. Morgan) denied this charge.

[32] *New York Times*, October 1, 1915, p. 1, column 1.

[33] See Nicolson, op. cit. p. 175.

[34] *Munitions Report*, Part 5, p. 16.

[35] *Chronicle*, op. cit. Vol. 103, November 25, 1916, page XXVII.

[36] *Munitions Report*, op. cit. p. 55.

[37] As early as July 23, 1916, President Wilson, in a letter to Colonel House, ex-

pressed irritation at the actions of the British government and stated that he was seriously considering asking Congress to authorize him to prohibit loans to the Allies. Ibid. pp. 16–17.

38 Willis, H. Parker, *Federal Reserve System*, New York 1923, p. 1095.

39 *Munitions Report*, part 28, p. 8552.

40 Reginald McKenna, then Chancellor of the British Exchequer, wired that he "did not wish to disregard the expressed wishes of the Federal Reserve Board" and requested Morgans not to issue the treasury bills. Lamont, op. cit. p. 207 ; Nicolson, op. cit. p. 176 ; Willis, op. cit. p. 1099.

41 Millis, Walter, "Morgan, Money and War" in the *Nation*, Vol. 142, January 22, 1936, p. 95 et seq. ; Willis, op. cit. p. 1099.

42 *New York Times*, December 22, 1916, p. 1, column 2.

43 Ibid. Index of stock prices, December 21 and 31, 1916.

44 Tardieu, André, *France and America*, Cambridge, Mass. 1927, p. 141. After three months of indecision, the Federal Reserve Board, on March 8, 1917, withdrew its opposition to the treasury bills in the statement that it desired "to make clear that it did not seek to create an unfavorable attitude on the part of American investors toward desirable foreign securities, and to emphasize the point that American funds available for investment may, with advantage to the country's foreign trade and the domestic economic situation, be employed in the purchase of such securities." *Federal Reserve Bulletin*, Vol. 3, April 1917, pp. 239–240.

45 Noyes, Alexander D., *The War Period of American Finance*, New York 1926, p. 139.

46 Borchard, and Lage, op. cit. p. 32. See letter from Ambassador Page to Colonel House, September 15, 1914. Seymour, Charles, *Intimate Papers of Colonel House*, Boston 1926, Vol. I, pp. 333–334.

47 See cable from Page to State Department, March 5, 1917. State Department, *Papers on Foreign Relations*, 1917, Supplement 2, Vol. I, pp. 516–18.

48 For criticism of the economic explanation of the entrance of the United States into the War see Baker, Newton D., "Why We Went to War," in *Foreign Affairs*, Vol. 15, October 1936, pp. 1–86. The inevitability of our entrance into the War is seen in testimony of President Wilson himself before the Senate Committee on Foreign Relations in the hearings on the Treaty of Versailles, in 1919 as follows :

Senator McCumber : Do you think if Germany had committed no act of injustice against our citizens that we would have gotten into this war—
The President : I do think so.
Senator McCumber : Do you think we would have gotten in anyway—
The President : I do.

Treaty of Peace with Germany, Hearings before the Committee on Foreign Relations, United States, 66th Congress, 1st Session, testimony of President Woodrow Wilson, p. 536.

49 Cited in Arnett, Alex Mathew, *Claude Kitchen and the Wilson Policies*, Boston 1937, pp. 220–221.

50 Ray Stannard Baker in his biography of President Wilson stated, "Thus by the end of the year 1914 the traffic in war materials with the Allies had become deeply entrenched in America's economic organization, and the possibility of keeping out of the war by the diplomacy of neutrality, no matter how skillfully conducted, had reached the vanishing point. By October, perhaps earlier, our case was lost." Baker, Ray S., *Woodrow Wilson, Life and Letters*, Vol. V, New York 1935, p. 181.

51 *Chronicle*, Vol. 103, October 28, 1916, p. 1553.

CHAPTER 13

1 The La Follette vote of nearly 5,000,000 in 1924 may be considered the strongest protest vote over these years.

2 Ripley, William Z., "Stop, Look, Listen!" in the *Atlantic Monthly*, Vol. 138, September 1926, pp. 380–399.

3 *Chronicle*, Vol. 123, September 4, 1926, p. 1201.

4 Ibid. Vol. 123, September 4, 1926, op. cit. p. 1202.

5 Ibid. Vol. 127, Part 1, September 8, 1928, p. 1336.

6 Appendix VI, columns 1, 2, and 3.

7 Ibid. columns 5, 6, 8, 9, 10 and 11.

[8] *Standard Statistics, Base Book,* 1930–1931, p. 130. Standard Trade and Securities Section, Vol. III, Statistical Section.

[9] Snyder, Carl, *Business Cycles and Business Measurements,* New York 1927, p. 31.

[10] *Standard Statistics, Base Book,* op. cit.

[11] Based on revenue ton mileage *Statistics of Railroads,* Interstate Commerce Commission.

[12] Persons, Warren M., "The Growth of the Nation," in *Barron's Weekly,* March 2, 1931, p. 3.

[13] Snyder, op. cit. p. 23; Dublin, Louis, "Birth Control, What it is Doing to America's Population" in the *Forum,* Vol. 86, November 1931, pp. 270–275. See also *Recent Social Trends in the United States,* Vol. I, New York 1933, pp. 1–3. Whelpton, P. K., "Trends in Population Increase and Distribution During 1920–1930," in the *American Journal of Sociology,* Vol. 36, May 1931, p. 867.

[14] Thompson, Warren S., "Population Trends in the United States and Their Effect on Industry," in the *Annalist,* Vol. 139, January 15, 1932, pp. 96–99.

[15] Colby, Benjamin, "City Debts and Financial Resources in the Light of Population Shifts and Losses," in the *Annalist,* Vol. 139, January 29, 1932, p. 227.

[16] Appendix VI, columns 13, 14, and 15.

[17] Mills, Frederick C., *Economic Tendencies in the United States,* New York 1932, p. 243 shows that from 1901 to 1913 the average annual rate of increase of employment in manufacturing industries was + 2.7 percent but for the years 1922–1929 was only 1.0 percent.

[18] Chase, Stuart, *The Nemesis of American Business,* New York 1931, p. 11.

[19] Quoted from Norman Hapgood's preface to the 1932 edition of Brandeis, Louis D., *Other People's Money and How the Bankers Use It,* p. lviii.

[20] Angly, Edward, *Oh Yeah,* New York 1931, p. 7.

[21] Ibid. p. 12.

[22] *New York Times,* October 25, 1929, p. 1, column 5; January 16, 1930, p. 1, column 4.

[23] Ibid. February 25, 1930, p. 1, column 2.

[24] Appendix VI, columns 3, 4, 5, 6, 8, 9, 11, 13, 14, and 15.

[25] *New York Times,* March 5, 1933; *Chronicle,* Vol. 136, March 11, 1933, p. 1658.

[26] Appendix VI, columns 1, 2, 3, 4, 5, 6, 7, 8, and 9.

[27] Ibid. columns 13, 14 and 15.

[28] In 1937 the United States was swept by labor unrest led by the Committee for Industrial Organization. The difference in the policy of banking and industrial capitalism toward the new organization was evidenced in the labor policies of the various steel companies in that year. On the one hand the United States Steel Corporation, related to the Morgan interests, came to an agreement with the C.I.O., while the independent steel companies generally opposed such agreements. *Chronicle,* Vol. 144, March 20, 1937, p. 1894.

CHAPTER 14

[1] See Appendix VIII, Ratio A.

[2] Ibid. Ratio B; for discussion see Hartzel, E., "Time Deposits," in the *Harvard Business Review,* Vol. XIII, October 1934, p. 33; also Williams, John H., "The Monetary Doctrine of J. M. Keynes," in the *Quarterly Journal of Economics,* Vol. XLV, August 1931, p. 564.

[3] Anderson, Benjamin, "Bank Expansion versus Savings," in the *Chase Economic Bulletin,* Volume VIII, June 25, 1928, p. 15.

[4] French, D. R., "The Significance of Time Deposits in the Expansion of Bank Credit, 1922–1928," in the *Journal of Political Economy,* Vol. 39, 1931, p. 782.

[5] Appendix VIII, Ratio C.

[6] See Appendix X.

[7] Computed from the *Report of the Comptroller of the Currency* for these years.

[8] *Hearings on the Operations of the National and Federal Reserve Banking Systems* Part VII, p. 1010, United States Banking and Currency Committee (Senate) 71st Congress, 3rd Session.

[9] Ibid. Part I, p. 151.

[10] Griffiss, Bartow, *The New York Call Money Market,* New York 1925, pp. 24–65; Mitchell, Waldo F., *The Uses of Bank Funds,* Chicago 1920, p. 35; *Hearings on the Operations of the National and Federal Reserve Banking Systems,* op. cit. p. 136.

[11] Ibid. Part VII; pp. 1016–1017; see comments of Dr. Adolph Miller, Part I, p. 151.

[12] Rogers, James Harvey, "The Effect of Stock Speculation on the New York Money Market" in the *Quarterly Journal of Economics*, Vol. XL, 1926, pp. 444–445 ; Hoover, Calvin, "Brokers Loans and Bank Deposits," in the *Journal of Political Economy*, Vol. XXXVII, 1929, pp. 713–727 ; Reed, Harold, L., *Federal Reserve Policy, 1921–1930*, New York, 1930, p. 168 ; Roelse, Harold V., "Security Loans in Recent Years" in the *Review of Economic Statistics*, Vol. XII, 1930, pp. 110–111.

[13] For technical explanation of definition of reserve assets, see footnote in appendix VIII. See also article by the author on "Liquidity and Solvency of National Banks 1923–1933," in the *Journal of Business of the University of Chicago*, Vol. VII, April 1934, pp. 161–172.

[14] See Appendix VIII, Ratio D.

[15] A Works Projects Administration study, conducted by the author, applied various statistical tests to determine the correlation between certain bank ratios and bank failures for the years from 1865 to 1934. This study showed a close correlation between the ratio of net capital to total resources and bank failures, and indicated that this ratio could be used to predict possible bank failures one or two years in advance.

[16] For full description of net capital see Edwards, op. cit. pp. 161–162.

[17] Appendix VIII, Ratio E.

[18] Ibid. Ratio F.

[19] Ibid. Ratio G.

[20] It is important to note that the decline in solvency continued after 1933 despite the efforts of the Reconstruction Finance Corporation in granting aid to the banks to increase their capital, and despite the exhortations of the Federal Deposit Insurance Corporation that the banks must maintain satisfactory capital structures. In fact the proportion of net capital to total securities fell from 24.14 percent in 1933 to 19.60 percent in December, 1936 or the lowest level in the history of the national banking system.

[21] Testimony of Allen M. Pope, President of the Investment Bankers Association of America, before the Senate Banking and Currency Committee, *Hearings* op. cit. Part IV, p. 539.

[22] Testimony of C. E. Mitchell, ibid. Part 2, p. 299.

[23] United States Banking and Currency Committee, Senate Report 1455, 73rd Congress, 2nd Session, on *Stock Exchange Practices*, ibid. p. 113.

[24] Ibid. pp. 164–165.

[25] Study of Terris Moore, *New Security Originations of Representative Investment Bankers and Security Affiliates of Commercial Banks*, Harvard Graduate School of Business Administration, 1933.

[26] *Recent Economic Changes in the United States*, National Bureau of Economic Research, New York 1929, Vol. II, p. 684.

[27] The latter is also known as the "shiftability" theory, but since this term applies to only the transferability of bank assets, it is better to use the expression "liberal" which may properly be applied to the broader issues involved in the conflict of the two opposing theories. As early as 1918 Harold G. Moulton, who may justly be called the founder of the liberal theory, demonstrated the flaws in the orthodox theory. See his "Commercial Banking and Capital Formation," in the *Journal of Political Economy*, Vol. 26, Washington 1918, pp. 484–508, 638–663, 705–731, 849–879. Benjamin Anderson expressed anti-classical views in 1909, *Value of Money*, New York 1917, pp. 514–517, but receded from this stand in his later writings. Chase Economic Bulletin, Vol. IX, October 1929, p. 3. For recent discussion see Harris, S. E., "Commercial Theory of Credit" in the *Journal of Political Economy*, Vol. 44, February 1936, pp. 94–105.

[28] 63rd Congress, 2nd Session, Chapter 16, 1913, Section B in United States Statutes at Large, Vol. 38, pp. 263, 275.

[29] Computed from the *Reports of the Comptroller of the Currency*. Other statistics on eligible paper are presented by the author in an article on "Liquidity and Solvency of National Banks, 1923–1933," in the *The Journal of Business of the University of Chicago*, Vol. VII, April 1934, pp. 162–166. These statistics on the volume of eligible paper most likely contain a margin of error, for, throughout the entire history of the Reserve system, there has been considerable confusion as to the exact volume of such paper due to the uncertainty as to the interpretation of the regulations governing eligibility. For discussion of this subject see Harris, S. E., *Twenty Years of Federal Reserve Policy*, Harvard University Press, Cambridge Mass. 1933. Vol. I, p. 301. A discussion of the relaxation of eligibility requirements after 1930 is found on pp. 294–295.

[30] Compiled from figures given in the *Wall Street Journal*, March 22, 1933, p. 10.

[31] Figure for 1912, as of November 12, from Secretary's Report, 1913.

Figure for main offices from September 13, 1912 to August 31, 1919 inclusive, from Secretary's report 1919, page 20.

Figure for main offices from 1921 to 1926 inclusive, from respective annual report of the auditor.

Figure for main offices 1927 computed from report of gain in membership over previous year in membership report.

Figure for branches August 31, 1913 from membership report of 1914.

Figure for branches in 1920 computed from membership report which states an increase of 17 new branch offices.

Branch office membership for 1916 and 1922–1924 inclusive unavailable.

All other figures from membership and audit reports of respective years in *Proceedings of the Annual Convention of the Investment Bankers Association of America.*

[32] From 1927 to 1931 inclusive Kuhn, Loeb and Company originated 54 issues of railroad bonds amounting to $1,137,429,000 and brought out 632,425 shares of railroad stock, while Morgans and Drexel and Company originated $732,165,023 of railroad securities. Senate report on *Stock Exchange Practices*, op. cit. p. 86. See pamphlet presented by Otto Kahn entitled "The Marketing of American Railroad Securities," Memorandum for the Interstate Commerce Commission, submitted by Kuhn, Loeb & Co., dated October 25, 1922, marked "Committee Exhibit I, June 27, 1933." U. S. Banking and Currency Committee (Senate) *Hearings* 73rd Congress, 1st and 2nd Sessions, *Stock Exchange Practices* Part III, pp. 1034–1052.

[33] Ibid. Part III, p. 964.

[34] *Chronicle*, Vol. 127, July 28, 1928, p. 317.

[35] United States Banking and Currency Committee (Senate) *Hearings*, 73rd Congress, 1st Session, Part I, p. 4.

[36] Edwards, George W. "4,398 Bond Issues" in the *Journal of the American Bankers Association*, Vol. 25, New York, November 1932, pp. 22 and 64.

[37] Adopted from report of Levison, Henry J., on *J. P. Morgan and Company from 1920 to 1935*, a thesis prepared for the B.B.A. degree at the College of the City of New York.

[38] *Chronicle*, Vol. 118, Jan. 26, 1924, p. 367.

[39] Ibid. Vol. 125, July 2, 1927, p. 16 and August 20, 1927, p. 1000.

[40] Ibid. Vol. 127, August 18, 1928, p. 901.

[41] Article by Paul Clay, *The New York Evening Post* February 16, 1929, section II, p. 1.

[42] *Chronicle*, op. cit. March 23, 1929, p. 1826.

[43] For description of the operations of the sale of securities see *Senate Report* No. 1455, *Stock Exchange Practices*, pp. 93–113.

[44] This practice continued even in 1936. *New York Times*, April 4, 1936, p. 25, col. 3.

[45] *Chronicle*, August 20, 1927, Vol. 125, p. 1000.

[46] *Stock Exchange Practices*, op. cit. June 28, 1933, Part III p. 1120.

[47] *Senate Report* No. 1455, *Stock Exchange Practices*, p. 99.

[48] Thus the Italian Government 7's in 1926 on the dissolution of the syndicate dropped from 94½ to 88½. *Wall Street Journal*, May 10, 1926, p. 4, col. 3. In the case of the German 5½'s offered at 90 on June 12, 1930, the syndicate bought approximately $9,000,000 of the bonds in the market for its own account at about the issue price over a period of eighteen days. Over this period the syndicate sold $98,000,000 of the bonds to the public at 90 or higher. After the withdrawal of the support of the selling group the bond dropped from 90 to 86. At the time of the Senate hearings on April 2, 1932, the bonds were quoted at 35. *Senate Report* No. 1455 on *Stock Exchange Practices* op. cit. p. 98.

[49] Sherrod, Julian, *Scapegoats*, New York 1931, p. 36.

[50] *New York Stock Exchange Bulletin*, Vol. III, February 1932, p. 1.

[51] *Report on Trading in Unlisted Securities upon Exchanges*, United States Securities and Exchange Commission, January 3, 1936, p. 33.

[52] Grebler, Leo, "The Changing Significance of the Stock Exchange," *Index*, Svenska Handelsbanken, April 1936, pp. 75–81.

[53] *New York Stock Exchange Bulletin*, Vol. III, February 1932, p. 1; *New York Stock Exchange Year Book*, New York 1936, p. 124.

CHAPTER 15

¹ To enable the reader to follow the tests used in this chapter a brief summary of the technique of corporate analysis in applied finance is herewith given.

The financial statement of a corporation is made up of an income account and a balance sheet which show respectively its earning power and its capital structure. Due to the lack of uniformity in corporate accounting, it is of course impossible to present a financial statement which will apply exactly to all corporations. Moreover, there is wide variation in the terminology used to describe even the same items. With these limitations in mind, there is given below the leading items to be found in most financial statements and the generally accepted term used to state each item.

ITEMS IN THE FINANCIAL STATEMENT OF A CORPORATION

NO.	ITEMS	EXPLANATION
	Income Account	
1	Operating revenues	
2	Operating expenses	
3	Operating income	1 — 2
4	Non-operating income	
5	Total income	3 + 4
6	Interest	
7	Sinking fund	
8	Fixed charges	6 + 7
9	Net income	5 — 8
10	Dividends paid	
	Balance Sheet	
11	Funded debt	
12	Capital stock	
13	Surplus and undivided profits	
14	Total capitalization	11 + 12 + 13
15	Property	
16	Reserves for depreciation	
17	Net property	15 — 16

A brief explanation of the meaning of these items is given below:

1. *Operating revenues* are the returns received by an enterprise from the sale of its goods or its services.

2. *Operating expenses* are the disbursements made in the conduct of the business for wages, raw materials and taxes as well as for maintenance and depreciation. Maintenance is the sum actually spent in keeping up the plant, while depreciation is the bookkeeping entry nominally made in writing down the value of the plant.

3. *Operating income* is the amount left over after deducting operating expenses from operating revenues.

4. *Non-operating income* is the return received from sources other than from the conduct of the business itself, as for example interest and dividends from securities of unaffiliated companies purchased with surplus funds as an investment.

5. *Total income* is the sum of the operating and the non-operating income.

6. *Interest* is the charge paid for the use of borrowed capital as represented by the funded debt of the corporation.

7. *Sinking fund* is a reserve into which the corporation annually contributes a fixed sum in order to have sufficient monies on hand to pay off the funded debt at maturity.

8. *Fixed charges* are the total of the interest on the funded debt and the annual contribution to the sinking fund.

9. *Net income* is the sum left over from total income after payment of fixed charges, and is the amount available for dividends.

10. *Dividends paid* are the sums actually disbursed on the common and on the preferred stock of the corporation.

11. *Funded debt* includes all obligations maturing after a year's time. It is generally the same as the bonded debt, for it consists largely of the fixed-interest bearing obligations of the corporation in the hands of the investing public.

12. *Capital stock* includes the common stock and the preferred stock of the corporation.

13. *Surplus and undivided profits* constitute the undistributed equity of the stockholders.

14. *Total capitalization* includes both funded debt and the total equity represented by the combined capital stock, surplus and undivided profits.

15. *Property* includes plant, equipment and other fixed assets.

16. *Reserves for depreciation* consist of bookkeeping entries that have accumulated over the years for the purpose of writing down the value of the property.

17. *Net property* is the value of property after reserves for depreciation have been deducted.

These items may be analyzed by the increase or decrease, the trend percentage and the ratio methods. For application of these methods see pp. 381–382 explaining the trend of railway finance, and for detailed discussion of these methods see Edwards, George W., *Investments II, Corporation Finance and Investments* written for the American Institute of Banking, New York, 1935, pp. 91–114. The increase or decrease method simply shows the net change in the dollar amount of each item. Thus if the X corporation showed a net income in 1935 of $200,000 and $300,000 in 1936, the increase would be $100,000. The trend percentage method merely presents these changes in percentages, and by this method the change in the net income of the X corporation would be expressed as 50 percent. These two methods analyze each item individually. An item may also be studied in relation to another item by means of a ratio which is a statistical device expressing the comparative relation between items in the financial statement of a corporation or of a government. The ratio may be expressed in dollars, in fractions, in number of times or in percent. Thus if the X corporation with net income of $200,000 had fixed charges of $100,000, the ratio of net income to fixed charges may then be expressed as $\frac{\$200,000}{\$100,000} = \frac{2}{1} = 2.00$ times or 200 percent. The ratio can therefore be stated as two dollars of net income for every one dollar of fixed charges, 2 over 1, two times or, 200 percent. The last method of expressing a ratio will generally be used in this study.

While a large number of ratios for corporate financial analysis may be used for the purpose of applied finance, only the following will be employed in this study since for the purposes of social finance we are interested only in problems relating to the earning power and capitalization.

RATIOS OF CORPORATE FINANCIAL ANALYSIS

	RATIOS	EXPLANATION[a]
A.	Operating expenses to operating revenues	2 ÷ 1
B.	Operating income to operating revenues	3 ÷ 1
C.	Total income to fixed charges	5 ÷ 8
D.	Net income to operating revenues	9 ÷ 1
E.	Net income to dividends paid	9 ÷ 10
F.	Funded debt to total capitalization	11 ÷ 14
G.	Total income to total capitalization	5 ÷ 14
H.	Net property to funded debt	17 ÷ 11

[a] Numbers refer to the items in the financial statement on pp. 370.

These ratios may be explained as follows:

A. *Operating expenses to operating revenues.* This ratio, generally called the "operating ratio," indicates the trend of the efficiency of the company, and shows the extent to which the operating expenses absorb the operating revenues of the corporation.

B. *Operating income to operating revenues.* This ratio, the converse of the above ratio, shows the extent to which the company is actually receiving income from its operations after the payment of operating expenses.

C. *Total income to fixed charges.* This so-called "times fixed charges earned" ratio is the generally-accepted test of financial practice for determining the investment status of the bonds of a corporation; it shows the extent to which the total income covers or protects the fixed charges.

D. *Net income to operating revenues.* This test supplements the previous test and shows the extent to which the operating revenues may fall before the protection of the fixed charges is impaired.

E. *Net income to dividends paid.* This ratio reflects the soundness of the dividend policy of a corporation, since it shows whether dividends are actually covered by net income or are merely paid out of surplus.

F. *Funded debt to total capitalization.* This ratio shows the extent of funded debt in the capital structure of a corporation.

G. *Total income to total capitalization.* This ratio reflects the extent to which the corporation is overcapitalized. As stated in the introduction, the basis of corporate valuation and therefore of capitalization is earning power. This ratio shows the total income, or earning power, to total capitalization of the corporation including both its bonds and stocks.

H. *Net property to funded debt.* This ratio shows the extent to which net property covers the funded debt. The theory underlying this ratio is the same as that behind the collateral loan, and rests upon the assumption that the claim of the creditor can in part be protected by requiring collateral with a sufficient margin, or excess value over the amount of the loan, to allow for shrinkage in the value of the collateral and still leave the principal of the loan protected.

2 See pp. 181–182.

3 Appendix IX. The trends and position of railway finance from 1890 to 1910 are discussed on p. 181.

4 Ibid. columns 1 and 2.

5 Ibid. Ratio A.

6 Ibid. Ratio B.

7 Ibid. Ratio C.

8 Ibid. Ratio D.

9 Ibid. columns 6 and 7, Ratio E.

10 *Investigation of Railroad Financing,* Hearings before the Committee on Interstate Commerce, United States Senate, 74th Congress, 1st session, p. 127.

11 Appendix IX, column 8.

12 Ibid. column 9.

13 Ibid. Ratio F.

14 See pp. 181–182.

15 Appendix IX, columns 1 and 2 ; Ratio A.

16 Ibid. Ratio B.

17 Ibid. columns 4 and 5.

18 Ibid. Ratio C.

19 Ibid. Ratio D.

20 Ibid. Ratio E.

21 Ibid. Ratio F.

22 Adapted from Clark, Evans, *Internal Debts of the United States,* New York 1933, p. 149.

23 Table 22, items 3, 4 and 5.

24 Ibid. Ratio A.

25 Ibid. Ratios B and C.

26 Ibid. Ratio D.

27 Adapted from Clark, Evans, op. cit. p. 152.

28 Table 23, Ratios A and C.

29 Ibid. Ratio A.

30 Ibid. Ratio C.

31 Ibid. Ratio D.

32 Compiled from the *Statistics of Income,* Treasury Department. Based on reports of taxable and non-taxable corporations.

33 Table 24, Ratio A.

34 Ibid. Ratio B.

35 Ibid. Ratio C.

36 Ibid. Ratio D.

37 *Statistics of Income,* op. cit.

38 Table 25, Ratio A.

39 Ibid. item 1.

40 Ibid. Ratio B.

41 Ibid. Ratio C.

42 Compiled from *Abstract of the Census of Manufactures,* 1919, p. 340, and for 1929 from Badger, Ralph E. and Guthmann, Harry G., *Investment Principles and Practices* New York 1936, p. 24.

43 *Statistics of Income,* op. cit. 1923, p. 118 and 1929, pp. 328–329.

44 See discussion by Copeland, Melvin, T., on "Marketing," in *Recent Economic Changes in the United States,* New York 1929, Vol. I, p. 343.

45 Ibid. Vol. II, p. 683. A study of 729 companies showed that from 1922 to 1928 the average bank loan declined from $929,000 to $582,000. Currie, Lauchlin, "The Decline of the Commercial Loan," in the *Quarterly Journal of Economics,* Vol. XLV, August 1931, p. 699.

46 A study made by Roy A. Foulke, *The Commercial Paper Market,* New York 1931, p. 51 showed that more than one-half of the paper then outstanding originated from medium sized corporations, or those with net worth between $500,000 and $2,500,000.

47 Federal Reserve Bank of New York *Monthly Review of Credit and Business Conditions,* October 30, 1920, p. 3 and July 1, 1933, p. 5.

48 *Journal of Commerce,* May 15, 1936, p. 4, column 2.

49 Clark, op. cit. p. 175.

50 Adapted from Clark, Evans, op. cit. p. 175. Unfunded debt here includes notes and accounts payable, and the funded debt includes bonds and mortgages.

51 Security valuation is difficult in any field, but it is especially so in real estate where valuation or appraisal is so largely a matter of personal opinion. Because of this uncertainty of valuation, lenders of funds on real estate attempted to develop definite standards. It became the accepted principle among experts that a real estate mortgage should not exceed more than 60 percent of the appraised value of the property even when it was improved property. This appraisal was to be based on earning power, and income from the operation of the property was to cover the fixed charges on the mortgage by at least 200 percent.

52 Adapted from Clark, Evans, op. cit. p. 66. Rentals refer to residential rentals only.

53 Table 26, item 6.

54 Ibid. item 1.

55 Ibid. item 2.

56 Ibid. item 6.

57 Ibid. items 3, 4 and 5.

58 Ibid. item 6.

59 Ibid. item 6.

60 Ibid. item 3.

61 Interim report. Real Estate Securities Committee, Investment Bankers Association of America "Future of Real Estate Financing" in *Investment Banking,* June 1931, pp. 7–10.

62 For discussion see Seagar, Henry R. and Gulick, Charles A., *Trust and Corporation Problems,* New York and London 1929, p. 307 et seq.

63 Stevens, W. S., "A Classification of Pools and Associations Based on American Experience," in the *American Economic Review,* Vol. III, September 1913, pp. 545–575.

64 For legal discussion of consolidations see Field, Kenneth "Nature of and Procedure for Direct Property Owning Consolidations," 6 *Rocky Mountain Law Review,* 232.

65 The Associated Gas and Electric Properties acquired the shares of beneficial interest in Manson Securities Trust at a cost of $544,500 and this interest was written up to $10,000,000. *Utility Corporations Report,* No. 45, p. 36.

66 Cited by John T. Flynn, "What Happened to Insull," in the *The New Republic,* Vol. LXX, May 4, 1932, p. 317.

67 *Utility Corporations Report* No. 45, op. cit. p. 50.

68 Statement of Harry M. Addinsell, President of the Chase Harris Forbes Corporation in an address delivered December 15, 1932 *New York Times,* December 16, 1932, p. 29, col. 8.

69 United States Senate Committee on Banking and Currency. Hearings on *Stock Exchange Practices,* 72nd Congress, 2nd Session, Part V., pp. 1589–1692.

70 Ibid.

71 Flynn, John T., *Security Speculation,* New York 1934, p. 159

72 United States Senate Committee, op. cit. 72nd Congress 2nd Session, No. 1455 on *Stock Exchange Practices,* p. 354.

73 Ibid. p. 355.

74 Ibid. pp. 348–349.

75 Ibid. p. 354.

76 Ibid. pp. 348–349.

77 Flynn, John T., *Investment Trusts Gone Wrong,* New York 1930, pp. 56–59.

78 *Stock Exchange Practices*, p. 344.
79 Standard Trade and Securities, *Investment Companies*, Vol. 2, section 2, March 17, 1936, pp. 1–53.

CHAPTER 16

1 A brief summary of the technique of governmental financial analysis is herewith given. As noted before in the case of corporate credit the income account and the balance sheet furnish the data from which an analysis can be made of the trend of the earning power and the capital structure of a corporation over a period of years. In like manner the financial analysis of government credit can be made from a study of the budget showing revenues and expenditures and from the financial statement showing the nature of the debt of the government. Just as the credit of a corporation depends upon its earning power, so the credit of a government rests upon its ability to obtain necessary revenues. There is of course a wide difference in the terminology used in the budgets and in the financial statements of federal, state, municipal and foreign governments, and it is therefore difficult to frame a single classification which exactly fits all these categories of governments. However, the following summarized budget and financial statement presents the separate items needed to understand the trend of government finance.

ITEMS IN THE BUDGET AND FINANCIAL STATEMENT OF A GOVERNMENT

	ITEMS	EXPLANATION
1	Revenues	
2	Total expenditures (includes 6)	
3	Balance	1−2
4	Interest on debt	
5	Public debt retirement	
6	Debt service	4+5
7	Unfunded debt	
8	Funded debt	
9	Gross debt	7+8
10	Deductions	
11	Net debt	9−10
12	Indirect debt	
13	Total debt	11+12
14	Debt base	

There is herewith given an explanation of the various items in the above statement.

1. *Revenues* are of various classes. These receipts include commercial revenues from rendering services, as those performed by a post-office, public bank, steam or electric railway, and from selling commodities, as water, gas or electric power. From exercising its functions, a government may also derive administrative revenues as fines, fees, licenses and special assessments. The third and most important class of revenue is raised from taxes which may be either direct in the form of property and income taxes or indirect in the form of excise duties on commodities and on services or of customs duties.

2. *Total expenditures* are the outlays made by the government to finance either current operations or permanent improvements.

3. *Balance* is the difference between revenues and expenditures, and may be either a surplus or a deficit.

4. *Interest on debt* is the charge paid for the use of borrowed capital as represented by the debt of the government.

5. *Public debt retirement* is the sum which the government is required to set aside for reducing the principal sum of its debt.

6. *Debt service* includes the interest on the debt and the public debt retirement.

7. *Unfunded debt* includes short-term loans, warrants issued to anticipate tax payments, floating debt or that not covered either by cash or by available debt retirement assets, and all other obligations payable within a year.

8. *Funded debt,* or the fixed, long-term debt, includes obligations payable after a year. Another distinction as to the maturity of the debt may be drawn at the five-year period, and obligations maturing after one year but before five years are sometimes described as the intermediate debt which may be included in the unfunded debt.

9. *Gross debt* is the total of the unfunded debt and the funded debt.

10. *Deductions* include the various items which may properly be subtracted from the gross debt as accumulated debt retirement assets actually held in a sinking fund to meet maturing obligations, and also debts which are no actual burden since they are based on self-supporting governmental properties.

11. *Net debt* is the balance of the gross debt after the above deductions have been made, and constitutes the actual direct debt of the government.

12. *Indirect debt.* Not only are there deductions from the gross debt, but there are also additions to the debt. The gross debt, as indicated above, constitutes only the direct debt of a government. There may also be additional obligations. A national government may assume or guarantee the obligations of other governments and even of public corporations. Likewise, a municipal government has not only its own direct debt but may also have an overlapping debt derived from other governmental bodies.

13. *Total debt* is the sum of the net debt and the indirect debt.

14. *Debt base* is the foundation upon which the structure of the government's debt rests. The debt base may consist of the taxable property within the jurisdiction of the government. In municipal finance this property is carried under the item of "assessed valuation." A broader debt base is the total wealth of the community within the jurisdiction of the government. In the past, wealth has been used as the debt base in judging the financial position of a national government, but usually has not been taken into consideration in state and municipal finance. In view of the fact that both state and municipal governments in recent years have been deriving a growing proportion of their revenues from sources other than the general property tax, it appears only logical to consider the item of wealth as a factor in determining the financial trend of state and municipal finance. The valuation of the debt base is generally difficult to ascertain with any degree of accuracy. The valuation of taxable property is necessarily indefinite since the methods of assessment are generally unscientific, and those of estimating wealth are still imperfect. Nevertheless, with these reservations, the item may be used as a means of studying the trend of government finance.

Based upon the items mentioned previously the following ratios may be used for the purpose of analyzing the financial trend of governments.

RATIOS OF GOVERNMENTAL FINANCIAL ANALYSIS

	RATIOS	EXPLANATION*
A.	Revenues to total expenditures............	$1 \div 2$
B.	Debt service to total expenditures.........	$6 \div 2$
C.	Unfunded debt to gross debt..............	$7 \div 9$
D.	Deductions to gross debt.................	$10 \div 9$
E.	Debt base to total debt..................	$14 \div 13$
F.	Net debt per capita [a]..................	

* Numbers refer to the items in the financial statement on page 374.
[a] Not a ratio but is expressed in money value.

These ratios may be explained as follows:

A. *Revenues to total expenditures* shows the extent to which the budget is or is not balanced. One hundred percent or more indicates a balanced budget.

B. *Debt service to total expenditures* indicates the extent of the total outlays absorbed by debt service. A high percentage indicates an unsatisfactory debt structure.

C. *Unfunded debt to gross debt* shows the extent of the short-maturing debt. A low percentage indicates a more satisfactory debt structure.

D. *Deductions to gross debt* shows the extent of the debt which is self-carrying and not an actual burden. A high percentage indicates a more satisfactory debt structure.

E. *Debt base to total debt* shows the extent to which taxable property or wealth covers the total debt. A high ratio reflects greater protection for the debt.

F. *Net debt per capita* shows the size of the net debt in relation to the population expressed in money value such as dollars. A low amount indicates a small pressure of the debt per person.

[2] For analysis of governmental securities see Edwards, George W., *Investments,* op. cit., chapters 12 and 13.

[3] The statistics used in this section are presented in Appendix VII.

[4] Ibid. column 6.

[5] Ibid. columns 9, 10 and 11.

[6] Ibid. column 14.

[7] Ibid. Ratios B and E.

[8] Ibid. column 3.

[9] Ibid. columns 9, 10 and 11.

[10] Ibid. columns 11 and 14, **Ratio E.**

[11] Ibid. column 2.

[12] Ibid. columns 1 and 3.

[13] Ibid. columns 4 and 5.

[14] Ibid. column 6, Ratio **B.**

[15] Ibid. columns 11 and 7.

[16] Ibid. Ratio C.

[17] Ibid. Ratio E.

[18] Ibid. columns 1, 2 and 3.

[19] Ibid. column 7.

[20] Ibid. Ratio C.

[21] Ibid. column 12. In addition, technically, the government also guaranteed postal savings deposits amounting to $1,218,000,000 and Federal Reserve notes amounting to $3,453,000,000. For description of guaranteed obligations, see the State and Municipal compendium of the *Chronicle.*

[22] Appendix VII, columns 2 and 6, ratio B.

[23] Ibid. Ratio E.

[24] *Financial Statistics of States;* Bureau of Census; United States Department of Commerce. This table continues the statistics on state debt given in Table 16 which presented the trend of the state debt from 1870 to 1913. (See p. 180.) For comments on the trend of state credit, see Raymond, William Lee, *State and Municipal Bonds,* 2nd ed., Boston 1932; Trull, Edna, *Resources and Debt of the Forty-Eight States,* Dun & Bradstreet, New York 1935.

[25] Table 27 items 1 and 2.

[26] Ibid. Ratio B.

[27] Ibid. Ratio C.

[28] Ibid. Ratio D.

[29] Ibid. Ratio E.

[30] Ibid. items 9 and 10.

[31] Ibid. Ratio F.

[32] These aggregate figures reflect only the general trend of state finance as a whole. Among these states there was considerable variation in financial trends. On the one hand, Connecticut paid off its debt entirely while on the other hand Arkansas increased its direct debt from $2,000,000 in 1923 to $164,000,000 by 1932. As a result, the State went into default on its debt and its obligations at one time fell in price to the low thirties. *Barron's Weekly,"* Vol. XIV, June 4, 1934, p. 15.

Source :

[33] *Financial Statistics of Cities,* Bureau of the Census, United States Department of Commerce. This table includes cities of 100,000 population and over. For comments on the trend of municipal finance see Rightor, C. E., "Bonded Debt of Cities," presented annually in the *National Municipal Review.*

[34] A distinction is here drawn between the term "city" and "municipality." The latter term, in technical finance, is more comprehensive and includes not only cities, but also other political subdivisions, as towns, villages and districts.

[35] Table 28, items 1 and 2.

[36] Ibid. item 3.

[37] Ibid. Ratio A.

[38] Ibid. Ratio B.

[39] Bird, Frederick L., *Trend of Tax Delinquency*, 1930–1935, Municipal Service Department, Dun & Bradstreet, New York 1936, p. 4.

[40] Table 28, Ratio F. Asheville, North Carolina, had a per capita total debt of $845.95, and Atlantic City, New Jersey, had a per capita debt of $504.67. Bird, Frederick L., *The Municipal Debt Load*, Municipal Service Department, Dun & Bradstreet, New York 1935, p. 16.

[41] Table 28, Ratio E.

[42] Miami was forced to reduce the assessed valuation of property within its jurisdiction by 73 percent, Atlantic City by 60 percent, Fall River by 50 percent and Asheville by 33 percent. In the case of Asheville the coverage of taxable property to total debt fell to less than 1½ times. Bird, op. cit. p. 9.

[43] *Financial Statistics of State and Local Governments, Wealth, Public Debt and Taxation for 1932*, Bureau of the Census, United States Department of Commerce, p. 62.

[44] Chatters, Carl H. *Municipal Debt Defaults* in Public Administrative Service Publication No. 33, 1933, p. 11.

[45] Ibid. p. 1.

[46] Shanks, Sanders, "The Extent of Municipal Defaults" in *National Municipal Review*, Vol. XXIV, January, 1935, p. 32. The financial situation was serious particularly in such cities as Cleveland, Chicago, Detroit, Toledo, Asheville, Atlantic City, Mobile and Pontiac. Hillhouse, Albert M., *Municipal Bonds*, New York 1936, p. 22.

[47] League of Nations *Statistical Yearbook*. Budgets for individual countries were also used. The figures for 1920 must be taken with reservation due to the incompleteness of South American budgetary statistics.

[48] Table 29, item 2.

[49] Ibid. item 1.

[50] Ibid. Ratio A.

[51] Ibid. Ratio B.

[52] Ibid. item 2.

[53] Ibid. item 1.

[54] Ibid. Ratio A.

[55] Ibid. item 6.

[56] Ibid. item 7.

[57] Ibid. item 3.

[58] Ibid. item 1.

[59] Ibid. Ratio A.

[60] Ibid. item 4.

[61] Ibid. Ratio B.

[62] Ibid. Ratio D.

[63] Conservative American bankers became concerned over the excessive lending to Brazil and hoped to check further loans. The author at the time was director of the Institute of International Finance sponsored by the Investment Bankers Association of America in cooperation with New York University, and in the name of the Institute issued a bulletin on the credit position of Brazil. This bulletin stated in part that "Brazil must, under present conditions, continue to import about $125,-000,000 of capital annually, either in the form of Government loans or as private investments in Brazilian trade and industry." *Institute of International Finance, Credit Position of Brazil*, Bulletin No. 3, March 17, 1927, p. 4. The overreliance of the country on coffee was shown by statistics, and the weakness of the plan for the stabilization of coffee prices was explained. The bulletin gave a detailed statement of the budget of the government and showed its continued deficits. It was also explained that the interest on a number of government loans still outstanding had been paid in script and that the sinking funds on 17 issues had been suspended for a period of 13 years. The conclusion was that "in the light . . . of the balance of international payments and the fluctuating position of the coffee trade the budgetary situation is uncertain. The addition of the sinking fund charges on the London and Paris issues is a substantial burden, but it is a small item compared with possible future charges on the treasury arising out of the currency stabilization proposal." Ibid. p. 7. The salient points of this bulletin were reproduced in the financial press and the bulletin was distributed among investment houses and their customers. Within a short time after this bulletin was released, a large Brazilian loan was successfully floated and in the following years additional issues of Brazilian bonds were placed. All eventually went into default.

[64] Table 29, item 6.

[65] Ibid. item 7.
[66] Ibid. Ratio D.
[67] Ibid. item 1.
[68] Ibid. item 3.
[69] Ibid. Ratio A.

CHAPTER 17

[1] Compiled from data in *Long Term Debts in the United States*, United States Department of Commerce, Bureau of Foreign and Domestic Commerce—Domestic Commerce Series—No. 96, 1937, pp. 52, 77, 163, 185. This table does not include domestic industrial or foreign bonds, as no complete study has been made of their distribution in this country. For a sample of the distribution of foreign bonds see statistics presented by Dwight Morrow in the *Chronicle* Vol. 119, September 27, 1924, p. 1455. The conclusions drawn from this chart are necessarily limited, because of the incompleteness of the data. The table has been included, however, since it is the only available study which attempts to show the entire field of security distribution.

[2] *Annual Report of the Federal Reserve Board, Federal Reserve Bulletin,* and *Annual Report of the Comptroller of the Currency.*

[3] Beckhart, Benjamin H., editor, *The New York Money Market*, Vol. IV, New York 1932, p. 315.

[4] In 1935 the federal government bonds accounted for 69 percent of the security investments of national banks, 54 percent of the state banks, and over 35 percent of the mutual savings banks. Computed from the *73rd Annual Report of the Comptroller of the Currency,* p. 100.

[5] Means, Gardiner C., "The Diffusion of Stock Ownership in the United States" in the *Quarterly Journal of Economics*, Vol. XLIV No. 4, p. 595. See also Berle, A. A. and Means, G. C., *The Modern Corporation and Private Property,* New York 1933, Chapter IV.

[6] McCoy, Joseph S., "The U. S. Legion of Capitalists" in the *Journal of the American Bankers' Association,* February 1927, p. 626.

[7] Twentieth Century Fund, Inc., *The Security Markets,* New York 1935, p. 50.

[8] Warshaw, H. T., "The Distribution of Corporate Ownership in the United States," in the *Quarterly Journal of Economics* Vol. 39, November 1924, p. 18.

[9] McCoy, op. cit. p. 626.

[10] "What Trends in Security Ownership" prepared by the Research Department of R. G. Dun & Company, May 16, 1932, reproduced in part in the *Chronicle*, Vol. 134, May, 1932, p. 3700.

[11] *New York Stock Exchange Bulletin,* February 1935.

[12] McCoy, op. cit. p. 628.

[13] Study of R. G. Dun and Company, op. cit. p. 3700.

[14] Appendix X.

[15] Computed from figures presented by Gilbert N. Riddle in Willis, H. Parker and Chapman, John W., *The Banking Situation,* New York 1934, p. 228.

[16] Computed from Riddle, Ibid. p. 229.

[17] Computed from Wood Struthers Co., *Trusteeship of American Endowments,* New York 1932, pp. 22–39. This study included an analysis of the holdings of thirty colleges and universities whose endowments were 74 percent of the combined investment of all the institutions of higher education in the United States, having endowments in excess of $5,000,000 each.

[18] Computed from the *Reports of the Comptroller of the Currency.*

[19] The statistics on the detailed distribution of the security investments of other classes of commercial banks are incomplete.

[20] Computed from the *Reports of the Comptroller of the Currency.* The reports for the years 1910–1924 contain apparent errors.

[21] *Proceedings, Association of Life Insurance Presidents.*

[22] The statistics on the holdings of philanthropic institutions in general are not published, but fragmentary studies have been made of the investment policies of particular institutions. These studies indicate that the depreciation in the value of securities after 1929 seriously reduced the value of the funds of these institutions and sharply reduced their incomes. In some cases these institutions found the income on their investments insufficient to permit the continuance of their work, and they were forced to draw on the principal, thus reducing the base for their future operations. Wood Struthers & Co., *Trusteeship of American Endowments,* New York

1932, p. 17. In the two years ending June 30, 1931, the endowment fund of Yale University, to which contributions of $17,500,000 had been made, suffered losses of $12,500,000 or 70 percent of the entire fund. *Report of the Treasurer of Yale University* cited in an article by Hopkins, Frances W., "Investment Operations of Universities" in the *Journal of Business of the University of Chicago*, Vol. V., p. 145. The market value of the investments of the University of Chicago, on June 30, 1929 exceeded book value by $15,000,000. The report a year later showed that this excess value was reduced to $11,000,000 and by the following year the excess had dwindled to $1,156,951. Ibid. pp. 145–146.

[23] *Annual Reports of the Comptroller of the Currency ; Proceedings, Association of Life Insurance Presidents.*

Since the reports of these financial institutions were made as of June 30 of each year, the security prices were likewise computed as of this date. In the case of the life insurance companies the fiscal year ends on December 31st, and so this date was taken in computing the changes in the value of the investments.

[24] This figure probably contains a margin of error, as the term "industrial" is loosely defined in the statistics on investment of these institutions.

[25] The financial position of the mutual savings banks was actually much stronger than that of other classes of financial institutions. The strength of the savings banks rested mainly in the fact that over the years they had accumulated large reserves through conservative dividend policies.

[26] Since 1906 only six life insurance companies actually failed. These were small institutions whose difficulties developed not so much from unsound investment policies but from unfavorable mortality experiences. However, the losses of the insurance companies on their securities have at times been very heavy. In the depression of 1921 the losses of the life insurance companies were severe and as a result, according to A. Vere Shaw, "more than a few life insurance companies in this country were actually insolvent. They had not succeeded in maintaining even the nominal value of their capital." Shaw, A. Vere, "Elements of Investment Safety," in the *Harvard Business Review*, Vol. III, July 1925, p. 447. In fact, one domestic life insurance company, in its statement as of December 31, 1921, reported a market value below cost of more than $63,000,000 on its bond holdings. Ibid. p. 449. In the depression following 1929 the position of the life insurance companies became even more uncertain. Not only was the decline in security values more precipitous, but in these low markets the insurance companies were forced to sell a large part of their securities in order to meet the pressing demand for loans on policies. Life insurance companies increased the cash surrender value of their assets from $6,300,000,000 in 1922 to $14,300,000,000 in 1933. See Berle, Adolph A., and Peterson, Victoria, J., *Liquid Claims and National Wealth*, New York 1934, p. 103; see also Sullivan, James P., "The Life Insurance Company as a Banking Concern" in the *Journal of Business*, October 1932, p. 346. By the end of 1931 the insurance companies had to apply a large part of investments to grant loans to policy holders. See testimony of Ecker, Frederick H., President of the Metropolitan Life Insurance Company before the sub-committee of the United States Banking and Currency Committee, *Hearings on the Creation of the Reconstruction Finance Corporation*, Senate Hearings, 72nd Congress, 1st Session, p. 130. The situation became serious in March, 1933, when the demands of policyholders for loans depleted the companies' holdings of cash and readily marketable securities at a time when the amount of new funds which they were receiving declined. Moreover, the companies were faced with extensive defaults on both their mortgage loans and their security holdings. Under these conditions, in March, 1933, the Superintendent of Insurance in New York, and in several other states, ordered the insurance companies to suspend the loan and cash surrender provisions of their policies.

In the post-war period fire and marine insurance companies increased their investment assets, and became virtually investment trusts. The investment experience of these companies in recent years has been unsatisfactory. A study of the period even from 1921 to 1925 by Nerlove showed that of 290 such companies, 206 incurred underwriting losses of $130,600,000 on business operations and on their securities while the remaining 84 showed profits of $28,300,000 or a net loss in all of $102,300,000. Nerlove, S. H., "Investments Subsidize Fire and Marine Insurance Business," *The Journal of Political Economy*, Vol. 35, February 1927, p. 128.

CHAPTER 18

[1] (a) National income: Kuznets, Simon, *National Income and Capital Formation*, New York 1937, p. 16.

(b) Saving funds: includes total of saving deposits of state banks, mutual savings banks, national banks, trust companies, private banks, aggregate reserves of life insurance companies and assets of building and loan associations, computed after the method used by F. C. Mills, *Economic Tendencies of the United States*, New York 1932, p. 425; sources, *Reports of the Comptroller of the Currency* and *Proceedings of Life Insurance Presidents*.

(c) New Securities: Table 39.

(d) Interest on Bonded Debt: Table 40.

(e) Bonded Debt: Table 41.

(f) Total Securities Outstanding: Table 42.

(g) National Wealth: *Standard Trade and Securities*, Vol. 3, Statistical section, p. D64.

[2] Table 38, column 1.

[3] Ibid. column 2.

[4] Fabricant, S., *Recent Corporate Profits in the United States*, p. 10 National Bureau of Economic Research, Bulletins 50 and 56; Ebersole, J. Franklin, "Income Forecasting by the Use of Statistics of Income Data," in the *Review of Economic Statistics*, November 1929, Vol. XI, p. 180; Nerlove, S. H., *A Decade of Corporate Incomes 1920–1929*, Chicago 1932; King, Wilford I., *The National Income and its Purchasing Power*, New York 1930, p. 280; Mills, Frederick C., *Economic Tendencies in the United States*, New York 1932, p. 429. For a consideration of the significance of corporate saving see Snyder, Carl, "Capital Supply and National Well Being," *American Economic Review*, Vol. XXVI, June 1936, pp. 195–224.

[5] A further deduction would be to omit the amount of investment trust securities, since the proceeds of such issues are applied to the purchase of other securities. This item is, however, included in Table 39 in order to show the relative importance of investment trust issues.

[6] The figures on corporate securities used in this table are compiled by the *Chronicle*. Although these are unquestionably the most comprehensive compilations of new security issues at present available, they are incomplete and do not represent the total demand for capital through the flotation of securities, since they do not include the issues of many local corporations. These issues in themselves are small in amount, but the total is large. Frederick C. Mills states that between December 31, 1928 and December 31, 1929 the total capital stock, plus bonds and mortgages of corporations submitting balance sheets to the United States Bureau of Internal Revenues increased by $17,183,000,000, while for the same period the new domestic capital issues as compiled by the *Chronicle* totalled only $9,425,000,000. This statement is questioned by Eddy, George A., "Security Issues and Real Investment in 1929," in the *Review of Economic Statistics*, May 1937, Vol. XIV, No. 2, pp. 79–91. Statistics on new security issues are also compiled by the *Journal of Commerce* and Moody's Investment Service.

[7] These amounts are based on the figures in Table 39.

[8] Computed from the *Chronicle*.

[9] (a) Federal Government — Moody's *Manual of Governments and Municipals*, 1935, p. 31; (b) State and municipal government — U. S. Bureau of the Census; Dept. of Commerce, *Financial Statistics of States; Financial Statistics of Cities;* (c) Corporate —United States Internal Revenue Office, United States Treasury Department, *Statistics of Income*.

[10] Table 41. These figures differ from those presented in the study of *Long Term Debts in the United States*, United States Department of Commerce, Series No. 95, Washington 1937, since this report includes not only bonded but also other long term debt.

[11] The figures for the securities of the Federal Land Banks, 1920 to 1924 inclusive, were obtained from the annual reports of the Federal Farm Loan Board for the respective years.

The figures for the real estate securities from 1920 to 1924 inclusive, were obtained from the estimates of Charles E. Parsons "Credit Expansion 1920 to 1929" in the *Quarterly Journal of Economics*, November 1913 Volume 45 Page 100.

All other figures were obtained from Moody's *Manual of Investment; Industrial Securities*. Since the figures were frequently revised in later editions, they were not obtained for the respective years but obtained from later editions of the manual, particularly 1924 (page LXV), 1925 (page LI), 1926 (page LI), 1927 (page XLIII), 1929 (page XLIV), 1932 (page LIV), 1934 (page A42), and 1936 (page A38–39).

The figures given by Moody's for state and municipal securities differ from those presented in other sources such as the *Bond Buyer* for January 1, 1936.

For the years 1920 to 1931 inclusive, Moody's figures are higher, while from 1932 to 1935 inclusive they are lower than the *Bond Buyer* statistics.

[12] 1925—Moody's *Manual of Industrials*, 1932, page LIV ; 1926–1935, 1936, page a-38.

[13] See Table 38 item 6 p. 279.

[14] Ibid. Column 7.

[15] See Weidenhammer, Robert, "Control of the Capital Market," in the *American Economic Review*, Vol. XXII, September 1932, p. 402 ; and Doane, Robert R., *The Measurement of American Wealth*, New York 1933, p. 111.

[16] See p. 8.

[17] Table 38, Ratio A.

[18] p. 232.

[19] *Standard Trade and Securities*, Vol. 3, Statistical Section.

[20] *New York Stock Exchange Bulletin—*Dec. 1931, p. 12.

[21] Ibid. *Federal Reserve Bulletin*, Vol. 16, January 1930, p. 13.

[22] Table 38, Ratio B.

[23] Ibid. Ratio C.

[24] Ibid. Ratio D.

[25] Conant, Charles A., "World's Wealth in Negotiable Securities," in the *Atlantic Monthly*, January 1908, p. 97.

[26] Table 38, Ratio E.

CHAPTER 19

[1] Since much of the confusion in monetary discussion has been due to the lack of clarity in terminology particularly with respect to the technical meaning of "money," "value of money," and "inflation," the definition of these terms as used in this analysis is herewith given. Money, in the broad sense, includes the means of payment held by the public for the purpose of discharging debt and price contracts. For amplification of this definition of money, see Currie, Lauchlin, *Supply and Control of Money in the United States*, Cambridge, Mass. 1934, especially Chapter II. Money is therefore composed of both currency and bank deposits. The expression "value of money" is used in the sense of both the external value and the internal value. The external value is expressed in terms of foreign exchange ; the internal value of money is stated not only in terms of commodities but also of securities. For the distinction between the external and the internal value, see study by Hardy, Charles O., *Devaluation of the Dollar*, in Public Policy Pamphlets, No. 8, University of Chicago Press, Chicago, 1933. Banking and monetary theory has in the past been overinfluenced by the restricted orthodox concept of the financial system. As in the case of banking theory, monetary theory has been largely based on the assumption that the financial system is still in the stage of individual capitalism, and has failed to appreciate the significance of security capitalism. As a result even leading monetary economists, not to mention popular writers, discuss the subject of the value of money almost exclusively from the standpoint of its relation to commodity prices.

The third term requiring definition is "inflation." It is used in this section to describe that economic condition caused by an increase in the means of payment in the form of currency and bank deposits in excess of the volume of goods and services offered for sale, and results in a decrease in the value of money expressed internally in terms not only of commodities but also of securities and externally in foreign exchange. Deflation is the opposite economic situation caused by a decrease in the means of payment in relation to the amount of goods and services offered, and results in an increase in the internal and external value of money.

Inflation may be either private or public. Private inflation may be largely commercial in nature when there is a maladjustment of the means of payment in relation to commodities. Private inflation may be largely investment in nature when the maladjustment in the means of payment is in relation to investment assets as securities or real estate. With the development of security capitalism, private security investment inflation caused by an excess of security investment over saving available for the security market has become of more pressing importance.

Public inflation may in turn either be domestic or international in nature. Both forms of inflation arise from an emergency, as war or depression, which necessitates outlays by the government in excess of revenues, and so leads to a deficit in the government budget. The simplest method of overcoming this fiscal problem is to balance the budget by decreasing expenditures and increasing revenues. Such a fiscal policy is generally impracticable in time of emergency, and so the government has recourse to the use of its credit. Such credit in turn may be either in the form of fiat money or of bonds sold to the investing public. With the development of security capitalism governments have made every effort to avoid the use of fiat money, primarily an instrument of individual capitalism, and have rather employed the device of issuing securities. When the sale of such securities is no longer possible and the country is not on the gold standard, inflation often takes place through the central bank and is partly bank note and partly deposit credit inflation.

International public inflation arises out of a deficit in the nation's balance of international payments. This deficit results from an excess of the international debits in goods, services and capital in excess of the international credits of the nation. Again, the simple policy is to overcome the deficit by decreasing debits and increasing credits through reducing the imports of goods and services and through stimulating exports. When this policy fails the nation makes use of its credit by placing its securities in foreign markets or as a last recourse by selling its fiat money abroad.

2 Technically Part III of the Farm Relief Act.

3 In addition to these statutes enacted by Congress, numerous additional proposals for monetary control were presented to Congress but were not enacted. These included the Fraser Bill for the Bank of the United States, 74th Congress, 1st Session, Senate Document 1869; the Somers Bill for the National Bank of the United States, 74th Congress, 1st Session, H.R. 3250; the Goldsborough Bill for Federal Monetary Authority, 74th Congress, 1st Session, H.R. 170; and the Cutting Bill for a Federal Monetary Authority, 73rd Congress, 2nd Session, 3744.

4 This structure, established by the Federal Reserve Act of 1913, was continually modified by subsequent legislation particularly the Banking Acts of 1933 and of 1935. The Banking Act of 1935 accomplished a sweeping revision of the Federal Reserve system, and went beyond the scope of the original Federal Reserve Act in broadening the function of the Reserve system in its relation to the economic life of the nation. An official review of the Banking Act of 1935 is given in the *Federal Reserve Bulletin*, Vol. 21, September, 1935, pp. 559–564; see also *Hearings on the Banking Act of 1935, 74th Congress, 1st Session*. The Act represented an effort to repair the banking system in the light of the unsatisfactory experiences of the post-war period. It consisted of three parts, Title I which placed the deposit insurance system on a permanent basis, Title II which revised the Federal Reserve system, and Title III which effected changes in the regulation of the individual banks of the country. This study will not consider Title III which deals with the technical regulation of banking practice.

5 See p. 193.

6 Willis, H. Parker, *The Federal Reserve System*, New York 1923, pp. 251–252, also Willis, H. Parker, "The Federal Reserve Act in Congress," in *The Annals of the American Academy of Political and Social Science*, Vol. 99, January 1922, pp. 36–49.

7 Federal Reserve Act, Section 10.

8 Senate bill 4412 as introduced in the 72nd Congress, 1st Session.

9 As a matter of fact, it had become the practice for the President to designate the chief executive officer of the Board only from year to year. See testimony of Governor Marriner S. Eccles, United States Committee on Banking and Currency, House, 74th Congress, 1st Session, *Hearings on the Banking Act of 1935*, pp. 189–190.

10 Clark, Lawrence E., *Central Banking Under the Federal Reserve System*, New York 1935, pp. 95–98.

11 It was first proposed that the position of Federal Reserve agent be abolished, but in the final act the office was continued and he still serves as chairman of the board of directors.

12 Harris, Seymour E., *Twenty Years of Federal Reserve Policy*, Cambridge, Mass. 1933, Vol. I, p. 145 et seq. gives an excellent account of this controversy between the Federal Reserve Board and the Federal Reserve Bank of New York.

13 Federal Reserve Act, Section 14.

14 *First Annual Report*, Federal Reserve Bank of New York, Washington 1916, p. 20.

15 *Federal Reserve Bulletin*, Vol. I, 1915, p. 360.

16 The effectiveness of the open market policies of the Reserve system has been subject to criticism. See comments of Dr. Adolph Miller, *Hearings before the Committee on Banking and Currency*, House, 70th Congress, 1st Session, Pursuant to H.R. 11806, 1928, p. 125; also Whitney, Caroline, *Experiments in Credit Control, The Federal Reserve System*, New York 1934, p. 28.

[17] The Federal Reserve Board refused to recognize the fact that in actual practice the banking system was turning toward the liberal rather than the orthodox theory. The Reserve Board scrupulously avoided public discussion of the broad principles involved in the changing character of the assets of the member banks. No public consideration was given to the serious problem as to whether the growing diversion of bank credit into direct and indirect security investment was in the interest of public welfare. If the individual members of the Federal Reserve Board were conscious of this actual revolution in the banking system, they gave no public utterance of it. Officially the Board chose to ignore the fact that the commercial banking system was changing as capitalism changed. The first official notice of the changing nature of the assets of the commercial banks did not come until 1926 when the Board made a brief comment on this trend. *Thirteenth Annual Report of the Federal Reserve Board*, Washington 1927, p. 10. In its annual report of 1928 the Federal Reserve Board made only a passing reference to the sweeping effect of security capitalism on the banking system. Ibid., *Fifteenth Annual Report*, op. cit., Washington 1929, p. 8.

[18] For discussion, see Harris, op. cit., Vol. I, pp. 291–311.

[19] *Hearings on Operations of the Banking System*, 71st Congress, 3rd Session, Senate, p. 712.

[20] United States Committee on Banking and Currency, *Hearings on Branch Banking*, House, 71st Congress, 2nd Session, 1930, Vol. I. p. 500 ; United States Committee on Banking and Currency, *Hearings, Operation of National and Federal Reserve Banking Systems*, 71st Congress, 2nd Session ; Appendix, Part 6, pp. 707–708.

[21] *Banking Act of 1932*, 72nd Congress, 1st Session, Chapter 58 of Revised Statutes, section 10b.

[22] *Summary of statements of Marriner S. Eccles on the Banking Bill of 1935 in reply to questions by members of the Committee on Banking and Currency of the House of Representatives at Hearings, March 4–20, 1935*, p. 18.

[23] Hearings: *Establishment of a War Finance Corporation*, 65th Congress, 2nd Session, 1918, pp. 38–39 ; United States House Ways and Means Committee, 1918, pp. 3–8, 23–26, 73, 108–110.

[24] Harding, W. P. G., "Suggested Changes in the Federal Reserve Act," in *American Bankers Association Journal*, Vol. 22, February 1930, p. 734. For further discussion see Mlynarski, Felix, *Gold and Central Banks*, New York, 1929, pp. 36–37 ; Kisch, Cecil H., and Elkin, W. A., *Central Banks*, London, 1928, p. 130; Mitchell, Waldo, *The Uses of Bank Funds*, Chicago 1925, p. 177; Watkins, Leonard, *Bankers Balances*, Chicago 1929, pp. 379–380.

[25] "Productiveness as the Test for Rediscount," *American Bankers Association Journal*, Vol. 22, June 1930, pp. 1178–1183 ; *Hearings : Operation of Banking System*, 71st Congress, 1st Session, op. cit. 1931, pp. 372–373.

[26] The hearings and the official documents relating to the Banking Act of 1935 contain no direct or indirect reference on this subject.

[27] United States Senate Committee, *Hearings*, Senate, Committee on Banking and Currency, 72nd Congress, 1st Session, 1932 on the Senate Bill 4115, p. 501.

[28] *Congressional Record*, Vol. 79, No. 153, July 25, 1935, p. 11827.

[29] Chapter 191, Section 2 (b) of the Banking Act of February 25, 1927.

[30] Banking Act of 1933.

[31] See ruling of December 27, 1934.

[32] See regulations governing the purchase of investment securities and further defining the term "investment securities," issued February 15, 1936.

[33] For statement of the statutes of the various states on the investment of savings and trust funds, see state and municipal section of the supplements to the *Chronicle* ; see also pp. 195–196.

[34] Reilly, Edward J., "Formulating a Sound Code Governing Legal Investments for Trust Funds," *Trust Companies*, February 1932, Vol. LIV, No. 2, pp. 233–238.

[35] *New York State Bar Association Bulletin*, Vol. 6, March 1934, p. 133.

[36] *Georgia Laws*, Sec. 2409, Acts of 1929 ; *Laws of Minnesota* 1929, Chapter III. For discussion see Halaas, E. T., "Legal Control of Life Insurance Company Investments," in the *Journal of Business*, Vol. 5, October 1932, p. 332.

[37] *Laws of Vermont*, 1929, Section 5580 ; *South Dakota*, see Comp. Laws, 1929, Section 4351a.

[38] Section 100 of Chapter 33 of the Laws of 1900 as amended.

[39] *Chronicle*, Supplement Vol. 107, October 12, 1918, p. 194.

[40] Ibid. Vol. 105, Part 2, November 17, 1917, p. 1939.

[41] *Chronicle*, Vol. 133, September 12, 1931, p. 1672.

[42] *New York Times*, January 1, 1932, p. 4 column 1.

43 Ibid.

44 *Best's Insurance Guide*, New York 1935, p. 7.

45 Kilbourne, R. D., "The War Finance Corporation" in the *The American Economic Review*, Vol. XV December 1925, pp. 810–20.

46 *Annual Report of the Secretary of the Treasury on the State of the Finances*, 1918, pp. 245–48.

47 War Finance Corporation, *First Annual Report*, Washington 1918, p. 9.

48 Corey, Lewis, *The Decline of American Capitalism*, New York 1934, p. 54.

49 This is well stated by Hugh Knowlton, an investment banker, who describes the loans of the Corporation as "not good enough for private capital but which the government was making as a rescue party." *Bulletin, The New York State Society of Certified Public Accountants*, Vol. 4, July 1934, p. 38.

50 *Banking Act of 1935*, Title I, section 101.

51 Computed from figures presented in the *Congressional Record*, House, May 4, 1935, p. 6945. Taggert, J. H., and Jennings, L. D., in their study on "The Insurance of Bank Deposits" in the *Journal of Political Economy*, Vol. 42, August 1934, pp. 508–516 present an actuarial study of the losses of both the State and national Banks. This study shows that over this period an assessment of even one-fourth of one percent would not have been sufficient to meet losses on total deposits.

52 *Hearings*, 74th Congress, 1st Session, Banking Act of 1935 op. cit. p. 28.

53 Massachusetts, Chapter 719 of the Acts of 1913 in the *Chronicle*, Vol. 97, August 23, 1913, pp. 487–488; see Secrist, Horace, "Constitutional Restrictions on Municipal Debt," in the *Journal of Political Economy*, Vol. 22, April 1914, pp. 365–383; Lancaster, Lane, *State Supervision of Municipal Indebtedness*, Philadelphia, 1923; Van de Woestyne, Royal S., *State Control of Local Finance in Massachusetts*, Cambridge 1935.

54 Ibid., p. 135. In 1926 the state of Massachusetts appointed a finance committee to take over and supervise the finances of the city of Lowell owing to its critical financial position. Ibid. p. 127.

55 For discussion see Frye, A., "State Receiverships of Insolvent Municipal Corporations" in the *National Municipal Review*, Vol. 25, June 1936, pp. 319–322.

56 Consolidated Statutes (1931) Chapter 60, (Sub-chapter 3).

57 Esch-Cummins Act, amending the Interstate Commerce Act of 1887.

58 In one case the Commission refused to permit a railroad to accept a price of 80 percent of par for a new issue, and insisted that the price be at least 90 percent of par. 70 *Interstate Commerce Commission*, 238.

59 For discussion of this activity of the Commission, see Frederick, John H., "Federal Regulation of Railway Securities Under the Transportation Act of 1920," in *The Journal of Political Economy*, Vol. 37, April 1929, p. 187.

60 Waltersdorf, Maurice C., "State Control of Utility Capitalization" in *Yale Law Journal*, Vol. 37, January 1928, p. 356.

61 See p. 165.

62 See pp. 204–205.

63 *Chronicle*, May 28, 1921, Vol. 112, p. 2248.

64 For explanation of the technical aspects of this ruling see analysis by Dulles John Foster, on "Our Foreign Loan Policy" in *Foreign Affairs*, October Vol. 5, 1926, p. 34.

65 *Chronicle*, Vol. 134, January 9, 1932, p. 209. The frequent statement made by governmental officers that the government never approved a foreign loan is untrue, for in the case of the Bolivian loan of 1917, the secretary of state in a letter to the Bolivian Government wrote "the loan is approved by the Government of the United States," and added that he was "glad that a satisfactory arrangement for this loan has been consummated." *Chronicle*, Vol. 104, June 23, 1917, p. 2500.

66 This term originated in a judicial decision where the court made a scathing criticism of "speculative schemes that have no more basis than so many feet of blue sky." *Hall vs. Geiger-Jones*, 242 U. S. 539. The first blue sky law was passed by Kansas in 1911 (Session laws of Kansas, 1911, Ch. 133), and in the following years similar statutes were passed by other states. United States Banking and Currency Commission, Senate 73, Cong. 1st Session, *Hearings on the Federal Securities Act*, p. 318.

67 *Hall vs. Geiger-Jones*, 242 U. S. 539.

68 See comments of Arthur Dean "The Lawyers Problems and the Securities Act" in *Law and Contemporary Problems*, Duke University Law School, Vol. 14, April 1937, p. 156.

69 *Hearings on Federal Securities Act*, op. cit. p. 106.

70 Address before National Association of Security Commissioners New York City, Ninth Annual Convention, 1926, p. 7.

71 Dalton, John E. "The Development and Future Trends in State Security Regulation," *Harvard Business Review*, October 1933, p. 26.

72 For reference to the work of the Capital Issues Committee, see Beckhart, Benjamin; Smith, James and Brown, William, *The New York Money Market*, New York 1932, Vol. IV, p. 295; Willis, H. Parker, *The Federal Reserve System*, New York 1923, p. 1294; Kilbourne, R. D., "The War Finance Corporation," in the *American Economic Review*, Vol. XV, December 1925, p. 812.

73 *Chronicle*, Vol. 104, June 9, 1917, p. 2268.

74 Ibid., Vol. 105, December 15, 1917, p. 2316.

75 Harding, W. P. G., *The Formative Period of the Federal Reserve System*, Boston 1925, p. 117. The plan received the active support of the two leading banking associations. As early as December 1917, the Investment Bankers Association appointed a committee to study the entire subject of the control of the capital market. *Chronicle*, Vol. 105, December 15, 1917, p. 2316. Mr. Allen B. Forbes, a member of this committee, served on both the informal committee of the Federal Reserve Board and later on the Capital Issues Committee. The Association therefore gave its full approval to the regulation of the capital market. *Chronicle*, Vol. 106, March 9, 1918, p. 978. Likewise the Administrative Committee of the American Bankers Association gave its approval to the Capital Issues Committee.

76 *Annual Report of the Secretary of the Treasury*, 1918, p. 61.

77 *Chronicle*, Vol. 105, November 24, 1917, p. 2047.

78 Ibid., Supplements, Banking Section, September 1918, p. 227.

79 Ibid., Vol. 106, February 2, 1918, p. 439.

80 See statement of general policies, as given in the *Chronicle*, Vol. 107, July 6, 1918, p. 25 ; see also Vol. 106, Part I, February 2, 1918, p. 439.

81 Ibid., Vol. 107, December 14, 1918, p. 2228.

82 Ibid.

83 Willis, H. Parker, *Federal Reserve System*, p. 1294.

84 *Report of the Capital Issues Committee*, 65th Congress, 3rd Session, House Document, 1485, December 2, 1918, p. 3 ; See message of President Wilson, August 8, 1919.

85 For a discussion of this bill, see *Hearings before the Committee on the Judiciary*, H. R. 188, 66th Congress, 1st Session, particularly pp. 11, 12, 19, 25, 50, 63, 124.

86 Ibid.

87 Senate Committee on Banking and Currency, 73rd Congress, 1st session 325–349, *Hearings on the Federal Securities Act*.

88 Public Statutes No. 22, 73rd Congress.

89 By the original terms of the Securities Act of 1933, the Federal Trade Commission was entrusted with the administration of the Act. However the Securities Exchange Act of 1934 created the Securities and Exchange Commission which was made responsible for the administration of both the Act of 1933 and that of 1934.

90 *Stock Exchange Practices*, Senate Report No. 1455, op. cit. pp. 100–101.

91 73rd Congress, 1st Session, *House Report* 85, May 4, 1933, p. 2.

92 Speech on July 25, 1934 reported in the *Chronicle*, Vol. 139, July 28, 1934, p. 525.

93 Even in 1928 and 1929 when the public absorption of securities was at its height, the total of all losses sustained by investors in cases investigated by the attorney general of New York State amounted to $52,000,000 in each of these two years. These sums in themselves were large, but constituted only a small fraction of the vast volume of securities issued in New York State in these years. New York State Law Department, *Reports of the Attorney General*.

94 Based on an unpublished report analyzing prospectuses over these years.

95 The insufficiency of the earning power of the issuing corporation was also stated in the case of the Federated Utilities, 3 year 5½% notes of November 1, 1927; American Utilities Co., 1st series, A, 6% bonds of December 1, 1925; Lexington Utilities, 1st refunding mortgage bonds, 5% series of February 1, 1927.

96 *New York Times*, May 31, 1928, p. 35.

97 *Stock Exchange Practices*, Senate Report No. 1455, op. cit. p. 73.

98 Ibid. p. 123.

99 A statement that the borrowing corporation reserved for itself, without restriction, powers which might adversely affect the investment position of the bond, was contained in the following issues : Southern National Corporation 6% debentures, issued March 15, 1929 ; Van Sweringen Corporation 5 yr. 6% notes of May 1, 1930 ; Texas Louisiana Power Company, 6% bonds series A, January 1, 1926 ; Paramount Publix bonds.

[100] This was the criticism of the Act made by the author in his article on "Control of the Security Investment System" in the *Harvard Business Review*, Vol. 12, October 1933. For discussion of this subject, see Dean, Arthur H., "Federal Securities Act" in *Fortune*, August 1933, Vol. VIII, pp. 50–55; Douglas, William, and Bates, George E., "The Federal Securities Act of 1933" in the *Yale Law Journal*, Vol. XLIII, December 1933, p. 171.

[101] See p. 25.

[102] Fortunately in the Public Utility Act of 1935 the Commission is given power to forbid a holding company to issue securities not approved by the Commission. Public Utility Act of 1935, Pub. No. 333, 74th Congress, 1st Session, 1935, 49th Stat. 803, 15 U. S. Code C, 2 C.

[103] *Chronicle*, Vol. 137, July 22, 1933, p. 581.

CHAPTER 20

[1] Hecht, Rudolph S., "A Banker Looks at Europe" in *Vital Speeches of the Day*, Vol. II, October 1, 1936, p. 797.

[2] *Chronicle*, Vol. 144, January 30, 1937, p. 701.

[3] European economists have long urged control over the quantity of investment credit. See Joseph Schumpeter, "Kreditkontrolle," *Archiv für Sozialwissenschaft und Sozialpolitik*, 1925, Vol. 54, pp. 289–328; Emil Lederer, "Das Kreditproblem" in *Der Weltwirtschaftskrise*, 1931, Vol. 66, pp. 247–283; Fritz Napthali, *Kapital Kontrolle*, Jena 1919; Bertil Ohlin in the *Index*, May 1932; Page, Kirby, Editor *A New Economic Order*, New York 1930, pp. 291–299; Hobson, John A., *Economics and Ethics*, New York 1929, pp. 284–287 ; Davenport, E. H., "The Control of National Investment" in the *New Statesman and Nation*, London, Vol. II, No. 33, new series, October 10, 1931, pp. 429–430 ; Report of the Liberal Industrial Inquiry *Britain's Industrial Future*, London, 1928, p. 111; Keynes, John Maynard, "A New Monetary Policy for England" in the *Economic Forum*, Vol. I, winter 1932–1933, p. 34; see the following studies by Keynes, John Maynard, *General Theory of Employment Interest and Money*, New York 1936, p. 164. *A Treatise on Money*, Vol. I, New York, 1930, p. 257. Keynes stated "I expect to see the State . . . taking an ever greater responsibility for directly organizing investment." He also stated "that the maintenance of equilibrium between saving and investment is a proper function of a 'currency authority.'" The need of control over the quantity of investment credit has been expressed by the following American writers : Berle, A. A., "Action to Avoid Another 1929" in *American Bankers Association Journal*, Vol. XXVI, July 1933, p. 17. Professor Berle urges a "Committee of Public Safety" conducted by investment bankers "to scrutinize every investment banking transaction of any public significance from the angle of the general public." See statement of Otto Kahn before Senate Committee on Banking and Currency, June 29, 1933, *Hearings*, U. S. Banking and Currency Commitee, op. cit. Part II, p. 1213; Fred Kent, a careful student of banking, urged some form of control over the quantity of investment. *Chronicle*, Vol. 129, November 23, 1929, pp. 2268–2270. Willis, H. Parker, "Reforms Due in Investment Banking," The *Annalist*, Vol. 35, January 17, 1930, p. 114; Meech, Stuart P., "The Investment Securities Business and the Future," *The Journal of Business*, Vol. V, July 1932, pp. 241–256; Weidehammer, Robert, "Control of the Capital Market," *The American Economic Review*, Vol. XXII, September 1932, pp. 389–402.

[4] Precedent for control of the quality of new financing is found in the Transportation Act of 1920, see p. 306, and in the Capital Issues Committee. In the administration of the state blue sky laws, the quality of investments has been regulated as in the case of real estate and investment trust securities. See p. 309.

[5] See idea as proposed by Paul M. Warburg in talk to the Bond Club of New York in 1919, quoted in Moulton, Harold G., *The Financial Organization of Society*, Chicago 1930, p. 221.

APPENDICES

These appendices seek to present the statistical data for studying the evolution of security capitalism. In interpreting these appendices certain qualifications must be kept in mind. Although every effort was made to select the most accurate and most reliable figures, many of them, such as national wealth and national income, can only be crude estimates. Furthermore, the farther back in time, the less reliable are these statistics, because of the inadequacy of the early data. Also, it cannot be taken for granted that governments have released accurate data with respect to certain items, such as expenditures for armament. For recent years, in the case of certain items, only estimated and not final figures were available, and so these were not included. Notwithstanding these limitations, the appendices bring together statistics which serve as a basis for undertaking a quantitative study of the subjects considered in this book.

APPENDIX I-A

Evolution of British Security Capitalism, 1820–1935
Economic Tendencies

| YEAR | PRODUCTION | | | | EXPORTS (million pounds) | COMMODITY PRICES (1910–14 =100) | UNEMPLOY-MENT (percent unem-ployed) |
	COAL (thousand tons)	PIG IRON (thousand tons)	STEEL (thousand tons)	INDUSTRIAL			
	1	2	3	4	5	6	7
1820	12,500	400			38	146	
1830		680			61	110	
1840	30,000	1,390			103	124	
1850	49,000	2,250			175	93	
1860	82,000	3,830			136	120	1.9
1870	110,000	5,960	215	43	200	116	3.8
1880	147,000	7,750	1,440	55	223	107	5.3
1890	177,000	8,250	3,670	67	264	87	2.1
1900	225,181	8,960	4,901	75	291	91	2.9
1910	264,433	10,012	6,515	87	430	94	4.7
1913	287,430	10,260	7,664	100	525	103	2.0
1920	229,532	8,035	9,057	90	1334	304	2.4
1921	163,251	2,616	3,763	63	703	188	15.3
1922	249,607	4,902	5,881	79	720	159	15.3
1923	276,001	7,441	8,489	84	767	156	11.5
1924	267,118	7,307	8,201	89	795	168	10.2
1925	243,176	6,262	7,385	86	773	165	11.0
1926	126,279	2,498	3,596	67	653	153	12.3
1927	251,232	7,294	9,099	92	709	148	9.6
1928	237,472	6,610	8,520	100	724	145	10.8
1929	257,907	7,589	9,636	106	730	139	10.5
1930	243,882	6,192	7,326	98	571	117	16.1
1931	219,459	3,758	5,176	84	391	100	21.7
1932	208,733	3,573	5,257	88	365	97	22.1
1933	207,112	4,124	7,003	93	368	96	19.9
1934	220,726	6,065	9,192	105	396	96	
1935	222,249	6,527	10,203	112	426		

Explanation and Sources

1. COAL PRODUCTION: Explanation: 1890 is 1889.

Sources:

1820, 1840–1890 — Mulhall, Michael George, *The Dictionary of Statistics*, London and New York 1899, p. 119.

1900 — Webb, Augustus D., *New Dictionary of Statistics*, London, 1911, p. 86.

1910 — *Statesman's Year Book*, London, 1912, p. 69.

1913, 1928–1930 — Moody's *Manual of Governments*, 1935, p. 1920.

1920–1922 — Ibid. 1926, p. 100.

1923–1927 — Ibid. 1930, p. 153.

1931–1936 — Statesman's, op. cit. 1937, p. 54.

2. PIG IRON PRODUCTION: Explanation: 1890 is 1889.
    Sources: 1820–1890   Mulhall, op. cit. p. 332.
                1900   Webb, op. cit. p. 353.
                1910   Statesman's, op. cit. 1912, p. xlviii.
                1913, 1928–1933 Moody's, op. cit. 1935, p. 1920.
                1920–1925   Ibid. 1930, p. 153.
                1926   League of Nations, *Statistical Year Book*, 1935/1936, p. 144.
                1927   Moody's *Manual of Industrials*, 1929, p. xix.
                1934–1935   Statesman's, op. cit. 1937, p. xix.

3. STEEL PRODUCTION: Explanation: 1890 is 1889, 1880 is 1881.
    Sources: 1870–1890   Mulhall, op. cit. p. 334.
                1900   Webb, op. cit. p. 353.
                1910   Statesman's, op. cit. 1912, p. xlviii.
                1913, 1928–1933 Moody's *Manual of Governments*, 1935, p. 1920.
                1920   Ibid. 1920, p. 34.
                1921   League of Nations, op. cit. 1927, p. 100.
                1922, 1923, 1927 Moody's *Manual of Industrials*, 1929, p. xix.
                1924–1926   Moody's *Manual of Governments*, 1930, p. 153.
                1934–1935   Statesman's, op. cit. 1937, p. xix.

4. INDUSTRIAL PRODUCTION: Explanation: Base for 1870–1927 is 1913 = 100; base for 1928–1935, 1928 = 100.
    Sources: 1870–1927   *Bulletin, Bureau de la Statistique Generale de la France*, 1928/1929, p. 106.
                1928–1935   Ibid. 1935/1936, p. 354.

5. EXPORTS:
    Sources: 1820–1910   Page, William, *Commerce and Industry*, London 1919, Vol. 2, pp. 71–73.
                1913–1925   Moody's, op. cit. 1926, p. 101.
                1926–1931   League of Nations, op. cit. 1935/1936, p. 218.
                1932–1935   Statesman's, op. cit. 1937, p. 57.

6. COMMODITY PRICES: Explanation: 1910–1914 = 100.
    Source: 1820–1934   Warren, George F. and Pearson, Frank A., *Gold and Prices*, New York, 1935, p. 87.

7. UNEMPLOYMENT: Explanation: Percent of trade unionists unemployed.
    Sources: 1860–1910   Webb, op. cit. pp. 610–612.
                1924–33   Moody's, op. cit. p. 1919, percentage unemployed of insured workers.
                1913–1923   Ibid. 1926, p. 101.

APPENDIX I–B

Evolution of British Security Capitalism, 1820–1935

National Finance

YEAR	NATIONAL DEBT (million pounds)	EXPENDITURES FOR DEBT SERVICE (million pounds)	EXPENDITURES FOR ARMAMENT (million pounds)	TOTAL EXPENDITURES (million pounds)	TOTAL REVENUES (million pounds)	DEBT SERVICE TO TOTAL EXPENDITURES (percent $9 \div 11$)	DEBT SERVICE TO NATIONAL INCOME (percent $9 \div 18$)	EXPENDITURES FOR ARMAMENT TO TOTAL EXPENDITURES (percent $10 \div 11$)	TOTAL EXPENDITURES TO NATIONAL INCOME (percent $11 \div 18$)
	8	9	10	11	12	13	14	15	16
1820	902	31	17	54	53	57.4		31.5	
1830	797	29	15	52	51	55.8		28.8	
1840	787	30	15	49	48	61.2		30.6	
1850	820	28	16	55	53	54.9		32.0	
1860	819	29	27	70	71	41.4	8.7	38.6	20.9
1870	800	27	24	68	74	40.3	6.1	35.3	15.3
1880	777	29	30	82	79	35.4	5.0	36.6	14.2
1890	698	25	33	86	89	29.1	3.7	38.4	12.9
1900	638	23	70	144	130	16.0	2.8	48.6	17.3
1910	754	22	63	158	131	13.9	2.6	39.9	18.9
1913	708	25	72	189	188	13.2	2.6	38.1	19.9
1920	7879	332	604	1666	1340	19.9	12.5	36.3	62.6
1921	7623	350	292	1195	1426	29.3	14.2	24.4	48.5
1922	7721	332	189	1079	1125	30.8	14.1	17.5	45.9
1923	7813	324	111	812	914	39.9	14.1	13.7	35.3
1924	7708	347	122	789	837	44.0	14.5	15.5	32.9
1925	7666	357	115	796	799	44.8	15.3	14.4	34.1
1926	7634	358	119	826	812	43.3	15.3	14.4	35.3
1927	7653	379	117	842	806	45.0	15.7	13.9	34.9
1928	7631	379	117	839	843	45.2	15.2	13.9	33.6
1929	7621	369	113	818	836	45.1	14.6	13.8	32.3
1930	7596	355	113	829	815	42.8	14.2	13.6	33.2
1931	7583	360	111	881	858	40.9	13.2	12.5	32.3
1932	7648	322	107	851	851	37.8	12.6	12.6	33.3
1933	7860	309	103	859	827	36.0	12.3	12.0	34.3
1934	8030	224	108	778	809	28.8		13.9	
1935	7902	224	114	797	805	28.1		14.3	

† 7700

Explanation and Sources

8. National Debt: Explanation: 1820 is the average of 1815–1820;
1850 is 1848; 1890 is 1889; 1900 is 1898; 1910 is 1909; 1913 is 1914.
Sources: 1820, 1850, 1870   Baxter, Robert Dudley, *National Debts*, London, 1871, pp. 76, 77.
     1830, 1840, 1860   Page, op. cit. Vol. 2, p. 44.
     1880   Mulhall, Michael George, *The Progress of the World*, London, 1880, p.41.
     1890   Mulhall, Michael George, *The Dictionary of Statistics*, p. 260.

	1900	Ibid. p. 699.
	1910	Webb, op. cit. p. 247.
	1913	Statesman's, op. cit. 1933, p. 30.
	1920	Moody's *Manual of Governments*, 1926, p. 104.
	1921–1923	Statesman's, op. cit. 1924, p. 41.
	1924–1925	Ibid. 1926, p. 36.
	1925–1932	Ibid. 1933, p. 38.
	1933–1935	Ibid. 1937, p. 40.

9. EXPENDITURES FOR DEBT SERVICE:

Sources:	1820–1910	Page, op. cit. Vol. 2, pp. 38–40.
	1913	Statesman's, op. cit. 1914, p. 44.
	1920–1923	Ibid. 1924, p. 41.
	1924–1925	Ibid. 1927, p. 38.
	1926–1928	Ibid. 1933, p. 38.
	1929–1933	Ibid. 1936, p. 38.
	1934–1935	Moody's, op. cit. 1935, p. 1926.

10. EXPENDITURES FOR ARMAMENT:

Sources:	1820–1913	Page, op. cit. Vol. 2, pp. 39–41.
	1920	Statesman's op. cit. 1921, p. 44.
	1921	Ibid. 1922, p. 46.
	1922	Ibid. 1923, p. 42.
	1923, 1924	Ibid. 1924, p. 37.
	1925	Ibid. 1926, p. 33.
	1926	Ibid. 1927, p. 35.
	1927	Ibid. 1928, p. 35.
	1928	Ibid. 1929, p. 35.
	1929	Ibid. 1930, p. 35.
	1930	Ibid. 1931, p. 35.
	1931	Ibid. 1932, p. 35.
	1932	Ibid. 1933, p. 35.
	1933	Ibid. 1934, p. 35.
	1934	Ibid. 1935, p. 35.
	1935	Ibid. 1936, p. 35.

11. TOTAL EXPENDITURES:

Sources:	1820–1913	Page, op. cit. Vol. 2, pp. 32–33.
	1920	Statesman's, op. cit. 1921, p. 41.
	1921–1926	Ibid. 1927, p. 32.
	1927, 1928	Statesman's, op. cit. 1929, p. 32 .
	1929–1931	Ibid. 1933, p. 32.
	1932–1935	Ibid. 1936, p. 32.

12. TOTAL REVENUES:

Sources:	1820–1913	Page, op. cit. Vol. 2, pp. 32–33.
	1920–1931	Moody's, op. cit. 1935, pp. 1925–1926.
	1932–1935	Statesman's, op. cit. 1936, p. 32.

FINANCE CAPITALISM

APPENDIX I-C

Evolution of British Security Capitalism, 1820–1935

Supply of and Demand for Capital

YEAR	NATIONAL WEALTH (million pounds)	NATIONAL INCOME (million pounds)	SAVING FUNDS (million pounds)	NEW SECURITIES (million pounds)	SAVING FUNDS TO NATIONAL INCOME (percent, 19÷18)	NEW SECURITIES TO SAVING FUNDS (percent, 20÷19)	NATIONAL DEBT TO NATIONAL WEALTH (percent, 8÷17)	GOVERNMENT BOND YIELDS (percent)	STOCK PRICES (1921 = 100)
	17	18	19	20	21	22	23	24	25
1820	2,600						34.7	4.42	
1830	3,750						21.3	3.49	
1840	4,100						19.2	3.35	
1850								3.11	
1860	6,113	335					13.4	3.19	
1870	8,548	445					9.4	3.24	
1880	10,037	577		84			7.7	3.05	
1890	9,400	669					7.4	2.85	
1900		833	187	166	22.4	88.8		2.76	
1910		838	221	192	26.4	86.9		3.08	
1913	14,310	951	256	197	26.9	77.0	4.9	3.39	
1920		2661	342	368	12.9	107.6		5.32	
1921		2462	357	389	14.5	109.0		5.21	100.0
1922		2353	366	574	15.6	156.8		4.43	113.2
1923		2303	376	271	16.3	72.1		4.31	112.8
1924		2401	387	209	16.1	54.0		4.39	117.5
1925		2337	396	232	16.9	58.6		4.43	116.5
1926		2337	394	231	16.9	58.6		4.55	118.0
1927		2416	399	355	16.5	89.0		4.56	122.8
1928		2494	409	369	16.4	90.2		4.47	127.3
1929		2531	409	285	16.2	69.7		4.60	121.0
1930	18,045	2497	423	268	16.9	63.4	42.0	4.46	114.4
1931		2725	432	102	15.9	23.6		4.53	98.5
1932		2554	460	189	18.0	41.1		3.74	109.4
1933		2505	498	245	19.8	49.2		3.39	117.6
1934			537	169		31.5		3.08	126.5
1935								2.91	126.4

Explanation and Sources

17. NATIONAL WEALTH: Explanation: 1820 is 1822; 1830 is 1833; 1860 is 1865; 1870 is 1875; 1880 is 1885; 1890 is 1888; 1913 is 1914.

Sources:

1820	Estimate by Lord Liverpool	in Mulhall, op. cit., p. 589
1830	Estimate by Pablo Pebrer	
1840	Estimate by Porter	
1860–1880	Estimate by Giffen	
1890	Estimate by Mulhall	

1913, 1930 Estimate by Josiah Stamp, *Journal of the Royal Statistical Society*, London, 1931, Vol. xciv, p. 20.

18. NATIONAL INCOME: Explanation: Prior to 1923, amount includes Irish Free State. Represents statutory income of taxpayers, after deductions of incomes of individuals below effective exemption limit.

Sources: 1857–1871 *Statistical Abstract for the United Kingdom*, Vol. 19, p. 15.
1880 Ibid., Vol. 42, p. 35.
1890 Ibid., Vol. 46, p. 36.
1900 Ibid., Vol. 60, p. 34.
1910 Ibid., Vol. 70, p. 143.
1913–1933 Ibid., Vol. 79, p. 195.

19. SAVING FUNDS: Explanation: Total of amount due to depositors at end of year from both Post Office and Trustee Savings Banks. The Post Office figures are supplied by the Postmaster and the Trustee figures by the Commissioner for the Reduction of the National Debt.

Sources: 1900–1934 Ibid., Vol. 79, pp. 244–249; Vol. 70, p. 187; Vol. 61, pp. 367–370.

20. NEW SECURITIES: Explanation: 1910 is 1908; 1880 represents yearly average from 1879 to 1882.

Sources: 1880 Mulhall, op. cit., p. 107.
1900, 1910 Webb, op. cit., p. 81.
1913–1934 *Economist*, Vol. 78, p. 88; Vol. 99, p. 659; Vol. 111, p. 634; Vol. 119, p. 642; Vol. 120, p. 376.

24. GOVERNMENT BOND YIELDS: Explanation: Average yield for year.

Sources: 1820–1933 Warren and Pearson, op. cit., p. 403 .
1934–1935 League of Nations, op. cit., 1935/1936, p. 261.

25. STOCK PRICES: Explanation: 1921 = 100.

Source: 1921–1935 *Banker's Insurance Manager's and Agents Magazine*, London, Vol. 141, p. 80.

FINANCE CAPITALISM

APPENDIX II–A

EVOLUTION OF FRENCH SECURITY CAPITALISM, 1820–1935

ECONOMIC TENDENCIES

	PRODUCTION				EXPORTS (million francs)	COMMODITY PRICES (1901–10 = 100)
YEAR	COAL (thousand tons)	PIG IRON (thousand tons)	STEEL (thousand tons)	INDUSTRIAL (1913 = 100)		
	1	2	3	4	5	6
1820	1,200	140				153
1830	1,990	220			573	130
1840	3,300	350			1,011	135
1850	4,400	570			1,435	111
1860	8,300	900			3,148	144
1870	13,300	1,180	84		3,456	133
1880	19,400	1,730	385		4,612	120
1890	24,600	1,720	530		4,840	100
1900	32,196	2,670	1529	66	5,522	99
1910	37,254	4,038	3450	89	8,105	108
1913	43,847	5,124	4614	100	9,260	116
1920	24,293	3,433	2706	62	36,625	589
1921	28,212	3,358	3098	55	25,244	399
1922	31,141	5,147	4464	78	27,217	378
1923	37,679	5,347	5302	88	41,554	484
1924	44,019	7,502	6906	109	57,170	565
1925	47,097	8,472	7330	108	62,010	636
1926	51,392	9,430	8386	126	77,967	812
1927	51,779	9,293	8306	110	57,254	713
1928	51,365	10,097	9387	127	54,429	716
1929	53,736	10,368	9696	139	52,751	706
1930	53,892	10,092	9396	140	43,502	615
1931	50,016	8,196	7812	124	30,879	523
1932	46,268	5,519	5604	96	20,035	461
1933	47,941	6,324	6485	107	18,772	440
1934	47,604	6,151	6194	99	17,850	415
1935	46,212	5,779	6216	94	15,473	393

EXPLANATION AND SOURCES

1. COAL PRODUCTION: Explanation: 1890 is 1889; 1830 is 1831.

Sources: 1820, 1840–1890   Mulhall, op. cit., p. 119.

1830   McCulloch, John Ramsay, *A Dictionary Geographical, Statistical and Historical*, London. 1862, Vol. 1, p. 858.

1900   Webb, op. cit. p. 86.

1910   Statesman's, op. cit. 1912, p. xlvii.

1913   Moody's *Manual of Governments*, 1931, p. 654.

1920   League of Nations, op. cit. 1926, p. 81.

1921–1925	Ibid. 1929, p. 103.
1926, 1928	Ibid. 1935/1936, p. 133.
1927	Moody's *Manual of Industrials*, 1932, p. xxiv.
1929–1933	Moody's *Manual of Governments*, 1935, p. 2447.
1934–1935	Statesman's, op. cit. 1936, p. xix.

2. PIG IRON PRODUCTION: Explanation: 1890 is 1889.

Sources:		
	1820–1890	Mulhall, op. cit. p. 332.
	1900	Webb, op. cit. p. 353.
	1910	Statesman's, op. cit. 1913, p. 802.
	1913, 1922–1924	Moody's *Manual of Industrials*, 1929, p. xix.
	1920–1921	League of Nations, op. cit. 1926, p. 86.
	1925, 1927, 1928	Moody's *Manual of Governments*, 1930, p. 619.
	1926	League of Nations, op. cit. 1935/1936, p. 144.
	1929–1932	Moody's, op. cit. 1935, p. 2447.
	1933–1935	Statesman's, op. cit. 1936, p. xviii.

3. STEEL PRODUCTION: Explanation: 1900 is 1899; 1890 is 1889.

Sources:		
	1870–1890	Mulhall, op. cit. p. 334.
	1900	Statesman's, op. cit. 1901, p. 564.
	1910	Ibid, 1912, p. xlviii.
	1913, 1929–1932	Moody's, op. cit. 1935, pp. 17, 2447.
	1920, 1921, 1923 1924, 1926, 1928	Ibid. 1930, p. 619.
	1922, 1925	Moody's *Manual of Industrials*, 1929, p. xix.
	1927	League of Nations, op. cit. 1935/1936, p. 145.
	1933–1935	Statesman's, op. cit. 1936, p. xviii.

4. INDUSTRIAL PRODUCTION: Explanation: 1913 = 100.

Sources:		
	1900–1929	*Annuaire Statistique de France*, 1929, p. 59*.
	1930–1934	Ibid. 1935, p. 72*.
	1935	Ibid. 1935, p. 73*.

5. EXPORTS: Explanation: In gold value.

Sources:		
	1830–1933	Ibid. 1935, pp. 124*, 125*.
	1934–1935	Statesman's, 1936, p. 893.

6. COMMODITY PRICES:

Sources:		
	1820–1933	*Annuaire Statistique de France*, 1933, pp. 441*–443*.
	1934–1935	Ibid. 1935, p. 441*.

7. UNEMPLOYMENT: This item is omitted since figures are unavailable for France, but the number of the column is included in order to retain uniformity with Appendices I and III.

APPENDIX II–B

Evolution of French Security Capitalism, 1820–1935

National Finance

YEAR	NATIONAL DEBT (million francs)	EXPENDITURES FOR DEBT SERVICE (million francs)	EXPENDITURES FOR ARMAMENT (million francs)	TOTAL EXPENDITURES (million francs)	TOTAL REVENUES (million francs)	DEBT SERVICE TO TOTAL EXPENDITURES (percent, 9÷11)	DEBT SERVICE TO NATIONAL INCOME (percent, 9÷18)	EXPENDITURES FOR ARMAMENT TO TOTAL EXPENDITURES (percent, 10÷11)	TOTAL EXPENDITURES TO NATIONAL INCOME (percent, 11÷18)
	8	9	10	11	12	13	14	15	16
1820	3,590	298		907	939	32.9			
1830	4,890	274		1,095	1,020	25.0			
1840	4,682	336		1,364	1,234	24.6			
1850	5,426	387	344	1,473	1,432	26.3		23.4	
1860	10,262	560		2,084	1,962	26.9			
1870	12,310	512	536	3,173	3,124	16.1		16.9	
1880	21,842	1,222	781	3,365	3,531	36.3		23.2	
1890	29,547	1,271	910	3,288	3,376	38.7	4.4	27.7	11.3
1900	30,428	1,240	972	3,747	3,815	33.1	4.8	25.9	14.4
1910	32,995	1,257	1,300	4,322	4,274	29.1		30.1	
1913	33,220	1,284	1,450	5,067	5,092	25.3	3.6	28.6	14.1
1920	240,242	15,098	5,005	30,688	22,505	49.2	13.7	16.3	27.9
1921	297,368	15,892	5,822	32,846	23,570	48.4	13.8	17.7	28.6
1922	316,984	18,169	5,027	35,187	35,426	51.6	15.3	14.3	29.6
1923	367,121	19,121	4,735	38,293	26,487	49.9	14.3	12.4	28.6
1924	409,708	20,155	4,510	30,921	30,568	65.2	13.0	14.6	19.9
1925	418,075	19,481	5,169	36,275	34,768	53.7	11.3	14.2	21.1
1926	488,915	23,729	5,729	41,976	43,064	56.5	11.4	13.6	20.2
1927	468,354	23,148	7,215	39,382	39,960	58.8	11.0	18.3	18.8
1928	479,587	22,908	8,482	42,445	42,497	54.0	10.1	20.0	18.7
1929	470,065	22,304	8,357	45,366	45,431	49.2	9.1	18.4	18.5
1930	480,173	22,654	10,970	50,398	50,465	45.0	9.3	21.8	20.7
1931	480,540	23,041	11,400	50,641	50,643	45.5	10.1	22.5	22.2
1932	481,115	23,660	9,456	41,083	41,087	57.6	11.5	23.0	19.9
1933	472,858	25,073	10,789	50,487	45,646	49.7	12.6	21.4	25.4
1934	486,278	27,323	10,803	50,163	48,281	54.5	15.4	21.5	28.2
1935	519,179		10,009	47,817	46,992			20.9	

†486

8. NATIONAL DEBT: Explanation: Total of interior debt (less debt Viegère), floating debt and external debt.

Source: 1820–1935 *Annuaire Statistique de France*, 1935, pp. 201*–202*.

9. EXPENDITURES FOR DEBT SERVICE:

Source: 1820–1924 Ibid. 1935, pp. 201*–202*.

10. EXPENDITURES FOR ARMAMENT: Explanation: 1850 is 1848; 1870–1880 includes expenditure for colonies. This item, however, was not very significant.

Sources: 1850   McCulloch, op. cit. Vol. I, p. 866.
      1870–1935 Statesman's, op. cit. cited in issue of following year.

11. TOTAL EXPENDITURES: Explanation: Expenditure for 1932, April 1st to December 31st. Prior to 1930 the financial year ran from April 1st, but in October 1931 it was reverted to the calendar year, therefore all budget estimates relate to the period from April 1st, 1932 to December 31st, 1932.

Sources: 1820–1926 *Annuaire Statistique de France*, 1935, pp. 203*–204*.
      1927–1932 Statesman's, op. cit. 1932, p. 858.
      1933–1935 Ibid. 1936, p. 885.

12. TOTAL REVENUES:

Sources: 1820–1926 *Annuaire Statistique de France*, op. cit. pp. 203*–204*.
      1927–1932 Statesman's, op. cit. 1932, p. 858.
      1933–1935 Ibid. 1936, p. 885.

APPENDIX II—C

Evolution of French Security Capitalism, 1820–1935

Supply of and Demand for Capital

YEAR	NATIONAL WEALTH (billion francs)	NATIONAL INCOME (billion francs)	SAVING FUNDS (billion francs)	NEW SECURITIES (billion francs)	SAVING FUNDS TO NATIONAL INCOME (percent, 19÷18)	NEW SECURITIES TO SAVING FUNDS (percent, 20÷19)	NATIONAL DEBT TO NATIONAL WEALTH (percent, 8÷17)	GOVERNMENT BOND YIELDS (percent)	STOCK PRICES (1905=100)
	17	18	19	20	21	22	23	24	25
1820	120						3.0		
1830								4.30	
1840			.2					3.90	
1850	125		.1					5.30	
1860	175		.4				5.9	4.30	56
1870	195		.6				6.3	4.80	59
1880	216		1.3				10.1	3.60	87
1890	243	29	3.0		11.4		12.2	3.30	96
1900	230	26	4.3		16.5		13.2	3.00	108
1910	287		5.6				11.5	3.10	118
1913	304	36	5.8		16.1		10.9	3.40	139
1920		110	8.1	11.8	7.3	145.7		5.30	208
1921		115	9.6	10.2	8.3	106.3		5.30	176
1922		119	10.8	14.2	9.1	131.5		5.10	176
1923		134	11.5	10.8	8.6	93.9		5.30	259
1924	797	155	12.0	6.5	7.7	54.2	51.4	5.75	314
1925		172	13.8	3.6	8.0	26.1		6.48	370
1926		208	15.7	4.6	7.5	29.3		6.17	444
1927		210	21.3	7.2	10.1	33.8		5.32	537
1928	1276	227	27.0	10.0	11.9	37.0	37.6	4.46	741
1929		245	32.0	14.4	13.1	45.0		3.98	965
1930		243	38.6	23.0	15.9	59.6		3.44	878
1931		228	50.9	16.3	22.3	32.0		3.48	656
1932		206	57.3	6.1	27.8	10.6		3.84	600
1933		199	59.5	3.9	29.9	6.6		4.38	
1934		178	60.7	4.7	34.1	7.7		4.14	
1935			62.8					3.88	

17. NATIONAL WEALTH: Explanation: 1913 is 1914; 1890 is 1892; 1910 is 1908.

Sources:	1850	Charguerant, A., *L'Economie Politique et L'Impot*, Paris, 1864, p. 47.
	1890	Théry, Edmond, *La Fortune Publique de la France*, Paris, 1911, p. 247.
	1910	Estimate by Théry, in Moulton, Harold G. and Lewis, C., *The French Debt Problem*, New York. 1925, p. 425.
	1913	Théry, Edmond, *Consequences Economiques de la Guerre pour la France*, Paris. 1922, p. 337.
	1924	Statesman's, op. cit. 1925, p. 882.
	1928	Dresdner Bank, *The Economic Forces of the World*, Berlin, 1930, p. 177.

18. NATIONAL INCOME.

Sources:	1890, 1900	Moulton and Lewis, op. cit. p. 425.
	1913–1932	*Revue d'Economie Politique*, 1933, Vol. 47, p. 659.
	1933–1934	League of Nations *World Economic Survey*, 1934/1935, p. 140.

19. SAVING FUNDS: Explanation: Represents savings deposits.

Sources:	1840–1910	*Annuaire Statistique de France*,1935, pp.3*, 186*.
	1913–1923	League of Nations, *Statistical Year Book*, 1926, p. 162.
	1924–1926	Ibid. 1932/1933, p. 243.
	1926–1935	Ibid. 1935/1936, p. 277.

20. NEW SECURITIES:

| Source: | 1920–1934 | *Bulletin, Bureau de la Statistique Générale de la France*, April–June, 1935, p. 430. |

24. GOVERNMENT BOND YIELDS: Explanation: Based upon Perpetual 3 percent rentes.

Sources:	1830–1923	*Journal de la Société de Statistiques de Paris*, May 1928, pp. 166–167.
	1924–1925	League of Nations, op. cit. 1932/1933, p. 250.
	1926–1935	Ibid. 1935/1936, p. 261.

25. STOCK PRICES: Explanation: 1905 = 100.

| Source: | 1860–1932 | *Bulletin, Bureau de la Statistique Générale de la France*, July–September 1934, p. 759. |

APPENDIX III–A

EVOLUTION OF GERMAN SECURITY CAPITALISM, 1870–1935
ECONOMIC TENDENCIES

| YEAR | PRODUCTION | | | | EXPORTS (million marks) | COMMODITY PRICES (1901–10 =100) | UNEMPLOY-MENT (percent unem-ployed) |
	COAL (thousand tons)	PIG IRON (thousand tons)	STEEL (thousand tons)	INDUSTRIAL (1913= 100)			
	1	2	3	4	5	6	7
1870	29,373	1,390	126	12	3,528		
1880	46,974	2,730	660	19	2,803	110	
1890	70,238	4,530	1,860	32	4,146	102	
1900	109,290	5,790	2,160	51	5,766	100	
1910	152,828	14,556	13,479	78	8,934	103	
1913	190,109	19,000	18,631	100	10,770	113	
1920	131,356	6,388	8,204	62	3,929	1,686	4.1
1921	136,227	6,096	8,700	78	5,732	2,169	1.6
1922	130,003	8,000	9,000	89	6,290	38,799	2.8
1923	62,225	4,400	5,900	56	6,150		28.2
1924	118,829	8,200	8,500	80	9,084	155	8.1
1925	132,729	10,018	12,004	94	12,362	160	19.4
1926	145,296	9,493	12,150	90	10,001	152	16.7
1927	153,599	13,089	15,937	117	14,228	155	12.9
1928	150,861	11,804	14,167	109	14,001	158	16.7
1929	163,441	13,240	15,863	110	13,447	155	13.1
1930	142,669	9,698	11,245	91	10,393	141	22.2
1931	118,640	5,964	8,136	75	6,727	125	33.7
1932	104,740	3,871	5,678	67	4,667	109	43.7
1933	109,692	5,125	7,430	75	4,204	105	24.7
1934	124,860	10,543	13,680	94	4,451	111	15.2
1935	143,016	12,800	16,175		4,269		

EXPLANATION AND SOURCES

1. COAL PRODUCTION: Explanation: Only anthracite and not lignite. 1870 is 1871; 1920–1934 excludes Alsace and Saar; 1935 includes Saar.

    Sources: 1870–1910   *Annuaire Statistique de France*, 1926, p. 268*.

                1921   Statesman's op. cit. 1924, p. 946.

                1913, 1922–1924   Ibid. 1925, p. xix.

                1920, 1925   League of Nations, *Statistical Year Book*, 1926, p. 81.

                1926–1932   Moody's *Manual of Governments*, 1935, p. 248.[8]

                1933   Statesman's, op. cit. 1935, p. xix.

                1934–1935   Ibid. 1936, p. xix.

2. PIG IRON PRODUCTION: Explanation: 1890 is 1889; 1895 is 1900.

    Sources: 1870–1900   Mulhall, op. cit., pp. 332, 757.

                1910   Statesman's, op. cit. 1912, p. xlviii.

1913, 1922–1924	Ibid. 1925, p. xix.
1920–1921	Ibid. 1924, pp. xix, 946.
1925–1926	Ibid. 1927, p. xxi.
1927–1930	Moody's, op. cit. 1935, p. 2488.
1931–1932	Statesman's, op. cit. 1934, p. xviii.
1933–1935	Ibid. 1936, p. xviii.

3. STEEL PRODUCTION: Explanation: 1895 is 1900.

Sources:	1870–1900	Mulhall, op. cit., pp. 334, 757.
	1910	Statesman's, op. cit. 1912, p. xlviii.
	1913, 1922–1924	Ibid. 1925, p. xix.
	1920–1921	Ibid. 1924, pp. xix, 946.
	1925–1926	Ibid. 1927, p. xxi.
	1927–1930	Moody's, op. cit. 1935, p. 2488.
	1931–1932	Statesman's, op. cit. 1934, p. xviii.
	1933–1935	Ibid. 1936, p. xviii.

4. GENERAL PRODUCTION: Explanation: 1913 = 100; 1932–1935 figures were shifted from 1928 base to 1913 base by author.

Sources:	1870–1927	*Bulletin, Bureau de la Statistique Générale de la France,* 1928/1929, p. 104.
	1928–1934	*Annuaire Statistique de France,* 1934, pp. 333*–334*.
	1935	*Bulletin, Bureau de la Statistique Générale de la France,* Supplement, September 1936, p. 16.

5. EXPORTS: Explanation: 1870 is 1875; 1920–1923 in gold marks.

Sources:	1870–1934	*Annuaire Statistique de France,* 1934, p. 430.*
	1935	Statesman's, op. cit. 1936, p. 969.

6. COMMODITY PRICES: Explanation: 1901–1910 = 100. 1923 unavailable.

Sources:	1880–1934	*Annuaire Statistique de France,* 1934, p. 441*.

7. UNEMPLOYMENT: Explanation: Number seeking employment. 1934 —first nine months only.

Sources:	1920–1921	League of Nations, op. cit. 1926, p. 34.
	1922–1928	Ibid. 1929, p. 44.
	1929–1934	Ibid. 1935/1936, p. 62.

APPENDIX III–B

Evolution of German Security Capitalism, 1870–1935

National Finance

YEAR	NATIONAL DEBT (million marks)	EXPENDITURES FOR DEBT SERVICE (million marks)	EXPENDITURES FOR ARMAMENT (million marks)	TOTAL EXPENDITURES (million marks)	TOTAL REVENUES (million marks)	DEBT SERVICE TO TOTAL EXPENDITURES (percent, $9 \div 11$)	DEBT SERVICE TO NATIONAL INCOME (percent, $9 \div 18$)	EXPENDITURES FOR ARMAMENT TO TOTAL EXPENDITURES (percent, $10 \div 11$)	TOTAL EXPENDITURES TO NATIONAL INCOME (percent, $11 \div 18$)
	8	9	10	11	12	13	14	15	16
1870	397								
1880	377	8	410	550	530	1.5		74.5	
1890	1,241	54	317	1,354	1,253	4.0	.3	23.4	6.3
1900	2,418	78	828	2,197	2,097	3.6	.3	37.7	8.8
1910	5,013	874	1260	3,024	2,943	28.9	2.9	41.7	10.1
1913	4,926	943	1960	3,521	3,384	25.8	2.1	55.7	8.0
1924	2,895	256	462	7,197	8,099	3.6	.9	6.4	24.0
1925	2,413	242	549	7,874	8,053	3.1	.4	7.0	13.1
1926	4,017	115	690	8,543	8,801	1.3	.2	8.1	13.6
1927	7,984	344	702	9,679	9,840	3.6	.5	7.3	13.7
1928	7,891	607	704	9,671	9,675	6.3	.8	7.3	12.8
1929	8,972	607	725	11,846	10,608	5.1	.8	6.1	15.6
1930	10,375	982	725	11,353	10,641	8.6	1.4	6.4	16.2
1931	12,090	982	716	11,740	10,646	8.4	1.7	6.1	20.4
1932	12,137	928	681	9,555	8,953	9.7	2.0	7.1	21.1
1933	12,331	917	671	8,219	8,219	11.2	2.0	8.2	17.7
1934	12,407	574	1004	8,232	6,024	7.0	1.1	12.2	15.7
1935	12,526	576	1130						

EXPLANATION AND SOURCES

8. **NATIONAL DEBT:**

Sources: 1870–1933   *Annuaire Statistique de France*, 1934, p. 486*.

1934–1935   Statesman's, op. cit. 1936, p. 964.

9. **EXPENDITURES FOR DEBT SERVICE:**

Sources: 1880   Ibid. 1881, p. 99.

1890   Ibid. 1891, p. 535.

1900   Ibid. 1901, p. 626.

1910–1913   *Annuaire Statistique de France*, 1934, p. 486*.

1924   Statesman's, op. cit. 1925, p. 953.

1925   Ibid. 1926, p. 926.

1926–1933   *Annuaire Statistique de France*, 1934, p. 486.

1934   Moody's, op. cit. 1935, p. 2491.

1935   Statesman's, op. cit. 1936, p. 963.

10. **EXPENDITURES FOR ARMAMENT:**

Source: 1880–1935   Statesman's, op. cit. cited in issue of following year.

11. **TOTAL EXPENDITURES:**

Source: 1880–1933   *Annuaire Statistique de France*, 1934, p. 489*.

1934   Statesman's, op. cit. 1937, p. 976.

12. **TOTAL REVENUES:**

Sources: 1880–1933   *Annuaire Statistique de France*, 1934, p. 489*.

1934   Statesman's, op. cit. 1937, p. 976.

8–12: Explanation: Because of the currency inflation, computations for the years 1920 through 1923 were omitted.

APPENDIX III–C

EVOLUTION OF GERMAN SECURITY CAPITALISM, 1870–1935

SUPPLY OF AND DEMAND FOR CAPITAL

YEAR	NATIONAL WEALTH (billion marks)	NATIONAL INCOME (billion marks)	SAVING FUNDS (billion marks)	NEW SECURITIES (billion marks)	SAVING FUNDS TO NATIONAL INCOME (percent, 19÷18)	NEW SECURITIES TO SAVING FUNDS (percent, 20÷19)	NATIONAL DEBT TO NATIONAL WEALTH (percent, 8÷17)	GOVERNMENT BOND YIELDS (percent)	STOCK PRICES (1913=100)
	17	18	19	20	21	22	23	24	25
1870			.5						
1880			1.6					4.00	
1890	200	21.5	3.3		15.3		.6	3.48	
1900	200	25.0	8.9		35.6		1.2	3.65	
1910	330	30.0	16.8	2.8	56.0	16.7	1.5	3.68	
1913	331	44.0	19.7	2.7	44.8	13.7	1.5		100
1924	150	30.0	0.6	.6	2.0	100.0	1.9		26
1925		60.0	1.7	1.7	2.8	100.0			
1926		62.7	3.2	4.6	5.1	143.8		7.98	
1927		70.8	4.8	4.3	6.8	89.6		7.32	158
1928	350	75.4	7.2	4.2	9.5	58.3		7.91	148
1929		75.9	9.3	2.7	12.3	29.0		8.28	134
1930		70.2	10.8	3.5	15.4	32.4		8.02	109
1931		57.5	10.1	2.0	17.6	19.8		7.95	85.
1932		45.3	10.2	1.0	22.5	9.8		8.72	54
1933		46.4	10.8	1.5	23.3	13.9		7.19	67
1934		52.5		1.0				6.49	77
1935								4.86	

Explanation and Sources

17. NATIONAL WEALTH: Explanation: 1890 is 1895; 1910 is 1907.
    Sources: In *Finanz-Archiv Zeitschrift für das gesammte Finanzwesen*, Stuttgart, Germany, 1928, p. 65:

1890–1900	Estimate of Schmoller.
1910	Estimate of Steinman-Bucher
1913	Estimate of Ballad.
1924	Estimate of Helfferich.
1928	*Economic Forces of the World*, op. cit. p. 177.

18. NATIONAL INCOME: Explanation: 1890 is 1895; 1910 is 1907; 1920 is 1919.

    Sources:

1890	Estimate of Helfferich	
1900	Estimate of Schmoller	
1910	Estimate of Reichsschatzent	Ibid.
1913, 1923	Estimate of Banker's Trust Co.	p. 66
1924	Estimate of Mundestens-Shirras	

1925–1926	*Europa Encyclopedia*, Vol. I, p. D536.
1927–1928, 1930	Moody's, op. cit. 1936, p. 2520.
1929, 1931–1933	Ibid. 1937, p. 2711.
1934	League of Nations, *World Economic Survey*, 1934–1935, p. 140.

19. SAVING FUNDS:
    Source: 1870–1933   *Annuaire Statistique de France*, 1934, p. 477*.

20. NEW SECURITIES:
    Sources:

1910	*Statistisches Jahrbuch für das Deutsche Reich*, 1913, p. 274.
1913	Ibid. 1920, p. 122.
1920–1921	Ibid. 1921–1922, p. 279.
1924–1931	League of Nations, *Statistical Year Book*, 1932–1933, p. 248.
1932–1934	Ibid. 1934–1935, p. 252.

24. GOVERNMENT BOND YIELDS:
    Sources:

1880–1910	National Monetary Commission, *Statistics for the United States*, 1869–1909, Washington, 1910. Dresdner Bank, *Germany's Economic Forces*, Berlin, 1913, p. 287.
1926–1934	League of Nations, op. cit. 1935–1936, p. 260.

25. STOCK PRICES:
    Explanation: 1913–1924   1913 = 100.
             1927–1934   Base 1924–1926 = 100.
    Sources:

1913–1924	*Statistisches Jahrbuch*, op. cit. 1924/1925, p. 322.
1927–1934	Ibid. 1935, p. 370.

APPENDIX IV

Evolution of World Capitalism, 1820–1935
Economic and Social Tendencies

YEAR	PRODUCTION				TRADE (million pounds sterling)	COMMODITY PRICES	EMPLOYMENT (percent, 1929 = 100)	POPULATION (million people)
	COAL (thousand tons	PIG IRON (thousand tons)	STEEL (thousand tons)	RAW MATERIAL (million dollars)				
	1	2	3	4	5	6	7	8
1820	17,200	1,010			341	131		732
1830		1,585			407	93		847
1840	44,800	2,680			573	108		1,009
1850	81,400	4,422	71	3,296	832	75		1,135
1860	142,300	7,180		7,187	1,489	90		1,288
1870	213,400	11,910	540	9,606	2,191	89		1,391
1880	340,000	16,140	4,255	13,645	3,033			1,456
1890	485,000	25,160	10,250	16,603	3,377			1,483
1900	771,100			23,991	5,500			1,512
1910	1,000,000	60,000	51,500	31,860	6,269			1,610
1913	1,216,097	77,714	74,687	35,449	7,331			1,657
1920		60,636	68,321	35,142	15,769			
1921		34,700	42,487	31,369	9,238			
1922	1,034,006	51,938	63,098	36,057	8,816			
1923	1,180,124	64,580	72,573	38,241				
1924	1,168,535	66,801	77,300	38,731	12,510			
1925	1,361,000	75,670	89,202	42,187	12,785			1,800
1926	1,365,000	77,573	91,898	41,319	12,739			1,895
1927	1,475,000	85,590	100,876	43,497	13,382			1,848
1928	1,444,000	87,070	107,477	45,942	13,709	100		1,962
1929	1,560,000	96,729	117,980	47,200	14,097	93.3	100	1,991
1930	1,414,000	78,360	93,057	44,799	11,416	71.7	164	2,013
1931	1,258,000	54,842	68,119	41,729	8,756	52.4	235	2,025
1932	1,124,000	39,244	49,836	39,957	7,664	42.5	291	2,042
1933	1,154,000	49,294	68,318	39,849	7,310	39.4	274	2,058
1934	1,102,000	62,250	80,880		7,774	36.8	221	2,100
1935	1,134,000	73,480	99,000		8,095	38.6	193	2,077

Explanation and Sources

1. Coal Production: Explanation: 1890 is 1889; 1910 is 1907.

    Sources:

1820, 1840–1890	Mulhall, op. cit., p. 119.
1900	Bukharin, Nicolai, *Imperialism and World Economy*, New York, 1929, p. 31.
1910	Webb, op. cit. p. 87.
1913, 1922–1924	Statesman's, op. cit. 1925, p. xix.
1925–1928	Moody's *Manual of Industrials*, 1929, p. xxi.
1929–1933	Ibid. 1934, p. a–10.
1934–1935	League of Nations, op. cit. 1935/1936, p. 133.

2. PIG IRON PRODUCTION: Explanation: 1890 is 1889; 1910 is 1907.

Sources:	1820–1890	Mulhall, op. cit. p. 332.
	1910	Webb, op. cit. p. 353.
	1913	Moody's, op. cit. p. a-32.
	1920	Statesman's, op. cit. 1922, p. xx.
	1921–1923	Ibid. 1924, p. xix.
	1924	Moody's, op. cit., 1933, p. a–96.
	1925–1931	Moody's, op. cit. p. a–32.
	1932–1934	Statesman's, op. cit. 1935, p. xviii.
	1935	League of Nations, op. cit. 1935/1936, p. 144.

3. STEEL PRODUCTION: Explanation: 1910 is 1907; 1890 is 1889; 1880 is 1881.

Sources:	1870–1890	Mulhall, op. cit. p. 334.
	1910	Webb, op. cit. p. 353.
	1913, 1925–1931	Moody's, op. cit. 1934, p. a–32.
	1920	Statesman's, op. cit. 1922, p. xx.
	1921–1923	Ibid. 1924, p. xix.
	1924	Moody's, op. cit. 1933, p. a–96.
	1925–31	Moody, op. cit. 1934, p. a–34.
	1932–1934	Statesman's, op. cit. 1935, p. xviii.
	1935	League of Nations, op. cit. 1935/1936, p. 145.

4. RAW MATERIAL PRODUCTION: Explanation: Excludes Russian production.

Source: Federal Reserve Bank of New York, Reports Department, Chart 2577, January 6, 1934.

5. TRADE: Explanation: 1890 is 1889; 1900 is yearly average of 1902–1906; 1913 is 1912; 1924–1928, converted from United States dollars into English pounds sterling, using average yearly rate of exchange for respective years as given in the *Federal Reserve Bulletin* for 1929, Vol. 15, p. 35; and for 1936, Vol. 22, p. 45.

Sources:	1820–1890	Mulhall, op. cit. p. 128.
	1900	Webb, op. cit. p. 94.
	1910–1922	National Association of Merchants and Manufacturers, London, *World Trade and the Standard of Living in Europe.* London, 1923, p. 2.
	1924–1925	League of Nations, *Memorandum on International Trade and Balance of Payments,* 1911–1925, p. 133.
	1926–1928	Ibid. 1926–1928, p. 17.
	1929–1934	League of Nations, *World Economic Survey,* 1934–1935, p. 157.
	1935	Ibid. 1935/1936, p. 158.

6. COMMODITY PRICES: Explanation: 1820 is 1819; 1830 is 1829; 1840 is 1839; 1850 is 1849; 1860 is 1859; 1870 is 1869.

Sources:	1820–1870	Mulhall, op. cit. p. 491. The base for these years is 1789 = 100.
	1928–1935	*Annalist*, September 18, 1936, p. 389. The base for these years is 1928 = 100.

7. EMPLOYMENT: Explanation: 1919 = 100

    Source: 1929–1935   League of Nations, *Statistical Year Book*, 1935/1936, p. 75.

8. POPULATION: Explanation: 1820 is 1822; 1830 is 1828; 1840 is 1845; 1850 is 1854; 1860 is 1859; 1870 is 1874; 1890 is 1886; 1900 is 1903; 1913 is 1914.

    Sources:

1820–1840, 1870, 1890	Mulhall, op. cit. p. 442.
1850, 1860, 1880, 1900	Australia, *Census and Statistics Office*, Vol. I, Appendix A, Census of 1911, p. 30.
1910	Webb, op. cit. p. 467.
1913	Bukharin, op. cit. p. 86.
1925	*Annuaire Statistique de France*, 1926, p.181*.
1926	*Journal des Economistes*, January, 1929, p. 16.
1927	League of Nations, *Memorandum on Production and Trade*, 1913 and 1923–1927, p. 12.
1928	Ibid. 1923 and 1928/1929, p. 12.
1929	Ibid. 1925 and 1929/1930, p. 12.
1930	League of Nations, *Statistical Year Book*, 1931/1932, p. 23.
1931	Ibid. 1932/1933, p. 23.
1932	Ibid. 1933/1934, p. 23.
1933	Ibid. 1934/1935, p. 23.
1934	*Annuaire Statistique de France*, 1934, p.229*.
1935	League of Nations, op. cit. 1935/1936, p. 24.

APPENDIX V

National Debts of Leading Countries, 1870–1935

(Percent, 1870 = 100)

YEAR	BELGIUM	FRANCE[b]	GERMANY [b]	ITALY	NETHER-LANDS[g]	RUSSIA	UNITED KINGDOM[b]	UNITED STATES[b]
1870	100.0	100.0	100.0	100.0[e]	100.0	100.0	100.0	100.0
1880	208.3	163.1	95.0	154.2[f]	98.7	132.1[h]	97.1	83.8
1890	295.5	194.1	312.6	195.4	114.7	246.5[i]	87.3	46.1
1900	396.6	206.9	609.1	212.2	119.7	334.0	79.8	37.7
1910	562.2	223.7	1262.7	206.6	115.9	487.1	94.3	18.8
1920	3356.5	1633.2	(d)	1176.9	266.0	1742.2[j]	984.9	997.9
1930	7722.1	3264.3	2613.4	1419.8	246.5	173.7	949.5	648.7
1935	8079.1[a]	3305.8[c]	3169.4	1691.6[g]	275.0	544.2[k]	987.8	1325.6

Explanation and Sources of Absolute Figures on Which Above Percentages are Based

Sources:

General Source: *Annuaire Statistique de France*, 1933, pp. 489*, 490*.
Ibid. 1935, p. 485*.

Individual Sources:

(a) *Statesman's Year Book*, 1936, p. 707, 1061.
(b) See Appendix for each country.
(c) 1935 is 1934.
(d) Not given because of currency instability.
(e) Statesman's, op. cit. 1872, p. 311, converted into lire from English pound sterling by author.
(f) Ibid. 1881, p. 310, January 1, 1879.
(g) Ibid. 1871, p. 333; 1881, p. 332; 1891, p. 759; 1901, p. 866; 1911, p. 1038; 1921, p. 1103; 1931, p. 1118; 1936, p. 1157.
(h) 1880 is September 1, 1878. Statesman's, op. cit. 1881, p. 377.
(i) Ibid. 1891, p. 863.
(j) 1920 is September 1, 1917. Statesman's, op. cit. 1936, p. 1271.
(k) Internal debt June 1, 1933. Statesman's, op. cit. 1936, p. 1272.

APPENDIX VI–A

Evolution of American Security Capitalism, 1906–1935

Economic Tendencies (Agriculture and Industry)

	AGRICULTURE			INDUSTRY						
YEAR	PRICES RECEIVED BY FARMERS (percent)	PRICES PAID BY FARMERS (percent)	PRICES RECEIVED TO PRICES PAID (percent)	INDUSTRIAL PRODUCTION (percent)	AUTOMOBILE PRODUCTION (thousand cars)	STEEL INGOT PRODUCTION (billion gross tons)	COAL PRODUCTION (percent)	CRUDE PETROLEUM PRODUCTION (million barrels)	BUILDING CONTRACTS (percent)	CONSTRUCTION COSTS (percent)
	1	2	3	4	5	6	7	8	9	10
1906				52.7	34	23.4	59.2	126.5		
1907				52.6	44	23.4	68.2	166.1		
1908				35.4	65	14.0	57.2	178.5		
1909				53.6	131	24.0	65.5	183.2		
1910	102	98	104	55.8	187	26.1	72.1	209.6		
1911	95	101	94	50.7	210	23.6	70.3	220.4		
1912	100	100	100	62.8	378	31.3	77.6	222.9		
1913	101	101	100	64.8	485	31.3	83.4	248.4		100
1914	101	100	101	52.1	569	23.5	73.5	265.8		88.6
1915	98	105	93	66.2	970	32.2	77.2	281.1		92.6
1916	118	124	95	85.0	1618	42.8	87.6	300.8		129.6
1917	175	149	117	86.8	1874	45.1	96.4	335.3		181.2
1918	202	176	115	82.2	1171	44.5	100.8	355.9		189.2
1919	213	202	105	71.7	1934	34.7	80.7	378.4	76.1	198.4
1920	211	201	105	80.1	2227	42.1	98.8	442.9	56.1	251.3
1921	125	152	82	57.3	1682	19.8	72.7	472.2	52.9	201.8
1922	132	149	89	77.9	2646	35.6	74.1	557.5	79.0	174.5
1923	142	152	93	92.9	4180	44.9	98.8	732.4	81.3	214.1
1924	143	152	94	87.1	3738	37.9	84.4	713.9	83.4	215.4
1925	156	157	99	95.7	4428	45.4	90.7	763.7	106.6	206.7
1926	145	155	94	100.0	4506	48.3	100.0	770.9	100.0	208.0
1927	139	153	91	97.2	3580	44.9	90.2	901.1	96.3	206.3
1928	149	155	96	101.0	4601	51.5	87.5	901.5	109.9	206.8
1929	146	153	95	108.1	5622	56.4	92.9	1007.5	89.6	207.0
1930	126	145	87	86.2	3510	40.7	80.7	898.0	57.7	202.9
1931	87	124	70	70.2	2472	25.9	66.9	850.3	41.2	181.4
1932	65	107	61	54.0	1431	13.7	53.6	785.2	17.5	157.4
1933	70	109	64	61.2	1986	23.2	58.4	898.9	16.5	170.2
1934	90	123	74	63.7	2870	26.1	62.9	908.1	17.1	198.1
1935	108	125	86	72.8	4120	34.1	64.3	993.9	28.0	195.2

Explanation and Sources

1. PRICES RECEIVED BY FARMERS: Explanation: 1910–1914 = 100.
   Sources: 1910–1919   United States Bureau of Agricultural Eco-
                             nomics, *The Agricultural Situation*, De-
                             cember, 1935, p. 23.
                 1920–1936   Ibid. December 1, 1937, p. 24.

2. PRICES PAID BY FARMERS: Explanation: 1910–1914 = 100.
   Sources: 1910–1919   Ibid. December, 1935, p. 23.
                 1920–1936   Ibid. December 1, 1937, p. 24.

4. INDUSTRIAL PRODUCTION: Explanation: 1926 = 100.
   Source: 1906–1935   Standard Statistics, *Trade and Industries*,
                             Vol. 3, p. D–25.

5. AUTOMOBILE PRODUCTION:
   Source: 1906–1935   *Statistical Abstract*, 1936, p. 363.

6. STEEL INGOT PRODUCTION:
   Sources: 1906–1909   Ibid. 1925, p. 719.
                 1910–1935   Ibid. 1936, p. 701.

7. COAL PRODUCTION: Explanation: 1926 = 100.
   Source: Ibid. 1936, p. 716.

8. CRUDE PETROLEUM PRODUCTION:
   Source: Ibid. 1936, p. 723.

9. BUILDING CONTRACTS: Explanation: Statistics for 37 states not compiled prior to 1925.   1926 = 100.
   Sources: 1913–1925   *Statistical Abstract*, 1925, p. 810.
                             Includes 27 northern and eastern states.
                 1926–1935   Ibid. 1936, p. 807, includes 37 states.

10. CONSTRUCTION COSTS: Explanation: Statistics for 37 states not com-
    piled prior to 1925.   1913 = 100.
    Sources: 1913–1925   Ibid.
                 1926–1935   Ibid.

APPENDIX VI–B

Evolution of American Security Capitalism—Economic Tendencies—
(Export Trade, Commodity Prices and Labor) 1906–1935.

| YEAR | EXPORT TRADE (million dollars) | COMMODITY PRICES (percent) | LABOR | | WAGES PAID BY ALL MANUFAC-TURING INDUSTRIES (million dollars) |
			EMPLOYMENT (percent)	PAYROLLS (percent)	
	11	12	13	14	15
1906	1743.9	61.8			
1907	1880.9	65.2			
1908	1860.8	62.9			
1909	1663.0	67.6			3,427
1910	1744.9	70.4			
1911	2049.3	64.9			
1912	2204.3	69.1			
1913	2465.9	69.8			
1914	2364.6	68.1			4,068
1915	2768.6	69.5			5,550
1916	5482.6	85.5			6,250
1917	6233.6	117.5			7,710
1918	6149.1	131.3			9,770
1919	7920.4	138.6	107.2	97.4	10,462
1920	8228.0	154.4	108.2	117.1	12,615
1921	4485.0	97.6	82.3	76.2	8,202
1922	3831.8	96.7	90.6	81.3	8,650
1923	4167.5	100.6	104.1	103.3	11,009
1924	4591.0	98.1	96.5	96.1	10.175
1925	4909.9	103.5	99.4	100.6	10,730
1926	4808.7	100.0	101.2	103.8	11,115
1927	4865.4	95.4	98.9	101.8	10,849
1928	5128.4	96.7	98.9	102.4	10,890
1929	5241.0	95.3	104.8	109.1	11,620
1930	3843.2	86.4	91.5	88.7	9,450
1931	2424.3	73.0	77.4	67.5	7,226
1932	1611.0	64.8	64.1	46.1	4,925
1933	1675.0	66.0	69.0	48.5	5,262
1934	2132.8	75.0	78.8	61.9	6,725
1935	2282.9	80.0	82.2	70.3	7,627

EXPLANATION AND SOURCES

11. EXPORT TRADE:
    Source: *Statistical Abstract*, p. 432.

12. COMMODITY PRICES: Explanation: Wholesale prices.
    Source: United States Department of Labor, Bureau of Labor
                   Statistics, *Handbook of Labor Statistics*, Bulletin No.
                   616, Washington, 1936, p. 674.

13. EMPLOYMENT: Explanation: Employment in manufacturing industries,
    1923–5 = 100.
    Source: Ibid., p. 132.

14. PAYROLLS: Explanation: 1923–1925 = 100.
    Source: Ibid.

15. WAGES PAID BY ALL MANUFACTURING INDUSTRIES:
    Source: *Handbook of Labor Statistics*, op. cit. p. 154.

APPENDIX VII–A

Evolution of American Security Capitalism, 1820–1935

National Finance (Budget)

(Million Dollars)

YEAR	TOTAL REVENUES	TOTAL EXPENDI-TURES	BALANCE (1–2)	INTEREST ON DEBT	PUBLIC DEBT RE-TIREMENT	EXPENDI-TURES FOR DEBT SERVICE (4+5) (percent)
	1	2	3	4	5	6
1820	17.9	18.3	−0.4	5.1		5.1
1830	24.8	15.1	9.7	1.9		1.9
1840	19.5	24.3	−4.8	0.2		0.2
1850	43.6	39.5	4.1	3.8		3.8
1860	56.1	63.1	−7.0	3.2		3.2
1870	411.3	309.7	101.6	129.2		129.2
1880	333.5	267.6	65.9	95.8		95.8
1890	403.1	318.0	85.1	36.1		36.1
1900	567.2	520.9	46.3	40.2		40.2
1910	675.5	693.6	−18.1	21.3		21.3
1915	697.9	760.5	−62.6	22.9		22.9
1916	782.5	734.1	48.4	22.9		22.9
1917	1124.3	1,977.7	−853.4	24.7		24.7
1918	3664.6	12,697.8	−9,033.2	189.7	1.1	190.8
1919	5152.3	18,522.9	−13,370.6	619.2	8.0	627.2
1920	6694.6	6,482.1	212.5	1020.3	78.7	1099.0
1921	5624.9	5,538.2	86.7	999.1	422.3	1421.4
1922	4109.1	3,795.3	313.8	991.0	422.7	1413.7
1923	4007.1	3,697.5	309.6	1055.9	402.9	1458.8
1924	4012.0	3,506.7	505.3	940.6	458.0	1398.6
1925	3780.1	3,529.6	250.5	881.8	466.5	1348.3
1926	3962.8	3,585.0	377.8	831.9	487.4	1319.3
1927	4129.4	3,493.6	635.8	787.0	519.6	1306.6
1928	4042.3	3,643.5	398.8	731.8	540.3	1272.1
1929	4033.3	3,848.5	184.8	678.3	549.6	1227.9
1930	4177.9	3,994.2	183.7	659.3	553.9	1213.2
1931	3189.6	4,091.6	−902.0	611.6	440.1	1051.7
1932	2005.7	5,153.6	−3,147.9	599.3	412.6	1011.9
1933	2079.7	5,143.0	−3,063.3	689.4	461.6	1151.0
1934	3115.6	7,105.1	−3,989.5	756.6	359.9	1116.5
1935	3800.5	7,375.8	−3,575.3	820.9	573.6	1394.5

1. TOTAL REVENUES:

    Source: 1820–1935   United States Treasury Department, *Annual Report of the Secretary on the State of Finances*, 1935/1936, pp. 357–359.

2. TOTAL EXPENDITURES:

    Source: 1820–1935   Ibid. pp. 360–363.

4. INTEREST ON DEBT:

    Source: 1820–1935   Ibid. pp. 360–363.

5. PUBLIC DEBT RETIREMENT:

    Explanation: This item consists of sinking fund; cash repayment of principal; bonds, etc., received as repayments of principal; bonds, etc., received as interest payments; bonds and notes received for estate taxes, franchise tax receipts, Federal Reserve banks; net earnings, Federal Intermediate Credit Banks, miscellaneous gifts, forfeitures, etc.; Ibid. p. 438.

    Source: 1918–1935.   Ibid. pp. 360–363.

APPENDIX VII–B

Evolution of American Security Capitalism, 1820–1935
National Finance (Debt)

YEAR	UNFUND-ED DEBT (9-8) (million dollars)	FUNDED DEBT (million dollars)	GROSS DEBT (million dollars)	SINK-ING FUNDS (million dollars)	NET DEBT (9-10) (million dollars)	INDI-RECT DEBT (million dollars)	TOTAL DEBT (11+12) (million dollars)	NA-TIONAL WEALTH (a) (billion dollars)	NA-TIONAL INCOME (b) (billion dollars)
	7	8	9	10	11	12	13	14	15
1820		91.	91.		91.		91.		
1830		49.	49.		49.		49.		
1840		4.	4.		4.		4.		
1850		63.	63.		63.		63.	7.1	2.2
1860	20.	45.	65.		65.		65.	16.2	3.6
1870	526.	1,910.	2,436.	1.	2,435.		2,435.	30.1	6.7
1880	1,096.	995.	2,091.	50.	2,041.		2,041.	43.6	7.4
1890	520.	602.	1,122.		1,122.		1,122.	65.0	12.1
1900	309.	954.	1,263.	346.	917.		917.	88.5	18.0
1910	234.	913.	1,147.	689.	458.		458.	186.3	31.4
1915	377.	814.	1,191.	991.	200.		200.	200.2	37.2
1916	421.	804.	1,225.	1,052.	173.		173.	251.6	43.3
1917	882.	2,094.	2,976.	1,120.	1,856.		1,856.	351.7	51.3
1918	2,623.	9,621.	12,244.	1,181.	11,068.		11,068.	400.5	60.4
1919	8,521.	16,961.	25,482.	1,460.	24,022.		24,022.	431.0	61.8
1920	8,271.	16,027.	24,298.		24,298.		24,298.	488.7	75.0
1921	8,050.	15,926.	23,976.	261.	23,715.		23,715.	317.2	59.4
1922	7,116.	15,848.	22,964.	276.	22,688.		22,688.	320.8	60.3
1923	5,930.	16,420.	22,350.	284.	22,066.		22,066.	339.9	70.8
1924	8,341.	12,910.	21,251.	296.	20,955.		20,955.	337.9	71.3
1925	7,160.	13,356.	20,516.	306.	20,210.		20,210.	362.3	75.6
1926	5,803.	13,840.	19,643.	317.	19,326.		19,326.	356.5	80.2
1927	6,037.	12,473.	18,510.	334.	18,176.		18,176.	346.4	78.1
1928	6,426.	11,178.	17,604.	355.	17,249.		17,249.	360.1	81.0
1929	5,406.	11,525.	16,931.	370.	16,561.		16,561.	361.8	84.1
1930	4,673.	11,512.	16,185.	388.	15,797.		15,797.	323.1	73.3
1931	3,894.	12,907.	16,801.	392.	16,409.		16,409.	275.1	56.0
1932	5,923.	13,564.	19,487.	413.	19,074.		19,074.	246.4	39.2
1933	9,013.	13,526.	22,539.	426.	22,113.		22,113.	252.3	38.8
1934	15,708.	11,345.	27,053.	359.	26,694.	691.	27,385.	289.2	47.8
1935	15,876.	12,825.	28,701.	573.	28,128.	4,151.	32,279.	308.9	53.1

Explanation and Sources

8. FUNDED DEBT: Explanation: Includes all bond issues whose date of maturity is five years after date.

9. GROSS DEBT:

| Sources: | 1820–1850 | United States Treasury Department, *Annual Report of the Secretary of the State of Finances*, 1900/1901, p. 101. |
| | 1860–1935 | Ibid. 1935/1936, pp. 411–412. |

10. SINKING FUNDS:

Sources:	1870, 1880, ⎫ 1900–1917 ⎭	Ibid. compiled from reports of treasury for respective years.
	1918–1919	Ibid. 1918/1919, p. 615.
	1921–1935	Ibid. 1935/1936, p. 438.

12. INDIRECT DEBT: Explanation: Consists of Federal Farm Mortgage Corporation, Home Owners Loan Corporation, Reconstruction Finance Corporation obligations.

Source: Ibid.

14. NATIONAL WEALTH: Explanation: 1910 is 1912.

| Sources: | 1850–1900 | King, Wilford I., *The Wealth and Income of the People of the United States*, New York, 1923, p. 13. |
| | 1910–1935 | Standard Statistics *Trade and Securities*, p. 64. |

15. NATIONAL INCOME:

Sources:	1850–1900	King, Wilford I., op. cit., p. 129.
	1910–1918	King, Wilford I., *The National Income and Its Purchasing Power*, No. 15, New York, 1930, p. 74, Publication of National Bureau of Economic Research.
	1919–1935	Kuznets, Simon, *The National Income and Capital Formation*, No. 32, New York, 1937. Publication of National Bureau of Economic Research.

APPENDIX VII–C

EVOLUTION OF AMERICAN SECURITY CAPITALISM, 1820–1935

NATIONAL FINANCE (BUDGET AND DEBT)

(Ratios A through E in Percent)

YEAR	BUDGET		DEBT			
	REVENUES TO EXPENDITURES (1÷2)	EXPENDITURES FOR DEBT SERVICE TO TOTAL EXPENDITURES (6÷2)	UNFUNDED DEBT TO GROSS DEBT (7÷9)	DEDUCTIONS TO GROSS DEBT (10÷9)	NATIONAL WEALTH TO TOTAL DEBT (14÷13)	GROSS DEBT PER CAPITA (in dollars)
	A	B	C	D	E	F
1820	97.8	27.9				
1830	164.2	12.6				
1840	80.2	0.8				
1850	110.4	9.6			11,269.8	
1860	88.9	5.1	30.8		24,923.1	2.06
1870	132.8	41.7	21.6		1,235.6	63.19
1880	124.6	35.8	52.4	2.4	2,085.1	41.69
1890	126.8	11.4	46.3		5,793.2	17.92
1900	108.9	7.7	24.5	27.4	9,651.0	16.56
1910	97.4	3.1	20.4	60.1	40,676.9	12.69
1915	91.8	3.0	31.7	83.2	100,100.0	11.83
1916	106.6	3.1	34.4	85.9	145,433.5	11.96
1917	56.8	1.2	29.6	37.6	18,949.4	28.57
1918	28.9	1.5	21.4	9.6	3,618.5	115.65
1919	27.8	3.4	33.4	5.7	1,794.1	240.09
1920	103.3	17.0	34.0		2,011.3	228.33
1921	101.6	25.7	33.6	1.1	1,337.6	221.09
1922	108.3	37.2	31.0	1.2	1,414.0	208.97
1923	108.4	39.5	26.5	1.3	1,540.4	200.10
1924	114.4	39.9	39.2	1.4	1,612.5	186.86
1925	107.1	38.2	34.9	1.5	1,792.7	177.82
1926	110.5	36.8	29.5	1.6	1,844.7	167.70
1927	118.2	37.4	32.6	1.8	1,905.8	156.04
1928	110.9	34.9	36.5	2.0	2,087.7	146.69
1929	104.8	31.9	31.9	2.2	2,184.7	139.40
1930	104.6	30.4	28.9	2.4	2,045.3	131.49
1931	78.0	25.7	23.2	2.3	1,676.6	135.37
1932	38.9	19.6	30.4	2.1	1,291.8	155.93
1933	40.4	22.4	40.0	1.9	1,141.0	179.21
1934	43.9	15.7	58.1	1.3	1,056.1	213.65
1935	51.5	18.9	55.3	2.0	957.0	225.07

EXPLANATION AND SOURCES

Source: F. Gross Debt per capita (1860–1936) United States Treasury Department, 1935/1936, op. cit. pp. 411–412.

APPENDIX VIII
Financial Position of National Banks, 1870–1935
(Percent)

YEAR	CIRCULATING NOTES TO TOTAL LIABILITIES	DEMAND DEPOSITS TO TOTAL DEPOSITS	SECURITIES TO EARNING ASSETS	RESERVE ASSETS TO TOTAL DEPOSITS	NET CAPITAL TO GROSS CAPITAL	NET CAPITAL TO TOTAL SECURITIES	NET CAPITAL TO OTHER SECURITIES
	A	B	C	D	E	F	G
1870	19.38	98.02	35.87	49.56	95.13	135.04	143.48
1875	17.31	98.27	30.64	36.48	94.04	154.30	160.37
1880	14.17	98.88	29.41	41.59	92.40	130.04	137.76
1885	10.89	98.66	23.51	30.80	93.06	168.72	174.06
1890	4.04	98.06	12.90	21.63	92.07	316.72	319.03
1895	5.41	99.21	17.33	20.30	89.55	208.79	213.10
1900	5.81	96.53	22.36	15.28	89.54	117.22	118.73
1905	6.42	98.49	14.24	13.23	89.14	190.05	193.04
1910	6.83	99.09	13.75	11.20	87.13	188.77	190.93
1913	6.43	98.18	15.04	8.06	86.16	159.97	160.87
1915	5.30	81.45	23.05	15.01	84.29	78.44	119.80
1920	3.25	71.20	24.85	13.36	84.40	57.09	118.23
1921	3.69	68.61	26.61	16.99	82.58	56.60	110.32
1922	3.29	67.34	29.74	20.36	81.32	47.47	101.20
1923	3.24	65.26	29.43	20.08	78.84	44.83	91.26
1924	2.93	64.37	31.05	19.91	76.96	38.95	71.71
1925	2.51	64.11	29.47	17.77	76.17	39.86	70.78
1926	2.52	61.74	29.60	16.46	75.56	40.33	66.81
1927	2.31	58.46	31.28	14.97	75.60	36.83	61.38
1928	2.13	58.11	31.12	17.97	76.29	38.40	66.32
1929	2.24	56.50	29.13	17.47	76.27	44.10	73.86
1930	2.23	54.48	32.18	18.10	75.37	40.15	64.09
1931	2.54	53.54	36.93	21.84	73.09	34.00	60.78
1932	3.35	46.82	43.04	30.83	69.78	28.29	56.06
1933	3.58	48.14	48.59	40.37	70.28	24.14	55.80
1934	2.55	49.46	57.82	53.49	71.73	19.80	59.19
1935	.85	51.33	57.56	50.84	72.00	21.17	59.73

Explanation and Sources

EXPLANATION:

Ratio C: *Earning Assets* include total securities and total loans and discounts.

Ratio D: *Reserve assets* include net cash (cash minus bills payable and rediscounts), bankers' acceptances, commercial paper bought in the open market, net loans to banks (loans to banks minus loans from banks), eligible paper, loans collateralled by United States Government securities, and United States Government securities.

Ratio E: *Net capital* is capital, surplus and undivided profits minus bank building, furniture and fixtures and real estate.

Ratio G: *Other securities* include securities other than those of the United States Government.

SOURCE: Compiled from the *Annual Report of the Comptroller of the Currency* for respective years.

APPENDIX IX–A

FINANCIAL POSITION OF THE RAILROADS, 1890–1934

(Percent, 1890 = 100)

YEAR	OPER-ATING REV-ENUES	OPER-ATING EX-PENSES	OPER-ATING INCOME	TOTAL INCOME	FIXED CHARGES	NET INCOME	DIVI-DENDS PAID	TOTAL DEBT	TOTAL CAPITAL-IZATION
	1	2	3	4	5	6	7	8	9
1890	100.	100.	100.	100.	100.	100.	100.	100.	100.
1895	102.3	104.8	97.5	99.0	113.1	56.4	97.7	120.8	115.9
1900	141.5	138.9	146.5	141.1	114.4	224.8	159.8	131.0	131.9
1905	198.1	200.9	192.8	184.5	140.1	323.8	273.6	169.6	159.3
1910	261.7	263.3	258.5	244.9	159.3	511.9	402.3	232.8	203.8
1915	273.2	292.1	239.3	207.5	174.0	312.9	297.7	215.0	182.4
1920	498.1	705.6	98.1	251.2	195.2	426.7	311.5	224.5	191.2
1921	524.8	659.3	265.7	226.1	199.4	310.9	459.8	226.4	191.5
1922	528.9	637.9	318.9	242.8	203.5	366.8	310.3	227.6	196.0
1923	598.4	707.4	388.3	289.6	206.7	548.5	397.7	238.5	203.0
1924	563.4	651.3	393.9	297.1	215.1	553.5	366.7	248.7	208.5
1925	582.5	655.5	441.8	330.7	214.4	693.1	394.3	245.9	209.8
1926	607.2	674.7	477.2	360.6	219.2	801.0	464.4	247.2	212.5
1927	583.8	661.0	435.1	329.2	221.2	666.3	571.3	245.2	213.7
1928	581.5	639.7	469.1	356.0	220.2	779.2	494.3	247.4	217.3
1929	597.4	651.2	493.9	385.0	223.4	888.1	562.1	249.6	220.4
1930	502.5	567.9	376.0	293.2	221.5	517.8	581.6	250.4	220.6
1931	398.5	465.8	268.8	196.1	217.0	133.7	379.3	250.0	217.0
1932	297.4	347.3	201.4	128.5	215.1	−137.6	106.9	252.1	215.5
1933	294.5	325.0	235.7	164.0	219.6	− 5.9	32.2	249.0	216.4
1934	311.3	352.9	231.2	158.9	216.3	− 16.8	152.9	247.4	215.6

EXPLANATION AND SOURCES

EXPLANATION:

(3) Operating income—technically called "net operating revenue."
(4) Total income—technically called "balance for fixed charges."
(5) Fixed charges—include lease rentals.
(8) Total debt—includes lease rentals capitalized at 6 per cent.

SOURCE: *Statistics of Railroads*, Interstate Commerce Commission.

APPENDIX IX–B

FINANCIAL POSITION OF THE RAILROADS, 1890–1934

(Percent)

YEAR	OPERATING EXPENSES TO OPERATING REVENUES	OPERATING INCOME TO OPERATING REVENUES	TOTAL INCOME TO FIXED CHARGES	NET INCOME TO OPERATING REVENUES	NET INCOME TO DIVIDENDS PAID	TOTAL DEBT TO TOTAL CAPITALI-ZATION	TOTAL INCOME TO TOTAL CAPITALI-ZATION
	A	B	C	D	E	F	G
1890	65.7	34.2	132.6	9.6	127.5	58.8	4.1
1895	66.5	32.6	116.1	5.3	67.0	59.1	3.5
1900	64.6	35.4	163.5	15.2	163.3	56.1	4.4
1905	66.7	33.2	174.8	15.7	137.6	58.7	4.7
1910	66.2	33.7	204.0	18.8	147.7	61.0	4.9
1915	70.3	29.9	158.1	11.0	122.0	63.1	4.6
1920	93.2	6.7	170.7	8.2	159.0	62.8	5.4
1921	82.7	17.3	150.4	5.6	78.5	62.4	4.8
1922	79.4	20.6	158.2	6.6	137.0	63.6	5.0
1923	77.0	22.2	185.8	8.8	160.1	64.3	5.8
1924	76.1	23.9	183.3	9.4	175.2	64.3	5.8
1925	74.0	25.9	204.6	11.4	204.0	64.1	6.4
1926	73.1	26.8	218.2	12.6	200.2	64.3	6.9
1927	74.5	25.5	197.5	10.9	135.4	63.8	6.3
1928	72.4	27.6	214.5	12.8	183.0	63.3	6.7
1929	71.7	28.2	228.7	14.2	183.0	63.4	7.1
1930	74.4	25.6	175.6	9.9	103.2	63.1	5.4
1931	76.9	23.0	119.9	3.2	40.9	62.4	3.7
1932	76.9	23.1	79.2	−4.4	−149.5	62.3	2.4
1933	72.7	27.3	99.1	−0.2	− 21.4	62.5	3.1
1934	74.6	25.4	97.5	−0.5	− 12.7	63.1	2.9
AVERAGES							
1890 to 1910	66.7	33.5	155.3	12.6	127.5	58.8	4.3
1911 to 1929	75.2	24.8	200.1	13.0	179.3	63.2	6.1
1930 to 1934	75.1	24.9	114.3	0.16	−7.9	62.7	3.5

EXPLANATION AND SOURCES

Explanation: Averages are for the averages of the individual years within each period.

Source: *Statistics of Railroads,* Interstate Commerce Commission.

APPENDIX X

PROPORTION OF SECURITY INVESTMENTS TO TOTAL ASSETS OF FINANCIAL
INSTITUTIONS, 1890 TO 1935

(Percent of Total Assets)

YEAR	NATIONAL BANKS	STATE BANKS	LOAN AND TRUST COM- PANIES	PRIVATE BANKS	STOCK SAVINGS BANKS	MUTUAL SAVINGS BANKS	INSUR- ANCE COM- PANIES	TOTAL
1890	5.0	4.6	19.5	3.6	11.8	45.8	35.3	18.0
1895	6.5	8.0	21.9	5.3	13.8	45.5		17.6
1900	7.8	10.8	24.4	4.7	25.7	48.3	46.0	23.2
1905	16.8	12.9	27.5	7.9	20.4	48.9	51.2	27.8
1910	16.3	8.2	23.7	6.3	14.6	45.9		24.7
1915	17.5	9.5	23.0	8.4	12.7	43.3	41.9	24.3
1920	18.9	15.9	22.8	15.0	21.5	48.4	48.4	25.0
1921	19.6	17.2	23.8	17.1	10.4	47.8	46.2	26.0
1922	22.0	17.6	27.1	18.8	20.6	47.3	44.3	27.6
1923	23.6	18.3	25.5	21.7	20.6	46.1	42.2	27.7
1924	22.8	18.4	26.6	22.5	19.1	43.7	41.3	27.3
1925	23.5	19.1	24.2	22.6	20.5	42.4	40.1	27.1
1926	23.1	19.4	23.0	20.0	23.0	40.5	38.1	26.5
1927	24.1	20.4	25.0	17.7	23.1	39.1	37.8	27.4
1928	25.1	21.7	25.4	19.5	25.1	38.7	37.8	28.2
1929	24.3	18.3	21.2	17.9	24.0	37.7	37.2	26.4
1930	23.7	19.3	21.7	19.1	24.9	37.6	37.5	26.6
1931	27.8	22.4	27.2	20.7	27.7	40.0	37.5	30.4
1932	32.2	23.9	32.0	21.8	32.2	37.7	36.6	33.0
1933	35.3	26.1	36.9	21.3	35.2	37.4	38.3	35.9
1934	39.1	31.3	38.4	48.8	39.0	38.5	43.3	39.3
1935	41.1	33.5	40.9	55.6	40.7	40.4	47.3	42.0

SOURCES: *Annual Reports of the Comptroller of the Currency.*
Proceedings of the Association of Life Insurance Presidents.

INDEX

Russia —
Germany } in spite of dictator control
Italy   do not issue currency direct
         to pay for expenditures but use
         capitalistic mechanism of bonds
         a sop to a former ideology